W9-DAR-013

CROSS EXAMINED

Putting Christianity on Trial

John W. Campbell

PB Prometheus Books

Guilford, Connecticut

Prometheus Books

An imprint of Globe Pequot, the trade division of The Rowman & Littlefield
   Publishing Group, Inc.
4501 Forbes Blvd., Ste. 200
Lanham, MD 20706
www.PrometheusBooks.com

Distributed by NATIONAL BOOK NETWORK

Copyright © 2021 by John W. Campbell

All rights reserved. No part of this book may be reproduced in any form or by any
electronic or mechanical means, including information storage and retrieval systems,
without written permission from the publisher, except by a reviewer who may quote
passages in a review.

British Library Cataloguing in Publication Information Available

Library of Congress Cataloging-in-Publication Data

Names: Campbell, John W, 1968- author.
Title: Cross examined : putting Christianity on trial / John W Campbell.
Description: Lanham, MD : Prometheus, [2021] | Includes bibliographical
   references and index. | Summary: "In Cross Examined, John Campbell
   applies his almost thirty years of experience as a trial lawyer to
   dissecting Christianity and the case of apologists for the Christian
   God. He addresses the best arguments for Christianity, those against it,
   and the reasons people should care about these questions. His purpose is
   to fill a void in books on atheism and Christianity by systematically
   taking Christian claims to task and making a full-throated argument for
   atheism from the perspective of a trial lawyer making a case"—Provided
   by publisher.
Identifiers: LCCN 2021001955 (print) | LCCN 2021001956 (ebook) | ISBN
   9781633886841 (cloth) | ISBN 9781633886858 (epub)
Subjects: LCSH: Apologetics. | Christianity—Controversial literature. |
   Christianity and atheism.
Classification: LCC BT1103 .C3625 2021 (print) | LCC BT1103 (ebook) | DDC
   239—dc23
LC record available at https://lccn.loc.gov/2021001955
LC ebook record available at https://lccn.loc.gov/2021001956

♾™ The paper used in this publication meets the minimum requirements of
American National Standard for Information Sciences—Permanence of Paper
for Printed Library Materials, ANSI/NISO Z39.48-1992.

CONTENTS

INTRODUCTION

The most fundamental of all questions that can possibly be asked is, "Does God exist?" That is not to say that it is the foremost question on everybody's mind. You may well have decided that there is a God and have other questions that are more important to you than this one: How can I find peace and happiness? What does the future hold? How can I solve my personal problems? Other questions of this sort may be far more prominent issues. However, the existence of God has huge implications for all these others.

—Joe Boot, *A Time to Search*

Is there a God? If so, what is the nature of this God, and what does He (or She) want? Which religion is right? Are any of them right? These are big questions—some of the biggest, most important questions around. How we answer them can profoundly affect just about every aspect of our behavior, including how we spend the majority of our time on Earth and how we treat other people.

Eighty-four percent of the world's population is affiliated with a religion: 32 percent are Christians; 23 percent, Muslims; 15 percent, Hindus; and 7 percent, Buddhists, with the remaining 7 percent split among various other sects. Mostly, these beliefs are mutually exclusive. They cannot all be right. And yet, the nature of religion is that the vast majority of religious adherents hold to their beliefs firmly, rarely acknowledging even to themselves that they may be wrong.

The adoption of religion is primarily an accident of birth, with the highest predictor of a person's religion being the religious persuasion of their parents. Religions are social memes passed within families based on the location and culture in which one was raised. Accordingly, religions congregate geographically. The Asia-Pacific region, for example, contains the vast majority of the world's Hindus (99 percent), Buddhists (99 percent), and adherents of folk or traditional religions (90 percent). In the United States, by contrast, 65 percent of Americans consider themselves Christians. Although most people adopt their religion as children well before they can critically evaluate their "decision," most will vigorously defend it into adulthood. Despite their awareness that man has created millions of gods, they will say, "Mine is different. Mine is real."

Religion is an emotionally charged issue. It is, for this very reason, infrequently discussed in polite company. It is considered common wisdom that spirited discussions about religion among the differently minded are likely to result in shouting matches and personal attacks. It is typically assumed that no opinions are changed by such discussions, which generate only offense and ill feelings. Even if one succeeds in changing the opinion of another, it is likely to cost the other's scorn; as Friedrich Nietzsche wrote, when another forces us to change our minds, "we hold the inconvenience he causes us very much against him." Frank discussions of religious differences are rare. Even rarer are discussions involving rigorous assessments of the truth of competing religious claims.

In today's world, however, these are exactly the type of discussions people should be having. When politicians defend their stands against gay marriage, global warming initiatives, and stem cell research by citing scriptural passages; when centuries-old land disputes are premised on religious texts; when terrorist groups justify their acts of violence by quoting religious holy books; isn't it worthwhile to discuss the legitimacy of those texts? The world faces many problems and conflicts inextricably tied to religious beliefs, and they can only be effectively addressed by publicly scrutinizing the source of those beliefs—the texts themselves.

Unfortunately, societal forces have erected formidable barriers against such discussions. Western democracies value cultural relativism over the quest for truth. The misplaced obsession with avoiding any risk of offense has led to a societally enforced directive that all religious beliefs be treated as valid and beneficial, with none being less legitimate than any other. But all opinions are not equally legitimate. Some are simply more grounded in reality and are thus more valid than others. Only by engaging in honest discussions on these matters can we assess the legitimacy of these beliefs, and this is something we should be doing, for as Thomas Paine observed, "It is error only, and not truth, that shrinks from inquiry."

In the academic community, this has conventionally been the work of philosophers, and there is no doubt that philosophy can boast a rich history of in-depth exploration of religious traditions. In the last hundred years, scientists and historians have also contributed much value to these dialogues, as their discoveries have provided ever more complete views of their respective fields—fields in which religion previously held a monopoly. Many feel that science has effectively rendered philosophy obsolete when discussing these issues. Philosophy has certainly ceded ground.

Regrettably, much of the relevant work of philosophers, scientists, and historians remains steeped in discipline-specific esoteric jargon that can seem impenetrable to those outside the respective fields, rendering it inaccessible to the average person. Also, much of this work has become outdated, making it difficult to find an appropriate starting point. No meaningful discussion among laypeople can occur without surveying the arguments, boiling them down to a manageable size, and putting them into plain English.

I have been a trial lawyer throughout my adult life, litigating cases across the United States. I recognize the core of that job to be something very different than I expected upon entering law school. It is explaining complicated things to ordinary people in ways they can understand. If you cannot explain your client's position to a jury, then you have little chance of persuading them that your client should prevail.

I have written this book to bring those same skills to answering the following question: Is Christianity a reasonable belief system to adopt and maintain? This question is, admittedly, of far narrower scope than those I presented at the beginning of this introduction. I have limited the scope for three reasons. First, Christianity is the belief system with which I was raised and am most familiar. Second, focusing on one religion keeps things manageable. Extending the scope beyond Christianity would increase the size of the book exponentially.

Third, and perhaps most important, while I believe all religions should be open to critical analysis, priority must be given to those with the most impact on our lives. In America, one stands above all others. Its members dominate every branch of government and regularly allow their religious beliefs to influence public policy, sometimes in dramatic ways. Any failures of Christianity to support its claims should, therefore, have enormous implications because Christianity is the foundation of so much of what our government does. In short, Christianity should be singled out because of its unique cultural and sociopolitical significance.

Many arguments for and against Christianity equally apply to other religions, especially other patriarchal ones as Islam and Judaism. Unless specifically addressed, however, I do not intend to suggest that Christianity is more or less warranted than any other religion. This is not a book about comparisons of religious systems. It is about whether Christianity is warranted on its own terms.

From a young age, I identified as a Christian. My father was a Baptist preacher, and my mother, a Methodist. I absorbed and internalized their beliefs. As I got older, I recognized that not everyone shared those beliefs and began for the first time to look for ways to defend them. I sought intellectual justifications that would persuade others that mine were the right beliefs. At first, I was delighted by the sheer abundance of material seemingly designed for this very purpose. But the more I read, the more disappointed I became. These sources provided weak arguments and rarely satisfying responses to my questions, which only increased the more I learned. The defenders of the faith rarely addressed the most powerful arguments against it, responding instead to misleading caricatures of those arguments. My quest to defend my faith resulted in abandoning my faith. I could not in good conscience defend it any longer.

To the extent I draw comparisons to Christianity, it is typically with atheism or naturalism. For reasons I explain later, I believe agnostic atheism to be the default position at which any reasonable person should begin when exploring whether a particular religious belief is merited. Only if that religious belief is warranted by reason and evidence should atheism be abandoned for belief. For reasons I explain in this book, I believe there is no good reason to abandon atheism, which is why I remain an atheist.

I draw many analogies from the American legal system, with which I am particularly well acquainted and conversant. While certainly not perfect, this is the best system we have for determining the truth of competing nonscientific claims (I get to those soon enough). Many of the sharpest minds in our nation's history have honed it for this very purpose. I have spent more than twenty-five years in that system, litigating cases in many jurisdictions. In each case, I have had to learn unique nuances, but I've been surprised how the basic rules remain the same. This is true because they work.

It must be acknowledged here that the term *Christianity* covers a wide spectrum of belief. Debating Christianity has been compared to boxing a bowl of jelly, as it can be a shifting, unclear, amorphous target. But one thing all versions have in common is that they are based to some extent on interpretations of canonical Christian Scripture—the Christian Bible. Obviously, I cannot address every possible interpretation or doctrinal position premised on such interpretations. For reasons I explain later, I focus on the Scriptures themselves, as well as arguments that theologians and Christian apologists, the intellectual defenders of the faith, have made from the dawn of the religion through today.

The defenders of Christianity have had almost two thousand years to construct arguments supporting their faith. It would be impossible to address them all comprehensively. Once one understands the landscape, however, it becomes clear that this isn't necessary. Many are premised on the same assumptions and are subject to the same objections. The same errors in reasoning arise repeatedly. By understanding these, one can recognize the flaws in many categories of arguments without the need to deconstruct each piece by piece.

My approach is to address the most popular, the strongest, and the most representative arguments made by Christian apologists, explaining my work along the way. In the process, I hope to provide the reader with the tools to continue effectively analyzing arguments long after reaching the final page. While Christianity is the focus of this book, I intend it also to serve as a survey course in critical thinking.

To the extent I find certain arguments for Christianity unconvincing or unreasonable, this should not be confused with saying it is unreasonable to be a Christian. I feel confident reasonable people are as common among Christians as any other group. Most Christians were raised as Christians and have presumably had generally positive experiences with Christianity. They have found community among Christians and people who share their basic values. Many have been comforted by their faith since they were children and have found it to serve important purposes in their lives. I would bet that virtually none became Christians because of the apologetic arguments I address.

I suspect that most have never drilled down and critically evaluated the arguments of natural theology, the domain of philosophers who maintain that Christianity rests firmly on sound principles of reason and rationality. And why would they, unless they felt a need to buttress their faith in this way? Perhaps it has always worked for them, and it is not unreasonable to continue doing something that seems to work. For many, religion is primarily about community. People are likely to belong to a religion, not because they have critically evaluated its doctrines and found them to be rationally sound, but because they were raised in that religion or they like a particular church they attended and found it to be a good fit for themselves or their family.

Most have never engaged in serious comparison shopping. Most have not studied the scripture of competing religions, such as the Koran, or the works of such atheist writers as Bertrand Russell and Robert Ingersoll. They have received their information about competing worldviews from other Christians within a Christian framework and evaluated it through a Christian lens. Having never been outsiders to the faith, those raised as Christians cannot see Christianity as an outsider sees it. They harbor assumptions developed in early childhood that frame and color every religious discussion. Unless those very assumptions are questioned, their beliefs will seem reasonable. But most have never been equipped to even identify the assumptions that may cloud their views—much less address them critically. None of us apply the same degree of skepticism to all ideas and beliefs. We are all more willing to accept and less likely to critically challenge those that are comforting or familiar. I, too, fall into this trap. This is not something to be shamed. It is just part of being human.

I am sensitive to the criticism (that will no doubt be raised) that I am attacking Christians. I am not. Knowing someone is a Christian by itself tells you nothing about their character, their values, or their position on any issue of importance. Christianity has evolved an enormous tent that can accommodate a vast array of beliefs. It exists in innumerable versions. There are no values universal to Christianity, just as there are no uniquely Christian values. My value system is virtually identical to many of Christians.

There is a huge difference, furthermore, between challenging the believer and the idea that person believes, just as there is a difference between respecting one's belief and one's right to believe. We might agree that horoscopes don't accurately predict the future, but that suggests no animus toward people who believe they do. Most likely, we believe those people are simply mistaken, which implies no fault. We all are surely mistaken about many beliefs we hold. I do not take it as an attack when someone points out that I may be wrong about something, which I'm sure I am about many things. If I have made an error, I would prefer that someone let me know so I don't persist in believing the wrong thing.

Our democracy was founded on the principle of free debate within the marketplace of ideas. All ideas must be open to criticism if we expect our knowledge to grow and improve. Science and history have effectively demonstrated that progress is made only when mistaken ideas are challenged and corrected. Astrophysicist and science popularizer Neil deGrasse Tyson said that some myths deserve to be torn apart out of respect for the human intellect. The believer of any idea should embrace criticism because it can only make his beliefs stronger or lead to better ideas. Criticizing the intellectual foundation of Christianity says absolutely nothing about any individual Christian or Christians as a whole.

Christianity in many respects represents a testable hypothesis about how the world works and how we should behave in it. It is, therefore, reasonable to question it, to debate it, and to point out when it doesn't fit the evidence or make sense. That isn't intolerance, and it isn't forcing ideas on anyone. We analyze and criticize every other kind of idea: science, politics, philosophy, medicine, art, sports, and who got cut from last night's episode of *The Bachelor*. There is no good reason religion should merit special treatment. The different religions of the world cannot all be right, but they can all be wrong. We can respect the freedom of religious belief while retaining the right to critically examine those beliefs and treat them the same as any other we consider mistaken. As H. L. Mencken wisely said, "We must respect the other fellow's religion, but only in the sense and to the extent that we respect his theory that his wife is beautiful and his children smart."

It is my strong conviction that no one should be criticized for their beliefs. People should only be criticized for their actions. But when bad actions are motivated by incorrect beliefs, the urgency of criticizing those beliefs goes up. When similarly motivated bad actions become widespread and the actions are causing significant harm, this urgency increases exponentially. I believe that in such situations, we have a moral imperative and civic duty to critically examine those beliefs. Maybe many people with those same beliefs are causing no harm, but that alone does not warrant suppressing the criticism, especially as it is reasonable to expect that incorrect beliefs will lead to more harm than good.

I am concerned about the future. I am concerned about the world my children and their children will inherit. I am concerned about the needs of the poor, the underprivileged, and the marginalized. For reasons I articulate later, I believe these all suffer when people believe things for the wrong reasons. As Matt Dillahunty has said, beliefs inform actions, and actions have consequences. If the past is any indication, and I think it is, the future is likely to suffer if people do not rethink their views on Christianity. Misguided Christian beliefs have led to enormous harm. Given the current state of the world, that harm is only likely to increase if not checked.

Combining evangelical officials at the state and local levels, the policy-making power of Christian conservatives is unprecedented in the history of our country. These officials share a governing approach that overtly incorporates a particular view of Christianity, meaning that their religious beliefs have an enormous impact on billions of people. If a policy is adopted because of a religious belief, then the policy debate must include whether that belief is justified. The arguments in this book will be increasingly important as the Christian Right increases its influence on US policy.

This book identifies the underlying assumptions of Christianity so they can be evaluated and then provides the tools to conduct that evaluation. No one can be expected to come to the right conclusion without relevant information, so I provide that, as well. An assessment of one's beliefs might not yield reassuring answers, but that does not make it any less justified. Sometimes the things we thought were true turn out not to be so, and we should see that revelation as a very good thing. I believe that for adults, truth is better than comforting fictions.

With that out of the way, let's begin.

1

STANDARDS

Every game has rules. Otherwise, how could we know who won? Likewise, when two people argue about something, there must be rules by which a third person can determine who is more likely to be right. If Joe says the traffic light was green when Sam entered the intersection, while Bob says it was red, how can we assess which of these competing claims is true? Should we side with Joe if he produces more people who agree with him? Should we side with Bob because he is a Nobel Peace Prize winner? Should it matter that Joe and Sam have been friends since grade school or that Bob has long hated Sam for stealing his high school girlfriend?

Whenever two rational people make competing claims, it is rarely a simple matter of choosing between them. Many considerations appear relevant, to which we must assign relative values. In the previous example, how important should it be that Joe has two witnesses on his side? What weight, if any, should be assigned to Bob's Nobel Peace Prize? If we are to navigate these waters with any hope of successfully reaching the right shore, then we need to apply the appropriate rules. We need to set standards.

Unless we obtain information directly through our senses, such as witnessing the accident in person, we must rely on other sources. Standards help us to assess which of these sources should be deemed trustworthy and under what circumstances. Without clear, mutually agreeable standards, it would be impossible for people to agree on just about anything.

LEGAL STANDARDS

The Anglo-American legal system has been specifically designed to assess competing claims. It has established objective standards to be used for this very purpose. These standards should apply equally to all parties, whether the action be civil or criminal. They are intended to protect the integrity of the truth-seeking process and ensure, to the extent reasonably possible, that justice is done. Litigation is the process by which competing claims are evaluated and a winner declared. In trials, disputed factual claims are typically decided by a jury. The jury comprises several people, usually nine to twelve, who listen to the parties' respective presentations and make a determination, known as a verdict, regarding which claim(s) should prevail.

A. Legal Evidence

Assume that you have been arrested for a murder you did not commit. You are brought to trial, where the prosecutor reads the charges against you. The judge immediately proclaims you guilty and sentences you to execution. You protest the judgment, arguing that the prosecutor has presented nothing to establish your guilt, and you can provide many witnesses and material objects to demonstrate your innocence. But the judge ignores your pleas and sends you to your death.

Regardless of your knowledge of the law, I expect you would find this scenario highly unfair. And this is because intuitively we feel it is unjust to punish someone without good reasons to believe they did something wrong. We would expect those reasons to include objectively verifiable information, tangible items linking the person to the crime, or both. We would likely feel it similarly unfair for the judge to side with one party over the other in a civil dispute without reviewing any information supporting that side's position. It is not enough to make a claim, such as that someone committed a crime. The person making that claim must back it up. The person opposing that claim should have the same opportunity to offer support for their position. We call the information offered by opposing sides of a legal dispute *legal evidence*.

Many standards applicable to litigation are concerned with legal evidence. Legal evidence includes every type of proof to be presented at trial and can take many forms, including the oral and written testimony of witnesses, documents, and physical objects. The American legal system is concerned not only with claims that are decided based on evidence but also with the quantity and quality of that evidence. It is important there be *enough* evidence, that it relate to the issues involved, and that it be sufficiently *trustworthy*. Such standards provide legitimacy to the judgment, demonstrating that it is justified rather than arbitrary.

The rules of legal evidence assign values to proof, separating the good, which is deemed admissible, from the bad. Admissible evidence is that which the judge finds may be presented to and considered by the jury in reaching a verdict.[1] Inadmissible evidence is that which cannot be considered. These admissibility standards are designed to ensure that the jury hears only evidence likely to lead to a valid and accurate result.

One category of evidence classified inadmissible by American rules of evidence is *hearsay*. Hearsay, in the legal sense, is a statement by someone other than a testifying witness to prove the truth of the matter asserted. If, in the earlier stoplight example, Joe testified that he knew the light was green *simply because a friend had told him so*, then Joe's knowledge would be based on hearsay. He would be attempting to establish a crucial factual issue, not through his own personal knowledge, but through the statement of another.

As to why the legal system bars hearsay, consider the children's game "Telephone." In "Telephone," ten or so kids sit in a circle. The first child whispers a story to the second, who then turns and repeats it to the third child. This continues until the final version of the story is repeated aloud by the final child. The enjoyment of "Telephone" comes from comparing this final version with the original story and noting how it has changed over the course of the game. If the story didn't change significantly in virtually every game, then "Telephone" would have lost its appeal long ago.

The recurrent popularity of this game demonstrates something we all know: Stories change in the retelling and change more the more they are retold. Each storyteller adds, subtracts, or modifies the tale they receive. Generally, this is unintentional, a natural result of the filtering and processing mechanics of the human mind. Maybe one or more of the "Telephone" participants simply failed to hear part of the story correctly. Maybe they paraphrased something too long to remember but in doing so left out a crucial piece of information. Or perhaps one or more players intentionally changed some of the story to make it more interesting. In any event, the result is the same: The final story is rarely an accurate or reliable version of the original.

If you were accused of a serious crime, how would it feel to learn that the only person to testify against you heard that you had committed the crime third- or fourthhand? It would be impossible for your attorney to effectively question the witness about the original source of this information because the witness could only testify about what was told to him. Perhaps the person who initially identified you as the culprit hadn't worn the correct prescription glasses that morning and had you confused with someone else. This detail would almost certainly be lost by the time the rumor made it to the person on the witness stand. This crucial piece of information that would severely undercut the reliability of the initial account would be unavailable to your attorney and thus to the jury. Or perhaps the initial witness didn't like you and was lying out of spite, or the information that ultimately led to the rumor was garbled and distorted. Many other possibilities are equally likely that would have resulted in the rumor being inaccurate, but the point is that this type of attenuated evidence is a weak indicator of guilt.

Hearsay is generally not allowed into evidence because it is inherently *unreliable*. The law recognizes exceptions to the hearsay rule, but they all involve unique circumstances in which there is some special reason to believe the hearsay testimony *would be* reliable despite the witness not being the original source, such as when the statement is against the interests of the speaker. It is not that such evidence as hearsay cannot be accurate or have any probative value. The problem is that it is categorically *less likely* to be helpful than other evidence. The law recognizes that certain types of evidence are simply of *higher* value—considered more helpful and thus *better*—than other types. Good evidence, such as the firsthand account of a witness, is simply more likely to lead to the right result than bad evidence, which is more likely to be inaccurate or misleading.

You might be questioning why judges are involved at all in separating good evidence from bad evidence. Why not just let the jury hear it all and sort it out? The reason is that prioritizing the value of different sources and types of information requires specialized expertise not possessed by the typical juror. Even if the jurors had such expertise, it would be asking quite a lot to require them to exercise it flawlessly in a trial in which they are bombarded with hundreds, if not thousands, of facts and arguments, many emotionally charged. Why add additional information that can be categorically classified as unhelpful? Judges play the role of gatekeepers, using common standards to ensure that jurors are presented only with relevant and reasonably reliable evidence.

Another example might be helpful. Assume a trial in which a doctor is accused of negligently prescribing a drug that caused a birth defect. Numerous studies found the drug highly dangerous and to have a 95 percent chance of causing defects in the children of pregnant women. A well-regarded doctor and medical researcher from Harvard Medical School testifies to the jury about these studies and explains why any competent doctor should have known the substantial risks of the drug.

The defendant seeks to have his own witness testify that this drug was safe. But the defendant's witness is neither a doctor nor a researcher. He never even graduated from high school. He plans to tell the jury that the drug does *not* cause birth defects, but he has no evidence to support his claim and nothing to rebut the plaintiff's witness or the numerous studies he cites. When pressed by the judge, he claims that his knowledge simply comes from a dream he had in which he was told by a golden unicorn that this drug is safe.

Should the judge allow the defendant's witness to testify to the jury? You might think it would do no harm because this witness's testimony would be so patently absurd. But by allowing this witness to testify, isn't the judge implicitly representing that the witness has something of value to offer? Isn't he signifying that the witness's testimony is comparable in value to that of the plaintiff's expert, suggesting an equivalence that isn't really there? And is it inconceivable that one or more jurors might then give his testimony more weight than it deserves?

Judges are entrusted to exclude from testifying any "expert" witness whose expertise cannot be demonstrated. Here, the defendant's expert would most likely not be allowed to testify because he doesn't have the knowledge and qualifications to provide reliable testimony that would assist the jury in making a well-informed and accurate decision. The defendant's evidence is *so much poorer* in quality than the plaintiff's that the jury is kept from hearing it at all.

But what if the defendant's witness *was* a doctor with training in the relevant field but not as prominent as the plaintiff's expert? Assume that rather than Harvard, the defendant's witness went to a small state school of little renown and had been practicing only half as long as the plaintiff's witness? What if his opinions supporting the safety of this drug were based on an alternate set of smaller-scale studies reaching different results? In such a case, all other things being equal, the witness would most likely be allowed to testify. It would be left to the plaintiff's attorney to point out these relatively minor distinctions through his examination of the defendant's witness and then to argue to the jury in closing argument that they should believe the plaintiff's witness over the defendant's. Lawyers describe these distinctions as going to the weight of the evidence, which is to be evaluated by the jury, rather than its admissibility, which is evaluated by the judge.

B. Burden of Proof

Related to the concept of evidence is that of the legal burden of proof. When one talks about the burden of proof in a legal context, one is referring to which party has the obligation to prove his or her position. In a civil case, in which a party (known as the plaintiff) is seeking money damages from another (the defendant), the plaintiff's lawsuit begins with a document called the "Complaint," which includes allegations of the defendant's wrongdoing.

The plaintiff, having made the allegations, carries the burden of proof with respect to those allegations. He or she has made a positive claim and must prove to the jury that the defendant actually did what the plaintiff has alleged. The defendant, on the other hand, need not prove anything. He carries what is known as the benefit of assumption, meaning he needs no evidence to support his denial of the allegations. In a criminal case, you have surely heard that the defendant is *presumed innocent* and must be *proven guilty*. This is because the criminal defendant, like the civil defendant, carries the benefit of assumption.

The *level* of proof necessary for the plaintiff to win is known as the standard of proof. This measure considers both the quality and quantity of the evidence. Different types of cases have different standards of proof. Two common and well-known standards are "beyond a reasonable doubt," which applies in most criminal cases, and "preponderance of the evidence," which is more common in civil cases. The different standards reflect the degree of concern collectively placed by society on the jury reaching the wrong result. We are less troubled with the wrong person paying a monetary judgment than with the wrong person losing their freedom or, sometimes, their life.

For a criminal defendant to be convicted of a crime, the prosecutor must prove her case to the point that the jurors have *no reasonable doubt in their minds* that the defendant did whatever he is charged with having done. Some doubt is inevitable because almost nothing can be proven with 100 percent certainty, and even in the strongest of cases there remains a theoretical possibility the defendant is innocent. This standard is designed to ensure the jury members are *reasonably certain* of the defendant's guilt. For example, while I am at work, I am reasonably certain my car is where I parked it that morning. Unless I regularly park in an area with an unusually high number of car thefts, it is not reasonable for me to insist on checking every hour to determine if my car is still there.

Preponderance of the evidence, the standard in most civil cases, means that the plaintiff must show it is *more likely than not* that her contention is true. Assume your two best friends come to you to settle a dispute. They

each present you with a different version of events that seems equally credible. There is, however, something you can't quite put your finger on in *the
way* one of your friends tells their story that makes her seem more credible
and thus tips the scales *ever so slightly* in her favor. That friend has established her case by a preponderance of the evidence. It has been said that
when two positions are equally weighted, a feather on the scale of either
position will satisfy the preponderance standard.

Civil claims and criminal charges are composed of *elements* that must
each be satisfied by the applicable standard if the plaintiff or prosecution is
to prevail. Assume a civil case in which the plaintiff alleges that the defendant's dog attacked and caused her serious injuries. The plaintiff, bearing
the burden of proof, must prove that (1) she was attacked by a dog, (2) the
dog belonged to the defendant, *and* (3) she suffered damages because of
the dog attack. On each point, she must present some affirmative evidence.

The first and third points could probably be established through the
plaintiff's own testimony, but the second—the ownership of this dog—will
most likely have to be established by testimony from someone else because
she would be unlikely to know of the dog's ownership. If she cannot find
someone with such knowledge willing to testify at her trial, then she will be
unable to satisfy her burden of proof on this issue, and she will lose the case.
While the defendant may present his own affirmative proof to rebut each
element of the plaintiff's case, he is not required to. If he doesn't believe
the plaintiff has enough evidence to convince the jury that each element is
likely, then he can sit silently, offering nothing in defense, and still prevail.

So what happens if the jury finds that both sides of an argument are
equally likely? For instance, what if the jury finds it is just as likely that the
defendant owned the dog as that he did not? This might occur if both sides
present a witness on this issue, the witnesses directly contradict each other,
and they are equally credible. In such a case, the defendant wins by default
because the plaintiff could not carry her burden of proof. A 50–50 tie goes
to the defendant.

The burden of proof is perhaps clearer in the criminal context applying
a reasonable-doubt standard. In such a case, the prosecution might present a mountain of evidence establishing the defendant's guilt. The jury
members may all believe that it is more likely than not that the defendant
committed this crime, but some or all may harbor doubts they believe to be
reasonable. In such a case, the jury is required by the law to render a "not
guilty" verdict because the prosecution has not met its burden of proof. The
prosecution's case was convincing but not convincing enough to meet the
higher standard.

So why must one party bear the burden of proof? An established legal maxim states, "The proof lies upon him who affirms, not upon him who denies; since, by the nature of things, he who denies a fact cannot produce any proof."[2] In other words, the one making the claim must bear the burden of proof because he is making the positive assertion, and one generally cannot prove a negative.

If someone alleged that you spread a lie about him, how could you definitively prove that you didn't? Assume that everyone agrees the lie was started and spread, but a serious dispute exists over who started it. You would need to round up every person you *could have spoken with* during this period and have each testify that you didn't tell them the lie. It would be virtually impossible to "prove" your innocence in this way because it could always be argued that you missed someone who might have heard the lie from you and passed it on.

By placing the burden on the one making the claim against you, he need produce only one person to testify that you told her the lie for a jury to find you guilty of the offense. If he can find no such person, then he cannot prevail. It is more reasonable to require the person making the allegation to produce evidence supporting it than the person denying the allegation to produce evidence negating it. Here, you can see how if neither of you can produce any evidence to support your claims, then you *should* be found innocent.

These are core principles of legal jurisprudence, not only in America, but also in developed countries throughout the world. There is little serious debate regarding the requirement or proper allocation of the burden of proof in legal proceedings.[3] Conservatives and liberals the world over typically agree.

SCIENTIFIC STANDARDS

The scientific method consists of the use of procedures designed to show not that our predictions and hypotheses are right, but that they might be wrong. Scientific reasoning is useful to anyone in any job because it makes us face the possibility, even the dire reality, that we were mistaken. It forces us to confront our self-justifications and put them on public display for others to puncture. At its core, therefore, science is a form of arrogance control.

—Carol Tavris, *Mistakes Were Made But Not By Me*

Men become civilized, not in proportion to their willingness to believe, but in proportion to their readiness to doubt.

—H. L. Mencken, *H. L. Mencken on Religion*

Science, like the law, is regularly confronted with competing claims to the truth. One person may claim that the Earth revolves around the Sun, while another may say the Sun revolves around the Earth. Science employs tools and standards analogous to those discussed in the legal context but also different, given the types of claims and evidence involved, the means available to test them, and the nature of scientific endeavors.

The first question we must answer is, What is science? The Oxford Dictionary defines it as the "intellectual and practical activity encompassing the systematic study of the structure and behavior of the physical and natural world through observation and experiment."[4] Systematic study is that which operates methodically, according to structure, reason, and logic. The purpose of science is to obtain, develop, and refine knowledge of the universe. Science does this through the collection and analysis of evidence; applying reason; observation and experiment; and the search for consistent, repeatable patterns.

Many people mistakenly look at science as a body of "facts" that cannot be questioned. Nothing could be further from the truth. Science is instead an *approach to resolving questions* about the world we experience. Science has no agenda other than revealing reality and uncovering mystery. Its conclusions are always provisional, never set in stone. It has no inherent direction other than the systematic elimination of propositions that are not true. It is officially agnostic on gods and religions. It is simply a tool, a process—but the best one mankind has ever developed for revealing Truth with a capital *T*.

When we talk about evidence in the scientific context, we mean something slightly different from in the legal one. Specifically, we are talking about *empirical evidence*, which is that which comes from sensory experience. This does not include a priori reasoning, intuition, or revelation, all of which are discussed later in this book. Scientific evidence is that which is equally accessible to the objective observer. You and I can discuss it intelligently from a common reference point because we share the same sensory mechanisms and have access to the same general pool of experience.

Also, when we talk about proof, we do not necessarily mean definitive proof that renders any competing hypothesis a logical impossibility; rather, we mean evidence so compelling that you would bet your life's savings on it. To say that science has "proven" the existence of gravity means that the evidence from many fields has converged so consistently in support of the phenomenon that it would be unreasonable to deny that gravity exists. Even that doesn't necessarily mean we fully understand gravity, but we can say with reasonable certainty it is there.

While science is, like the legal system, concerned with the value of the information it uses to form its conclusions, there is no judge assigned to evaluate that information and determine how it should be valued or weighted. Science as a discipline has had to develop its own standards by trial and error. In this way, science has organically arrived at a process of analysis and validation that represents one of the greatest achievements of mankind: the scientific method.

A. The Scientific Method

In modern use, *science* has become synonymous with *scientific method*. The Oxford Dictionary defines *scientific method* as a "method of procedure . . . consisting in systematic observation, measurement, and experiment, and the formulation, testing, and modification of hypotheses."[5] Wikipedia explains the distinguishing features of scientific methods of inquiry:

> The chief characteristic which distinguishes a scientific method of inquiry from other methods of acquiring knowledge is that scientists seek to let reality speak for itself, supporting a theory when a theory's predictions are confirmed and challenging a theory when its predictions prove false. Although procedures vary from one field of inquiry to another, identifiable features distinguish scientific inquiry from other methods of obtaining knowledge. Scientific researchers propose hypotheses as explanations of phenomena, and design experimental studies to test these hypotheses via predictions which can be derived from them. These steps must be repeatable, to guard against mistake or confusion in any particular experimenter. Theories that encompass wider domains of inquiry may bind many independently derived hypotheses together in a coherent, supportive structure. Theories, in turn, may help form new hypotheses or place groups of hypotheses into context.[6]

The scientific method is a way of learning about the nature of the universe by testing competing claims. For instance, Bob claims that a coin will rise when you release it, but Fred claims it will fall; this is a testable claim. One could easily devise an experiment to test the claim, such as dropping several coins and seeing what they do. If the coins remained motionless or moved side to side, neither claim would be supported by the experiment.

Assume that five coins are tested and all fall. Would this experiment conclusively prove that all coins fall when dropped? Certainly not, but because the results of the experiment are consistent with Fred's claim and inconsistent with Bob's, the experiment would give you a basis for believing that Fred's claim is more likely correct. You might, however, acknowledge that five coins is not enough to definitively test Fred's claim, so your belief is provisional—it is subject to change pending disconfirming evidence.

What would you need to do to strengthen your provisional belief? You would probably want to drop more coins—perhaps hundreds or even thousands. You might want to drop coins of different sizes and weights. You might want to drop them from different heights and different locations. These would further test Fred's claim, which is referred to in science as a hypothesis.

As each test yields consistent results—that is, if the coins all fall when dropped—then your confidence in Fred's hypothesis becomes steadily stronger. If, after millions of tests, the coins have fallen in *every test*, regardless of size or location, then your confidence can be said to be very strong. But have you proven Fred's hypothesis *conclusively*? Can you now say that "all released coins will fall" is a *fact* in which we can have *100 percent confidence*?

From a scientific standpoint, you have not and probably never can. The reason is that all hypotheses, no matter how consistent the data supporting them, are always provisional because they are always subject to revision. If a new test yields an inconsistent result, the hypothesis has potentially been undermined.

What if, for example, a researcher, Joe, after testing Fred's hypothesis, reports that a coin rose upward in one test? This would appear to be an anomaly because it conflicts with the results of all the other tests. In such a case, two possibilities exist: Either (1) a plausible explanation for the anomaly must be found that remains consistent with the hypothesis, or (2) the hypothesis must be revised. Where no plausible hypothesis can be derived that is consistent with our observations, we may need to abandon Fred's hypothesis entirely and start over with a new one.

So what are plausible explanations that might account for the object rising in Joe's tests? Perhaps Joe was innocently mistaken. You would need to assess the reliability of Joe's report. Alternatively, Joe might have deliberately falsified his findings. Perhaps Joe had a bias or other strong motivation to show that Fred's hypothesis was wrong. One way to assess such a thing is to attempt to replicate the test under conditions as close as possible to Joe's tests. If other researchers cannot replicate Joe's results, then there is reason to believe the initial results were innocent mistakes or deliberate frauds.

If years of testing yield consistent results, at some point your confidence in Fred's hypothesis becomes sufficiently strong that you are justified in treating it as a fact *for all practical purposes*. You may have recognized the similarity between our assurance and the reasonable-doubt standard of criminal law. Another way to express our confidence in Fred's hypothesis would be to say we are reasonably certain, or assured beyond a reasonable doubt, that Fred is correct.

While you may not be 100 percent sure, you are 99.99 percent sure, and that may be close enough to proceed assuming Fred's hypothesis to be true. If Fred's hypothesis continues to accurately predict all situations in which coins are released, that lends further credence and support. In such a case, your limited resources would probably be better spent testing other hypotheses with less support than Fred's. This is how science works. Scientists test hypotheses for validity by subjecting them to increasingly refined challenges.

The scientific process includes several features that work together to account for human mistakes and ensure accurate results. One of these is the peer-review process. Scientists who have conducted tests with significant or surprising results are encouraged to publish those results, along with their data and methodology, in respected scientific journals. Anyone reading the journal then has the tools to review and critique the tests and results. The more widely accepted the successfully tested hypothesis, the bigger name the scientist can make for him- or herself by demonstrating flaws in the testing that might lead to refutation of the hypothesis.

In relation to the previous example, assume that Fred publishes the results of thousands of tests supporting his hypothesis that coins fall downward when dropped. You are also a scientist, and when you read Fred's description of his tests and results, you immediately see a flaw in the design of his tests. You see that Fred failed to consider that all his tests occurred within the atmosphere of Earth, where there may be some force at work that wouldn't be present, say, in outer space. You propose a test to see if coins fall "downward" outside of Earth's atmosphere. If that test reveals that the coins don't fall downward when dropped in outer space, then you have pointed out an interesting exception to Fred's hypothesis that would likely yield better insights into gravity.

Likewise, if Joe published *his* findings in a scientific journal, you might discover that Joe conducted all his tests with steel coins in the presence of a superpowerful electromagnet in the ceiling. You propose this magnetic field could be the reason that the coins in Joe's experiments moved upward. This would again yield useful information explaining why Joe's tests didn't invalidate Fred's hypothesis.

Cognitive scientist Valerie Tarico explains,

> Our brains have built-in biases that stack the odds against objectivity, so much so that the success of the scientific endeavor can be attributed to one factor: it pits itself against our natural leanings, erects barriers across the openings to rabbit trails, and systematically exposes faulty thinking to public critique. In fact, the scientific method has been called "what we know about how not to fool ourselves."[7]

The scientific method has been designed specifically to minimize the error inherent in every human enterprise. That doesn't mean it eliminates all such error, but by openly acknowledging these problems and proactively addressing them, it goes further than any other system in removing them from the process.

Tarico also explains how science picks up where philosophy leaves off. Philosophy attempts to prove things by logic only. While logic is necessary for a successful argument, it is rarely sufficient, for a logical argument is only as valid as its premises and underlying assumptions. Even the most logically airtight argument will not be persuasive if its assumptions are faulty. Science confers validity on those theories that work. Biologist P. Z. Myers often tells the following parable:

> A philosopher designs a marvelous sausage machine. A scientist comes to marvel at this creation, and raises an eyebrow. The philosopher says, "Ah, behold the wonderful cogs and sprockets and temperature-controlled mixing chambers in my wonderful machine. Surely you can see how it must produce the most fantastic sausages!" The scientists says "Yes, that is all very interesting. Show me the sausages."[8]

Philosophers can endlessly pontificate, but scientists need to see the sausages.

B. Hypotheses and Theories

The scientific method works by comparing and contrasting hypotheses, which begin as guesses about how something works. These are subjected to ever more demanding proofs, which, outside the fields of mathematics and logic, refers to testing.[9] As the hypothesis makes its way through the scientific process, with more experiments yielding supporting results, the hypothesis grows ever stronger and more robust. It is entitled to increasing confidence that it represents reality. Often, robust hypotheses can reveal a bigger picture, like pieces in a jigsaw puzzle. This evolving puzzle represents a theory, which also grows stronger and more robust as additional pieces fill in the holes.

Science progresses not by proving things correct but by disproving the alternatives to those things. The scientific process works like a ratchet wrench, building on the strength of previously successful hypotheses and theories to increase understanding of the natural world. Each turn of the wrench involves testing new hypotheses and discarding what fails the tests. In this way, the scientist gradually strips away what doesn't belong to reveal what does. The key to the process is reliably identifying the good from bad hypotheses through testing. For the ratchets to take hold, the hypothesis must be falsifiable.

A falsifiable hypothesis is one that scientists can assess for value. It is clear, unambiguous, and precise in wording. It allows for specific predictions to be made that can then be verified by objective observers. In ideal cases, the phenomenon is observable and repeatable, though this is not necessary. In short, there is some mechanism by which everyone can agree, "That hypothesis is a good one."

The late Carl Sagan demonstrates the importance of falsifiability with his story "The Dragon in My Garage," in which he begins by positing that he has told you that a fire-breathing dragon lives in his garage:

> Surely you'd want to check it out, see for yourself. There have been innumerable stories of dragons over the centuries, but no real evidence. What an opportunity! "Show me," you say. I lead you to my garage. You look inside and see a ladder, empty paint cans, an old tricycle—but no dragon.
>
> "Where's the dragon?" you ask. "Oh, she's right here," I reply, waving vaguely. "I neglected to mention that she's an invisible dragon." You propose spreading flour on the floor of the garage to capture the dragon's footprints. "Good idea," I say, "but this dragon floats in the air."
>
> Then you'll use an infrared sensor to detect the invisible fire. "Good idea, but the invisible fire is also heatless." You'll spray-paint the dragon and make her visible. "Good idea, but she's an incorporeal dragon and the paint won't stick." And so on. I counter every physical test you propose with a special explanation of why it won't work.
>
> Now, what's the difference between an invisible, incorporeal, floating dragon who spits heatless fire and no dragon at all? If there's no way to disprove my contention, no conceivable experiment that would count against it, what does it mean to say that my dragon exists? Your inability to invalidate my hypothesis is not at all the same thing as proving it true. Claims that cannot be tested, assertions immune to disproof are veridically worthless, whatever value they may have in inspiring us or in exciting our sense of wonder. What

I'm asking you to do comes down to believing, in the absence of evidence, on my say-so.[10]

A nonfalsifiable hypothesis is worthless from a scientific perspective. What cannot be assessed for value must be assigned a value of zero in scientific deliberations. It plays no part in the ratcheting process, for no reliable foundation can be built on it. It can be safely ignored by science because it has no measurable impact on anything science studies.

With each test passed, each falsification attempt successfully navigated, and each line of supporting evidence, a hypothesis gains *epistemic weight*. Our justification for accepting it grows increasingly stronger. The higher the epistemic weight, the more confident we can be that the hypothesis accurately reflects reality. All nonfalsifiable claims, by contrast, have epistemic weights of zero. They float about like wraiths, with no mass or substance.

When robust hypotheses begin to consistently interlock into a tapestry of broader scope, a scientific theory comes into being. This occurs when different lines of evidence converge to support the same model of reality. When, for example, fossil evidence, genetic evidence, and anatomical evidence all appear to tell the same story regarding speciation, like separate strands combining into a strong rope, science recognizes the existence of a theory—in this case, evolution. The cumulative force of converging lines of evidence from unrelated sources and disciplines all leading to the same answer is known as consilience. A valid theory requires consilience.

Science prefers theories to be precise, predictive, and minimal, requiring the smallest amount of theoretical overhead. It is often not enough for a theory to explain past evidence or to explain things in a way that is convoluted or requires many unproven assumptions. Such theories are likely to be replaced by more elegant and streamlined ones, theories that allow us to forecast things we otherwise could not have known. These confirmed predictions give us ever greater confidence that the theory we've chosen is the correct one. Unsuccessful theories are never definitively disproven, as ad hoc explanations can always be concocted to save them. They simply fade into obsolescence as better theories gain acceptance.

To summarize, a scientific theory is expected to be

- consistent with other findings and disciplines, demonstrating consilience;
- parsimonious (see Ockham's razor, discussed later herein);
- useful (describes and explains observed phenomena and can be used to make predictions);

- empirically testable and falsifiable (see earlier);
- based on multiple observations (preferably in controlled, repeatable experiments);
- correctable and dynamic (can be modified given inconsistent observations);
- progressive (refines or corrects previous hypotheses and theories); and
- provisional or tentative (invites additional testing and does not assert certainty).

To be scientific, a theory must meet most, and ideally all, these criteria.[11] The more it meets, the better theory it is likely to be. Renowned physicist Richard Feynman gave the following example:

> If someone were to propose that the planets go around the sun because all planet matter has a kind of tendency for movement, a kind of motility, let us call it an "oomph," this theory could explain a number of other phenomena as well. So this is a good theory, is it not? No. It is nowhere near as good as the proposition that the planets move around the sun under the influence of a central force which varies exactly inversely as the square of the distance from the center. The second theory is better because it is so specific; it is so obviously unlikely to be the result of chance. It is so definite that the barest error in the movement can show that it is wrong; but the planets could wobble all over the place, and, according to the first theory, you could say, "Well, that is the funny behavior of the 'oomph.'"[12]

At some point, a consensus develops among scientists with relevant expertise. This means the theoretical model has successfully passed through the stringent scientific gauntlet and emerged unscathed from the other side. It means the model has, accordingly, earned the confidence of the relevant scientific community, representing the product of thousands of successful experiments and an enormous investment of brain power. It is no longer controversial among those with the appropriate knowledge and expertise. The scientific consensus cannot be treated as just another opinion among the noise. It is of a different character altogether. It is something of which we can be reasonably certain, treating it for all practical purposes as fact.[13]

This does not mean that the theory is complete or that it cannot evolve. Because theories generally cover a broad range of phenomena with a limited set of data points, additional data will always provide increased resolution. While one could arguably say the new data points rendered the old image wrong, it is not the type of wrong that justifies dismissing the theory. As explained by science fiction writer Isaac Asimov,

> In short, my English Lit friend, living in a mental world of absolute rights and wrongs, may be imagining that because all theories are wrong, the earth may be thought spherical now, but cubical next century, a hollow icosahedron the next, and a doughnut shape the one after. What actually happens is that once scientists get hold of a good concept they gradually refine and extend it with greater and greater subtlety as their instruments of measurement improve. Theories are not so much wrong as incomplete. . . . When people thought the earth was flat, they were wrong. When people thought the earth was spherical, they were wrong. But if you think that thinking the earth is spherical is just as wrong as thinking the earth is flat, then your view is wronger than both of them put together.[14]

In light of these considerations, scientists characteristically disdain the language of certainty even when speaking of robust theories. If you asked a layperson whether fairies exist, they would probably say, "No." But a scientist might say something more like, "I attach a very low probability to the existence of fairies," which doesn't answer the question but technically describes his position. This is simply the language of science, in which virtually nothing is categorically ruled out, no matter how improbable.

Scientists do not require absolute certainty. They simply develop models based on the best evidence available. So long as those models succeed, allowing us to make accurate predictions, they are considered worthy of tentative acceptance. Any model is always in danger, however, of being replaced by a better model. Through this process of comparing models, science advances. Bertrand Russell observes, "Science does not aim at establishing immutable truths and eternal dogmas; its aim is to approach the truth by successive approximations, without claiming that at any stage final and complete accuracy has been achieved."[15] In science, you are always trying to discover the truth. If you believe you know the truth, there is no role for science.

C. Science and Religion

While the value of the scientific method may seem fairly obvious today, it was not commonly employed until the late 1800s. Before that, there was no consistent way to test claims about the universe. There were millions of competing claims with no agreed-upon method to distinguish between

them. Religion was commonly accepted as the source of reliable explanations of natural phenomena, and where people's religions reached different
conclusions, there was little hope of resolution. Further progress on the
issue stood at a standstill.

Science and the methodology it employs changed all that. It allowed for
unprecedented advancement in many areas, including engineering and
medicine. Science's track record since then in uncovering the nature of the
universe is light-years ahead of any competitor. If we went about comparing
religion to science with intellectual honesty, we would determine what kind
of universe we would expect to live in if theism were true; then we would
do the same for the proposition that theism is false; and finally, we would
compare these two expectations to the universe we observe. But when we
do this, we find the theist models to lose out to the scientific ones time and
again.

Science begins with the fundamental presumption that nature operates
according to uniform laws. Our ability to control and use nature to our
benefit rests squarely on the truth of this presumption. It is verified every
minute of every day through the results of millions of scientific experiments
and observations. The presumption allows us to observe local phenomena,
make generalizations about it, and fashion and test predictive models that
can then be applied to similar phenomena elsewhere. Religion, by contrast,
requires accepting revelation that rests on the presumption that nature is
anything but uniform. With religion, truth is not discovered through observation and testing but through trust that certain ancient people claiming to
speak for invisible beings were sane, sincere, and correct. Gods, angels, and
other celestial minions constantly move in and out of our reality to tweak or
disturb the otherwise systematic flow of nature to bring about their desires.

Science is characterized by skepticism and a dispassionate weighing of
the evidence. It insists that all conclusions be evidence based, testable, falsifiable, published, and challenged. Science establishes facts by rigorously
trying to disprove them. Evolutionary biologist Jerry Coyne described his
introduction to the serious study of science as he entered his PhD program
at Harvard:

> Shy and reserved, I felt as if I'd been hurled in to a pit of unrelenting nega-
> tivity. In research seminars, the audience seemed determined to dismantle
> the credibility of the speaker. Sometimes they wouldn't even wait until the
> question period after the talk, but would rudely shout out critical questions
> and comments during the talk itself. When I thought I had a good idea and
> tentatively described it to my fellow graduate students, it was picked apart

like a flounder on a plate. And when we all discussed science around the big rectangular table in our commons room, the atmosphere was heated and contentious. Every piece of work, published or otherwise, was scrutinized for problems—problems that were almost always found. . . . Like Michelangelo's sculpturing, which he saw as eliminating marble to reveal the statue within, the critical scrutiny of scientific ideas and experiments is designed, by eliminating error, to find the core of truth in an idea.[16]

Science only proceeds by finding error in previously popular or accepted explanations. This is where all the glory is. Enrico Fermi notes about scientific experiments, "There are two possible outcomes: if the result confirms the hypothesis, then you've made a measurement. If the result is contrary to the hypothesis, then you've made a discovery."[17]

Religion is characterized by unwavering certitude and a passionate defense of belief. It insists its beliefs be accepted on faith but then attempts to validate those beliefs by citing any corroborating scientific observations while discounting, dismissing, or ignoring evidence to the contrary. Science and religion are different, in short, because only one incorporates a method by which to know it is wrong.

Science and religion come at the big questions from very different perspectives. Scientists construct models of reality and rigorously test those models against their observations. If the models pass all the tests, then they are accorded provisional acceptance and may then be used to generate other hypotheses or models. If at any point the model fails a test and the failure cannot be explained or accounted for, then the model must be abandoned. Accordingly, science is self-correcting. While this method will never provide complete Truth with a capital *T*, it provides us with increasingly accurate *approximations* of the Truth. Central to the concept of hypothesis testing is the underlying premise that the entire universe is natural and available, at least in principle, for human investigation. If one accepts this premise, then explanations are possible within the natural order through entirely human agency.

Rather than the bottom-up approach of science, the major religions come at the problem from the top down. They begin by treating as sacred some ancient texts. Those texts are considered the first and last word on any subject within their scope, including any issue concerning the nature of the universe. The texts are necessary because, from the supernatural paradigm of most religions, reality is presumptively not amenable to human explanation. The material world can only be explained by understanding a spiritual realm undetectable to human agency, and the Scripture is presumed the only reliable guide to that spiritual realm.

Scientific belief changes over time but remains static as to space, while religious belief changes over space but is static over time. In other words, scientific consensus evolves over time, but that evolution remains consistent among scientists all over the world. Religious belief changes from group to group and place to place but within any such group changes little over time. That is because scientific belief responds to evidence, while religious belief does not. George Bernard Shaw quipped, "What is wrong with priests and popes is that instead of being apostles and saints, they are nothing but empirics who say 'I know' instead of 'I am learning,' and pray for credulity and inertia as wise men pray for skepticism and activity."

Unlike in science, where no writing or conclusion is ever considered the final word and all are subject to modification if contradicted by reliable observation and experience, religious texts are not to be questioned. They begin with an irrefutable presumption of accuracy to which reality must conform. The problem with this approach is recognized by Arthur Conan Doyle, who writes for his character Sherlock Holmes, "It is a capital mistake to theorize before one has data. Insensibly one begins to twist facts to suit theories, instead of theories to suit facts."[18]

From the fifth century CE, when the church closed the Schools of Athens for teaching philosophy, right up through the seventeenth century, religion took the view it was right and science was wrong. Anyone who disagreed was considered a heretic, many of whom, such as Giordano Bruno, were put to death by the church. Others, such as Galileo, were only *threatened* with death. Luckily for him, Galileo escaped by recanting his groundbreaking scientific discoveries and conclusions. Luckily for us, they were preserved, to the benefit of the entire world.

Most of the scientific progress between the fifth and seventeenth centuries was in the Arabic world rather than the Christian one. Muhammad ibn Musa al Khwarizmi (780–850 CE) of Baghdad is credited with inventing algebra and the algorithm, both Arabic words. Hasan Ibn al-Haytham, known as Alhazen (d. 1040), of Cairo is among the first scientists to explicitly lay out the scientific method of hypothesis and experimentation and also the first to explain optics as light bouncing off an object and hitting the eye. Geometry was first used to solve algebraic equations by Omar Khayyam (d. 1131) of Iran. The Maragha Observatory in Iran made significant breakthroughs in planetary motion during the 1200s. Persian mathematician Ibn Sina (known as Avicenna) produced a medical textbook (c. 1012) that was translated from Arabic to Latin and used in European medical schools through the early 1700s. He is known as the father of early modern medicine and regarded as one of the most significant writers of the Islamic golden age.

Meanwhile, Christian churches were trudging through the Dark Ages, brutally suppressing open inquiry and science for religious dogma. It was only in the 1600s that the combination of the Renaissance focus on Greek learning and the movable-type printing press allowed renewed scientific discovery to flourish and spread in the Christian world. The Enlightenment of the mid-1700s allowed even freer inquiry. Though weakened in status, Catholic and Protestant churches continued to challenge any scientific discovery that conflicted with Scripture.

Even today, many Christian churches appear to be openly at war with science. Denominations refusing to adapt their beliefs to incorporate scientific discoveries find little choice but to attack science *as an enterprise*, claiming it to be, for example, just another worldview with no more legitimacy than embracing Norse mythology. If scientists reached a conclusion that supported their religious claims, they would be the first to trumpet that finding to the world. It is not science itself with which such denominations have a problem but the absence of validation from science.

Only relatively recently have the doctrines of some churches given up ground to scientific conclusions that appear to contradict scriptural passages, though only in those areas in which scientific theories have become robust and a strong consensus has formed so continuing to deny them would cause embarrassment and ridicule. Accordingly, most mainline Christian churches now accept evolution as a fact, though in a modified form, inexplicable to evolutionary biologists, that shoehorns in a place for undetectable divine guidance.[19] Many churches have attempted to harmonize the scientific findings with their Scriptures, with varying degrees of success.

The main point, however, is that religions get their Truth from Scripture and divine revelation, while scientists get their truth from analyzing observations and experiences. Scientists regularly change their models based on new information. Religions never change their scriptures or admit them to be in error. Scientists will read hundreds of books and still acknowledge they know very little about the universe. Many Christians will tell you they know everything of importance after reading just one.

Religion can be thought of as failed science. Despite thousands of years of religious explanations, none could hold a candle to those that developed once science took the wheel. Science came along and demonstrated how inadequate religion was at doing the primary job it had carved out for itself—explaining the natural world. This is why naturalism has pulled so far ahead of theism in the race to accurately model the universe.

If one's religion is based on claims of divine revelation—something anyone can claim and no one can ever conclusively refute—then it's virtually impossible to win an argument about who is right and who is wrong. Compare that to science, which is based on evidence and things that can be proven and, more important, disproven. Scientific investigation always converges on solutions, while as history shows, religious investigations lead to ever greater divergence. That is why there are 41,000 Christian denominations but not 41,000 versions of the theory of evolution or 41,000 scientific explanations for how the Sun produces energy.

Science yields stable truths that can be confirmed by anyone with the right equipment because they are based on repeatable patterns. Unlike religious "truths," scientific truths are often discovered independently, for the information supporting them is available to all. Who among us can verify that Paul had the correct understanding of grace and its connection to salvation? Any toddler, by contrast, can discover for him- or herself the concept of gravity. Penn Jillette observes, "If every trace of any single religion were wiped out and nothing were passed on, it would never be created exactly the same way again. There might be some other nonsense in its place, but not that exact nonsense. If all of science were wiped out, it would still be true and someone would find a way to figure it all out again."[20] Science was just waiting for people to discover it.

Whenever scientists have made important discoveries over the past four centuries, they have done so by ignoring God. The first accurate model of the celestial mechanics in our solar system was constructed by Pierre-Simon Laplace in 1799. Laplace's model overturned that of no less a figure than Isaac Newton, whose own model had allowed for periodic divine intervention to maintain stability. When Napoleon, upon hearing that Laplace's work made no reference to God, inquired how this could be, Laplace reportedly answered, "Sire, I had no need of that hypothesis." This has been the position of the scientific community ever since. Biologist J. B. S. Haldane cogently observes the following in relation to his own work: "My practice as a scientist is atheistic. That is to say, when I set up an experiment I assume that no god, angel or devil is going to interfere with its course; and this assumption has been justified by such success as I have achieved in my professional career. I should therefore be intellectually dishonest if I were not also atheistic in the affairs of the world."[21]

While science has yielded millions of significant insights into the nature of the world, religion has yielded exactly *none*. Physicist Steven Weinberg remarks on the joys of science, "[E]very once in a while someone finds a way of explaining some phenomenon that fits so well and clarifies so much that it gives the finder intense satisfaction, especially when new understanding is quantitative, and observation bears it out in detail."[22] This is a feeling never experienced by a theologian. Scientists have an advantage over religious mystics for the same reason computer manufacturers have one over crystal-ball makers—because computers work, and what works wins. As magician and paranormal investigator James Randi observes, "Science is best defined as a careful, disciplined, logical search for knowledge about any and all aspects of the universe, obtained by examination of the best available evidence and always subject to correction and improvement upon discovery of better evidence. What's left is magic. And it doesn't work."[23]

Science and religion are compatible only in the sense that religion occasionally relaxes its doctrinal positions to accommodate scientific conclusions so well established that continuing to ignore them would be profoundly humiliating. Their basic methods of determining truth and analyzing the world are inherently incompatible. Everywhere that science and education have advanced, religion has dwindled in influence. Where it retains a hold on the lives of people in more advanced and educated societies, it almost always does so in a much-modified form to make it more consistent with modern social norms and scientific understanding.

Given all this, it should be no surprise that American scientists are ten times more likely to be atheists than other Americans, a disparity that has persisted throughout more than eighty years of polling.[24] As we look at increasingly more accomplished scientists, the gap only widens. At elite research universities, an additional 20 percent of scientists lack any theistic belief. The crème de la crème of American scientists is represented by the National Academy of Sciences, where 93 *percent* are atheists or agnostics.[25] The better the scientist, the greater the likelihood they will be an atheist.

The most parsimonious explanation for this is that when one understands and applies the methods of science to their investigation of the world, it leads them to reject religious claims. Given science's successful history of distinguishing true claims from false ones, this sobering information should cause religious believers to pause before giving the claims of their own faiths the benefit of the doubt. At a minimum, it should demonstrate there is a wide disparity between how these claims are treated by science and religion. Science and religion employ different ways of coming to knowledge of reality and different ways of assessing the reliability of that information, which is why they ultimately arrive at different conclusions.

HISTORICAL STANDARDS

> Those of us who write and study history are accustomed to its approxi-
> mations and ambiguities. This is why we do not take literally the tenth-
> hand reports of frightened and illiterate peasants who claim to have seen
> miracles or to have had encounters with messiahs and prophets and
> redeemers who were, like them, mere humans.
>
> —Christopher Hitchens

Historians are engaged in an enterprise that rarely lends itself to even the approximate certainty possible with science. Historians often lack objective physical evidence and are forced to rely to some extent on reported testimony, which can be highly problematic. Rarely can they subject their hypotheses to testing or verify predictions their theories would suggest. They are typically forced to make guesses based on spotty information of questionable reliability. Under these less-than-ideal conditions, historians have developed their own standards for determining what actually happened.

The standards applied by historians are necessarily more subjective than those employed by scientists, especially where physical evidence is scarce or entirely lacking. Historians must often interpret ambiguous information and choose which among conflicting pieces of evidence to favor. Accordingly, their own preconceptions are likely to play a far greater role than among scientists in coloring their conclusions. Unlike in science, in which agreement regarding basic standards is virtually universal, disagreement among historians is ubiquitous. It is not so much the standards themselves that garner disagreement as the relative weight assigned to each and in what circumstances.

Historians are on firmer ground when they can point to objective evidence, such as dating pottery shards, in which scientific technology and methodology can play a part. Much of their work, however, necessarily depends on the writings of others, which are inherently plagued with issues of reliability, especially as we go further back in time and confirming accounts are unavailable. For this book, the relevant standards are those employed by historians *of antiquity*, where the issues discussed previously become especially troubling. Not only are firsthand witnesses unavailable, but so, too, are second-, third-, fourth-, and so on.

Historians of antiquity are often required to reach conclusions from isolated or conflicting written accounts by authors about which little or nothing additional is known. The modern genre of historical writing, in which writers attempt to present information as accurately and objectively as possible, is a recent invention. Ancient writers of history sought to accomplish many competing goals. For example, writers patronized by wealthy benefactors or governments, an exceedingly common practice, often glorified their benefactors and vilified their benefactors' enemies in their accounts. Historians have long recognized these cannot all be taken at face value.

While an exhaustive list of factors is impossible here, I briefly discuss three widely recognized among historians as valid considerations.

A. Multiple Independent Attestation

Where an event is described by multiple authors in unique, independent accounts and the accounts match on significant details, historians assign higher reliability to the matching details. The rationale should be fairly straightforward: Each story corroborates the other (at least on the common details), rendering it less likely that any one author was lying or mistaken.

There are two caveats to this factor. First, it must be clear that the accounts are in fact independent. If one copied from the other or they obtained their information from common sources, then they represent *dependent* accounts, with neither lending legitimacy to the other. To assess reliability, they should be treated as a single account.

Second, what we know of the authors should reflect no common bias that might lead them to provide inaccurate information. If two ancient writers were both known members of a political group that opposed a certain king, then historians would likely assign less weight than otherwise to their agreement that the king committed some atrocity, for they would share a common motivation to lie. With truly independent sources, whatever biases each may have should cancel each other out.

B. Principle of Dissimilarity

As briefly discussed earlier, historians openly acknowledge that ancient writers were regularly faced with competing interests that undermined their reliability. We might expect, for example, a writer commissioned by the king of France to present a rosier picture of the king's rule than his subjects actually experienced. When a writer we would expect to favor a certain spin on events reports something contrary to that expectation, historians are more likely to consider that report reliable. Why, after all, would this hypothetical French historian report the king having an embarrassing case of dysentery unless that actually happened? This is known as the principle of dissimilarity.

As with the first factor, however, historians must be cautious in applying this one. First, it assumes we know all the influences on the writer, so we can accurately predict their expected behavior. Rarely, in fact, do historians have this information. Second, it assumes we have such a clear understanding of surrounding circumstances that we can know whether the written account actually frustrates historical expectations. In the example of the French king, maybe dysentery was prevalent in the kingdom, and the historian fabricated an account of the king catching and then overcoming the illness to establish an empathetic connection to his subjects and demonstrate his hearty constitution. It is rarely a simple matter to reconstruct influences or expected biases long after the fact.

Good historians know to be cautious with dissimilarity and not accord it unwarranted weight. It is most helpful when we know much of the motivations of the writer from other sources. The Jewish historian Josephus, for example, is someone of whom we have a fair amount of biographical data, from which we can reasonably anticipate certain biases we would expect him to hold. The same could not be said of the typical anonymous writer for whom we have no biographical information. In such cases, dissimilarity becomes far less useful.

C. Principle of Analogy

Assume that you arrive home one afternoon and turn on the television. There you see a giant lizard rampaging through a Japanese city, destroying buildings with his fiery breath. Would you immediately assume you were watching *Headline News*? Probably not. Instead, you would likely assume someone had left the set on the Syfy Channel. Why? Because your day-to-day experience does not include newscasts of fire-breathing dinosaurs flattening modern cities, but it does include fictional "monster movies" in which such destruction is typical, even de rigueur.[26] Our conclusion is justified by drawing an analogy to our own experience.

Likewise, when faced with competing claims regarding an event, historians will prefer the claim that corresponds with their own collective experience. I would argue this is the most important factor because historical knowledge is only possible on the assumption that all events are, in principle, similar in nature. We assume that the way things work and the ways people behave are sufficiently similar that we can draw conclusions about the past from what we know of the present. All serious historical analysis ultimately draws on analogy.[27]

Historians are increasingly making use of a powerful mathematical formula of probability known as Bayes' theorem to evaluate competing historical claims. It is beyond the scope of this book to fully explain Bayes' theorem, but the principle of analogy plays a central role in determining an important component of the Bayes analysis: determining the prior probability of an event. Bayes' theorem requires us to begin with our background knowledge—our collective experience of how things work—to determine a prior probability for what we would expect to see in a particular situation. An explanation that fails the principle of analogy will always begin with a low prior probability, which will affect whether the historian will determine that claim to represent the best explanation.

When employing the principle of analogy, one must assess stories of ancient figures claim by claim. We can believe that Julius Caesar existed due to multiple contemporaneous accounts but rightly dismiss claims that he rode across the sky in a chariot of fire, even if found in those same accounts, because those claims fail the principle of analogy. We know that ancient sources commonly combined fact and fiction, history and legend. Our background knowledge tells us that flying chariots of fire would be, to put it mildly, extraordinary. Extraordinary claims require extraordinary evidence[28] and should be rejected when such evidence is lacking.

If I heard a historical account of a first-century rabbi giving sermons and having followers in Israel, I would probably find it a reasonable claim. It may or may not be totally accurate or even true at all, but I know it's at least plausible because it is consistent with my knowledge of reality. We know from multiple independent sources there were many such rabbis in Israel preaching the things rabbis preached about.

But if someone tells me that that same rabbi not only preached his religion but also walked on water, turned water into wine, raised the dead, and just happened to be God Himself in a logic-bending case of a god being his own son, well . . . those claims are quite a bit more far-fetched. I know that many people, including many people in my lifetime, have claimed to be miracle healers (such as Benny Hinn or Sathya Sai Baba), liaisons between the living and dead (John Edward), prophets, seers, sages, and all other manner of magical and mystical things. Few today consider their claims legitimate despite them being supported by contemporary eyewitness accounts. What plausible reason might I have to give biblical claims any more credence than I do these people? It needs to be evidence of a caliber far higher.

The corollary is that the frequency of incredible claims in our own time should rightly lead us to discount the reliability of any historical source to a proportional degree. As more and more claims from a particular source fail to satisfy the principle of analogy, we are justified in taking additional claims from that same source with an ever-growing grain (or even mountain) of salt. Just imagine a historical account that begins with a straightforward story of a young farmhand living with his aunt and uncle in the desert that then adds visits by strange wizards, flying spaceships, and laser swords. At some point, you would likely conclude that the account is not strictly historical and from that point on treat each succeeding fantastical claim less seriously, as well as the historical nature of the work as a whole.

D. Summary

These factors are by no means comprehensive. They should be sufficient, however, to demonstrate the difficulty historians face in reconstructing the ancient past. No historian of antiquity can justifiably profess "reasonable certainty" of any specific historical event, as that phrase is used by scientists, especially based on ancient writings alone. The quality and quantity of their evidence is simply not in the same ballpark and, accordingly, cannot warrant a similar degree of conviction. As the eighteenth-century theologian G. E. Lessing observed,

> We all believe that an Alexander lived who in a short time conquered almost all Asia. But who, on the basis of this belief, would risk anything of great, permanent worth, the loss of which would be irreparable? Who, in consequence of this belief, would forswear forever all knowledge that conflicted with this belief? Certainly not I. Now I have no objection to raise against Alexander and his victory: but it might still be possible that the story was founded on a mere poem of Choerilus just as the ten-year siege of Troy depends on no better authority than Homer's poetry.[29]

There are thousands of comparable claims throughout the historical record. Did Marco Polo really spend years in China as a confidante to Kublai Khan, or did he simply pick up fascinating tales on his journeys and weave them into a cohesive story? Did Plato make up Socrates as a literary device to illustrate his points? Was Robin Hood real? How about King Arthur?

This brief discussion should also clarify that no legitimate historian can begin with a preconception that any particular source is exceptionally reliable because it is the nature of the historian's job to assess the reliability of such sources. To say that any ancient source is inerrant or even divinely inspired, so it should be given special weight, is to step outside one's role as a historian and step into the role of devotional believer. All sources must be treated with the same skepticism and only trusted to the extent that trust is earned through independent verification. Assessing source reliability is an iterative process bound with the prior probability of the claims being made.

Likewise, it is rarely, if ever, warranted to treat any historical claim of the ancient world as certain. Our ancient sources aren't reliable enough to justify such certainty. To say I accept something as *historical* says nothing about how *certain* I am that it really happened. We tentatively accept many things simply because we have only one source, which supports the claim, and none to the contrary. Unless the prior probability for the event is low, the single source is sufficient reason to provisionally accept the event until we have additional information suggesting otherwise. But that doesn't mean we would bet substantial money that the claim is true. Our degree of certainty would depend on the reliability of the source, on confirming independent accounts, on dissimilarity, on analogy, and on other factors. The further back in time we go and the fewer sources we have, the less certain we would be—the less money we would bet on that account being factual. The factor looming perhaps largest in our analysis would be the prior probability, or plausibility, of the claim made.

When we look at stories about historical figures like George Washington, we are simply accepting what we have as the best evidence. We may acknowledge the potential for inaccuracy but still believe because the available evidence is the best we have. If new compelling evidence emerges to cause us to doubt certain claims made by or about George Washington, however, it would be unreasonable to hold dogmatically to our prior beliefs. We don't take our historical knowledge of George Washington to be absolute, infallible truth, and the further back we go in time, the less justified such certainty becomes.

Christianity, however, makes just such a claim regarding the historicity of Christ and the legitimacy of the biblical accounts. Even if more liberal Christians accept that there may be historically inaccurate pieces here and there, most of the fundamental claims—that Jesus was born of a virgin, performed miracles, died on a cross, rose from the dead, and ascended to heaven—are absolute pillars of the faith. Christians are expected to accept that these mystical claims are absolutely and infallibly true. Devout Christians could not imagine altering such major parts of the story, even if the evidence against them was overwhelming, because to do so would be to dismantle the pillars of the faith itself.

The pillars of Christianity are, for Christians, necessary truths. But due to the inherent unreliability of all historical truths, they can never be justified to nonbelievers as valid assumptions on which to premise a faith. This is the "ugly, broad ditch" of doubt spoken of by philosopher Gotthold Lessing that he could not cross.[30] Lessing explains,

> Miracles, which I see with my own eyes, and which I have opportunity to verify for myself, are one thing; miracles, of which I know only from history that others say they have seen them and verified them, are another. . . . But . . . I live in the 18th century, in which miracles no longer happen. The problem is that reports of miracles are not miracles. . . . [They] have to work through a medium which takes away all their force.[31]

For Lessing, the limitations of historical "knowledge" imposed an impenetrable barrier to accepting the very miracle claims that Christian theology demands one to accept as foundational "truths." These "religious truths" can never be established through historical inquiry.

If the consequences of mistaken belief are minimal, then we can make our best guess from the available historical evidence, step across the ditch, and move on. If the consequences are great, however, risking something of great value, then we must have very good reasons to step across the ditch, and "it would sure be nice to be on the other side" isn't such a reason.[32] The problem becomes even more acute when one can only reach the other side by climbing scaffolding that has been eroded away by critical historical and scientific scholarship. Once we recognize the deficiencies of that scaffolding, the wise choice is to exercise caution rather than unflinching certitude.

PHILOSOPHICAL STANDARDS

> All knowledge that is not the genuine product of observation, or the consequence of observation, is in fact utterly without foundation, and truly an illusion.
>
> —Jean-Baptiste Lamarck, *Systeme Analytique des connaissances positives de l'homme*

I began this discussion of standards with something specific and with which I hoped everyone could readily relate. I end it by discussing a topic that might seem esoteric but is nonetheless fundamental to the remainder of this book. Philosophy is the systematic study of what I call the "big issues," such as reality, existence, knowledge, values, reason, and mind. Philosophers attempt to break these into more manageable chunks and assess them from the ground up. They evaluate answers that have become popular and well established to determine whether those answers are logical and reasonable. Philosophy provides a rigorous framework for analyzing these issues, including mechanisms for identifying where one's reasoning is in error.

In this book, I am primarily concerned with the study of knowledge, which is known as epistemology. Epistemology derives rules leading to a reliable understanding of reality. Epistemological rules are analogous to the rules of evidence in the law. They serve the same function as a judge deciding what information is sufficiently trustworthy to go to the jury—what is actually useful and helpful in determining what is true. Epistemology tells us what's worth considering and what isn't.

Another field of philosophy that often arises in discussions of religion is ontology. Ontology is the study of existence. An ontological question is one regarding whether something, such as God, exists. To answer ontological questions, however, we must first agree on an epistemological framework— what should we legitimately count as proper evidence that *anything* exists? Only once we have agreed on such a framework can we get down to the business of determining what exists and what doesn't. The issues that arise when believers and nonbelievers discuss the existence of God are typically epistemological ones. They begin their discussions of ontology with very different epistemological assumptions and so start by talking past each other, with little hope of resolution.

You can see from the three previous sections the crucial role evidence plays in answering legal, scientific, and historical questions. This role is so well understood and so consistent with our collective experience that it is commonly taken for granted and rarely questioned. I maintain that, with two limited exceptions I discuss shortly, evidence must form the basis of *all justified beliefs*. As W. K. Clifford is quoted as saying, "It is wrong always, everywhere, and for anyone, to believe anything upon insufficient evidence."[33]

Most people live their lives as if this were so. If you asked them, they would probably agree that justified beliefs must be based on evidence, looking at you as if it were crazy to think otherwise. But when discussing religious matters, you will see many of them abandon that approach, implicitly if not explicitly. They readily adopt assumptions that cannot be justified by evidence. They open the door to competing epistemologies, such as faith, without ever demonstrating those epistemologies are warranted. When one bases unwavering metaphysical beliefs on such epistemologies, however, he has drifted from philosophy into religion. While philosophy poses questions that may never be answered, religion declares answers that may never be questioned.

A. The Foundations of Knowledge

How do we "know" anything? First, we must agree on what this question even means. Adequately defining knowledge has long presented a challenge for philosophers. A common definition, imperfect though it may be, is "justified true belief." It is crucial to understand the relationship between knowledge and belief before moving forward. Beliefs need not be true. Beliefs merely represent one's mental assent to a particular proposition. They are often cultural memes that get passed on from person to person based on many factors other than truth. To say one knows something necessarily means that one believes it, but the reverse need not apply, for one may believe something without having knowledge of it. One may sincerely believe something that is not true, but one cannot *know* something unless it is true. While all knowledge represents beliefs, not all beliefs represent knowledge.

To make things more interesting still, a belief may happen to be true and yet still not represent knowledge. Assume, for example, that I have erroneously believed my entire life that Elon Musk has a tattoo on his lower back. Assume further that just last week, Mr. Musk did get such a tattoo without telling anyone. My previously erroneous belief, by pure happenstance, now lines up with reality. But you cannot say this belief constitutes *knowledge* of Mr. Musk's tattoo. The problem is that my belief, though accurate, is not justified. My accuracy is due to chance alone. I *have no good reason* to believe it, and without such a reason, my belief fails the test of "epistemic reasonableness." It is coming to the correct conclusion *through good reasons* that generates knowledge.

The question this raises, of course, is what constitutes a good reason? The answer is the same as that for every system we've discussed: evidence. Specifically, we are talking once again about empirical evidence, which is considered *intersubjectively verifiable* because it can be checked and evaluated by anyone with working faculties, relevant education, and expertise. Such evidence is the rock on which is built all true forms of knowledge. Without it, any edifice rests upon shifting sands.

Earlier, I mentioned two exceptions to this rule. There are two required assumptions that cannot themselves be justified by empirical evidence. They are:

1. I exist.
2. My senses and memory generally provide me with reliable information.

Anyone who has seen *The Matrix* or read Plato's *The Allegory of the Cave* is familiar with the idea that reality as we perceive it is nothing more than an illusion. In the pages of science fiction, this idea has often been represented as humans existing as disembodied brains in jars, with all our experiences generated by alien scientists' experiments. How can we "know" these constructs don't reflect actual reality? After all, our sensory experiences would be identical in either event. The answer is that we can't. But fortunately, it doesn't matter.

One or both of these assumptions may be false, but there is *no good reason to expect that they are false*. For all practical purposes, we can treat them as true because they align with our experience, which is all we have to go on. More important, both assumptions are *necessary*. To deny them is to deny any *possibility* of obtaining reliable knowledge. Without them, we could not even construct a workable model of reality. We would be left with radical skepticism: the view that we can know nothing about anything. Epistemically, there would be nowhere to go. The assumptions are therefore justified by their practical necessity. So long as they remain consistent with our experiences and allow us to make accurate and useful predictions, we are further justified in retaining them.[34]

Because we cannot verify them empirically, the assumptions must remain provisional, always subject to revision or even abandonment if necessary. Nonetheless, they can be considered "properly basic"—*basic* in that they are foundational to knowledge and *properly* so because they represent the minimum necessary upon which to build an epistemic framework. They give us something upon which to attach the scaffolding supporting the models we build of existence. Once they are in place, empirical evidence can take over and carry us the rest of the way by applying the rules of logic and reason through which valid inferences can be drawn, either inductively or deductively.

Beliefs are considered basic in the sense that they are not inferred from other beliefs. Nonbasic beliefs all derive from previous beliefs, but the regress must end at properly basic beliefs, which are self-evident, incorrigible (incapable of being found in error, such as "I am thinking of an apple"), or pragmatically indispensable (i.e., necessary to render any understanding of the world coherent). Examples of the latter would be that we can generally trust our senses and memory, the reality of the external world, and belief in other minds. Such beliefs enjoy universal agreement across cultures. In other words, they are universally sanctioned.

Some people doubt that empirical evidence is adequate to model reality. They point to such conceptual ideas as truth or justice as not fitting the evidential paradigm. In fact, however, these fit quite well. Such concepts represent abstractions from experiences with which we are all familiar.

Each of us has faced a situation in which a lie caused injury or in which a person was treated in a way we intuitively felt was wrong. Later, I discuss the evolutionary origin of such intuitions, but for now, the key point is that it is a small mental leap for humans from the specific (treating her that way *feels* wrong) to the general (treating anyone in a similar manner *is* wrong) to an abstraction of the very concept (the treatment of people in a similar manner represents something I despise, which I call *injustice*). In this way, a series of concrete experiences builds on itself to form an abstract concept.

Mathematics, likewise, represents abstractions from our experiences. Looking at a complicated mathematical proof doesn't seem to match any experience with which most of us are immediately familiar. But while a mathematical proof may not be directly abstracted from our sensory experience, set theory, which describes the foundation of all mathematics, is. The world we live in is populated by discrete objects that can be grouped into numbered sets. These sets can share common characteristics, such as "plants," or represent arbitrary categories, such as "things I like." From these experiences, we can abstract the existence of conceptual numbered sets, and from here we can further abstract addition, subtraction, multiplication, and division of those sets. All mathematical proofs are built on these fundamentals. If we lived in a world in which everything blended into everything else, with no clear demarcation, we could not abstract numbered sets. In such a world, there would be no mathematics.

Another example is the "law" of causality: For every effect, there must be a cause. This principle is so familiar and unfailingly reliable that we assume it to be self-evident, never acknowledging that it may simply represent an abstraction of our common experiences that holds true only under a particular set of circumstances. In the quantum world, cause and effect do not adequately describe our observations. Virtual particles, nuclear decay, and quantum entanglement all defy the "law" of causality, as least as most people understand it. We must acknowledge that the frame of reference in which we have built our "self-evident" rules is limited and that even some concepts we treat as universal may not be so.

So what of beliefs? Is it possible to have beliefs without evidence? Assume a small child believes in Santa Claus. Obviously, the child's belief is not based on firsthand evidence that Santa exists. It is based on the statements of an authority, probably the child's parents. While the parents may attempt to support this belief with half-eaten cookies on Christmas morning, no one would consider the cookies the *reason* for the child's belief. The cookies would just be convincers used to support and strengthen a belief already introduced.

This calls into question the very definition of *belief* and whether it is even appropriate to say, for example, that a scientist "believes" in gravity. I would say there are certain things the scientist knows from empirical evidence and that she therefore concludes through reasonable and logical inferences that a force like gravity appears to exist. The term *belief* is used loosely to describe these types of conclusions, as well as conclusions reached from much less reliable forms of evidence, perhaps through a very poor and fault-prone process of reasoning. Obviously, all beliefs are not equal.

We all make observations, collect evidence, and use our experiences to draw what we consider justified conclusions. Philosophers call this a posteriori ("from the latter") knowledge. Other conclusions, called a priori ("from the former"), are drawn *before* considering the evidence and without reference to experience. Many apologetic arguments rely, either explicitly or implicitly, on the premise that true knowledge can be derived a priori or that a priori and a posteriori beliefs are equivalent, so these claims are worth a brief discussion.

In his *Critique of Pure Reason*, Immanuel Kant recognized a distinction between judgments reached through experience and judgments arrived at independently of experience. Kant used this distinction to explain the case of mathematical knowledge, which he regarded as the fundamental example of a priori knowledge. A priori justification rests on intuition or insight. Centuries before Kant, St. Augustine took this same concept and declared that such knowledge comes from God, who occasionally intellectually illuminates humans.

The rhetorical advantage of such an approach should be clear. It allows defenders of religion, such as Kant, to dispense with the need for evidential foundations and appeal directly to people's intuitions—elevating those intuitions to the same level as empirically derived scientific models. As demonstrated elsewhere in this book, however, this appeal to intuition is fallacious because intuitions are often wrong. As intuitions are uniquely subjective, they are useless for arguing the defensibility of a position. For that, you will need to reference empirical evidence, which is equally available to all.

A common approach of religious apologists is to argue that a priori intuitions should be given the same epistemic weight as a posteriori knowledge. One will often hear apologists claim that empiricists make the same types of assumptions as rationalists adopting an a priori epistemology or that empiricism is "self-defeating" because the premise that "true knowledge can only be obtained through empirical evidence" cannot itself be proven through empirical evidence. Such arguments improperly conflate the two approaches.

An empiricist makes a minimal number of provisional assumptions, those described previously as properly basic, and proceeds from there on the basis of evidence, logic, and reason. It is true that these assumptions cannot themselves be established by evidence, but their very nature is that they need not be. The empiricist makes no claim that these assumptions represent "truths" but only that they are useful and necessary. If they are true, he says, then so, too, is the information learned through evidence and experience. If they are false, then we can have no hope of knowing anything and must live in a state of radical skepticism regarding no belief as justified.

The apologist who relies on a priori justification, by contrast, labels his intuitions about the universe as necessarily true and impervious to all potential defeaters, known or unknown. This is very different from grounding a model in provisional assumptions. Significantly, no proponent of a priori knowledge has ever demonstrated that knowledge of the real world can be constructed without some combination of properly basic beliefs and experience. No conclusion reached solely through a priori knowledge has ever been conclusively verified through other means.

Returning to our initial definition of *knowledge*, "justified true belief," it should be apparent why, conceptually, knowledge can be so elusive. Who determines what is justified, and how do we know what's true? Regarding many things, we can never be perfectly certain and therefore should be hesitant to claim knowledge where we can at best put forward beliefs with various supporting arguments. While perfect "knowledge" may be impossible because we cannot know for certain what is "true," we can obtain a working form of knowledge that meets our needs. The path to this type of knowledge has always been blazed the same way.

In summary, there are very good reasons to believe that all knowledge ultimately comes from empirical evidence built on a pair of properly basic assumptions, a view known as *evidentialism*. An evidentialist worldview is justified by these reasons and *by our common experience*. It works. This is the epistemology that best reflects the world as we know it and best affords us opportunities for increasing our knowledge of that world. None other has come close to its success. We need not demonstrate that evidentialism is *true* in some metaphysical sense but only that it is profoundly *useful* in modeling the universe and that so far it has proven to be the *most useful* approach. It is with this in mind that I turn to an alternative a priori epistemology offered by many of the world's religions, including Christianity. That is faith.

B. Faith and Reason

> Faith can make no appeal to reason or the fitness of things; its appeal is
> to the Word of God, and whatever is therein revealed, faith accepts as
> true. Faith accepts the Bible as the word and will of God and rests upon
> its truth without question and without other evidence.
>
> —Edward McKendree Bounds, *The Resurrection*

Central to any discussion of Christianity is faith. Among Christians, faith
is almost universally heralded as a virtue, as something indispensable to
their belief system. Christian apologists all eventually appeal to the concept
of faith, as it supposedly allows them to transcend man's limited capacity
for rational thought. Philosopher George H. Smith observes, "Faith is the
epistemological underpinning of Christianity. If faith collapses, so does
Christianity."[35]

Evidentialists see no value in faith. They reject it as a valid means of
acquiring knowledge. They find reason, logic, and evidence to be entirely
sufficient and the only justified path to truth.[36] As the vast majority of atheists are evidentialists, this represents perhaps the principal conflict between
most Christians and atheists. The question, then, is whether there is any
valid place for faith in pursuing truth.

Before getting to that question, however, we must clearly define what
we are talking about, as faith is a subject rife with equivocation. The Bible
defines *faith* as "confidence in what we hope for and assurance about what
we do not see" (Hebrews 11:1). St. Augustine of Hippo said, "Faith is to
believe what you do not see."[37] French philosopher François-Marie Arouet,
better known by his pen name Voltaire, defined *faith* as "believing when
it is beyond the power of reason to believe."[38] In other words, it is the a
priori position of being sure of things we hope to be true but cannot verify
through empirical evidence. It is affirming such things, though they cannot
be deduced by observation, perception, and reason. It is assigning a proposition more confidence than our human faculties warrant based on some
alternative source of authority.

Obviously, words have different meanings, which is why dictionaries
list several. I am not claiming this is the only accepted meaning of *faith*. I
am referring to *theistic faith*, as it has been used since Paul's day to distinguish conclusions reached through empirical means, such as observation,
evidence, and reasoned deduction, from a priori conclusions reached in alternate ways, such as reliance on scriptural authority or subjective feelings.

Here are additional descriptions of religious faith by prominent religious believers:

- "Faith has to do with things that are not seen and hope with things that are not at hand."—Thomas Aquinas
- "I believe, though I do not comprehend, and I hold by faith what I cannot grasp with the mind."—Saint Bernard
- "It is the heart which perceives God and not the reason. That is what faith is: God perceived by the heart, not by the reason."—Blaise Pascal, *Pensees*
- "Faith is permitting ourselves to be seized by the things we do not see."—Martin Luther
- "Reason is our soul's left hand, faith her right."—John Donne
- "Faith is an oasis in the heart which will never be reached by the caravan of thinking. Faith is a knowledge within the heart, beyond the reach of proof."—Khalil Gibran

And here are a couple by religious skeptics:

- "The way to see by faith is to shut the eye of reason."—Benjamin Franklin, "July. VII Month," *Poor Richard's Almanac*
- "Faith, noun. Belief without evidence in what is told by one who speaks without knowledge, of things without parallel."—Ambrose Bierce, *The Devil's Dictionary*

The important thing to recognize here is that the believers and skeptics are using *faith* in the same way, to mean essentially the same thing. Each recognizes it as an approach to knowledge that is independent of reason and evidence. Repeatedly you see the juxtaposition of faith and reason, suggesting a stark dichotomy. This is the common understanding of religious faith that has persisted for centuries and allowed those on both sides of the debate to share the same assumptions.

It is instructive to contrast faith with an often-conflated concept: trust. To trust in something is to believe it based on the accumulation of supporting evidence. I trust that my mother loves me because she has repeatedly demonstrated it countless times throughout my life. I trust that the Sun will rise tomorrow because I have seen this occur every day of my life. The daily rising of the Sun has also been demonstrated scientifically, through millions of empirical observations and modeling employing the laws of physics.

A couple examples are in order. Assume I decide to conquer my fear of heights and enroll in a skydiving school. Before boarding the plane, I learn of all the precautions taken to ensure the safety of the skydivers. I learn of the school's fifty-year history in which no one has ever been injured. I learn of the extensive knowledge and expertise of their employees, including the people who will be packing my parachute and who will accompany me on the jump. If I decide to go through with my plan and jump from the plane, it would be a matter of trust rather than faith. I have acquired evidence that I am likely to land safely and used reasoned deductions to come to a justified conclusion based on that evidence.

But assume instead that I learn this is the first day the skydiving school has been in business. No one there has ever skydived before. None has even packed a parachute. None have pilots' licenses. They are, however, extremely enthusiastic and charismatic. I like them and am inspired by their passion. If I choose to go through with my plan under these circumstances, it could not be based on the same type of trust as described previously. I have no good evidence or reasons to believe I will reach the ground safely, so my decision cannot be grounded in such things. It can only be understood as an emotional response based on some positive intuition—as an act of faith.

Some Christians will object to defining faith in this way. They will claim that, as they define faith, it reflects beliefs reasonably inferred from available evidence. Defined in this ad hoc manner, however, the term is rendered superfluous. It would be indistinguishable from trust. If faith is to have a distinct meaning, then it must be something else entirely. It must be defined as it has been, both generally and specifically within Christian theology, as an epistemological approach independent of reason. What else could one be talking about when they say they have faith that, because they have accepted Jesus as their personal savior, they will go to Heaven when they die? This is the only meaning that makes sense in the religious context.

You will never hear scientists use faith to refer to beliefs based on evidence, such as faith the stars won't fall from the sky. As Bertram Russell says, "Where there is evidence, no one speaks of 'faith.' We do not speak of faith that two and two are four or that the Earth is round. We only speak of faith when we wish to substitute emotion for evidence."[39] To have faith is to convince oneself that what one merely believes is actually knowledge—that one is too smart to be wrong. Apologists who attempt to conflate theistic faith with some type of evidence-based trust are simply playing word games. They are trying to rebrand the word to make it seem more reasonable to "have faith." But it doesn't work that way.

One could say that theistic faith—the type that apologists have always relied on to justify belief when reason fails—is the opposite of reason, just as cold is the opposite of heat, and darkness, the opposite of light. They are mutually exclusive concepts, with no common ground. Faith is belief without, or in spite of, reason. It is unnecessary to quibble about the meaning of faith, however, to acknowledge the basic point: Christianity has always incorporated an evidence-free and reason-free epistemology as a key component of its apologetics, regardless of what we call it.

Faith can be thought of as shorthand for all the sources of nonempirical a priori "knowledge" Christians rely on to support their beliefs. These take many forms, including presuppositionalism, insisting on the authority of revelation available to us only through ancient unattested documents, or the authority of an intangible "Holy Spirit" that is available only through subjective experience. As I demonstrate, Christianity is based on the concept of belief without, or despite, reason and evidence—however it is labeled. Faith becomes a substitute for reason-based justification. In my experience, most Christians use faith in this way. Moreover, it has been used that way by Christian theologians and apologists since the dawn of Christianity. Accordingly, that is the way I use it here.

As stated earlier, the evidentialist puts no stock in faith. He requires evidence before committing to a position, and this evidence must be obtained from reliable sources. He then draws conclusions from this evidence, through a chain of inferences based on the rules of logic and reason. The confidence he places in these conclusions is in direct proportion to the quality and quantity of that evidence. As discussed, this paradigm provides the foundation for the American legal system and the scientific community. The scientific method is just a specialized application of evidentialism to the natural world.

Everyone uses an evidence-based paradigm in their daily lives, even devout Christians. We all trust our senses and our reasonable inferences from those senses. Likewise, we evaluate the reliability of information obtained from other sources and trust that information if it passes our internal "bullshit detector." Rarely, if ever, do we base everyday decisions on things we merely *hope* to be true but run contrary to the available evidence. We do not, for instance, set off into a driving rainstorm in our best attire, having "faith" the rain will stop the moment we step out the door.

For most Christians, however, their religion is different. In religious matters alone, they feel free to set aside evidentialism. They allow themselves to believe things for which there is no good evidence and which cannot be supported by any reasonable inferences. Why is this? Psychology suggests it is because they are wedded to the beliefs of Christianity for purely emotional reasons and recognize that such beliefs simply cannot be supported by reason. These beliefs are typically learned and incorporated into one's identity in childhood, before one develops critical thinking skills. Emotional attachments to these beliefs are formed, triggering mental defense mechanisms when threatened. Accordingly, Christians must appeal to an alternate means of establishing knowledge, and that is faith.

Faith and reason are, therefore, inherently at odds within Christian theology. This conflict can be seen in the writings of the father of Protestantism, Martin Luther, who called reason the "devil's bride," a "beautiful whore," and "God's worst enemy." According to Luther, "Faith must trample under foot all reason, sense, and understanding," replacing any deductions obtained through reason with the "Word of God."[40] According to Luther, this was because, by the standards of reason, the articles of Christianity must be acknowledged as "impossible, absurd, and false."[41] Tertullian, one of the so-called Church Fathers, embraced the irrationality he deemed essential to Christianity, stating that Jesus's Resurrection must be believed precisely *because it was absurd and impossible.*[42] This view that faith and reason are mutually hostile and that religion can be justified through faith alone is known as fideism.

Tertullian found reason irrelevant to belief, claiming that, given the truth revealed by the Gospels, there was no further "need of research."[43] Many of today's leading apologists likewise see reason and evidence as immaterial to Christian belief, as demonstrated by William Lane Craig's "internal witness to the Holy Spirit" or Alvin Plantinga's *"sensus divinitatis"* and view of Christian belief as properly basic, concepts discussed in more detail later in this book.[44] I do not mean to suggest that Christian theologians have been unanimous in their disdain for reason or that they are all strict fideists, but there has clearly been a long-lasting reluctance to claim that Christianity can be defended based on reason, logic, and evidence alone. Apologists have always left themselves the escape hatch of faith.

It is common for apologists to argue that reason isn't enough to meet humanity's needs for explanation, and it is certainly true that reason has not allowed humanity to answer all its questions. For faith to be considered a valid approach, however, it is not enough that reason be shown inadequate to explain everything or tell us all we want to know. Faith must *do a better job*. It must reliably increase our understanding of the world above and beyond what reason can accomplish, providing explanations *clearly and demonstrably superior*. And it must do so in a way that is objectively verifiable. We must be able to show that, at least sometimes, faith paints a more accurate picture than reason has or ever could. The role of reason is to allow us to reliably distinguish truth from falsity. Unless the Christian can demonstrate that faith can do the same and do it at least as well, if not better, faith must take a back seat to reason.

Rather than affirmatively demonstrating the efficacy of faith, which they cannot, Christian apologists point to questions that have not been definitively answered by science, such as the origin of life or consciousness.[45] To appeal to faith, they must first carve out some realm of knowledge inaccessible to science and reason. The need for faith is created by denying the adequacy of reason, and what better way than by declaring a body of "unknowable" knowledge where the light of reason can never shine? Faith can only play a role where reason fails.

But to acknowledge that reason has so far failed to provide an answer to some question is not to acknowledge that it never will or that it cannot. More importantly, it does not even remotely imply that faith in any particular set of religious doctrines *can do better*. We have repeatedly seen that where faith and reason have pursued answers to the same questions, reason has always come out on top when answers were ultimately found. There is not a single example in recorded history of any verifiable truth uncovered by faith alone.

While it may be true that some questions cannot presently be answered using reason and evidence alone, that doesn't mean the evidentialist framework must be rejected. In light of the inherent limitations in our collective knowledge, "I don't know" may simply be the best answer possible at a given time. Only if another framework can be shown superior across the board would we be justified in rejecting the current one. Faith has never demonstrated itself to offer such a framework.

Religions are virtually all antiempiricist because they hold that the real nature of the universe is hidden from us. Given such an assumption, empiricism becomes a fool's errand. What is the point of collecting and analyzing evidence when such an analysis bears no relation to the true nature of reality? In such a universe, we could only hope reasoned analysis to correlate to reality by chance and only when permitted by the supernatural agents ultimately in charge. But that is not what the history of science reveals. While it might have made sense to look for alternatives to an empiricist worldview when religions emerged, it makes sense no longer. We can now explain just about everything in the universe empirically or at least reasonably believe everything can be explained empirically as our scientific knowledge improves. That is the message and the lesson of science.

Faith can never provide an adequate alternative because faith can justify almost anything. If a process yields thousands of mutually exclusive answers to the same question, that process must be fatally flawed. The problem was well described by biologist Jerry Coyne: "The toolkit of science, based on reason and empirical study, is reliable, while that of religion—including faith, dogma, and revelation—is unreliable and leads to incorrect, untestable, or conflicting conclusions. Indeed, by relying on faith rather than evidence, religion renders itself incapable of finding truth."[46]

In online discussions, I have seen many Christians chastise one another for having "weak" faith, such as when biblical inconsistencies or scientific discoveries lead some to abandon certain fundamentalist positions. These "weak" believers are told that they would have held to their initial positions longer if their faith had been "stronger." *Strong faith* is defined as remaining steadfast in one's beliefs, even when faced with logical refutation or contradictory evidence. But how can this be deemed a virtue in any system that acknowledges value in reason? Can there be any justification for holding to a position after serious questions have been raised, for which one has received no satisfactory answers? This sounds more like closed-mindedness—being unwilling to admit one is mistaken. Such admonishments only make sense in a system that rejects reason entirely.

Likewise, any request to let oneself be "guided by the Holy Spirit" is just an appeal to a double standard. It is to say that if the evidentiary standards you employ in areas other than religion do not lead you to Christianity, then you should set those standards aside. You should employ a new standard, assuming the existence of something unsupported by evidence, and form beliefs based on that very assumption. I see such appeals as acknowledgments of the weaknesses inherent in the Christian position and concerns that, without the double standard, analysis of Christian arguments would likely lead to their rejection. Those promoting such a standard appear to agree with Abraham Lincoln, who recognized, "It will not do to investigate the subject of religion too closely, as it is apt to lead to infidelity."[47]

Many Christians encourage those with serious doubts to take a "leap of faith," a metaphor suggesting a bridge built of evidence, which unfortunately is only partially completed and does not extend to the desired destination. The metaphor suggests that one need not stop at the end of the bridge but should jump with eyes closed, hoping against all reason he will not fall but will reach the desired distant point. When applied to religion, I see myself at the end of that incomplete bridge, looking over at thousands of possible locations, being urged by people of all religions to take the leap to the one they favor. But what justifies one leap of faith over another? I would rather stand my ground.

Any principled Christian who claims to appeal to reason must avoid any appeal to faith and reject such appeals as fundamentally at odds with the pursuit of truth. Faith is a personal and subjective epistemology that has never revealed verifiable objective reliability. Reformed Christian evangelist Dan Barker observes, "Faith is a cop-out. It is intellectual bankruptcy. If the only way you can accept an assertion is by faith, then you are conceding that it can't be taken on its own merits."[48] Once a believer falls back on faith to support his or her views, he has abandoned any expectation of persuading nonbelievers, as any particular faith requires a set of assumptions that outsiders will never share. As Christopher Hitchens recognizes, that which is asserted without evidence can be dismissed without evidence—and typically should be.[49]

Faith has no place in the search for truth. It is a tool used by religions to shield their increasingly irrelevant doctrines from the ever-threatening onslaught of science and human reason. Likewise, it is employed by emotionally committed believers as a license to ignore all those unresolved questions about their religion and *just believe anyway*. It provides no answers but stops believers from asking the questions. While undeniably useful in maintaining religious institutions, it is intellectually indefensible. Believers may use it to fend off criticisms by nonbelievers, but in Pyrrhicly winning those battles, they give up the war.

C. Objective versus Subjective Worldviews

A crucial issue in religious discussions is whether one's worldview is objective or subjective. Reminiscent of the age-old question "Which came first: the chicken or the egg?" is the question "Which came first: existence (by which we mean the physical universe) or mental consciousness?" This is called the question of metaphysical primacy and so can also be expressed as which has primacy over the other or, the flip side, which depends on the other?

The term *objective*, used in this context, means "without reference to mental states."[50] Objective reality would be that which would exist whether any mental consciousness knew it or could know it. The objects of conscious thought are independent of anyone or anything's conscious activity. To believe in objective reality, one must believe in the primacy of existence over mental states. One must believe that the physical exists and that to the extent anything that we call "mental" exists is explained by the physical. We can refer to one with such beliefs as an objectivist.

A subjectivist, on the other hand, believes in the metaphysical primacy of mental consciousness. To the subjectivist, the objects of consciousness depend on a subject's conscious activity, either for the objects' nature, the actions they perform, their existence, or something else. He or she believes nothing is possible without conscious activity and therefore that physical reality itself could only have been created by an act of will of a necessarily immaterial consciousness. It follows from such a worldview that reality itself conforms to the whims, preferences, and commands of a consciousness, so merely wishing makes things so.

The only consciousness with which humans have any direct evidence is human consciousness. The objectivist worldview can account for human consciousness through the evolutionary process, at least theoretically, as discussed later in this book. The objectivist can also show that human consciousness is malleable and entirely dependent on the physical—specifically the condition of the human brain. As to human consciousness, therefore, the objectivist can clearly show the primacy of the physical over the mental.

The subjectivist, by contrast, cannot show that reality conforms itself to human intent or will. He cannot show that wishing makes things so or has any measurable impact on the physical world. Self-help gurus occasionally make such claims in books like the 2006 best-seller *The Secret* by Rhonda Byrne, but verifiable supporting evidence has never been demonstrated.

The Christian worldview is subjective, holding to the metaphysical primacy of consciousness over existence. The Christian Bible consistently describes God as having a consciousness in many ways recognizable and analogous to human consciousness. The Bible also makes clear, however, that God's consciousness is in other ways unlike human consciousness. One of these is that God's consciousness has primacy over existence, which obediently conforms to God's commands and carries out God's wishes. The key is that, under Christianity, everything is as it is for the sole reason that God has willed it to be that way.

The objectivist views things as being the way they are because those things have unique natures and exist in a universe governed by natural laws, which are just descriptions of observed regularities. The change in an object from one moment to the next can be accurately predicted if one knows the initial nature of the object and the conditions and forces that will act on the object over. The Christian must ultimately agree that no change can occur unless God either wills or at least allows it. Natural laws operate only at God's whim.

Both the objectivist and subjectivist make initial assumptions. The objectivist begins by positing existence as a brute fact. The subjectivist begins by positing a priori an incorporeal mental consciousness that somehow gave rise to existence, also as a brute fact. The Christian, in addition, must presume this consciousness possesses all the attributes assigned to the Christian God, such as omnipotence, omniscience, timelessness, and omnibenevolence.

D. Positing Belief in God as Properly Basic

Some apologists have argued that evidentialism is unjustified, maintaining that belief in God need not be supported by evidence because it is properly basic. Most notably, prominent apologist Alvin Plantinga makes this a centerpiece of his writings, using as an analogy of our belief in other minds, which he claims we accept despite being unable to prove it through empirical evidence. Plantinga states,

> There may be other reasons for supposing that although rational belief in other minds does not require an answer to the epistemological question, rational belief in the existence of God does. But it is certainly hard to see what these reasons might be. Hence my tentative conclusion: if my belief in other minds is rational, so is my belief in God. But obviously the former is rational; so, therefore, is the latter.[51]

In other words, if belief in other minds is rational, so, too, is belief in God. But the two are not analogous. There is enormous evidence for the existence of other minds. Our experience confirms this every day. We constantly interact with other people, and no competing hypothesis has been presented that parsimoniously explains the flood of evidence from our daily experiences. There is no corresponding weight of evidence for God. If there were, people would not doubt. How many people seriously doubt whether their loved ones have minds of their own? Trusting in one's senses differs greatly from accepting something based on a priori assumptions, despite Plantinga's attempts to conflate the two.

Plantinga, who rejects many of the traditional arguments for God as failures, subscribes to "reformed epistemology," which maintains that it is rational to believe in God simply because it remains possible that God created our minds to be disposed to believe in Him. The simple fact that people believe in God warrants their belief! Plantinga's argument fails because it assumes the species-wide existence of something that has never been demonstrated, an inner sense that God exists, known by apologists as the *sensus divinitatis*.[52] Another problem is that it provides no criteria by which to rule out other claims we all know to be absurd. If belief in the

Christian God is properly basic, for example, why not believe in Charlie Brown's Great Pumpkin? The Great Pumpkin, too, could have instilled in humans the belief that he exists. Where two people hold mutually exclusive religious beliefs, Plantinga's approach would require maintaining both are equally rational.

Still another problem is that, even if Plantinga is correct, he hasn't established an argument *for God* but merely a defense against those who claim his belief to be irrational. He is content retreating to the possible rather than attempting to demonstrate that God's existence is *probable*. What he is really saying is that *if* Christianity is true, then it is rational to believe in God. But of course, we don't know that Christianity is true. That is the *entire point of the exercise*. Because the same argument could be used to defend the rationality of millions of contradictory beliefs, it doesn't help us in determining which are actually true. For that, we require evidentialism. Reformed epistemology can accomplish nothing more than insulating one's belief from claims of *complete* irrationality. Plantinga conflates this with demonstrating affirmatively that such belief is rational, which requires more than showing one potential evidential path to belief. It also requires satisfactorily addressing all plausible defeaters to that belief.

The reformed epistemologist, content with demonstrating that his belief is rationally justified, offers little to nothing to engage a skeptic. To bridge the gap in their beliefs, believers and skeptics must begin with some common ground, which must be our shared reality. The language of shared reality is mutually verifiable evidence. If you refuse to speak that language, insisting instead on justifying your beliefs through subjective experiences or a priori assumptions I do not share, then you have created a wall between us rather than a bridge. Your wall may shield your beliefs from my evidence and logic-based criticism, but it fatally undermines your prospects of persuading me—or anyone—that your beliefs are true.

THE "SURPRISE FACTOR"

> If it looks like a duck, walks like a duck, and quacks like a duck, one can be reasonably certain it is not a rhinoceros.
>
> —Anonymous

There is an important concept that, if properly understood, assists greatly in evaluating the evidence for competing claims. It proceeds from the fact that weighing competing evidence is really a matter of assessing relative probabilities. A good way to understand probabilities is to think in terms of jars of marbles. A single black marble in a jar with ninety-nine white marbles would result in you having a 1 percent chance of blindly pulling a black marble from the jar on any given attempt and a 99 percent chance of pulling a white marble.

Assume a jar with one thousand marbles, composed of only two colors: black and white. Assume further that the jar is covered by an opaque cloth. You are told only that 10 marbles are of one color, while 990 are of the other. You are asked to guess which of two possibilities is true: (A) 10 are black, and 990 are white; or (B) 990 are black, and 10 are white. Initially, with no additional information, these options are equally likely. Assume, however, that before guessing, you are allowed to blindly select a marble from the jar. You do so, and it is white. How should this change your weighing of the two possibilities?

If possibility A were true, then you would have had a 99 percent chance of pulling a white marble, which would have made the selection of the white marble unsurprising. If possibility B were true, then you would have had only a 1 percent chance of pulling a white marble, which would have made the selection of the white marble surprising indeed. We can all see that the selection of the single white marble should cause you to weigh option A as more likely. I call this the "surprise factor."

Assume that you select a second marble, and it is also white. This significantly increases the weight you should place on possibility A because it would be very surprising to have pulled two white marbles in a row under possibility B. That probability would be 1 percent times 1 percent, or one in ten thousand. All the evidence you have acquired since the beginning of the experiment has supported possibility A over B. If you pull eight more marbles, and they are all white, then your confidence in possibility A should now be extremely high, as the odds against it given possibility B are astronomical. Even if one of the ten marbles you have pulled is black, your confidence in possibility A should remain very strong, for it remains a much better choice than option B.

If you are emotionally invested in possibility B, you can continue to believe B is correct even after ten white marbles are drawn, for B remains theoretically possible.[53] Maybe you just happened to pull the only ten white marbles from a one-thousand-marble jar. It would be obvious to any objective observer, however, that this belief is not a reasonable one. The surprise factor weighs so heavily for possibility A that one would have to ignore it completely to subscribe to possibility B. In other words, B is so *improbable* that one would have to abandon reason to maintain a belief in B.

In my analogy, atheism represents option A, while Christianity represents option B. Scientific observations and historical findings of the last two hundred years represent the selection of a consistent chain of white marbles. Each, while not necessarily invalidating Christianity, has made it more and more improbable. Each has contributed to the surprise factor supporting atheism because none would be expected if Christian doctrine were true.

But the problem is even worse for Christianity, for it is in competition with not only atheism but also many other belief systems that incorporate supernatural elements. Instead of only two possibilities, A and B, there are thousands. Some propose 800 black marbles; some, 990 green marbles; and others, 20 red marbles. All of these remain possibilities, but none are more likely than any other because all the marbles pulled to date have been white. All have reflected a purely naturalistic, materialist world.

2

DEFINITIONS

There are several terms and concepts that come up in the remainder of this book that either may not be familiar to the average reader or for which the reader may have a different understanding than the way I use them. Because it is important that we be on the same page about what these terms mean and what those meanings imply, I address them here.

A BRIEF DISCUSSION OF CHRISTIAN APOLOGETICS

I have found that a major barrier to Christians dealing seriously with skeptical arguments is the very existence of professional "apologists." Within Christianity, apologists are those who seek to defend Christianity from attack and to demonstrate that it is valid and "true." The apostle Paul employed the Greek term *apologia* in his trial speech to Festus and Agrippa in Acts 26:2, referring to his "defense," and employed a related term in Philippians 1:7, to reference "defending the gospel."[1] Religious apologetics is the attempt to show that the preferred faith is not irrational and that believing is not against human reason. Of course, defending a position already held is not the same as demonstrating that it is true.

Many apologists have impressive sounding academic degrees in, for instance, theology and philosophy. When confronted with a troublesome argument from a skeptic to which they can form no adequate response, certain lay Christians resolve their cognitive dissonance by reminding themselves there are very intelligent Christians out there who have devoted their careers to dealing with these same arguments, so they *must have developed good answers.* They assume that if such people can conclude Christianity is rationally justified, then it must be. The apologists thereby provide Christianity with a veneer of respectability.

To address this common misperception, it is important to understand the nature of apologetics and the perspectives apologists employ. It is also important to acknowledge that just because someone is intelligent doesn't mean they must be correct, especially when their initial opinions were formed early in life and strong emotional barriers exist to changing those opinions. In such cases, they may simply be better at constructing elaborate pseudointellectual defenses to protect what they already believe. Arthur Conan Doyle, the creator of Sherlock Holmes, was a brilliant man in many areas, but he believed in fairies and spiritualism, devoting a large part of his life to such pursuits. Likewise, Isaac Newton, one of the most intelligent men to ever live, spent the latter part of his life pursuing alchemy and searching for the fabled philosopher's stone that turned base metals into gold. Being brilliant did not protect either from believing in nonsense.

I do not believe that any apologetic argument or defense of the faith can survive rational scrutiny. Most are not inherently complicated and require no specialized expertise to understand. Their flaws are typically apparent to anyone with basic knowledge of logic. I have attempted to provide the only foundations required to assess their main arguments. There is no good reason to defer to an apologetic argument if one can properly assess it and understand why it is flawed. Nor should one concede the ultimate conclusion of apologists, that Christianity is rationally grounded, where it is apparent that conclusion rests on faulty arguments.

As demonstrated by Paul's letters, there have been apologists since the dawn of Christianity. All early Christians had to defend their faith, as Christianity was a fledgling religion attempting to establish a foothold among a vast marketplace of more established religions. These defenses would have been rough and ad hoc. As Christianity became more established and orthodoxy emerged, scholarly apologists appeared who offered more refined, philosophical defenses.

Early Christianity produced many famous apologists, such as Justin Martyr, Origen, Irenaeus, Augustine of Hippo, St. Anselm, and Thomas Aquinas. Well-known apologists from the modern age include C. S. Lewis,

N. T. Wright, Lee Strobel, Frank Turek, Alvin Plantinga, Josh McDowell, Gary Habermas, William Lane Craig, Dinesh D'Souza, Ray Comfort, and Timothy Keller. Christian enthusiasm for apologetics has not waned through the ages. In two thousand years, however, despite the best efforts of many brilliant Christian proponents, the argument has not been won. As discussed later, the apologists have lost the war among those most familiar with their arguments.

Modern apologists like to portray their discipline as something equivalent to science. It is, however, anything but. Science begins with a very limited set of necessary or self-attesting assumptions and builds testable models based on observable evidence and logic. If these models pass the tests, then they are provisionally accepted as accurate representations of reality, allowing extrapolations to be made and more elaborate models to be built around them. If the models fail the testing, they are rejected and abandoned. Science builds sequentially only on models that work, using those models to construct increasingly complete explanations.

No claim in science is privileged. All remain one test away from falsification. Any test that falsifies a widely accepted theory will be heralded among the scientific community because it leads to more knowledge and understanding. Science is not concerned with protecting *claims*. It is concerned with protecting the integrity of the *methods* used to separate true claims from false ones. Scientists are only too aware of the dangers of becoming attached to claims, which is exactly why they are dedicated above all to the methods of science.

Apologetics, by contrast, is a discipline entirely dedicated to *supporting and defending a specific set of claims about the nature of the universe*. The very word *apologetics* belies the true nature of the discipline, for it is exclusively concerned with *defense*. It is the antithesis of science and indeed of any legitimate academic discipline, as such disciplines are devoted to finding truth, wherever that path may lead and whatever that journey reveals. Science is about open-ended inquiry. Apologetics is about defending a position arrived at before inquiry begins. It incorporates an a priori commitment to justify one's preferred claims. There is nothing open-ended about it.

The Oxford Centre for Christian Apologetics notes that "apologetics is synonymous with evangelism," or preaching the Gospel to win converts. Apologetics is first and foremost a religious exercise, driven by the dictate to evangelize. This is where it departs from philosophy, which represents the critical examination of the rational grounds of humanity's most fundamental beliefs. In any discussion of the case for Christianity, if one is engaged in philosophy, then one has arguably ceased to do apologetics.

Apologists begin with a conclusion, which they take to be personally self-evident, and then devise ways to shield that conclusion against any attack. They work backward to mold the evidence and arguments to the conclusion, to which they are firmly anchored. The apologist is not allowed the luxury of questioning the conclusion, for it is his job simply to defend it. Imagine a knight tasked with defending the castle of the lord who employs him and has provided for the knight's family his entire life. The knight never considers whether the cause of his lord's attackers is just. He simply does whatever it takes to fend them off, to the point of laying down his life if necessary.

Apologists are defense lawyers for God, but God is not like the typical client. Lawyers are tasked with coming up with the best arguments for their clients' positions. But if the evidence, as it develops, fails to support those arguments or the opposing attorney otherwise undermines them, then the attorney can always go to her client and discuss reassessing their position. The lawyer and her client can concede certain arguments, settle claims on previously unacceptable terms, or take other actions to adapt to the new situation. Apologists don't have such options, for God doesn't compromise or reassess. They must proceed full steam ahead because to retreat would be unthinkable.

Humility appears nowhere in the apologists' playbook. Unlike scientists, who routinely admit their mistakes, apologists cannot admit to being wrong, as Carl Sagan observes:

> In science it often happens that scientists say, "You know that's a really good argument; my position is mistaken," and then they would actually change their minds and you never hear that old view from them again. They really do it. It doesn't happen as often as it should, because scientists are human and change is sometimes painful. But it happens every day. I cannot recall the last time something like that happened in politics or religion.[2]

If you doubt this, search for examples of well-known apologists conceding error on any significant point. Their jobs depend on them being dead certain of their position and right. An apologist faced with a strong argument that seems to undermine a crucial component of his faith cannot acknowledge that his own position may be flawed. If he cannot defeat his opponent's argument head on, then he must find a way around it that allows him, and the religion he defends, to save face. And as a last resort, he must simply *believe* anyway.

What if the evidence contradicting a key Christian claim, such as the Resurrection, were so overwhelming that no reasonable person could ignore it? William Lane Craig has famously said he would reject such evidence, no matter how compelling, because he prioritizes the "witness of the Holy Spirit" above all.[3] Theologian Justin Thacker of Cliff College takes a similar position: "Let's take the resurrection of Jesus Christ. If science somehow . . . told me that the resurrection of Jesus Christ was just categorically impossible, could not happen, I would disbelieve that and continue to believe what the Bible teaches about the resurrection of Jesus Christ, because if you take away the resurrection there is no Christian faith; it just doesn't exist."[4]

One must recognize the difference between *reasoning to a conclusion*, which is a valid approach, and *rationalizing from a conclusion*, which is not. The former is what scientists do. The latter is what apologists do.[5] Rather than clearly defining a concept of God, making predictions based on that concept, and then testing observations to see how well they fit those predictions, apologists take the world we see and craft ever-changing vague conceptions of God around it, relying heavily on cheats, such as logical fallacies, to fill in the gaps. Apologetics incentivizes and virtually requires such intellectual dishonesty. Accordingly, apologists excel in sophistry.

Logical fallacies allow the apologist to apparently save face without actually winning the argument or even moving the ball. Apologists use logical fallacies like magicians use smoke and mirrors because, like magicians, they are ultimately engaged in a game of deception. They are masters at incorporating hidden assumptions to frame issues so any answer works to their advantage. If they can get you asking the wrong questions, then they need not worry about the answers.

The same apologists who claim logic, reason, and evidence are on their side, however, are quick to devalue them when it is shown they are not. William Lane Craig is representative of the fickle value apologists place on such things, citing a commonly referenced "distinction" first recognized by Martin Luther:

> I think Martin Luther correctly distinguished between what he called the magisterial and ministerial uses of reason. The *magisterial use* of reason occurs when reason stands over and above the gospel like a magistrate and judges it on the basis of argument and evidence. The *ministerial use* of reason occurs when reason submits to and serves the gospel. . . . Should a conflict arise between the witness of the Holy Spirit to the fundamental truth of the Christian faith and beliefs based on argument and evidence, then it is the former which must take precedence over the latter.[6]

In other words, Dr. Craig will only acknowledge the validity of reason if it can be shown to support Christianity. If the arguments for Christianity are shown to be illogical and unreasonable, as I believe he ultimately knows they are, then Dr. Craig claims reason must be rejected for blind faith. For Craig and other apologists like him, non-Christian hypotheses aren't even "on the table" as options, which makes it laughable when he accuses atheists of closed-mindedness.[7] Craig has acknowledged that he would continue to believe despite the weight of rational arguments undermining Christianity, and he believes others should, as well. But could there ever be a legitimate justification for subjugating reason in this way?

Imagine you and I are playing a game like Monopoly, with clearly defined rules. I explain those rules will apply only if I remain ahead. If at any point you overtake me, then I will declare the rules void. You are simply to accept that I have won. Would you find this fair? Would you believe we were competing on a level playing field? That is the advantage that apologists like Craig demand for Christianity.

I would submit that if apologists require such an advantage, then they must recognize their position to be indefensible. They are requiring an exception to the rules that govern all other inquiry, a textbook example of special pleading. No one would demand such a thing unless they knew reason and logic were not on their side. The smarter apologists realize that while they can fool people with smoke and mirrors much of the time, they cannot demonstrate the reasonableness of Christianity against opponents adept at pointing out their sleight of hand. Accordingly, they must always allow themselves a "Get Out of Jail Free" card—the rejection of reason and appeal to blind faith. They must retain the ability to claim that if their arguments are shown to be unreasonable, belief is still warranted.

Christian apologists never provide opposing views a level playing field, for to do so would be giving up too much ground. They are never forced to admit defeat on any point because they haven't bought into the notion that the matter can be settled by reasoned argument. They will engage in discussions that employ reason only so long as their arguments are not effectively challenged. No one who takes this position can claim to be arguing in good faith.

Devout apologists can easily justify playing fast and loose with the rules of argumentation and debate because they believe they are fighting the good fight. In a battle for souls on God's behalf, shouldn't every weapon be at one's disposal, even pious deception? As Machiavelli would say, wouldn't such lofty ends justify any means necessary? The apologist must remain steadfast in his convictions and certain of his conclusions because just as a tiny chip can progressively spider across a windshield, so, too, can a hint of doubt crack the faith of believers until it is thoroughly shattered. It is this disaster against which the apologist stands guard.

All this demonstrates that apologists have strong incentives toward intellectual dishonesty. That does not necessarily mean they are all guilty of it, but like a stack of hundred-dollar bills sitting on the table before them, the motive is always there. My experience suggests this motive often gets the best of them. I have yet to read the work of any apologist not filled with fallacious reasoning, for which there can be only two explanations: incompetence or dishonesty. That they can typically adopt correct reasoning when convenient strongly suggests the latter.

In my studies of apologetics, I have observed a consistent pattern. Once arguments made in defense of Christianity are effectively refuted, apologists simply reframe the same arguments using additional fallacies. After these arguments are again refuted for essentially the same reasons, apologists reframe the arguments yet again, mischaracterizing the responses of their opponents, who continue to amass more evidence against them.[8] This cycle repeats ad nauseum. Most arguments employed by apologists today were effectively destroyed decades, if not centuries, ago, but from reading modern apologetics, it appears they failed to notice. Rarely do they seriously engage the arguments modern atheists make, preferring instead to battle straw men of their own construction.

Why do apologists take such positions? Why do they repeat the same discredited arguments rather than responsibly abandoning them? Why do they deliberately avoid addressing the most damning challenges to their faith? I think it is because they have enormously vested interests of their own and because they are heavily funded by others with the same interests. The endowments for many biblical institutions run into the millions or even *billions* of dollars per year.[9] This money is directed toward supporting vigorous defenses of the Christian faith. As Upton Sinclair writes, "It is difficult to get a man to understand something when his salary depends on his not understanding it."[10]

There is no analogous source of funding dedicated to undermining the Christian faith. Critical scholars have no common agenda—no story to confirm and no vested interest in any particular belief or interpretation of Christian Scripture. The only common motive with which they could reasonably be imputed is the search for truth, a motive that is neutral on the legitimacy of Christianity. This leaves us with an enormous resource imbalance: thousands to one for the defenders of Christianity against those impartially seeking truth. Under such a system, it is amazing any truth slips out.

A dispassionate search for the truth requires that we go where reason and evidence lead us, even if they lead us away from our most cherished beliefs. But this very approach is anathema to Christian apologists. Apologists are not skeptics, doubters, or seekers. They are deeply—personally, socially, and sometimes professionally—vested in defending a set of assumptions that, to anyone standing outside their insular belief system, look ridiculous. They are committed to the practice of thinking up excuses for believing in nonsense. To understand apologetics is to refute it.

I refer to various well-known apologists throughout this book, so I should introduce a few here. Perhaps the most often cited is Dr. William Lane Craig, who holds a doctorate in the philosophy of religion and runs an online apologetic ministry known as Reasonable Faith (https://www.reasonablefaith.org). Dr. Craig is extremely well known and influential due to his writings and series of debates, going back to 1991. Journalist Nathan Schneider says that in the field of philosophy of religion, Craig's books and articles are among the most cited. Sam Harris describes him as one of the most feared debaters among nonbelievers.

Richard Swinburne is a British philosopher at the University of Oxford. Professor Swinburne is a prolific writer always listed as one of the foremost Christian apologists in the world. Alvin Plantinga is an American philosopher at the University of Notre Dame described by *Time* magazine as America's leading orthodox Protestant philosopher of God. He has been regarded as the world's most important living Christian philosopher. While there are hundreds of living Christian apologists, these men represent the most modern and sophisticated approaches. They are all highly regarded within the Christian community, which is why I focus on them.

A BRIEF DISCUSSION OF CHRISTIAN THEOLOGY

> The study of theology, as it stands in Christian churches, is the study of nothing; it is founded on nothing; it rests on no principles; it proceeds by no authorities; it has no data; it can demonstrate nothing; and it admits of no conclusion. Not anything can be studied as a science without our being in possession of the principles upon which it is founded; and as this is not the case with Christian theology, it is therefore the study of nothing.
>
> —Thomas Paine, *The Age of Reason*, Part II, section 21

Christian theologians study the nature of God, using the Bible and other ancient writings as their primary guides. In this context, they attempt to construct a coherent system of Christian belief and practice. Some theologians consider themselves apologists but not all. It is important to understand, however, that professional theologians have dedicated their lives to a study that assumes the truth of Christianity. If it turns out the object of their study doesn't exist, then the entire discipline becomes meaningless, a subject without an object. The theologian might just as well have spent his or her entire life psychoanalyzing Tony the Tiger.

It should be apparent that strong institutional incentives exist to bias theologians toward conclusions that support Christianity. Theologians' attempts to systematize Christianity are themselves motivated by a desire to defend the faith from attack. The passages from the Bible are like bricks that they attempt to form into a building that cannot be toppled by even the strongest hurricane, much like the story of the three little pigs. Jonathan Haidt observes, "People who devote their lives to studying something often come to believe that the object of their fascination is the key to understanding everything."[11] This does not mean their opinions must be automatically discarded, but it warrants skepticism when encountering opinions that accord with Christian apologists. There are other problems with theological opinions, however, that are more serious.

One problem is that most of the big theological problems of the ancient world, such as "What does God do with the Sun at night?" have been conclusively solved—by science. Before science explained much of the natural order, such explanations were assumed to lie within the realm of theology. Theology and science were indistinguishable. Modern science has greatly eroded the very relevance of theology, leaving it to address only the most esoteric claims, searching for God in the gaps of science, or those related to the internal consistency of the Christian faith.

Unlike scientists, moreover, theologians do not employ empirical observations to guide them. While the object of their study is supposedly God, God has given none of them an interview. They are left to study the Scripture itself and the works of other theologians, operating in a continually reverberating echo chamber. Unlike with scientists, the esteem in which a theologian is held depends not on whether he has successfully proven or disproven anything but on how much he has read and how much he has written. With no way to measure the *quality* of output, one is left to go solely by *quantity*.

A major problem with theology is that it employs no consistent standards or methodology. It involves endless interpretations and reinterpretations of ancient texts, with no objective means of distinguishing who is right and who is wrong. Many disputes in the field involve assumptions based on pure speculation. People have long used a question posed by medieval theologians, "How many angels dance on the head of a pin?" as a metaphor for wasting time debating unanswerable topics of no practical value.

Theological constructs are not based on evidential discoveries but purely on human imagination. They result not from uncovering verifiable facts or building testable models from a cumulative body of knowledge but from people making things up out of thin air that are completely untestable and thus will remain forever debatable.

Given the speculative nature of their assumptions, it is impossible to demonstrate that theologians of today are any closer to the "truth" than were those of a thousand years ago. They deal in a hypothetical metaphysical realm that, even if it exists, lies beyond our ability to observe or study it. No theologian can reliably demonstrate that he has advanced the field or is more likely correct than any other, resulting in endless but ultimately pointless arguments. It is hard to see why a theologian should be accorded any expertise, except perhaps in the internal workings of his own discipline.

Perhaps the greatest problem with theology, however, is that it is entirely dedicated to understanding and explaining something that has never been established to exist. Psychologist Ray Hyman is well known for Hyman's maxim: "Do not try to explain something until you are sure there is something to be explained." Theologians jump the gun by assuming the existence of a particular god and then moving on to establish a scripturally consistent framework for that god without ever validating their assumptions.

After prominent atheist Richard Dawkins wrote his best-selling book *The God Delusion*, he was criticized by apologists for lacking a robust academic background in Christian theology, under the premise that this disqualified him from commenting on God's existence. Another well-known atheist, P. Z. Myers, responded to Dawkins's critics with what came to be known as the "courtier's reply." Comparing Dawkins to the truth-telling young gadfly of "The Emperor's New Clothes," Myers drafted the following response in the style of a pious Stephen Colbert:

> I have considered the impudent accusations of Mr. Dawkins with exasperation at his lack of serious scholarship. He has apparently not read the detailed discourses of Count Roderigo of Seville on the exquisite and exotic leathers of the Emperor's boots, nor does he give a moment's consideration to Bellini's masterwork, *On the Luminescence of the Emperor's Feathered Hat*. We have entire schools dedicated to writing learned treatises on the beauty of the Emperor's raiment, and every major newspaper runs a section dedicated to imperial fashion; Dawkins cavalierly dismisses them all. He even laughs at the highly popular and most persuasive arguments of his fellow countryman, Lord

D. T. Mawkscribbler, who famously pointed out that the Emperor would not wear common cotton, nor uncomfortable polyester, but must, I say must, wear undergarments of the finest silk. Dawkins arrogantly ignores all these deep philosophical ponderings to crudely accuse the Emperor of nudity.[12]

As Myers so effectively points out, theologians are like fashion commentators at the royal court, pontificating endlessly about the emperor's invisible attire. They scratch and claw to establish their superior knowledge and understanding of something that is simply unknowable. Someone must say, "The emperor has no clothes! There is nothing there! You are arguing over who best understands something you've never demonstrated to even exist!"

While one might find theological discussion enjoyable, that doesn't mean it is useful. Theology has solved no human problem and has contributed no valuable information to the human race. It has cured no diseases, alleviated no suffering, and yielded no "Eureka!" answers to any of the questions it was designed to address. It has yielded only discord and division. It is at best a form of intellectual masturbation and at worst a destructive pursuit that perpetuates and accelerates tribal hostilities among religious factions.

A BRIEF DISCUSSION OF ATHEISM, NATURALISM, AND HUMANISM

The atheist waits for proof of God. Until that proof comes, he remains, as his name implies, without God. His mind is open to every new truth, but only after it has passed the warder Reason at the gate.

—Annie Wood Besant, *The Atheistic Platform*

Skepticism is my nature. Freethought is my methodology. Agnosticism is my conclusion. Atheism is my opinion. Humanitarianism is my motivation.

—Jerry DeWitt, CNN Interview (July 22, 2013)

Before proceeding further, the reader should be familiar with three terms: *atheism*, *naturalism*, and *humanism*. Regarding these words, there is much confusion and misinformation. Some claim, for example, that atheists hate God and worship the devil (they don't), that naturalists reject supernaturalism a priori and out of hand (they don't), and that all humanists want to outlaw religion (they don't).

A. Atheism

An atheist is a person who does not believe in supernatural beings we commonly call gods. The atheist stands in direct contrast to a theist, who does believe in one or more gods. The atheist simply doesn't believe such beings exist or have ever existed. Of the atheist's beliefs, that is all that can be said with confidence.

Atheists have occasionally been further classified into gnostic (strong) and agnostic (weak) atheists. A gnostic atheist claims to know *with certainty* that gods do not exist. An agnostic atheist expresses no such certainty but nonetheless lacks belief because she does not feel such belief is justified by the evidence. The weakest possible atheist would see the scales as perfectly balanced, with the evidence equal on both sides, but concludes that due to theists' burden of proof to tip the scales, theism is not justified. So long as they conclude from this process there is no God and live their lives accordingly, they are atheists.

While gnostic atheists exist in theory, I have never in my life met one. I suspect the misperception among many Christians that most atheists are of the gnostic variety results from a psychological phenomenon known as projection, whereby theists with certainty in their own beliefs assume that atheists must be equally certain of theirs. Because the definitions and descriptions of gods are so vague and poorly defined, I don't think gnostic atheism is intellectually defensible, for how could one ever express certainty that no version of a god is even possible? Perhaps this is why, despite their regular use as straw men by Christian apologists, actual gnostic atheist sightings rank up there with Bigfoot and the Loch Ness Monster.

Theism and atheism represent a true dichotomy with respect to belief—you must be one or the other. There is no middle ground, for one cannot both believe and disbelieve in something simultaneously. Some use the term *agnostic* to avoid the atheist label, but these terms don't exist on the same scale. *Gnostic* and *agnostic* refer to one's *degree of certainty* or *claimed knowledge* in a position—not to the position itself. One can only be agnostic in reference to a held belief. Those claiming to be agnostics rather than atheists are merely erecting a linguistic smoke screen to avoid a socially undesirable label. As Madalyn Murray O'Hair said, the only difference between an atheist and an agnostic is guts.

William Lane Craig articulates a common "distinction" asserted by apologists. Craig labels agnostics as those who say there isn't a good reason to believe in God and atheists as those who say there is good reason *to disbelieve in God*. But this is nothing more than semantics, as the second position follows logically and necessarily from the first. If there is no good reason to believe in something (i.e., no good evidence for its existence, keeping in mind the inherent plausibility of the claim), then that itself is a good reason not to believe in it. It is the same position we would take regarding fairies or leprechauns. Would you be any less comfortable characterizing your belief in fairies in either way? These are just different ways of saying the same thing. I suspect Craig uses the latter description because it sounds more dogmatic, thus suggesting an equivalence between atheism and Christianity.

In the real world, I have found atheism a response to prevailing understandings of "God" in a given culture at a given time rather than a claim that no intelligible conception of "God" is conceivable. Generally, atheists don't believe in the God Christian theologians and apologists have traditionally tried to defend. To the extent one holds a unique customized view of God, atheists likely hold no opinion because they've never considered that version. In the Christian context, atheism typically means that one is *reasonably certain* that a being with the traditional characteristics of the Christian God does not exist.[13] In my own case, I am an atheist because I find most notions of God to be logically incoherent. To the extent models are advanced that are coherent, I don't find enough evidence to support them and much that defeats them.

Christians often charge atheism with being a religion, but such a charge reflects either an impossibly broad definition of *religion* that few would recognize or a profound lack of understanding of atheism. The common meaning of *religion* is a "belief system that incorporates supernatural elements, such as transcendent personal gods, as well as incontestable doctrines, rituals, and reality-encompassing narratives, which typically include a moral system."[14] Atheism entails none of these. It is the term we use to describe people who don't incorporate such things into their beliefs. It has been said, appropriately, that atheism is a religion like non-stamp-collecting is a hobby.

Every Christian knows what it's like to be an atheist because they already lack belief in every god but their own. They lose no sleep over whether they are following the dictates of Allah or Vishnu or Zeus. Atheists generally feel the same about the Christian God as Christians feel about the Greek gods and for many of the same reasons. Most of the arguments atheists use against the existence of the Christian God Christians already accept as compelling against the existence of all others. They take issue and sometimes offense only when those arguments are turned against the God they grew up with. An atheist can be thought of as someone who extends the same nonbelief Christians maintain toward the gods of other religions to one more god.

It is important up front to correct a common but entirely false charge leveled by many Christians against atheists: that they *reject* God. Atheists do not reject God; they simply don't believe in God, just as they don't believe in any other gods or other fantastical beings they conclude to have been invented by man. Few Christians would say they "reject" the Tooth Fairy. The very framing of this charge is loaded with the assumption that the entity being rejected actually exists, for one can only reject something they believe to be there.

Assume that Angela tells Bill he should go out with a friend of hers named Cheryl. Angela describes Cheryl as stunningly beautiful, whip smart, and otherwise perfect in every way. Bill declines Angela's invitation because he simply doesn't believe that Cheryl exists, at least as Angela has described her. Bill feels if it seems too good to be true, then it probably isn't. After Angela can produce no photos or other evidence of Cheryl's existence, he simply thinks Angela has made her up. If Cheryl does exist, then it would be absurd for her to become upset with Bill because he "rejected" her. Bill's disbelief must be laid at the feet of Cheryl's intermediary, Angela—she simply didn't give Bill a good enough reason to believe her. If Bill were to ultimately meet Cheryl, he likely would not harbor any feelings toward her other than perhaps surprise, for he never previously acknowledged her existence.

Christian fundamentalists often characterize atheists as the mortal enemies of Christians, as if the two sides were locked in a zero-sum game. But the dividing line is not between those committed to God and those committed to atheism. No one is "committed" to atheism. The line is between those committed to belief in God and those committed to finding the truth according to proven methods, even if that truth ultimately does not allow for God. Atheist activists generally push for paradigms that allow people's minds to roam freely, unconstrained by the rails imposed by religion or other strict dogmas. They are committed to open *processes* rather than any particular result, which is why they are also known as freethinkers.

Normally, we don't have names for people who *don't believe specific things*. We do so for atheists only because theistic belief is so widespread in many countries that the refusal to join in seems to many like aberrant behavior. It is the societal norm, and nonbelievers are the outliers. But if one can step back and look at it from a broader perspective, atheism is the appropriate default position. Sam Harris observes,

Atheism is not a philosophy; it is not even a view of the world; it is simply an admission of the obvious. In fact, "atheist" is a term that should not ever exist. No one ever needs to identify himself as a "non-astrologer" or a "non-alchemist." We do not have words for people who doubt that Elvis is still alive or that aliens traversed the galaxy only to molest ranchers and their cattle. Atheism is nothing more than the noises reasonable people make in the presence of unjustified religious beliefs. An atheist is simply a person who believes that the 260 million Americans (87 percent of the population) claiming to "never doubt the existence of God" should be obliged to present evidence for his existence—and, indeed, for his BENEVOLENCE, given the relentless destruction of innocent human beings we witness in the world each day.[15]

B. Naturalism

While atheism doesn't necessarily require any particular set of positive beliefs, my experience has demonstrated that the vast majority of atheists are also naturalists. Naturalists believe that nothing exists other than things and forces that are, from the proper vantage point, observable and measurable and thus can be studied by the natural sciences. Naturalists see the observable universe as a closed system in which, at least in principle, every aspect of the natural world can be explained by some other aspect of the natural world.

This view is known as metaphysical naturalism. The converse of this is supernaturalism—the belief there are things that cannot even in principle be studied by science. Anyone who is not a naturalist is a supernaturalist, positing the existence of entities and forces outside the natural world. Interestingly, the history of science is that of things being moved from the supernatural side of the ledger to that of the natural. We have never seen the reverse. As soon as something not yet understood becomes understood and incorporated into our collective knowledge, it becomes natural.

Due to the high correlation between atheists and naturalists, the terms are often used interchangeably, and I may do that occasionally. It is crucial to understand, however, that atheism need not *presuppose* or entail naturalism. The atheists with whom I am familiar reject supernatural claims not because they presuppose such claims *cannot be true* but because such claims are indeterminate—they are either poorly structured (hopelessly vague or containing logical inconsistencies), or they lack supporting evidence. There is, therefore, *no good reason* to believe they are true.

To postulate supernatural realities, we must conceptualize them in a familiar framework: that of the material world. But of course, we have no reasonable expectation that the supernatural, to the extent it exists at all, can be understood within such a frame—no expectation that the natural and supernatural share any qualities by which analogies of one can be drawn from the other. It is nonsensical to talk of things beyond the physical universe as though they were bound to the same rules and framework as the physical universe. Supernatural concepts are thus *fundamentally incoherent.*

Due to the intrinsic incoherency of supernatural concepts, naturalists can justifiably acknowledge our epistemic horizon (the limits of what we can hope to know) while affirming a *provisional assumption* that the natural world is all that exists. The concept of provisional assumptions is crucial. When considering a proposition, one is not limited to (1) demonstrating its falsity or (2) accepting it as true. One can also acknowledge that evidence for the proposition does not meet a reasonably acceptable threshold and thus operate under the provisional assumption the claim is false, dismissing it until it is demonstrated otherwise. This is the default position of naturalists. Outside of their own theology, theists do this as well. Most easily dismiss, for instance, the notion we are mere brains in a jar or simulations living in the Matrix, despite being unable to definitively disprove either. Without such provisional assumptions, none of us could operate effectively in the world.

It should be clear that one need not subscribe to the kind of ontological naturalism that theists generally accuse atheists of subscribing to—a belief that supernatural things *cannot* exist. But if one's epistemology is grounded in the physical universe, talk of supernatural things is at best speculative and meaningless and at worst, destructive to acquiring new knowledge and understanding. Assuming only the things for which we have good evidence has always proven the most useful approach for building those foundations.

It should be apparent that naturalism does not represent a positive a priori claim about the universe adhered to as doctrine. Nor is it a philosophy. It is instead an observational conclusion because everything we study appears to have a natural or material explanation. This conclusion results from an evidentialist worldview in which reason and evidence matter. Naturalists typically come to their position because that is where the evidence has led them, not because they have presumed it before even evaluating the evidence. In my experience, most naturalists would agree with Richard Carrier:

> Though I am an atheist, in the basic sense that I do not believe there are any gods, you will find that whether God exists or not really doesn't matter all that much. Every component of my philosophy can be arrived at independently and stands on evidence and reasoning that would not change tomorrow if a god announced himself to the world today. Rather than being a starting

assumption, my atheism is but an incidental conclusion from applying my worldview to the current state of evidence.[16]

Christian apologists like to claim that naturalists are closed-minded and express an *antisupernatural bias*. To make such a claim, however, one must first clearly define what is meant by *supernatural*, which they never seem able to do. One could, of course, define it as everything beyond the realm of the natural, but that is just a meaningless tautology. If the definition includes observable phenomena, then those are within the bounds of science. Naturalism allows for consideration of even the most unusual explanations, even those one might consider supernatural, so long as they can meet the standards required of *all other claims*.

Like the best physicians, who practice evidence-based medicine, prescribing only treatments shown to be effective through reliable methodologies, naturalists employ evidence-based metaphysics. Should medical schools still teach the demon theory of disease, given our knowledge of germs? Should they teach alchemy along with chemistry? And what of more esoteric hypotheses, such as divine creation of the universe? Claims that cannot be verified or tested are treated not as necessarily false but as indeterminate. Either way, they are necessarily ineligible for consideration in the modeling of reality. Only testable claims can provide a foundation for the erection of further knowledge. When asked whether, as a scientist, he would deny the possibility of Jesus having changed water into wine, Carl Sagan aptly responded, "Deny the possibility? Certainly not. I would not deny any such possibility. But I would, of course, not spend a moment on it unless there was some evidence for it."[17]

Apologists often claim that naturalists employ faith just as they do, but this is a false equivalence. Naturalists do not rely on religious faith but on trust in reliable processes like the scientific method. A clever apologist might respond that he is doing the same thing, but the reliable source in which he places his trust is the Bible. If he takes this route, however, he directly places into issue the reliability of the Bible, as the question then becomes "Which is the more reliable basis of accurate information about the nature of the universe: science or the Bible?" As discussed herein, the Bible is spectacularly inaccurate and unreliable as to just about every testable claim it makes, the opposite of the basis for naturalist beliefs. Geoff Mather observes, "To say that atheism requires faith is as dim-witted as saying that disbelief in pixies or leprechauns takes faith. Even if Einstein himself told me there was an elf sitting on my shoulder, I would still ask for proof, and I wouldn't be wrong to ask."[18]

Those who castigate naturalist scientists for too quickly dismissing supernatural claims also fail to consider the practical problem of resource
allocation. Assume your daughter was abducted in a small town with an
understaffed sheriff's department. What if four of the five deputies on
duty pursued such supernatural explanations as ghosts, demons, and evil
fairies rather than following up on leads leading to natural possibilities?
What percentage of their resources would you want the department to
spend exploring these supernatural options as opposed to natural ones?
Would you be upset if the department failed to follow up with someone
who witnessed your daughter being abducted by a suspicious but otherwise ordinary-looking man because they were all busy looking for a werewolf? If one officer dropped the werewolf chase for the more mundane
abduction report, would you accuse them of manifesting a "nonsuper-
natural bias"?

Every observation science has made has demonstrated the presence of
matter and energy. They have also demonstrated that every effect in the
known universe can be attributed to a cause generated by interactions of
matter and energy. In not a single case has that interaction been found
insufficient. In none has a third force been necessary to explain it. In other
words, all our evidence demonstrates that matter and energy are all there is.
Not a shred demonstrates the existence of anything other than matter and
energy. So the evidence for supernatural forces is exactly zero.

Only in a predominantly religious society would it be controversial to
claim that what we can see and observe is probably all there is. The evidence for this proposition is all around us and continuously subject to all
our senses and instruments of measurement. Therefore, naturalists maintain it should be the default position of mankind. If someone wants to demonstrate otherwise, then he or she is making a positive claim contrary to our
collective observations, which is why we demand specific evidence for such
claims. If it were any other way, then we would all have to acknowledge the
existence of invisible dragons, despite the lack of evidence in their favor,
simply because their nonexistence couldn't be disproven.

All supernatural claims rest on equal footing because they are equally unfalsifiable. Naturalism is the only framework that allows us to sort claims by
plausibility because it employs rules. The natural world is bound by impersonal laws that can be demonstrated to exist and that dictate the operation
of everything we experience. With those rules in place, we can test claims to
identify which are more likely to be true and build our base of knowledge.
With no such rules, any supernatural claim for the Christian God must be
considered as likely as the myths of any culture or religion.

It is important to distinguish metaphysical naturalism from *methodological naturalism*. Methodological naturalism is a disciplinary method used by scientists that categorically excludes interventionist supernatural forces from consideration of scientific questions. Scientists assume *for purposes of their research and methodology* that the universe works regularly according to rules and that if we can identify these rules, then we can reliably predict how things will behave. They focus on identifying causes that can be measured, quantified, and studied methodically rather than vague "supernatural" forces that lack such qualities.

For example, when measuring the distance of another galaxy to our Sun, scientists assume that light travels at a constant speed, as all our known experiments have demonstrated. They do not assume the light may have been arbitrarily sped up or slowed down along the way by some mysterious supernatural force. Allowing for the latter assumption would prevent one from reaching any conclusion about the distance because there would be no reliable rules to apply. Without the assumption of methodological naturalism, science as we know it would not be possible because all known physical laws would be invalidated as unreliable.

Scientists don't even have tools to test for causation by supernatural agency, as the very concept is incoherent. This necessarily limits scientists to natural explanations. Methodological naturalism is therefore justified by its prudential value and practical necessity. It is further warranted by its stellar record of results. Employing methodological naturalism in scientific research does not, however, commit one to metaphysical naturalism. The former is merely a tool rather than a philosophical position, limited in scope to a particular enterprise, and as such is employed by both religious and nonreligious scientists alike.

C. Humanism

The last topic for this chapter is humanism, also known as secular humanism.[19] Humanism represents an ethical and philosophical outlook that focuses on the well-being, flourishing, and thriving of humans. It emphasizes human needs and seeks rational ways to solve human problems, preferring critical thinking and evidence over ancient dogmas or faith. Humanism grew out of the eighteenth-century Enlightenment once people began to widely question religious dogma and the many ways it edged out and arguably perverted human-based ethical considerations. It reflected a new system of values stripped of supernatural components, focusing solely on practical, earthly concerns.

For humanists, every person has intrinsic value simply by being a member of the human race rather than their value being defined by their worth to a transcendent god. Unlike in Christianity, humans are not considered inherently evil, requiring external salvation. Everyone is given the benefit of the doubt unless and until they demonstrate otherwise. Humanists do not judge people by their piety or their adherence to any "divine" code. They are judged by their actions, their accomplishments, and how they treat others. To humanists, beliefs don't make you a better person. Behavior does.

Humanists do not try to appease supernatural agents and do not allow for the possibility that wrongs unpunished in this life may be punished in the next one. For humanists, this is the only life we have, so we must work to make sure justice is done here. Likewise, humanists believe this is the only world available to us, and we as a species will likely live on it unless and until we seriously screw things up. Humanists take a long-term view as opposed to the short-term view advocated by many Christians who posit the imminent Second Coming of Christ. Humanists therefore recognize a serious need to protect our planet's resources so they are preserved for future generations.

If we were to name a mythic hero of humanism, it would be Prometheus, the character from Greek mythology who defied Zeus to bring fire to mankind. For this "transgression," he was punished horribly by the gods but remained a hero to the Greek people. Prometheus represents down-to-earth compassion in the face of divine dictates and concerns of no value to man. The next Promethean character of mythology is Lucifer ("light bringer") in John Milton's *Paradise Lost*. Through the lens of Christianity, however, this character represents the ultimate embodiment of evil because rather than defying Zeus, he defies God. Author Janet Fitch observes, "If evil means to be self-motivated, to be the center of one's own universe, to live on one's own terms, then every artist, thinker, every original mind, is evil. Because we dare to look through our own eyes, rather than mouth the clichés lent us from the so-called Fathers. To dare to see is to steal fire from the gods. This is mankind's destiny, which fuels us as a race."[20]

Not all atheists are humanists, but as with naturalism, my experience reflects that most are. Like materialism, humanism flows naturally though not quite as directly from an evidentialist worldview. Once supernatural considerations are set aside for failing to meet the standards of epistemic reasonableness, one is left to mold an ethical system around natural concerns. As all humans share similar practical concerns, along with empathy for others, it follows that ethically minded atheists would be drawn to humanism.

Humanism is not itself an ethical system but rather a framework by which certain values are prioritized, which can then be incorporated into an ethical system. There are many entirely secular ethical systems consistent with humanism. Humanism would be inconsistent with ethical systems of certain conservative religions that focus heavily on doctrine and spiritual concerns divorced from human experience but could be consistent with more liberal religions that concentrate more on earthly human problems. An example in which conservative theists and humanists would likely disagree would be voluntary euthanasia. Humanism is not, therefore, inconsistent with Christianity per se but only with certain strains of Christianity and certain dogmas to the extent they conflict with human welfare or flourishing.

Humanism also represents no religion or specific political ideology. Unlike religions, humanism entails no creeds, sacred texts, or rituals. Unlike political parties, humanists have no common platform or position on most political issues. They can be Democrats, Republicans, Libertarians, Socialists, or many other political persuasions. Something all humanists do share is strong support for democracy, freedom, and human rights. Lists of humanist values include freethinking, fair and equal treatment of all people, and commitment to reason. Accordingly, humanists are opposed to such totalitarian systems as communism or fascism.

The US Constitution and Bill of Rights are steeped in humanist principles, which is not surprising since they were drafted by people well versed in Enlightenment thinking and writings, such as those of Thomas Jefferson and Thomas Paine. The original American values were Enlightenment values, and the Enlightenment was defined by its opposition to and deconstruction of Christian Scripture. Unlike comparable documents of just about every other nation of the day, the Constitution makes no reference to God, Christianity, or any other religion or supernatural concept. The remarkable thing about the United States is *precisely that it was created as a secular republic organized around the rights and freedoms of its citizens* rather than any divine authority. In 1797, the US Senate *unanimously* passed a treaty, signed by President John Adams, declaring that the "government of the United States is not in any sense founded on the Christian religion."[21] You can't get much clearer than that.

Because personal freedom is valued so highly by humanists, it would be inconsistent with their principles to demand their government to advocate their worldview or to punish or silence those who disagree with them. Humanists believe governments should be neutral on "spiritual" issues and that all religious, political, and philosophical positions should be open to debate and discussion without censorship on an equal playing ground. Only with a free marketplace of ideas can the best be expected to consistently win out.

Naturalism, humanism, and ultimately atheism can be seen as logical though not inevitable results of adopting an evidentialist worldview.

AVOIDING ERRORS
IN LOGIC AND REASON

Logical errors are, I think, of greater practical importance than many
people believe; they enable their perpetrators to hold the comfortable
opinion on every subject in turn.

—Bertrand Russell, *A History of Western Philosophy*

I assume we all agree that the evidentialist paradigm represents a legitimate epistemological framework, if not the only legitimate framework. We
also agree on what constitutes evidence and on the importance of distinguishing good evidence from bad. But this is not enough to guarantee we
reach valid conclusions. We must also understand how to tie this evidence
together. We must recognize how to draw the appropriate inferences.

This is the role of logic, the study of valid reasoning. Logic is a field unto
itself, on which volumes are written and to which entire college courses are
devoted. It is beyond the scope of this book to provide an in-depth discussion of logic. It is crucial, however, to develop a basic understanding of how
reasoning can get off the tracks. A logical argument is one in which each
step justifiably follows from the preceding step. Given certain premises,
certain conclusions must follow.

If I tell you that all Martians are aliens and that Marvin is a Martian, then
it logically follows that Marvin is also an alien. Given the two premises, the
conclusion is warranted and even required. Certain conclusions would not,
however, follow from the two given premises. If you concluded that Marvin

was a mechanic, that would not be a reasonable inference. It might be true, but the conclusion would not be compelled or even warranted by the available information. Given this information alone, you would have no logical basis to convince me that Marvin *must be a mechanic.* An argument that lacks logic is a failed argument.

Logic represents the rules that allow us to get from discrete pieces of information to a valid conclusion. If your beginning information is accurate and your logic is sound, then you will reach a valid conclusion. If either is lacking, you will not. Your conclusion may be correct by chance, but it will not be valid. What's more, you would have no ground to convince others that it is true, as any good argument must rest on sound logic. That is why good debaters focus on attacking either their opponent's premises or his logic.

A good example of an illogical argument from popular culture is the "Chewbacca Defense" from the popular show *South Park*. In a parody of Johnnie Cochran's closing argument in the O. J. Simpson trial, a fictional Cochran, in defending a record company from a claim of copyright infringement, presents the jury with a picture of the *Star Wars* character Chewbacca and says,

> I have one final thing I want you to consider. Ladies and gentlemen, this is Chewbacca. Chewbacca is a Wookiee from the planet Kashyyyk. But Chewbacca lives on the planet Endor. Now think about it; *that does not make sense!* Why would a Wookiee, an eight-foot-tall Wookiee, want to live on Endor with a bunch of two-foot-tall Ewoks? That does *not make sense!* But even more important, you have to ask yourself: What does this have to do with this case? Nothing. Ladies and gentlemen, it has nothing to do with this case! *It does not make sense!* . . . And so you have to remember, when you're in that jury room deliberatin' and conjugatin' the Emancipation Proclamation, does it make sense? No! Ladies and gentlemen of this supposed jury, it does not make sense! If Chewbacca lives on Endor, you must acquit! The defense rests.[1]

The fictional Cochran's closing sways the jury, and his client wins the case—despite the other party's well-reasoned arguments and substantive evidence. While this scene was obviously written for comic effect, it is eerily similar to arguments I've heard from other attorneys.

Another example comes from the movie *Animal House* in which the pre-law character Otter makes an impassioned defense of his fraternity, the Deltas, when they are brought before the dean for violation of college rules:

> Ladies and gentlemen, I'll be brief. The issue here is not whether we broke a few rules or took a few liberties with our female party guests—we did. But you

can't hold a whole fraternity responsible for the behavior of a few sick, twisted individuals. For if you do, then shouldn't we blame the whole fraternity system? And if the whole fraternity system is guilty, then isn't this an indictment of our educational institutions in general? I put it to you, Greg—isn't this an indictment of our entire American society? Well, you can do whatever you want to us, but we're not going to sit here and listen to you badmouth the United States of America. Gentlemen! [leads the Deltas out of the hearing, humming the "Star-Spangled Banner"][2]

Rather than trying to actually defend the actions of his fraternity, Otter turns the situation into a test of patriotism. Who wants to be known as badmouthing America? This is, of course, irrelevant to the issue at hand, but it is intended to stir the emotions, and emotions can lead us to conclusions, just as reason can.

Illogical or irrational arguments are considered "fallacious" and categorized into specific "logical fallacies."[3] It is the job of attorneys to identify and point out fallacious arguments in a trial, so the jury does not get off track and decide based on irrelevant considerations. Attorneys who employ such arguments generally do so when they have no good arguments to make, as a type of smoke screen. A common saying among lawyers is "If the facts are with you, argue the facts. If the law is with you, argue the law. If neither is with you, just argue." Fallacious arguments are just that: arguments without substance.

But just because they have no substance does not mean they can't be persuasive. Such arguments often appeal to emotions or to commonly held misconceptions or assumptions. Or, as in the previous examples, they may just distract from relevant issues. It is crucial to understand, however, that logical fallacies never legitimately advance an argument. A position supported only by logical fallacies is in actuality supported by nothing.

Recognizing and understanding logical fallacies is not easy or intuitive. It takes study. Psychologist Alfred Mander recognizes,

> Thinking is skilled work. It is not true that we are naturally endowed with the ability to think clearly and logically—without learning how, or without practicing. . . . People with untrained minds should no more expect to think clearly and logically than people who have never learned and never practiced can expect to find themselves good carpenters, golfers, bridge-players, or pianists.[4]

I address many fallacious arguments in this book. Why? Because I believe Christianity rests on a foundation of fallacies. Those who defend the Christian faith, Christian apologists, pepper their writings with them. I can think of no well-known Christian apologist who does not rely heavily on fallacious reasoning and arguments. Why is this? As discussed in the previous chapter, like in economics, it comes down to incentives.

LOGICAL FALLACIES AND CONCEPTS COMMON TO APOLOGETICS

> The tough mind is sharp and penetrating, breaking through the crust of legends and myths and sifting the true from the false. . . . Rarely do we find men who willingly engage in hard, solid thinking. There is an almost universal quest for easy answers and half-baked solutions. Nothing pains some people more than having to think.
>
> —Dr. Martin Luther King Jr., *Strength to Love* (1964)

When attempting to determine the truth of a claim, one should look for supporting arguments that are solid and strong. A good argument combines demonstrable facts and sound reasoning. What constitutes a demonstrable fact is relatively straightforward and noncontroversial. What constitutes sound reasoning, though, is anything but.

Sound reasoning uses the principles of logic to connect facts and propositions so one follows appropriately from the other, from factual premises to a conclusion. Sound reasoning is the stock in trade not only of lawyers but also of those seeking to responsibly persuade others of their positions. Reasoning can go wrong, however, in many ways. Common reasoning errors are known as "logical fallacies."

Because logical fallacies arise repeatedly in the works of Christian apologists, I address them early on, so I digress less frequently when discussing the substance of the arguments. Logical fallacies are not factual mistakes but rather mistakes in connecting the factually established "dots" from a premise to a conclusion. If not identified, they can make the argument persuasive for the wrong reasons. They fool the critical faculties of your mind much like an optical illusion fools your eyes. Sometimes, these fallacies are offered innocently, while other times, they result from deliberate attempts to mislead.

The fallacies I discuss are known as "informal." Such fallacies are context-sensitive rather than form-based and do not necessarily require that the proposition for which they argue be false. They are based on faulty reasoning rather than faulty logical deduction. Nevertheless, to the extent an argument is based on an informal fallacy, that argument does not render the proposition any more likely than before the argument was made. The fallacious argument should have no persuasive effect because it does not legitimately advance the ball for the person making it, and an unpersuasive argument is a failed argument.

Fallacious arguments can often be identified without a thorough understanding of the content. Once an argument has been demonstrated to be fallacious, there should be no need to otherwise respond to it. Some complex arguments can appear very compelling because they involve numerous steps, many of which may be based on sound logic and reasoning. As with a physical chain, however, any such argument is only as strong as its weakest link. If a link can be shown to be fallacious, then the entire argument may fail. I suspect that is why arguments from such literate apologists as C. S. Lewis remain so popular, for given the often-unwarranted assumptions Lewis demands, the arguments otherwise seem logically sound. If you miss the fallacy underlying those assumptions, then the arguments appear entirely convincing.

Some examples may help demonstrate the concept. Assume that Alex proposes to Bill that the grass at their feet is green. His argument for this contention is that when he looks down, the grass appears green to him. Alex acknowledges that he assumes his eyes are working properly and that they accurately reflect the true nature of the world. If we accept Alex's assumptions as true, then there is nothing obviously fallacious about his argument. It proceeds from mutually recognized facts through logical inferences to a reasonable conclusion.

Now, let's assume that Bill disagrees with Alex. Bill proposes these counterarguments:

1. *Alex is wrong because Alex is a jerk.* This argument demonstrates the *ad hominem fallacy*. It is an attack on Alex's character. It is unnecessary to know whether Alex is a jerk. To say this would not address or even engage with Alex's argument. It is intended to make people dislike Alex and therefore reject his argument regardless of its merits.

2. *Alex only claims the grass is green because it appears that way on television. But television programmers can and often do change the colors of things through editing and camera tricks.* Here, Bill uses a *straw man*. He has mischaracterized Alex's argument, claiming it to be something Alex never actually argued but that Bill could more easily rebut. Alex never argued that the grass was green *because it appeared green on television*. He relied instead on his own firsthand

sensory experience. Disingenuous debaters frustrated by the strength of their opponents' *actual* arguments use straw men to create the appearance of an easy win. If one accepts Bill's mischaracterization of Alex's argument, then Bill's response will seem persuasive because his other points follow logically. An honest approach would be for Bill to obtain Alex's agreement to his summary of Alex's position before addressing it. If that is not possible, then Bill should at least attempt to state Alex's position in the most charitable way possible, an approach known as "steel-manning."

3. *If you accept that the grass is green, then what will prevent you from thinking everything is green? Soon, you will cease to recognize other colors entirely.* This is the *slippery slope fallacy*—claiming that accepting something seemingly benign (A) will necessarily lead to other things that are highly undesirable (B). The first problem with this fallacy is the typical failure to demonstrate that A *necessarily* leads to B. It has been said that a valid slippery slope requires strong gravity and weak friction, two assumptions rarely demonstrated or justified. The second and more fundamental problem is that even if A does lead to B, it does not mean that A is untrue or unethical. Fundamentalist Christians use this argument against gay marriage, claiming it will lead to families falling apart and people marrying their pets, farm animals, or toasters—never with any supporting evidence for such claims. Each move along the slope must be justified for the argument to be a valid one.

4. *Either the grass is blue, or the moon is made of cheese. Because we know the moon isn't made of cheese, the grass must be blue. It therefore cannot be green.* This is a *false dichotomy*. A limited set of options is presented as the only set of possibilities, when in fact there are many others. For instance, the grass could be green and the moon *not* be made of cheese. The argument can seem valid, unless one points out other options.

There are dozens of logical fallacies. Apologetic literature may appear compelling to the uninitiated reader because it is loaded with such fallacies, often constructed ingeniously to build on one another. Many are hidden within assumptions built into the Christian worldview that people have accepted since childhood without ever critically analyzing them. In the appendix to this book, I explain in detail some of the more common fallacies employed by Christian apologists, and I highly recommend reviewing that now. Here, I discuss concepts that are not all fallacies per se but are crucial to understand before proceeding further.

A. The Argument from Ignorance

Also known as the "God of the gaps," the argument from ignorance, as employed by apologists, posits that any time science can't provide a definitive answer to a question, the answer must be God. It posits the Christian God as the default explanation for any and all unanswered questions. It is amazing and instructive how often Christian apologists resort to arguments from ignorance. Most apologetic arguments fall into this category.[5] All these arguments have the same fatal objections, though I spend additional time on each to demonstrate additional reasons why they fail.

The argument from ignorance is based on a false dichotomy that things are either explained in their entirety by a comprehensive and consensus-based scientific theory or they are explained as the work of God. It can be summarized as "If we don't know with certainty how something happened, then God must have done it." It consists of nothing more than giving our ignorance a name—that name being "God."

An example of how the argument from ignorance typically plays out is this: Scientist Alex explains his naturalistic theory of how consciousness works. He says he can explain just about every step in the process. He can definitively show how A leads to B leads to C and so on, through the final step Z. He says he and his team aren't exactly sure of the mechanism for moving from P to Q, though they have some pretty good ideas and are far along in testing those ideas. The testing looks promising. The supernaturalist stands and says, "Oh, you can't explain P to Q? Then you fail. God did it. Case closed."

As explained in more detail elsewhere, there is no justification for making the Christian God the default position. Any religion could claim the same in a game of "King of the Hill." Where we don't know something, agnosticism ("We don't know") is the only rationally justified default position. The move from ignorance to knowledge can only be justified through evidence. We should accept and believe only claims supported by evidence. Until that happens, we should withhold judgment—not jump to the conclusion that the deity of one's preference is the true cause.

The argument from ignorance also rests on the false assumption that what we know now is all we'll ever know—that the "as yet unexplained" should be treated as "forever unexplainable" and that if no satisfying natural explanation is currently at hand, then such an explanation is impossible.

Accordingly, it posits, we are justified in throwing up our hands, ending our quest for knowledge, and simply concluding that "God did it." It implicitly proposes an end to scientific inquiry in favor of blind acceptance of theological causation.

I suspect that people so easily fall prey to this fallacy because of two characteristics common to the human condition: (1) arrogance in our own individual abilities to make unaided sense of nature and (2) discomfort with uncertainty. Many feel that if they can't understand how something works, then it must be because *no one can understand it*. It must be beyond the human capacity to comprehend. As French author Henri René Albert Guy de Maupassant writes in his short horror story "Le Horla," "How weak our mind is; how quickly it is terrified and unbalanced as soon as we are confronted with a small, incomprehensible fact. Instead of dismissing the problem with: 'We do not understand because we cannot find the cause,' we immediately imagine terrible mysteries and supernatural powers."[6]

As discussed, the best approach when confronted with a scientific question for which no clear scientific consensus has emerged is simply to acknowledge that we don't know the answer *yet*. As history has demonstrated again and again, science will eventually plug the gaps in our knowledge. It is reasonable to wait for that to happen rather than inject an unnecessary and unjustified hypothesis (God) out of a desire for immediate certainty.

Because I find it more descriptive, I often refer to the argument from ignorance as the "God Default" argument. The alternative to the God Default is the Naturalistic Default. That means that if we don't know the answer to some scientific question, then we should assume the question has an answer found within the natural world unless proven otherwise. What, you may ask, justifies the Naturalistic Default over the God Default? Only that whenever a natural explanation to a scientific question has been assumed, that assumption has *always* turned out to be correct once more knowledge was obtained.[7]

By contrast, *every time* a supernatural explanation has been assumed for something we now understand, that assumption has been proven wrong. There are innumerable examples of the former but none of a supernatural explanation proving to be correct. *Ever.* As Neil deGrasse Tyson observes, "I have yet to see a successful prediction about the physical world that was inferred or extrapolated from the content of any religious document. Indeed, I can make an even stronger statement. Whenever people have used religious documents to make detailed predictions about the physical world, they have been famously wrong."[8] Naturalism's 100 percent success rate should be justification enough.[9]

If science has taught us anything, it is that the unknown and the unknowable are different things, and the first does not imply or require the second. Science has made a practice of identifying the unknown and explaining it. History is strewn with those claiming the unknowable, only to find the fact was merely unknown, and temporarily at that. As scholar Robert Price says, "Experience tells us that whenever a scientist or historian has stopped short, shrugged, and said, 'Well, *I* can't explain it! I guess it must be a miracle!' he has later regretted it. Someone else was not willing to give up, and, like a detective on a *Cold Case Files* show on TV, he or she did manage to find the neglected clue."[10] It has never been profitable to bet against the power of science to explain the natural world.

Given that we have no experience with supernatural explanations, we would need to eliminate all-natural explanations decisively before defaulting to a supernatural one. The burden, then, is always on the apologist to eliminate *every possible naturalistic explanation* before arguing for a supernatural one. "We don't know, therefore God" is not sound reasoning. "We don't know" is never a good reason for believing *any particular theory*. All we can say within the bounds of reason is "We don't know; therefore, we don't know." Meanwhile, we are justified by analogy in assuming the world works according to natural laws and that a natural solution will be found if given enough time. The god of the gaps posited by the argument from ignorance is merely a pocket of scientific ignorance always diminishing.

The biggest problem with the argument from ignorance, however, is that, as used by apologists, God represents no alternative explanation, at least not in any meaningful sense. The purpose of an explanation is to dispel mystery. No valid explanation introduces an *even more mysterious concept* to explain the first. Assume you witnessed a man pull a rabbit out of an apparently empty hat and asked him to explain how he accomplished this feat. In response, he simply says, "It's magic." I doubt this would satisfy you. To say something is magic amounts to another way of saying we have no explanation. Likewise, to identify the explanation of something as God without clearly defining God and the process by which God accomplishes this result is no different. It represents a glib and ultimately meaningless tautology—a placeholder for those lacking the courage or intellectual honesty to admit they don't know. By invoking the supernatural, anything can be "explained" in this sense, but such an explanation is worthless because it tells you nothing of value.

To compare explanations, furthermore, they must be roughly equivalent. Arguments from ignorance can, at best, poke holes of ignorance in the positions of others. But that isn't enough to win the argument. One must build a comparable explanatory theory of one's own to replace the one he is attempting to tear down. Scientific theories provide testable models that describe how things currently work and allow for predictions of how they *will* work under different conditions. Religious "explanations" do neither.[11] How can they when God and his ways are considered forever unexplainable? These arguments can never justify nor legitimately advance belief in the Christian God. Religious explanations never serve as anything but rationalizations for our ignorance, which is why, when contrasted with real scientific explanations, they can and should be rejected out of hand.

B. Shifting the Burden of Proof

Percy Bysshe Shelley recognized, "God is an hypothesis, and, as such, stands in need of proof: the *onus probandi* (burden of proof) rests on the theist."[12] The burden of proof is always on the one making the affirmative claim, especially when arguing over the very existence of something. It is axiomatic that you can't prove a negative, but that isn't to say that the negative may still not be the most reasonable conclusion. A negative position is supported by a lack of proof for the positive position to which it is opposed. To demonstrate, assume I claim to own a rare baseball card worth thousands of dollars. When you question my claim and ask me to produce the card, I demand instead that you prove me wrong—right there, right then. You would be at a loss. Does that mean you must accept my claim as true? Of course not. The logic is the same when theists demand the atheists prove God doesn't exist.

When apologists attempt to shift the burden of proof, they are asking atheists to prove there is no needle in the haystack. As the atheist nears the bottom, sifting through every strand and finding no needles, the apologist returns with truckloads more hay to add to the pile, repeating until the atheist collapses in exhaustion. Once the atheist has gone through a few tons of hay without finding a needle, however, I maintain he would be well justified in jumping onto the ever-growing pile without fear of impalement.

Someone claiming the existence of a supernatural deity with specific characteristics must provide evidence this being is likely to exist. This burden is further justified by the fact that the apologist makes an extraordinary claim—one that contradicts natural law and thus the principle of analogy. Because we see natural law in action every day, every observation affirms it as the only game in town. Scientists have recorded no observation that cannot be explained by natural law. All of science is thus evidence for naturalism.

If I walked up to you and said, "Prove I can't fly," I'm guessing you would respond, "What do you mean, prove you *can't* fly? Show me you can!"[13] Your skepticism would be well justified. I'm the one making the extraordinary claim, so why shouldn't I have to prove it? How would you feel if I went around telling everyone that your failure to definitively disprove my claims demonstrated that I could in fact fly? But apologists do this every day. They demand of their opponents, "Disprove my unproven and unprovable argument."

Defending a position as a logical possibility differs greatly from demonstrating that it is true. If I firmly believe that my invisible incorporeal dragon exists with no supporting evidence, then there is probably little you can do to convince me otherwise. By accepting an unfalsifiable premise, I have created my own airtight excuse to continue believing. Without positive evidence supporting my position, however, I could not reasonably expect to convince anyone else of my claim. The burden of proof tells us who must support their claim with evidence.

A murder trial provides an apt analogy. Assume the defendant establishes through several reliable witnesses that he was across the city only seconds before the crime was committed and also seconds afterward. In response to this evidence, the prosecution argues that he must have magically teleported to the location in the intervening seconds, committed the murder, and then teleported back. In America, the law places the burden of proof on the prosecution. The defendant, therefore, need not call an array of scientific experts to the stand to demonstrate that teleportation is impossible. Nor must the defendant prove an alternate theory of how the murder occurred. In fact, the defendant does not have to put on any proof. If the jurors feel no compelling case has been made for the prosecution's legal theory, then they *must* find the defendant innocent.

The prosecution would need to make a compelling case for his claim, demonstrating that it is not only plausible but also likely. He would need to show the mechanism by which the teleportation occurred. He could not simply say, "It's a mystery," leaving it to the jury to speculate on the means. He would then have to demonstrate that no more mundane explanation is remotely plausible. If the prosecution fails to meet his burden of proof, then the defendant must be found innocent. Technically, this represents a finding not that the prosecution's position was necessarily false but that it was simply unsupported.

For another example, assume our mutual friend Joe tells us he was abducted by aliens, anally probed, and returned to his bedroom with no time having passed. You maintain that Joe's story lacks credibility, presenting me with evidence that Joe is a schizophrenic, with a history of visions normally controllable with medication, but he went off his medication on this night. You haven't conclusively proven that Joe's story is false, but you have called into question the reliability of his testimony. Because the event is so inherently implausible, most people would find this enough to conclude that Joe is mistaken. Likewise, the way to demonstrate something like Jesus's Resurrection never occurred would be to show (a) the event is highly improbable and (b) the sources for it are not sufficiently reliable to overcome the inherent implausibility. As I demonstrate later in this book, both have been done.[14]

As a final example, imagine you and I are debating the existence of leprechauns to an audience of sugary-cereal lovers. I go first and tell the audience I will attempt to show that leprechauns exist, but you must show they don't. I then relate my evidence—the testimony of a classmate, John Smith, who claims to have seen a leprechaun once as a child. I explain that all John Smith's classmates and teachers regard him as honorable and reliable, and therefore we must accept his written account of his visitation by a leprechaun as factual, for it is more likely that Smith is telling the truth than lying. In fact, there is no evidence he was lying. I claim the only way you can win the debate is to prove Smith is lying.

This would, of course, be impossible, but the very fact his testimony is *about the existence of leprechauns* calls it into serious question, regardless of his character witnesses. It is far more likely that he acted out of character on this occasion or that his character witnesses were wrong or lying than that leprechauns actually exist. This is because, applying Bayes' theorem, given the low prior probability for that claim, the evidentiary standard is proportionately high. Most people today don't think of the standard being that high for the Resurrection of Jesus simply because they have grown up with this claim unchallenged, and it is familiar to them. But to an outsider, the Resurrection is no different from the existence of leprechauns.

When presented with an extraordinary claim, it is simply not reasonable to accept the claim unless another can definitively prove it impossible. There are endless such claims that cannot be proven impossible. The claim should be rejected once found to be *implausible*. Because extraordinary claims are inherently implausible, they should not even be open to consideration unless and until the proponent first demonstrates that all natural possibilities are less probable than magic. Supernaturalism should always be the explanation of last resort.

The supernatural represents that which cannot be disproven, for it is exempt from the rules of proof. And if it cannot be disproven, then it cannot lead anywhere because it is only by disproving hypotheses that we find the path to Truth. Questions regarding such supernatural entities as God are ultimately meaningless because we have no evidence to support the proposition and no means to obtain any evidence about the matter. We therefore have no reason to even consider the question, much less presume to answer it affirmatively. All supernatural theories are equal in terms of their plausibility.

It is extremely important to understand this concept because many of the arguments raised by apologists get into areas outside the bounds of reliable scientific knowledge, such as how the universe came to be. In those areas, we can only speculate. But not all speculations are equal, and this is where the burden of proof tentatively settles which should be preferred. The burden must always be assigned to the one making the positive claim. And when that claim is extraordinary, the level of required proof should be very, very high.

When a scientist says, "God does not exist," she means something similar to when she says, "Aether does not exist," "Psychic powers do not exist," and "Life does not exist on the moon." All such statements are casual shorthand for a more elaborate and technical statement: "This alleged entity or thing has no place in any scientific equations, plays no role in any scientific explanations, cannot be used to predict any events, and does not describe any thing or force that has yet been detected, and there are no models of the universe in which its presence is either required, productive, or useful." In other words, it has never been shown to affect anything, and because God fails this test of impact, we have no good reasons to believe such an entity exists. And if we have no good reason to believe, then why should we?

While placing the burden of proof on believers may seem unfair to Christians, it isn't. Placing the burden on nonbelievers would amount to a truly impossible standard because they could never prove a negative. But believers can always defeat the naturalistic hypothesis with good evidence. The naturalistic hypothesis is unforgiving. It can be rebutted with any good evidence of a violation of the regular patterns predicted by natural laws. Naturalists find common ground with Albert Einstein, who remarked, "No amount of experiments can ever prove me right; a single experiment can prove me wrong."[15] Unfortunately for Christians who object to naturalism, they have never produced such evidence.

The bottom line is that in any debate over the existence of a supernatural being, such as the Christian God, the burden of proof *must be assigned to the believer*. Any other approach would require us to accept every supernatural claim at face value, making it impossible to ever discern reality from fantasy.

C. Retreating to the "Possible"

Once the burden of proof is appropriately in place, the person making the claim must demonstrate that his position is *probable*, meaning it is more likely than not. This is why apologists seek to avoid the burden of proof like the plague. They know they cannot effectively demonstrate that the core claims of their religion are probable, as probability requires appeal to evidence they don't have. Instead, they are forced to retreat to the position that their claims are merely *possible*. They saddle their opponents with the burden of disproof and then express contentment with a reasonable doubt that the position they have been advocating so vehemently just *might be true*.

To establish that something is possible isn't persuasive that it is true. Very few of the things we discount out of hand represent logical impossibilities. For example, it is not a compelling argument to claim that it is *possible* for a fully formed McDonald's to exist on the surface of Titan. Everyone could readily agree that this is logically possible, but it is so highly improbable that no one would seriously entertain it for a moment. Likewise, saying that God is logically possible doesn't move the ball down the field if the apologist is interested in persuasion because you win no argument by showing your position *might be true*. Such possibilities are cheap. The proponent of a position must convince you that his is the *most likely* among all possible alternatives, and this can only be done through mounting evidence. The opponent need not demonstrate that the position cannot possibly be true but merely that the arguments and evidence presented *do not demonstrate it to be true*.

The apologist, furthermore, includes within his definition of the possible *magic and miracles*—for neither of which modern man has any good evidence. This is merely equivocation because most people have a very different concept in mind when they talk about what is possible and what is not. If I ask you whether it is possible for a rhinoceros to appear out of thin air, you would most likely respond, "Of course not," for that would contravene your experience and everything science has revealed to us about how the universe works. If apologists are asking us to leave these behind and speak of *logical possibilities*, then it makes no sense to even ask what is possible because it would include virtually anything and everything one could imagine. The answer would always be yes and also "So what?"

This might also be described as a retreat to metaphysics, which is the branch of philosophy dealing with such abstract concepts as being, knowing, substance, identity, and time and space, with no necessary grounding in reality or evidential support. This explicitly occurs when your debate opponent dismisses your takedown of all the evidence supporting his claim, demanding that in addition you demonstrate that, given the possibility of magic and a supernatural world unfathomable to us, his claims cannot be true. In other words, your evidence means nothing once we untether the argument to the rules we apply in the real world. But why should we ever do this?

When encountering such a response, the principles of parsimony and analogy come into play. A claim that something is possible by natural forces with which we are familiar and have common experience is categorically superior to a claim that something is possible only by means of supernatural forces with which we have neither familiarity nor experience. Our knowledge and experience justify confidence in option A over option B, which requires assumptions we likely do not share and which have no independent justification.

There is a vast gulf between conceding something is possible and taking it seriously. We cannot definitively disprove that we are in the Matrix, that we are brains in a vat, that external reality is an illusion, or that we will ride on magic potatoes through rainbow-colored clouds when we die. And yet, these are not propositions to which many people, aside from a few people wandering Hollywood Boulevard in tin-foil hats, devote any serious thought. These possibilities violate Ockham's razor, which experience tells us leads us in the right direction far more often than not.

One may only legitimately resort to possibilities when responding to a specific claim that one's proposition is logically *impossible*. Apologists implicitly presume that their opponents have made such a claim regarding the existence of God. But this is a straw man, for most atheists rest their beliefs not on the theoretical impossibility of theism but rather on apologists' failure to evidentially support theism. This argument can only be countered by evidence.

Establishing the possibility of one's position is worthless as persuasion. It cannot advance the ball. Only properly supported *probabilities* do that. Relying solely on a possibility is essentially a concession and should be treated as such.[16] Ultimately, a retreat to the possible is not something that can establish a reason for believing. It can only serve as an *excuse* for continuing to believe—and a weak one at that.

D. Ockham's Razor

Ockham's razor (also known as the "principle of parsimony") is a principle used in logic and problem solving stating that among competing hypotheses, the one with the fewest new assumptions is generally correct and therefore preferred.[17] It is often paraphrased as "The simplest explanation is usually right" or, as Albert Einstein is said to have explained, "Everything should be made as simple as possible, but not simpler."[18] These statements can be misleading, however, unless one understands *simpler* to mean the explanation with the least assumptions—the one that invokes no more presuppositions than necessary. It does not mean the explanation that takes the shortest time *to explain* or is the *most intuitive* but instead the most parsimonious one. Each new assumption multiplies the possibilities of error, increasing the probability that the proposition is false. Parsimony is therefore directly related to reliability.

Another way of understanding Ockham's razor is by asking if the additional assumptions required by the more complicated theory add any explanatory advantage or value. Are they required to explain something not otherwise explained? Do they allow us to make predictions that are more accurate than the simpler theory? If not, then they have no value and can probably be safely abandoned. Some say that Ockham's razor "shaves off" the extraneous assumptions.

An example of Ockham's razor would be the explanation for most diseases. In ancient times, as reflected in the Bible, such illnesses were thought to be caused by evil spirits. The Bible even suggests this may have been the primary function of demons: causing disease. Biblical healing rituals involved exorcising the demons from the body of the afflicted. Modern science and medicine have revealed that such illnesses are instead the result of purely natural processes, resulting in the now universally accepted germ theory of disease. The common cold, for example, can be fully explained by the germ theory. A virus invades the body and causes such symptoms as coughing and runny noses. Such an explanation is based on millions of observations and experiments. It explains everything about the common cold with no need for additional assumptions. The explanation is airtight.

But what if you were a doctor, and your patient claimed that he believed his cold was actually caused by demonic possession, and he planned to engage in a very dangerous exorcism ceremony to rid himself of the cold? As you have no doubt guessed, his argument violates Ockham's razor. The problem is that it requires additional assumptions (the existence and possession of demons) that are unproven and, more important, unnecessary to explain the disease. The disease is already explained by observable natural phenomena. The additional assumptions have no additional explanatory power (they clarify nothing not already adequately explained by the existing theory) and are therefore superfluous. Furthermore, as we know nothing about demons, we have injected into a known process something that is completely unknown, rendering the explained inexplicable.

Another example is the concept of the "aether." This was a material hypothesized by medieval philosophers to explain several natural phenomena, such as the traveling of light through space. Though no material could be observed or measured, an undetectable substance was the only thing the philosophers could postulate to make sense of light's otherwise strange behavior. Ultimately, more precise theories were developed that required no such assumptions and had far greater predictive power. The existence of the aether was never actually disproven. It was simply unnecessary and thus ultimately discarded, shaved off by Ockham's razor.

Once, belief in God appeared to provide the most parsimonious explanation for many natural phenomena, but that time has long passed. Science has provided us reliable and verifiable knowledge that offers simple and clear explanations requiring no supernatural intervention. Science has destroyed the apparent parsimony of theological explanations. The success of methodological naturalism is a testament to Ockham's razor as applied to the hypothesis of an interventionist God because by not factoring it in as a possibility, we can safely assume the regularity of nature, and that assumption has consistently allowed us to make accurate scientific predictions. Without that assumption, such predictions would be impossible. Any irregularity in the laws of nature would be compelling evidence for an interventionist God, but no such irregularity has ever been observed.

Adding God to any explanation adds not just a single assumption but many. For instance, we must assume that incorporeal minds exist, that matter can be wished into being, that a sentient being can exist timelessly, and all the other features of God never observed to exist in any sense. If considering two potential explanations for something difficult to explain, such as human consciousness, the first of which requires assuming something inexplicable even in principle (e.g., a disembodied mind that can wish things into existence) while the second does not, then the second explanation is preferred.

As with science, Ockham's razor has a place in the law. Many legal disputes turn on the interpretation of words within a statute or a contract. The law typically requires the application of the plain meaning rule to such situations. According to the plain meaning rule, one must begin by applying the words according to their plain and ordinary meaning—that apparent from the text taken at face value. In applying the plain meaning rule, one is not to read into the text unstated assumptions or motivations.

This is not an absolute rule, but if one argues for violating Ockham's razor, he should have a very good argument as to why the violation is justified. In legal parlance, Ockham's razor creates a presumption in favor of the most parsimonious explanation. This presumption can be rebutted only with a strong, properly supported argument. If one wishes to argue for a meaning of a contract other than its plain meaning, for example, then one must present strong evidence the author intended the words to mean something other than what they appear to say. Apologist arguments regularly violate Ockham's razor with no justification. They are content to show that the less parsimonious hypothesis remains *possible* and appeal to their audience's faith to carry them the rest of the way.

Ockham's razor is related to a fallacy known as the "far-fetched hypothesis," in which one skips over hypotheses that are more inherently probable and parsimonious, without giving them due consideration, to reach an inherently implausible hypothesis likely consistent with one's existing beliefs. People believe far-fetched hypotheses out of desire, emotion, or faith, but they are never justified based on reason. Miracle claims, including but not limited to Jesus's Resurrection, all fall into this category.

Ockham's razor and the far-fetched hypothesis often come up when apologists appeal to what they call "explanatory scope." They may argue, for example, that the explanation that makes the most sense of Jesus's Resurrection stories is that Jesus actually was God because no other single explanation can cover all the evidence. This would be equivalent to arguing that the best explanation for stories of UFO abduction stories is that UFOs are actually abducting people and sexually probing them because reports of such activity are common to all, and any alternative hypothesis we propose would need to be supported by evidence, which will vary from case to case.

Explanations that appear to cover a broad range of reports are intuitively appealing, but that doesn't render them more likely—especially when they appeal to a far-fetched hypothesis, or they violate Ockham's razor due to all the additional assumptions that must be smuggled in to make them work. Sometimes, the best explanation is many different explanations, each of which is limited in scope. In such a case, a single overarching theory is not the most parsimonious one.

E. Ad Hoc Explanations

Ad hoc literally means "for this [special purpose]" but could more colloquially be translated as "thrown together," usually after the fact. In context, it refers to reactionary explanations manufactured specifically to address a single argument or item of evidence in a piecemeal fashion rather than as principled parts of a greater argument or model proposed in one's initial argument. These are common when people are put on the spot to explain or support a position that does not fit into the framework of arguments previously advanced. The "explanation" in such cases is just a way to rationalize away valid criticisms of an argument when well-reasoned counterarguments are unavailable.

The problem is these explanations typically fail to fit together in any logical way and produce glaring inconsistencies when applied beyond the immediate argument. They lack coherence or explanatory value. Regularly using ad hoc arguments demonstrates that someone is not arguing in good faith. They are being intellectually dishonest, trying to insulate their position from criticism and render it nonfalsifiable rather than honestly accepting the paradoxical implications of their explanations and abandoning them.

The invisible dragon conversation previously discussed presents a textbook example of someone giving a string of ad hoc explanations, resulting in a nonfalsifiable hypothesis. Here is another example:

ALEX: I prayed to God and he healed my cancer. It was a miracle that proves the existence of God.

BILL: I know other cancer sufferers who also prayed but were not healed.

ALEX: They must not have prayed hard enough.

BILL: I know several who prayed every day for years—far more than you.

ALEX: They must not have been good enough.

BILL: Some were missionaries who devoted their entire lives to God and helping the poor in his name.

ALEX: They must not have been sick enough.

BILL: Some of them died while praying for a cure.

ALEX: Well, the Lord works in mysterious ways. We cannot expect to know why he answers some prayers but not others.

Notice how in this conversation Alex begins by positing that his "miraculous" recovery from cancer proves the power of prayer and thus the existence of God. When confronted with a series of increasingly inconvenient truths that undermine his hypothesis, Alex offers a string of rationalizations, each time moving the goalpost further downfield so his opponent cannot score. When those also fail in the face of contradictory evidence, Alex retreats further, ultimately to where his hypothesis cannot be falsified by any evidence in a classic example of special pleading. Arguments like these seem persuasive only to those already committed to accepting them.

A valid explanation is part of a coherent, consistent framework. It applies beyond the issue at hand and explains more than it must to address the immediate argument. It builds on other hypotheses and theories and helps to incorporate them into a greater whole. It can be established proscriptively so it can be honestly evaluated rather than after the fact, when it can be endlessly modified. It allows for predictions to be made, the fulfillment or nonfulfillment of which would either support or discredit the explanation. It is falsifiable. And one who offers such an explanation in good faith will abandon it if the explanation is indeed falsified.

Well-known magician, skeptic, and paranormal investigator James Randi in numerous interviews discussed another good example of ad hoc reasoning. From 1996 through 2015, Randi offered a "Million Dollar Challenge" to anyone who could demonstrate "supernatural" powers under a mutually agreed-upon scientific protocol.[19] No one ever passed the test and claimed the money. According to Randi, the would-be "psychics," after failing at the very experiment to which they agreed, offered such explanations as "There were too many people around" or "I can't perform under pressure or stress." No such limitations were ever mentioned before the test—only after they failed. If, for instance, the room was cleared of people for their next trial and they failed again, then the participants always came up with a new explanation until ultimately arriving at one that could not be addressed within the protocol.

A common example of ad hoc argumentation relates to the thousands of contradictions found within the Bible. Theologians holding to some version of biblical inerrancy have discussed and debated these for centuries. Many mutually exclusive rationalizations have been developed that address one contradiction or a small subset of them, but no true explanation has ever been developed that accounts for them consistently. For atheists, these contradictions are easily explained in a simple, coherent, and parsimonious way: The Bible is an entirely human work with human errors. The contradictions defeat the position of early apologists that the Bible was perfectly true and thus divinely inspired. Isn't this the most plausible explanation? Another example is the long trend among liberal denominations of redefining God in ways increasingly vague and incomprehensible, with each redefinition designed to address a new argument.

A common catalyst for producing ad hoc arguments is the strategy of *moving the goalposts*. This refers to repeatedly changing the objectives your opponent must satisfy, demanding that they clear ever-higher bars, before you accept their argument or concede your initial position. Where one's opposition is especially strong, this strategy concludes by moving the posts off the field entirely—demanding that your opposition disprove a hypothesis that is unfalsifiable, a requirement that is literally impossible.

Moving the goalposts is only possible when one's initial position is, at least to some extent, vague and ill-defined. This is why science requires hypotheses to be stated clearly and specifically: so they cannot escape falsification through creative reinterpretation. Theologians and apologists refuse to apply such standards to theological positions, always leaving themselves the escape route of driving the post farther and farther downfield.

The history of Christian apologetics is a case study in moving goalposts. As science, philosophy, and history have invalidated more and more of Christianity's falsifiable claims, apologists have increasingly retreated to theoretical positions that can't be falsified, disingenuously claiming victory. Theologians have moved from anthropomorphic to increasingly inscrutable models of God. Christian culture warriors have shifted their focus from creationism to "intelligent design," embracing the inherent ambiguity and concomitant defensibility such a move entails. Whenever one spots someone moving the goalposts in an argument, red flags should go up.

One reliable way to spot ad hoc arguments is to observe when people add assumptions, moving in the opposite direction of the parsimony demanded by Ockham's razor. These assumptions invariably generate more complexity and conflict than clarity, revealing their true goal of defense rather than explanation. Ad hoc arguments can rarely be reconciled or harmonized. You can rarely derive a coherent argument from them, which is why they cannot be taken seriously.

Creating your own unfalsifiable belief through ad hoc arguments is easy. Simply express a belief, and then when someone proposes a way in which the belief can be tested, add to or change some attribute or assumption of the belief to render the proposed test invalid. Repeat until no test is possible. If all else fails, appeal to mystery. Any time you detect such a pattern in your opponent's argument, you can be reasonably assured his argument is worthless or at least that he believes so because he is not arguing in good faith.

Pierre Abelard, a well-known Christian thinker from the medieval period, noted that the fathers of the Christian Church issued contradictory statements on a wide variety of theological issues. He collected many of these in his famous scholastic text *Sic et Non*, which means "Yes and No." Abelard invited his readers to find some way to harmonize these sayings, unintentionally emphasizing the ad hoc nature of Christian apologetics up through Abelard's time. No one has ever met Abelard's challenge. Nothing has changed.

F. Appeal to "Cumulative" Arguments

A common apologetic strategy is to claim that one is sequentially build-ing a case for the Christian God through "cumulative" arguments. A well-known proponent of this cumulative case approach is William Craig. Dr. Craig attempts to use arguments from ignorance, such as the kalam and fine-tuning, to establish the existence of a nondenominational "first mover" before finally turning to an argument for the historicity of the Resurrection to link his earlier arguments to the Christian God.

There are several problems with such an approach. To begin, first mover arguments are consistent with thousands of hypotheses inconsistent with Christianity. The vast majority of religions posit a supernatural first mover of some type. Even Deists propose a first mover, though this would be a distant god far removed from that of Christianity, practically indistinguish-able from none at all. Atheism, too, could allow for a first mover, perhaps a supercomputer with the power and processing ability to create but lacking personal agency. An argument consistent with all these competing claims cannot support a cumulative case for any of them against the others. It can-not be treated as a foundation for an argument for Christianity if it would likewise serve as the foundation for an argument against Christianity.

The second problem is that a cumulative case can never be established by merely establishing necessary conditions. At some point, one must establish conditions *sufficient* to render the hypothesis true. If I claimed that dragons exist, then it would not be enough for me to show you that green lizards ex-ist or that some animals fly or that fire can occasionally be created through organic materials. While these would all be necessary for dragons to exist, none are sufficient to establish my claim. Even establishing them all to your satisfaction would make you no more likely to believe in dragons. They do not build on one another so much as establish independently necessary conditions, of which there may be thousands more.

The truth of Christianity requires the truth of many other propositions, all of which must be established as true before a persuasive case can be made. To use an example from the world of law, the prosecutor in a crimi-nal trial must prove *all elements of the crime charged*. Regardless of the strength of the prosecution's evidence of the defendant's motive and intent to steal, she cannot convict for theft without evidence that something was actually stolen. To say that the motive and intent evidence represents a "cumulative case" against the defendant is absurd. Nine-tenths of the pros-ecution's case equals no case. Without this final element, stolen property, the strength of the prosecution's case is not 90 percent but *zero*.

Likewise, establishing conditions necessary for Christianity to be true does not build a progressively stronger case. Each element of the Christian case must be established independently, with the arguments for each succeeding on its own terms. No argument can make up for the weaknesses of another. Only through successful arguments independently supporting every element can the apologist expect his audience to seriously consider his proposal. Establishing the existence of an all-powerful being, for example, is useless if one fails to demonstrate this being is good, for perfect goodness is an essential quality of the Christian God. Nine-tenths of God is not God.

The third problem is that this argument fails to properly account for the risk of error in each link of the cumulative case. Unless an argument is airtight, leading to a conclusion that is 100 percent certain and inescapable, some risk of error must be acknowledged. Where a larger argument rests on the success of other arguments, the cumulative error rates of those foundational arguments must be accounted for in determining whether to accept the larger argument. In discussing metaphysics, where solid evidence is impossible to come by, there is always a risk of error.

Assume I claim that Bill Gates walked into the First National Bank of Seattle on January 1, 2015. I present a security camera photo that looks a lot like Bill Gates, from which you are 70 percent sure it is him. I then reveal that the photo came from a common feed that covered several banks but contains details suggesting it was *most likely* taken at First National, leaving you 75 percent sure it came from the right bank. I explain that the feed also covered several days but point out some good reasons to believe it was taken on January 1, 2015, leaving you 80 percent certain of this. After presenting my evidence, I will have successfully convinced you that each link necessary to establish my claim is more probable than not. So what is the probability that my claim, as a whole, is correct? The answer comes from multiplying the probabilities of each successive link ($0.7 \times 0.75 \times 0.8$), which yields 42 percent. While each link independently may be highly probable, the end result is improbable. You would *not* be reasonably justified in believing that Bill Gates was in the bank that day.

This makes sense when you consider that for my claim to be true, three separate conditions must be satisfied. Satisfying three conditions will always be more difficult than satisfying one, and the claim can be no stronger than the weakest (i.e., least probable) condition, just as no chain can be stronger than its weakest link. Any proof of the Christian God must establish *many conditions*. Even if one agrees with Christian proponents of the cosmological argument, for example, that a transcendent personal being has been demonstrated to be more likely than not based on the existence of our universe, some risk of error must be acknowledged. That the vast majority of people with relevant expertise disagree with you, as discussed later in this book, should cause you to hold off on treating your conclusion as anything close to a certainty. Failing to make this allowance renders the cumulative approach fallacious.

The truth of Christianity is predicated on at least hundreds of necessary conditions for which our evidence is far less than certain. Even generously assuming 95 percent certainty for each condition (a mere 5 percent possibility of error), Christianity becomes a bad bet (less than 50 percent probability of it being true) after a mere fourteen conditions have been satisfied. As I demonstrate later in this book, the odds are far, far worse than that.

The final implication of probability theory is that if any necessary condition of Christianity is shown to be impossible or even highly improbable, then the argument for Christianity collapses. It is a house of cards in which removing one condition results in the entire edifice crumbling. That is why apologists must be so uncompromising, for a single successful argument by their opponents results in them losing the entire war.

G. Appeal to Mystery

> But though every created thing is, in this sense, a mystery, the word mystery cannot be applied to moral truth, any more than obscurity can be applied to light. . . . Mystery is the antagonist of truth. It is a fog of human invention that obscures truth and represents it in distortion. Truth never envelops itself in mystery, and the mystery in which it is at any time enveloped is the work of its antagonist, and never of itself.
>
> —Thomas Paine, *The Age of Reason*

> [M]ystery is made a convenient cover for absurdity.
>
> —John Adams

This is a specific argument, representing a combination of fallacies, that merits its own short discussion because it is so widely relied on by apologists. It serves as a catchall when all other arguments fail or no others can be imagined. The appeal to mystery (ATM) represents the apologists' trump card. It is the final stage of a strategy based on moving the goalposts and ad hoc argumentation. Once the apologist is stumped for a reasoned response to the skeptic's argument, finding no move to play on the chess board of the debate, he simply flips the board over and declares the rules of the game no longer applicable. The ATM is nothing more than smoke and mirrors—a vacuous "argument" that ultimately serves merely as a misleading way of dodging valid arguments.

Imagine a criminal trial in which the prosecution, during closing argument, simply says, "The circumstances of this crime are a complete mystery to me. I cannot tell you what happened or how it happened or demonstrate that the defendant was even involved. I expect the jury will understand this because the defendant is a very clever criminal. He could find many devious ways to cover his tracks and apparently has done so, for I have no evidence that he did it, only my heartfelt belief. Please find him guilty." Any competent judge would not hesitate to throw the case out, for the prosecutor has effectively conceded he has no case.

Now suppose a troublesome Bible passage is presented to an apologist as evidence against divine inspiration. The essence of the argument is that the passage is more consistent with what we would expect ignorant Bronze Age men to write than an eternal, all-knowing god. Assume the apologist responds by appealing to mystery, claiming we can have no reasonable expectation of what God would write because He is ineffable. This provides an ontological bomb shelter to the apologist, for how can you object to an ineffable concept? This response can have no weight, however, unless you agree with the assumption that God is in fact ineffable—that we can know nothing of substance about God. But this is contrary to the teachings of virtually every Christian denomination.

The ATM allows the apologist to halt critical conversation with a tautology: "One cannot say anything about that for which nothing can be said." But of course, they do then go on to say quite a bit about God, such as that he exists, has a very definite nature, is omniscient, is omnipotent, is perfectly good, and even *exactly what God expects of mankind and why*. Apologists claim that religious skeptics cannot pin God down based on scriptural passages. But they then use the very same Scripture to make specific claims about God that fit their specific theology.

The ineffability claim simply contradicts the fact that most religions have scriptures and additional writings that say a great deal about their divine beings. If apologists were serious about ineffability, they wouldn't attempt to say much of anything about God *because they couldn't*. They use this tactic with skeptics likely to poke holes in their substantive claims about God's qualities, returning to those claims upon addressing the believing fold. Once the skeptics have left the building, they return to their more traditional version of God, with all the anthropomorphic qualities that entails. This is a textbook ad hoc argument.

No one begins believing in an ineffable God. No one is told as a child we can know nothing of God's nature or motives or that we can have no expectations of God. Why would anyone worship a god one knows nothing about, who operates by no comprehensible rules, or who could change the rules at any time? All begin with very clear notions of God with very specific qualities and motives, such as that He is perfectly good (as we understand good), that He loves us, and that He wants the best for us. The inscrutable God of apologetics is merely a debating tactic, used to deflect criticism when faced with insurmountable counterarguments to specific qualities of God. It is the ultimate example of moving the goalposts.

Think about trying to get an investor to put money into a scheme that cannot be described or coherently discussed. The effort would be a complete failure. Throughout history, Christianity has never been presented this way. Christian evangelists have always sold a specific picture of God with clearly defined qualities. The appeal to mystery cannot be squared with this picture. The apologists suddenly tell us we can know nothing about God, except perhaps that which supports whatever argument they may be making at the moment. This approach is their way of having their cake and eating it, too.

Philosopher Karl Popper famously remarked that a theory that explains everything explains nothing because a good theory specifies what would refute it. The ATM does just the opposite. What one is saying by making this argument is that when it comes to explaining or understanding God, there are no rules. But if God cannot be explained or understood, then he cannot be justified within the bounds of reason and logic. If one agrees to discuss or debate God's existence within those bounds, then he cannot step outside when pressed into a corner. In every other context, stepping outside the ring results in disqualification.

Crucial to the ATM is first shifting the burden of proof onto the skeptic. Accepting the burden of proof while simultaneously appealing to mystery are inherently inconsistent. To appeal to mystery is to acknowledge one's inability to build a case for one's position and rely exclusively on the inability of one's opponent to definitively defeat it. Masking one's position in vagueness and obfuscation is a low bar that is child's play to meet.

There are certainly questions, such as "How did consciousness or life or the universe begin?" to which naturalists must honestly answer, "I don't know." But it isn't as though Christians have a better answer. A real answer would look like a hypothesis or theory, allowing predictions to be made and verified. "God did it, but His methods are a mystery" is no answer. It is simply another way of saying, "I don't know, either." Accordingly, it cannot be used to support an argument for God's existence.

The ATM is not constructive of knowledge. Rather it is destructive of knowledge. It is a roadblock on the path to progress placed strategically to protect established beliefs. The ATM applies an inconsistent and arbitrary standard, whereby God is knowable only to the extent it supports the apologist's claims. The theist can't have it both ways. Use of this argument betrays the apologist's attempts to obfuscate God rather than explain Him. I agree with Daniel Dennett: "I think we should stop treating ['God works in mysterious ways'] as any kind of wisdom and recognize it as the transparently defensive propaganda that it is. A positive response might be, 'Oh good! I love a mystery. Let's see if we can solve this one, too. Do you have any ideas?'"[20]

Apologists appeal to mystery when reality fails to confirm what Christianity would predict. They retreat to it when the overwhelming evidence stands in stark contradiction to what any reasonable person would expect if Christianity were true. It is a disingenuous way to explain why the evidence doesn't support their position. But such an explanation is convincing only to those already convinced. To others, it is the equivalent of raising the white flag—an acknowledgment that no legitimate explanation is available and so none will be offered. It is an admission that evidence has failed the apologist, leaving only empty conviction.

4

ARGUMENTS FOR CHRISTIANITY

No one infers a god from the simple, from the known, from what is understood, but from the complex, from the unknown, and incomprehensible. Our ignorance is God; what we know is science.

—Robert Green Ingersoll, *On Gods and Other Essays*

I begin by addressing the so-called positive evidence for the Christian God and the Christian belief system—the arguments Christian apologists put forward to demonstrate that their God exists. Most of these arguments suffer from the same fatal flaw. They are arguments from ignorance. They attempt to exploit scientific questions to which no clear consensus answer has emerged and insert one. In each case, scientists have formulated hypotheses and sometimes theories to resolve the issues, but they have yet to definitively agree on a common resolution. This is how science works. It often requires a steady pace in which scientists test hypotheses, reject some, and continue testing others, gradually refining the successful ones until broad agreement can be reached.

Apologists, however, cannot wait for science to parse through the competing hypotheses and theories. Where they see an area of uncertainty, they must posit their preferred deity, the Christian God, in its place. This is the god of the gaps. In doing so, they are merely replacing one unknown with another, for scientists have no understanding or explanation for God. God defies scientific explanation—or explanation of any kind—so using God as a default adds nothing to our understanding. It has no explanatory value. God can serve only as a placeholder until scientists reach broader agreement—the same role that other gods have always served.

Science has made enormous progress in explaining virtually everything we observe. The primary gaps left are the origin of the universe, the origin of life, and consciousness. These are exceptionally difficult areas to study due to such factors as the inaccessibility of relevant data or ethical implications of doing human research. Nevertheless, scientists are making steady progress on all these fronts, and there is every reason to expect better scientific understanding of these issues in the future. There is no need to insist on any supernatural "explanation" while we wait for a universally satisfying natural one.

NATURAL THEOLOGY

> Natural theology accepts empirical science but views it as a means to learn about God's creation. And so, religion in general goes much further than science in giving credence to additional sources of knowledge such as scriptures, revelation, and spiritual experiences that are not based on verifiable empirical evidence. This credence is never tested.
>
> —John Loftus

Several arguments in this section fall within the realm of "natural theology." Natural theology is the branch based on reason and ordinary experience, as opposed to revealed theology, which is based exclusively on Scripture and religious experiences. Apologists who work in the realm of natural theology attempt to use common observations of the world to argue the existence of God. They attempt to infer God's existence from observed phenomena that allegedly cannot be explained naturally. They begin with the assumption that God exists and cherry-pick the scientifically derived facts and holes in scientific understanding to construct scaffolding upon which to build their theistic arguments.

Many observation-based scientific models of the universe are consistent with naturalism. Far fewer would potentially be consistent with Christianity. Christianity is constrained by Scripture, so each Christian model would need to be internally consistent and coherent within a Christian worldview. Unfortunately, though not surprisingly, Christian natural theology has never generated a testable model that meets these qualifications. Rather than proposing its own comprehensive model, natural theology operates by exploiting the gaps in existing scientific knowledge to serve a preset agenda that has nothing to do with knowledge.

Arguments based on natural theology can only, if successful, yield the lowest common denominator of a god—a transcendent "something" that set the universe into motion long ago and need not even still exist—a prime mover. Such arguments would support the views of thousands of religions with mutually exclusive claims. They would also support the existence (in the distant past) of an unconscious and impersonal force much like a computer algorithm. None can be considered arguments for the Christian God per se. Philosopher George Smith observes, "We have now returned to 'god' with a lower case 'g.' If valid, the arguments of natural theology will verify supernaturalism in some form, but they cannot establish the existence of a creature with the muddled and contradictory attributes of the Christian God."[1]

The god advanced by natural theology is also known as the philosophers' god because it is and always will be beyond empirical detection. It can only be discussed and debated in philosophical terms. It can never be definitively proven or disproven. But this god is not the God of Christian theology. It bears little resemblance to the God that Christians recognize and worship. It is merely a philosophical abstraction.

Though these arguments could only warrant a type of Deism, the apologists wielding them are usually Christians, Muslims, or Jews—people whose theological commitments include claims about sin, salvation, and the relationship between humans and the divine. Many apologists seem under the impression that if they can convince their audience that *some type of supernatural force* is likely to exist, then this will start a chain reaction that will lead to the automatic acceptance of their theologically specific claims.

All arguments from natural theology fail for the same reason. Each proceeds from the premise that the unknowable somehow *explains* something currently unknown. But how could this possibly be? How can we derive knowledge from ignorance? How can the mere acknowledgment of holes in our understanding justify plugging those holes with anything? The very structure of the argument defies logic.

Another problem for natural theology is that the philosopher's god from which it argues is ineffable and inscrutable—a being about which nothing meaningful can even be said. It can only be defined in terms of what it is not. The appeal to an ineffable god lacks any explanatory power. It is no more than an acknowledgment that we have no explanation at hand. It uselessly adds a supernatural component to an unsolved mystery, moving no further toward a real solution. Accordingly, it violates Ockham's razor. But naturalism is not superior to supernaturalism simply because it is the more economical explanation. It is superior because it is the only framework in which explanation is *even possible*. The supernatural, if it exists, is a realm whose rules are forever outside our grasp. To punt to supernaturalism is to concede forever the quest for explanation.

Humans, operating entirely within the natural world with natural brains and natural tools of observation, would have no means to evaluate the supernatural, even if it existed. We could at best identify anomalies—events that appear to defy natural explanation—and simply label them as supernatural because they don't fit the paradigms with which we are familiar. We could not expect to arrive at a specific supernatural explanation, however, because we have no basis to presume the rules of a supernatural world. If we are to conclude that the explanation for an event must be supernatural because we have ruled out every possible natural explanation, then that must be the end of our inquiry. We don't have the tools to proceed further. What we do know is that if God intervenes in any way in the physical world, then such intervention would leave traces that could be investigated by science, and no such traces have ever been found.

I know that these arguments are unlikely to have led anyone to Christianity. People believe because they were raised that way and have always believed or because the Christian faith filled a need in their life or because they had an experience that led them to feel that God was real. These often-complicated philosophical arguments are just post-hoc rationalizations for previously formed beliefs. They do, however, form the bedrock of the defense mounted by modern Christian apologists. They are what defenders of the faith fall back on when called on by skeptics to justify their beliefs. They are what believers rely on to provide their faith intellectual legitimacy. Although what I've said so far should be enough to categorically dismiss them all, I feel it is important to address the specific arguments in more detail.

THE EXISTENCE OF THE UNIVERSE (COSMOLOGICAL ARGUMENTS)

> If the existence of the universe is supposed to be evidence for the existence of God because everything comes from something else, then what does the existence of God evidence? Where does God come from?
>
> —Anonymous

One of the principal arguments used by Christian apologists concerns the very existence of the universe. Before going further, it is necessary to clearly define what is meant by "the universe." Physicist Brian Greene writes,

> There was once a time when "universe" meant "all there is." Everything. The whole shebang. The notion of more than one universe, more than one everything, would seemingly be a contradiction in terms. Yet a range of theoretical developments has gradually qualified the interpretation of "universe." The word's meaning now depends on context. Sometimes "universe" still connotes absolutely everything. Sometimes it refers only to those parts of everything that someone such as you or I could, in principle, have access to. Sometimes it's applied to separate realms, ones that are partly or fully, temporarily or permanently, inaccessible to us; in this sense, the word relegates our universe to membership in a large, perhaps infinitely large, collection.[2]

Physicist Lawrence Krauss echoes the same sentiment:

> Talking about many different universes can sound like an oxymoron. After all, traditionally the notion of universe has become synonymous with "everything that exists." More recently, however, universe has come to have a simpler, arguably more sensible meaning. It is now traditional to think of "our" universe as comprising simply the totality of all that we can now see and all that we could ever see.[3]

Unless I indicate otherwise, I use the term in the modern sense, to refer to all contiguous physical reality, sometimes known as the "local universe." If we had an interstellar spaceship and all the time in the world, then this is the area we could theoretically traverse. Only in this local universe are empirical observations even possible. As I discuss shortly, there may be realms whose space and time are disconnected from our own. Adding these would expand the definition to "all there is," which I refer to separately as the "global universe" or the "cosmos." Understand, however, that anything beyond the local universe is purely theoretical. The local and global universes may be the same, but they are *not necessarily* the same.

Christian appeals to the existence of the universe represent variations of the cosmological argument. All forms of this argument cannot be addressed in the space allowed. I, however, address what I have found to be the most popular and well-regarded form of the argument today. Known as the kalam cosmological argument or simply the kalam, this version forms the centerpiece of many modern arguments for God. Interestingly, the kalam originates with Muslim theology. It is posed as a syllogism with two premises leading to a single conclusion:

1. Everything that began to exist had a cause.
2. The universe began to exist.

Therefore,

3. The universe has a cause.

Even if successful, the kalam does not establish the existence of the Christian God, the Muslim God, or any other god. Nor does it establish or even point to any characteristics of the cause of the universe. It would establish only that something outside the universe somehow brought it into existence, a first mover. Such Christian apologists as William Lane Craig, who has done much to popularize the argument that he considers his favorite, argue that the cause would have to be not only transcendent (outside the universe itself, transcending both space and time) but also personal (capable of making decisions and interested in doing so). As the Bible arguably describes God in these terms (biblical descriptions of God are all over the place, but this certainly falls within that range), the apologist claims it is reasonable to believe the cause to be God. There are many problems with this argument, from both logical and scientific standpoints. Let's begin with the premises.

A. Everything That Began to Exist Had a Cause

This premise would, at first glance, seem noncontroversial. After all, in our everyday experience, things do not happen without being caused. Items do not pop into being, for example, for no reason. Humans share a common experience of causality based on observations of the physical world. Accordingly, the premise seems intuitive. But this is one of those times in which our intuitions and common experiences may lead us astray.

This sounds radical to many but *maybe not*. The very notion of cause and effect may only apply on a certain scale and within a certain temporal frame. Because humans evolved within that scale and frame, causality has always been part of our experience, and our minds developed to intuitively accept it as universal. But within the last fifty years, scientists have demonstrated many reasons to suspect this traditional view may not be warranted, at least when extended beyond the local universe, which the kalam requires us to do.

Philosophy recognizes several types of causation, but in the theological context, we are speaking of "event causation." This describes a relationship between events that take place in space and time. Pursuant to this relationship, effects always follow causes, and causes always precede their effects. If a physicist could know everything about a given point in time, then he could arguably predict what would happen next with perfect accuracy. With all potential causes at hand, he could determine all their effects. This thought experiment is known as "Laplace's Demon," named after the nineteenth-century French scholar Pierre-Simon Laplace. Laplace hypothetically posited the existence of a being that could know with certainty the precise location and condition of every atom in the universe. Laplace concluded that such a being could predict the future and read the past with perfect accuracy. This was the first published articulation of causal determinism.

Science has revealed that the causation required by the apologists to validate their first premise simply doesn't apply in certain circumstances. At the quantum level, for instance, the entire concept of causation as most of us understand it breaks down. Causality, in the classical sense of the word, does not apply to the field of quantum mechanics. No cause, for instance, is evident in the decay of a radioactive nucleus. Likewise, scientists have observed quantum particles appearing from a state of apparent "nothingness" with no cause. If quantum particles, then why not the universe?[4]

When we talk about causality, furthermore, we are strictly talking about a phenomenon *within* the known universe, which is all that humans have ever observed. We have no epistemic grounds to make assertions about what kinds of laws hold *outside* of that universe, such as before the big bang. But for the first premise of the kalam to work, it has to presume that the laws of causality we know from our observable local universe also hold independently of and outside it. The argument is already presuming, in part, what it is trying to prove—begging the question.

The universe itself may simply differ from anything *within the universe*. Time as we know it began with the big bang and, with it, temporal concepts like causality. Apologists who use analogies of familiar objects to argue that the universe itself requires a cause are employing the fallacies of false equivalence and composition, for they are assuming that what applies to the parts applies equally to the whole. What could it possibly mean to talk about "cause" where there is no space, no time, no matter, no energy, and no physical laws at all?

Prior to the expansion of the universe, time could have operated very differently, perhaps nonlinearly. The model of time relied on by such apologists as Dr. Craig to support the kalam, the A-theory, is rejected by 85 percent of academic philosophers.[5] The alternative theory embraced by these philosophers is known as the B-theory, or "tenseless theory of time," and has been considered "almost the default view in contemporary debates."[6] According to Craig,

> From start to finish, the kalam cosmological argument is predicated upon the A-Theory of time. On a B-Theory of time, the universe does not in fact come into being or become actual at the Big Bang; it just exists tenselessly as a four-dimensional space-time block that is finitely extended in the earlier than direction. If time is tenseless, then the universe never really comes into being, and, therefore, the quest for a cause of its coming into being is misconceived.[7]

Under the B-theory, therefore, the universe would never "begin to exist." This doesn't necessarily mean the A-theory is false but does mean this crucial premise is sufficiently uncertain to undermine the kalam's conclusion. If linear time did not precede the big bang, then asking about the universe's cause would be no more meaningful than asking what is south of the South Pole. Outside space and time as we know them, causality is simply undefined.

While causality *might* transcend the known universe, we have no evidence it does, and to assume as much is no more than wanton speculation. Such assumptions as "everything requires a cause" and "something cannot come from nothing" are based on our collective observations. We are therefore justified in assuming them to apply within the confines of our empirical experience but not beyond that. We cannot justifiably take an inference based on our experience and convert that into an immutable truth that transcends that part of the universe observable to us. The premises in a sound deductive argument must be unequivocally true—not speculative, not *merely possible*, not "true in one meaning of the term but false or speculative in another"—but well-established empirical facts. The transcendent causality posited by the first premise fails this requirement. It cannot be assumed.

Moreover, it should be noted that we have no basis to conclude this because we have no experience of something "beginning to exist," as apologists use this phrase. All our experiences of apparent beginnings are actually observations of preexisting things *changing from one state to another*. This is guaranteed by the law of conservation of mass and energy. Things move, come to rest, get larger or smaller, combine or divide in half, and so on. But we have no experience of things coming into existence *from nothing-*

ness. We don't even know if this is possible. If we have no experience with anything beginning to exist, then we cannot assume that a cause must be involved.

In fact, we have no experience with "nothing," as apologists use the word. They suggest what is known as "philosophical nothingness," meaning a complete absence of *anything.*[8] No one has ever observed such a state. When physicists talk about nothingness, they are referring to quantum vacuums, which have been observed and are testable. We know that things appear "uncaused" from quantum vacuums, suggesting that the universe also could have appeared uncaused if nothingness is defined in such a way. The concept of philosophical nothingness is arguably more comprehensive than a quantum vacuum, but it is impossible to get a handle on such a concept as it is so poorly defined. What, for instance, would philosophical nothingness exclude that would be present in a quantum vacuum? No one has ever provided a clear answer, leaving our practical understanding of philosophical nothingness empty.

A rhetorical question often posed by apologists is "Why is there something rather than nothing?" But this question is premature, for one must first answer the question "Should we reasonably expect something or nothing?" If *something* is more likely, then there is no problem to be solved. What justifies treating nothing as the default? The apologists' very question presupposes transcendent causality, but as we have seen, that cannot be simply assumed.

This question poses no problem for physicists. Everything in the universe can, in a sense, be seen as another form of nothing. Einstein showed us that matter can be converted to energy and vice versa. The universe consists of both positive and negative energy, which, when aggregated together, cancel each other out and leave us with a total energy of zero—the state of a quantum vacuum. As Stephen Hawking explains,

> In the case of a universe that is approximately uniform in space, one can show that the negative gravitational energy exactly cancels the positive energy represented by the matter. So the total energy of the universe is zero. Specifically, within small measurement errors, the mean energy density of the universe is exactly what it should be for a universe that appeared from an initial state of zero energy within a small quantum uncertainty.[9]

All that we observe is simply another form of "nothing," just unevenly distributed.

As late physicist Victor Stenger notes furthermore, a state of nothingness is inherently unstable. You may have heard the statement "Nature abhors a vacuum," and the same is true of a quantum vacuum. A universe with zero total energy is highly likely to result in positive energy and matter alongside negative energy rather than both being locked in perfect equilibrium as "nothing." The natural state of affairs is therefore something rather than nothing. It is what the naturalistic hypothesis predicts. Supernatural intervention would be required to maintain a state of nothingness.[10] The existence of something defeats the God hypothesis. No miracle or transcendent agent is required to explain why there is something rather than nothing.[11] This is unsurprising given the naturalistic hypothesis. It is exactly what we should expect—a logical corollary to a naturalistic universe.

Before demanding the cause of the universe, we must first answer the question "Does the universe even require a causal explanation?" to which the only responsible answer is "We don't know." We have no broader context in which to develop such expectations. Maybe some things just are, representing brute facts. The very question may be rooted in a baseless assumption. Apologists posit God as the solution to the metaphysical problem supposedly raised by the question "What caused the universe?" but they have established no such problem even exists. God represents a solution to a problem of their own making.

B. The Universe Began to Exist

Once again, this premise would appear intuitive at first glance, but as stated previously, we have no experience with anything actually *beginning to exist*. That alone should give us pause. It is highly debatable whether our universe began to exist. It may, for instance, have always existed.

The common understanding that our universe began to exist, and that this is noncontroversial among physicists, likely stems from a misunderstanding of the big bang theory. This theory posits that our universe is rapidly expanding, and this expansion began from an incredibly dense point approximately 13.7 billion years ago. We know from Einstein's theories that matter causes space-time to curve, and if we went back in time toward the big bang, the matter in the universe would become increasingly dense, and space-time, more and more curved. Eventually it reaches a point of *infinite curvature*. This is known as the *cosmic singularity*.

People often colloquially call this the "beginning" of the universe because that is where the laws of classical physics, derived from Einstein's theory of general relativity, break down and lose their utility. Because of this, we have no information before the moment of the big bang, a period known as the Planck epoch. The big bang event is not really an event at all but rather a placeholder for our lack of understanding. It does not represent a beginning to the universe but an end to our theoretical comprehension of the universe's history.

What we *do* know is that the laws of physics do not require the universe to have a beginning. Maybe it did, maybe it didn't, but the laws of physics *do not require it*. When physicists say our universe "began" at the big bang, they are referring to the *observable expansion of our observable universe*. We know that at the big bang, our local universe began rapidly expanding outward. But we don't know what was or wasn't there before this expansion. The Planck epoch and beyond remain a mystery, and until we have a successful theory of quantum gravity, theologians simply don't have the epistemic grounds to declare, unequivocally, that the universe had a beginning.

Likewise, we have no reason to believe that "before" the big bang there was only philosophical nothingness, as apologists routinely suggest. Physicist Alan Guth explains,

> [T]he standard big bang theory says nothing about where the matter in the universe came from. In the standard big bang theory all the matter that we see here, now, was already there, then. The matter was just very compressed, and in a form that is somewhat different from its present state. The theory describes how the matter evolved from one form to another as the universe evolved, but the theory does not address the question of how the matter originated.[12]

Another reason people look at the big bang as the "beginning" of the universe relates to the second law of thermodynamics. This postulates that within a closed system, entropy will increase over time. Entropy can be thought of as a tendency toward randomness and away from order. In fact, the arrow of time can be defined in terms of whether we see entropy increasing or decreasing. Observations have demonstrated that the entropy of the universe at the big bang was lower than at any time thereafter. Accordingly, the big bang appears to be the beginning of time as we know it.

But, as with cause and effect, our intuitive understanding of time may be a relic of our evolutionary heritage. After all, our ancestors have always experienced time as we experience it today, as a linear arrow, having no means of seeing it any other way. Science has provided physicists with a much broader perspective, and learned cosmologists now understand that time is not so simple. It does not necessarily proceed forever forward in a straight vector. It may stop and begin again. It may proceed in different directions at once. It may be circular. It is certainly much more complicated than our limited experience with it would suggest, and it is far too early to be making confident claims as to how it operates.

> The origin of the arrow of time turns out to be very similar to the origin of the arrow of space. We have an arrow of space telling us the difference between up and down because the Earth is influencing how we think about space. We have an arrow of time telling us the difference between the past and the future because we live in the aftermath of the big bang. All of the differences between the past and the future are going to be ultimately traced to what happened at the origin of our universe. They are not traced to the laws of physics themselves. That's the great mystery we need to confront.[13]

As Sean Carroll explained in his February 2014 debate with William Craig, many models of the universe are consistent with our knowledge of physics and cosmology that do not require the universe to have a "beginning," as any of us would understand that term. The apparent persuasiveness of Dr. Craig and other apologists disappears when one recognizes that they are simply cherry-picking naturalistic models to attack as straw men.

So what does this all mean? It means we have no good reason to believe that the universe "began to exist." Physics allows for the possibility that the universe has always existed, though perhaps not in its present form. It could be like standing on an enormous circle. We can say that something comes before us and something comes after, but we cannot say, without seeing the entire circle, that there is *always* something before and *always* something after. Nor can we say that the line composing the circle begins to exist at some point. Time may not be linear, so there may be no valid basis to talk about cause as we do. While it is difficult for us to wrap our minds around the idea of an eternal universe (or series of local universes), is it any easier to grasp a universe that began to exist, preceded only by nothingness?[14] Bertrand Russell observes, "The idea that all things must have a beginning is really due to the poverty of our imagination."[15]

Imagine ancient times, when humans thought the Earth was flat. There were two possibilities: that the Earth went on forever or that it had a boundary or "edge." But we now know there was a third possibility: that the surface of the Earth is finite but has no boundary or edge. Similarly, a picture of the universe in classical physics gives us two possibilities: the observable universe is past-eternal or it has a beginning. But quantum mechanics reveals a new possibility: that the universe is finite but has no boundary— much like the surface of the Earth.

This is precisely what prominent physicists Stephen Hawking and James Hartle describe in their no-boundary proposal. We know that, at least in the formulation of general relativity, the universe has a past boundary at the big bang. We know the *observable* universe could not have gone infinitely into the past, though it could be part of a cycle of infinite expansion and contraction. The "boundary" could be merely an artifact of our limited understanding, and a quantum theory of gravity will erase it.[16] The no-boundary proposal is testable and has to date passed the tests to which it has been subjected.

Physicists as prominent as Hawking, Victor Stenger, Sean Carroll, and Lawrence Krauss find absolutely no problem with a universe that has always existed. In fact, this is the current scientific consensus, based on the wave function of the universe, which suggests it is *highly probable* (near 100 percent) that a universe with the characteristics of our own would exist without a "cause." All four are atheists and see no reason to postulate a preexisting intelligent agent. As Hawking says, "[I]f the universe is really completely self-contained, having no boundary or edge, it would have neither beginning nor end; it would simply be. What place then, for a creator?"[17]

For now, all we can say is the moment of the big bang and before must be treated as an unknown. We cannot say the universe began. We cannot say it had a cause. Viable models exist that require no beginning and no cause. Unless apologists can definitively invalidate all these models, they cannot state either with certainty or even with any measurable probability. More important for present purposes, they cannot use them as premises for any argument.

If this were such a compelling argument, furthermore, you would expect cosmologists and physicists to be lining up behind it—flocking to Christianity as the evidence rolled in. But that isn't what you see. Cosmologists and physicists are far more atheistic than the general public. The last definitive survey on this topic was published in *Nature* in 1998 by Edward J. Larson and Larry Witham. Questioning the several hundred members of the National Academy of Sciences, Larson and Witham found "near universal rejection of the transcendent by NAS natural scientists. Disbelief in God and immortality among NAS biological scientists was 65.2% and 69.0%, respectively, and among NAS physical scientists [including astronomers] it was 79.0% and 76.3%. Most of the rest were agnostics on both issues, with few believers."[18] This can plausibly be attributed to their being in the best position to understand these very complex areas of science and seeing no compelling evidence for any God there.[19] That so many experts find no evidence for God in the cosmos should be deeply troubling to any Christian who clings to the cosmological argument.

C. The Christian God Is the Cause

Even if one were to concede the first two premises, this argument does not lead to the Christian God. If the universe came into being and was caused to do so, then it simply implies some preexisting agency that transcends the observable universe. Such an agent, known as the first mover, could be an impersonal force; a giant supercomputer; an alien being; or, if we feel a god must be posited, any one or several of millions of gods that have been dreamed up by humans since the dawn of time or even one not yet dreamed of by man. Nothing in this argument would remotely suggest the Christian God as a possibility more likely than any of these.

The Christian apologist must first prove that the Christian God exists, along with all His incompatible qualities, before nominating Him as a candidate for personal creator of the universe. To use the kalam as a proof for this specific god gets the entire analysis backward. You must first establish the need for a personal god and then bring in all the gods you've independently established to exist for an interview. You can only then whittle them down based upon how well their qualities and revelations match the empirically observable evidence.

The cosmological argument can only argue for a first cause—a transcendent (existing outside of known time and space) something that started the ball of causation rolling that led to the creation of the universe. But while God would be a first mover under Christian doctrine, not every first cause would be God. A first cause could have many characteristics inconsistent with the Christian God. Many existing religions, for example, posit the existence of a first cause, but acceptance of those religions would require rejection of Christianity. To simply call the first cause "God," as in the Christian God, requires a jump that must be independently justified.

Furthermore, there is absolutely *zero* independent justification for saying that the first cause must be supernatural, that it is eternal, or that it is some anthropomorphic deity. Perhaps, for instance, the cause is a natural one that we simply don't yet understand. One purely naturalistic model, proposed by physicist Neil Turok, is that the universe is in an infinite state of expansion and contraction. Because entropy only increases *within* the local universe, time would essentially "reset" at every boundary condition. There would be no "absolute time" or "master time" over the expansion and contraction; time could still be said to exist within the local universe. This universe would still be finite into the past, have a beginning, and have a cause, and yet there would be absolutely no kind of deity or "eternally existing cause."

Likewise, there is no good reason to believe the first cause to be personal. William Craig argues that the universe must have a personal cause because only a personal cause can make a choice. But because God's "decision" to create must be an eternal or timeless decision (existing, as it did, before time), it is equivalent to a nonpersonal cause. There can be no temporal gap between the willing and the willed before the existence of time because time did not yet exist. Yet it is impossible to conceive of a decision that doesn't incorporate such a gap. It is implicit in the very word. A timeless personal cause is no different from a nonpersonal cause.[20] Ockham's razor therefore leads us to the conclusion that an impersonal first cause, entirely consistent with atheism, is more likely than a personal one.

If the first premise is accepted as true, furthermore, then even this transcendent agent must have had a cause. If *everything* must have a cause, then what caused God? And what caused the cause of God? We end up with an infinite regression of agents and causes. Christian apologists posit that, by definition, God is uncaused (the "uncaused cause") and therefore an exception to the rule of causation that is otherwise absolute. They build into the definition of God that He had no beginning and thus is not subject to the first premise of the kalam. As discussed, this is simply special pleading. What independent evidence do we have that the Christian God is uncaused? Simply labeling God as "uncaused" is certainly convenient for the purpose of argument but doesn't make it so. There is no more reason to believe in an "uncaused" God than my pet invisible dragon.

If God can be considered eternal, furthermore, then why can't the universe be eternal, as a great many physicists believe it is? If an end to the regression of causes is required, then why not the universe itself rather than God? Why can't the universe be uncaused? Unless we grant God some unwarranted exception to the rules of causation that make up the first premise, the entire argument falls apart.

God is posited as a being with no spatial or temporal qualities that nevertheless acts within space and time. But any attempt to work out how this interaction takes place is doomed to descend into incoherency. What could it possibly mean for a nontemporal being to act, a concept that relies exclusively on concepts of temporality? And what does an "action" look like when time itself doesn't exist? Unless one can answer such questions coherently, they cannot reasonably expect anyone to accept an argument based on this assumption.

Another problem is that positing God as the cause of the universe doesn't resolve anything or increase understanding. The real question is "How did our universe come to be?" Saying the Christian God was responsible doesn't get us any closer to answering that question, for due to God's in-scrutable nature, no one can even begin to explain how this occurred. It simply adds another layer of mystery, for how did God come to be? With no hint of irony, apologists claim to "explain" the universe as the creation of a being they in turn refuse to explain. Rather than explaining the mystery away, we have only increased it. This is obfuscation rather than explanation.

Our knowledge will always have its limits, and at some point we reach the end of the road and must say, "I don't know." We might call this our episte-mological horizon. That has always been the point at which Christians have inserted God, only to have science explain the phenomenon in question and push the horizon back further. Currently, our epistemological horizon for the history of the universe is the big bang. Christians arguing that God "caused" the big bang are not basing their argument on any knowledge that would extend our epistemological horizon. Even if it did, that would only push the horizon back another step and leave us with the question "So how did God happen?" This vacuous exercise would gain us nothing.

Claiming God as the cause of the universe is an unnecessary, unwar-ranted, and useless hypothesis, violating Ockham's razor. An infinite universe is a simpler explanation (which also accords with the consensus of cosmologists) than a finite universe brought into existence by a transcen-dent, personal, all-powerful being that was previously just hanging out in "nothingness," whatever that could possibly mean, until deciding to make something. Unlike the Christian hypothesis, the naturalistic explanation requires no violations of the known laws of physics, no supernatural conjec-ture, and no endless parade of paradoxes. Admittedly, scientists don't have all the pieces yet to describe *with certainty* how the universe came to be as it is, though there is no shortage of naturalistic theories. If one remains unconvinced by any current theory, however, that doesn't justify leaping to the conclusion that it must have been a supernatural event caused by the Christian God.

The universe we see is not the universe we would expect the Christian God to create. According to the Bible, all of creation was made to benefit man. This is why the Christian orthodoxy defended the Earth-centered view of cosmology so aggressively and for so long—because it is exactly the cosmos described and predicted by the Bible. What use has man for distant nebulae he can never visit or even see? What use for billions of light-years of empty space? Why would God create a universe in which over 99.999999 percent will be forever inaccessible to man?

Finally, if the Christian God were the cause, why does God's explanation of the Creation, as found in Genesis, bear absolutely *no relation* to what science tells us about the origin of our universe and our planet? I explore this matter in greater detail later in the book, but for now, it is sufficient to say that Genesis *could* have provided accurate details unknown to the people of the day that would leave no doubt that the author had some unique and special knowledge about the Creation. Instead, we find a story (three, actually) closely related to creation myths of neighboring Bronze Age tribes, reflecting a scientifically inaccurate view of the Earth common to ancient people. As the late Victor Stenger observes,

> [T]he biblical story of creation bears no resemblance whatsoever to the Big Bang as described by modern cosmology. Genesis describes a creation taking place in six days a few thousand years ago. According to Genesis, Earth was created before the sun, the moon, and the stars within a fixed firmament. In contrast, scientific cosmology describes a universe tunneling out of chaos 13.7 billion years ago and an expanding universe, certainly not a "firmament," in which the solar system appeared 4.6 billion years ago, followed by the formation of the sun and Earth in the next 100 million years or so.[21]

You would think that if God were there, He at least would have gotten the details right.[22]

D. The Modal Cosmological Argument

Another version of the cosmological argument is known as the modal cosmological argument (MCA), or the argument from contingency. This version requires no universe that "began" in time and is thus consistent with an infinitely existing universe. The argument draws on the distinction between things that are necessary and things that exist contingently. Something is necessary if it *must* exist—if it could not logically fail to exist. By contrast, everything not necessary would be contingent. We can imagine a set of circumstances or even an entire world or universe in which that thing did not exist. Ultimately, this argument also relies on temporal causation because necessity and sufficiency as used in this argument are temporal concepts.

This argument rests on the claim that the universe and everything in it is contingent because we can imagine a state of affairs in which nothing exists. That there is something rather than nothing, proponents claim, demands an answer. The only plausible explanation, they argue, is that there exists a necessary being on which the universe's existence rests. A contingent cause of the universe would lead to an infinite regress, which cannot be the answer because it would leave the existence of contingent things unexplained. The MCA can be stated more systematically: (1) Everything whose existence is contingent has a cause; (2) nothing can be the cause of its own existence; (3) the existence of the universe is contingent; therefore, (4) the universe must have a cause that is necessary, the existence of which is explained by its own necessity.

One can see this argument is not based on any empirical observations but rather on words and definitions. It is equivalent to saying, "The existence of caused things means there must necessarily be uncaused things, and only such an uncaused thing could have brought about the caused things." It is these uncaused things the proponent identifies as "necessary," though it takes only a little thought to see the circularity of this definition.

Proponents of the MCA demand that everything has a cause. They reject the existence of so-called brute facts—facts we are justified in accepting even without an explanation—*unless that brute fact is the Christian God.* They cannot accept the idea, with which most physicists and secular philosophers are comfortable, that something like the universe might not have a cause in the sense we commonly use that word—that the universe *might simply exist.*

Unfortunately for its proponents, who offer it as a more powerful argument than the kalam, the MCA ultimately represents a distinction without a difference. It is subject to the same objections as the kalam because causation is a temporal concept. If the universe is indeed eternal and has no beginning, then it cannot have a cause because *nothing could have occurred before the universe existed.* There was no "before the universe existed." This is true even if the universe "began" at the big bang, as the very concept of cause arose simultaneously with the universe. Temporality is built into the definition of "cause," and we cannot discuss it outside a temporal frame. But according to the MCA, time itself is contingent, so the first premise leads us to the impossible conclusion that time must have a cause. The very notion of contingency rests on temporal causation.

If one is to argue that even an eternal universe must have a cause, then she is using the word *cause* in a novel manner—a manner that strips it of any temporal qualities and thus any recognition. But for the argument to have any weight, the "cause" of the universe must be understood in the familiar way. It must explain why the universe exists. The success of the argument thus requires equivocation, which dooms it at the starting gate.

Another problem with the MCA is that no proof is ever offered for the existence of a necessary "being." Other than the unsupportable claim that logically contingent things must have causes, no reason is ever given to compel the conclusion that some transcendent intelligence must be logically necessary. It is easy for me to imagine a "world" with no God, just as it was for John Lennon, thus demonstrating that God is unnecessary. The MCA merely represents wordplay without substance.

E. Philosophical First Cause

Like the modal cosmological argument, this argument is based not on evidence per se but on philosophy. Proponents, such as conservative writer Ben Shapiro, typically cite Aristotle, who posited that the universe consists of a series of events stretched across a long, causal chain, with each event caused by some previous event. In such a world, Aristotle concluded, there must be a first mover that set the entire chain of events in motion. The first mover, by definition, could not be a part of the chain, so must exist outside of it. This first mover, Christian proponents claim, must be God.

This argument suffers from the same primary flaw as the cosmological argument—the presumption of temporal causation up to a point arbitrarily designated as God when other possibilities are possible and, given Ockham's razor, far more plausible. Also, as discussed earlier, even if a first cause is granted, there is no reason to expect it to be a personal one with thoughts, hopes, and desires, such as the Christian God. The first cause is just whatever initiated the arrow of time as we know it. It is a necessary but far from sufficient condition of the Christian God.

THE ARGUMENT FROM APPARENT DESIGN (TELEOLOGICAL)/ARGUMENT FROM COMPLEXITY

> The contest between evolution and Christianity is a duel to the death. If evolution wins . . . Christianity goes—not suddenly, of course, but gradually, for the two cannot stand together.
>
> —William Jennings Bryan

Perhaps the most popular argument for God that purports to be based on empirical data is the argument from apparent design, also known as the teleological argument. *Teleology* is a philosophical term for describing something in terms of the purpose it serves, and this argument is premised on the intuitive concept that everything serves a purpose. In the largely man-made world we live in, after all, we are surrounded by items that were designed to serve very specific functions. We have been conditioned to see things in these terms.

The argument stems from an analogy to items we know were designed by human intelligence. The apologist argues that when we see natural phenomena and living organisms (or components of living organisms) that appear to have some clear function, we can reasonably assume they were designed by an intelligent personal agent. Our first question should be "Is this analogy warranted?"

The first known use of this argument is by William Paley in his book *Natural Theology* (1802). Paley uses the analogy of a pocket watch found on the beach to demonstrate that humans and their components (such as the eye) show the same evidence of design. Paley concludes that the designer must be God and thus that the apparent design of humans served as an argument for God's existence.

There are several problems with Paley's argument. First, the watch has a clear purpose that does not benefit itself, for the watch is not alive. The watch performs a single function—telling time—which can only be of use to an intelligent agent. Second, every component of a watch has a specific use that advances the watch's utility to such an agent—all are means to the end of accurately telling the time. No component is extraneous to that purpose. Third, we know of no plausible mechanism whereby a watch can come into existence, fully formed, unless assembled by an intelligent agent.

None of these is true for humans. Humans have no clear external purpose. To claim the purpose of humans is to serve God is simply begging the question. It is a circular argument because it assumes the existence of God and the truth of the Bible. It is not the type thing that an objective observer from another planet could ever discern from simply observing humans. None would say, "The only possible reason those beings could be here is to serve an all-powerful creator." From a naturalist's viewpoint, humans as a species have no common purpose, for none is apparent. The most that can be said from an objective viewpoint is that *we don't know* whether humans even have a purpose, much less what it is. Without clear evidence of a purpose, one can't assume humans were designed with any particular purpose in mind.

Second, humans exhibit many features that appear to have no function, much less a function that can be tied to a common external purpose. Such organs as the appendix and features like the tailbone, wisdom teeth, and male nipples may have once served crucial purposes for humanity's ancestors, but we cannot determine that they benefit modern humans at all. Such features are classified as "vestigial." Watches have no vestigial parts.

Third, science has provided a plausible mechanism for humans in their current form, as well as every other species of living creature on the planet—evolution by natural selection. I discuss this in more detail later, but the point here is that, unlike Paley's watch, evolution perfectly explains how humans arrived at this point with no need for an intelligent agent at any point.

Likewise, evolution explains how the *components* of living creatures, such as eyes, livers, and kidneys, came to exist in their present forms. Traits that benefit the organism, either directly or indirectly, are naturally selected for over millions of years. Beneficial mutations are passed along to more descendants, who themselves procreate, while less beneficial ones die out. Over time, it was beneficial for organisms to become more complex, with different components of their anatomy taking on specialized functions. Unlike the components of a watch, which cannot serve the watch itself, human organs evolved to do exactly that.

Intimately related to the apparent design argument and arguably subsumed by it is the argument from complexity. Using analogies like Paley's (paintings, Boeing 747 aircraft, or skyscrapers springing out of thin air), many modern apologists argue that complex beings like humans or complex molecules like DNA simply could not have come about without a designer. Anything complex arising out of thin air is a false analogy, however, because no one claims biological complexity arose spontaneously. Just because two things share one quality (complexity) doesn't mean they share another (design), especially when that complexity has another explanation.

Natural selection and large time periods adequately explain how the complexity we see in nature builds gradually from relatively simple origins. Human DNA, for example, results from genetic material growing steadily more complex over hundreds of millions of years. The most obvious flaw, however, is that this argument requires special pleading. It posits that complexity requires a designer yet exempts the most complex being imaginable—God. If humans are so complex as to require design and humans are made in God's image, then who or what designed God? Only by exempting God from this otherwise universal rule can the argument proceed. But by this point, it has refuted itself.

In short, Paley provides a false and misleading analogy while also failing to account for alternative explanations that neither require nor even suggest a designer. Paley should not be faulted for this latter failing too harshly because Darwin's theories had not been publicized when Paley's book was published. Those who argue for Paley's design hypothesis today, however, have no such excuse.

A. Charles Darwin Provides a Viable Alternative

Until Charles Darwin published *On the Origin of Species* in 1859, it was commonly understood, even in scientific circles, that the various species had always existed in their present forms. Such arguments as Paley's for a designer, therefore, had great persuasive force, for how else could one account for the wide variety of species?

This particular hypothesis is a good fit for Christian theology, which posits a six-thousand-year-old Earth in which each species were brought into existence by God in its present form. Even Deists of the Enlightenment who rejected Christianity, such as Thomas Jefferson, found the design argument compelling for *some type of intelligent designer*, though not necessarily the God described by Christian Scripture. Absent an explanation that could account for different species without top-down directed design, the "intelligent designer" hypothesis was the only game in town.

But then along came Mr. Darwin, and he changed everything by offering an alternative and then compelling evidence in its favor. Almost twenty-three years after returning from a five-year voyage of painstaking observation and scientific discovery aboard the HMS *Beagle*, Darwin published his groundbreaking work, *On the Origin of Species*. The ultimate cataclysmic impact of this book and the theories Darwin proposes within it, as well as the even more shocking *The Descent of Man* in 1871, cannot be overstated.

In these books, Darwin proposes that all living creatures had, over vast spans of time, descended from simpler ancestors, with all sharing a common ancestor at some point. While distinct species could be identified, those distinctions arose only through millions of years of changes, in which members of the same species became isolated from one another and one or both adapted to a new environment, so eventually their descendants were too dissimilar to procreate.

The most important aspect of Darwin's theory is the mechanism he proposes to explain these changes: *natural selection*. By purely natural variation, certain members of a species will be born with traits different from their brethren—longer tails, better eyesight, and so on—that are better adapted to their environment. Such fortunate creatures will enjoy a selective advantage over their less fortunate brothers and sisters. They are likely to live longer and enjoy more breeding opportunities. This means their genetic material is more likely to be passed along to future generations, which will themselves enjoy the same advantages. In this way, species develop that are better and better adapted to their environments, generally growing more complex with more specialized organs and anatomy.

We are all familiar with how this can be accomplished artificially from dog breeding. By deliberately breeding dogs with certain traits, we can create new breeds with a wide variety of specific desired characteristics—larger, faster, more docile, and so on. The insight of Darwin's theory was that this same selection *occurs naturally* due to the survival pressures of different environments. The survival advantages of certain traits favor creatures born with such traits, causing those traits to be relatively overrepresented in the genetic pool. Because what was advantageous for a population living under one set of conditions might not be so for a population living under different conditions, the traits of those populations would diverge over time, until ultimately they would represent different species.[23]

As Darwin describes it, evolution itself is not random. The mutations themselves might be random, but the natural selection of specific genes or alleles is not. They are driven by the imperative of survival. Natural selection works like a ratchet wrench, preserving only those features that are adaptive and beneficial to survival. While this is admittedly an over-simplified summary of Darwin's theory, it captures the key point: Darwin provides an explanation for the diversity of life on Earth that requires *no intelligent designer*. The mechanism of natural selection worked *automatically*, allowing for millions of species to develop from the bottom up, driven by environmental conditions, with no need for any top-down intervention or guidance by an external creative agent. No teleological force is evident or required. This renders all creator-deities, including the Christian God, unnecessary and irrelevant for explaining biological design.

Though Darwin began his voyages as an orthodox Christian, regularly quoting Bible verses and expecting to find evidence for God in nature, he ultimately gave up Christianity and ended his life as an agnostic. Darwin lost his strong faith through contemplating the implications of his work and other scientific discoveries of the time, which were casting more and more doubt on established Christian doctrine. His gradual disenchantment resulted from his increased knowledge and understanding of nature.

Thinkers of ancient Greece and the Enlightenment both considered the design argument for theism a persuasive one, but both groups recognized that its power rested on there being no viable alternative explanation. It seems highly likely that had they lived to see the publication of Darwin's seminal works, such Enlightenment thinkers as Jefferson, Madison, Washington, and Benjamin Franklin would have been atheists rather than Deists.

Besides undermining the argument from design, Darwinism, as Darwin's collective theories began to be called, directly rebut two bedrock principles of Christianity. First is the reliability of the Bible. No one could argue that the Bible states or even remotely implies anything similar to Darwin's explanation for speciation. The story of Adam and Eve, among many others, could no longer be taken seriously. If Darwin is right, then the Bible must be wrong. And if the Bible is wrong about something so fundamental as this, then how far can it be trusted about other things? If it is mistaken in telling us where we come from, then how can we trust it to tell us where we are going?

Second, Darwinism undermines the Bible's claim that man is special—somehow qualitatively different from every other living creature on Earth. According to the Bible, man was made in God's own image to rule over all the other creatures.[24] But Darwinism tells us that our species, like every other species on Earth, developed gradually from humble origins, only recently (by geological standards) taking its current form. It reveals that we are merely one branch on an interconnected tree of life rather than something wholly new and unique. We are less the first telephone created by Alexander Graham Bell and more the iPhone 11.1.

Darwinism teaches that modern humans and apes share a common ancestor in the recent past. It also demonstrates this ancestor descended from a chain including mammals, amphibians, and fish. How, then, could man have been created in God's image? What image would that have been? At what point in man's evolutionary history could he first be regarded as "man," qualitatively distinct from other creatures?[25] At what point was man infused with a "soul"?

As Daniel Dennett points out in *Darwin's Dangerous Idea*,

> It's the loss of teleology, or purpose, that makes evolution such an uncomfortable fact for even liberal theologians. Evolution removes human beings from any privileged place among the animals, and its nonrandom selection of randomly varying genes shows that if we were to start the clock of evolution from the beginning again, all probability is that the resulting biodiversity would not even include humans at all. Quite simply, evolution is not a process designed to produce humans.[26]

Dennett's point is that evolution by natural selection (EBNS) inherently contradicts the end-result-driven, top-down purpose that underlies Christian Creation. To the extent EBNS can be described as purposive in any sense, it is in the bottom-up one. EBNS brings about organisms increasingly better adapted to survive in their environments simply because adaptation and survival are linked. Where that process ends up, however, depends on an endless number of variables over millions of years. If we started the process over again tomorrow, the chances it would generate anything approaching a human within the same time frame are vanishingly small.

Yet another implication of Darwinism is that complexity arises from simplicity. A superintelligent god existing prior to the known universe is contrary to what we know about biology because it presumes complexity without antecedents. If you accept the implication of Darwinism that complexity and probability are inversely related, then God, being infinitely complex, is also infinitely improbable. God thereby violates the principle of analogy established by EBNS. It was these conflicts that created such tension between early Darwinians and Christians and that still plague the discussion between evolutionists and fundamentalist Christians today.

B. The Theory of Evolution Evolves

Darwin's writings provide a good start to the discussion of speciation by laying out a conceptual framework and providing evidence-based theories, but his work is far from complete. Darwin was working from a limited data set and with no knowledge of genetics as science understands it today. Of course, scientists wasted no time subjecting Darwin's theories to the broader scientific process—testing them, refining them, and expanding them.

One hundred sixty years later, it is astonishing how well Darwinism has held up. Darwin's core ideas have been verified by millions of tests and observations in virtually every field of science. The basic theory has been in a state of continuous reconfirmation since Darwin first proposed it, with biology, geology, anthropology, and every dinosaur bone ever found providing a nonstop barrage of additional proof points and astounding consilience. As the theory has matured, it has become only more robust.

Evolution, referring to the process by which modern species developed to their current form, is a fact. This process undeniably happened but should be distinguished from the *theory of evolution*, which is a model of *how* evolution occurred and occurs. The theory of evolution can be thought of as a jigsaw puzzle in which we have about 90 percent of the pieces. We have more than enough to tell what the ultimate picture will generally look like but not all the details. We have been able to predict with startling accuracy many of the missing pieces. For instance, if you have all the pieces surrounding the eye of a cat, you could predict that when you find that missing piece, it will be the cat's eye. If you have a piece from the iris of the eye, you can anticipate that the remainder of the iris will be same color.

It is the same with the evolutionary theory, which is one way we know it is accurate. To use the previous analogy, because the theory has grown robust, scientists have never predicted that the missing piece would be an eye but then came to learn it was actually an ear. They never anticipated the eye would be blue and then found it to be green. Two fossils in the same chain of evolution can tell us what the intermediate fossils should look like. When we have found such intermediate fossils, we have consistently found the predictions of evolutionary biologists validated, linking the chain.

Creationists often argue that evolution is disproved because scientists haven't found the "missing link" between some arbitrary modern species and another, such as crocodile and a duck. The specific example of a "crocoduck" was posited by creationist Ray Comfort in a televised presentation with like-minded Christian actor Kirk Cameron as a mic-dropping defeater of evolution and is still raised today for that same purpose. This is a classic straw man, however, because it completely mischaracterizes evolutionary theory. Biologists would not expect to see a link between a crocodile and duck because ducks did not descend from crocodiles or vice versa. Evolution tells us that both descended *from a common ancestor* millions of years ago that was neither a crocodile nor a duck. The theory predicts that we would find transitional fossils revealing the gradual development of crocodiles and ducks from that common ancestor. And that is exactly what we have found.

If you think of "missing links" as transitional fossils detailing the gradual development of modern species from common ancestors, then the fossil record is replete with them. An internet search for "transitional fossils" yields thousands of results documenting the gradual development of speciation across the tree of life. In response to the oft-repeated argument that evolutionists could not identify missing links between reptiles and birds, a post from *Scientific American* offers the following rebuttal:

Actually, paleontologists know of many detailed examples of fossils intermediate in form between various taxonomic groups. One of the most famous fossils of all time is Archaeopteryx, which combines feathers and skeletal structures peculiar to birds with features of dinosaurs. A flock's worth of other feathered fossil species, some more avian and some less, has also been found. A sequence of fossils spans the evolution of modern horses from the tiny Eohippus. Whales had four-legged ancestors that walked on land, and creatures known as Ambulocetus and Rodhocetus helped to make that transition. Fossil seashells trace the evolution of various mollusks through millions of years. Perhaps 20 or more hominids (not all of them our ancestors) fill the gap between Lucy and the australopithecine and modern humans.[27]

From our findings of transitional fossils between dinosaurs and modern birds, scientists predicted that transitional fossils would reveal dinosaurs with feathers. That is just what they discovered in 2016, when a dinosaur tail was found preserved in amber, revealing the same feathers predicted by evolutionary biologists.

Just as the transition from reptiles to birds has been reflected by the fossil record, so, too, has the transition from fish to land dwellers. A great example, dubbed Tiktaalik, was discovered in 2004. Tiktaalik contains spiracles, suggesting primitive lungs along with gills, and fins that were weight bearing, with rays similar to fingers. It is the earliest fish to have a neck, which would allow it more freedom to hunt prey on land. It was just the type of thing scientists expected to find at just the right place in the layers of the Earth, where evolutionary theory predicted it would be.

Like the rings of a tree, the sedimentary layers of the Earth reveal a record of development. Those layers, known together as the geologic column, go back millions of years, forming a progressive timeline as each hardens into rock. The deepest layers are the oldest, while those on top are the most recent. Evolutionary theory tells us we should expect no fossils of modern animals at the deepest levels but that as we move up toward the surface, we should find fossils of fish, then amphibians, then reptiles, birds, and finally modern mammals—*in that exact order*. And that is just what we have found. Never have scientists discovered a single fossil out of the sequence evolution demands. Never have they found a mammal in the age of reptiles or a reptile in the age of fish. Each fossil has been found in the geologic column just where evolution requires it to be.

The fossil record, however, is only the beginning of the story. Since Darwin's time, the findings of all relevant fields of science have converged to support evolutionary theory. Examples include the following.

1. Comparative Anatomy

Many groups of species share the same body structures. Vertebrates, for example, share internal skeletons with the same basic features. The arms of humans, forelegs of dogs and cats, and flippers of whales and seals all contain the same types of bones (humerus, radius, and ulna), which only makes sense if they shared a common vertebrate ancestor. These would not be optimal designs if engineered from the ground up but would be necessary in a system that must build on what came before rather than starting from scratch with each new species. That is the very system employed by evolution.

2. Comparative Embryology

Humans, dogs, snakes, fish, monkeys, eels, and many more life forms are all considered chordates because they belong to the phylum *Chordata*. One feature of this phylum is that, as embryos, all have gill slits, tails, and specific anatomical structures involving the spine. For humans (and other nonfish) the gill slits reform into the bones of the ear and jaw at a later stage in development, but initially, all chordate embryos strongly resemble each other and begin development in much the same manner. Pig embryos are often dissected in biology classes because of how similar they look to human embryos, and they have recently been found capable of hosting human cells in a human-pig hybrid. This is another instance of a system that builds on what came before rather than beginning anew. These common characteristics could only be possible if all members of the phylum *Chordata* descended from a common ancestor.

3. Vestigial Structures

These are structures, including genes, muscles, organs, or even behaviors, that provide little or no useful function in their current form but would have served a necessary role in evolutionary development. They would likely have been functional—even necessary—in an ancestral species but are now either nonfunctional, semifunctional, or repurposed. Their existence makes no sense if each species was designed independently but perfect sense if speciation entails common descent, with later species built on the designs of older ones. There are thousands of examples across the animal kingdom. In humans, vestigial structures would include the appendix, wisdom teeth, sinuses, tonsils, the tailbone (coccyx), goosebumps (arrector pili muscles), and male nipples.

4. Biogeography

This refers to the geographical distribution of species. Under evolutionary theory, we would expect distinct species to emerge in conditions of geographical isolation, where conditions differ substantially from those in which their ancestors lived. In this way, a single population is split into two or more smaller populations that develop independently. That is exactly what we find. Without evolution as an explanation, we would expect the same species to exist wherever in the world conditions are the same, but we don't. For example, marsupials like kangaroos, bandicoots, and quolls make up about half of Australia's indigenous mammal species but are found nowhere in Africa, which occupies the same latitude. Likewise, until introduced by humans, Australia lacked many of the placental mammals common on other continents, such as squirrels, rabbits, and foxes. Evolution leads us to expect unique species on an isolated continent, such as Australia, and that is just what we find.

5. Genetics

The entire field of genetics was unknown in Darwin's day and could have shattered Darwin's theories. Instead, it affirms them at every turn. We can now trace the development of speciation through the genetic codes of different species, living and extinct. We can see how, as species evolved from simple to more complex forms, much of the coding from the prior forms was retained but supplemented. Much like vestigial organs, we have identified "junk DNA" existing in the genetic code of all living species that serves no present function, being merely a remnant of our evolutionary past. We have found we share genes with other species in direct proportion with how long ago our genetic lines diverged. For example, we share 99 percent of our genes with chimpanzees, 90 percent with cats, 80 percent with cows, and 75 percent with mice, percentages that correspond to speciation in the fossil record. These shared genes demonstrate common ancestors just where we would expect to find them. The genetic evidence alone provides sufficient support for evolution beyond a reasonable doubt.

6. Observations of Natural Selection at Work

Natural selection, the primary driver of speciation, is not simply an academic theory. It is observed and documented every day by scientists. One of the most familiar and disturbing examples is antibiotic resistance in bacteria. Scientists developing antibiotics have repeatedly been stymied by the speed at which new strains of bacteria evolve with the ability to resist them. The appearance of the deadly vancomycin-resistant *Staphylococcus aureus* (VRSA) results from EBNS. In fact, all classes of microbes have been observed to develop resistance, including fungi, viruses, protozoa, and bacteria. Natural selection has also been observed in fish, lizards, and even humans. Lactose tolerance, for example, results from natural selection.

7. Computer Modeling

Computers have given us unparalleled abilities to test and compare theories involving complex systems. Models can be constructed based on those theories and known rules of how things behave. We can model, for example, how subsequent generations of genetic material would change over time based on random mutations and environmental pressures and then compare those models to real-world observations. We can ask the computer, "Given the rules of evolutionary theory, what should we expect to see?" When we plug those rules in, what we see is the world around us. Such modeling has consistently confirmed evolutionary theory. No other theory has ever been proposed that would pass this test.

Every scientific field with anything relevant to add has confirmed evolutionary theory. All these strands have converged to create a steel cable of unparalleled strength. The predictive value of Darwinism has been astonishing. One example relates to chromosome 2, the second-largest human chromosome. All hominids have twenty-four pairs of chromosomes, except humans, which have twenty-three. Genetic coding revealed this twenty-third chromosome, known as chromosome 2, represents a fusion of two virtually identical chromosomes found in humanity's closest living relative, the chimpanzee. This is just as we would expect it to be if humans and chimpanzees descended from a common ancestor and is inexplicable otherwise.

It is not a stretch to say that modern biology and even most of medical science is built on the foundation of Darwinian evolution. A well-known essay written in 1973 by Eastern Orthodox Christian biologist Theodosius Dobzhansky is titled "Nothing in Biology Makes Sense Except in the Light of Evolution," and that is indeed the consensus view of the relevant scientific community today.[28] This has only become clearer in the years since Dobzhansky penned his essay. If Darwin was wrong, then there is simply no way to explain modern biology or medicine. No theory has been proposed that even begins to make sense of it all, much less *explains it all*, as evolution does so elegantly.

This is not to say that Darwin was right about everything. Given his limited knowledge and perspective, it would have been virtually impossible to have made no errors. But where science has shown Darwin to have made mistakes, none have undermined the core theory that all species, including man, evolved over time from simpler species through a process of natural selection. This is the core of modern evolution, and it is accepted as fact by virtually every legitimate biologist (and anyone else with relevant expertise) in the world.

C. The Rise and Fall of Intelligent Design

Despite the overwhelming scientific consensus on evolution, fundamentalist Christians have mounted a long and well-funded battle to prevent it being taught in public schools. The first publicized battleground occurred in Dayton, Tennessee, in 1925 and was known colloquially as the Scopes

Monkey Trial. The defendant was a high school teacher, John Scopes, who was accused of violating Tennessee's Butler Act, which made it unlawful to teach evolution in any state-funded school.

The trial, later dramatized in the play and movie *Inherit the Wind*, was deliberately staged to attract as much attention and publicity to the issue as possible, with the sides each represented by a nationally known personality of the day. Scopes was ultimately found guilty and fined one hundred dollars, but the trial was widely recognized as a public defeat for the forces of creationism. Scopes's attorney, Clarence Darrow, levied devastating attacks on the creationist position, undermining it at every point and demonstrating its complete lack of any scientific foundation. Scopes's conviction was overturned on appeal.

The national ridicule, however, only galvanized the creationists. Following Scopes, they continued their battle against evolution unabated. They mounted fundraising drives in conservative areas of the country, citing the fear of "atheistic" evolution invading the classrooms of America. This led to passing laws in primarily southern states to prevent public school teachers from teaching evolution. The Supreme Court ultimately struck down all these laws as violations of the First Amendment Establishment Clause. The Establishment Clause, as interpreted by the courts, prevents the government from promoting or favoring a particular religion. The courts found the purpose of these state laws was to shield children in public schools from established scientific ideas that might erode their faith in Christianity. Creationism was a uniquely Christian teaching.

In the late 1980s, the creationists changed their tactics. They began using scientific jargon and focusing on the fallacious argument from ignorance. They would attempt to identify areas of minor disagreement among evolutionary biologists, mischaracterizing them as catastrophic failures of evolutionary theory, and to make scientific-sounding claims to undermine public acceptance of evolution. If they could convince the public there was a legitimate scientific dispute regarding whether evolution occurred, then they could appeal to the public's sense of fairness to have other theories (i.e., creationism) taught alongside evolution ("Teach the Controversy"). This tactic had a name—the Wedge Strategy—given to it by a conservative think tank known as the Discovery Institute. The very name belies the movement's recognition that a direct assault on evolutionary theory through traditional channels would be untenable, leaving the only feasible strategy to sow enough doubt to get their foot in the door.

The Discovery Institute pushed a proposed alternative to evolution known as intelligent design (ID). Unlike evolution, ID was not a scientific theory capable of falsification or making predictions. It made no attempt to meaningfully explain anything about speciation. It was instead a simple assertion: Modern species *must have been* deliberately designed by a superior intelligence because that's all that makes intuitive sense. ID proponents appealed to teleology—that things happen by design and for a purpose. Paley had long ago demonstrated how emotionally appealing such a claim could be. To the extent ID proponents advanced any arguments, they were aimed solely at poking holes in evolution rather than laying out a compelling case for ID.

The primary such "argument" focuses on irreducible complexity—the claim that certain biological features are too complex and improbable to have resulted from natural selection. Proponent Michael Behe defines an *irreducibly complex form* as "comprised of several well-matched, interacting parts that contribute to the basic function, whereby the removal of any one of the parts causes the system to effectively cease functioning."[29] ID proponents argue that such structures as the eye could not have evolved naturally because the gradual evolutionary stages preceding the development of a fully functioning eye would have had no utility to the organism and thus could not have been the product of natural selection.

This argument has been debunked repeatedly by the scientific community. Features might provide one advantage when they initially appear but then confer a different advantage once they develop past a certain point. Also, even a slight advantage can be naturally selected. In the case of eyes, cells with slightly higher light sensitivity can provide an advantage without being a fully formed eye. Through a process known as scaffolding, a structure may increase in complexity through mutation or duplication of its parts, which are later knocked out through more mutations, leaving a structure with no direct linear relationship to the original structure. Function shift, or exaptation, involves features shifting from one function to another, such as the feathers of a bird, which originally evolved to keep dinosaurs warm but turned out to be useful in flight and so evolved further to aid that function. ID proponents have never identified a single biological feature for which biologists cannot demonstrate an evolutionary path. Quite simply, there are no legitimate examples of irreducible complexity in nature.

ID was given its day in court in the 2005 case *Kitzmiller v. Dover Area School District*. The ID proponents put on their best experts to show that ID was legitimate science. They presented their case to a conservative judge, John E. Jones III, appointed by Republican president George Bush. At the end of the proof, Judge Jones ruled against them in a harshly worded order. Judge Jones ruled that intelligent design is not science but merely creationism in disguise. Regarding irreducible complexity, Judge Jones concluded it had "been refuted in peer-reviewed papers and . . . rejected by the scientific community at large."[30] Judge Jones's order described the history of fraud and "outright lies" that characterized the tactics of the ID proponents, ultimately ruling that teaching ID, like creationism before it, violated the First Amendment.

D. Not-So-Intelligent Design

Despite being thoroughly discredited within the scientific and legal communities, intelligent design and creationism in all its forms remain popular with the general public. Well over 50 percent of Americans believe some form of creationism should be taught in public schools.[31] Because the ID movement persists within American culture, having a corrosive effect on scientific literacy throughout the country, I include one additional section to demonstrate just how hollow this movement is. The premise of ID is that evolution cannot explain the variety of organisms and features we see in nature. ID proponents argue this demands one to accept the alternative explanation that an intelligent designer purposefully crafted every organism and every feature of every organism for its highest and best use.

One need take only a cursory look at nature to see that this alternative explanation does not hold up. If a designer is postulated, then virtually all creatures show evidence of poor, if not completely incompetent, design. They all possess features that are at best redundant and unnecessary and at worst highly disadvantageous, but all represent an expected by-product of evolutionary development. Humans alone possess numerous such features, including the following:

- The existence of a cavity between the ovary and fallopian tube in human females allows fertilized eggs to implant outside the uterus, resulting in an ectopic pregnancy. Prior to modern surgery, such pregnancies invariably caused the death of mother and child.
- A single passageway, the pharynx, is used for both ingestion and respiration in humans, resulting in a dramatically increased risk of choking.
- The human appendix is a vestigial organ with no known value to modern humans, though it is crucial to the digestion of plant material in some herbivores. The organ can and often does become infected, however, leading to appendicitis. Prior to modern surgery, appendicitis resulted in certain death for millions.

- The human eye is structured so the optic nerve and blood vessels lie on the surface of the retina rather than behind it, as with many invertebrate species. This gives all humans a blind spot, rendering human vision far from optimal.
- The size of human brains has resulted in skulls so large that, before modern medicine, billions of women died in childbirth when the infant's head became lodged in the birth canal.
- Because humans share basically the same set of teeth with their primate cousins but have evolved flatter faces, they have crowded teeth and poor sinus drainage. Anyone who has had to have their wisdom teeth removed has experienced this flaw firsthand.
- Humans exhibit goosebumps when cold or frightened. This would have provided a defense mechanism to our hairier ancestors by raising their hairs to make them appear larger or to trap heat close to the surface of the skin. For today's relatively hairless humans, it is merely a useless curiosity.
- Male humans have nonworking nipples that represent genetic traits left over from fetal development. This makes sense only if human sexual characteristics were scaffolded on as natural selection would require and not if humans were designed from the ground up as Christianity teaches.
- All organisms, including humans, possess much nonfunctional junk DNA (approximately 90 percent of human DNA) that evidences their gradual evolution but serves no present purpose. As with redundant computer code, elimination of this junk DNA serves no detrimental effect. There is no coherent reason for an intelligent designer to pack our DNA with so much superfluous junk.

Obviously, human design is suboptimal to say the least. If God directly designed and constructed man in his current form or even guided evolution toward his preconceived design, then one must acknowledge that He could have done a *much* better job. The evidence of poor design is everywhere and extremely surprising, given the Christian hypothesis. Within the context of gradual evolutionary development, however, in which more recent features had to be adapted or repurposed from earlier ones rather than designed from the ground up, all these features make perfect sense. They are just what we would expect, given the truth of naturalism.

Apologists typically respond by retreating to the "mystery" position, arguing that one cannot assume God would select the optimal design for his creations. Of course, this renders the design argument unfalsifiable because it uses apparent good design to support its argument while rationalizing away evidence of poor design. Through this strategy, apologists seek to avoid answering such questions as "Why would God design things to appear indistinguishable from what we would expect to see from purely natural processes?" This boils down to arguing that God would purposefully design man to appear as though He didn't design man. Ockham's razor again leads us to the more parsimonious explanation.

As for the claim that evolution is insufficient to explain the natural world, this can be easily refuted by the fact that ID proponents have never pointed to any feature or organism for which a plausible naturalistic process, consistent with evolution, has not been identified. Evolution is perfectly sufficient to explain the entire spectrum of life we have observed, and no one has ever demonstrated otherwise.

ID proponents limit their efforts to trying to point out weaknesses in evolutionary theory. Typically, this involves fraudulently manufacturing a "weakness" that doesn't exist, such as irreducible complexity, while ignoring the scientific literature that effectively rebuts their claims. It is significant that ID proponents *never* attempt to provide an alternative theoretical framework for speciation that might be testable. This is why ID is not science. The US National Academy of Sciences (a collection of the top 2,350 scientists in America) disregards intelligent design as unscientific and pseudoscience.[32] Intelligent design is just old-school creationism dressed up in modern clothing. It is religion grossly masquerading as science.

ID proponents argue that they should be entitled to "equal time" in public school science classes. In other words, those representing less than 0.01 percent of the relevant scientific viewpoint should be entitled to 50 percent of the time. They likely think because science conflicts with the Bible on these questions that those representing the majority religious view should get equal time to rebut science. But in science class, the curriculum must not be determined by those holding the most popular religious views. In science class, as in the scientific community, the science curriculum must only be modified when warranted by better science. American author Judith Hayes recognizes, "If we are going to teach creation science as an alternative to evolution, then we should also teach the stork theory as an alternative to biological reproduction."[33] Bill Maher characteristically puts it more bluntly: "You don't have to teach both sides of a debate if one side is a load of crap."[34]

Ultimately, creationism in whatever form represents a massive conspiracy theory because it would require widespread collusion of virtually every biological scientist in the world to distort the truth to deny God's existence.

But creationists fail to recognize the implications of this. For all the evidence to fit together so perfectly, to tell the same story, and to consistently lead to the same conclusions would require a calculated, coordinated scheme on a scale that only God could accomplish—a conspiracy by God to purposefully deceive mankind into believing He didn't exist.

Even previously resistant religious institutions have taken notice. In 1996, Pope John Paul II said,

> Today, almost half a century after publication of the encyclical, new knowledge has led to the recognition of the theory of evolution as more than a hypothesis. It is indeed remarkable that this theory has been progressively accepted by researchers, following a series of discoveries in various fields of knowledge. The convergence, neither sought nor fabricated, of the results of work that was conducted independently is in itself a significant argument in favor of the theory.[35]

In February 2014, intelligent design spokesman Ken Hamm debated Bill Nye (the "Science Guy") at the Creation Museum in Kentucky. Both were asked what it would take for them to change their mind. Nye responded, "Evidence." He would change his mind immediately if presented with *just one piece of good evidence* that he was wrong. Hamm simply stated, "I'm a Christian." In other words, *nothing would change his mind* because his creationism is a matter of faith impervious to evidence. And that, summed up, is the difference between the two positions.

E. Theistic Evolution

The fallback position for Christians who concede the evidence for evolution but insist on a place for God in the process is known as theistic evolution—the idea that *God guided the evolutionary process* for the purpose of ultimately producing man. Such Christians are willing to live with some of the disconcerting implications of evolution but treat as non-negotiable the idea that God was in control of the outcome all along. Theistic evolution allows those unsatisfied with creationism or intelligent design to adopt what they see as a middle ground, accommodating the general thrust of evolutionary theory as they understand it while shoehorning into the process a place for God.

Theistic evolution is supported by 33 percent of Americans and represents the official position of the Roman Catholic Church.[36] Recent popes have made numerous statements on the subject. What is missing from them all, however, are any specifics. At what points, for example, did God supposedly intervene into the process, and what did that intervention accomplish? What part of the evolutionary process requires an explanation, and how is that explanation accomplished through invoking God? Theistic evolution is never presented as a testable model but only as a series of vague generalities to plug supposed gaps never identified.

Theistic evolution is not a hypothesis proposed to solve any scientific problem with evolutionary theory. Rather, it is a proposed solution to a *theological problem* with accepting evolution by natural selection—that the scientific theory eliminates the crucial role Christianity insists must be played by God. Alvin Plantinga states the problem,

> What is not consistent with Christian belief, however, is the claim that evolution and Darwinism are unguided—where I'll take that to including being unplanned and unintended. What is not consistent with Christian belief is the claim that no personal agent, not even God, has guided, planned, intended, directed, orchestrated, or shaped the whole process. Yet precisely this claim is made by a large number of contemporary scientists and philosophers who write on this subject.[37]

Plantinga is, if anything, underinclusive in his estimates. In fact, *virtually every contemporary scientist and philosopher not already a devotional Christian makes this claim.* And that is because the evidence overwhelmingly supports that evolution through the development of modern man was indeed an unguided process. All available evidence compels that *it must have been unguided.* That is what the words *natural selection* entail.

Evolution relies on mutations, which we know to occur randomly due to processes we now understand. There is no discernable direction in the type or rate of mutations along our evolutionary path. Such teleological force would be trivially easy to detect, for we would see pure directionality rather than responses to shifting environmental contingencies. What you see instead are millions of mutations over untold generations, the vast majority of which died out immediately. Others led to new genetic structures that were more lasting, some persisting for hundreds of generations before dying out, some even longer. A small sliver continued until they led to new mutations, which had fates similar to their ancestors. The only common thread was that the mutations that survived were adaptive, and adaptivity defies top-down direction. A good analogy is provided by neuroscientist Rodolfo Llinas:

> If you let something tumble long enough, it comes out almost perfect. Such is the power of random collisions and patience, and that constitutes the sum

total of nature's intelligence. All the rough edges, the flaws, the things that don't work are systematically dispatched by natural selection. What remains and carries on into the next generation and the next after that and so on are the advantageous aspects, what *does work what makes survival easier. And survival is the fuel of natural selection.*[38]

If we propose that the end result of evolution was designed to be man, then the path looks fantastically circuitous. Rather than a straight line or anything close to it, with each adaptation steadily bringing our ancestors closer to our current form, we see thousands of fits and starts—movement forward, movement backward, movement sidewise, and dead ends galore. Rather than a freeway from LA to New York City, man's evolutionary path represents a drunken road trip passing through thousands of towns all over the United States, often backtracking or veering off-road into rambling wilderness.

Theistic evolution is an unnecessary hypothesis, adding nothing to our understanding of the theory of evolution. At no point, from the earliest single-cell organisms all the way through the rich tapestry of life we now observe, is a supernatural intervention apparent or necessary to explain any element of the theory. The evolutionary process shows no evidence of any guidance or planning. Evolution is fully explained by the mechanism of *natural selection*, which leaves no role for God to play. This was, in fact, Charles Darwin's primary contribution to the theory: demonstrating that evolution could occur naturally, with no intervention by any intelligent agent. As with germ theory, the theory of evolution is airtight in this respect. Nothing is left to explain.[39]

This doesn't, of course, rule out the possibility that some omnipotent entity *could have been* intervening in the process at key points or even all of them. This remains logically possible, but significantly, there is *no evidence* for this. This more complicated theory requires additional assumptions (the existence and regular involvement of a tinkering God) that are unproven and unnecessary, just as with the demon theory of disease. It also presupposes this entity intervened so his intervention would be entirely undetectable—completely indistinguishable from naturalistic processes.

If God did direct evolution in such a way to significantly shortcut the developmental path of modern humans, then this would be detectable through various means. We could see, for example, a streamlined path from the earliest forms of life to modern humans, with no unnecessary detours or dead ends. But what we see is the opposite. If evolution was guided with modern humans in mind, then it was done so with a deliberate design to cover the creator's tracks by rendering the path impossibly circuitous. It requires a god that *bent over backward* to make it appear he played no role, a motivation inconsistent with the God described in the Bible. Accordingly, there is no *good reason* to believe that any such entity was involved. Naturalism provides the more parsimonious explanation—by far.

The God of Christianity could have used any method to create and sustain the life of every creature existing on Earth today. He could have merely willed it, and it would be. Likewise, He could have used an infinite array of approaches that would be entirely inconsistent with naturalism. But if naturalism is true, then evolution by natural selection is the only possible explanation. Given naturalism, evolution must be true. Given theism, evolution seems highly contrived and unnecessarily complicated—a divine Rube Goldberg machine. Could this have been God's plan? Of course. Is this the type of plan anyone would honestly expect of a perfect God? Of course not.

Theistic evolution also generates a host of new theological problems for Christian believers. Why, for example, would a loving, all-powerful God choose a methodology that would cause so much suffering for so many? More than 99 percent of species that have existed on Earth have gone extinct. The process of (apparent) natural selection would have to be considered a horrifically cruel one if deliberately designed, requiring an endless parade of extraordinarily painful illnesses and death for billions of sentient creatures. For every adaptive mutation along the circuitous path to humans, there were billions of maladaptive ones, causing agony, death, and ultimate extinction. This would all be an unfortunate but expected consequence of purely naturalistic evolution but highly surprising if the all-loving Christian God were in charge.

THE FINE-TUNING ARGUMENT

Another version of the design/teleological argument expands the scope to the entire universe. It argues that the specific characteristics of our universe suggest that it was "fine-tuned" for human life.[40] William Lane Craig's website identifies this fine-tuning argument as "one of the primary arguments Dr. Craig offers as evidence of God's existence."[41] Another strong advocate of this argument is apologist Lee Strobel.

The beginning proposition is that according to the Bible and the basic tenets of Christianity, God created the universe *to benefit man*. Man was God's highest creation, with all God's other creations intended to support and serve him. Apologists then point to the characteristics of the universe and claim they must have been fine-tuned by an intelligent creator for man to even exist.

Apologists correctly point out that there are innumerable theoretical possibilities for what kind of *universe might exist* but then go on to argue that our universe seems exceptionally hospitable to human life—far more so than we could expect by chance. Apologist Tim Keller calls this the "Cosmic Welcome Mat."[42] Because we purportedly find ourselves in a universe so hospitable to human life, Keller argues, we must assume that this was by design. And where there is design, there must be an intelligent designer. The premises are:

1. the universe is exceptionally hospitable to human life;
2. the probability of this occurring by chance are extremely low; and
3. we would expect God to create a universe hospitable to human life.

Accordingly, apologists argue that we can reasonably conclude that our universe was designed by the Christian God.

This argument is fraught with problems throughout, including unwarranted assumptions, misleading use of statistics, fallacious reasoning, and even blatantly false claims. I find it illuminating that the same apologists who appeal to mystery when confronted with the problem of evil or a universe whose properties don't correspond to biblical predictions have no difficulty intuiting God's purposes with certainty when it suits their own. It should go without saying that unless we can all agree on God's purposes, there is no way to determine whether any particular observation corresponds with those purposes and thus can count as evidence of God's existence. If God's motives and plans are inscrutable, then we can't say we would expect Him to create the universe we see. In fact, we can't say we should expect anything at all.

Even if all these problems were ignored, however, it would remain nothing more than an argument from ignorance, another example of defaulting to God as an explanation just because science hasn't yet definitively put all the pieces together. As I show, however, the pieces *are* coming together, and we know enough to make the God hypothesis highly unlikely.

A. Our Universe Is Not Especially Hospitable to Human Life

The first problem is that our universe *isn't* particularly hospitable to human life. In fact, the vast majority of it is absolutely toxic to human life.

Moreover, so much of the universe is simply unnecessary and unusable for human life. In other words, the stage is far too large for the drama for which Christians claim it was designed.

Assume that you were to take just the space we know of the universe and shrink it to the size of a house—not just any house but the largest mansion on Earth, one with thousands of rooms extending for acres in all directions. Now, assume you were assigned to wander through the house and locate the area that could sustain life. You would never find it. It would be a sub-microscopic speck smaller than a single proton. Would it make any sense to conclude that the entire house was built to serve and benefit an organism that could survive only within that speck?

If an intelligent designer did intend to create an environment solely to benefit mankind, then why would He create trillions of galaxies filled with billions of stars apiece, all inaccessible to man? Nothing outside our solar system could be said to be of any direct benefit or use to man's survival. The vast majority will remain forever beyond human observation, much less use. All of this would appear superfluous to God's purpose and, moreover, a tremendous waste of space and resources.

And why would God require so much *time* before allowing man to take the stage? If we created a timeline the length of a football field representing the age of the universe (13.75 billion years), with the big bang at one goal line and our present day at the other, humans would not appear until a point immediately before the present goal line, *less than the width of a human hair*.[43] To the immediate left of that hair, Neanderthals were walking erect.

Another analogy, employed by Carl Sagan and Neil deGrasse Tyson in the television series *Cosmos*, is that of a "cosmic calendar." If the known history of the universe were compressed into the space of a single year, then primitive man would not have appeared on the scene until 10:24 p.m. on December 31, the final day of the calendar. Jesus would not have appeared until the final seven seconds.

If the real show involved the creation of man and the climax involved the Resurrection of Jesus (only two thousand years ago), then why the incredibly long prologue? If the universe was created with man in mind and exclusively *for man*, then why has virtually its entire existence been human-free? Drawing on the previous analogies, what was the rest of the football field or the rest of the calendar for? This doesn't even consider the remaining life of the universe. If you imagined watching the life of the universe as a movie, beginning with the big bang and ending with the death of the final black hole, then all the visible stars will have died before the first frame of film. Virtually the entire life of our universe will be populated only by black holes. The Christian hypothesis must explain *all* the attributes of the universe—not just that it allows for human life.

Saying that something is fine-tuned means that the parameters are *exactly* what they need to be—no more and no less. But that is not what we see. Not only are the size and age far greater than necessary given the Christian hypothesis, but so, too, are the initial entropy of the universe, the generations of elementary particles, and countless other factors whose values are far from what we would expect in a universe finely tuned for human or any other life. Maybe the value of the constants must be within a *certain range* for life to exist, but why should we expect a range at all? Why would they not all be set at the ideal value and naturally constrained to that value? The apologist cannot appeal to mystery here because he makes a very specific claim. Man is a speck on a speck on a speck—not only within the vast vacuum of the universe but also within the time span in which the universe has existed. To say that the universe was created for man under such circumstances seems the height of arrogance and is completely dismissive of reality.

According to renowned physicist Lee Smolin, the particular characteristics of our universe make it ideal not for producing human life but for *producing black holes*. Our universe contains more black holes than all the humans who have ever existed. We could reasonably expect an efficient black-hole-generating universe to be naturally selected for if, as Smolin also theorizes, ours is one of a virtually infinite number of local universes throughout the cosmos produced by black holes. According to Smolin, an inevitable consequence of an ideal black-hole-producing universe are conditions allowing for chemical life such as our own. This suggests that such universes as ours have evolved within the cosmos to perpetuate themselves, and we are but a necessary by-product.

Regarding Smolin's findings, scholar Richard Carrier remarks,

> If you found a pair of scissors and didn't know what they were designed for, you could hypothesize they were designed as a screwdriver, because scissors can, after all, drive screws. In fact, there is no way to design a pair of scissors that would prevent them from being used as a screwdriver. But as soon as someone showed you that these scissors were far better designed to cut paper, and in fact were not the best design for driving screws, would you stubbornly hang on to your theory that they were designed to drive screws?[44]

If any relatively clear purpose can be derived from our observations of the universe, it would be that it is efficient at producing black holes. This is what a naturalist might reasonably expect in light of what we know of evolution and natural selection, applying the principle of analogy. While this type of universe might also very rarely allow for human life, it would be absurd to claim this was its *primary purpose*. If human life would be a necessary by-product of such a universe, then naturalism would also predict that our universe would allow for it. Christian theology does not explain why the universe God created to generate human life would be so much exponentially better at producing black holes.

The Christian hypothesis, by contrast, predicts the very universe that such early Christians as Paul believed in. In that universe, the only places that existed were Earth, Heaven, and Hell. Men, as well all other creatures, were created almost immediately after the creation of Earth. The Earth was flat and covered by a dome in which the stars, pinpoints of light, existed within the dome and could be moved at will by God. According to the Bible, the Earth is both stationary and flat. Most pointedly, there are at least two passages in which a single point is visible to the whole world (Daniel 4:10–11 and Revelation 1:7) and one (Matthew 4:8) in which the whole world can be seen from a single point—an obvious impossibility unless the Earth is flat. The Bible reflects a view shared by the ancient Egyptians and Babylonians, and there is a wide range of scriptural passages to prove it. The Bible is far clearer in its support for flat-Earthism than in opposing abortion.

Paul would deny God would ever use billions of years of meandering and disastrously catastrophic trial and error to figure out how to make a human. God would simply make them on the first try, as Genesis says He did. Paul actually believed in God *because of the evidence of the universe as he understood it* and condemned nonbelievers for rejecting this evidence. (Romans 1:18–22). It was the conformity between the Scripture and his own observations that Paul found so compelling. We now know that Paul was completely wrong about the nature of the universe in every relevant respect, as his observations lacked the perspective today's science provides. If we take Paul at his word, then modern scientific discoveries would have seriously undercut his faith, likely causing him to abandon Christianity altogether. If Paul knew what we know, then by his own account he would be an atheist.

This flawed understanding of the universe was crucial to the church and its apologists for centuries precisely because it seemed to fulfill what the Bible predicted. This is why the Catholic Church held to this party line so long, denouncing anyone claiming differently as a heretic, often with fatal consequences. As scientific discoveries became increasingly difficult to stifle or explain away, the church grudgingly accepted those it could harmonize into its evolving theology through ever more contrived means. For those it couldn't, sentence of death remained an effective deterrent, as Galileo discovered when he challenged the position that the Earth was the center of the universe.[45]

Today, science has gained such credibility among the general public that the major churches accept most of the broad conclusions of science about the universe, such as its approximate age and expanse. When called to harmonize these with biblical teachings, apologists routinely retreat to the "mystery" defense: We don't know why the Bible describes and predicts a different type of universe than the one we observe, but we must defer to God's mysterious plan. No apologist since the dawn of time has come up with a good explanation for why the universe looks as it does rather than as we would expect it to look from a biblical perspective. A failed prediction amounts to a failed hypothesis.

B. We Cannot Say Our Universe Is Finely Tuned for Any Life

Some apologists will step back from claiming that the universe is exceptionally hospitable to human life and merely claim it to be exceptional that it *allows for life at all*, human or otherwise. They contend that, given the myriad possibilities, even this is too remarkable to be anything but the result of an intelligent designer. An example comes from William Lane Craig, who defines his version of the fine-tuning argument: "[T]he fundamental constants and quantities of nature fall into an exquisitely narrow range of values which render our universe life-permitting. Were these constants and quantities to be altered by even a hair's breadth, the delicate balance would be upset and life could not exist."[46]

The "constants" Craig talks about are things like the speed of light, the rate of expansion of the universe, the force of gravity, and other such parameters of our observable universe. For instance, if matter had not expanded at the rate it did after the big bang, then stars and solar systems would not have formed. Craig claims it is extremely unlikely that these would fall into ranges that allow for life by chance and that it is therefore reasonable to assume they were fine-tuned by an intelligent designer.

Craig's reasoning, which echoes that of many other apologists on this issue, is problematic on many levels. First, he has absolutely no basis to make claims regarding competing probabilities about what is likely or unlikely. Second, he has no basis for drawing conclusions about the *range* of conditions that would allow for life. We simply *don't know* what conditions would allow for life within the universe. We don't know what the universe would look like if the parameters of the standard model were different. We don't know the necessary conditions for life. And we don't know the range of possible parameters.

Knowing none of these variables, it would be complete speculation to claim that ours is the only possible universe that could support life or that the parameters of our universe should be considered improbable or remarkable. Even within the standard model of physics, the late physicist Victor Stenger identifies numerous examples of constants that could range significantly in value and still allow for life.[47] There is simply no scientific support or justification for the proposition that any alteration in the characteristics of the universe would render it lifeless.

C. Probability Arguments Are Red Herrings

Proponents of the fine-tuning argument like to support their position by appeals to probability. They begin at the big bang and postulate all the myriad possibilities for how the universe could have developed, only one of which they claim would result in life. A common analogy is that the universe we live in is roughly equivalent to being dealt a royal flush (odds of 1 in 649,740) from a single deal of five cards, though, of course, the proponent always states the odds to be exponentially higher for our "fine-tuned" universe.

This is an entirely disingenuous use of probability theory. The problem is that the proponent is beginning with a known end result and trying to extrapolate toward it after the fact. Every day, millions of things happen that would seem highly improbable had you predicted them the day before, but after they have occurred, their probability becomes 100 percent. Take the lottery. The odds of any one specific person winning the lottery are astronomically low. But someone does always win. We don't immediately invoke divine intervention to explain this because inevitably *someone* would win. Only had the winner been predicted *before the lottery began* would we find this extraordinary. The winner might find the result extraordinary because it is uniquely significant to him or her, but the rest of us do not.

A deck of cards allows for another analogy. Before the deck is shuffled, the odds it will end up in any particular order are vanishingly low—orders of magnitude lower than a specific person winning the lottery. There are *billions* of possibilities. But the deck always ends up in some order, and this is rarely questioned. Again, only if the particular order of every card had been predicted in advance would we become suspicious—assuming the shuffler to be a magician or a card cheat.

With those two examples in mind, let's look at a royal flush. The dealing of a royal flush in any five-card poker game would be considered extraordinary, regardless of whether anyone had predicted this beforehand. But this is because the value and significance of a royal flush are predefined by the rules of poker, giving that particular set of cards intrinsic value. If the game were different, those same cards might be worthless. But given their intrinsic value *in poker*, being dealt a royal flush is considered amazing and highly improbable. It is crucial to recognize that the rules of poker are set *before the game begins*. If this were not the case, then the dealer could simply wait until his hand was dealt, note the values of his cards, and arbitrarily invent some game or rule in which his hand is the winner. ("A two, four, seven, eight, and jack unsuited! Just what I needed!")

You simply cannot assess something as improbable *after the fact* unless significance has been established beforehand. As seen in the poker example, every specific hand is equally probable and equally improbable before the deal. Only if significance is assigned to certain hands before the deal can one assess whether a particular result is unusually improbable because you can then compare the significant possibilities with the insignificant possibilities. The question, then, is whether life *as we know it* should be considered like a royal flush.

It should not. There is nothing intrinsically significant about life as we understand it because we don't know what could have been. Had the universe formed differently, perhaps there would be different forms of life. We simply don't know what all possible universes different from ours might look like. Nor do we know the requirements for all possible forms of life. We don't even have a clear definition of life. Perhaps a universe with different constants would yield a form of life radically different from our own, even with moral agency like our own or greater. If we existed as that form of life rather than this one, then would we not likewise conclude that the universe had been fine-tuned for us?

Isaac Newton explained why he found the fine-tuning argument compelling: "Atheism is senseless. When I look at the solar system, I see the earth at the right distance from the sun to receive the proper amounts of heat and light. This did not happen by chance."[48] The late author Douglas Adams has the perfect response:

> Imagine a puddle waking up one morning and thinking, "This is an interesting world I find myself in—an interesting hole I find myself in—fits me rather

neatly, doesn't it? In fact it fits me staggeringly well, must have been made to have me in it!" This is such a powerful idea that as the sun rises in the sky and the air heats up and as, gradually, the puddle gets smaller and smaller, it's still frantically hanging on to the notion that everything's going to be alright, because this world was meant to have him in it, was built to have him in it; so the moment he disappears catches him rather by surprise.[49]

We are like the puddle or the lottery winner. We look around and observe that things seem to have come together in our favor, concluding this could only have been by design. Apologists fail to consider that our species may have adapted to its surroundings, as evolution shows it did, rather than our surroundings being customized for us. Also, there is no good reason to privilege our perspective. When viewed from a higher level, the results we see may lack significance at all.

A final example is instructive. Assume that you are asked to roll ten dice, giving you the possibility of arriving at any number from ten to sixty. It turns out that any number you roll will have some unique and interesting quality, not possessed by the others. If it is twenty-five, for instance, it is the only perfect square which is itself the sum of two squares (nine and sixteen). Twenty-seven is the only perfect cube of all of them. Eleven is the smallest palindromic number, and fifty-five is the largest. Forty-two would be the answer to life, the universe, and everything.[50] And so on.

So no matter what number comes up, we can justifiably say, "How amazing! Not only was this number initially highly improbable (they were all equally improbable), but this is the only one that . . ." followed by the unique characteristic of that number. So while our universe might be unique in supporting life as we understand it, perhaps others would be unique in some equally amazing and interesting way. Often, what appears to be purpose, where it looks like object X has feature F to secure some outcome O, is better explained by a filtering process: that is, object X wouldn't be around if it did not possess feature F, and outcome O is only interesting to us as a human projection of goals onto nature.

To claim our universe is amazing because it supports carbon-based life is the equivalent of a card dealer calling the game after the cards have been dealt and then marveling at his luck. We can't say that carbon-based life is extraordinary because we don't know what all the other possibilities might be. Perhaps another form of life would allow for beings more complex and intelligent than humans, but the constants of our universe wouldn't allow it. That life form might be a royal flush, while human life would be pair of twos. We simply cannot say that something is improbable unless we knew what result we were looking for in advance.

Another problem with attempting to assess the probability of the universal constants being of certain values is that we don't know their possible ranges. If we deemed six to be an inherently intrinsic value, then it might seem amazing if six were randomly generated from a billion ping pong balls with unique values written on each. It would not seem nearly so amazing if it were generated from a six-sided die. Apologists like to assume an infinite number of possibilities, but we simply don't know how many sides the universal die contains.

These points deal only with the difficulties of calculating the prior probability of the universal constants being set at their existing values naturally. But ultimately, this argument must come down to *comparing* prior probabilities—the probability of the universe obtaining its constants by natural processes versus the probability of it obtaining them from the will of the Christian God. Even if we could calculate the probability of the former, how could we possibly calculate the probability of the latter? We have absolutely no basis to determine this probability, especially as it is based on such unproven assumptions as the very existence of God (which, of course, is what the argument is attempting to prove). While the prior probability given naturalism might be low, it might be even lower given theism. This is especially true where the apologist appeals to an inscrutable God, whose existence cannot be independently verified. Any argument that assumes the existence of such a God must also include an argument for that God that is not circular. ("The universe could only have come from an all-powerful God, the existence of which is established by the fact we have a universe that could only have come from an all-powerful God.")

Whenever you hear apologists resort to probabilities of this type, therefore, you can be sure it is nonsense. No one has sufficient information to come up with reliable probabilities behind the universal constants, much less compare them and conclude that one hypothesis is more likely than the other. This is especially true when assessing inherently implausible supernatural causes, such as God, for which no independent explanation is ever offered. *How* did God create such a finely tuned universe? Magic. As with the origin of the universe, all we can say with any reliability is that we don't know why the constants are what they are. There is simply no way to construct a logical argument that the Christian God (or any intelligent designer) is a more probable explanation for the universal constants than purely natural processes.

D. God Would Have No Need for a Finely Tuned Universe

There is a simpler objection to the design argument that in its simplicity may be the most powerful. God wouldn't create a finely tuned universe *because He wouldn't need to*. If God is indeed omnipotent, as Christianity maintains, then He could arrange for humans to live in a universe with any features. Any god that can suspend or modify the laws of physics at will would not require a universe with any particular characteristics to create or sustain life. Only a god *without the ability to miraculously intervene*, such as the God posited by the Deists, would need to make sure he got everything just right on the front end. But that is not the God of Christianity. From a Christian perspective, therefore, the argument is self-refuting.

A universe with constants that allow for human life is exactly the universe predicted by naturalism. Naturalism allows for no supernatural intervention, so the only way life could develop in such a universe is for the constants to either be life-consistent from the beginning or to develop that way. Christianity has no need for such conditions because God could create and sustain life regardless of the initial or any subsequent settings. If we expand the definition of life to include incorporeal souls, such as those that populate Heaven, then God would require no conditions at all. You might say that given the qualities of God, there are more than a trillion ways He could have organized the universe that would have allowed for life, while the naturalistic hypothesis allows for only one—the one we see. Taking a cue from the apologists, this means the odds are more than a trillion to one for naturalism over theism.

The existence of human life in a universe that would not otherwise allow it would be the ultimate evidence of God's existence. Instead, however, we see a universe with the opposite characteristics, the only type of universe in which life would require no God. This is extremely surprising under the theistic hypothesis but obvious and necessary given naturalism. As Richard Dawkins observes, "The universe that we observe has precisely the properties we should expect if there is, at bottom, no design, no purpose, no evil, no good, nothing but pitiless indifference."[51] Once again, the Christian hypothesis requires a God that bends over backward to make it appear He doesn't exist.

E. Positing the Multiverse

Even if we assume the constants of the universe could have fallen into a vast range and that they therefore seem uniquely calibrated to allow for life, physics offers a simple, naturalistic solution: Ours is but one of billions of local universes that has existed throughout the cosmos, perhaps even an infinite ensemble, each with different constants. Some of these universes would permit carbon-based life, while others would not. Obviously, we live in one with constants that allow for life. This array of universes is known as the multiverse.

If indeed we do live in a multiverse, then the fine-tuning argument is rendered moot. While a royal flush might seem unlikely given a single deal, it becomes a certainty given an infinite number of deals. Likewise, life-permitting parameters would be completely unsurprising for one universe among a virtually infinite panoply. This may at first sound like science fiction, but most physicists consider it plausible, even likely. Sean Carroll and Victor Stenger describe the multiverse hypothesis as the simplest and most elegant explanation on paper. Other prominent proponents include Stephen Hawking, Brian Green, Max Tegmark, Alexander Vilenkin, and Steven Weinberg—giants in their fields. Hawking, for example, says, "Science predicts that many different types of universe will be spontaneously created out of nothing. It is a matter of chance *which* we are in."[52]

The principle of analogy demonstrates why, between a multiverse and a single divinely tuned universe, the multiverse is the more plausible option. We know that this universe exists. Nothing we know from science suggests that other universes cannot exist, and a significant number of physicists believe there are good reasons to believe they do. This provides a reasonable explanation for why this universe appears as it does. We are observing this universe because this is one of the universes that allows for observers. Why would we need to posit an unknown entity for which we have no evidence and no explanation?

Apologists have quickly responded to the multiverse hypothesis, claiming it is special pleading because it is untestable and a violation of Ockham's razor, all of which I find highly amusing, given their common use of the former and blatant disregard of the latter. As to the claim that the multiverse represents an untestable hypothesis, many types of tests address different aspects of the hypothesis. Various models of the multiverse have been tested mathematically and been found consistent with our knowledge of physics. To have value, a hypothesis need only be testable in theory, and the multiverse is that.

Physicists have also identified observations that would be more likely if we lived in a multiverse than if we did not, and we can test for those. This allows scientists to assess relative probabilities of the theory being true or false. If these observations consistently point in one direction, then this increases confidence in the theory. In fact, the observations made have pointed consistently to the multiverse.

According to Sean Carroll, "The multiverse is not a theory; it is a prediction of a theory, namely the combination of inflationary cosmology and a landscape of vacuum states. Both ideas came about for other reasons, having nothing to do with the multiverse. If they are right, they predict the existence of a multiverse in a wide variety of circumstances." Furthermore, "Given inflation and the string theory landscape (or other equivalent dynamical mechanisms) a multiverse happens, whether you like it or not."[53] In other words, if two of the leading theories in cosmology are correct, then we live in a multiverse. Period. Not that we are in a position to definitively answer the question or even to weigh in with confidence. Our tools and perspective are limited, and there is only so far we can see through space and time. But the unavailability of the definitive test does not render the hypothesis worthless.

The second objection is that the multiverse violates Ockham's razor. One must keep in mind that two theories are being compared here: the divine creation theory and the multiverse theory. The first requires supernatural intervention, while the second does not. Scientists have never observed divine intervention, which its proponents cannot even adequately define. They have, however, observed every necessary condition for the formation of a multiverse. The multiverse is, therefore, the "simpler" theory and the one preferred by Ockham's razor.

It may seem counterintuitive because the multiverse theory results in multiple universes rather than one. But this confuses quantitative with qualitative parsimony. Ockham's razor addresses the simplicity of the *theory*—not the simplicity of the results. In this way, it is comparable to evolution. Evolution is a messy process, resulting in unbelievably circuitous routes through time, with millions of dead ends. But the underlying theory in which natural selection provides a ratcheting mechanism for cumulative change is an elegant one. So it is with the multiverse.

Even if the multiverse hypothesis were completely untestable, it would still be more plausible than the Christian alternative. The former is consistent with all known laws of physics, while the latter is not. The former requires no additional assumptions, while the latter requires numerous assumptions that have failed testing in other areas (the Christian God has repeatedly failed the test of impact, meaning that God has never been shown to have any demonstrable effect on *anything*). Accordingly, if the only two options were the Christian hypothesis and the multiverse hypothesis (they aren't, by the way), then the multiverse would be the more plausible.

Scientists view the multiverse as a very plausible hypothesis. It is well-regarded by many relevant experts and represents the favored view of theoretical physicists. If we indeed live in a multiverse, then it makes no more sense to ask why the universe seems fine-tuned for life than to ask why the Earth, of all the planets in the universe, seems fine-tuned for life. With many options available, we would expect some to be life-permitting, and where else would we expect to find ourselves than in such a life-permitting universe and on such a life-permitting world? It is not necessary to believe we live in a multiverse, however, to conclude that it is necessarily a more probable hypothesis than that proposed by Christianity.[54]

F. A Finely Tuned but Ultimately Baseless Argument

The fine-tuning argument begs the question from the outset "Why is the universe fine-tuned?" It comes loaded with the assumption that the universe is in fact fine-tuned, and once that assumption is accepted, then by definition, there must be a fine-tuner because tuning is a purposive process. The proper, nonloaded, question is "Why are the conditions of the universe what they are?" and the fact is that we simply don't know. It is fortunate for us that they allow for human life, or we would not be here to ponder these questions. But there are many possibilities for why the universe looks the way it does that don't require the intervention of an intelligent agent, much less the Christian God.

A key assumption of the fine-tuning argument when used to support Christianity is that our universe is exactly what the Bible predicts. But this simply isn't so. It's true that our universe allows for moral agents, in the tiniest fraction of its spatial and temporal expanse, and that this is one necessity for Christian Scripture. But other than this, the features of our universe cannot plausibly be said to have been predicted by the Bible or to bear any relationship to the model described by the Bible. Until the modern age, no Christian writer argued for an interpretation that would encompass anything like what we now know of the universe. It was simply not part of the Christian hypothesis. Taking the Bible at anything approaching face value, Christianity simply isn't compatible with the nature of our universe.

Unlike Christian theism, naturalism is not bound by Scripture to a specific theory of the origin or nature of the universe. There are many naturalistic theories under which it would not be surprising to find a universe such as the one we observe. Only if our observations were incompatible with all natural laws and theories could we say those observations were so surprising as to suggest that naturalism could not provide an adequate explanation and simply conclude "God did it."

No answer is better than a glib answer. I do not know how this universe came to exist or why it has the properties it does. But neither do Christian apologists. Neither of us has sufficient bases to make claims regarding either with anything close to certainty, but only one institution is actively working to come up with answers and making progress, while the other rests, treating its ignorance as knowledge. Christian apologists argue that scientists should stop looking for answers and just accept their nonexplanation explanation. Until scientists throw up their hands and give up on the possibility of a natural explanation, there is no good reason to choose a supernatural one.[55] If history is any guide, that will not happen soon.

The fact that scientific findings and observations have forced modern Christians to dramatically revise their doctrines regarding the universe since St. Paul shows that the surprise factor has consistently weighed against Christian theism. It is only because current Christian doctrine is so vague and poorly defined that anyone can even make the claim that our observations are consistent with Christianity. The more literally and specifically one reads the Scripture, the more obvious it becomes that science and Christianity are incompatible in how they describe and explain the universe. Of course, the vague, inscrutable God approach also means that fine-tuning can't be used as an argument for God's existence because we can have no reasonable expectation of what kind of universe such a God would create, if any.

THE ARGUMENT FROM LIFE

In the same breath as arguing that the universe is finely tuned for life, many apologists turn around and argue that the origin of life on Earth required the active intervention of God—that it *required a miracle*. They appear not to realize that only if the conditions of the entire universe made life *impossible* would a miracle be required to explain it. That our universe allows for life makes it far from surprising that we should see it somewhere just as a matter of probability. Naturally occurring life is just what we would expect to find in a vast universe that allows for it.

A bigger problem is that the fine-tuning theory is simply inconsistent with the argument from life. If the universe was finely tuned for human life, then it would have occurred naturally with no need for divine intervention. The whole concept of divine intervention presumes that the universe was not capable of producing life on its own, but wasn't this the very reason God created it as He did? The need for a miracle disappears if you take the design argument at face value, which places the proponent in the same position as the religious skeptic, in which we would expect life to arise from ordinary, natural processes.

As with evolution, the apologists' argument is purely a negative one: A scientific consensus has not formed explaining the exact mechanism by which life originated on Earth; therefore, God did it. Apologists make no attempt to provide their own detailed, competing mechanism. Instead, they simply work at poking holes in existing naturalistic theories, hoping people will simply default to God as the "explanation" after becoming dissatisfied with what's on the table. Once again, God serves the same function as magic.

It is true that scientists have not reached a consensus regarding the origin of life or abiogenesis. But once again, there is no shortage of plausible God-free theories. Scientists have demonstrated that the building blocks of life, amino acids, can be synthesized in conditions similar to those of the early Earth, and they have shown how those amino acids could ultimately lead to life as we know it. Scientists have shown that every step necessary for life to develop *could have occurred naturally*. No theist, by contrast, has ever explained how God engineered any step in developing life or, given the implications of the design argument, why He would even need to.[56] It is true that the scientific community has yet to agree about the exact process, but it is making progress toward doing so. As with the previous arguments from ignorance, there is no need to default to God in the meantime.

Anyone arguing that the beginning of life is so improbable that it requires the existence of God, furthermore, must weigh that probability against the probability of God existing. If simple life coming into being is improbable, then God coming into existence (something far more complicated) is exponentially more improbable. Using a more improbable thing to explain something less improbable represents a travesty of human reasoning.

CONSCIOUSNESS, THE SOUL, AND MIND-BODY DUALISM

It used to be obvious that the world was designed by some sort of intelligence. What else could account for fire and rain and lightning and earthquakes? Above all, the wonderful abilities of living things seemed to point to a creator who had a special interest in life. Today we understand most of these things in terms of physical forces acting under impersonal laws. We don't yet know the most fundamental laws, and we can't work out all the consequences of the laws we do know. The human mind remains extraordinarily difficult to understand, but so is the weather. We can't predict whether it will rain one month from today, but we do know the rules that govern the rain, even though we can't always calculate their consequences. I see nothing about the human mind any more than about the weather that stands out as beyond the hope of understanding as a consequence of impersonal laws acting over billions of years.

—Steven Weinberg, *A Designer Universe*

We all experience a sense of an incorporeal "me" who thinks, exercises free will, and directs our body in its daily activities. It is what we think of as our true "self," feeling somehow independent of our physical bodies and outside of them. Though technical definitions vary, we generally call this sense *consciousness*. Consciousness is an extraordinarily complex topic that has to date proved an elusive target for scientists. Because of this uncertainty, many apologists argue that the existence of consciousness supports belief in God.

Richard Swinburne is a well-known proponent of this argument. He finds it personally incredible that mental events can be reduced to physical causes and also that consciousness could have arisen naturally by evolutionary processes. Neither Mr. Swinburne nor any of the apologists who promote this argument are biologists or neurologists or otherwise possess any expertise in the science of the human mind. Their incredulity, as Swinburne candidly acknowledges, is based solely on intuition. The line of demarcation between Christian apologists and secular thinkers on consciousness typically correlates to how amenable each side is to the concept of dualism.

A. Dualism and the Mind-Body Problem

The idea that an incorporeal "mind" exists separate and distinct from the physical brain and body is known as Cartesian, or substance, dualism, which for short I call *dualism*.[57] Dualism posits that the mind comprises something entirely different from the brain or anything else in the material universe. This something is often called a *nonphysical substance*, without further explanation of how something can even qualify as a substance without physical properties. Christians would call this a *soul*. Dualism is typically contrasted with monism, the view that the mind and brain represent two ways of describing something composed of the same substance.

Dualism is an intuitive concept that virtually everyone grasps at an early age, when each of us recognizes a sense of an independent "self" that controls our body. Body swap comedies, such as *Freaky Friday*, tap into this idea that our true conscious self and the body it inhabits are different things. Viewing the mind as something outside the body that controls it makes sense of the way we perceive our thoughts and movements. It also seems inextricably bound up with traditional notions of free will, for how can I be in control if *I* is just another way of saying an "emergent concept created by a group of living cells"? Dualism also addresses the apparent disconnect between our physical bodies and our identities. We can see our bodies change, for example, but we feel that we retain our personal identities. If our bodies are truly the source of our identities, then how can this be so? We must postulate an immaterial self that endures through bodily changes.

Dualism has been posited to address what philosophers have labeled the "mind-body problem." Seventeenth-century philosopher René Descartes describes the "problem" this way:

> [T]here is a great difference between the mind and the body, inasmuch as the body is by its very nature always divisible, while the mind is utterly indivisible. For when I consider the mind, or myself in so far as I am merely a thinking thing, I am unable to distinguish any parts within myself; I understand myself to be something quite single and complete. . . . By contrast, there is no corporeal or extended thing that I can think of which in my thought I cannot easily divide into parts; and this very fact makes me understand that it is divisible. This one argument would be enough to show me that the mind is completely different from the body.[58]

In other words, because Descartes could not imagine the mind being broken into parts, even in concept, he concluded it must be of an entirely different nature than the body, which is divisible.

Eighteenth-century philosopher Gottfried Leibniz expands on Descartes, employing the following analogy: If we could take a machine that could think and we examined each of its parts, then we would find nothing that explained how this thinking took place. None of the individual components could think, so (rhetorically) how could any compilation of these components think? Alvin Plantinga summarizes Leibniz by saying a quality lacking in the parts cannot be present in the whole and because organic parts don't think, thinking can't be a function of the brain alone. It must arise by a different process altogether.

Another way of looking at this is to distinguish between the qualitative and quantitative. The external world can be measured quantitatively. With mathematical precision, we can describe physical objects in terms of their size, weight, and so on. These descriptions are objective and meaningful across populations. But our thoughts don't seem to fit this paradigm. Our experiences of, for example, emotion can't be reduced to objective measurement. Even our mental impressions of physical objects seem to defy such measurement. When I picture a coffee mug in my mind, that picture lacks any qualities we would associate with the cup itself. My mental image has no measurable size, weight, or structure. And yet my subjective experience of that cup is very real to me. From this, dualists conclude that internal qualia and external matter must represent entirely different things.

B. Conceptual Problems with Dualism

Before we can assess whether dualism provides a plausible, much less likely, solution to the mind-body problem, we must determine whether any such problem exists. Maybe the real problem is with the way dualists frame the discussion. For example, does the fact that we *perceive* our "selves" to be indivisible and unchanging mean this is true? In what sense is this intended, and what objective evidence do we have that it is correct? Is subjective introspection really a reliable source for how our minds operate? If we are going to posit a problem based on the mind and body being fundamentally different, then how can we be sure they really are?

Leibniz proposes a model of the mind that many of us *feel* to be accurate intuitively but should not be accepted as accurate without some external verification. Leibniz also presupposes a conceptual roadblock that science has since demonstrated to be no roadblock at all. Leibniz's analogy fails to consider the concept of *emergence*, in which components that do not themselves possess a quality can come to possess that quality when brought together. Neither hydrogen nor oxygen atoms, for example, can be described as wet. When bound as H_2O, however, wetness emerges. Water has qualities possessed by neither of its components. Likewise, there can be no conceptual objection to organic components of the human brain coming together to create a sense of consciousness.

Just because we haven't determined how to accurately measure qualia or correlate it to specific physical objects or events doesn't mean we never will. Maybe this qualia can be represented by specific patterns of brain waves that are reproducible and predictive. This represents not a conceptual hurdle but a scientific one, capable in theory of empirical resolution. The ethical, legal, and expense issues of conducting widespread scientific research in this area suggest that the answer will continue to evade us for the near future.[59] There is no good reason to believe, however, that it will do so forever.

The real question should be, between dualists and monists, who is most successful at constructing a model of the mind that accounts for qualia with maximum parsimony, considering what we now know of the brain's interaction with the body? Dualists immediately face a problem because any model they construct must assume the existence of some nonphysical and previously undetected substance that somehow interacts with the physical brain in a way that has never been demonstrated. Dualists have consistently failed to posit any specifics regarding this substance or to agree on what it does or how.

The interaction problem is highly significant, for we know our ability to think is affected by physical interactions with the human brain. Even dualists acknowledge that the brain is at least heavily involved in the thinking process. Any role for dualist's nonphysical substance, whether you call it a soul or otherwise, must include "pushing the buttons" of the brain—operating as the ghost in the machine. Scientists know that the nonphysical cannot cause physical phenomena without violating the laws of conservation of mass, energy, and momentum. This creates a dilemma for the dualist, as he must be able to empirically model mind-body interaction in a way that such interaction is entirely undetectable. The process can neither inject nor extract energy from the brain-body system.

Other questions arise, such as "How could an immaterial soul be tethered to its physical host?" "How would we know that a person's behavior is caused by *their soul* rather than someone else's?" Dualists should be able to provide hypothetically testable models to answer these questions, but they never have. Their response has always been, essentially, "It's magic." Dualism therefore remains conceptually incoherent.

Regarding the existence of the soul, the argument of dualists boils down to "It must exist because there is no other explanation for consciousness." Once again, we can see that their definition of *explanation* is suspect because the very concept of the soul is inherently vague and undefined. This position sets up as defeater any alternative theory that can account for qualia within the natural world. If your best argument is the implausibility of any other explanation, then your position is a fragile one indeed. And given the strength of other explanations, discussed later, dualism is left with little to recommend it.

Dualism also leads to solipsism, the untenable position that nothing exists outside of one's own consciousness. The only thing of which a dualist can be sure is his own incorporeal mind. The principle of analogy, by which we can infer the thoughts of others from the similarity of their behaviors to ours, is unavailable to the dualist because he denies any connection between the mind and body. The dualist would therefore not be warranted in concluding from others' physical behaviors that they share minds like his because those behaviors might just as easily result from purely physical processes. There is no good reason to believe they aren't just mechanical zombies, possessing the mere appearance of independent minds. There is, therefore, no principled way for dualists to avoid sliding off the cliff into solipsism.

C. What the Science Reveals

As science and medicine have advanced to where we can meaningfully study the brain, scientists have conducted experiments to test whether human intuitions of dualism reflect reality. Without exception, those tests have demonstrated the opposite. They have shown dualism to be an illusion—a powerful and persistent one but an illusion nonetheless.

If dualism were true, then that would mean our conscious mind, the mind that purportedly transcends the body at death and survives forever in an immaterial form as a soul, would be independent of the physical. We would expect the mind to be indivisible into pieces or parts, that damage to the physical brain would not affect consciousness, that we could not determine what people are thinking by merely observing their brains, and that we could not generate conscious experience or behavior by stimulating the brain. We now have answers to these questions, and in each case, the answers undermine and ultimately defeat the dualist hypothesis. Instead, they point consistently to monism and physicalism, the position that the sum of our mental processes is the product of and controlled by our physical brain.

One line of evidence that flies in the face of dualism is work with people whose corpus callosum, the pathway connecting the two hemispheres of the brain, has been severed. Known as split-brain patients, these individuals act as though independent minds control different parts of their bodies. Each hemisphere has been shown to be unaware of information presented to the other, as if two minds inhabited the same body. If dualism were true, then we would not expect damage to organic tissue to have such a profound effect on the mind, effectively creating a new mind in the process.

Splitting the brain can also result in a person's body parts acting outside their conscious control. Patients suffering from alien hand syndrome, for example, watch helplessly as one of their hands unexpectedly and involuntarily reaches for objects, manipulates them, and sometimes even attacks the person. There seems to be no relation between the movement of the hand and the person's conscious thought, as if the hand were thinking for itself.

If our thoughts originate beyond our physical brains in immaterial souls, then it would be impossible to "read" the mind by merely observing the brain. But scientists can do this very thing by employing an fMRI machine. Simply by looking at a subject's brain, a trained fMRI reader can determine with near perfect accuracy what the subject is observing. Brain imaging can thus provide intelligible snapshots of a person's consciousness, something highly surprising, given the required assumptions of dualism.

By directly stimulating or neutralizing discrete brain tissue, scientists can change everything about a person's experiences and even their entire personality. Brain manipulation can also induce false memories or disrupt real ones. Scientists can cause people to distrust and fear their families and loved ones, as occurs with the Capgras delusion. Every aspect of conscious thought can be altered and controlled through such techniques. Even the ability to reason itself can be stripped from a person through manipulation of the physical brain. Where every recognizable human character trait and ability can be overwritten entirely by manual manipulation of physical tissue, what place is left for a soul?

Other experiments have demonstrated that our bodies take action before we have "consciously" decided to do so—before we are even aware we have made a choice—further calling into question whether humans have free will, in the commonly understood sense. People can be caused to desire or intend things simply through electrical stimulation of the brain. Through transcranial magnetic stimulation, scientists can even affect how people respond to questions reflecting their ethics and morality, demonstrating that our moral compasses are not fixed but subject to external manipulation. It would appear, at a minimum, that much of what we consider conscious thought is really the result of unconscious feelings and impulses we do not purposefully direct and of which we are generally unaware.

These experiments have demonstrated that, rather than the mind and the body being detachable, our consciousness is simply an emergent property of our brains. The physical brain gives rise to conscious awareness, which in turn allows us to store and interpret sensory information and create mental concepts from that information. The mind is how we describe the workings of the brain at a certain level of abstraction. It is the process of cognition. The mind is what the brain does.

Dualist beliefs likely result from what philosopher Gilbert Ryle (1900–1976) calls a category mistake. Ryle provides the following analogy: Assume a stranger from a foreign land arrives in America and wishes to visit our institutions of higher learning. You take him to visit the campus of your alma mater, showing him the academic buildings, the library, the dorms, the cafeteria, the administration buildings, and everything between. At the end of the tour, he says, "Those are all nice buildings, but now I would like to see *the university*." You are initially confused and taken aback, until it becomes apparent that the visitor has made an error in thinking. He has failed to recognize that a university is merely an abstraction from a group of concrete structures. In the same way, when scientists refer to the mind, or consciousness, they are referring to an abstraction from purely organic biological processes.

Philosopher George Lakoff suggests that the very process of human reasoning results from the way our brains process information and the fact that they are embodied—integral parts of our organic human systems. Lakoff suggests that the many abstractions we use in reasoning result from concrete metaphors based on physical properties and relations, such as spatial relationships. For example, from the spatial concept of things being "near to" or "far from" us, we describe people we love as "close to us," while more casual acquaintances are considered "distant." Likewise, emotional "closeness" gives us "warm" feelings, representing a metaphor for physical warmth, which is typically comforting, allowing us to conceptualize more abstract concepts, such as love. This accounts for widespread cultural agreement on metaphors for abstract concepts. It also leads to the conclusion that speaking of consciousness outside the context of a human brain makes no sense, as consciousness depends entirely on the brain's human embodiment.

One consequence of the embodiment of human reasoning is that most of it occurs outside our conscious awareness, which is extremely surprising, given the assumptions of dualism. Consider all the things that take place when you have a conversation, as identified by Lakoff:

- Accessing memories relevant to what is being said
- Comprehending a stream of sound as being language, dividing it into distinctive phonetic features and segments, identifying phonemes, and grouping them into morphemes
- Assigning a structure to the sentence in accordance with the vast number of grammatical constructions in your native language
- Picking out words and giving them meanings appropriate to context
- Making semantic and pragmatic sense of the sentences
- Framing what is said in terms relevant to the discussion
- Performing inferences relevant to what is being discussed

- Constructing mental images where relevant and inspecting them
- Filling in gaps in the discourse
- Noticing and interpreting your interlocutor's body language
- Anticipating where the conversation is going
- Planning what to say in response

All are crucial components of our reasoning through any discussion, and yet the vast majority, if not all, are directed unconsciously. Rather than some external (to our bodies) consciousness directing the brain through the reasoning process, the brain is directing most of the reasoning process behind the scenes without "our" input, only letting our consciousness in on the tip of the proverbial iceberg of what is really going on. This is disconcerting to some but entirely in line with what the science has revealed.

Another implication is that because our perceptions are shaped by our brains and bodies, we can never lay claim to *absolute knowledge* of reality because all our perceptions are filtered by our embodied brains. For example, we think in terms of metaphors to experiences and concrete observations; we thus cannot conceive of anything we cannot analogize. This represents a significant limitation on our ability to perceive the world perfectly accurately—a limitation that is inexplicable given a Christian worldview. God could easily provide humans perfect perception.

Outside of neuroscience, the social sciences provide ample evidence that our thoughts are entirely embodied and determined by processes and stimuli outside our conscious awareness and control. The entire field of psychology is premised on millions of experiments manipulating human behaviors through external stimuli, each further undermining the notion of libertarian free will that underlies dualism. There is no shortage of studies demonstrating that opinions and behaviors can be changed in predictable ways, with the subject having no idea any manipulation is occurring. None of this makes sense given dualism.

Many converging lines of evidence all point in the same direction with remarkable consilience—there is no "ghost in the machine." As science has advanced, the realm of the soul has receded until there is effectively nothing left. Science provides all the tools we need to model the brain, if not perfectly, then with at least enough detail to be remarkably predictive. Neuroscientist Steven Novella explains it this way:

> In science theories are judged not only by how well they fit the data, but by how useful they are as predictive models—and the materialist position that brain function is the mind has been fantastically successful. There does not

appear to be any intrinsic limit to our ability to map and alter anything considered to be part of our subjective experience. Damage or alteration to the brain can change your sexual identity, your moral decision making, your personality, your ability to even think about the world. Patients with non-dominant hemisphere strokes, for example, often have what is called neglect—they do not know that the left half of the world even exists. There is no model inside their brain for the left half of their body or the world, so they cannot even think about it. Non-materialists often dismiss this as mere correlation, but that is not fair, in my opinion. The correlation is incredible, and predictive.[60]

Science has conclusively shown us that brain activity not only correlates with subjective experience but also causes it.

Scientists have more than enough puzzle pieces to conclude there is no place for an incorporeal mind or self-aware soul within the picture of consciousness. They may not know exactly how all the pieces fit together, but they at least know there isn't a big one missing. The brain is all we need to explain consciousness. Any theory of mind-body dualism violates Ockham's razor in the same way as the demon theory of disease. This is why physicalism is by far the mainstream position among scientists of the mind, both secular and Christian.[61]

Regarding the emergence of consciousness, biologists have identified many evolutionary mechanisms that would provide adequate explanations. Consciousness appears to develop once the brain reaches a certain level of complexity. While no one particular region of the brain can be identified as the source of consciousness, the same could be said for processes that no one claims to exhibit a nonphysical component, such as digestion, which requires the interaction of many biological systems working in concert.

Some claim that dualism is proven by evidence of near-death experiences (NDEs, as they are commonly known). Such "evidence" consists solely of anecdotal reports of people leaving their bodies or visiting Heaven while in altered states of consciousness. Despite decades of testing, no credible scientific evidence has ever come close to validating these claims. In 2007, researcher Keith Augustine comprehensively compiled and reviewed all the evidence for NDEs in the *Journal of Near-Death Studies*, ultimately concluding that such evidence provides no support for souls or the afterlife. The experiences reported by those claiming NDEs can be induced by researchers and have been shown to be explicable through natural neurological mechanisms, such as Cotard's syndrome or hypnagogia.

The human soul has the same properties as the emperor's new clothes: It cannot be seen, observed, or otherwise demonstrated to exist. It serves no apparent function, explains nothing previously unexplained, and fills no gap in our collective knowledge. It gives us no predictions or falsifiable claims. It is true that scientists have yet to settle on a comprehensive theory that explains human consciousness. But, as with the previous issues, there are many plausible hypotheses vying for dominance, none of which require an immaterial mind. In light of the science, which provides adequate naturalistic explanations for all the brain activity observed, we are not warranted in deferring to God as the most likely solution.

MIRACLES

According to a 2009 survey by the Harris Poll, 76 percent of adult Americans believe in miracles, as do 95 percent of born-again Christians. The existence of miracles is regularly cited as a primary reason for belief in God. William Lane Craig, like many apologists, cites miracles and fulfilled prophecies (addressed in a later section) as the evidential link that breaks the circularity of his arguments from scriptural authority:

> Thomas's [Aquinas] procedure, then, may be summarized in three steps: (1) Fulfilled prophecies and miracles make it credible that the Scriptures taken together as a whole are a revelation from God. (2) As a revelation from God, Scripture is absolutely authoritative. (3) Therefore, those doctrines taught by Scripture that are neither demonstrably provable nor empirically evident may be accepted by faith on the authority of Scripture.[62]

In other words, because we know that Jesus performed miracles and fulfilled Old Testament Scriptures, we can trust the Scriptures. Once we can trust the Scriptures, we can use them as a springboard for Christian faith where supporting evidence is lacking. The reliability of Scripture therefore depends entirely on the case for miracles and fulfilled prophecy.

To discuss miracles intelligently, it is necessary to first agree on a definition. The Oxford Dictionary defines *miracle* as an "extraordinary and welcome event that is not explicable by natural or scientific laws and is therefore attributed to a divine agency."[63] While some might use the term to refer to things that are statistically unlikely, such as surviving a natural disaster, or simply wonderful or awe-inspiring, such as the birth of a baby, those types of events are perfectly compatible with naturalism and so are outside of this discussion. I am talking about events that defy all known natural laws and thus demand an alternate explanation. This is how Craig, Aquinas, and other apologists use it because no other definition could justify an argument for scriptural reliability.

One problem with identifying seemingly unlikely events as miracles is that few of us can effectively assess whether these events are truly unlikely, in the sense that they *should be unexpected*. With 7 billion people on Earth engaged in 1,000 events per day, a one-in-a-billion event would still happen 7,000 times a day and 2.5 million times per year. Mathematician J. E. Littlewood suggests that each one of us should expect one-in-a-million events to happen to us about once every month. These may seem like miracles in retrospect, but unless the specific event was predicted in advance, it cannot be considered unexpected. We should expect some exceedingly unusual events to happen to us regularly, just given the sheer number of events we engage in and the laws of probability.

The first question we must ask is "Do we have any good evidence that a miracle has occurred?" To answer that question, we must ask another: "What type of evidence, and how much should suffice?" The quality and quantity of the evidence must be directly proportional to the inherent implausibility of the claim. As Carl Sagan eloquently says, "Extraordinary claims require extraordinary evidence."[64] A not-so-eloquent statement of this rule is "If you tell me something that sounds crazy, then you had best expect me to ask you to prove it; and the crazier your story sounds, the more proof I'm going to need." As to why this must be so, I quote an excellent explanation by Richard Carrier:

> If I say I own a car, I don't have to present very much evidence to prove it, because you have already observed mountains of evidence that people like me own cars. All of that evidence, for the general proposition "people like him own cars," provides so much support for the particular proposition, "he owns a car," that only minimal evidence is needed to confirm the particular proposition.
>
> But if I say I own a nuclear missile, we are in different territory. You have just as large a mountain of evidence, from your own study as well as direct observation, that "people like him own nuclear missiles" is *not* true. Therefore, I need much more evidence to prove that particular claim—in fact, I need about as much evidence (in quantity and quality) as would be required to prove the general proposition "people like him own nuclear missiles." I don't mean I would have to prove that proposition, but that normally the weight of evidence needed to prove that proposition would in turn provide the needed background support for the particular proposition that "I own a nuclear missile," just as it does in the case of "I own a car." So lacking that support, I need to build at least as much support directly for the particular proposition "I own a nuclear missile," which means as much support *in kind and degree* as would be required to otherwise prove the general proposition "people like him own

nuclear missiles." And that requires a lot of very strong evidence—just as for any general proposition.

We all know this, even if we haven't thought about it or often don't see reason—because this is how we all live our lives. Every time we accept a claim on very little evidence in everyday life, it is usually because we already have a mountain of evidence for one or more of the general propositions that support it. And every time we are skeptical, it is usually because we *lack* that same kind of evidence for the general propositions that would support the claim. And to replace that missing evidence is a considerable challenge.

This is the logical basis of the principle that "extraordinary claims require extraordinary evidence." A simple example is a lottery. The odds of winning a lottery are very low, so you might think it would be an extraordinary claim for me to assert, "I won a lottery." But that is not a correct analysis. For lotteries are routinely won. We have observed countless lotteries being won and have tons of evidence that people win lotteries. Therefore, the general proposition "people like him win lotteries" is already well-confirmed, and so I normally don't need very much evidence to convince you that I won a lottery. Of course, I would usually need more evidence than I need to prove "I own a car," simply because the number of people who own cars is much greater than the number who win lotteries. But still, the general proposition that "people win lotteries" is amply confirmed. Therefore, "I won a lottery" is not an extraordinary claim. It is, rather, a fairly routine claim—even if not as routine as owning a car.

In contrast, "I own a nuclear missile" would be an extraordinary claim. Yet, even then, you still have a large amount of evidence that nuclear missiles exist, and that at least some people do have access to them. Yet the Department of Homeland Security would still need a lot of evidence before it stormed my house looking for one. Now suppose I told you "I own an interstellar spacecraft." That would be an even more extraordinary claim—because there is no general proposition supporting it that is even remotely confirmed. Not only do you have very good evidence that "people like him own interstellar spacecraft" is *not* true, you also have no evidence that this has ever been true for anyone—unlike the nuclear missile. You don't even have reliable evidence that interstellar spacecraft[s] *exist*, much less reside on earth. Therefore, the burden of evidence I would have to bear here is enormous. Just think of what it would take for you to believe me, and you will see what I mean.[65]

A miracle is the quintessential extraordinary claim. It is in fact more extraordinary than claiming to own an interstellar spacecraft. We know that interstellar spacecrafts *can* exist. We may even be able to build one with present technology. But we have no comparable knowledge supporting the existence of miracles. A miracle would mean that, contrary to what science has consistently told us through billions of observations and experiments, the universe does not obey regular and systematic laws—that what we perceive as laws are just conditions that can be suspended, negated, or simply ignored based on the whim of an invisible being.

So the evidence for a miracle must be orders of magnitude greater than what we would require of one claiming to own an interstellar spacecraft. But that does serve as a useful starting point. What would it take for you to believe that I have an interstellar spacecraft in my garage? Would you trust my word? Would you trust the word of your closest friend? Would you trust an internet blog posting? Or a news report from CNN or Fox News? Or all of the above?

Due to the inherent implausibility of this claim, you would be right to begin as very skeptical. In evaluating my evidence, you would likely be sensitive to such things as whether the person supporting my claim (the proponent) had any incentive or bias to distort the truth. Or perhaps the proponent wasn't qualified to determine whether a vehicle in my garage was capable of interstellar travel. What if the proponent was reporting something second- or thirdhand? What if he had never even been to my garage?

My guess is that before you would believe my claim, you would have to see it for yourself. Unless you worked for NASA designing spaceships, you would probably also require input from various experts in relevant fields with opportunities to do hands-on testing. Even with all that, you might still doubt me until you or someone you found highly reliable observed the spacecraft travel to another star system. I would suspect you would laugh in my face if I told you to accept my claim simply on "faith."

Now, contrast this with the evidence for any miracle. Does any of it meet the standard discussed previously? Most of the evidence is anecdotal—stories passed from one person to another, sometimes through a long and tenuous chain. Rarely are any of us in a position to evaluate the credibility of the person initially making the claim. And even if they were credible, couldn't they have been mistaken? As Isaac Asimov explained when asked about his supernatural beliefs, "I believe in evidence. I believe in observation, measurement, and reasoning, confirmed by independent observers. I'll believe anything, no matter how wild and ridiculous, if there is evidence for it. The wilder and more ridiculous something is, however, the firmer and more solid the evidence will have to be."[66]

Now let's talk about miracles in the religious context. Regarding plausibility, let's think about what is being claimed when one says that a transcendent agent acted in some causal fashion. First, this is a supernatural being that cannot be directly observed empirically but nonetheless has both a mind and the capability of causally affecting the physical world. Second, this agent did, in fact, transcend whatever boundary there may be between the natural and supernatural worlds and produced an observable effect in the natural world. The mechanism by which the agent transcends its supernatural nature and interacts with physical objects and forces is never explained. Presumably, a being that can causally affect the physical world could in principle be examined using the tools of science. Alternatively, the being can't be examined using the tools of science precisely because it doesn't interact with the physical world. Theists insist on having it both ways without ever justifying this proposition. Finally, this effect was made specifically to one person or perhaps to a relatively small group of people (such as everyone in a church); that is, it is revelatory. The being has chosen, for some unknown reason, not to share this stupendous feat with the rest of the world. If you were presented with such a claim outside your religious tradition, how plausible would you find it?

No miracle claim has ever been substantiated by scientific standards. From 1964 through 2015, skeptic and magician James Randi offered a large cash prize, ultimately one million dollars, to anyone who could demonstrate a supernatural or paranormal ability, something that would clearly be defined as a miracle, under agreed-upon scientific testing criteria. More than one thousand people applied to take the challenge. None succeeded.

When looking at claims reflected only in ancient documents, keep in mind that they can never rise to the level of scientific facts, especially when our evidence for them is limited to recorded human testimony. Even calling them facts simply reflects a subjective judgment regarding the relative reliability of the sources. When historians debate whether something happened, they are just discussing relative probabilities of the likelihood of that event having occurred based on what they know of the sources. Even the most reliable literary sources, however, cannot be trusted absolutely. Historical facts and scientific facts are very different things.

Essential for assessing the relative reliability of competing sources or explanations of an event is the principle of analogy. Assume the historian comes across two sources describing the final stages of a siege. In one, victory is attributed to the inhabitants of the sieged city running out of food and surrendering. In the other, victory is attributed to winged dragons attacking the city. Historians are aware of many examples of the first scenario, even in modern times. They have no comparable experience with the second. The principle of analogy suggests that the first source should be preferred to the second. The first source and the explanation it provides are inherently more plausible.

Crucial to the principle of analogy is the use of background knowledge. This can be described as the sum and substance of our reliable knowledge and experience before looking at this claim. Background knowledge is cumulative. As a society, we have a better understanding of how things work now than we did one thousand or even one hundred years ago. All of this is useful when evaluating claims of historical happenings. Background knowledge is a key component of Bayes' theorem, discussed earlier, because it allows us to weigh the probability of historical claims based on mountains of accumulated evidence. Employing the principle of analogy has consistently led historians to results later confirmed to be accurate. That is why it is considered essential to historical analysis. Many apologists, however, strongly disapprove of using it for studying the Bible because, they claim, the Bible is unique.[67] This special pleading suggests their selective application is driven by ideological concern rather than any true methodological flaws in the theorem itself.

One area in which apologists often criticize the use of analogy is when assessing the possibility of miracles. Miracles are by definition extremely unlikely, and the sources available to historians will never be so reliable as to rule out all competing natural explanations. If the apologist finds the principle of analogy unappealing because it does not allow room for serious consideration of miracle claims, then what filter would he suggest for distinguishing certain incredible-sounding claims in ancient documents from others? None is ever offered.

Philosopher David Hume rhetorically asked in 1748 whether it was more likely that the laws of nature should be violated or that people would lie. Hume answered his own question: "There is not to be found, in all history, any miracle attested by a sufficient number of men, of such unquestioned good sense, education and learning, as to secure us against all delusion in themselves."[68] In a similar vein, American patriot Thomas Paine stated, "We have never seen, in our time, nature go out of her course. But we have good reason to believe that millions of lies have been told in the same time. It is therefore at least millions to one that the reporter of a miracle tells a lie."[69] These points are as applicable today as when Hume and Paine first made them. Untrustworthy testimony is the simplest explanation and the one compelled by Ockham's razor.

A fatal problem for apologists of any particular religion claiming a miracle is that *many religions make miracle claims*—relying on the same type of evidence. If you take one miracle claim at face value, then you have to take *all miracle claims* at face value. You don't get to pick just the ones from the religion you already believe in—that's special pleading and cherry-picking. Religious miracles are reported in the sacred books of many religions and each year by numerous believers. Each uses this evidence to support his or her own religious claims, which often stand in direct opposition to the followers of other religions. Any evidence that can support mutually exclusive claims cannot by itself justify any of them. Any apologist who argues for relaxing the standards by which historians should accept the miracles of his religion must be prepared for an opening of the floodgates for similar claims of all religions. For them, such technology would represent the very definition of supernatural.

If we hear of a miraculous event for which no natural explanation is immediately apparent, then the only reasonable conclusion is that the event is provisionally unexplained. Science and history do not justify jumping to the conclusion that the event was *in fact a miracle*, much less that it was performed through, and therefore evidence of, any particular deity. Only if all naturalistic possibilities, as well as all competing *supernatural* explanations, could be *definitively ruled out* could we reasonably reach such a conclusion. Throughout the long history of Christianity, this has never been done.

MORALITY

Can we be good without God? Can there even be goodness without God? Or is God necessary for us to hold onto any intelligible sense of "goodness" and morality? Many apologists argue this very thing—that our intuitive sense of morality is itself powerful evidence for God. This argument from morality is one of the most popular among modern apologists. It generally takes three forms.

1. God is the only explanation for the intuitive sense of right and wrong that seems to apply across human cultures.
2. Morality is self-evidently objective, and only a transcendent personal being such as God can provide a transcendent objective standard for morality.
3. Without Christian morality, people would descend into moral anarchy.

I address these in order.

A. God Is the Only Plausible Explanation for the Intuitive Sense of Right and Wrong That Seems to Apply across Human Cultures

The first premise of this argument is that there is a common cross-cultural sense of right and wrong agreed upon by virtually all people in all places. This leads to the conclusion that this can be explained only by a transcendent standard that all people can intuitively access. The argument continues to posit God as the author of this standard because God has all the necessary qualities (transcendence, agency, absolute morality, etc.) to create the standard and transmit it to all of humanity.

This argument fails with the initial premise. A survey of cultures demonstrates that any cross-cultural agreement on issues of morality would be limited to a narrow range of issues, and these are far better explained naturalistically. For instance, most cultures agree that indiscriminate murder is wrong, but there is widespread disagreement on such related issues as abortion, physician-assisted suicide, and capital punishment. Likewise, there is common agreement that pedophilia is wrong but widespread disagreement regarding the appropriate age of consent and other sexual practices, such as homosexuality. Many issues recognized as settled in some countries, such as equality of racial minorities and women, remain the subject of much strife and dissent in others. When one specifically sets about the task, it is more difficult than one might first think to arrive at a definitive list of moral issues on which there is widespread cross-cultural agreement. But some do demand such agreement. The question is whether naturalism can plausibly explain these. The answer is yes.

Wherever we see such agreement, naturalism provides a satisfactory explanation. People are ultimately animals and so operate according to a hierarchy of needs. They seek food, shelter, sleep, and sex, not necessarily in that order. Being intelligent and socially adapted, humans also long for social connections and recognize the best way to maintain access to food, shelter, sleep, and sex is to actively participate in society and encourage and enforce social norms. Such actions as killing and stealing are inconsistent with these norms and thus contrary to survival needs.

As humans evolved, they found it advantageous to protect their families. Those with protective instincts were more likely to pass along their genes through natural selection. Humans later found it advantageous to live among and within groups for additional protection. People often had to sacrifice their individual wants and needs to benefit the group to retain that protection. Extending social instincts cultivated in family life to larger groups would have come easily to some. These individuals would have thrived in group settings and thus been more likely to pass their genes along. Those unable to adapt would have been more likely to face ostracism or banishment from the group, which would decrease their chances for survival, as banishment was typically a death sentence. Morality might be better understood as an evolutionary imperative to propagate genes and ultimately reproduce.

Anthropologist Frans de Waal has devoted a considerable part of his professional career to researching these issues. In *Primates and Philosophers*, de Waal's central thesis is that morality is a means by which social-living creatures cooperate for mutual benefit. We have evolved as interdependent individuals living in a complex social hierarchy, with moral norms serving as a mechanism that allow us to cooperate and thrive. According to de Waal, "We come from a long lineage of hierarchical animals for which life in groups is not an option but a survival strategy. Any zoologist would classify our species as obligatorily gregarious."[70] De Waal rebuts the thesis that morality is a triumph of human reason, arguing instead that it is an evolution of more primitive social behaviors in our evolutionary ancestors that can still be observed in our modern evolutionary cousins today.

De Waal demonstrates there is nothing uniquely human about impulses toward reciprocity, empathy, and fairness, as these are found in many other animal species. These impulses evolve as group living becomes increasingly effective as a survival strategy. In humans, these developed further, becoming the foundation of increasingly complex moral behaviors, but de Waal reminds us there is no clear line of demarcation: "We start out postulating sharp boundaries, such as between humans and apes, or between apes and monkeys, but are in fact dealing with sand castles that lose much of their structure when the sea of knowledge washes over them. They turn into hills, leveled ever more, until we are back to where evolutionary theory always leads us: a gently sloping beach."[71] Moral differences between human and monkey are not in kind but in degree.

De Waal shows that chimpanzees would slow their pace so as not to leave injured friends behind. He documents bonobos tending to one another's wounds and comforting each other after traumatic events. With each example observed and documented, it became ever clearer to de Waal that the moral authority reserved by humans to their own species is not so limited. Creatures other than humans regulate their group conduct by many of the same moral norms.

De Waal's views have been supported by recent work by others in the field. Felix Warneken, for example, a professor of psychology at Harvard

University, demonstrates that chimpanzees often perform spontaneous altruistic acts absent any reward—even to assist those of other species.[72] These observations all point in the same direction: that our moral intuitions are inherited from our primate ancestors. They are neither learned nor imbued by any supernatural force.

The history of moral progress reflects not so much a change of moral norms as an ever-increasing extension of those norms beyond the immediate self and family—a gradual widening of the circle of interest and concern. The earliest cavemen found killing and stealing objectionable when others killed or stole from their families, and this was surely true of every caveman of every culture. As one's protective group extended from family to tribe to nationality, so, too, would the reach of those norms have expanded. Modern societies have increasingly extended prohibitions against these behaviors across the lines of nationality, gender, race, and sexual orientation. A progressive society can be identified by how broadly it extends civil liberties and protections, even to the most marginalized.

So wherever we see areas of cross-cultural moral agreement, we see what is predicted by evolutionary theory. Murder and theft, for example, completely contradict a functioning group dynamic. No family or group will survive long, moreover, if its children are not adequately protected. It is no surprise that love and protection of children extend across cultural borders and are two of humanity's most powerful moral instincts. Because of the importance of children, a widespread lack of concern for them would defy evolutionary predictions. But of course, we see exactly the opposite.

The adaptive value of a moral instinct that extends beyond direct self-interest is apparent in a beehive. It might even be an evolutionary necessity. Bees work together for the good of the colony and protect the queen at all costs. Ants do the same. At a certain level, the interest of the self and that of the group overlap to such a degree that they are effectively identical. Any social organism with the ability to coexist and copulate displays the instinctual need to protect others within the community.

There are other reasons to reject the premise of a divinely imbued morality. The existence of a "universal" code of right and wrong magically grafted onto the brains of every human by God is contradicted by those exhibiting such low-spectrum empathy disorders as narcissistic and borderline personality disorders and sociopathology. These people lack the cognitive pathways that allow them to empathize with others. Their actions are not constrained by any empathy-driven conscience, leaving them with no internal compulsion to subscribe to commonly recognized codes of conduct. Sociopaths, for example, may feel nothing like guilt for torturing another human being—for reasons that are entirely biological. People with injuries to the same areas of the brain inactive in sociopaths likewise lose their ability to feel empathy.

We might characterize such people as morally handicapped. They are less likely to make morally appropriate choices simply through accidents of birth and biology. Christianity requires us to conclude that God deliberately creates people with moral handicaps, recognizing they are more likely to harm others through no fault of their own. The existence of morally handicapped people is highly surprising, given theism.

Moral handicaps are just what we would expect, however, given naturalism, which is indifferent to the moral consequences of brain abnormalities. They suggest that the moral instinct is driven by evolutionary psychology, which, unlike an omnipotent God, would not produce perfectly consistent results. These exceptions to the apparent uniformity of cross-cultural moral imperatives demonstrates that we are not dealing with anything like a divine mandate but rather with something predicted by naturalistic evolutionary theory.

And what of altruism? First, we must be certain that we are interpreting the evidence correctly before reaching any conclusions about the prevalence of altruism. Many apparently altruistic acts can be motivated by ultimately selfish reasons, such as the desire for social approval or a heightened sense of self-worth. The people performing such acts may receive a jolt of dopamine in their brains that acts like a street drug when they perform some action they perceive as altruistic. It makes them feel good to do good. In such cases, can we really consider their actions selfless?

A thorough body of scientific evidence tells us that a great deal of moral behavior in humans can be explained by reciprocity, the expectation that one will receive kind for kind. A compelling motive for bringing soup to a sick friend, whether conscious or unconscious, is likely to be the obligation this creates in the receiving party to return the favor if and when you become sick. This motive need not be a conscious one, as even subconscious motives drive many, if not most, of our actions. Reciprocity drives an incalculable range of human cooperation, and it's an essential component of social behavior, given our obligatory interdependence. The Golden Rule itself is a maxim of reciprocal altruism, essentially saying, "I will respect your needs and interests, as I wish you to respect my own."

Of course, sometimes a person makes a sacrifice for another in which the personal cost is clearly greater than any possible reward. We are all familiar, for example, with parents being willing to, and sometimes actually, sacrificing their lives for their children. But even here, one can see how strong evolutionary pressures would create internal motivators for such behavior. As Richard Dawkins explains in his seminal work *The Selfish Gene*, natural selection favors the preservation of *genetic material*, not necessarily the organism itself. It also favors those who act to benefit their tribal group, for reasons discussed previously. Accordingly, we would expect evolution to favor those willing to sacrifice themselves to protect their offspring or their tribe and to select for those self-motivated to such behavior.

It is far rarer, though not unprecedented, for people to make extreme sacrifices for those not within their immediate family or tribe—even complete strangers. Is it really that great a stretch, however, to imagine that in those situations, one's natural drive to protect family or tribe members could extend to others? Alternatively, it may be that the preprogrammed *expectation of social reward* overrides the real danger in a moment of crisis. In such cases, we might be seeing an extrapolation of a naturally selected instinct to cover something other than that for which it strictly developed. Such extrapolations are not uncommon in evolutionary theory and are, once again, predicted by a naturalistic model.

So there is nothing about common moral instincts or altruism, whether real or merely apparent, that contradicts naturalism. Natural selection favored social cooperation among mankind's ancestors and ultimately in man himself. We are, after all, social creatures, and as Aristotle observes, "Without friends no one would choose to live, even if he had all other goods."[73] This led to a moral sense that came to be shared almost universally among humans. It is that moral instinct that guides our respective consciences, separating proposed actions into right and wrong. The explanation requires no God.

All of this supports the understanding of common moral instincts as naturally developed through evolution and natural selection. Morality results not from universal truths or divine attribution but from common embodied moral programming. Such programming is at least species-wide and apparently applies even beyond that, having evolved from more rudimentary traits of empathy, cooperation, and sympathy.

Even in light of the compelling naturalistic explanations for areas of moral agreement, such as the common evolutionary formation of moral intuitions, some Christians refuse to accept these were not imbued by God. Christians are especially ill-positioned to argue that common human intuitions provide evidence for objective moral values, however, because they must acknowledge many situations in which God commanded his followers to do things that run counter to our common cross-cultural intuitions, such as murdering children. If God was right, then our intuitions regarding the justness of his commands must be wrong. This requires acknowledging that human moral intuitions are unreliable and thus cannot reflect objective moral truths.

But even if one is not convinced that naturalism can conclusively explain some human instinct or another, that does not justify concluding that they must have a supernatural explanation. Appealing to ignorance is really the sum and substance of the apologists' entire line of reasoning on this subject.

B. Morality Is Self-Evidently Objective, and Only God Can Provide a Transcendent Objective Standard for Morality

This is a centerpiece argument of many modern apologists. Accordingly, I spend some time explaining the argument before deconstructing it. What is important to understand is that the argument is built on assumptions that appear intuitive but are unproven and highly suspect. Even if the assumptions hold, the argument falls apart when applied to Christianity.

The premise of the argument is that moral values—what is right and what is wrong—are objective. By this, Dr. William Lane Craig, a major proponent of this argument, means these moral values are true independent of the belief *of humans*. As an example, Dr. Craig posits that the Nazis had won World War II and brainwashed everyone on Earth into thinking the Holocaust was morally justified. If we are to maintain that the Holocaust would still have been wrong despite every single person on Earth believing it to have been right, we must appeal to a transcendent standard of right and wrong—one that takes no account of human opinion or beliefs.

Once Dr. Craig has convinced his audience to accept the existence of objective moral values (OMV) as he has defined them, he targets naturalism as inadequate to account for or provide such a transcendent moral code. Such a code, he argues, can only be provided by a transcendent *lawgiver*. As the Christian God is by definition personal and transcendent, all knowing and all good, and has offered mankind a written code as found in the Bible, He is the best candidate for this lawgiver. Christianity then best explains the existence of OMV.

1. There Is No Evidence That Moral Values Are Objective

The argument fails at the outset because it cannot establish its foundational premise: that moral values are indeed objective. First, it is important to agree on a workable definition of *objective*. Philosophers have used the term to mean different things, which muddies the water when attempting to discuss the existence of such things as objective moral values. Secular philosophers often acknowledge belief in objective morality but mean something different from Christian apologists when they employ the term.[74]

Philosophical objectivity refers to the quality of existence or truth that is independent of perception or opinion. Logically, this would include any being capable of perception or opinion, which would encompass all sentient beings. In other words, something is objectively true if it is true *regardless of what any sentient entity thinks or knows*. It transcends any decision-making actor.

Within the scope of sentient decision-making actors is God. The Bible tells us that God, like man, makes decisions, regrets decisions, changes His mind, has opinions, and otherwise acts as a thinking person. God has discussions and arguments with several figures in the Bible, including Abraham and Moses, and is said to have been persuaded to new courses of actions by these interactions. God's mind is distinct from the minds of others. His thoughts, perceptions, and beliefs, therefore, must be considered subjective. If morality can be defined and redefined by an intelligent agent such as God, then it, too, must be considered subjective—subjective to God. So for something to be objectively good, it must be good despite what anyone thinks, *including God*.

Here is where apologists typically employ special pleading. They need to exclude God from the list of actors who can destroy objectivity. Accordingly, they redefine objectivity so it includes *only humans*. William Craig defines it this way: "To say that something is objective is to say that it is independent of what people think or perceive. By contrast, to say that something is subjective is just to say that it is not objective; that is to say, it is dependent on what human persons think or perceive."[75] Craig attempts to define *objectivity* so it *arbitrarily excludes God*. This way, if he can simply convince people that moral values are objective, *as he defines it*, then God is the only candidate left as the source and arbiter of such values. But neither Craig nor any apologist has ever provided any justification for excluding God from the scope of subjectivity. Allowing God to arbitrate "objective" morality turns the entire concept on its head. Under such a system, morality would not be objective in the traditional sense but would instead be simply exogenous; that is, external to humanity. These are different things, and any argument that conflates the two is guilty of equivocation.

A concept of God that allows Him to distinguish right from wrong contradicts objective moral values, for these must be timeless and universal and not subject to whim or caprice. It cannot be wrong to murder one moment but then right to murder the next simply because God decrees it. If objective moral values exist, then God is bound by them just like everyone else. I return to this later in relation to the Euthyphro dilemma, but for now, it is sufficient to recognize what we mean by objective moral values.

Despite what Craig says, it is far from self-evident that values and normative duties exist independent of what anyone thinks. Apologists attempting to establish this typically provide such examples as torturing babies. These examples appear designed to elicit universal revulsion, presumably under the premise that if no one can conceive of a world in which this could be considered acceptable, then it is not just bad but objectively bad. But this does not necessarily follow. All such examples can hope to demonstrate is that some values enjoy an almost universal consensus of human belief.[76] To say that the consensus view determines objective truth, however, renders objectivity dependent on human belief—which it cannot be. Objective truths must be independent of any consensus, rendering any appeal to consensus irrelevant.

Craig's view of objective moral values is known as moral realism. The legitimacy of moral realism depends on its ability to distinguish the subjective consensus-based view of morality from a truly objective moral code. Moral realists should easily be able to identify examples of behaviors that are objectively good *despite* widespread consensus that they are morally wrong. The only alternative is that objective moral values line up perfectly with the consensus values of modern society at this exact moment (for we have seen how the moral zeitgeist evolves over time). Here, our definition of objective moral values would simply be the modern consensus, with no need to appeal to any metaphysical certainty or objectivity.

a. Morality Is Necessarily Subjective   The perspective of all humans is necessarily subjective. We can only perceive and interpret things from our own unique points of view. Even our values are inherently subjective because they are constructed from our entirely subjective experiences. When I say I prefer honesty over deceit, isn't this really an extrapolation from my own experiences in which honesty has served me and others better than its opposite? As philosopher Richard Garner observes, "When people complain about the lack of values, they are usually complaining about the fact that other people fail to value the things they value, and they are presupposing that the things they value are the things that are truly valuable."[77]

But there are some things, such as basic mathematics, that we can *treat* as objective truths *for all practical purposes*. They appear to apply universally and consistently based on mankind's collective experience, independent of anyone's unique perspective. Two plus two equals four regardless of who you are, where you were born, or what path your life has taken. Moreover, treating two plus two as if it *would always* equal four has allowed us to make consistently accurate predictions.

Though mathematics appears to be based on objective truths, we can never say *for certain* that it is because our perspective is limited. Even if we combined the collective experience of every human who has ever lived, and it consistently validated a particular "truth," it would remain a subjective judgment, for every brick of its foundation would be subjective. No quantity of such bricks can magically convert a subjective truth to an objective one. They are qualitatively different.

This does not mean we cannot have confidence in mathematics or consider it a reliable system. Just because something is subjective does not mean or even suggest that it is arbitrary. Unanimously consistent collective experiences can justify enormous confidence. They can even justify us treating something like mathematics as objective for all practical purposes. But we must never make the mistake of saying with absolute certainty it truly is objective. We simply don't have the perspective or evidence to say so. Unanimously consistent collective experiences would be necessary but not sufficient to state with complete confidence that something is an objective truth. That is why mathematics can approximate objectivity but never definitively reach it.

Let us now contrast mathematics with morality. Can we ever say that something is *morally wrong* with anything close to the same confidence we can say two plus two equals four? We may feel that with certain moral questions, we can approach such confidence. But if morality is truly objective, then it must be so for *all moral questions*. Is it wrong to view pornography? To smoke marijuana? To engage in premarital sex? To lie? Is anyone comfortable saying there are moral absolutes regarding each of these questions that will apply in *every possible circumstance*? If not, then, unlike mathematics, you don't even have a necessary condition for objective morality, much less a sufficient one.

But what about those things that just about everyone agrees are wrong? In the previous section, I discuss the naturalistic explanation for developing widely shared moral values and transgressions. As predicted by a naturalistic model, such values are those that would be important and necessary to a functioning and flourishing society. They would reflect high values for individual autonomy and, to a lesser extent, for social order.

No society can thrive in which its members indiscriminately murder each other. Or steal from each other. Or victimize their children. All humans evolved in similar circumstances and so are likely to have developed common instincts condemning such actions. Likewise, such actions remain at odds with the well-being of individuals and the societies in which they live. We would expect them to be universally condemned based on their consequences, and that is indeed what we see. We also evolved to understand the best way to achieve pleasure and avoid pain for ourselves and our families was to cooperate and establish rules and norms of behavior to encourage behaviors leading to these goals.

Carl Jung, the father of analytical psychology, introduced the concept of psychological archetypes, which are patterns and images that have through evolution been imprinted on human brains. Snakes were one of man's earliest predators, and today almost all humans begin life with an instinctual fear of, or at least discomfort with, snakes. It should not be surprising that in myths and legends across cultures, we see snakes representing evil and malevolent forces. The snake as evil is an inherited archetype passed down to modern man. Other archetypes would be wizened old men as sages and mentors or young adventurous boys as heroes. These archetypes help explain why so many cultures and religions share commonalities.

There is good reason to believe morality works in much the same way. Such useful psychological traits as empathy, reciprocity, and even altruism helped social societies, and thus the individuals living in those societies, thrive. So, too, did the instinct to create and enforce norms of behavior to reward helpful behaviors and discourage negative ones. Those behaviors along with archetypes representing them in action were passed down evolutionarily to the present day. Our common moral instincts can be explained by what worked for our ancestors.

Professor of cognitive science George Lakoff approaches this issue from a slightly different but related perspective. Lakoff argues persuasively that all human cognition, even abstract reasoning, depends on the organic structure of the brain and can only be understood by incorporating that structure. Lakoff sees disagreements over moral issues as resulting from conflicting metaphors. Humans mostly share values, interests, and responsibilities because they share the same physiology and collective experience. Often, they also share and build on the same metaphors.

Consider a family governed by strict authoritarianism versus one that is more egalitarian and nurturing. The members of these families are likely to derive very different metaphors. The authoritarian family, for example, is more likely to see power and strength as associated with good and submission to an authority as a good in itself. When extrapolated from the family, in which the father is the authority, to the state, the members of the authoritarian household would more likely become political conservatives because conservatism prioritizes these same values. If Lakoff's model is correct, then this would demonstrate that values derive from our makeup and experiences, both those common to humanity and those unique to each of us. This defies the very possibility of such values, or the behaviors they bring about, being classified as objectively right or wrong.

Regarding behaviors considered immoral or unlawful by most modern societies, it is unnecessary to say they are objectively wrong to condemn them. Our ethical principles can be universally subjective across humanity, meaning common to all humans of sound mind but with no claim to metaphysical objectivity. They may represent the overwhelming consensus of morally conscious agents, justified on that basis alone. As with mathematics, we can acknowledge the limitations of our perspective and yet maintain that acts condemned by the human consensus be *treated as objectively wrong* for all practical purposes because they serve goals we all find valuable. Doing so allows us to maintain our intellectual integrity but also to make consistent value judgments across societies and cultures. Significantly, it does not require positing a supernatural lawgiver standing outside of and above humanity.

Of course, that leaves many difficult moral questions for which there are no definitive universal answers. Such questions typically involve trade-offs between two or more things considered good, and the answers depend on how different people value these competing goods. In certain circumstances, a man might have no other choices than breaking a law or watching his family starve. Though he may value and respect the law, can we consider his choice to steal food wrong if he values the lives of his family more? Where one comes down on this question is likely to depend on the relative importance one places on the rule of law and a parent's responsibility to provide for his family.

That might seem like a trite example, but what about decisions made by politicians every day that help one group at the expense of another? Should the United States open its doors to refugees of war-torn countries? On one side are innocent families displaced from their homes and under imminent threat through no fault of their own; on the other are Americans concerned for their jobs, benefits, and security. There are no political decisions without winners and losers. How one judges such decisions depends on how one feels about these groups and the respective interests they represent. It is absurd to think any objective standard could apply to all such situations or that the values or preferences involved could apply regardless of what anyone thinks.

Most people would agree that such values as honor, loyalty, and sacrifice are good and important. If faced with a decision that required you to choose which of these was *most* important, however, could there ever be a controlling objective standard? A morally complex television show like *Game of Thrones* demonstrates how such values as honor and love might give way depending on the circumstances. Different people always place different weights on such values, and those weights always depend on their unique experiences and the situations in which these people find themselves. We have no problem with shared ideas of courage, justice, charity, hope, patience, humility, greed, and so on. None of these has an objective grounding, and no one argues that they do. Why should it be different for morality?

Lying is forbidden in the Ten Commandments. But few of us would object to those who, in Nazi-occupied Poland, lied to authorities to protect the lives of Jewish people. Sometimes, lying is the most compassionate thing to do. This means that lying cannot be objectively, absolutely wrong. There are circumstances in which we recognize it as not only permissible but even morally obligatory. Lying is clearly not *absolutely* wrong. Neither is taking someone's life. We can probably identify any atrocity, no matter how disgusting and awful, and then imagine a situation in which it was the lesser of evils—though admittedly for some we must get creative.

That is precisely what Christian apologists do when they defend genocide commanded by God: They're arguing that, while not pretty, it was the best and most moral course of action under the circumstances. They pull justifications out of the air—such as that death would be preferable to growing up in such moral decay—apparently not recognizing that objectively good acts require no justification. Justifications are only necessary where morality is subjective and legitimate differences of opinion are recognized so that arguments over the morality of an action are even possible. Even where morality is defined by the consensus of opinion, such a consensus is always subjective and relative. Without acknowledging it, these apologists are undermining the argument for objective morality.

b. Two Approaches to Ethics and Morality It is important to distinguish here between the two approaches to ethical questions. Those subscribing to systems of *deontological ethics* judge the morality of one's actions based on their adherence to preestablished rules. Such rules establish duties and obligations through which we can assess one's moral worth. The Christian Bible approaches ethics deontologically, setting rules to be obeyed and a system of rewards and punishments for compliance. Humans are not accorded the freedom to assess the real-world consequences of their actions in assessing moral worth. They are instructed that their actions will be judged by adherence to biblical rules and that they are to defer to the interpretations of church-ordained interpreters when those rules seem unclear.

Consequentialist systems of ethics, by contrast, judge the morality of one's actions by their real-world consequences, which are in principle subject to quantification. Consequentialism is the class of normative ethical theories holding that the consequences of one's conduct are the ultimate bases for any judgment about the rightness or wrongness of that conduct. In other words, such normative properties as right or wrong depend solely on the consequences of the action rather than, for example, whether the action fits within a classification of prohibited conduct. By comparing the number of people a particular action would hurt or help as opposed to a different action, I can rationally choose the "best" ethical option. This is in theory an objective approach because it relies on measurement and comparison. Unfortunately, that theory assumes perfect information and predictive ability, which we never actually have. Because we are always working from incomplete information and because people value consequences differently, consequentialism always entails subjectivity.

Whether one looks at ethics from a consequentialist or deontological viewpoint has enormous impact on how one assesses moral worth. Consider the vast disconnect between people regarding abortion. Consequentialists will speak of the societal costs of denying legal abortions for unwanted pregnancies. They will talk of the mothers whose educations and prospects will be cut short, leading to underemployment and depression. They will speak of the children who will grow up unwanted and often neglected, leading to increased involvement in criminal activities. They will raise the specter of back-alley abortions with the inevitable pain, suffering, and death these will inflict on the desperate.

Those who think deontologically find such concerns irrelevant. For them, the question is simple and straightforward: Is a human life being taken? If so, then this is murder and therefore intrinsically wrong. Murder cannot be justified by an uptick in a mother's employment prospects, whether it is one mother or one million. Murder is wrong, and that's all there is to it. Immigration represents another example. One inclined to think consequentially will focus on weighing the societal costs versus benefits of different policies toward undocumented immigrants. One who thinks deontologically, however, will be inclined to halt the conversation after declaring the immigration illegal. This fact outweighs all others, rendering discussion of other considerations moot. Not surprisingly, two people coming from opposing camps on these ethical approaches seem to talk past each other. It helps explain why conservatives, generally prone to think deontologically, and liberals, seeing things consequentially, run into problems discussing issues of values and ethics. Their assumptions are very different, leading to different paths to approaching these problems.

The apparent simplicity of deontological ethics, however, can be deceiving. First, such systems depend on the legitimacy of the rules one is employing. Why should we be using this rule book rather than that? Because the entire ethical system is premised on the rules, justifying them as valid becomes of primary importance. With so much at stake and consequences be damned, that justification must be rock solid.

The second problem is that no set of rules in existence has ever been sufficiently comprehensive to address all situations and therefore will always demand interpretation and elaboration. The interpreters become crucial to the exercise, and unless they can be deemed highly consistent and reliable, the system quickly loses its legitimacy. Fallible humans interpreting a deontological framework of rules will always be the weakest link in the chain.

Third, deontological systems inevitably break down when two or more ethical rules or principles come into conflict. As in the earlier example, for instance, should I lie to prevent a murder? In such cases, one must come up with another system to determine which principle takes priority, and that involves considering consequences. The disagreements among those claiming to adhere to deontological systems demonstrate just how much context matters.

In *Star Trek II: The Wrath of Khan*, Mr. Spock explains his decision to sacrifice himself for the crew of the *Enterprise*: "The needs of the many outweigh the needs of the few."[78] This is a consequentialist viewpoint but one uniquely relevant to Christianity. Would it be morally justifiable to sacrifice one innocent person to save a thousand? Or a million? Or an entire planet of people? At what point would it no longer be justifiable? Would it be acceptable, for instance, to sacrifice five people to save six? Does it matter how old the people are? Or how morally righteous? Do one's intentions matter? Does the effect on others and the overall moral landscape? What other factors might relate to the decision? Among any group of people, even ardently avowed Christians, you will find different answers to these questions, which should demonstrate just how futile it is to break ethical questions into a set of simplistic rules.

Unless two people can agree on a rough hierarchy of values, it makes little sense to engage in discussions of policy or ethics. What is the point of debating the universal "single best route from Cleveland" if you want to go to New York while I want to go to Dallas? There is no single route that most efficiently meets both our goals. This is another reason discussions about such issues as abortion break down so quickly and are rarely productive: The parties begin with different core values. While each likely places some value on the unborn fetus and the rights of the mother, the different values they assign those rights means that from their first steps, they are moving in different directions.

There are countless examples of complex moral issues without obvious answers. If you need more, just watch a season of such television shows as *Breaking Bad*, *Game of Thrones*, or *The Wire*. But I hope this brief discussion highlights why objective morality, as intuitive as it might first seem, is highly unlikely to actually exist, much less exist *self-evidently*. The very concept of objective moral values is incoherent. *Morality* is a conceptual term that presupposes relationships between and among sentient, social beings. The term *value* is inherently subjective. We must always ask, "Value to whom?" It makes no sense to talk about value in the abstract. There must always be a personal reference point.

Morality only makes sense in a human context and will always be dependent to some extent on the respective preferences of individuals within a social environment. In a lifeless universe, what would be the "value" of a rock? Of a planet? What could right or wrong even mean in such a world? The destruction of an entire solar system via a supernova would represent merely a rearrangement of atoms, with no moral quality whatsoever.

Even if moral values were objective, furthermore, we could never confirm this. Our limited perspectives do not allow us to see beyond how morality plays out in the world of human beings. We have no direct access to any objective code of values and, even if one exists, no way to compare it to those we have reached by consensus to see if they line up. The very existence of objective moral values must, therefore, remain speculative, and this alone dooms the moral argument for God. If we cannot confirm the key premise of Dr. Craig's argument, then we cannot be justified in reaching his final conclusion—nor that of the many apologists who follow his lead.

2. Even If Moral Values Were Objective, That Would Not Make the Christian God More Likely

Dr. Craig's morality argument is based on semantics. Craig first defines *objective moral values* in such a way that they cannot be the products of human imagination but must necessarily be the products of a transcendent being.[79] Next, he takes objective moral values as a given based on intuition and cross-cultural agreement on certain moral issues. Finally, he posits the Christian God as the most likely author of this objective moral code, thereby providing support for God's own existence. Upon closer inspection, however, regardless of how one defines *objective morality*, its existence would not support the existence of God.

As demonstrated, the Christian God, given the vast number of unproven metaphysical assumptions necessary for His existence, is very unlikely indeed. Accordingly, any argument for the Christian God based on the claim that God is the true explanation is immediately refuted by *any other plausible explanation*. To defend the argument from morality, for example, the apologist must do more than show a God-ordained objective morality is possible. He must show it is the *only reasonable possibility*.

Prominent Christian apologist Richard Swinburne believes in objective moral values but rejects the claim that such values must be anchored in the Christian God. Swinburne believes that basic moral principles are necessary truths that would hold whether God existed or not. The idea of God grounding all morality is, in Swinburne's view, logically incoherent. Accordingly, he sees no force in an argument to the existence of God from morality.[80]

It is theoretically possible for absolute morality to exist as mathematics exists. Morality may be a methodology for evaluating claims but need not have an independent existence like chihuahuas do. When we say there are 4 items on the table, it is unnecessary that there be a "4 giver" to ensure that when we count out the objects, they don't spontaneously burst into 15,000 or −1 million.

As another example, all humans experience hunger; hunger thus exists as an abstraction. It doesn't exist spatially, of course. Nor is hunger created by an independent entity; rather, it is how we describe the sensation caused by the interaction between our stomachs and our brains. And we can see hunger in other mammals, too. Thus, hunger is objective. It means the same thing from person to person. It is real. It exists. But we do not posit a "hunger giver" to explain why all people feel hunger. In this sense, morality could be the by-product of a brain capable of rational self-reflection evolving in a social environment. All beings with such a brain would experience morality; morality would exist objectively across them all but not require any independent causation outside the brain.

If we look at objective morality as generally agreed-upon societal norms based on widely shared human values, then it becomes completely explicable through naturalism. We all experience moral impulses and moral reasoning subjectively. However, we have *nonarbitrary* reasons for adhering to norms of moral behavior. There are rational reasons for treating others fairly, for doing acts of goodwill, and even for sacrificing ourselves for the good of others. The very notion of grounding morality in God's commands, by contrast, *necessarily* makes morality arbitrary. If even the indiscriminate killing of children as a part of a hostile military conquest can be viewed as circumstantially moral, then what act *can't* be circumstantially moral?

Outside the religious context, humans don't base morality on revelation from authority. That would render us merely obedient. Moral behavior is doing what's right—not simply what we're told. There must be something to be said for or against a given action other than that it is forbidden by authority. If intuition tells us that something is immoral, then we must ask what triggers the intuition. Once we do this, we are dealing with valid reasons. Once we're discussing reasons, we have no valid basis to refer to Scripture.

3. The Christian God Cannot Be Considered Good in Any Meaningful Sense

A major problem for the Christian apologist is that the God portrayed by the Bible cannot be considered good, much less perfectly good, in any recognizable sense. Our only common source for the nature of God is the Christian Bible, a source considered authoritative by virtually every Christian denomination. If one takes an impartial view of the God portrayed by the Bible, however, then it is obvious that this character comes nothing near any reasonable ideal of good. He is far closer to the embodiment of evil.

The Old Testament provides many stories and examples by which the character of God can be assessed. God is repeatedly portrayed in very human terms, as a being with emotions, wants, and needs. God is presented as analogous to a powerful human king, with many of the traits ancient people respected and feared in such kings, as well as their character flaws. Many have chronicled the moral atrocities either committed, ordered, or allowed and implicitly ratified by God in the Old Testament, and I do not intend to provide an exhaustive list here. By way of example, however, consider the following.

God sent a flood to drown every man, woman, and child on the planet except Noah and his family. God's flood also would have killed every land animal except those lucky few taken aboard Noah's ark (Genesis 6:11–13, 7:21–23). At this point, God had provided mankind no laws or rules of behavior, so it cannot be said humans were disobedient. They were simply acting in accordance with the nature God had given them and thus free of moral accountability. That is a mass murder of innocent life on a massive scale. Millions would have died.

God sent a plague to kill every firstborn child (and cow) in Egypt simply because Pharaoh wouldn't accede to God's demands to release the

Israelites (Exodus 20:29–30). In other words, God murdered thousands of innocent children to persuade Pharaoh to do something God could have done directly. To make this act more atrocious, God first "hardened Pharaoh's heart" so that none of God's persuasive "efforts" would succeed and this murder of innocents would be a foregone conclusion, thus putting on display God's great power to the world (Exodus 10:1, 10:20, 10:27, 11:10).

After wandering in the Sinai Desert for forty years following their escape from Egypt, the Israelites returned to Canaan and went to war with the inhabitants to take the land for themselves. The Israelites claimed a right superior to that of the native inhabitants simply because God decreed it. This was a war in which the Israelites were to take no prisoners but were ordered by God to slaughter every native man, woman, and child they came across, as well as most of their animals (Joshua 6:20–21; Deuteronomy 2:33–35). Occasionally, God allowed the Israelites to take women and children to enjoy for themselves as slaves and spoils of war (Deuteronomy 20:10–17). God clarified that virgins, in particular, should be kept by Israelite men for their enjoyment (Deuteronomy 20:14; Numbers 31:18). This is a God in favor of the rape, slavery, and the murder of innocents.

A particularly gut-wrenching example of God's "objective" value system comes from Exodus. The Israelites had just attacked and defeated the town of Midian. Pursuant to God's command, they had killed every adult Midianite male. But some Israelites took women and children *captive* rather than killing them as God had commanded. Moses was furious and, to comply with God's orders, ordered that the Israelites immediately kill every male *child* and every nonvirgin woman. But as for "all the young girls who have not known man by lying with him, keep alive for yourselves" (Numbers 31:1–18). For issuing and presumably enforcing these commands to murder children and rape women, God was pleased with Moses.

Moderate Christians today extol the virtues of religious tolerance, but the Old Testament presents a God that had no use for tolerance. God begins the Ten Commandments by stating that He is a jealous god and that the people shall have no gods before Him. The penalty for breaking this commandment (as well as any of the others) was *death*—typically by stoning. God commanded that anyone among his initial Israelite followers choosing to worship other gods be killed, as well *as their wives and brothers* (Exodus 32:26–28). God ordered his followers to murder anyone who even encouraged them to follow a different religion (Deuteronomy 13:5–15). The post-Exodus period is the story of God repeatedly commanding his people to kill anyone who did not worship and follow Him (e.g., 1 Kings 18:17–40; Joshua 8:1–29; Deuteronomy 12:2–3). This is a God of intolerance and genocide.

While God is today often presented as supremely merciful and compassionate, the Old Testament reveals a very different reality. As to those who worshipped other gods, the Christian God ordered them decapitated (Numbers 25:3–4), buried them alive (Numbers 16:32–35), and acquiesced in their violent torture by His trusted servants (2 Samuel 12:31). On numerous occasions, God explicitly ordered that the *infants and children* of nonbelievers be murdered along with their parents (1 Samuel 15:2–3; Deuteronomy 2:34, 3:6–7). Of the Babylonians in particular, God promised to have their children smashed into pieces and their wives raped before their eyes (Isaiah 12:16). Several times, God ordered the Israelites to show *no mercy* to unbelievers (Deuteronomy 7:2, 20:16–18; Joshua 8:25–28, 10:28–40; Ezekiel 9:5–6). God counsels that righteous believers should rejoice in the blood of "wicked" unbelievers (Psalms 58:10). This is a God of cruelty.

To the extent one believes in objective moral values or even values treated as objective for practical purposes, one would almost certainly include the murder of children, rape, slavery, torture, and genocide objectively wrong. Could there be any clearer moral question than whether it is right to own another human being? And yet, the Bible presents God as repeatedly committing, commanding, or ratifying these very things. Nowhere in the Bible is slavery prohibited or identified as immoral. As Robert Ingersoll discovers, "The Bible is not inspired in its morality, for the reason that slavery is not moral, that polygamy is not good, that wars of extermination are not merciful, and that nothing can be more immoral than to punish the innocent on account of the sins of the guilty."[81] If God were the author of an objective moral code, then why would He violate it repeatedly throughout the Old Testament? If objective moral values exist, then the Christian God cannot be their source.

And it is not as though Jesus changed the game. Jesus fully accepted Old Testament laws (Matthew 5:17, 15:4) and explicitly approved of the killing God performed in the Old Testament, stating that he would do the same when his turn came (Matthew 10:14–15, 24:37; Luke 17:26–32, 19:27). Jesus surpassed the God of the Old Testament in cruelty by establishing a system of eternal torture for those without the right beliefs (Matthew 13:41–42, 13:49–50, 25:41–46).

The standard response of Christian apologists is the appeal to mystery. They claim that God is ineffable and cannot be judged by human standards. Presumably, if God came down and brutally flayed a thousand toddlers before their eyes, these apologists could register no surprise, for by their own admission, we can have no reasonable expectations about what God would do. They would simply have to say, "Well, that's just God being merciful and just in His way." That no apologists take such a glib approach suggests this argument is insincere. Their attempts to rationalize God's behavior indicate that they do in fact recognize standards by which they expect God's conduct to conform.

Unable to harmonize God's actions and commands with any recognizable deontological code of morality, many shift to a consequentialist approach, claiming that we must simply have faith that God's biblical actions were in the service of a greater good beyond our feeble capacities to understand. Apologists can't have it both ways: claiming God's morality is absolute and paradoxically asserting that God's atrocities are circumstantially justified. And what possible good could be worth the murder of millions of innocent children? Or the rapes of thousands of young women? With all God's powers, is it really possible there could have been no other way for Him to accomplish His goals? Without identifying these goals or showing how they justify God's apparent atrocities, these apologists leave us with an argument devoid of content.

4. Goodness Defined by Divine Command

Another approach is to completely redefine what objective morality even means. This approach, favored by Dr. Craig, among others, defines as *good* whatever God commands. If God orders someone to rape, murder, or steal, then raping, murdering, or stealing must be good precisely *because God commanded it*. Fittingly, this is known as divine command theory (DCT). DCT is not unique to Christianity but has been adopted by many prominent Christian theologians, including St. Augustine and Thomas Aquinas, in one of several variants. It is supported by the traditional Christian view of God as both omnipotent and omnibenevolent, as the Creator of all things would reasonably be expected also to be the Creator of moral truths.

DCT is problematic, however, for numerous reasons. First, from a human perspective, which is all that is available to us, it renders moral values arbitrary. If literally anything commanded by God can be good, then what can *good* possibly mean? The term is stripped of any useful meaning because it can be used to characterize any action, regardless of how intuitively appalling we might find it. It becomes divorced from how people understand the term and is thus unrecognizable.

It would no longer make sense to state categorically that a serial killer was wrong. Many serial killers claim they were told by God to kill. If we subscribe to DCT, then can we justifiably call their actions immoral? No, we cannot, for what can be more moral than following God's direct commands? How would we expect such people to distinguish right from wrong? And could it ever make sense to say that the Israelites' slaughter and rape of the Midianites was *objectively good*, so we are silly to even question it? DCT posits that it must have been. It is instructive that when asked for examples of acts that are objectively good, apologists favoring DCT never use those such as the Midianite massacre or any other act that people typically find morally abhorrent. If DCT were correct, however, any Old Testament atrocity could be used to demonstrate what is objectively good. God's command would represent the beginning and end of the inquiry.

DCT removes moral reasoning from the equation of determining what constitutes a good act. Secular ethical systems would look to the tremendous pain and suffering caused by rape and conclude that rape is bad. But for DCT adherents, rape is bad *solely because God commanded us not to rape*. The harm caused by rape becomes irrelevant. If God commands us to rape, as he did throughout much of the Old Testament, then rape *must be good*, even if it violates some of our strongest moral intuitions.[82] You can't argue why an action is good or a person is good because these concepts are devoid of content. Nor can theologians argue that God is good because this would require appealing to things outside of God to ground the concept, which DCT prohibits. Good is simply what God says it is.

A parent who teaches their morality based on DCT is not really teaching morality. The child is given no tools by which to assess difficult moral choices except to refer to Scripture and attempt to work out its interpretation and application to the matter at hand. If the child comes under the sway of a charismatic cult leader who claims to hold the proper interpretation of that Scripture, then the cult leader will hold the child's moral compass in his hands, for the parents will have relinquished it to him. Anyone making a persuasive claim to proper scriptural interpretation can likewise usurp that moral authority, causing the child to commit any act—even those that contradict their moral intuitions in the most egregious ways.

If you believe that what makes an action wrong has something to do with whether it causes harm to conscious beings, then you must acknowledge that DCT is off-base, as it takes no account of this. Such factors as the quantity and quality of harm imposed on others would be considered "morally relevant facts" in secular systems of morality, but they are entirely irrelevant to DCT proponents. The methodologies of these systems share no overlap. Arguing to a DCT proponent that a certain action should be taken because it will bring peace and well-being to every inhabitant of Earth would be pointless because the question of what should be done is solely whether it accords with God's commands.

DCT begins with the premise that God exists and is completely good. But as discussed in this section and a later one, the available evidence contradicts this conclusion. If we continue to ascribe some understandable and consistent meaning to *good*, then we cannot hold onto the notion that God, as described in the Bible, is entirely good. That apologists wedded to DCT must redefine a commonly understood English word so it can mean anything (and therefore nothing) suggests that we are dealing with rationalization and intellectual dishonesty rather than reasoned argument.

The problem of reconciling the concept of objective moral values with deities behaving badly is not a new one. It was notably dealt with by the Greek philosopher Plato in his dialogue *Euthyphro*. Plato posed what became known as the Euthyphro dilemma, which in the Christian context can be stated as, beginning with the assumption that whatever God wills is good, is something good because God wills it (as maintained by DCT adherents), or does God will it because it is good?[83]

The problem with the first option has been addressed. It would render the concept of *good* arbitrary and therefore practically meaningless. When we say that people are good, we mean we can predict with reasonable certainty what they would do and how they would act in certain situations. We would not expect a good person to, for instance, rape and murder an innocent child he finds wandering across his lawn. But for DCT adherents, calling God good provides no useful information or insight on what God might do, for a "good" God might just as easily feed starving refugees or slaughter them mercilessly. Each would follow from their view of "good" because it is God's actions that determine what we even mean by good. To say that God is good becomes a meaningless tautology: Good is what God commands; God only commands what is good. It may be true as far as it goes, but because God defines what it means to be good, it tells us nothing of God's character.

Option 1 also undermines any meaningful concept of objective morality. We cannot say that anything is intrinsically wrong. By labeling something wrong, we are saying nothing more or less than "God prohibits it." If God changes His mind tomorrow, then it is no longer wrong. An objective morality would require moral truths to be as set as $2 + 2 = 4$. But DCT entails that God could do the equivalent of declaring that $2 + 2 = -5879$, and "objective" truth would change on a dime. Clearly, this would contravene any principled definition of *objectivity*.

As problematic as the first option is, however, the second is worse for Christianity because it renders God *superfluous to morality*. If there are moral standards independent of God, then to be good, God is bound by those laws rather than being their establisher. God's "goodness" can be evaluated by the extent to which He conforms to these independent moral standards. God is no longer sovereign or omnipotent, for as to remain good, He would be limited by these independent standards. Morality would retain its authority even if God did not exist.

In this scenario, God is not the lawgiver but the law transmitter, merely passing along a set of standards that exist independently of Him. God is a middleman—an unnecessary cog in the wheel and not necessarily a reliable one. To determine what is right, we could bypass God and go straight to the standard. Objective morality would exist with or without Him. If God is unnecessary to morality, then morality cannot be an argument for God. Our moral landscape would look the same whether God existed or not. This is why Christian DCT is committed to option one of the Euthyphro dilemma. Dr. Craig explains,

> I think that a good start at this problem is to enunciate our ethical theory that underlies our moral judgments. According to the version of divine command ethics which I've defended, our moral duties are constituted by the commands of a holy and loving God. Since God doesn't issue commands to Himself, He has no moral duties to fulfill. He is certainly not subject to the same moral obligations and prohibitions that we are. For example, I have no right to take an innocent life. For me to do so would be murder. But God has no such prohibition. He can give and take life as He chooses.[84]

Christian apologists have done their best to address the arbitrariness objection by proposing variants of DCT. The most popular, stemming from the work of Robert Adams, involves claiming that God's goodness flows from his nature. Because God's *nature* is good, the argument goes, his commands *must necessarily be good*. God cannot be otherwise, so neither can his commands. Dr. Craig puts it this way: "God's moral nature is expressed in relation to us in the form of divine commandments which constitute our moral duties or obligations. Far from being arbitrary, God's commandments must be consistent with his holy and loving nature."[85]

This is merely a distinction without a difference. The semantics have changed, but the two options, with their inherent problems, remain. The dilemma is simply rephrased as "Is God responsible for God's nature (in which case God could have made Himself evil and called it good—rendering goodness arbitrary), or is God's nature determined independently (in which case, an exogenous standard applies, and God is, again, unnecessary to the equation)?" It is absurd and incoherent to imagine God determining His own nature for one would have to *have* a nature before determining anything, so we are left with the second option.

But relocating the standard to God's nature yields the same result: God is bound to act according to something over which He has *no conscious control*, whether we call it His nature, or an independent standard of goodness. Rather than being bound by an external standard of good, God is now bound *by His good nature*, which He did not choose but cannot disregard. His nature just happens to correspond to the independent moral code, which would exist with or without God, *but this is not God's doing*. It is simply a brute fact. The existence of objective morality ceases to be an argument for God. The argument is also a textbook example of circularity. God is good because it is His nature to be good. We as humans can only define *good* by what God says and does. We know that God's nature is good because He says so. Notice that at no point in this circular chain is there any possibility of independently assessing what is good. No useful information is conveyed about the meaning of *goodness*.

If we are to assume God exists, then there are only two options to explain His apparently immoral behavior. God is either in violation of a truly objective moral code, or the "objective" moral code posited by Craig and others is actually arbitrary and of no value to any human. In the latter case, common cross-cultural intuitive values would cease to provide any evidence for objective morality because the moral code would be independent of human intuition and sometimes directly opposed to it. Because a truly objective moral code would render God superfluous, apologists are left with the untenable position of doubling down on DCT or some variant thereof. To claim that morality leads to God, they must claim that God defines what is good. In doing so, however, they give up on objective morality because morality becomes subjective to God. However you look at it, God cannot be the basis of objective morality.

5. Objective Morality, If It Existed, Would Be Useless to Humanity Because We Have No Access to an Objective Moral Code

Dr. Craig claims that without objective morality, one could not effectively argue with a Nazi that the Holocaust was wrong because there would be no objective standard to which to appeal. This is just a fallacious argument from final consequences, premised on the unsupported belief that there can be no legitimate moral code unless it is laid down, policed, punished, and rewarded by a deity. But it is worth addressing to demonstrate why, besides being irrelevant, it is also wrong.

If there is an objective moral code, whether truly objective or objective as defined by Dr. Craig, then humanity has no direct access to it. All we have are people's interpretations of what they think God's moral code is.

And there are thousands of such interpretations across Jewish and Christian denominations. Thomas Paine observes, "That God cannot lie is no advantage to your argument, because it is no proof that priests cannot, or that the Bible does not."[86] Why would God create a code whereby every action could be classified as right or wrong but provide no definitive guide to that code?

If Christianity and the Bible provided a clear guide, then why is there virtually no important social or moral question on which all Christians agree? People who find moral absolutes in God's revelations have never agreed on those absolutes. Despite using the same book as their guide, Christians are all over the map on the big moral issues of the day. Take any such issue, and you will find devout, God-fearing, Bible-believing Christians coming down on opposite sides:

- capital punishment
- abortion
- divorce
- physician-assisted suicide
- gay rights
- women's rights
- corporal punishment
- war (hawks vs. doves)
- birth control
- fetal tissue research
- cloning
- separation of church and state
- slavery (especially in the nineteenth century)

Much of the Bible's appeal depends on its countless moral inconsistencies, which allow almost anyone to find passages that endorse his or her gut viewpoint. Making images is both forbidden (Exodus 20:4) and commanded (Exodus 25:18–20). We are told to stone others to death (Deuteronomy 21:21) and then not to throw the first stone (John 8:7). Good deeds are to be shown (Matthew 5:16) and not shown (Matthew 6:1). Books that endorse all viewpoints ultimately endorse none. It is no help to claim that the right answer is a matter of interpretation because no one can agree which interpretation is correct.

The Bible is filled with relatively clear proscriptions ignored by the vast majority of modern Christians. Despite what most Christians were brought up to believe, there is only one set of rules in the Bible carved in stone and explicitly referred to as the Ten Commandments. It is found at Exodus 34:10–28.[87] Virtually all are disregarded by modern Christians. A few examples:

- Always keep the feast of unleavened bread, eating only unleavened bread for seven days.
- Ensure that all male children appear before me three times a year.
- Sacrifice to me every male firstborn cow, ox, and sheep.
- Never offer me a sacrifice with leavened bread.

Had God intended for anything to serve as a moral code, you would expect it would be here—in a set of commandments He carved in stone and singled out for special treatment. And yet Christians do not treat it as one.

Even if we use the Decalogue as our guide, as most modern Christians do, we can see that much of it is now irrelevant. How useful, for instance, is the commandment against making graven images? While it may have been helpful in seventh-century BCE Judah, where graven images of Baal were all the rage, it is virtually obsolete today. Wouldn't that slot have been better used to say something about rape or slavery or abortion? Clear guidance on any of these would have prevented much suffering and conflict. That these were not considered immoral at the time (but are now) shows that the Decalogue was a creation of men of their time rather than an eternal all-knowing God.[88]

Regarding abortion: To the extent any guidance can be obtained from the Old Testament, it is prochoice. Exodus 21:22 imposes merely a fine for a man who causes a woman to miscarry. This is in stark contrast to the prescribed punishment for murder, which was death by stoning, and thus inconsistent with the view that God considers unborn fetuses humans with all such rights fully vested. The biblical definition of *life* is, furthermore, tied to breath, as described in Genesis 2:7. As unborn fetuses do not "breathe," it is most reasonable to conclude that the biblical writers did not consider them alive. And why would we expect them to? They had no understanding of conception as we know it today or of fetal development. There would have been no way for them to conceptualize either process to make any call on when human life began outside of birth.

For those who maintain that the Ten Commandments (the Decalogue version) represent the foundation of the American legal system, consider that these things are not illegal anywhere in the United States:

1. Worship gods other than YHWH
2. Make/worship idols

3. Use God's name however you want
4. Ignore the Sabbath
5. Mistreat and disrespect your parents
6. Lie (unless you're in court)
7. Cheat on your spouse
8. Want things you don't have

The only commandments that made it into modern laws are prohibitions against stealing and killing, both of which are necessary for the functioning of any civilized society and cannot lay claim to any uniquely biblical origin.

If we adopt a historical perspective, then it is instructive how Christian morals have evolved over time and across different cultures. In ancient times, for example, menstruation was misunderstood and considered unclean, and it is so categorized throughout the Bible. In the writings of primitive societies, God's morality was also considered more primitive and barbaric. God valued what the kings and rulers of that time valued. God's character reflected that of the civilizations of the time and place. But as cultures evolved, so, too, did the morality ascribed to God. The texts did not change—only the emphasis placed by the people interpreting them.

Christian morality is neither timeless nor absolute. A mind experiment proposed by author Alan Jeskin demonstrates this point:

[J]uxtapose a pious and genteel gentleman from Williamsburg, Virginia in the early 1800s, and a pious and genteel Christian co-ed from Virginia's College of William and Mary in the early 2000s. Imagine if the two were to meet on a warm summer day, he in his breeches, stockings, shirt, waistcoat, and silk cravat, she in a t-shirt, shorts, and flip-flops. Before the first words are exchanged, he would probably regard her as a woman of ill repute for shamelessly exposing almost the entire length of her legs and arms in public. He would likely be shocked she is a Christian, as no moral woman of God would parade around in broad daylight in attire barely adequate for the boudoir. Likewise, after a bit of conversation she would likely regard him as a shameless racist and male chauvinist for his support of slavery and open disdain at the thought that women could have a right to vote, fight in the armed forces, and date outside their station or race. She, like he, would regard her new acquaintance as highly immoral. Again, these would be two pious Christians, each with supposedly timeless moral standards.[89]

Christianity has throughout recent history closely mirrored the dominant moral values of the culture immediately surrounding it. The greatest change took place in the eighteenth century, when an intellectual movement known as the Enlightenment swept through Europe and America. Philosophers and scientists began to challenge conventional wisdom and think critically, looking beyond religious texts and tradition to find answers that made rational sense from a secular perspective. This movement would have profound effects on politics, science, religion, and art. It was a dominant inspiration among America's founding fathers, the influence of which is readily apparent in such documents as the Declaration of Independence and the Constitution.

The Enlightenment's effect on concepts of morality was especially powerful. The perspective shifted from focusing on God to focusing on humans and their welfare. Whereas "goodness" had been primarily measured by obedience to God, it now meant respecting the rights of your fellow man. People were increasingly judged based not on their adherence to Scripture but on their treatment of other people. Since the Enlightenment, morality has become more human-based, and Christian morality has been forced to change with it.

But this has not been without a dogged fight. Conservative Christians have been on the losing side of every moral shift in the United States since its founding. From the beginning, they stood against exclusion of references to Christianity in the founding documents and against any separation of church and state. Having lost that battle, they stood against freeing slaves, allowing women to vote, and protecting the freedom of minorities with civil rights legislation. Today, they continue to oppose humanity-based morality and lobby against gay marriage, reproductive freedom, and euthanasia. The basis for their opposition has nothing to do with alleviating human suffering or promoting human dignity. It is based solely on their interpretation of God's will from Bronze Age Scriptures.

Slavery and segregation were repeatedly and regularly justified by reference to biblical passages in churches throughout the United States (with the obvious exception of African American churches, which had compelling self-interested reasons to interpret Scripture differently) well into the maturity of both these movements. Both movements owe their success primarily to secular activists, who were not beholden to religious dogma, such as Ralph Waldo Emerson, William Lloyd Garrison, Robert Ingersoll, Jeremy Bentham, and John Stuart Mill. It was only after such secular movements found success that the mainstream churches in America jumped on the bandwagon, so to speak, and began the process of rewriting history. Every argument made by a religious group was preceded by years, if not decades, by a secular group. This information is even more important today, as the wall between church and state is under siege.

There are many passages in the Bible that promote what virtually all of us would agree to be positive moral values, though they are by no means unique to Christianity and did not originate with Christian writings. Liberal Christians of today might identify forgiveness as a Christian value and could point to biblical passages that support this claim. But members of the Westboro Baptist Church could also identify hatred of gays and religious intolerance as Christian values, and they, too, could point to Bible verses to back up their claims. If you, the reader, can distinguish the morally admirable passages of the Bible from the barbaric Old Testament passages, then that is clear evidence that your moral judgment originates outside of the Bible.

Looking to the New Testament, consider the "greatest commandment": *Love your neighbor as yourself.* I can't imagine that anyone believes God arbitrarily came up with this as a test for getting into Heaven. I think most Christians would agree that the rationale for such a commandment is that living by this principle results in a better world for everyone. It is a commonsense sentiment that, even in writing, precedes its biblical expression by more than a thousand years.[90] But if that's the case, then it need not be commanded—we can arrive at such a moral obligation through reason alone. What need, then, for God?

Returning to Dr. Craig's example of arguing with the Nazi, I would say that the secular humanist has a distinct advantage over Dr. Craig. The humanist can at least say that his moral standard is consistent, in that, for example, it logically follows the principles of increasing human happiness and decreasing human suffering, which benefits both individuals and society as a whole. The Nazi agenda runs directly counter to those goals and thus must be condemned. In response to Dr. Craig, the Nazi could easily point out the hypocrisy of Craig's DCT-based code. He could reference the myriad examples of God ordering genocide and condoning other atrocities no less horrible than those committed by the Nazis.[91]

A major problem for those claiming that Christians derive their moral code from God is psychological research showing the arrow instead points the other way. According to a 2009 study, when asked about God's position on a moral issue, Christians consulted that part of their brains used to determine *their own beliefs*. First manipulating the subjects' beliefs influenced their views on God's position.[92] The study suggests that when people say they are consulting God's code, they are really just asking themselves what *feels* right and then cherry-picking biblical verses to rationalize that position. Religion can make no claim to being a moral compass if religious people faced with moral choices simply mold religion to fit their own biases.

If an objective moral code exists, then no one knows what it is. And of course, no one can demonstrate that it does. So the entire discussion is moot because in the end, we are left to figure morality out for ourselves. That such ancient texts as the Bible provide a rough moral code of sorts is not helpful because these sources are highly limited in scope, ambiguous, self-contradictory, and allow for endless interpretations. If the code follows commonly recognized, consensus-based norms of behavior, then the Bible (and thus Christianity) provides no consistent guide to it.

Accordingly, we are forced to work out a system of rules and laws on which most of us can agree, which leads us to ethics and philosophy. All that is necessary to speak meaningfully of morality is that one be able to come up with a coherent concept of ethics, a system to help people make good decisions when the best decisions aren't always clear. Many philosophers have developed such systems that have no use for God or any requirement of metaphysical "objectivity." Philosophical morality is far closer to the objective ideal praised by apologists than any religious-based system because it follows a transparent and logical process. It may not be perfect, but it need not be perfect to be useful, and it is the best we have.

C. Without Christian Morality, People Would Descend into Moral Anarchy

This third argument may be the most common, though it is just an appeal to final consequences, that the argument that leads to the most psychologically comfortable outcome must be the correct one. Many apologists have argued that people need religion, and Christianity in particular, to make good moral choices. And because a society of people making good moral choices is preferable to one in which they don't, Christianity must be true. But the conclusion doesn't follow from the premise. There are other problems with this argument.

As many a theologian has claimed, citing Fyodor Dostoyevsky, "without God, all is permitted."[93] Based on this claim, Jordan Peterson maintains that all atheists who make good moral choices must be secretly or unknowingly religious because this is the only explanation for their moral code. But this simply isn't true. The premise is that there are only two choices available to those who seek moral guidance: religion and nihilism. But this is a false dichotomy. Many ethical systems and philosophies exist independently of religion, such as social contract theory, utilitarianism, virtue ethics, Kantianism, and John Rawls's theory of justice. Where this claim is made referring to Christianity, it is especially specious. There is no indication that such great ethical thinkers as Aristotle and the Stoics knew anything resembling Christian morality.

This claim also ignores the crucial role that moral decision making has played in man's long evolutionary history. We are part of a species that is innately interdependent; none of us has the luxury of moral autonomy because we are all dependent on one another for all aspects of our mental and physical well-being. Our tendency to feel empathy toward one another is deeply embedded in our biology—something that can be observed even in the behavior of toddlers or in our simpler evolutionary cousins.[94] Were they not, we wouldn't have survived long enough to evolve rational thought. As the late Christopher Hitchens was so fond of pointing out, if the Israelites thought murder and theft were permissible before God decreed it, then they wouldn't have survived long enough to make it to Mount Sinai.

Many of the greatest societies known to man made their accomplishments without Christianity: Greece during the Golden Age, the early Roman Empire, several dynasties of China, the Islamic Empire under Muhammad, and the historic Japanese culture. While such apologists as Ben Shapiro and Jordan Peterson claim that the core values of Western civilization are uniquely Judeo-Christian in nature, the truth is that none can trace their roots to anything Judeo-Christian, a term only invented in the twentieth century as a marketing term for Christians trying to convert Jews. Laws against murder and theft date back at least four thousand years, long before the birth of Judaism. Laws abolishing slavery date back only two hundred years, long after the birth of Judaism and Christianity. Democracy and freedom of speech were planted in ancient Athens and the Roman Republic and only blossomed during the early Enlightenment around 1700, opposed by the Christian Church.

Those who claim society should be based on Christian Scripture can look to medieval Europe to see how this played out. This period, in which Christianity exercised complete control, had a name: the Dark Ages. It was a time in which many of the previous societal advances were overturned. Universities were condemned for teaching anything that conflicted with church teaching. Scientific books were banned, burned, or overwritten for copies of religious text. Those expressing views opposed by the Orthodox Church were branded heretics and persecuted mercilessly. The loss of knowledge set Western civilization back centuries. Slavery was accepted without question. Rule was vested exclusively in monarchies. No laws contemplated equal treatment of women, gays, or ethnic minorities. When it comes to slavery, wars, inquisitions, witch hunts, and scientific progress, Christians who've been handed the reigns have a terrible track record.

So why prefer a religious basis for morality, such as that derived from Christian Scripture, to a secular one? The primary argument I've seen from apologists is that a secular system can't ground prescriptive rules of behavior because it can't justify an objective moral code—which they consider a necessary condition of a moral society. David Hume articulates this through what has come to be called the "is/ought" distinction. Hume concludes there is a boundless gulf between positive factual statements about *what is* and normative statements about *what ought to be*, so the former cannot justifiably lead to the latter. The severing of *is* statements from *ought* statements is known as Hume's guillotine.

The problem for secular systems, apologists argue, is that in refusing to recognize anything beyond the natural world (what is), naturalists can appeal to no transcendent standard. If we can know things only through observation of what is and logical deductions from those observations, then there can be no objective moral knowledge. Accordingly, no secular system of morality can be valid. But this requires false assumptions: (1) that the validity of a system is unrelated to its social utility and (2) that a society cannot justly impose rules of behavior without a transcendent objective standard of morality.

A valid secular ethical system is one that provides rules that make our lives and the lives of those around us better than alternative systems. Human morality is defined by our shared experiences and common values. All humans value the life and the welfare of themselves, their families, and their close friends. As John Donne famously wrote, "No man is an island."[95] Clearly our fortunes are tied to the remainder of humanity, suggesting that the flourishing of humanity should also be highly valued. Once we agree on these values, the means of achieving them are objectively measurable and can be assisted by science. This is how we can derive our *oughts*. As Albert Einstein notes, "Science has been charged with undermining morality, but the charge is unjust. A man's ethical behavior should be based effectually on sympathy, education, and social ties; no religious basis is necessary. Man would indeed be in a poor way if he had to be restrained by fear of punishment and hope of reward after death."[96]

Admittedly, goals are subjective things. But there are certain goals that, if we correctly apply reason and logic, should be noncontroversial for human societies. Human welfare is one of these, as it benefits both the individual and the group with no negative externalities. If we can agree on a goal like human welfare, then that goal can lead to objective rules. Take, for example, the rules of football. That these rules are what they are is purely subjective—they're merely the way the inventors of the game wanted them to be.

There is no objective reason, for example, that a first down must be ten yards rather than nine. Yet within the rules of football, we can *objectively* determine whether a team has made a first down. Similarly, the goal of human well-being may be entirely subjective to humans (alligators care nothing for our welfare), but that subjective framework enables us to create objectively measurable *oughts*, and these *oughts* comprise what we call morality.

The system must balance competing subgoals and values considered important by humanity, such as societal flourishing and individual autonomy. This is often elusive in practice because these values are weighted differently by different people, but that doesn't suggest the task is impossible. Some ethical rules are necessarily situational, meaning that the same action can be right or wrong depending on the context.[97] Even if it were impossible to create a perfect system, that doesn't mean we cannot approximate increasingly better systems or that such systems lack validity. Their validity is established by how well they accomplish the goals we set for them. Because human flourishing is a goal shared by virtually all humans, it is not unreasonable to establish moral codes based on such a goal, even if we cannot in doing so ground it in a technically objective standard.

Christian morality, by contrast, is completely divorced from social utility and human welfare. According to the apologists who make the moral argument, it is irrelevant whether a Christian moral code makes life better for humans. Its validity is established not by reference to its consequences but because it complies with God's commands. A rule to stone unchaste women need not be justified on the basis that it would improve anyone's life or even that it is fair or just, but solely that it reflects a reasonable interpretation of the Bible. The only valid objection under such a system is that the biblical interpretation is flawed. A system of morality requires nothing other than common agreed-upon goals. With Christianity, that goal is simply to please God. But such a goal is entirely removed from the human relationships that govern our intuitions. Consequentialist secular morality, by contrast, is more in line with our common moral intuitions than deontological biblical morality, with its countless paradoxes.

A system of secular ethics is not improved by adding divine commandments or promises of celestial rewards and punishments. Atheists would be sufficiently motivated not to steal from friends and family by their love for those very people and desire not to hurt them. Humans have evolved to recognize all relationships as part of an interconnected web in which disrespecting others ultimately affects us all. Human empathy and solidarity are entirely sufficient motivators without the veneer of divine threat. Divine sanction only cheapens moral choices.

As an example, assume that before being killed in a terrible Wonkavator accident, Willie Wonka created the most beautiful and delicious piece of candy ever made. The candy sits on a table in a small room as plans are hatched for a world tour in which everyone can witness this miracle of confection. While the adults deliberate, a small boy, Charlie, is told to wait in the room for ten minutes alone. He is politely asked not to devour the tantalizing treat before him. It is explained to Charlie that this would destroy the wonderful experience of everyone to come after him, who would never know the joy he is feeling just observing this marvel.

Next, assume another boy, Augustus, is given the same opportunity. He is told all the same things as Charlie, but in addition, he is told that his school principal will be watching from a peephole near the top of the room. If he even touches the candy, the principal will see it, and Augustus will be horribly punished. If Augustus refrains from touching the candy for ten minutes, then he will be given all the delicious candy he can ever eat. If neither boy eats the candy, which would you conclude to be more virtuous? If you chose Charlie, then you have everything you need to see why the Christian system of morality is hopelessly flawed.

Avoiding a behavior for fear of punishment by an authority figure is not morality but subservience. Christian moralists turn morality into obedience, but obedience represents the *abdication of moral responsibility*. It is moral outsourcing. The story of Isaac and Abraham, in which God commands Isaac to kill his most beloved son, perfectly illustrates this. What message can this horrible story possibly be intended to convey except that when our moral intuitions conflict with the will of God, we must abdicate the former for the latter? We must be willing even to kill our most beloved family members if God commands it. It was this very willingness that delivered Abraham, and thus all his descendants, into God's favor.

Adopting a moral system based on obedience means that a Christian cannot justifiably condemn serial killers or even the 9/11 hijackers if the hijackers honestly believed they were following God's commands. They may be faulted for choosing the *wrong* God (though given what we know of the effect of demographics on religious beliefs, it would be a stretch to call this a choice), but every action from that point forward would be equally justified by Christian DCT. Those who quote Dostoyevsky have it backward: Only with God is all permitted.

One claim is rarely explicitly made by apologists but nonetheless follows inevitably from their logic. If Christians hold as their standard the one and only true moral code, then we would reasonably expect Christians to act significantly better than non-Christians as a group. A good basis of comparison would be atheists because they treat neither the Christian code nor any other divine code as authoritative. If Christianity provides the only true basis of morality, then atheists could only hope to make morally correct choices by random chance. And if humans are naturally evil and tainted by sin, then one would expect atheists to be wildly immoral by nature, having nothing to constrain them.

By Christian logic, atheists would have neither the incentive nor means to be good and thus should be expected to be make far fewer morally "right" choices than Christians. This doesn't mean that one would never expect to see a Christian make poor moral choices. No one is perfect, and we can reasonably expect even well-intentioned Christians to fall along the path of righteousness occasionally. But one should surely expect to see *far more* Christians on that path than atheists, who don't even acknowledge that the path exists. The unrestrained sinful nature of atheists would predispose them against the morally righteous choice the vast majority of the time.

That is not what we see *at all*. By any reasonable measure, atheists are at least as likely to make morally appropriate choices as Christians. Sociologist Phil Zuckerman, who has studied this issue extensively across many cultures, concludes that "high levels of organic atheism are strongly correlated with high levels of societal health."[98] The least religious countries are better off than most religious countries. Atheist countries have a higher life expectancy, lower infant mortality, less crime, fewer suicides, fewer homicides, higher literacy, less poverty, greater gender equality, better health care, and so forth. Atheists, furthermore, are almost completely absent from the American prison system, especially in contrast to Christians.

Some studies appear to have demonstrated a positive correlation between religiosity and such prosocial behaviors as helping the disadvantaged. When analyzed more closely, however, it is not the uniquely religious aspects of the religions, such as supernatural beliefs, that are positively correlated but those aspects that religious groups share with nonreligious but equally cohesive groups, such as shared community, regular socialization, and common purposes. Once these are considered, this correlation fades away.

In their book based on two of the most comprehensive surveys on American religious attitudes, Robert Putnam and David Campbell conclude that it is religious "belongingness" rather than religious *belief* that matters for positive socialization, especially in a predominantly Christian country.[99] After reviewing the literature on the effects of religion on prosocial behavior, psychologist Paul Bloom concludes there is "surprisingly little evidence for a moral effect of specifically religious beliefs."[100]

A common apologetic tactic is to reference such brutal dictators as Joseph Stalin, Mao Zedong, and Pol Pot, who shared a lack of theistic belief, as if such examples represent atheist value systems. There are several major problems with this. First, these examples are far from representative of atheists, the vast majority of whom demographics confirm to be well-adjusted law-abiding citizens. Second, as previously discussed at some length, atheism entails no particular system of morality or values. Apologists are suggesting that Stalin, for example, wouldn't have been such an awful guy if he had simply adhered to a Bible-based version of morality.[101] The only way to evaluate this claim would be to determine what system of morality Stalin *adhered to* and then compare that to a Bible-based system.[102] It could have been one of many recognized secular systems of ethics or perhaps one unique and proprietary to him, such as "might makes right." Only equivalent ethical systems and those atheists who explicitly subscribe to them, can provide a legitimate basis of comparison, and even then it wouldn't provide a referendum on atheism. Otherwise, one is comparing apples to oranges.

Third, one would require evidence that Stalin's atheism somehow influenced his actions. But because atheism represents a negative position, a lack of belief rather than an affirmative one, this would be virtually impossible to do. There are surely many things Stalin didn't believe that played no role in his decision making. One might as easily maintain that nonbelievers of UFOs are terrible people because Stalin also didn't believe in UFOs—or nonbelievers of Bigfoot or the Loch Ness Monster. There is no legitimate way to connect the dots. And what if Stalin adhered to a xenophobic form of Christianity, such as that practiced by the Westboro Baptist Church or the leaders of the Spanish Inquisition? Is there any reason to think that in such a case, his faith would have deterred him from committing the atrocities attributed to him? Does anyone believe Westboro founder Fred Phelps would have been more restrained if he had wielded Stalin's power?

What such dictators as Stalin, Mao Zedong, and Pol Pot did share was a state-sponsored dogma that required obedience without question or dissent. In this way, such systems were similar to monotheistic religions, such as Christianity and Islam, which are exclusionist and based on revealed Scripture rather than freethought. Such systems require people to override their moral instincts and do things they might otherwise find abhorrent if commanded by an authority, an element not only lacking but also universally condemned by secular humanism and every significant system of secular ethics. One cannot legitimately blame the atrocities of fascist dictators on their atheism. A more apt comparison would be between dogmatic governments and secular democracies. Here, the contrast could not be starker. Secular democracy has been the most successful and morally upright form of government the world has ever known, and it fits hand in glove with atheism. The problems with the systems of these men were things that conflicted with the values of secular democracy.

The late Christopher Hitchens regularly challenged Christian apologists to name one moral act only a Christian believer could take. Hitchens would then offer many examples of *immoral* acts that could only be justified by Christian Scripture. His point was that Christians can demonstrate no point on which Christianity yields a higher level of morality than its alternatives, but the reverse is not true. If looking for ways Christianity degrades morality, examples abound.

There is simply no good evidence that belief in God or adherence to a Bible-based system of morality is necessary for or even positively correlated with better moral behavior. Many secular ethical systems are available to atheists with values very similar to those of liberal Christian denominations. The question before us as humans is simple: Which type of system do we prefer? Would we rather ground our morality in such goals as human flourishing or in the words of a book written more than two thousand years ago?

THE TRANSCENDENTAL ARGUMENT (TAG)

Appearing to gain steam within apologetic circles, especially the presuppositionalists, is the transcendental argument for God (TAG). Presuppositionalists Greg Bahnsen, John Frame, and Cornelius Van Til have written extensively about it. Frank Turek dedicates most of his book *Stealing from God* to it. This argument, first proposed by Immanuel Kant in 1763, posits that reason and logic themselves must have come from God *necessarily*. Anyone using reason or logic to argue against God's existence is in effect proving that God exists! Without God, the apologists claim, atheists would not have these tools at their disposal.

TAG represents an interesting attempt to end-run opposing arguments entirely without ever having to address them on their merits. Apologists who resort to TAG often refuse to engage with their opponents until they provide a nontheistic explanation of the origin of logic and reason. It differs from many of the other arguments because it is not based on inductive reasoning but simply on acceptance of the supposedly self-evident premise that knowledge, reason, and logic could not exist without God. In this way, it is similar to the argument from moral absolutes, and subject to some of the same criticisms.

The TAG proponent begins with the premise that there are such things as logical, scientific, and moral *absolutes*. The proponent would say the "laws" of logic represent logical absolutes, such laws as identity (A = A), noncontradiction (A cannot be not-A), and the excluded middle (everything must be either A or not-A). The proponent posits these absolutes are immaterial and unchanging and thus require an immaterial and unchanging source that transcends our material reality. In other words, they require the existence of something with the claimed attributes of the Christian God.

There are many problems with this argument, but the biggest is there is no reason to accept its premises. No one has ever demonstrated the existence of a logical, scientific, or moral absolute. This term does not exist in science or academia but only in Christian apologetics, where it is never meaningfully defined, much less demonstrated to exist. Instead, it is employed without proof, explanation, or justification to beg the question, for if we accept the existence of transcendent standards the universe is bound to obey, then we must accept the existence of some transcendent realm from which they came. But there is no need to accept such standards or such a realm and therefore nothing for the naturalist to account for.

The naturalist begins with the assumption that reality exists and has certain properties. Logic and reason do not represent prescriptive rules, such as traffic laws, as if the universe must be told what to do. Rather, they represent *descriptions of how reality appears to work*. We have always observed that a rock is a rock and cannot be a nonrock. We have made similar observations about everything else we have encountered in the Newtonian world, from hydrogen atoms to spiral galaxies. This has led us to conceptual abstractions describing these apparently consistent properties, which we call the laws of logic. The key is that we have built them from the ground up based on our sensory data, and we justify them daily based on their pragmatic utility. They work.

There is a difference between the laws of logic and the circumstances to which they refer. Our reality appears to have consistency as a property, meaning a thing's attributes do not arbitrarily change. This is a property *described by the laws of logic*. These descriptions are useful as guidelines to shepherd our thinking *so it conforms with reality*. But that doesn't mean these descriptions are themselves metaphysical absolutes, universally applicable throughout the cosmos from every point of reference. In modern times, for reference, we have observed that at the quantum level, things act in ways that defy common understandings of causality. As with objective morality, we simply lack the perspective to make such a claim. Accordingly, there is no transcendent absolute, in the sense of a prescriptive rule, for which the naturalist must account and no basis to posit that logic and reason presuppose God.

Even if the axioms of logic apply universally throughout the cosmos, that wouldn't require a personal lawgiver. It would just mean these axioms are qualities of existence we humans have come to recognize. Just because something appears to be this way or that doesn't mean someone or something made it to appear this way or that or required that it be that way. The qualities of the universe we observe may simply be brute facts. They are what they are. We have no grounds to assume otherwise.

TAG proponents refuse to accept this answer. For them, the source of everything must ultimately be a personal one. But this places them into the same inescapable dilemma as Euthyphro. Logic and reason are independent of God, in which case God is superfluous, or their very existence is subject to God's whim. If the latter is true, then God is not subject to logic or reason, including the law of noncontradiction. God can therefore exist and not exist simultaneously, which sends apologists spiraling into the abyss of absurdity.[103] Neither path leads to the existence of God.

THE ARGUMENT FROM REASON

Related to TAG is the argument from reason, or the evolutionary argument for God. This argument, advanced by C. S. Lewis, Alvin Plantinga, Frank Turek, and Lee Strobel, among others, claims that humanity's ability to reason and make accurate sense of the world is itself evidence for God. Plantinga claims that naturalism cannot adequately explain these faculties because natural selection is primarily concerned with genetic survival rather than accuracy.[104] Specifically, Plantinga summarizes his argument this way:

First, the probability of our cognitive faculties being reliable, given naturalism and evolution, is low. (To put it a bit inaccurately but suggestively, if naturalism and evolution were both true, our cognitive faculties would very likely not be reliable.) But then according to the second premise of my argument, if I believe both naturalism and evolution, I have a defeater for my intuitive assumption that my cognitive faculties are reliable. If I have a defeater for that belief, however, then I have a defeater for any belief I take to be produced by my cognitive faculties. That means that I have a defeater for my belief that naturalism and evolution are true. So my belief that naturalism and evolution are true gives me a defeater for that very belief; that belief shoots itself in the foot and is self-referentially incoherent; therefore I cannot rationally accept it. And if one can't accept both naturalism and evolution, that pillar of current science, then there is serious conflict between naturalism and science.[105]

C. S. Lewis explains the argument this way:

> One absolutely central inconsistency ruins [the naturalistic worldview]. . . . The whole picture professes to depend on inferences from observed facts. Unless this inference is valid, the whole picture disappears. . . . [U]nless Reason is an absolute—all is in ruins. Yet those who ask me to believe this world picture also ask me to believe that Reason is simply the unforeseen and unintended by-product of mindless matter at one stage of its endless and aimless becoming. Here is flat contradiction. They ask me at the same moment to accept a conclusion and to discredit the only testimony on which that conclusion can be based.[106]

Plantinga, Lewis, and other proponents argue that naturalism is self-refuting because it requires rational beliefs to be inferred from nonrational processes. They claim that the arguably haphazard and arbitrary processes of evolution by natural selection cannot be considered a trustworthy method of creating a reliable means (the human brain) for engaging in rational thinking. Nonreason, they posit, cannot lead to reason. Accordingly, the argument goes, no belief is rationally inferred if it can be fully explained in terms of nonrational causes. The reasoning used by atheists to argue for naturalism, they posit, must then have come from a non-natural, entirely rational source. The only credible candidate for this source is God.

Proponents of this argument misrepresent the evolutionary process and ignore the adaptive value of accurate modeling. Evolution by natural selection is not random and purposeless. Though it involves and builds on random mutations, natural selection blazes a nonrandom path toward maximum survivability in the environment in which the organism finds itself. This isn't antecedent purpose of the type a Christian would assign to a Creator God but rather a direction imposed on the development of the organism over time by the naturally occurring correlation between survival and adaptability.

Clearly, an organism that can construct true beliefs and accurate models of reality will have significant survival advantages over those that can't. It can make predictions that lead it to catch prey and avoid being preyed upon. We would expect evolution to build increasingly precise sensory mechanisms that would provide successive generations with better model-making abilities than their ancestors. The ability to accurately reason would be especially valuable and would grow stronger with successive generations.

While natural selection may not directly forge true beliefs, it would be expected to shape the sensory and mental mechanisms *that lead to true beliefs*. Because we should expect naturalistic processes to imbue humans with minds capable of producing reasonably accurate models of reality, naturalism does not provide a "defeater" to the belief that our cognitive faculties are reliable or that naturalism and evolution are true. Contrary to Lewis's and Plantinga's assertions, there is no conflict between naturalism and evolutionary science.

The greatest weakness in the argument from reason, however, is that human minds *don't model reality perfectly*. We are prone to many cognitive weaknesses and blind spots, which are exactly the types of imperfections predicted by naturalism but extremely surprising given theism. We are, for example, prone to ad hoc reasoning and ex post facto explanations. Stephen Pinker identifies many common false beliefs based on cognitive flaws inherent in the human brain:

> Members of our species commonly believe, among other things, that objects are naturally at rest unless pushed, that a severed tetherball will fly off in a spiral trajectory, that a bright young activist is more likely to be a feminist bank teller than a bank teller, that they themselves are above average in every desirable trait, that they saw the Kennedy assassination on live television, that fortune and misfortune are caused by the intentions of bribable gods and spirits, and that powdered rhinoceros horn is an effective treatment for erectile dysfunction. The idea that our minds are designed for truth does not sit well with such facts.[107]

Under naturalism, human minds evolved to maximize survival in a particular environment—one of limited numbers of medium-sized objects traveling at medium speeds. Our ancestors had no experience with anything at the quantum or cosmic level or of exceedingly large numbers. And unsurprisingly under naturalism, our intuitions and understanding fail us when attempting to grasp these scales. We are consistently better at intuiting whether our neighbor is angry with us, for example, than at approximating the volume of Lake Mead. Naturalism predicts that we would do a good but not perfect job at approximating reality, with our accuracy increasing in direct proportion to how valuable it would have been for our ancestors to model a particular situation, given the experience they encountered in their lives. And that is just what we find.

Luckily, we can supplement our collective understanding and complement our cognitive limitations through such man-made constructs as scientific methodology, an intersubjective activity that systematically corrects for the unreliability of our intuitions and cognitive faculties. Our collective cultural achievements have, in this way, outpaced our genetic limitations and allowed us to obtain reliable knowledge that would have been impossible for prior generations.

Christianity predicts that God would invest even the earliest humans with perfectly functioning brains with no cognitive limitations that might lead them astray. According to Christian doctrine, man was made in God's image, which would presuppose that all human brains model reality flawlessly. There would be no reason to expect the accuracy of intuitive beliefs to be directly correlated to their survival value, becoming increasingly faulty as the relationship to our ancestors' survival becomes more tenuous.

These imperfections also raise a troubling question for apologists. Why would God build any faults into our brains or our senses? Only if our brains work as faultless truth detectors could God assign any blame to us when we don't accept Christianity. Only if we all reached conclusions through perfect logic could we be faulted for reaching the "wrong" conclusion. Free will can't be considered truly free if our decisions are hampered by imperfect brains. Our flawed cognitive mechanisms get humans entirely off the hook for rejecting Christianity and make a mockery of the idea that Heaven and Hell represent any recognizable form of justice. If our minds were designed to perfectly perceive truth, then why are there so many conflicting and incompatible religions? What truth could be more important than the right religion?

THE ARGUMENT FROM DETERMINISM

Closely related to the argument from reason is the argument from determinism, which is directed to the subset of atheists who consider themselves determinists. Proponents claim that determinism defeats atheism because it posits that we do not choose our beliefs and therefore we cannot come to them rationally. And if atheists cannot show that their beliefs are derived through reason, proponents argue, then they cannot justify them. Accordingly, proponents say, one cannot be both an atheist and a determinist. But this is a misreading of determinism. Determinism holds that at the lowest level of abstraction, the most reductive point, we are in a closed system, where all effects are determined by preexisting causes in a way that is theoretically perfectly predictable. But this does not accurately describe our world at higher levels of abstraction, the ones that matter to our lives.

I am a determinist, but I would acknowledge that, in the commonly understood colloquial sense, we do make decisions. We do employ logic and reason. At that level, it is not helpful to talk of the interactions of protons, electrons, and quarks, even though those do affect our decision making in predictable ways. The deterministic processes are under the surface outside our awareness. In the way people typically think about decision making, we decide things based on any number of factors.

Determinism simply doesn't entail all that apologists say it does. That the ultimate mechanism of the universe and thus the mind is deterministic does not necessitate that human decisions are irrational. As discussed previously, natural selection molded the human brain to recognize and employ reasoning due to its inherent survival advantages. If one can describe his or her beliefs and their genesis in terms of good evidence and reasonable inferences, then they are rationally justified—by definition.

The mind-brain distinction and consciousness make a good analogy. As discussed in more detail herein, the workings of the mind can be fully explained by the workings of the brain. But that doesn't mean we can't call what the brain does "thinking" or "decision making," even if it can ultimately be reduced to a series of neural firings. It is two ways of describing the same thing at different abstraction levels. Consciousness, likewise, is a higher-level abstraction of brain activity. If apologists cannot provide a plausible alternative explanation for the way our minds work, including all their imperfections, then they cannot justifiably criticize determinists. There is simply no conflict between determinism and a justified atheist worldview.

THE *SENSUS DIVINITATIS*

Sensus divinitatis ("sense of divinity"; SD) is a term first used by John Calvin to describe a hypothetical human sense that gives humans knowledge of God. Calvin claims this sense manifested itself universally in an instinctual knowledge that God exists. By positing such a sense, Calvin could claim there were no true atheists, in that no one could truly disbelieve in God. The only explanation for the existence of non-Christians is that they are *actively refusing* to follow God and thus actively rejecting Him. This also conveniently offers Calvin an argument *for God* because, he claims, there is no other plausible explanation for the existence of the SD than the existence of God. As explained by Calvin,

There is within the human mind, and indeed by natural instinct, an awareness of divinity. This we take to be beyond controversy. To prevent anyone from taking refuge in the pretense of ignorance, God himself has implanted in all men a certain understanding of his divine majesty. Ever renewing its memory, he repeatedly sheds fresh drops. Since, therefore, men one and all perceive that there is a God and that he is their Maker, they are condemned by their own testimony because they have failed to honor him and to consecrate their lives to his will. . . . Therefore, since from the beginning of the world there has been no region, no city, in short, no household, that could do without religion, there lies in this a tacit confession of a sense of deity inscribed in the hearts of all. . . . Men of sound judgment will always be sure that a sense of divinity which can never be effaced is engraved upon men's minds. Indeed, the perversity of the impious, who though they struggle furiously are unable to extricate themselves from the fear of God, is abundant testimony that this conviction, namely, that there is some God, is naturally inborn in all, and is fixed deep within, as it were in the very marrow.[108]

Calvin claims the existence of the SD to be "beyond controversy," which conveniently absolves him of the need to provide any evidence supporting it. In fact, however, the biggest problem with this argument is there is *no evidence* for any SD. The evidence is overwhelmingly against it. The argument requires that every human on the planet have this sense, but this is demonstrably false. It would be simple to devise surveys to put this to the test, but none have provided support for this claim. Surveys of religious beliefs suggest a wide variety of mutually exclusive ones, with many people having no such beliefs. This is just what we would expect if there were no SD.

Atheists throughout history have written extensively about their beliefs, and these writings confirm no "God-shaped hole" in their lives, which we would expect of someone rejecting a divinely imbued knowledge. They have confirmed living happy and meaningful lives, with no need for any spiritual component, much less one that could be filled only by the Christian God. They report no "endless searching" for spiritual sustenance that can only be satisfied through Christianity. Unless one claims that all the survey participants and atheist writers are deliberately lying, no universal SD exists.

Apologist Alvin Plantinga takes this argument to heart and goes back to the drawing board through a complex argument he calls "reformed epistemology." He champions a modified form of the SD, in which everyone has the sense, but due to sin, *it does not work properly in some people*. This allows Plantinga to account for everyone who *claims* not to have the SD without retreating from his position that it is universally imbued. Everyone manifests the SD, he claims, except those who don't.[109]

This is called having your cake and eating it, too, which is another way to describe special pleading. Besides negating God's omnipotence, Plantinga redefines the SD to effectively render the hypothesis unfalsifiable. If you feel an intuitive sense of God, then that counts as evidence for the SD. If you don't, then that just means there's something wrong with you because you don't share the SD. With this unfalsifiable version "established," Plantinga uses it to argue that knowledge of God is properly basic and should be assumed without evidence before beginning any religious argument. Plantinga maintains that if the SD is real, then beliefs formed through it would likewise be warranted and must be considered *knowledge* without further justification. The SD is a form of a priori knowledge not based on experience but on intuition. This conflicts with the evidentialist view that the reliability of all "knowledge" exists on a continuum in direct proportion to the quantity and quality of supporting empirical evidence. Though there is no evidence that sin can impair one's inner SD "God detector," as Plantinga claims, it seems there is substantial historical evidence that piety can impair one's inner BS detector.

Plantinga also modifies the definition of the SD in another important way. Rather than the SD providing knowledge of the *Christian God*, he claims it simply necessitates an intuitive sense of something "godlike," such as a personal supernatural force that pervades existence—something greater than us. This allows Plantinga to use the followers of many contradictory religions and denominations as supporting evidence—even "new-agers" who identify with no particular organized religion. Essentially, Plantinga argues that the common tendency of humans to gravitate toward religion and spirituality *in general* is evidence for the Christian God in particular.

Plantinga's argument conveniently ignores that most claims of competing religions, and even many denominations within their religions, are mutually exclusive. Plantinga never convincingly explains how an innate tendency toward a religion that denies the existence of the Christian God is evidence *for the Christian God*. What possible reason could God have for imbuing those He wishes to follow Him with a strong sense to believe in and follow other gods, especially where such belief precludes belief in Him? In seeking to make SD more plausible, Plantinga succeeds only in making it laughably nonsensical.

Another apologist who relies heavily on this line of reasoning is William Lane Craig. Dr. Craig often acknowledges that his faith is ultimately based not on any objective evidence for God but on a strong feeling he has that

God exists. Dr. Craig refers to this, circularly, as the "internal witness of the Holy Spirit," which he describes as a "kind of elevating feeling of blessed assurance . . . that one is rightly related to God."[110] To Dr. Craig, this "self-authenticating" feeling is a trump card that can single-handedly deflect any evidence proffered against it. "It doesn't matter what you show me," Craig can say, "because I know it to be true in my heart." Craig's position is the very definition of closed-mindedness. Craig is basically saying that if the feeling causes him to believe it is coming from God, then it must be. But there is simply no way for Dr. Craig, or any other Christian, to know this. There are countless naturalistic explanations for "transcendent" feelings, so no one can say with reasonable certainty they arise from any supernatural source.

It is true that religion and spirituality have been common features of cultures throughout recorded history. It is also true that many people intuitively feel there is an intangible personal force at work in the world directing and influencing things. But as I pointed out previously, human intuitions, even widespread ones, often do not reflect reality. The question that comes to mind is whether there is a plausible explanation for these widespread intuitions that does not require the existence of a God. There is.

Human brains evolved two specific traits that aided our survival but can also be detrimental in constructing accurate models of the world. The first is pattern recognition—the ability to make sense of apparent randomness and to separate potentially meaningful patterns from their less meaningful surroundings. A prehistoric man hunting a wild animal would be aided greatly by the ability to identify areas of the landscape in which the natural layout was interrupted by unique signs of recent activity. This would make it far easier to track the animal back to its lair and kill it. Likewise, the ability to identify the eyes and face of a predator under cover of the forest, because they break an otherwise familiar pattern, would help ancient man stay alive in the presence of constant danger. This same ability to recognize and distinguish faces would aid primitive man in distinguishing friend from foe and the aggressive from the passive, even within his own species and tribe, leading to the formation of cohesive groups.

The second trait conferring a significant survival advantage is agency detection. An agent is anything capable of intention, which in our world would be other living creatures. The ability to distinguish a living creature from an inanimate object would be crucial both in hunting prey to eat and avoiding being eaten oneself. Those incapable of distinguishing fish from rocks would make few contributions to the genetic pool.

An interesting feature of both these traits is selective evolutionary pressure toward overinclusiveness. The survival advantages of an overactive detecting mechanism far outweigh its disadvantages. Failing to identify a pattern or agency that existed was far more dangerous than mistakenly identifying a pattern or agency that didn't. Assume, for example, that you are a caveman and mistakenly conclude an unexpected sound is a predator when in fact it is merely the wind rustling the branches. There would be no harm done, and you would probably forget the incident almost instantly. But assume instead that you incorrectly conclude the sound is a rustling branch, but it is instead a hungry tiger. That's the type of mistake that could wipe out your bloodline early.

Due to these selective pressures, humans developed brains overactive in both pattern recognition and agency detection, something that has been repeatedly confirmed through psychological studies. Our brains are hardwired to find patterns and to assign agency, *even when they aren't there*. It has developed a bias toward false positives. One interesting and well-documented result of the former is pareidolia, a tendency to attribute meaning or significance, such as human faces or familiar objects, to random but visually ambiguous visual stimuli. As Carl Sagan writes,

> As soon as the infant can see, it recognizes faces, and we now know that this skill is hardwired in our brains. Those infants who a million years ago were unable to recognize a face smiled back less, were less likely to win the hearts of their parents, and less likely to prosper. These days, nearly every infant is quick to recognize a human face, and to respond with a goony grin.[111]

This explains why so many people see faces in clouds, rock formations on Mars, and even slices of toast.

Hyperactive agency detection (HAD) is a natural result of our brains erring on the side of caution throughout our evolutionary history. As a result, people improperly ascribe commonly occurring events to the behavior of nonexistent intentional agents. Even today, it is natural for people to intuitively feel fear when they hear a strange sound at night, as if the sound were caused by an intelligent agent, even when but a moment's reflection allows them to acknowledge less-threatening and far more plausible alternatives, such as creaking boards. HAD helps to explain why so many people believe in ghosts. Along with hyperactive pattern recognition, it also explains why so many people accept conspiracy theories. A series of unrelated events will never seem as compelling an explanation to our intuitions as the intentional work of purposeful agents.

Because of our common human experience, the most likely candidate for an unknown purposeful agent will be a human, or at least a being with very humanlike qualities. Philosopher David Hume recognized the following in the late 1700s:

> There is a universal tendency among mankind to conceive all beings like themselves, and to transfer to every object, those qualities, with which they are familiarly acquainted, and of which they are intimately conscious. We find human faces in the moon, armies in the clouds; and by a natural propensity, if not corrected by experience and reflection, ascribe malice or goodwill to everything, that hurts or pleases us.[112]

From what we know of psychology, it is unsurprising so many religions have anthropomorphized natural forces and objects like lightning, thunder, drought, and fertility into gods. As I discuss later in this book, that is how the Christian God started, as part of a pantheon of humanlike gods representing the forces of nature.

No one can doubt it is common for people to experience feelings of awe and wonder that seem to transcend ordinary, everyday experience. The real questions are how we interpret these feelings and to what do we attribute them. Every interpretation depends on our cultural upbringing. The religious are likely to interpret the experience through the lens of their faith as evidence for transcendent gods. The nonreligious are unlikely to come to the same conclusions. That these experiences lead us all in different directions should tell us they shouldn't be considered evidence for anything in particular in the real world.

Many scientists have concluded that belief in gods is an evolutionary by-product of our hyperactive agent detection and pattern recognition. Our brains are hardwired to find patterns in chance events and assign personal meaning to them, so that they relate specifically to us. They are likewise hardwired to posit agents behind these events with humanlike thoughts and emotions. These biases explain why many of us want and expect the course of events to be divinely guided. It is merely our prehistorically evolved intuitions leading us astray.

And so it is with gods and God. One raised a Christian would interpret his or her intuitive sense of agency in the forces of nature as evidence of the Christian God. Adherents of other religions do the same, confirming the beliefs their parents taught them as children. But there is no justification for treating this sense as evidence of either. It is merely an illusion developed through the process of natural selection, one far from surprising, given naturalism.

THE POPULARITY OF CHRISTIANITY

> If we go back to the beginning, we shall find that ignorance and fear created the gods; that fancy, enthusiasm, or deceit adorned them; that weakness worships them; that credulity preserves them and that custom, respect and tyranny support them in order to make the blindness of men serve their own interests. If the ignorance of nature gave birth to gods, the knowledge of nature is calculated to destroy them.
>
> —Baron D'Holbach, *The System of Nature* (1770)

Another argument is so related to the SD that I include it immediately afterward. It is that the very popularity of Christianity is evidence for its truth. In other words, if God doesn't exist, then why do so many people believe in Him, and if Jesus wasn't God, then why are so many people Christians?

It is true that Christianity can claim more worldwide followers than any other religion, but this can't be considered a legitimate argument for its validity.[113] It is instead a textbook example of the argument from popularity. To say an idea is popular is simply to say it has ignited the public's interest, which can occur for many reasons. An idea that has remained popular for many generations across many cultures can plausibly be said to have broad intuitive appeal, along with perhaps an effective marketing campaign, but that doesn't make the idea any more likely to be true.

What determines which beliefs survive the test of time? A crucial factor is the utility of that belief. Does it assist the organism to survive and propagate? Truth is certainly relevant to utility, but it is not the only factor, and sometimes can even be detrimental. Studies have shown, for example, that people who overestimate their own abilities and prospects are more successful than those with more accurate self-evaluations. Donald Trump is surely not as good at everything as he thinks he is, but his inflated self-assessment has clearly been a major factor in his success. Overconfidence can become a self-fulfilling prophecy.

The most successful beliefs are self-replicating. In other words, there is something about the content of the beliefs that make them more likely to flourish. An example would be the belief that having children is beneficial. If you don't share this belief, then your genetic material is probably making its farewell performance. Another is a belief that includes the importance of teaching that belief to one's children or that one should engage in regular reinforcement of that belief or form social networks to reinforce the belief. Religion fits these requirements perfectly, regardless of its accuracy.

The allure of Christianity is, furthermore, completely understandable given human psychology. The religion has certain unique elements, some present from the beginning and others developed over time, that have given it broad marketing appeal and a major competitive advantage. Comparing Christianity to other religions is beyond the scope of this book, so I focus instead on comparing the intuitive appeal of Christianity with that of naturalism and providing other reasons for the popularity of the religion.

A. Christianity's History of Conquest and Political Power

> Here commences a new dominion acquired with a title by divine right. Ships are sent with the first opportunity; the natives driven out or destroyed; their princes tortured to discover their gold; a free license given to all acts of inhumanity and lust, the earth reeking with the blood of its inhabitants: and this execrable crew of butchers, employed in so pious an expedition, is a modern colony, sent to convert and civilize an idolatrous and barbarous people!
>
> —Jonathan Swift, *Gulliver's Travels*

> They came with the Bible and their religion, stole our land, crushed our spirit, and now they tell us we should be thankful to the Lord for being saved.
>
> —Chief Pontiac

Many Americans have grown up with Christianity as the norm. They argue it could not have become the dominant American religion without divine assistance. This view ignores the very human history of brutal and bloody conquest by which Christianity gained its position atop the heap.

Christianity started from humble roots as a fringe and occasionally persecuted sect, but that all changed in 320 CE with the conversion of Holy Roman Emperor Constantine. Some apologists claim that Christianity grew exponentially prior to Constantine's conversion, but the support for such a claim is virtually nonexistent. The evidence reveals that while Paul and other Christian missionaries succeeded in starting Christian communities in several cities bordering the Mediterranean Sea, those communities remained quite small. Throughout this period, Christians represented an insignificant cult, probably numbering no more than several thousand people (less than a fraction of 1 percent of the Roman Empire) prior to 320. After that date, however, everything changed dramatically.

First, Emperor Constantine bestowed official recognition upon Christianity, ending all persecutions. One of Constantine's successors, Theodosius, made Christianity the official religion of the empire, after which his son commissioned the Theodosian Code, which legislated competing religions out of existence. Thereafter, pagan temples were torn down or repurposed as Christian churches. From that point onward, Christian rulers systematically tortured and killed those following other religions. It was now the Christians doing the persecuting. This continued for more than a thousand years. The largest repositories of pagan literature and art, such as the library of Alexandria, were destroyed. Likewise eradicated were the works of early Christians who disagreed with the orthodoxy of the day.

The Crusades of the Middle Ages saw the military enforcement of Christianity against other cultures, such as the Jews, Muslims, and remaining European pagans. Hundreds of thousands of non-Christians were slaughtered by Christian soldiers on orders from the pope. The Inquisitions saw official enforcement throughout Europe of conformity with the "correct" Christian beliefs. To openly identify as anything other than a committed Orthodox Christian meant certain torture or death for most inhabitants of Western Europe for hundreds of years. Rather than relying on the persuasive strength of their arguments, Christian leaders spread and maintained their religion through force, intimidation, and subjugation. Their methods were extremely effective.

Once the Europeans arrived in the Americas, they brought their religion with them and once again enforced its adoption by force. They were guided by a papal bull issued in 1452 CE, forty years before Columbus set foot in the Americas. The church mandate declared war on all non-Christians throughout the world and specifically sanctioned and promoted the conquest, colonization, and exploitation of non-Christian nations and their territories. Christians were directed to put all non-Christians "into perpetual slavery" and "to take all their possessions and property."[114] This directive, by which indigenous people were classified as the lawful spoils of their Christian conquerors, became known as the discovery doctrine.

The discovery doctrine and related concept of manifest destiny legitimized Western expansion and the rape, pillage, displacement, and slaughter of Native Americans, who were required to adopt Christianity or die.[115] This started with Christopher Columbus himself, who, in addition to his widespread torture, rape, and murder of the Native population, set the stage for the African slave trade, writing, "Let us in the name of the Holy Trinity go on sending all the slaves that can be sold."[116] According to Ward

Churchill, a professor of ethnic studies at the University of Colorado, the reduction of the North American population from about 12 million in 1500 to barely 237,000 in 1900, a death toll of more than 98 percent, represents a "vast genocide . . . the most sustained on record."[117] In 1992, the National Council of Churches acknowledged as much by adopting a resolution criticizing the European conquest, driven by Christian doctrine, for causing the "slavery and genocide" of the Native people.

Those Native Americans who survived the European genocide were isolated on reservations. On a massive scale, their children were taken from them and placed into Christian boarding schools. There, they received military-style discipline and Christian indoctrination to "kill the Indian in the child," a practice labeled by the Canadian Truth and Reconciliation Commission "cultural genocide." Until 1935, traditional non-Christian religions were banned on reservations, and Native Americans practicing their religious beliefs could be fined and sent to prison. Even after 1935, many traditional religious rituals remained illegal. Christianity was simultaneously forced on the Native Americans by missionaries. It took a special act of Congress, the 1978 American Indian Religious Freedom Act, to affirm religious freedom for the Native nations. In 2009, the US government passed a resolution formally apologizing for its treatment of Native Americans.[118] In 2015, Pope Francis finally acknowledged openly the church's widespread atrocities against indigenous people during the colonization of the Americas. He sought forgiveness, on behalf of the church, for the "grave sins committed against the native peoples of America in the name of God" and for the "pain and suffering" caused by the church throughout the conquest of the Americas.[119]

Not surprisingly, given its bloodstained history of intimidation and persecution both inside and outside the Americas, Christianity was very successful.

B. The Need for Certainty, Simplicity, Understanding, and Closure

> Doubt is not a pleasant condition, but certainty is an absurd one.
>
> —Voltaire, Letter to Prince Frederick William
> of Prussia (28 November 1770)

Many psychological studies have demonstrated that people are uncomfortable with ambiguity and with their own ignorance. As the *New Yorker* reported in 2013,

The human mind is incredibly averse to uncertainty and ambiguity; from an early age, we respond to uncertainty or lack of clarity by spontaneously generating plausible explanations. What's more, we hold on to these invented explanations as having intrinsic value of their own. Once we have them, we don't like to let them go. In 1972, the psychologist Jerome Kagan posited that uncertainty resolution was one of the foremost determinants of our behavior. When we can't immediately gratify our desire to know, we become highly motivated to reach a concrete explanation. That motivation, in Kagan's conception, lies at the heart of most other common motives: achievement, affiliation, power, and the like. We want to eliminate the distress of the unknown. We want, in other words, to achieve "cognitive closure."[120]

Christianity meets these needs. If you buy into Christianity fully, then the world becomes a much simpler place in which off-the-shelf answers are available to otherwise tough or unanswerable questions. How did the universe begin? God made it. How did we get here? God made us. Why are we here? To serve and worship God. There is no need to look further. If it can't be readily explained, then the question can be safely shelved because God has chosen for it to remain a mystery. In either event, we can stop racking our brains for answers. Of course, for reasons already discussed, "God did it" isn't really an explanation. It provides no real intellectual understanding. But that isn't the point because for many, it *feels as though it does*. And it is this emotional feeling that punches the right buttons. It provides closure.

Naturalism fails to provide the same cognitive comfort. The explanations of science are often counterintuitive and require specialized knowledge to understand. For example, the Christian explanation of how the universe began, why it exists, and how it will end can be given in five minutes. Any attempt at a naturalistic explanation would require at least a rudimentary understanding of theoretical physics, which takes years to acquire. Scientific explanations are not always simple or elegant. Many scientific questions still lack definitive answers, and the answers we have remain provisional and continually subject to reevaluation.

In argument, the person who appears certain of her position and can explain it simply and intuitively always has a rhetorical advantage over those who can't, as Donald Trump's opponents discovered in the 2016 Republican primary. The nature of science makes naturalism a much tougher sell for this reason alone. People intuitively but incorrectly correlate reliability and accuracy with certainty—a simple certainty naturalism can never provide. Scientists openly acknowledge their limitations and qualify their conclusions, for it is doubt rather than certainty that drives science. However intellectually defensible this may be, doubt doesn't make for a compelling argument in the culture wars. Doubt is most often the subject of ridicule.

C. The Need for Coherence

[T]he main thing that I learned about conspiracy theories is that conspiracy theorists actually believe in the conspiracy because that is more comforting. The truth of the world is that it is chaotic. The truth is, that it is not the Jewish banking conspiracy, or the grey aliens, or the twelve-foot reptiloids from another dimension that are in control, the truth is far more frightening; no-one is in control, the world is rudderless.

—Alan Moore, *The Mindscape of Alan Moore*

An exceptionally strong cognitive bias common to all humans is the need for coherence. It is incredibly important to us that explanations fit together in a consistent and readily understandable way. Our minds strongly, though mistakenly, correlate coherence with truth. They prefer a *seemingly* coherent story over the alternative and will almost always ignore objective evidence supporting the accuracy of claim A over claim B if claim B allows for a story that seems to make more sense. We all possess a strong systemic bias for claims suggesting coherence over those that don't.

As appealing as this relationship seems, it is fallacious. Given enough time and imagination, anyone can generate a coherent story from just about any set of random facts. The coherence of that story says nothing, however, about its truth. For examples, we need only look to thousands of myths created by long-dead religions. Those religions provided stories that were internally consistent yet are recognized by virtually every living person today to be false. Given this logic, the Bible proves the existence of God just as the *Odyssey* proves the existence of Odysseus or *Star Wars* proves the existence of Darth Vader. While incoherence does suggest falsity, the reverse is not necessarily true. Coherence is just one of many necessary conditions for reasonably believing a story to be true. Though necessary to an accurate worldview, however, it is by no means sufficient.

Christians have had two thousand years and a great deal of incentive to develop a coherent theological narrative around their Scripture. There have been many wrong turns and dead ends along this path, but a strong narrative did eventually emerge and gain powerful cultural traction. As discussed elsewhere, modern science and archeology have discredited many foundations for this narrative. But given its prodigious momentum, the narrative itself remains robust.

Naturalism, by contrast, lacks a narrative of comparable coherence. It relies on science, which is merely descriptive. Science observes and seeks to explain an incredibly complex and chaotic universe piece by piece. Naturalists, like Christians, experience a sense of awe when confronted by the beauty of nature, but while Christians interpret this as consistent with a narratively compelling story, naturalists do not. While naturalists hope (and justifiably expect) a coherent global narrative will one day come together, that is likely a long way off. Meanwhile, Christianity will maintain a strong intuitive advantage over naturalism based on our inherent cognitive biases alone. People prefer coherence. People prefer certainty. Christianity provides both.

D. The Satisfaction of Emotional Needs

> Religion is an illusion and it derives its strength from the fact that it falls in with our instinctual desires.
>
> —Sigmund Freud, *New Introductory Lectures on Psychoanalysis* (1933)

Perhaps the greatest advantage of Christianity is the way it satisfies powerful emotional needs, such as the need for purpose, the desire for justice, and the relief from the fear of death. Christianity provides responses that are highly comforting. We are special, the crown jewel of Creation, made by a perfect God in His own divine image.[121] We have a clear and common noble purpose: to help God usher in a kingdom of everlasting happiness. The wicked will be punished, and the good, rewarded, if not in this life, then the next. And we will never truly die. Our souls will live on forever, to be reunited with all our loved ones for eternity. As Mark Twain observes, "Man is a marvelous curiosity. . . . [H]e thinks he is the Creator's pet. . . . [H]e even believes the Creator loves him; has a passion for him; sits up nights to admire him; yes and watch over him and keep him out of trouble. He prays to him and thinks he listens. Isn't it a quaint idea?"[122]

Humans thrive on validation. We all want our lives to be meaningful and exceptional. That is why we work so hard to stand out and gain recognition and approval of family; friends; complete strangers; and, in the case of believers, God. Every trophy, degree, or autographed photo or selfie with a celebrity is a testament to our uniqueness. We display them to remind others how special we are. The idea that we will someday cease to exist and ultimately be completely forgotten, with every trace of our existence erased, is extremely disturbing.

Christianity has evolved to meet human emotional needs very effectively. It provides certainty in a world teeming with ambiguity, relieving believers from dealing with often difficult shades of gray. It offers ready answers to otherwise tough or unanswerable questions. For many, it validates their very existence by assuring them they are far more than just intelligent animals. It provides comforting rituals to mark life's transitions; satisfaction for the human desires for justice and purpose; and, crucially, an escape from the fear and finality of death. Many would agree with William Craig that, "If there is no God, then man and the universe are doomed. Like prisoners condemned to death, we await our unavoidable execution. There is no God, and there is no immortality. And what is the consequence of this? It means that life itself is absurd. It means that the life we have is without ultimate significance, value, or purpose."[123] Craig believes, like many, that a "universe without moral accountability and devoid of value is unimaginably terrible."[124] The Christian's emotional investment in maintaining a worldview committed to the contrary is likely to increase exponentially each year closer to death.

For atheists, the story is very different. From a naturalistic worldview, we must assign purpose and meaning to our own lives.[125] There is no ultimate reconciliation of rights and wrongs, leaving injustice often unredressed. And our deaths represent the end of all we are or ever were. For many, these are troubling implications, likely to discourage those contemplating leaving Christianity for intellectual reasons. Many ex-Christians have reported years of living with a worldview they found increasingly indefensible simply to avoid the emotional discomfort they expected if they abandoned it. Those who strongly desire their lives to have meaning and purpose on a cosmic scale, for instance, and cannot imagine how that is possible without God have a potent incentive to hang onto their belief or at least the pretense of it. There is, furthermore, an endorphin rush that comes with being part of a crowd with a common purpose. Weekly visits to church reinforce this feeling, with the added benefits of providing a sense of metaphysical certainty and moral superiority.

If you think about it, however, the Christian's incorporation of purpose isn't that comforting. Is living life according to someone else's plan really more fulfilling than living life according to a plan that fits you? When Christians talk about the joys of handing their lives over to God or of letting Jesus "take the wheel," I want to ask them why they consider this to be so desirable. I can't help but feel they have forfeited an essential part of what makes them unique for a pedestrian role in someone else's drama. The ultimate purpose provided by Christianity is to serve God—the same purpose as a slave. The Christian view is that we serve and must profess eternal loyalty to a mercurial master known to slaughter all His subjects for the most trivial of offenses. The atheist worldview, by contrast, is that we are our own masters, creating our own purposes in life based on our unique qualities and experiences. Being in control and creating one's own purpose can be a scary thought, but ultimately, which is more appealing?

And what of guilt? Each of us falls short of our own standards from time to time. Each of us gives in occasionally to anger or fear or plain laziness. Many Christians see these struggles with their own desires and natures as part of the cosmic war with Satan, who is always working behind the scenes to tempt them away from God. Without the cosmic scapegoat of Satan, these people might have to take responsibility for their own actions. They might have to change their ingrained destructive habits on their own rather than just pray about it.

One might validly point out that the comforts Christianity provides are solutions to problems created by its own narrative. Christianity teaches us that we are born corrupted with a stain of sin we cannot remove without supernatural aid, that we are doomed to a meaningless existence in this life and an eternity of horrific torture in the next if we do not follow the Bible's directives, and that we are locked in a daily struggle with evil forces intent on leading us to destruction that we are ultimately powerless to resist without God's help. Even if false, however, once that narrative has been learned and deeply ingrained in one's worldview, that comfort is no less real.

I strongly suspect that the greatest obstacle to people leaving Christianity behind is the fear of death. There may be no stronger motivator for humanity than avoiding death. We collectively spend billions each year just trying to delay it, extending our earthly stay a little longer. Psychologists have long recognized the elaborate coping mechanisms humans use to manage their thoughts about death, which could otherwise become a constant, paralyzing terror.

Christianity takes mankind's most visceral fear head-on, offering a vision whereby death loses its sting. In Christianity, death represents merely a change in state and, for the believer, a magnificent *promotion* to an eternity of blissful happiness. Christianity offers a chance, in the afterlife, to reunite with lost friends and loved ones, who are never truly gone. This has often throughout history resulted in Christian martyrdom or even suicide, demonstrating that commitment to these beliefs can even render death *attractive*. Once one has bought into that view, it is difficult to let go.

As with purpose, however, further reflection may suggest this idea is not as appealing as it first appears. Would it really be that great to live forever?

There must be a limit to the number of experiences a disembodied soul could have. What happens once you've done them all a trillion times? Would the next trillion be just as satisfying? Would you not feel deprived of challenges, of hardship overcome, of loss, of failure, and of all the ways those experiences make us grow? As philanthropist John Shedd observes, "A ship in harbor is safe—but that is not what ships are for."[126]

Or would you spend all eternity endlessly praising God? Does that sound like fun? How much time would you spend mourning those friends and family members who didn't make it to Heaven but instead are, every moment, experiencing horrific tortures in Hell? Or would God magically render you pleased with their torment so as not to interrupt your bliss? Would you live out eternity as one of Odysseus's crew in the land of the Lotus Eaters? As Deepak Chopra acknowledged on the *Colbert Report*, "In [H]eaven, you would be doomed to eternal senility."[127]

But even if it is all rainbows and butterflies and that is to your liking, to accept any worldview simply because it is more appealing is to fall prey to the fallacious argument from final consequences. What sounds most appealing is no more likely to be true. Being an adult often means facing up to reality, even when that reality might be unpleasant. This is crucial because only by accepting how the world is will we work to make it better. To hold out for an afterlife that may never come often means neglecting the present, which may ultimately be all we have.

There is absolutely no good evidence that people's lives conform to any divine plan or that any form of existence transcends death. Accepting these as truths may initially be hard, but it can ultimately yield great benefit, both individually and for society. Contrary to Dr. Craig's dire conclusions, the lack of external meaning can grant us freedom to set goals that are individually meaningful to us. And acknowledging death forces us to maximize and fully enjoy the time we have, knowing that our lives are uniquely valuable precisely because they have an expiration date.

E. Cognitive Biases

> The most difficult subjects can be explained to the most slow-witted man if he has not formed any idea of them already; but the simplest thing cannot be made clear to the most intelligent man if he is firmly persuaded that he knows already, without a shadow of doubt, what is laid before him.
>
> —Leo Tolstoy, *"The Kingdom of God Is within You":*
> *Christianity Not as a Mystic Religion but as a New Theory of Life*

Christianity is perfectly adapted to take advantage of certain flaws in human decision making. These flaws, known as cognitive biases, systematically predispose us all to certain patterns of thinking that do not necessarily correspond to reality. We all, for example, have a need for cognitive closure. It is uncomfortable to leave open big issues like "Why are we here?" even when clear answers are virtually impossible to come by. Our minds push us to land on some belief so we can move on. Unfortunately, this can lead us to positions we can't intellectually defend. As Bertrand Russell notes, "Man is a credulous animal, and must believe something; in the absence of good grounds for belief, he will be satisfied with bad ones."[128]

One of the most powerful human predispositions is confirmation bias: the tendency to selectively filter new information based on whether it supports or undermines one's existing views and thus to believe what we find comforting. A major factor supporting confirmation bias is the human desire to avoid what is known as cognitive dissonance: the unpleasant anxiety and tension associated with trying to hold two inconsistent positions simultaneously. This leads to motivated reasoning: the tendency to scrutinize ideas inconsistent with existing beliefs more carefully and skeptically than those that are consistent. These three biases acting together lead us to easily and noncritically accept information that confirms our opinions while ignoring, distrusting, or outright rejecting information that challenges them.

A related source of cognitive waywardness is congruence bias. This is the tendency to look only at hypotheses that support our existing views and failing to consider those that don't. The classic example is the researcher who gives subjects the number sequence "2, 4, 6"; tells them this sequence follows a particular rule; and instructs them to identify that rule. Most respond by quickly deciding that the rule is "numbers ascending by 2," testing only sequences concordant with this rule, such as "3, 5, 7." While this sequence does follow the experimenter's rule, "numbers ascending by 2" is not *the rule*. It turns out that by testing other sequences, such as 9, 14, 52, the subjects would have learned these fit the rule as well, for the actual rule is simply to list ascending numbers. Once finding a sequence that works, most are loathe to test it further or to attempt to invalidate it, leading them to the wrong answer.

Rather than incorporating controls to guard against such biases, as science does, Christianity adds fuel to the fire. The concept of faith justifies ignoring or discounting troubling information. Analysis of noncongruent hypotheses, such as other religious claims equally supported by many of the arguments of Christian apologists, is actively discouraged as potentially corrosive to Christian belief. The Bible itself counsels strongly against listening to any views that might lead the believer astray. Unlike in science, there are no systemic checks within the Christian worldview designed to challenge previously accepted beliefs, leaving cognitive biases to run roughshod in a self-reinforcing loop.

F. Childhood Indoctrination

> Give me a child until he is seven and I will give you the man.
>
> —Jesuit motto, attributed to founder of the Jesuit order

> We will never have the media on our side. . . . We will never have the elite, smart people on our side. . . . American values will always be sustained through two institutions—the church and the family.
>
> —Rick Santorum, Republican presidential candidate

Few, if any, Christians come to their faith through reasoned, logical arguments. The vast majority are born into Christian families and indoctrinated into the religion well before the age of reason. Most can't recall a time they didn't consider themselves Christian. It becomes an integral part of their identity from their earliest memories. Christianity becomes their tribe. Most Christians will thereafter associate primarily with other Christians.

Christianity, like many religions, places a strong emphasis on bringing children into the faith at the earliest possible age. This is long before the age that children think through things rationally and independently. It is instead the time they are most receptive to ideas from such authoritarian figures as parents and teachers. The child's Christian faith and identity will typically be reinforced regularly through attendance at weekly Sunday school and church services. Rarely if ever do they hear opposing viewpoints, and simply hearing the same things repeatedly without contradiction will burrow the belief more deeply. For some, doctrines of Heaven and Hell instill internal rewards for belief and fears for thinking too critically about the faith.

As Christian children grow, strong psychological influences, such as confirmation bias, cognitive dissonance, and the need for coherence and personal consistency, erect formidable barriers to opposing views. Also at play is the sunk-cost fallacy, which occurs when one has incurred a cost that cannot be recovered and doubles down on that position to avoid the psychological impact of acknowledging the loss. None of these represent volitional mental processes. All operate behind the scenes of conscious awareness.

No one can be blamed for being strongly predisposed to Christianity (or any other religion) and holding onto such beliefs. It is just how our minds work. And after a while, the mind naturally erects barriers to protect these beliefs. As Carl Sagan observes, "One of the saddest lessons of history is this: If we've been bamboozled long enough, we tend to reject any evidence of the bamboozle. We're no longer interested in finding out the truth. The bamboozle has captured us. It's simply too painful to acknowledge, even to ourselves, that we've been taken. Once you give a charlatan power over you, you almost never get it back."[129]

By the time a cradle Christian reaches adulthood, the inertia behind his belief is enormous. He probably sees it as an integral part of his identity and also as highly useful. Why would such a person actively seek to challenge his worldview? Under these circumstances, it is rational to continue believing as he has always done.

There is no comparable process for atheism. As discussed elsewhere, atheism does not represent a worldview that even could be taught. To the extent naturalism could be called a worldview, it represents more a commitment to a process rather than any particular set of conclusions. There is no doctrine. There is no church or Sunday school—no systematic indoctrination. The focus of naturalists is likely to be on freethinking and rational inquiry, which can lead in many directions. These are not qualities that lead to followers, causing many to compare organizing atheists to herding cats.

Perhaps the most important aspect of childhood indoctrination is that it provides the norm by which everything else is thereafter measured. It establishes Christianity as the base belief system, presumptively setting the challenge for competing beliefs to knock it off the mountain, something very difficult to do if their arguments are no more compelling. Marketers selling everything from soda to cigarettes have long recognized the value of establishing strong brand loyalty as early as possible. If you begin as a Marlboro toddler, bombarded with prosmoking images, cigarette companies know you are far more likely to become a Marlboro man and to remain so until lung cancer cuts your life short. Meanwhile, you are far less likely to give competing products a fair chance.

G. Social Acceptance

Humans are social animals that live their lives within communities. We depend on others for support, guidance, conversation, and many other things. Our professional fortunes are almost universally governed by how others—bosses, customers, coworkers—perceive us. Social acceptance is crucial for both our personal and professional well-being. Even if we are personally comfortable with social or professional rejection, we must consider the effects such rejection will have on our spouses and our children.

Christianity is the dominant religion in many countries, including the United States. In such countries, it represents the social norm. Psychology tells us that anyone professing Christianity in a predominantly Christian country will enjoy the many benefits of tribal acceptance. We would expect to see the opposite for those perceived to have rejected Christianity, and that is just what we see.

Public opinion polls have consistently revealed widespread distrust and rejection of atheists within the United States. I use the example of atheists because most Christians I've met do not consider the followers of other religions to have rejected Christianity, as they consider atheists. They find common cause with the followers of other religions because they are involved in a common project of pursuing spiritual truths through faith and acceptance of the supernatural. Atheists reject the entire paradigm employed by the alliance of the faithful.

A 2006 survey by the University of Minnesota put atheists atop the list of minorities considered least American, least desirable to join one's family through marriage, and least acceptable as political candidates.[130] President George H. W. Bush told the president of the American Atheist Press he didn't think atheists should be considered patriots *or even citizens*.[131] Forty percent of Americans said they would refuse to vote for an otherwise qualified presidential candidate *simply because he was an atheist*, the lowest of any religious affiliation.[132] In other studies, participants equated the trustworthiness of atheists with rapists.[133] Several commentators, referring to consistent poll data over the last fifty years, recognize atheists to be the "most hated" group (religious or nonreligious) in the United States.[134]

Not surprisingly, polls also reveal that those with no belief in God are hesitant to label themselves as atheists, even anonymously. In a 2007 survey from the Pew Forum on Religion and Public Life, only 1.6 percent identified themselves as atheist, while a Gallup poll taken the same year showed 7 percent of respondents stating they did not believe in God.[135] As discussed, there should be no difference in these numbers because they represent the same position, the only difference being that the first requires acceptance of a maligned label. Atheism continues to carry a powerful social stigma. This stigma undermines the happiness and flourishing of nonbelievers in countries with religious social norms because they are not free to openly acknowledge their beliefs.[136]

Where Christianity represents the social norm and atheists are widely distrusted and demonized, massive incentives are in place to identify as Christian. We would expect the forces of social conformity to act as a dam preventing Christians from publicly crossing the divide over to atheism. The wide spectrum of belief among Christian denominations allows Christians who have lost their faith to slip into more liberal denominations without abandoning their identity as Christians. Social conformity also results in gross underrepresentation of the actual number of nonbelievers, perpetuating negative stereotypes of atheists as extreme outliers.

Some studies have shown believers to be happier or more adjusted than nonbelievers. It is not clear how this represents an argument for Christianity because, as recognized by George Bernard Shaw, the "fact that a believer is happier than a skeptic is no more to the point than the fact that a drunken man is happier than a sober one. The happiness of credulity is a cheap and dangerous quality."[137] Nevertheless, it is important to point out that these studies do not suggest that Christian belief leads to greater happiness.

Instead, they demonstrate that any happiness benefits associated with Christianity result from the establishment and leverage of an in-group/out-group hierarchy in predominantly Christian countries. Where Christianity represents the social norm, those belonging to that in-group are accorded many benefits, to the detriment of the out-groups. This can be why many Christians see their way of life as superior—because in their communities, Christians enjoy many social advantages that are very real, even if no more than historical inheritances. In Muslim communities, Muslims enjoy the same type of advantages. We should expect that in communities of nonbelievers, the flow of in-group benefits would be reversed. This says nothing, therefore, about the inherent legitimacy of any particular belief system.

Contributing to the river of social acceptance carrying Christianity downstream is the paradigm supported by both the liberal Left and conservative Right (though for different reasons) of exempting religion from public criticism. Anyone raising the slightest objection to a religious claim or belief is reflexively vilified as a bigot, regardless of the potential merits of their claim. No other subject can claim such protection. This allows religious claims, and only religious claims, to go unchecked and unrebutted whenever made, giving them a patina of legitimacy they have never earned.

Nonreligion, furthermore, is not evangelical like many forms of religion. There is no call to convert. The nonreligious rarely push their views about religion on others. Most simply don't think about religion because it isn't a part of their lives. Also, due to the stigma attached to being atheist or agnostic, most do not speak publicly of their lack of belief. The public gets a false sense there is no real dissent from the religious views of the majority.

H. Cultural Momentum and Tradition

> A long habit of not thinking a thing *wrong*, gives it a superficial appearance of being *right*, and raises at first a formidable outcry in defense of custom.
>
> —Thomas Paine, Common Sense

The long-term acceptance of Christianity throughout the Western world has provided it a strong cultural momentum. Christian language and symbolism are tightly interwoven into much of American society, just as such common words as faith are loaded with unique meanings derived from centuries of Christian writings and teachings. The general familiarity of Americans with Christianity lends it a protective varnish against critical inquiry. Beliefs that might seem bizarre if held by a new or unfamiliar religious group rate no second glance in America, where Christianity is ubiquitous.

These factors render American Christianity into a massive glacier, crawling slowly but steadily across the land. Having grown up with that glacier always visible, most Americans hardly notice it anymore. Even strange and unusual features are ultimately taken for granted. Its very familiarity makes it seem comfortable and unthreatening. People are likely to think, "It's always been there and has done no harm. Why should I be concerned now?" It has become so massive, its inertia so great, that no single blow can appreciably affect its progress.

Christianity has become a national myth rooted in beliefs that went largely unchallenged for hundreds of years. It is an intellectual comfort food that affects our tastes for everything else at the table. But this food is far from harmless. As John F. Kennedy observed, "The great enemy of truth is very often not the lie—deliberate, contrived and dishonest—but the myth—persistent, persuasive and unrealistic. Too often we hold fast to the clichés of our forebears. We subject all facts to a prefabricated set of interpretations. We enjoy the comfort of opinion without the discomfort of thought."[138]

Related to this is that Christians dominate the major institutions and organizations of power within the United States and other Western countries. This allows them to put policies and procedures in place that ensure the continued dominance of Christianity. This is not an advantage inherent to

Christianity but simply a result of the privilege to which Christianity has been accorded for centuries in the Western world. To assume the validity of Christianity based on the societal prominence of Christian leaders would be like saying Whites are genetically superior to other races because they have all the power.

Interestingly, much of the cultural connection between American values and Christian values is of relatively recent vintage. While Christianity has had a significant presence and influence since the first American colonies were established, it did not attain full dominance of the political sphere until the Red Scare of the 1950s, in which Christianity was explicitly tied to patriotism to combat communism. Before that, American politicians were more open about their rejection of Christianity. For example, consider the following:

> [T]he day will come when the mystical generation of Jesus, by the supreme being as his father in the womb of a virgin will be classed with the fable of the generation of Minerva in the brain of Jupiter. But we may hope that the dawn of reason and freedom of thought in these United States will do away all this artificial scaffolding.
>
> —Thomas Jefferson, Letter to John Adams, April 11, 1823

> During almost fifteen centuries has the legal establishment of Christianity been on trial. What have been its fruits? More or less, in all places, pride and indolence in the clergy; ignorance and servility in laity; in both, superstition, bigotry, and persecution.
>
> —James Madison, *Memorial and Remonstrance to the General Assembly of Virginia on the Religious Rights of Man* (1785)

> My earlier views of the unsoundness of the Christian scheme of salvation and the human origin of the scriptures have become clearer and stronger with advancing years and I see no reason for thinking I shall ever change them.
>
> —Abraham Lincoln, Letter to Judge J. A. Wakefield after the death of his son in 1862

The unfortunate result is that these perceived traditions form a bulwark against any change that appears to challenge Christian teachings and values, be it LGBTQ rights or simply a critical approach to inquiry. As Maurice Polydore Marie Bernard Maeterlinck comments, "At every crossroads on the road that leads to the future, tradition has placed against us ten thousand men to guard the past."[139]

I. Malleability

The world's cultures did not independently arrive at religious beliefs and stick with them, unchanged. Instead, religions were formed through complicated circumstances, including invasions and militaristic takeovers. Ideas were stolen, borrowed, modified, and repurposed by conquering nations. The religions we have today are a tiny fraction of all religions that have existed throughout human history. Those remaining have survived because they more effectively adapted to attract and hold the allegiance of many people. Like Madonna (the pop star, not *the* Madonna), they repeatedly reinvented themselves to remain relevant. It is likely that religious beliefs today are so widespread because they tap into the psychological desires of many people, not because there is any external proof of their truth.

Christianity has proven itself exceptionally malleable to changing cultural tides. It has long been recognized by religious scholars that many core Christian doctrines represent the melding of Greek philosophy, such as the concept of the Logos, with a Jewish worldview, making the new religion comfortable and recognizable to both groups. Much of Jewish Scripture, in turn, can be traced back to roots in Babylonian and Canaanite mythology, making it palatable to those living at its inception. As science and archeology have invalidated many of Christianity's teachings, it has liberalized, attempting to reconcile the conflicts through metaphorical interpretations.

In college, I had an English teacher who loved poetry. He viewed it as an emotional opiate, the effectiveness of which was due to its ambiguity. He strongly opposed the claim that the meaning of any poem could be pinned down. Any time a student asked about a poem's meaning, his response was always the same: "What does it mean *to you*?" To him, it was this encompassing subjectivity that elevated poetry among all other forms of writing. Christianity's apologists have for centuries treated Christian Scripture as my English teacher treated poetry.

Christianity's widely divergent Scriptures allow for endless interpretations that can fit many worldviews and value systems, something that is evident simply by observing the incredible array of Christian denominations. The seemingly endless interpretive avenues available to Christians due to the inconsistencies and ambiguities of their Scripture has, in this sense, been a great strength. At some point, however, one has to acknowledge that while this may be an effective survival strategy for the religion, it is hardly an intellectually defensible one.

J. Conclusion

Given all these factors, we would expect Christianity to be far more popular than naturalism as a worldview, regardless of any evidence in its favor. To become an atheist in a predominantly Christian country, one would typically have to start in a religious family, resist all the emotional and psychological incentives, learn to think critically (something not taught in school and actively discouraged by most religions), and give up the community aspect of religion. One would have to accept: (1) life as a relative outsider, (2) the often-noncomforting and complicated realities taught by science, and (3) being part of the most hated and distrusted minority in the country.

Under such circumstances, it is amazing that *anyone* would openly consider themselves atheist or agnostic. The fact that millions of Americans do openly identify as atheists demonstrates there is something extremely powerful there that religion, with all its advantages, still cannot overcome. I would suggest it is that the atheist's beliefs consistently conform to observed reality in the most parsimonious manner. There is repeated confirmation from the natural world that atheists are correct, and being consistently right is a powerful convincer.

Nevertheless, given these advantages, we would expect Christianity to be more successful than it is—especially if, as Christians claim, it represents the correct worldview advocated by the one true God. Why isn't everyone a Christian by now? After two thousand years, it's reasonable to assess how successful the belief system has been. If the Truth were as compelling as Christianity predicts, surely the world would have noticed, and literally everyone would be Christian. And yet, Christians represent less than a third of the world's population. These are numbers we might reasonably expect of a man-made belief system with strong marketing advantages but highly surprising for one with the blessing of the most powerful being in the universe and a lock on the Truth.

What is crucial to understand, however, is that Christianity's marketing advantages, whatever they may be, say nothing about whether its claims are true. It has been wisely said that a lie can travel halfway across the world while the truth is still donning its shoes. The rapid spread of an idea may evidence only its intuitive, broad-based appeal. Truth is not decided by such means.

SOCIETAL VALUE

> [T]he strategy of apologizing for Christian faith by trying to demonstrate its social utility is always eventually self-liquidating. Sooner or later people realize that a great many of the supposedly practical and secular benefits of the Christian religion can be had more easily without religion. . . . The logic of practical atheism may well be more deeply ingrained in the evangelical tradition than conservatives perhaps have realized.
>
> —Craig M. Gay

One common argument for Christianity is that it provides some unique value to society. This can't be considered an argument for the truth of Christian claims, as it simply appeals to final consequences. Nevertheless, I think it is important to address the claim of some apologists that Christianity causes people to behave better or to be happier.

The first question I would pose to anyone arguing for the societal value of Christianity is "Which Christianity?" As discussed, Christianity takes on as many forms as there are people willing to interpret Christian Scripture. History has seen Christianity used to support moral progress and inclusiveness but also to justify hatred, bigotry, and war. Is there societal value in Pat Robertson's brand of Christianity, equating homosexuality and feminism with evil? What about that of Fred Phelps and the Westboro Baptist Church? Should we heed Martin Luther's rampant anti-Semitism? Any appeal to societal value must take all these permutations into account.

The second question I would ask is "What is your evidence?" This is one area in which the hypothesis under consideration is actually testable and, if true, should be supported by a mountain of evidence. We would expect to see societies composed mainly of Christians fare far better on every scale of societal well-being than those composed of non-Christians. Furthermore, if Christianity did provide a superior framework for moral guidance, then Christians would always be at the forefront of positive social change.

An example that directly addresses the claim that Christianity provides measurable societal value is Europe, in which many nations are now more than half atheist or agnostic. According to social scientist Phil Zuckerman in his groundbreaking work on the subject, countries with high rates of atheism are the happiest and highest-functioning on Earth.[140] Their residents score at the top of the "happiness index," and their societies can claim some of the lowest levels of corruption and violent crime, excellent educational systems, strong economies, well-supported arts, free health care, and egalitarian social policies. By these criteria, Scandinavia and northern Europe rank far higher in well-being than the United States, which among the seventeen First World countries included in Zuckerberg's surveys ranked *dead last*.[141]

In 2005, freelance researcher Gregory Paul published the results of several surveys correlating religiosity with social health. He concluded that "in almost all regards the highly secular democracies consistently enjoy low rates of social dysfunction, while pro-religious and antievolution America performs poorly."[142] Paul found that higher levels of belief in a Creator correlated with higher rates of homicide, juvenile and early adult mortality, STD infection rates, teen pregnancies, and abortion.[143] Clearly, religion in general and Christianity in particular is unnecessary or even unimportant for a happy and healthy society.

PERSONAL EXPERIENCE

> If you don't believe in transcendent experience, you haven't been to the right concert, you know, you haven't used the right drugs, you haven't had sex with the right partner.
>
> —Bart Campolo, *Why I Left, Why I Stayed*

> One ape's hallucination is another ape's religious experience—it just depends on which one's god module is overactive at the time.
>
> —Charles Stross, *Accelerando*

Perhaps the most intuitive argument, and the one most resistant to counterargument, is that from personal experience. Many Christians claim to remain Christians because of something they experienced that convinced them their religion was the correct one. These are subjective experiences that are as unique and personal as the people experiencing them, so it is impossible to generalize about them based on substance. All that can be said is, they were sufficiently compelling to convince those experiencing them they were on the right track. While the individuals who experience these things might find them powerful proof to validate their own beliefs, their power to persuade others not similarly inclined to believe is highly limited. The subjective experiences of others rarely translate across the divide of culture and belief. Personal experience represents the ideal defense against alien beliefs but has little to recommend it as a tool of persuasion.

Several things can be said about the argument from personal experience. First, it is undisputed that we all experience things at some point in our lives that take us out of the mundane. We have all experienced awe and transcendence, such as when looking over a beautiful landscape or contemplating the vast cosmos. Many of us also have had experiences that can be described as altered states of consciousness. These can be induced through drug usage but also may occur naturally through combinations of chemicals in our brains. Scientists have demonstrated that around 40 percent of people experience hallucinations, seeing things that simply aren't there. The experiences are not in dispute. The real question is how they are interpreted.

Research has consistently shown that people interpret these experiences through culture and context. Where cultures worship animist gods, people see animist gods. Where cultures teem with stories of ghosts, people see ghosts. During the space race of the 1960s and the flood of science fiction stories of alien species and extraterrestrial contact, people saw UFOs and alien visitors. Never do you hear of a Hindu viewing an angel or of a Christian seeing Brahma. But you often hear of the reverse. The point is that personal experiences are always subjective. The fact that so many similar experiences are interpreted so many different ways and that those ways are so culturally dependent should cause the rest of us to pause before taking them as proof of any deity or any supernatural claim. As evidence, their value is negligible.

ARGUMENTS AGAINST CHRISTIANITY

I have now addressed the primary arguments of Christian apologists *for* Christianity. These represent the apologists' big guns. I know of no apologist who does not rely heavily on one or more of these arguments. They represent the intellectual foundation upon which theologians have built the edifice of their faith and which they have used to defend it against external criticism. But as should be apparent by now, each is a house of cards built upon porous sandstone that washes way when exposed to the tide of reason.

I now want to discuss serious problems with Christianity that have caused many atheists to leave the faith and others never to embrace it in the first place. These are arguments *against* Christianity, in that they affirmatively demonstrate why Christianity is unlikely to be true. Apologists have, of course, attempted to respond to these arguments, but I think you will soon understand why those responses have been so unpersuasive to nonbelievers. I believe no apologist has ever effectively addressed them.

GOD'S SILENCE REGARDING HIS EXISTENCE AND EXPECTATIONS

Billions of years ago, God was creating universes and life; thousands of years ago he was creating angry floods, sin-saving human sacrifices, and audible burning bushes. Today he occasionally appears on a piece of toast. To state that God has become reclusive over the years would be an overwhelming understatement.

—Trevor Tremaine, *How to Prove God Does Not Exist*

I'm sure many reading this book have children of their own. For those who don't, please imagine that you do. Parents know there is nothing more precious than their children, on whose behalf they routinely make enormous sacrifices. Parents generally want nothing so much as to see their children grow up healthy and happy.

Christianity tells us we are all God's children. He is our heavenly father. He loves us unconditionally and, presumably, wants the same general things for us that any earthly father would want for his children—only more so because He is the *perfect* father. Christians are told God is also perfectly just. He will always treat us fairly and with compassion. Christianity predicts we will see ample evidence of this when we look at God's treatment of mankind. But that is not what we see.

Assume you are a wealthy and powerful father, the king of a small country, conversing with your estranged teenage son, whom, due to your extremely pressing schedule, you have met for the first time:

You: Son, I know I've never actually spoken with you directly in your entire life, but I'm doing so now because I understand you have disobeyed me.

Son: I'm so happy that you are finally speaking with me! I have so many questions! But what do you mean I've disobeyed you?

You: Well, I know you ate oatmeal on Thursday. I hate it when people do that.

Son: I'm so sorry. I never knew that. You never told me.

You: Not directly, but I've indirectly passed it along. There was that book that about two hundred people put together after I talked to them separately about what I liked and didn't like. You should have been able to figure it out from that.

Son: But that book said so many contradictory things. One section said you shouldn't ever eat oatmeal on Thursday, while another said that it pleased you to no end. How was I to know which you preferred?

You: I know it might have been difficult to interpret on your own, but I gave some people the right interpretation. You should have listened to them.

Son: Thousands of people claimed to correctly interpret your rule book—all with different interpretations of almost every passage. How could I have known who had the right one?

YOU: Not my problem. You should have figured it out. What about the fact that my invisible, incorporeal dragon never eats oatmeal on Thursday? Shouldn't that have clued you in?

SON: I have no evidence that such a creature even exists! I've heard people say it does, but I've found nothing that supports their claims. If this were important, then couldn't you have given me better evidence of the dragon?

YOU: That's not my job. Look, I'm sorry, but you really screwed up. I love you, but I'm going to have to send you to the dungeon and have you tortured horribly every day for the rest of your life. Goodbye. We won't meet again.

Is this your idea of a just, loving father? Is it anyone's? I can't imagine so. But it is an accurate analogy for God's treatment of mankind. For like the father in this example, God does not speak directly to his children. God is highly concerned that they follow his rules but provides no clear guidance on what those rules are. He requires his children to believe certain things but provides poor, if any, supporting evidence for them. And if his children fail to believe the right things or to follow some crucial doctrine, then they are horribly punished for all eternity.

A just God would leave no doubt as to His existence. It would be obvious to everyone and irrefutable. God could write us a message on the Moon in real time. He could appear to everyone on Earth and answer all their questions with unfailing accuracy. Or He could simply provide one piece of objective, intersubjectively verifiable evidence that could be explained in no other way. It is remarkably easy to come up with countless ways God could conclusively and inarguably establish His existence. As Thomas Paine recognized in his day,

> Had the news of salvation by Jesus Christ been inscribed on the face of the sun and the moon, in characters that all nations would have understood, the whole Earth had known it in twenty-four hours, and all nations would have believed it; whereas, though it is now almost two thousand years since, as they tell us, Christ came upon Earth, not a twentieth part of the people of the Earth know anything of it, and among those who do, the wiser part do not believe it.[1]

Likewise, God's rules on everything of any significance would be perfectly clear. If God is so concerned with people understanding and following His instructions, as Christianity claims, then why has He made or allowed them to be so confused and contradictory? Why would He leave the job of interpreting these instructions to fallible, sinful humans? Why would

He not deliver the message directly to every human on Earth in terms we would implicitly understand? Why doesn't God simply buy ad time during the Superbowl and lay out the reasons everyone should buy into His plan? If GoDaddy can do it, then why can't God?

When a church leader or theologian tells Christians that "God says X," what he is really saying is, "I say, God says X." Because God does not speak with His children directly, they are left to consult other humans like themselves as God's interpreters, none of whom can boast even the simplest credentials. That these interpreters far more often disagree than agree should give pause to anyone who believes this is the approach that would be taken by a supremely wise God.

If you wrote a book that attracted a following and you saw that your followers were, out of misunderstanding of what you wrote, using your book to justify genocide and other atrocities, would you not step in to point out the error of their misunderstanding? Would you not, at the least, in your next edition clarify the passage(s) that led to the confusion? If you stood by and did nothing, then what should we think of you? Under such circumstances, is it not reasonable for atheists to find the biblical God morally repulsive? And is it not also reasonable for the atheists to believe, based on the inconsistency between the actions or inactions of this God and the "all-good" God advocated by Christians, that the Christian-advocated God simply doesn't exist?

If God wanted us to follow a specific path, then there would be no more dispute about which religion or doctrine is correct than there is about the fundamentals of math, physics, or engineering. All these issues would be as repeatedly demonstrable as simple addition. And unless things were precisely this clear, God would not punish us for making the wrong choice—much less eternally. This is what a loving parent would do. Should we expect any less of God?

This is a vexing problem for apologists, who have engaged in a variety of mental gymnastics attempting to address it. I discuss each of their arguments here.

A. Apologetic Responses: Free Will

The typical apologetic response is that God is trying to "protect our free will" because our love for and devotion to Him means nothing unless they are freely given. Whenever I hear this, I wonder if the speaker even understands what it means to exercise free will, for nothing I've suggested previously would impair it.

As I've discussed elsewhere, belief in something's existence is generally not a voluntary action. It is an involuntary compulsion based on convincing arguments and evidence. I am compelled to believe what I genuinely think is true. That which convinces me justifies my belief. I do not set the criteria by which my mind accepts a belief but only evaluate whether a particular claim satisfies it. As Robert Ingersoll observes, "It seems to me that evidence, even in spite of ourselves, will have its weight, and that whatever our wish may be, we are compelled to stand with fairness by the scales, and give the exact result."[2] No amount of evidence will impair your free will to believe in something. The evidence either meets your internal criteria, or it doesn't.[3]

Assume a friend tries to convince you to believe in a large werewolf allegedly roaming your neighborhood. You are skeptical. In response to your skepticism, your friend shows you footprints, photographs, and finally video of the beast. Your skepticism softens, and you become more open to the idea this monster might actually exist. Is it accurate to say that your friend has deprived you of your free will? Of course not. Your will remains entirely free. Your initial belief has simply changed in response to new evidence.

We don't think of an attorney presenting mounting evidence to a jury as depriving the jurors of their free will. Every juror processes the evidence differently and applies a unique set of cognitive filters based on their own nature and nurture. But the processing of this evidence itself occurs automatically, behind the scenes. No amount of evidence can impair your free will to believe because *belief is not a question of free will to begin with.*

Some apologists claim that God's primary goal is not for us to believe in Him but for us to have a "personal relationship" with Him. This ignores that you cannot have a personal relationship with someone *unless you first believe that he or she exists.* You cannot, for instance, have a personal relationship with the Easter Bunny, no matter how much you want him to exist. If I want to have a personal relationship with a person I see walk outside my window every day but have never met, then wouldn't step one be to walk out one day and introduce myself? We can't expect a person to initiate the relationship with us without knowing we are there. Belief is a necessary prerequisite to any relationship and not one within our conscious control. So if God wants so desperately to have a personal relationship with us, then He would have to begin by providing us with unassailable evidence of His existence.

God would also clearly communicate His rules, desires, and instructions to us. How would doing so undercut anyone's free will? Once you understood God's expectations, you would remain free to accept or reject them.

Don't we all try to do this with our children? And aren't clear expectations a basis for just punishments when people don't meet those expectations?

How would we feel about a person fired for failing to meet some employment obligation never clearly communicated to her? Assume, for example, a woman is terminated for parking in a particular space but was never told this was prohibited. In my years of handling lawsuits like this, I can tell you that juries favor the employees in such matters. Employers who fail to provide clear expectations are considered unfair. Would it be any less unfair for God to do the same? Free will is the ability to choose between options. For a choice to be truly free, one must be presented with clear options that are demonstrably distinct. How does hiding information about one option make the choice *more* free? Doesn't it actually make it *less* free?

Assume you are given a choice between two medications, one of which you are told is far more effective at treating your illness than the other, but you are not told which one. Would you not expect your doctor to provide you with all the information he has regarding the relative effectiveness of each? While your choice might rightly be called free if you were forced to choose based upon the bottle colors alone, is your free will impaired if you are provided with more useful information? What about if you are provided with incomplete information that could be misleading, such as only side effects? The more effective medication might also have more side effects, but how could you possibly make an informed decision unless you are told about their relative effectiveness? For your doctor to provide anything less than full disclosure of all the information available to him would be malpractice and almost certainly immoral. So it is with God.

Another example should make this clearer. Assume a scientist conducts an experiment with identical twins. Each is raised separately in a controlled environment. The first is exposed solely to information suggesting that governments are evil and the source of all misery. The second is exposed solely to information that governments are good and the source of all well-being. As adults, is there any doubt these men will possess opposing political beliefs? To what extent can we characterize their choices of political party to be free?

The problem is that they were each exposed to limited information. By doing so, the scientist effectively controlled the twins' decision-making processes, leading each to a predetermined conclusion. You could not blame either twin for having the "wrong" political views because neither was provided with all the relevant information. The freedom of their decisions is directly proportional to the quality and quantity of information at their disposal. So contrary to what the apologists argue, God would be *decreasing* man's free will by withholding evidence—not increasing it. If God sought to preserve man's free will, then He would make sure that everyone on Earth had rock-solid evidence of His existence and expectations.

Another problem with this argument is that it ignores clear biblical evidence to the contrary. While apologists claim we should not expect God to provide clear evidence of His existence or expectations, this concept of God contradicts what we see in the Bible. Throughout the Old Testament, God regularly speaks directly to humans, providing direct evidence of His existence and clearly communicating His expectations.

Would God's punishment of Adam and Eve be considered remotely just if His instructions were considered vague or contradictory? What if God had told Adam on one day that he should eat from the Tree of Knowledge but on another that he shouldn't? If God provided only conflicting or indirect signs that could be read differently by reasonable people, then could we legitimately fault Adam and Eve for eating of the tree? The story retains its punch and instructive value only because God's instructions were *so clear and free of ambiguity.*[4]

Likewise, God directly commanded Abraham to kill his child, Isaac. God left Abraham with no ambiguity as to His existence or desires. If He had, then given the love and devotion the story demonstrates Abraham had for Isaac, Abraham would have rationalized a reason to avoid murdering his child. But God did not allow Abraham this out. Crucial to the story is that Abraham *continued to exercise his free will* and chose to follow God's wishes. Had Abraham simply been God's puppet, he could not have earned God's approval.

Another recurring theme of the Old Testament is God's exhibition of power to prove His existence and to demonstrate His dominance over other gods, the existence of which these passages clearly support. In Exodus, God inflicted plagues on Pharaoh *expressly for this purpose.* God even hardened Pharaoh's heart to prevent him from releasing the Israelites early *so that* God could engage in additional public exhibitions of power. On several occasions, God accepts challenges from the followers of other gods. The story of David and Goliath tells of an army of Philistines that openly defies God's people and how God works through a mere shepherd boy to prove that He is greater than the Philistine gods (1 Samuel 17–51).

In Exodus, Pharaoh challenges God's authority through his court magicians, who can turn their staffs into snakes through the power of their respective gods. God turns Aaron's staff into a snake that eats the other snakes, thus proving God's power and dominance over competing deities (Exodus 7:8–13). God's prophet Elijah engages in a competition with the prophets of competing Canaanite gods Baal and Asherah to cause a sacrificial fire, which God causes Elijah to win, thereby proving God's existence and dominance (1 Kings 18:20–40). If there were any doubt about God's intent here, the story explains that following the win, all those in attendance, including the followers of other gods, fell to the ground, crying, "The Lord is God." In another story, God accepts a challenge from a believer, Gideon, to prove himself by creating dew on an otherwise dry fleece (Judges 6:36–38). The common theme of these stories is that God is not only willing but eager to demonstrate His power in clear and unambiguous ways *so that people will believe and follow Him.*

The New Testament continues this theme of God (and Jesus) recognizing that people are justified in expecting good evidence for their beliefs and God providing it. Jesus states throughout the Gospel of John that he performs miracles *so people will believe.* Jesus recognizes that people need proof to believe his claims, and so he offers it. Likewise, after Jesus's death, he returns to the disciples in human form, but they still doubt him (Matthew 28:17; Luke 24:11). Jesus allows Thomas to feel his wounds to *prove* his bodily Resurrection. Rather than reject Thomas for requiring tangible evidence, Jesus gladly provides it to him (John 20:24–29). Jesus clearly recognized his disciples were entitled to actual firsthand evidence of his Resurrection. Why should we be entitled to any less? And if it didn't violate their free will, then why should it violate ours? As Thomas Paine said, "Thomas did not believe the Resurrection and, as they say, would not believe without having ocular and manual demonstration himself. So neither will I, and the reason is equally as good for me, and for every other person, as for Thomas."[5]

The apostle Paul represents another example. Paul did not come to believe in and follow Jesus based on written texts and oral accounts, as today's Christians expect atheists to do. He had a vision of Jesus in which *Jesus spoke directly to him.* If we assume Paul was being honest and this vision was not the result of a psychiatric abnormality or hallucination (a very questionable assumption), then we would have to say that God recognized a skeptic like Paul could only be swayed with direct evidence and so provided it. By his own account, Paul would never have become a Christian if required to rely on the type evidence available to religious skeptics in the twenty-first century. Only his profound, earth-shattering vision on the road to Damascus could have done this. And if Paul merited such a demonstration, then why don't the rest of us?

Apologists argue that protecting human free will is supremely important to God. Alvin Plantinga argues it is *so important* that God would rather allow the endless suffering endured since the dawn of man than to impair man's free will *in any way*. He says,

> A world containing creatures who are significantly free (and freely perform more good than evil actions) is more valuable, all else being equal, than a world containing no free creatures at all. . . . To create creatures capable of *moral good*, therefore, He must create creatures capable of moral evil; and He can't give these creatures the freedom to perform evil and at the same time prevent them from doing so.[6]

But this is not what the Bible tells us. According to the Bible, God has no problem overriding or removing the free will of his subjects as he sees fit, which is often.

According to the Bible, God killed millions of people. That obviously interfered with their free will, considering they did not want to die. God did many things, some quite spectacular, to cause observers to believe certain things or take certain actions. Furthermore, the Bible suggests that God knows the future and predestines people's fates. That, too, at best interferes with and at worst obliterates human free will. In addition, there are many obstacles to free will in our present world (famine, mental retardation, grave diseases, premature death, etc.) that God does little or nothing to prevent. This is not conclusive proof that God does not have human free will as a high priority, but it does count pretty heavily against it.

God's disdain for free will is obvious from the numerous biblical cases in which God exerts *mind control* to cause people to make the decisions that accord with God's plan. For example, God "hardens the heart" of the Pharaoh in Exodus so the Pharaoh will not free the Israelites until God finishes his plagues (Exodus 4:21, 9:35). Similar biblical evidence of God interfering with human free will can be found at Deuteronomy 2:30; Joshua 11:20; Proverbs 16:1, 16:9, 16:33, 19:21; Job 42:2; Isaiah 64:8; Jeremiah 1:4–5, 10:23; Daniel 4:35; Galatians 1:15; Romans 9:18; and Ephesians 1:4–11.

As for the New Testament, there is no better example than Jesus's "betrayer," Judas Iscariot. Jesus makes it clear to his disciples that all the events leading to his Crucifixion, including his betrayal, are part of God's divine plan for salvation. All these events have been prophesied by Old Testament Scripture, which Jesus came to fulfill. According to Luke, Jesus is fully aware of this plan and gladly accepts his role in it. Moreover, according to Jesus, everyone had an assigned and predetermined role to play in the drama, including Judas, the betrayer.

If Judas had free will, then he could have avoided betraying Jesus. But that was never a possibility, for such a decision would have defeated God's plan for salvation. No one thinks Judas was powerful enough to single-handedly subvert God's plan by deciding not to go along with it. God must have overridden Judas's free will to bring about God's divine plan. Those who demonize Judas are missing the point. *Judas was God's vessel for bringing about human salvation.* There was never any chance of Judas avoiding this destiny. Judas can be blamed no more than a puppet on a string, and his free will was of no more value to God than a speck of dust in the wind.

Finally, there is the problem of Heaven. Christian theologians maintain that once a human soul is admitted into Heaven, it remains there for eternity. The soul need not regularly prove itself. But this can only be correct if Heavenly human souls lack free will. If they can choose to disobey God, then they remain always on probation and subject to banishment. Heavenly residence is no more a permanent state of affairs than life on Earth. This leads to the paradoxical conclusion that the ideal state of affairs for human souls *is to lack free will.* If God strips us of free will in our exalted state, then He either considers it trivial in value or of no value at all. In either case, the apologists' argument collapses.

For the sake of argument, let's assume that providing good evidence of God's existence and expectations would violate man's free will. Let's also assume God's biblical accounts can be rationalized to explain why He repeatedly provided this same type of evidence through the time of Jesus and then stopped. The question then becomes whether protecting free will is likely to be so important that a loving God would withhold evidence necessary for his children's salvation. *Should free will be that important?*

According to the Bible, if one does not believe in God or if one follows the wrong doctrine, then he will be eternally damned. By the apologists' account, God ensures that people receive incomplete and thus inaccurate information, leading them to make poor choices because they never understood the options, all in the service of protecting these people's "free will." I think that if presented in this way, most people would tell God He can keep His free will. If given the option, I, for one, would rather have all the information clearly presented (a claimed violation of free will) than to be damned based on confusing or contradictory information. What could possibly be so great about free will as to justify God sending billions to their eternal damnation?

We need only return to our parent analogy for the answer. As a parent, would you withhold crucial information from your child if it meant they would be forever damned for making the wrong, uninformed decision? No loving parent would. If God existed and were truly the all-good and all-loving parent apologists claim, then He wouldn't either.

B. Apologetic Responses: The Stubbornness of Nonbelievers

Another response is related to free will but sufficiently distinct to merit its own section. Many apologists claim that God has purposely provided *just enough* evidence of His existence that those who *want to believe* will accept it. The only reason more people haven't become Christians, according to this view, is their own stubborn resistance. For selfish reasons, non-Christians simply don't want to believe, and this motivated reasoning leads them to reject good evidence. This conclusion is entailed by the *sensus divinitatis*, discussed previously. William Lane Craig makes this claim:

> Therefore, when a person refuses to come to Christ it is never just because of a lack of evidence or because of intellectual difficulties: at root, he refuses to come because he willingly ignores and rejects the drawing of God's Spirit on his heart. No one in the final analysis fails to become a Christian because of a lack of arguments; he fails to become a Christian because he loves darkness rather than light and wants nothing to do with God.[7]

This argument puts the blame squarely on the nonbeliever, claiming she is guilty of "willful blindness" and thus *rejecting God*. It argues that there are no true good-faith atheists—no one who disbelieves in God for principled reasons. Atheism is a disingenuous position asserted from sinful pride. Those claiming disbelief are lying, using their professed but false disbelief as an excuse to avoid following God's rules and free up their Sundays. They just want to go on living their hedonistic lifestyles without pesky interference from God. They are in open rebellion against God, which is why this position has been called the "rebellion thesis."[8]

Christian apologist Randal Rouser, who has effectively detailed and documented the widespread acceptance of the rebellion thesis in modern Christianity, defines it: "While atheists profess to believe that God does not exist, this disbelief is the result of an active and culpable suppression of an innate disposition to believe in God which is borne of a hatred of God and a desire to sin with impunity."[9] Rauser demonstrates that where Christians explicitly rely on the rebellion thesis, they often bypass justifying it with evidence and instead simply accept it a priori based on such scriptural passages as Psalms 14:1 ("The fool says in his heart 'there is no God'") or Paul's epistles, such as Ephesians 2:12 or Romans 1:18–21. Rauser shows these passages were not intended as critiques of the intellectual atheism that has flourished since the Enlightenment and that defines atheist thought today. No such thing even existed in Paul's day or before. They were instead addressed to the hypocrisy of Jews who lived as if God didn't exist *while professing He did.* In Paul's view, furthermore, all humans were equally culpable and foolish, Jews and Gentiles alike, because they all had turned from God.[10] Paul makes this clear in Romans 3:10–12, which quotes from Psalm 14, where he writes, "There is no one righteous, not even one; there is no one who understands; there is no one who seeks God. All have turned away; they have together become worthless; there is no one who does good, not even one."

Proponents of the rebellion thesis cannot rest on vague Scripture. They must support their argument with evidence. They must establish that no nonbeliever is really interested in the truth and that to the extent they may claim otherwise, nonbelievers are deliberately lying or at least self-deluded regarding their own intentions.[11] But where is that evidence? How can these apologists demonstrate that nonbelievers are operating in bad faith, from anything other than a neutral application of objective evidentiary standards? The simplest way would be to demonstrate some inconsistency in applying the nonbeliever's evidentiary standards, for which there should be ample evidence if true—some hypocrisy that reveals their true intentions. But the apologists never show anything like this.

This argument can be perfectly understood however as a rationalization for demonizing nonbelief and for the validity of the Christian scheme of salvation. It is necessary for many Christians to represent atheists as consciously resistant to portray them as deserving of punishment. The representation of evil throughout the Old Testament is one of rebellion against God *by people who know Him to exist.* From Adam on, it is a story of people consciously rejecting God's plan for them and choosing to go their own way.

But the modern atheist does not fit this paradigm, for to rebel against something, you must first believe that something *exists.* Just because I don't follow the directives of the Elf King, one cannot say I am *in open rebellion against the Elf King.* That would be absurd. I simply don't believe any such being exists because I have seen no good evidence for an Elf King. A lack of belief in something differs greatly from rejecting its authority.

Not until the New Testament did belief itself suddenly take on moral significance. But most people today look critically at the claim that it can be more morally correct to believe one thing over another regardless of the respective supporting evidence provided. On what general principle other than evidence and reason can one rely to sort truth from nonsense?

If a nonbeliever states he is ready to give God a fair hearing but that God simply needs to be more direct, such as speaking to him, as God did to countless people throughout the Bible, then who can say this is unreasonable? If it were true that God loved this person and wanted him to be saved, then God would grant this request and provide the necessary evidence. This is what is predicted by Christianity. If God does not speak, then isn't it reasonable to assume this is because there is no God? Otherwise, one must demonstrate the nonbeliever is insincere and that he wouldn't believe despite the evidence provided.

Many Christians feel they need show only that belief in God is reasonable, in that it is not logically absurd. But this is backward. Only atheists are justified by demonstrating that their position (nonbelief) is *reasonable* for they make no claim regarding a salvation scheme. According to the Christian scheme, God could justly punish atheists for disbelief only if that belief were unreasonable. Christianity requires that *all available evidence compel belief beyond a reasonable doubt*. Christians must demonstrate that anyone not accepting their particular theology has no legitimate excuse and *is therefore worthy of punishment*.

I'm very clear about the standard I use to evaluate evidence and determine what merits my belief. It is the same standard the vast majority of theists use in all areas *other than their own religion*. Unless a theist can show I have been inconsistent in applying that standard, he cannot say I am *to blame* for my atheism. If God exists, then it would be ridiculously easy for Him to provide me evidence that met that standard, so either no God exists, or He has deliberately chosen not to provide evidence. If God exists and wants me to believe, then He has no one to blame for my disbelief but Himself. If God were indeed perfectly loving, then there would be no "nonresistant" nonbelievers. God would be a light in the darkness that could only be missed if one deliberately closed one's eyes. The existence of even a single nonresistant nonbeliever therefore disproves the existence of a loving God.

And there are many examples of nonresistant nonbelievers. Believers often forget that most atheists used to be religious and that many used to think they had a personal relationship with God. You can go to the internet and search for books by former believers who loved their Christian faith and valued it above everything in their lives but were gradually forced by their intellectual integrity to leave it.[12] Their stories are typically heartbreaking ones in which they left behind many of the things that mattered most to them, such as friends, family, and a supporting community, as well as a sense of certainty and purpose. These people had an intense desire to believe and every motivation to do so. But their desire for truth and need for intellectual honesty compelled them to leave that belief behind once they found they could only hold onto those things by deceiving themselves.

And how can the rebellion thesis account for substantial disagreement *among believers* on the correct church doctrine? These people have heard

God and chosen to accept Jesus as their shepherd, but they disagree in often substantial ways on God's message, expectations, or both. They can't agree on some of the most basic rules of the game. Therefore, either God is deliberately telling them different things to sow confusion, which contradicts what Christianity predicts and teaches to be God's nature and desire, or no one is receiving legitimate information from God, which indicates there is no God.

Those who claim to have heard God directly must distinguish their experience from those of Hindus, Muslims, or Mormons who claim the same thing. If they cannot do so objectively, then all such experiences stand on the same footing. Because the "inner voice" communications are inherently contradictory and there is no valid way to privilege one over any other, one can only reasonably conclude that they are all equally illegitimate. And what of those nonbelievers who have become Christians? If all had been motivated by rebellion, then wouldn't we expect them to unanimously cite that as their basis upon their conversion? I've never seen even one give such an explanation.

In response to this argument, some apologists have maintained that all atheists and mistaken theists are resistant, *even if they don't recognize it themselves*. Unable to square their all-loving God with nonresistant nonbelievers, they simply deny their existence. They claim that while these people may *think they would be receptive* to the existence for God, the very fact they *don't* see it is evidence they aren't *willing* to see it. They are deluding themselves.

This effectively nonfalsifiable response strikes me as absurd. This book demonstrates that the evidence for God is at best unclear and highly ambiguous. Even a believer, if she is being honest, must admit there are many legitimate reasons for not believing, even if they themselves are not convinced by those reasons. To say all nonbelievers are deliberately shutting their eyes is, given the state of the evidence, an extraordinary claim. And yet it is a claim for which no evidence is ever offered. Unless that evidence is provided, the existence of nonresistant nonbelievers stands as powerful evidence against the Christian God.

Even if one accepts that all atheists and mistaken theists are stubbornly irrational, then wouldn't Christian theology require that God go the extra mile to prevent these people from making choices that lead to their eternal damnation? Good people don't give up on their friends and family until their resistance becomes intolerable. When we hear of spouses and parents of alcoholics who stood by their loved ones for years, often staging interventions, we think of them as good and committed. Would the Christian God do any less?

In his book *Why I Am Not a Christian*, Richard Carrier provides the following example of how humans act when they *really* care about saving someone with mistaken beliefs from harm:

> Back in my days as a flight-deck firefighter, when our ship's helicopter was on rescue missions, we had to stand around in our gear in case of a crash. There was usually very little to do, so we told stories. One I heard was about a rescue swimmer. She had to pull a family out of the water from a capsized boat, but by the time the chopper got there, it appeared everyone had drowned except the mother, who was for that reason shedding her life vest and trying to drown herself. The swimmer dove in to rescue her, but the woman kicked and screamed and yelled to let her die. She even gave the swimmer a whopping black eye. But the swimmer said to hell with that. I'm bringing you in! And she did, enduring her curses and blows all the way. Later, it turned out that one of the victim's children, her daughter, had survived. She had drifted pretty far from the wreck, but the rescue team pulled her out, and the woman who had beaten the crap out of her rescuer apologized and thanked the swimmer for saving her against her will. Everyone in my group agreed the rescue swimmer had done the right thing, and we all would have done the same—because that is what a loving, caring being does. It follows that if God is a loving being, he will do no less for us. In the real world, kind people don't act like some stubborn, pouting God who abandons the drowning because they don't want to be helped. They act like this rescue swimmer. They act like us.[13]

C. Apologetic Responses: God's Evidence Is Only Available to Those with the Right Frame of Mind

Closely related to the "stubborn nonbeliever" response is the argument that only those in the "right frame of mind" can see the evidence God has provided. If one comes to the question in this frame of mind, then he will find the evidence of God's existence and His expectations compelling. If he doesn't find this evidence compelling, then he never had the right frame of mind to begin with.

I believe this argument is intended to address the inconvenient fact that nonbelievers are generally more knowledgeable about Christianity than Christians are and yet still reject it. In attempting to explain why a large-scale survey reflected this very thing, Alan Cooperman, associate director for research at the Pew Forum, concludes that American atheists tend to be people who grew up in a religious tradition and consciously gave it up, often after a great deal of reflection and study. "These are people who thought a lot about religion," he says. "They're not indifferent. They care about it."[14]

It is exactly because they care about it and take it seriously that they cannot accept it unless they can do so without the cognitive dissonance that comes with believing contradictory things.

This suggests that once Christians accept their faith, usually at a young age, most stop examining it. Consistent with the Dunning-Kruger effect, they thereafter mistake their vague familiarity with Christianity for true understanding, even feeling very confident in a level of comprehension that is actually an illusion.[15] Meanwhile, those with the most knowledge of science, philosophy, and comparative religions—even Christianity itself—continue to reject it.

The response apologists propose is that those rejecting Christianity simply aren't beginning from the right place. They claim that one must be persuaded that God exists prior to examining the evidence in order to properly hear God and understand what the evidence is saying. To these apologists, I would ask, "On what reasonable basis is one warranted in being persuaded *before examining the evidence*?" Shouldn't we strive for objectivity and open-mindedness before considering any argument? Doesn't persuasion then entail one party making a better argument or more justified claim than another? How can one be persuaded unless the evidence supports that position? To reach a conclusion before evaluating the evidence is the antithesis of rational inquiry.

Different people can make sense of the same data in various and mutually exclusive ways based on their respective initial assumptions. But the assumptions must be justified before one can argue that a specific interpretation is correct, especially if the interpretation depends on the assumptions. Scientists recognize that one must bring no assumptions to the table in evaluating a hypothesis unless the assumptions themselves are justified by previous testing or are properly basic.

Would it be better for someone to take these questions seriously, come up with an objective standard by which to evaluate them, and reach a good-faith conclusion that God doesn't exist or to simply accept what her parents told her and believe by "faith" without ever exploring the matter independently? Assume you have two people: Barbie and Jeff. Barbie is told as a child to believe in God and Jesus. She does so at age five and never looks back. She doesn't critically read the Bible for herself. She never questions anything her pastor says. She considers herself a good Christian.

Jeff also becomes a Christian at a young age by accepting the teachings of his parents and other Christian authority figures. But as Jeff approaches his twenties, he looks at all the other religions of the world and begins to question whether his is correct. It becomes very important for Jeff to determine whether Christianity is true and justified, so he researches the issue and applies an objective standard to the claims of all religions. He examines the claims of Christianity critically, from an outsider's viewpoint. He ultimately concludes that Christianity is false and becomes an atheist. Between Barbie and Jeff, who is more intellectually honest? For those who believe Jeff is worthy of blame, where has he gone wrong? What did he do that is worthy of punishment?

Perhaps I hear inner voices I cannot readily explain. If I am a Christian, then I might interpret these "voices" to emanate from God. If I am a Hindu, then I might interpret them to come from Vishnu or Brahma. If I am a UFO believer, then I might believe the voices come from extraterrestrials. If I am a naturalist, then I might consider them misfirings of a complex but imperfect brain developed through millions of years of evolution.

That is just what anthropology tells us will happen. People in different cultures interpret inner voices in ways unique to their cultural and religious identities, suggesting that none of these voices has a single supernatural, faith-specific cause. So while it may be accurate to say I would be more likely to hear God if I accepted that God exists, this doesn't make it any more likely that the voices I hear *actually* come from God but only that I'm more likely to *believe* they do.

This cannot be the only valid way to know God, furthermore, because this very method (being first convinced of a deity) has led to thousands of contradictory beliefs. This method cannot distinguish true beliefs from false ones, as it can be used to justify and support *any belief*. A just God wouldn't require one to accept His existence on weak or nonexistent evidence before one could hear Him.

In light of the the previous discussions, it should be apparent this is a circular argument that creates its own cocoon of nonfalsifiability. You must first believe to believe. This line of reasoning is nothing more than an excuse for Christians to lower their standard of proof for Christian claims alone, a textbook example of special pleading.

D. God Is Limited

Some apologists take a different approach. They acknowledge that if God possesses the attributes traditionally ascribed to Him, then He could easily provide better evidence of His existence and expectations and would do so. To save their beliefs, they are willing to handicap God. They claim that God must not actually be all powerful and therefore *cannot* directly communicate His message or provide better evidence of His existence. Rabbi

Harold Kushner, for example, in his well-known book *When Bad Things Happen to Good People*, takes the position that God is not omnipotent and thus cannot prevent human suffering.[16]

This is an interesting approach that brushes aside more than a thousand years of theology with a hand wave. Aside from the many doctrinal issues this raises, it suffers from a more serious problem. God cannot struggle under any limitations greater than those upon us. Any of us with the power to will the entire universe into existence and direct the course of events to any significant degree would be capable of providing direct evidence of his or her existence. Any of us without those abilities could surely do the same. Surely a God could clarify it enough that Christians would not still be attempting to persuade the majority of the world of this foundational fact. It would take far less than the power God has already demonstrated to accomplish this.

Some will even go so far as to construct a version of the Christian God indistinguishable in all relevant details from the Deist god—one that simply set the creative forces of the universe in motion and then retired to an eternity of inactivity. Such an entity would certainly allow for the full panoply of modern scientific discoveries without conflict, but of what value would this God be to humanity? He would be the perpetual chairman of the universal board of directors, holding an office of fine title but no powers. He would certainly not be the God at least 99.9 percent of Christians recognize. All the ad hoc excuses offered for God's inaction amount to nothing more than claiming that different rules apply to God, without justifying such an exception or explaining those rules.

THE FUTILITY OF PRAYER

> Give a man a fish, and he will eat for a day; teach a man to fish, and he will eat for a lifetime; give a man religion, and he will die praying for a fish.
>
> —Anonymous

Christianity posits a God interested in our personal affairs and who intervenes in the natural world upon request. The Bible clearly tells us multiple times that if there is anything we want—literally *anything*—we need only ask in Jesus's name, and God will provide it. ["What things you desire, when you pray, believe and you shall have them" (Mark 11:23–34); "Ask and it will be given to you" (Matthew 7:7, 21:21–22); I will do/give you "whatever you ask in my name" (John 14:13, 15:16, 16:23)]. This promise is direct and unconditional. But as every new Christian learns almost immediately, it is a promise far more often broken than kept.

Virtually every Christian denomination engages in intercessory prayer. Priests and pastors lead public prayers in church while encouraging their congregants to pray privately at home.[17] Christians are encouraged to pray for everything from world peace to health and wealth to winning the Tuesday night Little League game or finding their keys. Prayer lists are maintained and systematically updated to leverage the value of sheer numbers in making divine appeals. A full 88 percent of Christian Americans pray to God, and 76 percent consider prayer an important part of their daily lives.[18]

The premise behind this is that God cares about our personal pleas and will intervene on our behalf to ensure our wishes are granted, much like a genie or at least a medieval king granting an audience to his favored subjects. This is one area in which Christianity provides a testable hypothesis because we can look at those who engage in such prayer and those who don't and compare the results.

Thanks to an extensive study performed in 2006, we now have a definitive answer to the question of whether Christian prayer works.[19] The experiment was funded by the Templeton Foundation, whose explicit mission is to show that science supports religion.[20] The Templeton experimenters took roughly 1,800 patients scheduled for coronary bypass surgery at six US hospitals and divided them into three groups of approximately 600 each. One was prayed for but not told. Another, the control group, was not prayed for. The last was prayed for and told.

The results showed *no difference between the first two groups*. The prayers had no statistically significant effect. The patients in the control group did just as well or better as those for whom Christians were offering systematic pleas to Heaven. Interestingly, the last group showed more complications, suggesting that praying for people and then telling them about it, as is the practice with most prayer lists, did more harm than good. The takeaway would seem to be, don't bother praying for someone, but if you do, at least don't tell them about it because this may make them worse. If God were interested in encouraging more people to pray, as you expect He would be, then He would have ensured this study would unambiguously show just that. If prayer does have a measurable effect, then one must once again conclude that God has gone out of His way to hide that fact by ensuring this study does not support it. God has again taken extreme measures to support the atheistic hypothesis that He doesn't exist.

Suppose we could identify the most important and deserving prayer request of all and measure its effectiveness objectively. Consider the prayer of a mother as she embraces her suffering and dying baby: "Please, God, save my baby. Don't let her die." This is about as sincere and unselfish as any prayer can be. But in the developing world, we know it is either refused or ignored millions of times each year. The poor are more religious and pray more often than the wealthy. If prayer works, then we should see the most religious societies on Earth as the most secure places to live with the lowest infant mortality, but that is not what we see. The most religious places appear to be the most hellish places to live, in which children die annually by the thousands. Prayer appears to have no noticeable effect.

Save the Children, a charity organization that focuses on the world's poorest children, produced the "mother's index," revealing the best and worst places to be a mother. According to this index, the best countries to raise children are those with the lowest rates of religious belief, ranking highest in atheism. At the bottom are the most intensely religious countries.[21] Religious belief and prayer do not save the lives of babies or ease their suffering in any detectable way. Malnutrition, malaria, and other parasitic diseases, common causes of infant death in these countries, are horrible ways to die. In virtually every case, the children suffer terribly and die slowly. And yet these deaths occur most where Christian belief and prayer is strongest. Either no God exists, or God chooses not to answer the most sincere, important, and just prayers in the entire world.

Another knock against Christian prayer is its failure to generate any clearly supporting data, which by this point should be exceedingly voluminous and obvious. If there were a system by which people could obtain things they desired simply by asking for them and this system worked better than random chance, then it would be child's play for statisticians to prove that it works. This would unquestionably lead to a worldwide rush of people clamoring to adopt it. If Jesus is listening and does fulfill the wishes and prayers of Christians to any measurable degree as the Bible tells us he does, then wouldn't the entire world have noticed it by now? The reality, however, is that the majority of the world's religious people are not Christians. One must acknowledge this as, in part, a consequence of the failed hypothesis of Christian prayer.

Why do so many stories cited for the success of prayer involve self-limiting conditions or vague and subjective initial diagnoses? The website Why Won't God Heal Amputees? cleverly pokes fun at apologetic rationalizations for why all God's healings seem limited to situations in which His intervention is neither observable, measurable, nor otherwise unambiguous. It often appears that God, like the great and powerful Oz, is limited to giving people things they already had or would have gotten anyway.

Most Christians, if they are honest with themselves, will recognize these results as consistent with their own experience. They have prayed enough to recognize that prayers seem to come true to the same extent as wishes and to the same degree we might expect without appeals to divine intervention. We get far more found keys than ponies or superpowers. Accordingly, more sophisticated believers shy away from crediting prayer with every lucky break that falls their way, perhaps implicitly recognizing that Ockham's razor compels a more mundane explanation.

Apologists have, unsurprisingly, come up with an ad hoc solution to this problem. They claim that while God does answer all prayers, He doesn't always answer them as we would like because He knows best and our desires might interfere with His divine plan. His answers, like a cosmic Magic 8 ball, may consist of "yes," "no," or "wait." By directly contradicting Christian Scripture (which states clearly that just asking merits a yes—see earlier), apologists have rendered the previously falsifiable hypothesis unfalsifiable. Any state of affairs would be consistent with "Yes/no/wait God."

The same state of affairs would also be consistent with a belief system based on praying to a jug of milk. When they say God works in mysterious ways, what they really mean is mysteriously similar to random chance. With their falsifiable hypothesis falsified, apologists have once again moved from an argument *for God* to an argument that simply provides a weak excuse for believers to continue believing. The absurdity of this position was best demonstrated by comedian George Carlin:

> Long time ago, God made a Divine Plan. Gave it a lot of thought, decided it was a good plan, put it into practice. And for billions and billions of years, the Divine Plan has been doing just fine. Now, you come along, and pray for something. Well suppose the thing you want isn't in God's Divine Plan? What do you want Him to do? Change His plan? Just for you? Doesn't it seem a little arrogant? It's a Divine Plan. What's the use of being God if every run-down shmuck with a two-dollar prayer book can come along and fuck up Your Plan? And here's something else, another problem you might have: Suppose your prayers aren't answered. What do you say? "Well, it's God's will." "Thy Will Be Done." Fine, but if it's God's will, and He's going to do what He wants to anyway, why the fuck bother praying in the first place?[22]

This isn't the only reason prayer would be pointless. An omniscient God would know all our needs and desires before we would. There would be no need for prayer. Shouldn't God do the right thing even if we never prayed? If it isn't the right thing, then why would God allow it at all, regardless of our pleas? A good God would do good regardless of whether people begged Him to or not. What difference should it make to God if one or more people pray for a little girl dying of leukemia if God has decided she should die? Should it matter how many people pray for her? If not, why do we have prayer lists? Does God operate like a teenager paging through her social media, reserving His blessing for those who give Him the most Instagram "likes"? Is this the way a perfectly just being would operate—like a capricious king who hands out scraps of mercy in proportion to his subjects' groveling? Prayer simply sets up and reinforces a dynamic of begging that churches have perpetually exploited to benefit their very human leaders.

Adopting a belief system that incorporates prayer, furthermore, can warp one's sense of empathy and cause serious psychological damage. Such a system presumes that everything that happens is to some extent within our control. If God is all powerful and prayer can sway God, then every terrible event or circumstance could be thought of as something that happened because one or more people didn't pray hard enough or with enough conviction. Every tragedy takes on a moral component in which the victims are at fault for their own misfortune. A child who prays her mother will recover from terminal cancer will have only herself to blame if her mother dies anyway. In such a world, there are no true accidents—only consequences of inadequate piety. What a terrible psychological burden to bear—or to impose on others.

Finally, a belief in the power of prayer renders people otherwise impotent. If you believe God has things under control and your role in the process is simply to appeal for His intervention, then there is no incentive or even reason for you to do *anything* to fix the situation yourself. Once you've turned over the wheel to Jesus, you can't very well take it back. If you give God all your worries, heartaches, and fears, then you're not dealing with them. Teaching kids to pray to solve problems creates adults who can't solve problems.

EVIL AND SUFFERING

Imagine, if you will, a young woman living in rural Africa—perhaps the same one referenced in the previous section. Tears stream down her gaunt face as she rocks back and forth. She is weeping uncontrollably. In her arms is a frail baby. His bones protrude from his stiff, tiny frame. His glassy eyes stare off into space, unblinking. Her baby has died and in a most horrifying manner.

The child was a victim of starvation and disease. And that baby is not alone. Before the modern historical age, *50 percent of children* died before reaching their fifth birthday. Today, nearly 40,000 people, mostly children, die *every day* around the world due to hunger and malnutrition. The Holocaust left some six million Jews dead. But nearly double that number of children die *every year* in the developing world, many in great agony. Their parents pray furiously for them, but their prayers go unanswered. Their deaths leave behind anguish and despair—intense and unyielding pain.

You can say they died because there wasn't enough food or rain or medical care. But if you believe in the Christian God, you must acknowledge that God either caused those children to die or allowed them to die when He could have intervened. Either behavior is simply inconsistent with the loving God posited by Christianity. Nearly all the things for which men are hanged and imprisoned are everyday performances for nature. Nature impales men, breaks them as if on a wheel, casts them to be devoured by animals, burns them to death, crushes them with stones, starves them with hunger, and freezes them with the cold. This is the same nature the Bible identifies as the instrument of God. And that, in nutshell, is the problem of suffering.

Suffering is everywhere. Those of us in the developed world can deceive ourselves that it is not that common or that terrible because our exposure to it is limited, but the truth is just a Google search away. Suffering is real, it is intense, and it is going on all over the world in appalling numbers. Millions of sentient creatures suffer terribly every day. And that is how it has always been.

Suffering is a huge problem for Christian apologists. I would estimate they have devoted more attention to this issue than any other—and for good reason. It represents a devastating refutation of Christianity by shining the spotlight on a feature of the world that is completely inconsistent with Christian claims. It is often called the "evidential problem of evil" because the vast evidence of suffering (or evil) so markedly contradicts what Christianity predicts.[23] If Christianity is assumed to be true, then the existence of such suffering is *extremely surprising*.

An entire subfield of apologetics exists to respond to the problem of suffering. It is known as theodicy, with the apologetic responses themselves labeled "theodicies."[24] Despite more than a thousand years of effort, however, no apologist has come up with a theodicy convincing those outside the insular circle of other apologists and Christian theologians. Though I cannot address them all in this limited space, I hope my brief survey of the most popular theodicies demonstrate why I find each unconvincing and why you should, too.

Many recognize this issue as the problem of "evil," and it can be thought of that way. But *evil* is a theologically loaded word. It suggests there exists a measurable, palpable force with agency and purpose of its own—a sinister force that guides and cajoles human behavior.[25] Numerous religious belief systems are built on such an assumption, as it represents a primitive, prescientific way to explain terrible events that tap into our cognitive inclination to assign agency to impersonal forces.

Today, however, there is no good reason to think of evil in this way. No such force has ever been demonstrated to exist. Our understanding of human behavior has revealed a complex web of motivations for all behaviors. Everyone who commits bad acts justifies and rationalizes them to himself as "good" in some way. Some have said that there are no true heroes or villains, only people with different assumptions and motives. Such motives permit no simplistic approach, such as attributing all antisocial behaviors to a singular, nefarious force called "evil."

When I use the term throughout this discussion, I am referring to bad things that happen to sentient creatures. I generally use the term *suffering* because this adequately captures the concept from the appropriate perspective but without the theological baggage associated with the term *evil*. When I use *evil*, I mean it only in the descriptive sense, to characterize some action that causes suffering without a clear and legitimate justification.

Moreover, evil as typically used doesn't capture suffering caused by such natural forces as earthquakes and disease. A hurricane is not normally thought of as evil, as it has no agency, but it can cause enormous suffering just the same. Positing the question in terms of evil is therefore underinclusive. The real question that must be answered by the apologists is not whether there is evil in the world (for it isn't clear such a thing even exists) but why, if God exists, there is so much *suffering*.

The problem of suffering can be thought of as a subset of the previously discussed problem of God's silence. Once again, apologists face explaining why God sits idle where we would expect, from his biblical biography, to find him more involved than a Little League parent. According to Christian theology, for example, Jesus has been present in every room in which a child was sexually molested or otherwise physically abused and failed to stop it. Why? Other religions must occasionally explain the inaction of their gods but not to the same extent as Christians.

The pervasiveness of suffering is a uniquely Christian problem because other religions do not claim for their deities the remarkable qualities attributed by Christians to theirs. Other religions do not claim their gods to be all-powerful, all-knowing, and all-loving. They do not claim their gods to be perfect defenders of justice. *Christian theodicy* has been defined as the attempt to reconcile God's omnipotence, omniscience, and omnibenevolence with the prevalence of suffering, an issue that simply doesn't arise for non-Christians.[26]

The Bible assigns these qualities to God. See, for example, Matthew 19:26, 1 John 3:20, and Psalm 145:9. Many Christian doctrines are premised upon God possessing all three. Yet no principled response to the problem of suffering *allows for all three*. God must either be ignorant of human suffering, powerless to stop it, or indifferent. Indifference to human suffering would contravene a loving God. Few Christians would be comfortable with a God who simply doesn't care about them.

Under Christianity, we would expect God to produce pain and pleasure only when He has morally sufficient reasons to do so. If God guided evolution, then we would expect the pain and pleasure of sentient beings to be tied inextricably to actions with moral consequences and in direct relation to the moral quality of their choices. Under naturalism, we would expect pain and pleasure to be tied directly or indirectly to reproduction and survival, incentivizing behaviors that lead to reproductive success, which is what we observe. Even seemingly gratuitous pleasure, such as the sexual pleasure of infertile couples, can be understood as side effects of connections evolved to serve reproductive functions. Such side effects are just what we would expect in a naturalistic world with no mechanism for fine-tuning. They are inexplicable in a theistic world governed by an all-powerful God. In such a world, every connection must have an explanation based on moral significance. Christianity must resolve this glaring imbalance in favor of naturalism.

Any effective Christian theodicy must not just reconcile the attributes essential to a recognizable and consistent vision of God. It must also (1) account for all the suffering in the world; (2) maintain consistency with widely held scientific and historical opinion; (3) not rely on the unknown and unknowable; and (4) incorporate coherent, plausible, and recognizable moral principles. Let's look at the most well-regarded theodicies and see how they fare.

A. Apologetic Responses: Suffering Is Necessary for the Greater Good

The first response I heard to the problem of suffering and one I still hear regularly is that suffering is necessary for the "greater good." Though it may seem to us mere mortals that suffering is a bad thing, that is only because our perspective is limited. If we could see things from a more cosmic perspective—God's perspective—then we would understand where suffering fits into the big picture and why it must exist to further God's ultimate divine plan, which is righteous and good.

The "greater good" argument is also known as "philosophical optimism." It was notoriously advocated by French philosopher Gottfried Leibniz—and challenged by Leibniz's contemporary Voltaire most brilliantly in his book *Candide*. Leibniz maintained that if God were indeed omniscient, omnipotent, and omnibenevolent, as Christian doctrine maintains, then any world He created must necessarily be the best of all possible worlds. Accordingly, anything we perceive as bad cannot *really* be bad, as, after all, it was *intended by God*. If we had God's knowledge, then we would understand how and why what we perceive to be bad is actually good. In other words, whatever is, is right. Voltaire brilliantly demonstrated the many absurdities this view entailed, describing parades of miseries inherent in the human condition, juxtaposed with the endless optimism of his protagonist, certain of his place in the best of possible worlds.

The question that initially comes to mind when I hear something like this is "On what basis can you make such a claim?" The only perspective available to us is our own. Without a full understanding of God's plan, how can anyone possibly say this plan is ultimately good or that all the suffering in the world (or *any* suffering) is necessary to its success? Assuming God exists and has a plan, that plan is an unknown quantity. To say we can be sure God's plan is good because the Bible tells us so is circular reasoning. And to say its success requires vast suffering is so beyond speculative as to be absurd.

If we observed someone engage in numerous criminal acts, such as rape and murder, would we immediately assume this was actually a good man committing such acts for a noble cause? Of course not. We would take his actions at face value and assume his character to be in line with his actions. Only if presented with compelling evidence that these actions were out of character, along with specific justifications for each, would we consider changing our assessment. Only if we saw how these criminal acts were warranted by consequences not otherwise obvious could we be expected to think differently about this man's character.

No such evidence is ever presented to justify the world's suffering. Apologists simply assume there *must* be good reasons for all the suffering because God *must* be good, once again beginning with a conclusion and sticking with it despite all evidence to the contrary. The apologists, wedded firmly to an a priori position immune to argument, meet overwhelming evidence with a mere assertion. Bob the atheist says, "Suffering is bad; see examples 1 through 1 billion." Alex the apologist says, "Suffering is ultimately good; see . . . nothing. Just trust me. Have faith."

Assume you live in a totalitarian regime in which the king imposes and brutally enforces crushing taxes and people are dying in the streets, with no public assistance. The need for the taxes has never been explained. Neither you nor anyone you know has seen any evidence of the king providing positive aid to help his subjects, despite having the resources to do so. What would you think of such a king?

Further assume someone approaches you and says, "Perhaps the king is doing this for a greater good. You don't know what his plan might be, so you shouldn't protest against him but simply be happy to live in his kingdom. You should trust that his tactics are justified, even though, for whatever reason, he isn't explaining them to us." Would that satisfy you? Would it cause you to simply accept things as they are?

Occasionally, someone identifies a "silver lining" to an apparent tragedy. Perhaps after running over a child while driving drunk, Peter quit drinking and became a better father. Or perhaps after surviving a horrible disease, Carol stopped obsessing over trivial details, relished life more, and became more "spiritual." It is not surprising that some good would occasionally come from otherwise terrible circumstances. But it is ludicrous to think that all suffering can be justified in this way. There is no sound basis for extrapolating from a few anecdotes to all the suffering of the world. Could there ever be any benefit that the survivors of a deadly tsunami would consider worth the loss of their families? What good came to those millions of Jews murdered in the Holocaust?

And that is just the problem with this response. The proponents can identify no specific good resulting from even a small percentage of the suffering in the world. I don't mean in a purely hypothetical way but in a real-world, demonstrable way. As apologist Richard Swinburne acknowledges, claiming greater goods justify the presence of widespread suffering is worthless unless one can point out exactly *what they are and how they fit into the big picture*.[27] You could just as easily make the claim that all the good in the world is for a greater evil, thus demonstrating that God is evil.[28] The evidence would look the same.

Nor can any apologist provide a plausible *framework* by which such suffering could be justified. They simply ask us to have faith that it is all part of God's plan—that God could not accomplish His goals without inflicting or allowing massive anguish. Ultimately, this response is just another version of the appeal to mystery. The response violates Ockham's razor because it requires the assumption that God has good reasons for the world's suffering but has mysteriously chosen to hide them from us. How are hidden and unknowable reasons different in practice from no reasons at all? Why posit the existence of reasons when none are apparent to even the most dedicated and astute theologians?

Another flaw in the apologists' reasoning is that they inappropriately treat the entire human race as if it were a single organism. They claim, for instance, that allowing some suffering will lead to improvement or advancement, such as some degree of enlightenment. This might make sense were we talking about a single creature that can progressively learn from mistakes. But humans are individuals. Suffering borne by one individual cannot be justified by the enlightenment of another individual or even a group of individuals.

And that is not the lesson we learn when looking at the history of civilization. If the wages of sin were intended to be instructional, then why has humanity still not learned its lesson? If the atrocities of the last two thousand years were some type of divine lesson plan leading people to Christianity, then why have we not seen a steady increase in Christian ranks with virtually the entire world now Christian? If this was God's method of teaching, then it has been spectacularly unsuccessful.

Such a response is also insulting to those who have experienced suffering. It suggests their pain is ultimately insignificant: "I understand that your baby has died, but your pain is nothing when compared to the goal her death has served." I suspect you could forgive the grieving parent from asking questions that no apologist can answer, such as "What goal?" and "How?" The parent is essentially being told that their grief is misplaced because their suffering is part of a mysterious, undefinable cosmic plan to make things better for *someone*. They should be happy for the opportunity to contribute!

As Voltaire points out in *Candide*, furthermore, philosophical optimism leads to fatalism—the conclusion that we should take no action to alleviate suffering or stop evil. If the current state of the world is right in the eyes of God, then whatever *will be* is also right. If all suffering happens according to God's plan, then by working to alleviate it, aren't we undermining God's will? By preventing suffering, we are also preventing the greater good for which it is required. And by extension, we can rationalize any act, no matter how horrendous. For if God does not actively prevent you from performing it, then God has permitted it, so it must be for the greater good.

Let us assume for a moment that all this suffering is in fact necessary to serve God's plan. Would a just God require His children to endure horrendous pain and suffering without (1) an understanding of why their pain was necessary and (2) the opportunity to choose whether to endure the torment? No good human would do this. But God provides no one that information. And God provides no one a choice. In any other context, this would be universally condemned as highly immoral. Why should it be different with God? Any God who employs such a plan cannot be good.

The argument that God may have an unknown purpose that justifies our suffering, furthermore, is just another way of saying that the end always justifies the means. This Machiavellian position is poorly regarded by ethicists today. Assume that you can build a happy, thriving society but only by making a little girl suffer every day in agonizing torture with no hope of relief. Would you do it? If not, then you have answered whether a justification for the world's suffering can exist, for God does much, much worse.

Perhaps the biggest problem for apologists who make this argument is that they must deny God's omnipotence. A truly omnipotent God could accomplish whatever ends He desires *with no* negative consequences. It makes no sense to say that suffering is an unfortunate means to God's ends because the Christian God doesn't require means. One cannot say of an omnipotent being that he requires A to accomplish B because an omnipotent being *requires nothing* to accomplish B. That is what being omnipotent means. So ultimately, suffering cannot be justified by God's divine plan because if God were omnipotent, *He would need no such plan.* Any God who would require the suffering humans observe daily cannot be the God of Christianity.

In summary, the "greater good" is a deficient rationale for evil and suffering. It requires one to assume something (good reasons for all suffering) for which there is no evidence and acquiesce to a framework that violates widely accepted ethical norms. It is not enough for the apologist to claim that God *may have* morally sufficient reasons for allowing suffering in the world, for it is the burden of the apologist to show that God *does have morally sufficient reasons*, and this he cannot do. Such a proposal denies God's omnipotence by assuming that God cannot stop the suffering without tanking His divine plan or even that He would require any such plan when He could simply accomplish His ends directly. Finally, there is the problem that "greater good" theodicies are compatible with every possible state of affairs—with any piece of evidence that could be presented. They are nonfalsifiable and render any notion of God's "goodness" ultimately meaningless.

B. Apologetic Responses: Suffering Is Necessary So Man Can Exercise Free Will

Probably the second-most common response is that God must allow suffering to afford man free will. C. S. Lewis writes, "Try to exclude the possibility of suffering which the order of nature and the existence of free wills involve, and you will find that you have excluded life itself."[29] Lewis and like-minded proponents posit that God did not want people to be robots, doing everything He commanded without thought. He created them to be morally accountable agents. Such agents can express love and affection, which God values. But this ability is a double-edged sword with the potential for abuse, as when humans choose not to act morally. The good of allowing humans to exercise free will outweighs the bad, but some suffering is a necessary by-product. Lewis offers the following example to demonstrate the necessity of free will in any divine plan:

> In a game of chess you can make certain arbitrary concessions to your opponent, which stand to the ordinary rules of the game as miracles stand to the laws of nature. You can deprive yourself of a castle or allow the other man sometimes to take back a move made inadvertently. But if you conceded everything that at any moment happened to suit him—if all his moves were revocable and if all your pieces disappeared whenever their position on the board was not to his liking—then you could not have a game at all. So it is with the life of souls in a world: fixed laws, consequences unfolding by causal necessity, the whole natural order, are at once limits within which their common life is confined and also the sole condition under which any such life is possible.[30]

The first problem with offering free will as the justification is that it only addresses a *tiny fraction* of the suffering in the world—that directly caused by morally significant choices of humans. This would include such things as war and first-degree murder. But it would not include famine, disease, or other natural causes. Nor would it account for the billions of years of horrendous animal suffering before humans arrived on the scene or the animal suffering today not caused by humans. How would it jeopardize human free will for God to prevent a chimpanzee from slowly starving to death in remote Africa?

The second problem is that allowing people to do evil itself often deprives others of free will. For example, the murder of a young child would prevent the child from ever exercising their free will. The sexual molestation of a child will deeply affect their psyche, affecting all their subsequent choices.

Likewise, allowing a totalitarian regime, such as the Third Reich, to thrive would deprive millions of opportunities to make free moral choices. The Jews of Nazi Germany were placed into concentration camps, where they had virtually no choices to make. What's more, millions were killed—preventing any additional exercise of free will. By not intervening, God simply favors the free will of bad people over the free will of their victims. This response must ultimately concede that God is not all good, for no "good" father would allow a child to die simply to preserve a soldier's autonomy. A God who allows not only the actions of evil but also all its consequences is effectively the noninterventionist God of the Deists, but this is not the God of Christianity.

Third, given God's alleged omnipotence, there is no reason He could not allow for free will without suffering. For example, God could intervene immediately after a poor moral choice to prevent that choice from causing actual harm. You could freely choose to shoot your cable repairman, but God could instantly vaporize the bullet before it reached its target. Your free will has not been impaired, and no suffering has resulted. Because God is timeless, He knows what we would do in every situation. He knows if we will steal that iPhone when no one is looking. Why would it be necessary to allow these situations to play out when they would cause harm to others?

God could also incentivize good moral choices far more directly, discouraging behaviors that lead to suffering without affecting free will. He could, for instance, make good moral choices more pleasurable to us, so we would be encouraged to do them. If anything, the opposite seems true. Our physical pleasure centers seem primed for self-indulgent behaviors. Alternatively, He could punish immoral actions immediately and unambiguously, as parents do with their children—instilling a strong moral code through carrots and sticks in real time. A God who despises suffering could accomplish either without disturbing free will. But God does neither.

Those who claim God could not provide incentives for good behavior or punish bad behavior directly must account for the many Bible stories in which God does just that. On many occasions, God "hardened the hearts" of Israel's enemies, pushing them to commit wrongful acts that would justify God's retribution. Why could God not similarly "soften" the hearts of otherwise bad people to prevent them from causing suffering? On other occasions, such as that of Paul of Tarsus, God directly intervened in the life of a man who persecuted others to set him on the right path. Paul's conversion is universally heralded by Christians, despite the fact that it counts as divine interference. If these stories are true, then God shouldn't hesitate to do the same regularly to prevent suffering on a mass scale. But He doesn't.

Apologetic responses to these arguments presuppose a cosmic playing field with the same rules as the world we live in, but that would not be the only option to an omnipotent God. A possible better world that preserves free will without unnecessary suffering would be one in which people suffer for their own bad choices but others do not. Video gaming provides us with such a world, where we can make bad decisions that do not actually harm real people. The film *The Matrix* also presents such a world—one of virtual reality, in which actions and consequences could be distanced and isolated from one another by the controllers of the world. Though *The Matrix* is science fiction, there is nothing about such a reality that would be impossible for the Christian God.

God could also create a world in which there are more direct consequences for people who do harm to others, as opposed to the world we live in, where there seems to be very little, if any, correlation between being good, as Christians define it, and earthly rewards or punishments. Once the atheist identifies this as a possible world, the apologist must demonstrate that such a world is logically impossible. He may not justifiably shift the burden of proof and require the atheist to provide the particulars of such a world. If God is omnipotent, as Christians claim, then He can create any world not logically impossible. The apologist must explain why He doesn't.

Christian appeals to free will drastically underestimate the gap between God's understanding and human understanding, which is supposedly infinite. A far lesser gap exists between an adult and children in nursery school. But suppose I give a class of toddlers guns, knives, and explosives, leaving it up to the children to use the weapons as they choose. Should I escape moral accountability if someone is hurt? If you think I should be held accountable, then why not God, who has left His children with the means to inflict far more carnage upon one another?

Finally, this argument values free will far more highly than anyone can reasonably justify. Why should we expect that an additional degree of freedom would more than compensate for all the suffering we see in the world? The suffering is a known, and it is immense. The advantages of the marginal increase in "freedom" are a complete unknown, so the two cannot be compared, but no one has come up with a plausible basis for assigning it such value. There is no recognizable version of good that would privilege autonomy so highly or so cavalierly disregard the rights of the innocent. The preservation of free will simply cannot account for the prevalence of suffering.

C. Apologetic Responses: Suffering Represents the Necessary Casualties of a Cosmic War

A response that has gained traction among certain apologists of late, such as Alvin Plantinga and Gregory Boyd, is that suffering (especially from natural causes) is the result of a "cosmic conflict" between the forces of good and evil. As Boyd puts it, "My claim, then, is that the earth is a battlefield. We are, like Normandy in World War II, caught in the cross fire of a cosmic battle. And on battlefields, as you know, all sorts of terrible things happen. In such a situation, everything becomes a potential weapon, and every person a potential victim."[31] Humans are simply "collateral damage" in a war between God and Satan.

The first thing to point out about this position is that it lacks virtually any biblical support. It is a Zoroastrian concept borrowed from the religion of ancient Babylonians. There is nothing in the Bible about an ongoing cosmic war between good and evil. Second, it entirely concedes God's omnipotence, for an omnipotent God could instantly destroy the forces of evil with a mere thought. The image it proposes is of God and His army of angels in a pitched battle with Satan and his demons. The battle rages every minute of every day. Ground is gained and then lost. God may claim victory in one battle, but Satan claims it in the next. The result of every skirmish is uncertain. The God of this scenario is not in control. He is merely a combatant against an equally matched opponent. And He is powerless to stop the carnage of their war.

If taken to its logical conclusion, this view would render Christianity a very risky bet. For if the outcome of the war is so uncertain, then why should one be so quick to bet on God? If God cannot assure a victory in any particular battle or even control the body count, then how can anyone be sure He will come out on top in the ultimate war? The apologetic response breaks down into clearly ad hoc reasoning, for no apologist can concede that the cosmic war might be lost! Boyd claims that God merely *delegates* some of His power, perhaps to preserve the free will of such spiritual beings as demons, as if God were more concerned about the free will of demons than innocent human children. This simply opens up the apologists' response to all the objections to the "free will" response discussed previously.

If God can delegate his power, for example, then He also has the power to rescind that delegation. So this doesn't get God off the hook for the world's suffering, for He always can end it by taking back the power He ceded. If Satan was overly ambitious, then it is only because God made him that way and can just as easily unmake him. God wrote and directed the play, so how can one blame the actors? To the extent there is a cosmic war going on, it is all part of God's plan, including all the collateral damage. So depending on how you look at this response, God is either impotent or ambivalent to human suffering. In either case, this would be a God foreign to mainstream Christianity.

D. Apologetic Responses: Suffering Is Temporary and Justified by the Afterlife

Perhaps, say such apologists as Randy Alcorn, all human suffering is justified by the afterlife. After all, Heaven is forever. Any suffering we experience on Earth is trivial when viewed from this eternal perspective. For the righteous, their pain will be more than compensated for by a subsequent eternity of blissful pleasure. Philosopher Stephen Maitzen calls this the "Heaven swamps everything" theodicy.[32]

The first problem with this response is that it is based on a circular argument. It assumes the existence of something (Heaven), for which we have no evidence but the Bible.[33] If there is no Heaven, then Heaven cannot justify earthly suffering. Likewise, if Heaven exists but is not as great as the Bible claims it to be, then it cannot justify earthly suffering. But we have no good evidence for either the existence or nature of Heaven! We have only claims made about Heaven in the New Testament of the Bible, for the Old Testament does not mention Heaven at all. While human suffering may be temporary, it is still real. If there is an afterlife, then we have no concept of how it compares with the reality of this world. We're not justified in using this afterlife, of which we know nothing and have no evidence, to justify the real, known suffering of this world.

Second, the response conflates compensation with justification. The claim is that the sheer volume of bliss you will experience in Heaven will *more than compensate you* for the suffering you experienced on Earth. But that is not the same as demonstrating that your suffering was *justified*. Would any payment justify causing a child to be born into prostitution, tortured daily for years, blinded, starved, and then subjected to a horribly painful disease? Justification and compensation represent entirely separate issues.

Assume you live in a medieval fiefdom and learn that the king has brutally raped and killed one of your three children. The king offers to compensate you with riches beyond your wildest dreams. He will offer you a kingdom of your own. Your remaining children will grow up well educated and without a care in the world. The king will even ensure that each is likewise well appointed with an amazing job when they reach adulthood. Would you feel that these overtures *justified* the king's prior actions? Would you take his offer and consider all forgiven? Would you now recognize the king as a good and just man?

I expect your answers to these questions would all be the same: of course not. This is because human morality does not allow a legitimate moral complaint to be erased by any subsequent compensation—regardless of the amount. We judge the morality of an action by whether it was justified *when it was taken*. Where we have not specifically agreed to the terms on the front end, God cannot be absolved of evil acts by "buying us off" after the fact. So even if Heaven exists and it is as wonderful and eternal as claimed, it cannot justify earthly suffering. If God exists and is truly good, then He would never have allowed it in the first place.[34]

E. Apologetic Responses: Suffering Is Justified by the Fall of Man

Many apologists lay all human suffering on mankind's common ancestors, Adam and Eve. Because they made a bad decision, God is absolved of responsibility. God allowed humans to determine their own fate, and their representatives, the first human couple, screwed it up for everyone. All sentient creatures have been paying the price ever since. Apologist and author Tim Keller explains it this way:

> One of the greatest barriers to belief in God is the problem of suffering and evil in the world. Why, people ask, did God create a world in which violence, pain, and death are endemic? The answer of traditional theology is—he didn't. He created a good world but also gave human beings free will, and through their disobedience and "Fall," death and suffering came into the world.[35]

This response parsimoniously presumes a literal reading of the book of Genesis, in which Adam and Eve disobeyed God and were cast out of the Garden of Eden. God also cursed them and all their descendants with sin and death. Their sin was inherited by and imputed to all humans, justifying all the suffering of the human race from that point forward. This point is made explicitly by Paul in Romans 5:12–21. It is also presupposed by such passages as John 3:3; 2 Corinthians 5:17; and Colossians 3:10, in which humans are said to be in need of being made anew, or Hebrews 12:23, in which our final state is described as one in which our spirits are perfected.

I pass quickly over the objection that evolution assures us that the literal story of Adam and Eve could not have been true.[36] Let's move to the more troubling aspect of this story: that a just God would allow the act of an ancestor to condemn all their descendants. Can anyone think of an analogous situation today that we would consider morally just? A virtually universal moral precept is that people can be held accountable only for their own acts. The justice system of every civilized country is based on the shared assumption of personal responsibility. We are responsible only for our own actions and deserve no punishment for those of another. If you must get your morality from the Bible, then it even says it there: "The son shall not suffer for the iniquity of the father, nor the father suffer for the iniquity of the son. The righteousness of the righteous shall be upon himself, and the wickedness of the wicked shall be upon himself" (Ezekiel 18:19–20).

Even if God did curse mankind, then He holds it within his power to lift that curse. But He chooses not to. So we are just back where we started—trying to provide a legitimate justification for God failing to stop human suffering.

F. Apologetic Responses: Suffering Should Be Expected Because God Doesn't Owe Us Anything

Some apologists, citing such passages as Romans 9:20, maintain that we have no right to question human suffering or indeed to any explanation for anything because God doesn't owe us anything. Everything He has given is a gift we don't deserve (grace), including our health and happiness, so He is always justified in taking that gift away for any reason. We aren't entitled to expect God to prevent our suffering because God is so much greater than us that we can only defer to His judgment.

The first problem with this view is that it contradicts the biblical narrative of the relationship between God and mankind. The Bible doesn't present humans as God's playthings, as Greek mythology does with its gods. It presents God as the loving father of mankind. At a minimum, that should mean we should expect God to adhere to the universal norms governing parent-child relationships. We do not absolve a parent from any duty to her child because the parent gave that child life. The child did not ask to be born. The act of creating a human life imposes upon the parent the responsibility to properly care for that life, at least until it can properly care for itself. Parents who fail in this duty, such as mothers who habitually neglect their babies, are subject to criminal liability and public shame. Likewise, a just God would properly look after the living beings He caused to exist and not treat them wantonly.

The second problem is that this view of gift giving is not consistent with modern morality. If I give someone a gift, then I can't rightfully take it back. Doing so is both immoral and illegal. I cannot, for instance, give blood to save someone's life and then demand it back later. Nor can I fund a lifesaving medical procedure as a gift and then raid that person's bank account for the funds or forcibly take their life because I saved it. Would you think it moral for a man to save a woman's life and then demand she be his sex slave? If Christians maintain that God's gifts have strings attached, such as our obedience, then He never truly gives us anything. Even if our life is a gift, then why should we be grateful when God literally has everything and these gifts cost Him nothing? Should a beggar be grateful to the multibillionaire who buys him a fast-food meal and in return demands his eternal subservience? The creation of an obligation must involve a real sacrifice by the one giving the gift. But God makes no sacrifice. Man, therefore, bears Him no obligation for the mere unrequested "gift" of being born.

G. The Bible Addresses Suffering: The Book of Job

One might rightly inquire why apologists must spend so much time and effort dealing with this issue when the Bible devotes an entire book to it. The book of Job is addressed to the problem of suffering and divine justice, and no discussion thereof would be complete without examining it. This book promises to take us behind the "mystery" of God's plan, so it is crucial to look at how it addresses this most intractable of problems.

The character of Job is by all accounts a model servant of God. When God brags on Job to Satan (they appear to be essentially drinking buddies in this account), Satan suggests that Job's goodness results from his tremendous wealth and prosperity. God therefore proposes a wager: Satan may afflict Job with every form of misfortune, and they will see whether Job turns away from God. God will allow Satan to cause Job tremendous suffering, putting Job's faith to the ultimate test, so God can prove his point and win . . . bragging rights? The stakes are not revealed.

Satan sets upon his task almost immediately. Job's cattle are slaughtered; his fields are burned; his slaves are killed; all his wealth is destroyed in a single day. But Satan is not done. In an act of savage cruelty, Satan causes Job's house to collapse, crushing all Job's children beneath it. Job is of course horribly distraught, but he does not turn away from God.

God wins this first round, but Satan wants to go double or nothing. So God allows Satan to turn the screws tighter and ratchet up Job's misfortunes to see if this will finally cause Job to crack. While previously preventing Satan from causing Job physical harm, God now removes this restriction. Satan runs with this, inflicting Job with agonizing boils across his body, resulting in horrific suffering. Seeing her husband's severe distress, Job's wife is so distraught that she prompts Job to "curse God and die." But Job's faith is steadfast.

The main "instructive" part of the tale then begins, in which Job's "friends" attempt explanations for his precipitous change of fortune though literary dialogues. They argue that Job must have committed great evil, for which he is being punished—the only way they can retain their image of a just God, given Job's situation. Job knows this isn't the case and so posits God must be unjust, effectively winning the bet for Satan by essentially turning against God. One friend argues that neither Job nor his friends are correct.

Finally, God appears to Job in a whirlwind. Rather than provide Job with the explanation Job and his friends have been seeking, however, God reprimands Job for his insolence. God seems upset that Job has begun trash-talking God, proving Satan's point. Like the Wizard of Oz, God essentially bellows, "Who are you to question me? I am great and all powerful, while you are but dirt. I own you and can do whatever I want with you. I don't owe you anything, much less an explanation of my actions." Job agrees with God that he is not entitled to an explanation for God murdering his entire family or inflicting him with horrible pain and disease, and he simply grovels before God. Job's obsequiousness pleases God. God "rewards" Job with twice the wealth he had before and with new sons and daughters to replace the ones God killed by proxy. The end.

From the standpoint of a Christian trying to resolve the problem of suffering, the book of Job must be quite a letdown. God simply refuses to explain himself and then attempts to buy Job off with new wealth and children, invoking the whole justification-versus-compensation issue discussed in section D. No wonder apologists find this book unsatisfactory and unsatisfying for harmonizing suffering with Christianity.

But while God doesn't explicitly reveal his reasons to Job, we can see, from the omniscient narrator approach of the author, that God had *very clear motives* for allowing Job's suffering. Like the two investment banker villains in the 1980s movie *Trading Places*, the Duke brothers, God just wanted to prove he was right in a friendly argument with his adversary, Satan, and win a bet. In *Trading Places*, wealthy Wall Street broker Randolph Duke bets his equally wealthy brother Mortimer that a trader's success was entirely due to his fortunate upbringing and circumstances. The Dukes therefore arrange for the trader to lose everything while replacing him with a poor, streetwise con artist. Once the trader's life falls apart, proving Randolph correct, the bet is settled—for one dollar. The villainous character of the Duke brothers is driven home by the negligible worth they place upon destroying another person's life.

I suspect knowing this would have upset Job greatly, as it should upset anyone reading the story. God's motives were petty and callous, with no regard for the suffering He caused His most loyal servant. The Duke brothers received their due comeuppance at the end of *Trading Places*. Why should we look at God any differently? The book of Job, the Bible's most direct response to the problem of suffering, clearly shows God to be of the same character as the most vile and cartoonishly evil movie villains.

H. Suffering Cannot Be Coherently Harmonized with Christianity

I hope it is clear by now that each of the previous responses fails to explain the evil and suffering of the world satisfactorily. If Christianity is true, then we simply shouldn't see widespread suffering. An all-powerful, all-loving God would ensure that it didn't exist. Under Christianity, such suffering is extraordinarily surprising, for it is incompatible with any plausible model. Apologists attempting to build a defense to the problem of suffering must tear so many blocks from the foundations of Christianity that it falls apart around them.

But let us now consider the competing hypothesis: naturalism. According to naturalism, there is no overarching plan. There is no master intelligence guiding things along—no captain of the ship. According to naturalism, the world comprises billions of independent agents and natural forces indifferent to human and animal suffering. If it is true, then we would expect to see great good and great evil and everything between. As Arthur C. Clarke points out, the problem of evil would simply be an "inevitable consequence of the bell-shaped curve of a normal distribution."[37] We would expect there to be no apparent rhyme or reason to the infliction of suffering. We would expect it to appear random and chaotic. And *that is just what we see*. Naturalism is the most parsimonious explanation for the suffering we observe in the world. It is the conclusion demanded by Ockham's razor.

Looking at suffering through the lens of naturalism is liberating: The reason natural suffering looks random and meaningless is because *it is* random and meaningless. No one is being punished; it's not anyone's fault; no greater good is being served. A child who suffers and dies from a horrible disease did nothing to deserve her ailment, and there is no God for whom we must make excuses and rationalizations. This explanation makes perfect and efficient sense. It satisfies Ockham's razor. Why need we look any further?

I. Fairness and Justice

Similar to the problem of suffering is the problem of fairness and justice. We have become used to people saying "Life's not fair" as a truism. We all acknowledge that life isn't fair. But if God is truly just and all powerful, then *life should be fair*. A just God would create a just world. What explanation allows for a perfectly just God but such unjust conditions here on Earth?

Some will say we should not expect fairness in our lifetimes but only after death. This is a convenient rationale because we have no access to an afterlife through which to evaluate the claim. If that is the case, then the rules governing how we spend our postmortal eternities must accord with some recognizable sense of fairness. Any system of reward and punishment in the afterlife must incorporate proportionality and avoid excess. If it is to remotely model the best systems humans have created, then it must punish and reward only voluntary actions and not mere thoughts or beliefs, especially those over which one has no control. But that is not the system Christianity teaches. I address these issues in greater detail in a later section dealing with Hell. The bottom line here is that the world's inherent unfairness and injustice are highly surprising given Christianity but expected under naturalism, providing yet another reason to prefer the latter over the former.

CHRISTIANITY DOESN'T MAKE SENSE

> I do not feel obliged to believe that the same God who has endowed us with sense, reason, and intellect has intended us to forgo their use.
>
> —Galileo Galilei, Letter from Galileo Galilei to Grand Duchess Christina (1615)

This should not surprise anyone, but for a belief system to be valid, it must make sense. It cannot be premised on incoherent concepts or filled with internal inconsistencies, for coherence is a necessary condition of believability. Core concepts must fit together like pieces of a jigsaw puzzle. If the system is based on Scripture, then the Scripture must be consistent and coherent and convey unified themes. Christianity fails these tests.

Before going any further, I should point out that, though necessary, internal consistency is not sufficient to establish a valid belief system. I could come up with a system that is completely consistent, with every component fitting together perfectly, but it might still be false. If my system is not internally consistent, however—if it doesn't make sense—then it *must be false*. If Christianity fails the test of internal consistency, then it must be abandoned.

A. The Nature of God

> If he is infinitely good, what reason should we have to fear him? If he is infinitely wise, why should we have doubts concerning our future? If he knows all, why warn him of our needs and fatigue him with our prayers? If he is everywhere, why erect temples to him?
>
> —Percy Bysshe Shelley, *The Necessity of Atheism*

The first point at which Christianity fails the test of internal consistency is in formulating the nature of the Christian God. As defined by Christian apologists and theologians, God represents a mixture of known and unknown qualities, which ultimately breaks down into an ineffable entity about which nothing can be reliably said. The *National Catholic Almanac* defines God as possessing these attributes: "almighty, eternal, holy, immortal, immense, immutable, incomprehensible, ineffable, infinite, intelligent, invisible, just, loving, merciful, most high, most wise, omnipotent, omniscient, omnipresent, patient, perfect, provident, self-dependent, supreme, true."[38] This list is representative, though not exhaustive, of how other Christian denominations describe God. It does, however, illustrate the serious problems that arise when Christians attempt to move from vague generalities to specifics in defining their hypothesis.

I believe the vast majority of disputes between Christians and atheists begin and should probably end with the Christian's inability to clearly define the God he seeks to defend. An undefined and inscrutable God cannot be argued into existence through evidence because such a vague concept is both consistent and inconsistent with any evidence presented. Unlike a naturalistic model, the Christian concept of God does not allow us to know what evidence to even expect. While such an approach immunizes the theistic claim to evidentiary argument, it simultaneously divorces it from any reasoned defense.

Apologists often claim that atheists have been trying to disprove the existence of God for years, without success. But that isn't true because to make that statement, one must begin with a consistent definition of God and of success. A theistic god with defined traits who interacts with the physical world in observable ways has been disproven by atheists again and again, simply by demonstrating that none of the things we would expect to observe if such a God existed have ever been. If something is claimed to exist and that thing has consequences, then the consistent absence of those consequences should lead us to disbelieve. What atheists have clearly done is effectively refute and render untenable, again and again, standardly held definitions and conceptions of God. Using the tools of science and history, they have pummeled these down, forcing Christians to repeatedly redefine those concepts so much that what they've been left with so little resembles what they started with as to be unrecognizable.

The end result of centuries of criticism has been the apologetic embrace of a vague ineffable God—one defined more by what it is not than by what it is. When skeptics have latched onto some claim about God and directed arguments to refute it, the claim is dispersed into the untargetable cloud of metaphor. What's left has been, as philosopher Thomas Nagel describes it, an "unspecified purposiveness that itself remains unexplained."[39]

A claim that something exists can never be proven false unless that something is defined so clearly that certain demonstrable circumstances would contravene its existence. The inability to conclusively disprove some abstract, nebulously defined concept does not give us sufficient grounds to deem it worthy of consideration. Just as no atheist has ever definitively disproved the existence of the God of Abraham, no Christian has ever disproved the existence of millions of gods various other religions have believed in throughout history. Does that count in those gods' favor? Is it reason to lend them belief? The only options are that *most* gods are the subject of human fantasy or that *all* gods are the subject of human fantasy, and the more one considers these options, the more it should become apparent that they are not so far apart.

There is an irreconcilable conflict among Christians in how they attempt to conceptualize God. On one hand, they agree that man can have no direct knowledge of God's nature. God's nature must ultimately be unknowable to man. But if God's nature is truly unknowable, then how can we reliably say *anything* about God? How can we say, for example, that He cares for mankind or is good in any meaningful sense? If God is defined with such negative attributes as ineffable (indescribable), immutable (changeless), or eternal (not subject to temporal succession), then He is indistinguishable from nonexistence. These tell us nothing affirmative about God and in fact make it *impossible* to say anything affirmative about Him. We could not infer His motives or nature, even in the most general sense. This will not do for theologians and apologists. One cannot base a religion around an ineffable God. There must be some meat on the bone.

But a problem arises once one attempts to positively define God, for this very process limits God's nature. To say that God has characteristic A necessarily means that He lacks the characteristic of non-A. If God is just, for example, then He cannot simultaneously be unjust. In certain cases, God's attributes conflict indirectly: To be perfectly merciful must at times conflict with being perfectly just, as sometimes justice does not entail mercy. To avoid this problem, theologians long ago introduced the notion of "unlimited attributes"—characteristics of God that purportedly do not limit His nature. Hence, we have such traits as omnipotence, omniscience, and omnibenvolence, which define the Christian God of classical theism.

These unlimited attributes, however, represent a contradiction in terms. A trait such as "powerful" indicates a certain *quantity* of power, and any quantity, no matter how large, is necessarily limited. What could it possibly mean to have unlimited power if we must do away with the idea of quantities entirely, leaving no scale by which to judge? It is meaningless, for we have abandoned all criteria that could give it meaning.

These traits cannot be defined in terms of analogy. One cannot say, for instance, that God's omnipotence can be thought of in terms of a powerful human, just to a greater (in fact, an infinitely great) degree. If gods are defined in terms of degree, then man would be a god to a dog. A dog would be a god to a slime mold, and so on, to absurd extremes. Any creature superior to another would become a "god" at some point. Despite their relative superiorities, what all known creatures (and even aliens, should we ever encounter them) have in common is that they are bound by the same natural laws of the universe. Those laws are what we use to measure their relative superiority. But this is not true of God. It can't be.

The difference between God and anything within the natural world therefore must be one of *kind*, not merely degree. God is not bound by natural laws. He is, by definition, *supernatural*. He cannot even be placed on the same scale. There is no scale on which to hang such words as *more* or *most*. But this raises a new problem, for what could we possibly mean by a supernatural or transcendent being? To exist outside natural law means to exist beyond the realm of human knowledge. As we cannot know even the basics of such a being, we can have no legitimate basis to assign attributes to it, even unlimited ones.

Whatever term we assign does nothing to increase our understanding of the being in question. To say that God is "good" for instance, says nothing more than that an unknowable being possesses an unknown quality in an unknowable way. Assigning qualities that have meaning in a human sense to an unknowable God results in a God who is no more knowable than before. Such qualities provide no useful information and thus no explanation. Theologians are left with a God about which nothing meaningful can be said. Back to the drawing board.

To be intelligible, an attribute must be meaningful and understandable. Lewis Carroll's poem "Jabberwocky" became famous for his brilliant use of words that in context sounded like they made sense but were devoid of actual meaning. If we are to accept the use of such words to support an argument, then we might as well demand answers to such questions as "What is the color of irony?"

The point of all this is to demonstrate that all concepts of the Christian God advanced by theologians and apologists are incoherent. It is impossible to square an ineffable God with one about whom anything meaningful can be said. To say that God is just or merciful in one breath and beyond man's comprehension in the next is to talk nonsense. Where is the basis for either claim, and how can they possibly be reconciled? Any support for one claim would negate the other. The concept of the Christian God fails at the starting gate.

These problems are encompassed by such pretentious-sounding terms as *ignosticism* and *theological noncognitivism*. *Ignosticism*, a term coined in the 1960s by humanistic Jew Sherwin Wine, refers to the position that one cannot plausibly argue for the meaning of God without a clear, agreed-upon definition, but no such definition exists. Theological noncognitivists similarly argue that none of the language theologians use to describe God is meaningful, making every attempted definition incoherent. Such definitions are circular ("God is that which caused everything but God"), ambiguous, equivocal, self-contradicting, or any combination of these.

The conclusion an ignostic or theological noncognitivist must draw is that it makes no sense to take a strong position that God either exists or doesn't exist because there is no way for humans to make sense of the term *God*. One can say that Christian apologists are *not even wrong* because to be wrong about something, one must first have a position that is clear and definite. In failing to meaningfully define their God, however, they have waived the right to step into a proper argument.

This is where the burden of proof becomes central and further explains why apologists fight so hard to avoid it. The burden of proof is the death knell of an incoherent concept. Step 1 in proving a position is clearly de-fining and explaining it. A failure at this step dooms the exercise. If you can somehow convince your opponent to shoulder the burden of proof instead, however, then your fatal weakness becomes a perfect defense. An unprovable incoherency is equally impossible to definitively disprove. Your opponent can only strike at the air while you claim victory. The concessions apologists have made in assigning even unlimited attributes to God have, however, been their undoing, even where they have sought to foist the bur-den of proof on their opponents.

With these points in mind, I address the traditional unlimited attributes assigned to God to demonstrate the specific problems each entails for the apologist. I define a defensible concept of God that incorporates these at-tributes, beginning with the assumption that this task is at least possible. Keep in mind that any argument demonstrating that God does not possess one or more of these qualities necessarily negates the existence of God or requires a radical redefinition of God that is inconsistent with every major denomination of Christianity. Either would destroy the validity of Christi-anity as we know it. Only a concept that coherently incorporates all these attributes would be consistent with Christianity.

1. Omnipotence

According to virtually all Christian theologians and apologists, God can do *anything*. There is general agreement this doesn't include things that are logically impossible, such as creating a square circle, but means anything conceivable—anything that can be represented, for example, through ani-mation, such as drawing a cartoon.

To believe in an omnipotent God is to believe that anything can become anything else. This is regardless of that thing's initial nature and based simply on God's whim. The existence of such a God would negate causal-ity—the premise that one thing necessarily leads to another—making it im-possible to reliably know anything. To accept omnipotence would be to ac-cept effects without causes and consequences without means. It would be, as philosopher George H. Smith notes, a "Walt Disney wonderland where pumpkins can turn into coaches, oranges into spaceships, and women into pillars of salt."[40]

Such a God would have no need for the natural laws and systematic regularity that form the basis of science, for causality would not apply to Him. Why should we expect mathematical relationships between physical constants and forces when an omnipotent God could assign them randomly and then change them from moment to moment? It would be pointless for scientists to attempt explanations or predictions assuming natural consistency because that very assumption would be invalid. No observation or group of observations could have any predictive or explanatory value. It would undermine every possible means by which man could acquire knowledge except divine revelation.

Nor would it be necessary for God's creations to employ means, such as a digestive system or even the consumption of food and water, to attain their ends. This observation rebuts arguments for God based on apparent design in nature. To say that birds appear designed is to say that their bodies seem well suited to their goals and functions within the natural world. Their feathers, for instance, allow them to fly. But in the universe of an omnipotent God, there would be no need for such contrivances because God could easily bring about the ends directly. Birds could be made of solid lead and still fly, if God willed it. Elephants could float around like butterflies. As John Stuart Mill so aptly points out, "every indication of design in the cosmos is so much evidence against the omnipotence of the designer."[41]

An omnipotent God could not experience desire or such feelings as love, anger, and disappointment. Each of these presupposes limitations that such a being could not have. How could a being with the power to do and have everything desire anything? If He wishes it to be, it simply is. God could instantly reverse any result that displeased Him. Anger and disappointment require surprise at unexpected events, but for God, nothing could be unexpected. To love someone is to want such things for them as happiness, but an omnipotent God cannot want. No such desire could ever materialize, for it would be instantly fulfilled.

The whole idea of a salvation scheme makes no sense for an omnipotent God. Why would such a being require such convoluted means to achieve His ends? Why would the scheme require billions of years to reach fruition and the condemnation of billions of souls to Hell as collateral damage? Why would it involve impregnating a virgin in a small backwater of the Middle East, allowing the child to grow to maturity, torturing that child, killing him, and then raising him from the dead? If God wanted good souls to join Him in Heaven, then why not simply create them there? Why wouldn't God simply rid the world of sin, destroy the devil, and make everyone happy? Why the need for sin in the first place? The universe can only be understood as an elaborate Rube Goldberg machine using trillions of steps to topple every domino simply to drop the last one. Why wouldn't God just flick it over?

Finally, omnipotence would conflict with other qualities of God. For example, unlike humans, God could not commit suicide, for this would violate God's eternal nature. Nor could God be both omnipotent and omniscient.

If God knows the future with certainty, then He cannot change it. If He can change it, then He cannot know it with certainty. One or the other attribute must give way to make any sense of God's nature.

2. Omniscience

Almost certainly God is not in time. His life does not consist of moments one following another. . . . Ten-thirty—and every other moment from the beginning of the world—is always present for Him. If you like to put it this way, He has all eternity in which to listen to the split second of prayer put up by a pilot as his plane crashes in flames.

—C. S. Lewis, *Mere Christianity*

Omniscience means that God knows everything there is to know, past, present, and future. This "timeless" knowledge of God is a most interesting quality. For a timeless God, every moment from the big bang through the final death of the universe is laid out before Him on a huge, multicolored diagram. From the vantage point of a modern human, we can say that God can see everything that has happened and that will happen all at once. He can see every decision we will make and the results of those decisions. And God can step into the diagram at any time, as often as He likes, to alter the course of events, moving images around on the page.

If so, then it cannot be squared with the God who appears in the Bible. That God regularly experiences surprise, anger, jealousy, disappointment, and regret, emotions only triggered by the disappointment of expectations. The very decision to send Jesus to Earth is prompted by a long string of disappointments with the Jews, leading God to try a new approach. An omniscient God would have gotten everything just right from the beginning and never needed to change course. What is the story of Noah if not God registering profound disappointment in the way the human race had turned out and correcting His mistake in a horrifying way through genocide? The biblical God often appears constrained by the same temporal laws as the rest of us—forced to slog sequentially forward through time from one moment to the next, never knowing for certain what is around the corner. For examples, see Genesis 22:12; Deuteronomy 13:3; Jeremiah 3:7, 3:19–20, 26:3, 32:35; Ezekiel 12:3; and Jonah 3:10.

What would be the use of praying to a timeless, omniscient God? Such a God has everything laid out just as He wants it. He knows the beginning, He knows the end, He knows everything in between, and it is all perfectly to His liking because He arranged it that way. And then someone comes along and prays that something be changed—that God step in and modify something in His divine plan. Again, as comedian George Carlin points out, why would God ever do that?

Many Christians dismiss the God of the Old Testament as essentially irrelevant to their theology. But a timeless God is an unchanging God. The Old Testament and New Testament Gods are one and the same. The Sermon on the Mount must be read alongside the massacre of the Amalekites. There is no justification to claim that one represents God's values any better than the other. These cannot be read as successive events, for from God's perspective, they occurred simultaneously, brought about by the same unchanging being.

Omniscience, furthermore, does not allow for human free will. If God knows the future with certainty and incorporates it into His divine plan, then every man's future *must be predetermined*, and he is powerless to change it. God merely pulls the strings for humans to dance *Swan Lake* for his amusement. Volition becomes an illusion, rendering morality meaningless. Man cannot be blamed or praised for actions over which he has no real control. The Christian scheme of salvation must be a farce because men are destined to Heaven or Hell from the moment they are born. Not only must God have known who would go where from the beginning, but also He must have arranged it to be just so.

Some apologists argue for a modified version of omniscience, whereby God can see some things but not anything that results from human free will. A moment's reflection, however, reveals that such a constraint would limit God's foresight to virtually nothing. For example, God could not have known how the events leading up to Jesus's Crucifixion would have played out due to the vast number of human players involved who could have frustrated God's divine plan at any moment with an unexpected decision. God's plan could only have succeeded if He had known exactly what every player would do in advance.[42] Also, under this modified approach, how could God be the source of prophecies of things not to occur for hundreds or even thousands of years, given the billions of intervening human decisions?

If God were omniscient, furthermore, then God himself could not possess free will. To know everything is to know every consequence of every possible action. It is also to know what path one *will* take through the end of time. In such a case, one's actions involve no meaningful choice. God would be nothing more than an automaton going through the motions He has known He must make from the dawn of time and cannot help but make. An omniscient God is a robot God working from a script He is powerless to change.

Finally, God's omniscience cannot relate to knowledge as humans understand it. Man obtains his knowledge through acquisition of information and then through verification to ensure the reliability of that information, the process we call learning. Man employs mental processes over the course of time to increase and refine that knowledge, constructing more elaborate and abstract concepts from simpler, more concrete ones. Many use this accumulating knowledge to create increasingly detailed models of the world.

But none of these processes would apply to God, for He must have had full and complete knowledge of all things throughout time. God's knowledge could not have been cumulative or the result of conceptualization. God cannot learn. There could never have been a time when God's knowledge was simpler or less complete. God's knowledge must therefore differ from man's in kind rather than degree, with an epistemic chasm between them. This renders it unintelligible and no more meaningful than the "slithy toves" of "Jabberwocky."

3. Omnibenevolence

Men rarely (if ever) manage to dream up a god superior to themselves. Most gods have the manners and morals of a spoiled child.

—Lazarus Long, from Robert Heinlein's *Time Enough for Love*

I don't know if God exists, but it would be better for His reputation if He didn't.

—Jules Renard, *Journal*

This is perhaps the most important attribute of God to modern Christians but also the most problematic. It is crucial for Christians to believe that God is the pinnacle of goodness and morality in a way that corresponds with what we all mean when using those terms. It is the cornerstone of the argument from morality and the ultimate foundation of Christian ethics. Apologist Richard Swinburne writes, "In our sense of 'moral,' all theists hold that God is perfectly good, and *this is a central claim of theism.*"[43] If God does not represent the moral ideal, then where can Christians derive any standards for right and wrong?

The first problem we encounter is that the God of the Bible is not a character that any objective observer would ever describe as good, much less the *ultimate ideal of good.* Thomas Jefferson describes God, as portrayed in the Bible, as "cruel, vindictive, capricious and unjust."[44] Mark Twain describes Him as an "irascible, vindictive, fierce and ever fickle and changeful master."[45] Anyone who describes God as good must be talking about something very different than when we describe a person by the same word.

a. The Old Testament God Is Anything but Good   Throughout the Old Testament, God is described as jealous, wrathful, and "drunk with blood."[46] God considers jealousy so essential to his nature that he claims *his very name is "Jealousy"* (Exodus 34:14). These are characteristics universally despised in civilized societies and attributed to those of weak character. God is also described by his designated prophets as the source of all evil, anguish, and misery (Amos 3:6; Lamentations 3:38; Isaiah 45:6–7). On multiple occasions, God sends "evil spirits" to cause confusion and desolation (Judges 9:23; Samuel 16:14, 18:10). On others, he engages in deliberate deceit (Ezekiel 14:9; 2 Thessalonians 2:11). We can see that by God's own acknowledgment, he is not good in any traditional sense.

But there is no need to rely on how God describes himself through the writers of the Bible. To determine the character of a man, we look to his values and his actions. The same should be true of God. Throughout the Bible, God provides many examples of His values through His actions. A common theme is that "might makes right" and that God should not be questioned—only obeyed. God repeatedly threatens the vilest of punishments for those who disobey Him in the slightest, without consideration of their motives or reasons (e.g., Leviticus 26:14–28).

Nowhere does God evidence a respect for intrinsic fairness or human worth. God views humans as intrinsically evil and unworthy of respect. Throughout the Old Testament, they are His servants, who must subordinate all their own needs to praise Him. One example is His requirement that people be stoned to death for doing anything other than worshipping Him on the Sabbath (Numbers 15:32–36). Others evidencing God's values include the following:

- God demands and sanctions human sacrifice (Leviticus 27:28–29; Judges 11: 29–40; 2 Samuel 21:1–9).
- God sanctions slavery (i.e., keeping humans as property; Leviticus 25:44–45), the beating of slaves (Exodus 21:2–6, 20–21; Leviticus 25:44–46), and the selling of one's *daughter* into slavery (Exodus 21:7). Male children are exempt from this injunction.
- God requires intolerance of other religions, going so far as to prohibit intermarriage or even fraternization (Corinthians 6:14). Anyone who worships another god is to be put to death (Exodus 22:20).[47]
- God prohibits fraternizing with the disabled—the blind, lame, or deformed (Leviticus 21:18–23).
- God's system of justice involves punishing the innocent children and grandchildren of those who have sinned against Him, a system He describes as "merciful" (Exodus 34:6–7).

- God commands wildly disproportionate punishments, such as that people be put to death for failing to show him the proper respect (Leviticus 24:16), dabbling in witchcraft (Exodus 22:18), cursing their parents (Leviticus 20:9), committing adultery (Leviticus 20:10), or having sex with someone of the same sex (Leviticus 20:13). Any woman who has sex prior to marriage must also be burned or stoned to death (Deuteronomy 22:20–21; Leviticus 20:9). No such punishment applies to men.

- God ordains that rapists of young women need pay only fifty pieces of silver to the woman's father, after which the woman must marry the rapist and never be allowed a divorce (Deuteronomy 22:28–29).

Above all, the Old Testament describes God as *bloodthirsty*. The prophet Isaiah's description (Isaiah 34:2–7) is characteristic of God through much of the Old Testament: "The Lord is angry with all nations; his wrath is on all their armies. He will totally destroy them. He will give them over to slaughter. Their slain will be thrown out. Their corpses will stink. The mountains will be soaked with their blood. . . . The sword of the Lord is bathed in blood."

In his book *Drunk with Blood*, Steve Wells catalogs the killings attributed to God in the Bible.[48] These are killings either committed by God, directed by God, or approved by God. The total, using only exact numbers provided in the Bible, is 2,821,364. If reasonable estimates are allowed (such as assuming 1,000 kills when the Bible records the destruction of a city, such as Sodom, without providing a specific death toll), then God's killings swell to *25 million*. By contrast, Satan is credited with only ten kills throughout the entire Bible (in the book of Job), and even these were with God's approval.

The vast majority of God's killings suggest the actions of an all-powerful psychopath with no moral compass and a hair-trigger temper. For example, God is reported to have killed 70,000 men simply because David took a census of Israel (2 Samuel 24). On another occasion, God sends two bears to tear apart forty-two children for mocking the prophet Elisha's bald head (2 Kings 2:23–24). Some additional examples include the following:

- Because He regrets His creation and mistakes in dealing with humanity, God floods the entire Earth, drowning all but a select few men, women, children, and animals (Genesis 6:6–7, 6:17, 7:4, 7:21–23). This is one of many examples in which God punishes people for His own mistakes.

- Rather than target just the bad people living in Sodom and Gomorrah, God destroys both cities entirely, killing all inhabitants: men, women, and children (Genesis 19:1–29). This is one of many examples of God killing indiscriminately, manifesting wanton disregard for human life.

• Because a group of farmers is excited to see the Ark of the Covenant as it passes through the countryside after a great Israelite victory and look into it, God kills them and 50,000 of their countrymen, who did nothing wrong (1 Samuel 6:13–19). These are just a few of many examples in which God kills people for the most trivial infractions and innocent people due only to their associations.

• God kills the first-born of every Egyptian family as a show of power, so that not a single family is without a dead child (Exodus 12:29–30). This is one of many examples in which God kills people to buttress His reputation among non-Christians.

• God forces three thousand friends and family members to kill *each other* for worshipping a golden calf (Exodus 32:26–28). This is one of many examples in which God exacts unusual and horrible punishments out of jealousy toward other gods (the existence of which the Old Testament explicitly acknowledges).

• When the Israelites experience hardships in the wilderness, God burns alive those who complain (Numbers 11:1–2). When others complain of no meat, He makes them eat meat until it becomes "loathsome" and comes out of their noses and then sends a plague to kill them (Numbers 11:4–33). When they complain of no bread or water, God sends fiery serpents to kill them (Numbers 21:5–6). When they complain about His killings, God sends another plague and kills 14,700 more (Numbers 16:42–49). God does not tolerate whining.

• After scouts return from Canaan with bad news, which they honestly report, God kills them with a plague (Numbers 14:36–37). This is one of many examples of God punishing people for events over which they have no control.

• To punish David for committing adultery with Bathsheba, God has David's wives raped by a neighbor while others watch and then kills David's baby progressively over the course of seven days (2 Samuel 12:11–19). This is one of many examples of God punishing innocent parties for the sins of others, whom God favors.

• On many occasions, the Bible records the Israelites, with God's blessing and endorsement, indiscriminately slaughtering men, women, and children. Repeatedly, we read accounts in which they "utterly destroyed all in the city, both men and women, young and old, oxen, sheep, and asses, with the edge of a sword" (Joshua 6:21). On several occasions, God directly commands such atrocities, such as when He orders Saul to destroy the entire Amalekite nation—men, women, children, babies, cattle, sheep, camels, and donkeys (1 Samuel 15:2–3).

In one of the most horrifying biblical stories, God orders Moses to kill the Midianites because some Israelites had sex with Midianite women and began worshipping their gods. Moses later becomes furious with Israelite officers for taking some captive rather than killing everyone, as God had commanded. He orders, "Now therefore, kill every male among the little ones, and kill every woman who has known man by lying with him. But all the young girls who have not known man by lying with him, keep alive for yourselves" (Numbers 31:17–18). After murdering the Midianite wives and male children, the Israelites took 32,000 virgins, presumably to be sex slaves for life (Numbers 31:32–35).

William Lane Craig provides an insightful apologetic response to the Canaanite massacres:

> So whom does God wrong in commanding the destruction of the Canaanites? Not the Canaanite adults, for they were corrupt and deserving of judgment. Not the children, for they inherit eternal life. So who is wronged? Ironically, I think the most difficult part of this whole debate is the apparent wrong done to the Israeli soldiers themselves. Can you imagine what it would be like to have to break into some house and kill a terrified woman and her children? The brutalizing effect on these Israeli soldiers is disturbing.[49]

If, like Dr. Craig, you are comfortable with God ordering the rape and slaughter of thousands of women and children, then at least consider the poor Israeli soldiers who had to carry these orders out, the ones *truly brutalized*.

Interestingly, during the Exodus, God regularly starts down one violent path and has His mind changed by Moses, who suggests a more benevolent approach.[50] Often, Moses's justification is to protect God's reputation among neighboring tribes. Moses plays the part of God's Jiminy-Cricket-like conscience, or at least the cool-headed advisor to an impetuous and bloodthirsty king, much like Robert Duvall in the *Godfather* saga. Given God's initial inclinations, I was, when first reading these accounts, concerned what would happen once Moses died. As it turned out, I was right to be concerned, for with Moses's death God's rage spirals out of control.

Numerous times throughout the Old Testament, we see that God must use mind control to force the Israelites' enemies into taking unreasonable positions, specifically to provide an excuse for killing them and their people. For example, God "hardens the heart" of Pharaoh *eight times* to prevent him from backing down, for the express purpose of allowing God to complete His horrific plagues on the Egyptian people (Exodus 4:21, 7:3, 7:13, 9:12, 10:1, 10:20, 10:27, 11:10). Presumably, Pharaoh would have released the Israelites much sooner, avoiding much bloodshed, if God had not turned him into a puppet to justify the theatrical display of God's power.

On another occasion, God hardens the heart of a king expressly so the Israelites will be justified in killing the "men, women, and little ones" of his cities (Deuteronomy 2:30–36). God employs this same tactic with *twenty other kings* during the conquest of Canaan: "For it was of the *Lord* to harden their hearts, that they should come against Israel in battle, that he might destroy them utterly" (Joshua 11:20). God turns otherwise reasonable leaders unreasonable to superficially justify killing them, their followers, and their families.

After reading the Old Testament, Founding Father Thomas Paine understandably concludes,

> Whenever we read the obscene stories, the voluptuous debaucheries, the cruel and torturous executions, the unrelenting vindictiveness, with which more than half the Bible is filled, it would be more consistent that we called it the word of a demon, than the word of God. It is a history of wickedness, that has served to corrupt and brutalize mankind; and, for that part, I sincerely detest it, as I detest everything that is cruel. . . . To believe, therefore, the bible to be true, we must unbelieve all our belief in the moral justice of God; for wherein could crying or smiling infants offend?[51]

To call this God good is to bastardize the term. The God described in the Old Testament is a monster and anything but good.

b. The New Testament God Is Even Worse: The Problem of Hell

> In the New Testament [of Jesus], death is not the end, but the beginning of punishment that has no end. In the Old Testament, when God had a man dead, he let him alone.
>
> —Robert Ingersoll, *Orthodoxy*

Despite the claims of Christian theologians that the God of the New Testament represents love and mercy, He is in fact even more obscenely cruel.[52] The Old Testament God inflicts his wrath only on the living during the short span of their earthly existence. The New Testament God, however, in the guise of Jesus, reveals an entirely new scheme in which rule breakers will be tormented *for eternity*. Their suffering will last more than a trillion times as long as any of those killed by the Old Testament God. This is the doctrine of Hell.

The entire concept of Hell is an affront to human dignity and the universally esteemed principle of proportional punishment. The Bible describes a terrible place in which those found wanting by God are banished to eternal torment, never to escape. There is no opportunity for rehabilitation or redemption. There is only everlasting pain. Evangelical scholar Dan Carson has this to say: "The New Testament speaks far more directly and frequently about Hell. And the person who has the greatest variety of images of Hell—all of them horrifying in one fashion or another is Jesus himself. There are some passages that are so horrific it is hard to read them in public."[53]

Prominent evangelical preacher Carlton Pearson found it so disturbing that he could no longer reconcile the concept of Hell with a loving God and so stopped believing in Hell. He explains his decision after many years of wrestling with the biblical accounts of God and Hell:

> The God we've been preaching is a monster. He's worse than Saddam. He's worse than Osama bin Laden. He's worse than Hitler because Hitler just burned 6 million Jews, but God is going to burn at least 6 *billion* people and burn them forever. He has this customized torture chamber called Hell, where he's going to torment, torture, not for a few minutes, or a few days, or a few hours, or a few weeks, but *forever*.[54]

Ironically, the Bible teaches that eternal suffering awaits anyone who questions God's infinite love. God will burn you forever for not loving Him enough, which must be the most abusive relationship ever.

Many apologists today reject the view that Hell is a place of endless suffering, thereby rationalizing their belief in an omnibenevolent God. Some claim, for example, that Hell represents mere *separation from God*, freely selected through the cumulative effect of one's earthly choices. For example, according to Pope John Paul II, "Rather than a physical place, Hell is the state of those who freely and definitively separate themselves from God, the source of all life and joy," and "Damnation consists precisely in definitive separation from God, freely chosen by the human person, and confirmed with death that seals his choice for ever."[55] Billy Graham preached, "Could it be that the fire Jesus talked about is an eternal search for God that is never quenched? Is that what it means? That, indeed, would be Hell. To be away from God forever, separated from His Presence."[56]

To accept this "mere separation" model, however, one must ignore biblical passages that explicitly describe Hell, such as Matthew 25:46, which make it crystal clear that Hell is a place of eternal, visceral torment, from which there is no escape. Here are a few other Bible verses that describe Hell:

- "And His winnowing fork is in His hand, and He will thoroughly clear His threshing floor; and He will gather His wheat into the barn, but He will burn up the chaff with unquenchable fire" (Matthew 3:12).
- "The Son of Man will send forth His angels, and they will gather out of His kingdom all stumbling blocks, and those who commit lawlessness, and will cast them into the furnace of fire; in that place there shall be weeping and gnashing of teeth" (Matthew 13:41–42).
- "[The damned] will be tormented with burning sulfur in the presence of the Holy angels and in the presence of the Lamb and the smoke of their torment will rise for ever and ever" (Revelation 14:10–11).
- "[They] shall be tormented day and night forever and ever" (Revelation 20:10).

A place in which people are burned continuously with unquenchable fire, forever weeping and gnashing their teeth while experiencing perpetual torment, is obviously a place of torture, and as the Revelations passage states, God is right there the entire time! The Bible does not define Hell in terms of separation from God or as a place people voluntarily choose. It is a place to which God/Jesus permanently expels those who do not meet His standards, condemning them to unending agony. Hitler's concentration camps, by contrast, would be Disneyland.

Subjecting conscious creatures to physical and mental torture for all eternity is clearly sadistic and represents a punishment far in excess of anything that any human being could possibly deserve. Rehabilitation isn't on the table if one's sentence is to be tortured "forever and ever." The only purpose of this horrific place is vengeance, something incompatible with a benevolent God. If, before God made the world, we were to speculate on what perfect justice is, we would *never* come up with Hell. It is far from the measured responses required by the penal systems of all Western democracies. If that is what perfect justice looks like, then our human systems are way off the mark. That this would be so surprising to us just highlights how foreign it is to our common moral intuitions and to our secular systems of justice.

And we must keep in mind how God determines who will be banished to Hell. Because the Christian scheme is based on *belief* rather than behavior, all those who have in good faith found the evidence for Christianity wanting will be condemned to eternal torture. That means a lot of very good people will burn forever: Gandhi, Einstein, Mark Twain, and all non-Christian charity workers and social reformers. With the stakes so high, a truly compassionate God would owe us better evidence.

Likewise, those who have never been given the opportunity to believe will also be condemned. For centuries, the official position of the Catholic Church was that all nonbaptized infants went to Hell, a position well supported by Scripture. But this caused an enormous amount of pain for families whose babies died either in or shortly after childbirth. The clear injustice of this fueled many criticisms of Catholic theology. Finally, Catholic theologians informally created the concept of Limbo out of thin air to deal with what was becoming a major public relations problem.[57] Hell, taken to its theologically required conclusion, was just too disturbing to those who actually thought through the implications.

Meanwhile, anyone can dodge Hell by simply repenting their sins before death and accepting Jesus. It doesn't matter how horrible a person was in life or what they did, as belief and acceptance trump everything. This would include someone with as many mortal sins on record as Adolph Hitler or Joseph Stalin. Any system that would allow a Catholic Hitler into Heaven while condemning a Jewish Anne Frank to Hell cannot be said to represent perfect justice.

Some apologists, such as Randall Rouser, object to the interpretation of hellish torment as eternal. They subscribe to a position known as annihilationalism, in which God eventually snuffs the doomed sinner out of existence. They take an ad hoc approach and simply ignore all the passages that describe God's punishment as eternal, such as Matthew 25:46. Unfortunately for them, however, if you ignore it for Hell, then you would have to ignore it for heavenly pleasures as well because the same word, *aionios*, is used to describe both. This same word is also used to describe God, so if Hell's torments aren't everlasting, then neither is God. St. Augustine had the final word on this argument more than 1,500 years ago: "To say that life eternal shall be endless, [but that] punishment shall come to an end is the height of absurdity."[58]

Many protest that Jesus's moral teachings were at least admirable. I explore Jesus's role as a moral teacher in a later section. For present purposes, however, I mention only a few points. First, Jesus is the Bible's biggest proponent of Hell. He explicitly refers to it thirty-seven times in the Gospels, making it a central tenet of his teaching. If you deny the existence of Hell, then you are rejecting one of Jesus's primary messages.

Second, Jesus reaffirmed all the laws of the Old Testament referenced in the previous section, making it crystal clear that none *would ever pass away*

(Matthew 5:17–19; Luke 16:17).[59] Third, Jesus never spoke out against the great moral scourges of our time, such as slavery, class-based poverty, or discrimination against women. A few brief comments on human equality or the moral repugnance of owning another person would have avoided untold horrors. Instead, Jesus's teachings have lent support to those on the wrong side of these issues for the last two thousand years.

Jesus said nothing to suggest that his followers be more tolerant of other religions. In fact, his teachings simply extend the Old Testament theme of religious intolerance: "But those mine enemies, which would not that I should reign over them, bring them hither, and slay them before me" (Luke 19:26).[60] In case he was unclear there, Jesus affirmed twice more that his mission was not a peaceful one: "I came not to send peace, but a sword" (Matthew 10:34), and "He that hath no sword, let him sell his garment, and buy one" (Luke 22:36). So while *some* of Jesus's teachings were indeed admirable, it would be absurd to call Jesus the pinnacle of morality, as least by modern standards. As many have recognized, if your every action were governed by "What would Jesus do?" then you would quickly find yourself in prison, perhaps even on death row.

Contrary to what Christian leaders tell their flocks, the very message of the New Testament is not about love, as any reasonable person understands it. Former evangelical preacher Dan Barker concluded this after decades as a committed Christian:

> I do understand what love is and that is one of the reasons I can never be a Christian. Love is not self-denial. Love is not blood and suffering. Love is not murdering your son to appease your own vanity. Love is not hatred or wrath, consigning billions of people to eternal torture because they have offended your ego or disobeyed your rules. . . . Love is not obedience, conformity, or submission. It is a counterfeit love that is contingent upon authority, punishment or reward. True love is respect and admiration, compassion and kindness, freely given by a healthy, unafraid human being.[61]

The type of love described in the New Testament is none of these things.

c. The Problem of Evil and Suffering   When arguing for omnibenevolence, one ultimately must face the problem of evil and suffering. I address that issue at length in an earlier section, and therefore I do not expound on it here. It is relevant, however, in that any resolution of this problem must involve relaxing, if not completely invalidating, the standards by which mankind has always distinguished good from evil. But if we cannot use human standards, then by what means can we possibly conclude that God is good? The answer is that we can't. If the condition of the world is to lead us to any conclusion about God's nature, then it can at best be said that God is apathetic.

The problem of evil and suffering also highlights the inherent conflict between God's omnipotence and His omnibenevolence. If God has morally justifiable reasons for allowing natural suffering, for instance, then it follows that this must be for some greater good and part of his divine plan. But this would mean that God was incapable of accomplishing the goals of this divine plan without all the natural suffering, which means He cannot be omnipotent. However, if God could accomplish His goals without the suffering but chooses not to, then He cannot be considered omnibenevolent. One of God's core characteristics must give way.

d. An Omnibenevolent God Is an Amoral God The final problem with omnibenevolence is that it removes God from the moral playing field entirely. The entire concept of morality rests on choice. We describe someone as having good morals when they consistently *choose* the path of good over that of evil, especially when faced with strong incentives to stray. One cannot be described as good until he has heard the siren call of temptation, struggled with his desires, and successfully resisted it. There can be no true virtue without the pull of vice.

To claim God is good *by nature* and in fact the very essence of good is to say that God can be nothing other than good.[62] He is good *by definition* and incapable of evil. But this is to say that God has *no choice* but to be good. He does not *choose* the right path; He simply trailblazes a route, and it *becomes* the right path because that is how the right path is defined. What criteria would God even use to choose between good and evil? God cannot be tempted to do evil because God has everything and is omnipotent. God will continue to have everything regardless of what He chooses to do in any situation. God is therefore neither moral nor immoral. He is simply *amoral*.

An amoral God is not a God to be respected, must less praised or worshipped. He is certainly no role model, as God's path to righteousness bears no relationship to our own. As philosopher Gottfried Leibniz wrote long ago, "In saying that things are not good by any rule of goodness, but merely by will of God, it seems to me that one destroys, without realizing it, all the love of God and all his glory. For why praise him for what he has done if he would be equally praiseworthy in doing exactly the contrary?"[63] We might just as well praise water for being wet.

If one is to maintain that God is supremely good, then that term is being used in a novel way. If God's goodness is to be considered consistent with the widespread atrocities reported in the Bible, the alleged existence of Hell, man's experience of vast evil and suffering in the world, and God's inability to act in any other manner, then it must be different in kind from goodness as humans comprehend it. But to say that God is good in some unknowable way is to deprive the word of any conceivable, much less recognizable, meaning. We might as well make up a new word altogether and say that God is "mogly." Assigning such an attribute does not help to explain God.

4. Perfection

Most theologians assign one final attribute to God—perfection. They consider God to be perfect in every way, to in fact represent the ideal of perfection. While this would certainly seem to flow naturally from the previous attributes, it poses serious problems for anyone attempting to coherently argue for God's existence.

The first problem comes in defining *perfection*. A typical definition includes "having all the required or desirable elements, qualities or characteristics."[64] But this requires an ideal model against which to grade the degree of perfection. If we are going to claim that something represents such a model, then we must have ways of describing it other than "perfect," or we are merely begging the question, creating a useless tautology.

A perfect square has four sides of equal length at right angles to one another because that is how a square is defined. If you attempted to draw a square freehand, you might approximate but would never reach this ideal. But you would know what you were striving for because a perfect square has attributes that are clear, concrete, and definite. These provide independent standards against which we can measure to determine how close our drawing comes to perfection, how close our drawing of the square comes to what a square is *supposed to look like*. Here, we can see that perfection is only meaningful when the ideal is clearly defined—when we can know with no doubt what our own attempts are supposed to match. Speaking of perfection only makes sense when discussing an ideal whose exact parameters are objectively clear in every way.

What would a perfect cloud look like? This question is impossible to answer because there is no clear definition of an ideal cloud. Unlike a square, a cloud is not defined in such a way that we could ever objectively assess what would count as perfection. Would it be big and fluffy or thin and wispy? There can be no resolution because even if one has in mind an ideal cloud, that concept is necessarily subjective and changes from person to person. If I say, "That cloud is perfect," each person would have to create his own concept of an ideal cloud and compare the actual cloud to that one to evaluate my statement. In a crowd of a thousand, I would expect those agreeing with me to number no more than one or two.

This example demonstrates why the concept of perfection, applied to God, cannot be meaningful. When we say that God is perfect, we must ask, "Perfect compared to what?" God is supposed to be the ideal of perfection, but because God is so poorly defined, there is no way to make sense of God's perfection. Is God perfectly good? As discussed previously, not according to the standards applied by every civilized society. So what could perfection mean in this context? The term is equivocal and therefore useless.

There is a sense, however, in which the concept of perfection can be meaningful, but in that sense, God cannot qualify. A secondary definition of *perfect* is "absolute, complete."[65] A perfect being, therefore, is a complete being. To be perfect means you need nothing. What's more, a perfect being would desire nothing, for nothing could advance its completion. Such a being would not demand love, obedience, or weekly worship, as the insecure Christian God does. Such a God would simply be.

A perfect being cannot grow or change, for that would mean it was previously less than perfect. An omnipotent perfect being would exist in a state that likewise would not change. It would be inconceivable for a perfect being to exist beside imperfection of any kind at any point because it could will such imperfection out of existence with but a thought. Imperfections would never arise. There would be nothing for an omnipotent perfect being to do because it would have been in complete control of the cosmos throughout eternity.

The very existence of our universe contradicts a perfect God. It must be possible for God to exist in a reality consisting of only God. Why would God degrade that perfect world by creating a universe filled with imperfections, including imperfect beings such as ourselves? To replace a universe consisting solely of perfection with one containing horror, suffering, and pain would be not just profoundly surprising but also contrary to all logic and reason. A perfect God would have created nothing at all. Our very presence demonstrates conclusively that no such God exists.

B. The Bible Is a Hodgepodge of Inconsistent Ideas

Christianity is a religion of Scripture. The central document that defines the faith and sets forth all its core beliefs and doctrines is the Bible. Some Christians maintain the Bible is literally true, while others allow for a more liberal interpretation. But central to all Christian denominations is that the Bible is divinely inspired and constitutes the central (perhaps only) narrative and "rule book" for the religion. We would expect these rules would adhere to a common framework and, at a minimum, be consistent with one another. If these are the words of God, furthermore, then they should, from beginning to end, reflect a coherent and a steady voice.

But that is not what we find. The Bible was compiled by many authors, often separated by centuries, something that becomes immediately evident upon reading it and further evident upon studying it. These authors express distinct ideas on countless issues of theological importance. They contradict each other repeatedly—not just on factual details but also on crucial doctrinal points, such as the nature of God, what God expects of us, and what is necessary for salvation.

Since the late nineteenth century, critical scholars have recognized that the first five books of the Bible, the Pentateuch, were compiled from at least four sources combined together to appear a cohesive whole.[66] Each source was independent, revealing a complete narrative on its own. The sources overlapped in the telling of certain stories, which explains why we see parallel tales of, for example, the Creation—contradicting each other from verse to verse. But each of the sources, when separated from the rest, presents distinct theological and historical views unique to the time and place in which it was written and the unique concerns of the authors.

We also now know from the recovery of documents dated to the first three centuries of the Common Era that early Christians disagreed vehemently on many crucial issues. These included whether Jesus was divine and not simply a human servant of God (Arianism), whether Jesus was born as an ordinary man later adopted by God (Adoptionism), whether the God of the Old Testament was the same as that associated with Jesus (Gnosticism and Marcionism), and whether Jesus's Crucifixion and Resurrection was merely an illusion (Docetism), along with many others.

In 325 CE, Emperor Constantine the Great convened the First Council of Nicaea to address some of these competing views and define "official" church doctrine. The council did so and drafted the Nicene Creed to memorialize its conclusions and labeled opposing viewpoints as heresies. Historians have dated the first list containing the twenty-seven books of the New Testament to 367 CE. They appear to have been first officially accepted as canon in 393 CE.

The twenty-seven books of the New Testament were selected for inclusion from hundreds of writings. This process began before the Council of Nicaea, but there can be little doubt the men involved wanted a final product that (1) appeared coherent and (2) reflected their own views on theological disputes of their day. They purposefully left out such writings as the Gospel of Thomas, which is very different in tone and philosophy from the four canonical Gospels, and the Gospel of Peter, which includes an account of the passion that differs significantly from the canonical Gospels. They also left out contemporary writings that reflected Arian, Adoptionist, Gnostic, Marcionite, and Docetist positions.

You would think a concerted effort to compile a uniform and harmonious final product, especially with divine guidance, would be more successful. But since the Enlightenment, when they first dared to engage in critical examination of the Bible, scholars have recognized that the Bible is chock full of irreconcilable contradictions and inconsistencies. In the seventeenth century, philosopher Baruch Spinoza called the Bible a "book *rich in contradictions*."[67] In the eighteenth century, American patriot Thomas Paine compiled many of the Bible's self-contradictions in his influential book *The Age of Reason*.

Apologists have mostly acknowledged that the Bible contains many contradictions. They maintain, however, that these can be safely ignored by the faithful. Some claim that focusing on inconsistencies is just nitpicking, for believers should be concerned only with the overall gist of what the Bible tells them. To understand why this is a ridiculous request, consider a trial in which a key witness testifies for the prosecution, detailing how he personally witnessed the defendant commit the crime. On cross-examination, the defense attorney demonstrates inconsistencies in every aspect of the witness's story. He shows, for example, that the witness wasn't even in town on the day of the crime and so couldn't have witnessed it. Assume further that in closing argument, the prosecutor asks the jury to ignore all the inconsistencies and just accept the gist of the witness' testimony, which is that the defendant is guilty. I suspect the jury would waste little time discounting the witness's testimony entirely and issuing a verdict of innocence.

Apologists seem to forget that for those not already deeply wedded to Christianity, a primary question is whether the Bible is a reliable source of information. Those evaluating Christianity objectively against other religions are looking to see whether Christian Scripture is credible and trustworthy. Nothing undermines credibility more than repeated inconsistencies. For this reason alone, these inconsistencies matter.

Alternatively, apologists may argue that all biblical discrepancies are of little consequence because they do not bear on any issues of true *importance* to Christians. To that, I say, "Really?" What can be more central to the Bible than the correct path to salvation? Are good works required, or may salvation be obtained by faith alone? The necessity of good works is attested to by, among others, these passages: Psalm 62:12; Ecclesiastes

12:14; Jeremiah 17:10; Ezekiel 18:27, 18:30; Matthew 5:20, 16:27, 19:17, 25:41–46; John 5:29; Romans 2:6, 2:13; 2 Corinthians 5:10, 11:15; James 1:22, 2:14, 2:17, 2:21–25; 1 Peter 1:17; and Revelation 2:23, 22:14. But hold on. These passages make it just as clear that good works are *irrelevant to salvation*, for it is obtained through faith alone: Mark 16:16; John 3:3, 3:18, 3:36; Acts 16:30–31; Romans 1:16–17, 3:20, 3:28, 4:2, 4:13, 5:1, 10:9; Galatians 2:16, 3:24; Ephesians 2:8–9; and Titus 3:5. Many of these passages appear specifically intended to rebut and counter those who claim works are necessary.

This has been called the most important question in all of Christian theology. And yet the Bible is wildly unclear on the point. This ambiguity has caused the Reformation, the split between the Protestant and Catholic Churches, and the splintering off of too many Christian denominations to count. Even if you are swayed by the often-clumsy apologetic attempts to harmonize these passages, you must admit that a divinely inspired work could have been a lot clearer on this.

And speaking of what counts for good works, are Christians bound to follow the law given by God in the Old Testament? Absolutely, according to these passages, for those laws apply to the end of time: Genesis 17:19; Leviticus 23:14, 23:21, 23:31; Deuteronomy 7:9; 1 Chronicles 16:15; Ecclesiastes 12:13; Matthew 5:17–19; Luke 16:17; John 7:9, 14:15; Revelation 22:14. Absolutely *not*, according to these letters of Paul, for the Resurrection of Jesus has rendered the law obsolete: Romans 3:28, 6:14, 7:4, 10:4; Galatians 2:21, 3:13, 3:23–25, 5:18; Ephesians 2:15; Colossians 2:14. You may justifiably say that because Jesus himself clearly proclaimed the law still in effect, it should trump Paul's claims to the contrary well after Jesus's death. But again, the Bible could, and should, have been clearer on such an important point.

There are many places to find lists of biblical contradictions. One good source is the Skeptic's Annotated Bible (skepticsannotatedbible.com), which has compiled almost five hundred of them, with references. Here are a few more examples, from that list, in which the Bible speaks with conflicting voices:

- Is God the source of evil? Yes!—according to 2 Kings 6:33; Isaiah 45:7; Job 2:10; Lamentations 3:38; and Amos 3:6. No!—according to Psalm 5:4 and 1 John 4:8.
- Does God lie and deceive us? Yes!—according to 1 Kings 22:23; 2 Chronicles 18:22; Jeremiah 4:10, 20:7; Ezekiel 14:9; and 2 Thessalo-

nians 2:11. No, God cannot and does not lie—according to Numbers 23:19; 2 Samuel 7:28; Psalm 119:160; Titus 1:2; and Hebrews 6:18.

- Does God cause atheists to disbelieve just so He can send them to Hell? Absolutely!—according to John 12:40 and 2 Thessalonians 2:11–12. No, atheists' disbelief is the fault a different god(!)—according to 2 Corinthians 4:3–4.

- Does God make mistakes, change his mind, and repent like ordinary humans? Yes, God makes hasty decisions and then regrets them—according to Genesis 6:6; Exodus 32:14; 1 Samuel 15:11–35; 2 Samuel 24:16; 1 Chronicles 21:15; Isaiah 38:1–5; Jeremiah 15:6, 18:8, 42:10; Amos 7:3, 7:6; and Jonah 3:10. No, God is perfect, unchangeable, and always gets it right the first time—according to Numbers 23:10; 1 Samuel 15:29; Ezekiel 24:14; Malachi 3:6; and James 1:17.

- Does God punish otherwise innocent people for the sins of their ancestors? Yes!—according to Genesis 9:21–25; Exodus 20:5, 34:7; Numbers 14:18; Deuteronomy 5:9, 23:2, 28:18; 1 Samuel 3:12–13; 2 Samuel 12:14, 21:6–9; 1 Kings 2:33, 11:11–12, 21:29; 2 Kings 5:27; Isaiah 14:21; Jeremiah 32:18; Zephaniah 1:8. No!—according to Deuteronomy 24:16; 2 Kings 14:6; Jeremiah 31:29–30; and Ezekiel 18:20.

- Is divorce ever permissible? No, divorce is *never* permissible; divorcees who remarry are committing adultery and must be stoned to death—according to Matthew 19:6; Mark 10:11; and Luke 16:18. Yes, but only if the wife is unfaithful—according to Matthew 5:32 and 19:9. Yes, if either partner isn't a Christian, or if the husband is displeased with his wife—according to Deuteronomy 24:1–2 and 1 Corinthians 7:15. If the wife is displeased with her husband, she'll just have to suck it up.

- Should Christians accumulate wealth? No, they should sell everything they own and give it to the poor—according to Luke 12:33, 14:33, 18:25; and Matthew 6:19 and 6:24. Yes, for money is the answer to everything—according to Ecclesiastes 10:19.

- Does man have free will? Yes, God allows us to make free choices—according to Deuteronomy 30:19; Joshua 24:15; and Revelation 22:17. No, God has predetermined every move we make and decided before we were ever born who is saved and who is damned—according to Jeremiah 10:23; Acts 13:48; Romans 8:29–30, 9:11–22; Ephesians 1:4–5; and Jude 4.

- Do born-again Christians sin? Yes, according to 1 John 2:1–2. They sin constantly and must be redeemed through Jesus. No, according to 1 John 3:6 and 3:9, for whoever has been born of God forever after has God's seed in him and cannot sin.

- Should gays be exiled or put to death? Exiled!—according to 1 Kings 15:11–12. Killed!—according to Leviticus 20:13.
- Should anyone who works on the Sabbath be exiled or put to death? Exiled!—according to Exodus 31:14. Killed!—according to Exodus 31:14–15, 35:2; and Numbers 15:32–36. Any gay man who works on the Sabbath is pressing his luck.

It is hard to believe that anyone today could maintain a straight face when saying that the Bible is internally consistent. Christian denominations number in the tens of thousands and have proliferated since the dawn of the religion. According to the Center for the Study of Global Christianity (CSGC) at Gordon Conwell Theological Seminary, there are approximately 45,000 Christian denominations and organizations in the world.[68] All are mutually exclusive on at least one doctrinally significant point. All are supposedly based on scriptural authority.

The only reasonable conclusion is that the Bible provides no unified voice. If God inspired it and intended it to provide clear and consistent guidance, then He failed spectacularly.

C. Doctrinal Inconsistencies

Next, I turn to some of the central doctrines of Christianity. We would expect that if these doctrines were indeed important to human salvation, then they would make clear sense and be easy for humans to understand. What would be the point of doctrines that couldn't be easily grasped by the dimmest human mind? If salvation depends on whether someone accepts Christianity, then why wouldn't God want it to be as simple as possible to understand?

However, if these doctrines resulted from theologians trying to piece together something coherent from diverse, often-contradictory sources, then we would expect them to be messy, vague, and difficult to grasp. We wouldn't expect them to fit together nicely or to be easily explicable. We would expect them to appear ad hoc. And that is just what we find.

The plethora of Christian denominations, mentioned several times previously, attests to this so powerfully that no further discussion should be required. But a purely high-level discussion would fail to address the apologists' refrain that doctrinal inconsistencies are trivial—that the denominations are making mountains of molehills. Accordingly, I discuss a few examples that prove the greater point.

1. The Trinity

> One may say with one's lips, "I believe that god is one, and also three," but no one can believe it because the words make no sense.

> —Leo Tolstoy, *What is Religion*

What could be more central to Christianity than the very nature of God and the relationship between God and Jesus? All the major Christian traditions maintain the doctrine of the trinity—that God is defined as three entities: the Father, the Son (Jesus), and the Holy Spirit. The three entities are distinct and yet one in "substance, essence or nature."[69] They are coequal, coeternal, and cosubstantial. Each is God, wholly and completely. Despite this, however, the Son was "begotten" of the Father, and the Holy Spirit "proceeds" from both.

The Bible contains no express formulation of the Trinity.[70] Instead, the Trinity was developed by Christian theologians over several hundred years attempting to explain the perplexing relationship described by the Bible among God, Jesus, and the Holy Spirit. Many biblical passages describe God as the only divine being, while others suggest that Jesus was also divine. Some passages appear to describe Jesus as fully human, while others appear to describe him as an incorporeal spirit. Some passages suggest that Jesus was created by God, while others indicate that Jesus, like God the Father, was eternal.

According to theologian Alister McGrath, the doctrine of the Trinity was necessary to harmonize these apparently contradictory passages. The God described throughout the New Testament writings could only be understood in "Trinitarian terms."[71] Faced with a mishmash of apparently inconsistent biblical claims about God, Jesus, and the Holy Spirit, theologians had to invent a doctrine that appeared to make sense of it all and manufacture a mechanism by which they could all be rationalized. Thus was born the Trinity.

The Trinity didn't gel until the fourth century, before which various other solutions were proposed, such as Binitarianism (one deity in two persons, or two deities), Unitarianism (one deity in one person), and Modalism (one deity manifested in three separate aspects). The church leaders of the day, however, ultimately rejected all these, awarding Trinitarianism the brass key as the best of the lot.

From the beginning, this was a fuzzy concept. St. Augustine, one of the most influential Christian theologians writing in the early fourth century, was one of the earliest proponents of the doctrine. But even he acknowledged that it could not be coherently explained. According to Augustine, an explanation was beyond human comprehension, so one simply had to accept it on faith. For someone tasked with explaining a previously unknown doctrinal construction, this may have been the biggest loophole in history, and one that started a growing trend among apologists of appealing to faith and mystery.

Since the fourth century, nothing has changed. The *Oxford Dictionary of the Christian Church* defines the *Trinity* as a "mystery of faith revealed in scripture, historically being deemed unknowable by unaided human reason and not capable of logical demonstration once revealed, being above reason without being incompatible with the principles of rational thought."[72] In short, no one has made sense of it to date, and there is no reason to expect that anyone ever will.

Not that many modern apologists haven't taken a crack at a coherent explanation. You can read many online. But I'll save you some time. They're all over the place. To say they've failed to reach a consensus is a vast understatement. You would be hard-pressed to find *any significant agreement* among them. Something so confusing as to defy explanation for two thousand years by the best experts in the field may properly be called incoherent.

It is incoherent for a very good reason—because it was never intended to be so. It was always meant to wave away obvious inconsistencies among the biblical writers in describing God and Jesus. It was meant as a way to say "Don't think about those inconsistencies. Don't focus on them. Don't let them distract you. They are separate, yes. They are the same, yes. They are all of it and none of it. Just accept this as a great mystery and move on." It is the same sleight of hand used to explain something as magic. The purpose is not to explicate. The purpose is simply to end the inquiry.

And I ask, if God existed, would He be okay with the fact that all of humanity is hopelessly confused over His very nature—especially when this confusion stands as a deal-breaking obstacle to many accepting His existence? Why would anyone worship a God they have no hope of understanding? And yet God provides no guidance—no intelligible explanation.

To accept the Trinity, we must adopt a position that makes no sense to us. But what justifies us in adopting an incoherent position when a coherent, parsimonious, and plausible one is available? Isn't it more likely that the entire notion of the Trinity is a hopelessly convoluted but completely human attempt to make sense of disparate and unrelated biblical passages—ideas never intended to be read together in the first place?

2. Sin and Salvation

The incoherent nature of the Trinity becomes a real problem (as opposed to merely a theoretical one) when it comes to sin and salvation. The central message of the New Testament is that Jesus died for the sins of humanity and that, through the resurrected Jesus, we can all be saved from eternal damnation. Anyone who looks at this objectively and analytically will recognize the many problems this presents.

Let's begin with the concept of sin. The traditional Christian view is that sin is hereditary. It originated with the first humans, Adam and Eve, who did not know good (right) from evil (wrong). God created a tree, the fruit of which would bestow such knowledge, but God forbid Adam and Eve from eating of it. God also created a snake, which He knew would tempt Eve to eat of the tree.[73] God knew Eve would do so and would encourage Adam to do the same, as God created them and knows everything of their natures. Upon eating of the tree, their eyes were opened, as the snake had promised. For their insubordination, however, God cursed Adam, Eve, and all their descendants with original sin and exiled them from the heavenly Garden of Eden.

Anyone looking at this story in a book of Greek myths rather than the Bible would surely conclude that God was in the wrong here. He entrapped Adam and Eve, whose innocence must have equaled that of newborn babies, into disobeying His instruction. They had no concept of right or wrong until they ate of the tree, so the whole scenario would have been child's play to arrange from beginning to end. God created the test and then set up the perfect conditions for Eve to fail. Everything about the story reads as if God were manipulating events to guarantee a fall. Even if there had been no overt manipulation, God must have known in advance how things would turn out. Whatever Adam and Eve did, it was because that was how God made them, and as Gene Roddenberry observes, "We must question the story logic of having an all-knowing all-powerful God who creates faulty humans and then blames them for his own mistakes."[74] The Fall of man and all man's resulting misery can be squarely laid at God's feet. It was a script played out for God's amusement, with the actors merely playing the parts assigned.

Rather than using this as a teaching moment, like responsible parents of young children would, God levies the ultimate punishment: pain and death for everyone. Even the strictest parent would recognize the severity of such a punishment as far greater than warranted by the "crime." Can you imagine banishing your toddler from your home forever, leaving her to die in the wilderness, for eating a piece of cake, even if you had instructed her not to? Given Adam and Eve's lack of knowledge of right and wrong, how could they even be blamed? It would be like mercilessly torturing a new puppy for peeing on the carpet.

If original sin was an unjust punishment for Adam and Eve, then it was infinitely more so for their descendants. As discussed, a universally recognized moral precept is that people are held accountable only for their own actions. But according to Genesis, God punished *all of humanity* for the actions of two people. What could be more unfair than that? It doesn't help to say that sin is baked into human DNA, for if this is true, then how can God be justifiably angry about it? No one should be faulted for an immutable characteristic.

Following the story of Noah, the remainder of the Old Testament describes God's on-again, off-again relationship with the Jews. Beginning with Abraham, God selects the Jews to be His "chosen people" but is repeatedly disappointed when they worship other gods or otherwise fail to meet his expectations. God makes a covenant with the Jews in which they will worship Him alone and ritualistically slaughter animals at their holy temple in return for His divine favor (grace).

Unfortunately, the Jews fail to uphold their end of the bargain again and again. The Old Testament reflects a repeating cycle in which God arranges for the Jews to be sold into slavery, then to escape and kill their enslavers. Finally, according to the Christians, God decides that he has had enough of this cycle. Despite being omniscient and a perfect planner, things didn't work out as he'd hoped with the Jews, so he is ready to create a new covenant—this time with all of mankind. God decides to lift the generational curse of original sin, allowing people to be judged individually for their own actions. But there are prerequisites. And there are conditions.

First, there must be a blood sacrifice, for as we all know, only the blood of an innocent can atone for the wrongs done by others. And only the blood of an innocent can lift a curse. Blood tainted by a curse has no power. But what to do? For all of mankind is tainted by the stain of original sin, inherited from their ancestors, Adam and Eve. None are innocent. None could serve as an appropriate sacrifice.

God arrives at a solution. As a perfect being—the only perfect being—God alone is innocent. So, God sends Himself, in the form of Jesus (also his "Son") to be sacrificed to Himself. For some unstated reason, Jesus must reach a certain age before the sacrifice, so he bides his time, performing miracles, collecting disciples, and teaching about the coming Kingdom of God. Finally, as meticulously arranged and orchestrated by God the Father, God the Son is tortured and killed by the Romans.

Jesus remains dead for a respectable period, three days, after which God (the Father) resurrects Himself (the Son). Jesus makes a few appearances (the Gospels differ on how many, where, and to whom) and then ascends to Heaven (in some versions) with the promise to return soon, bringing with him the kingdom of God. Jesus further promises that those who believe in him will be free of original sin and, upon his return, will live forever. The rest will burn forever in Hell. And man, will they be sorry.

In the meantime, humans can gain salvation by simply asking God directly for forgiveness and being sincere. This requires that you believe in Him and "bend the knee" to His total authority. In return, God will grant you His grace, which is another way of saying His divine favor—He gives you what you've asked for. This is just an interim arrangement, though, that God acknowledges is far from perfect. For that, we'll all just have to wait for the kingdom of God to arrive, in which, following an epic battle with the Devil or something, the Earth will be destroyed and remade, all in accordance with God's convoluted divine plan.

The first problem with this scenario is that it depends on literally interpreting Genesis, which any scientifically literate person recognizes as absurd. The concept of original sin makes sense only if there had been an actual Adam and Eve. Also, they must have been the first humans, so the curse would be inherited by all mankind. If not, what was the point of Jesus's death and Resurrection? Without original sin, there would have been nothing for Jesus to atone. This is why biblical literalists are so adamant that Genesis be read nothing but literally. Only a literal translation gives meaning to Jesus's sacrifice.

The second problem is that there should have been no need for a blood sacrifice. Such sacrifices were common among many religions in ancient times based on the belief that gods enjoyed such things. A description of the specific ritual used by the Jews is contained in Leviticus 4:13–21, and it is horrific by today's standards. Many times, the Bible describes how God enjoys the smell of burning flesh from animal sacrifices. The value of such sacrifices was understandable among ancient people, who attributed human qualities to their deities. If humans liked burning meat, then so, too, must their gods.

Today, however, Christians enjoy a modern scientifically informed perspective. Does anyone today believe that the same God who created the vast cosmos would care about animal sacrifices? That a being who modeled billions of galaxies and set them in motion would delight in the smell of a roasting bull? Virtually all modern human societies today recognize human sacrifice as barbaric. The need for a blood sacrifice to atone for sins is something we can understand making sense to people of the Bronze Age, but it makes no sense today.

Even if it did, however, the point of the sacrifice was that the person making it was giving up something *of value*, for which he expected to receive something from the deity in return. But this makes no sense with Jesus. Because Jesus and God represent *different aspects of the same being*, God was merely sacrificing Himself to Himself. If God is both the giver and receiver of the sacrifice, then nothing of value has changed hands. There has been no loss to God and no benefit to God. The analogy of a human father allowing his human son to die, often used by apologists, is inappropriate, as God and Jesus were not separate beings and were never actually separated. They were always one, and after all, where could Jesus go to be away from God who is literally everywhere?

Even if we assume for present purposes that we can treat God and Jesus as separate beings, you still cannot say that any true sacrifice has occurred. Both God and Jesus always knew that Jesus would be resurrected and return to Heaven after three days, where he would ultimately reign as king. This was the plan all along. If you were offered that deal, wouldn't you take it? Anyone would because *you would have lost nothing*. You would be better off in the end. To Jesus, death was just a three-day sabbatical, after which he would return better than ever. Jesus had a bad long weekend for your sins but started off the next week in peak form. Implicit in the concept of a sacrifice is loss, but Jesus had none, and neither did God the Father.

I suspect this is why many Christians like to focus so much on the events *leading up to Jesus's death*, highlighting the indignities he suffered. Passion plays (*passion* comes from the Greek word meaning "to suffer") depicting the last few hours of Jesus's life are a common feature among Christian churches and have been for hundreds of years. Mel Gibson's *The Passion of the Christ* is the highest-grossing R-rated movie of all time in the United States, despite consisting of more than two hours of brutal torture scenes. Christians must feel that God sacrificed *something* in the process—perhaps comfort or dignity.

But even this is nonsensical. Throughout the passion, Jesus knew his suffering was temporary and just a brief stop he had to pass through on the road to his ascension, at which point everything would be restored and exponentially improved. According to John's and Luke's Gospels, Jesus *experienced no mental distress* over any of it. There would have been physical discomfort for a few hours, but what is this to God? And crucifixion, though certainly not pleasant, would have been an extremely mild form of torture by Inquisition standards, in which people were tortured horribly *for months, if not years*, in God's name, to the point of begging for death. If you knew what Jesus knew, wouldn't you gladly go through what he did?

And what theological purpose could the *Resurrection* have had? It was Jesus's *death* that provided atonement for man's sins, after which the process of atonement was complete. The Resurrection effectively undid that act of sacrifice. If anything, the Resurrection cheapened Jesus's "death" and his suffering. In Christianity, there is no inherent tragedy in death, for our sentience survives it through our soul. As demonstrated by the parable of Lazarus and the rich man, tragedy only results if our soul ends up in the wrong place. It makes no sense to claim that the Resurrection represented a triumph over death because according to Christian theology, death is neutral or even a positive doorway to better things. So what does the Resurrection defeat?

If the point was to provide definitive proof that Jesus was indeed God, then the entire affair must be viewed as a colossal failure. The vast majority of the world still doesn't believe Jesus was resurrected, and the Bible provides only the weakest evidence to support it. If the Resurrection was intended to provide such proof, then it would be supported by evidence incontrovertible to any modern skeptic—not conflicting hearsay from a handful of heavily biased Iron Age sources.

The Resurrection makes far better sense from a naturalistic context than a theological one. We have many precedents for people inventing fantastic claims to make their gods more impressive. This is called legendary accretion. Overcoming death would be a powerful claim in favor of Jesus's divinity in the time his followers were recruiting converts. The Resurrection has no equal theological context. It adds nothing to atonement theology. It serves no clear theological purpose. Were God using it to prove Jesus's claims, He could have done so far more effectively.

The next problem is that God set up the entire scenario and made the rules. Original sin was God's curse. He could have lifted it any time for any reason. Had God wanted to forgive mankind, either for past sins or future ones, He simply had to do it. Humans forgive people all the time. Jesus encouraged his disciples to forgive all slights against them and ask nothing in return. Why couldn't God do the same? Why would God require the playing out of such an elaborate and brutal ritual before offering His forgiveness (for the mistake of an ancient ancestor)? Why does He have to kill *anyone* to forgive?

And what was God saving mankind from? He was saving us from *Himself*. The God of the New Testament is a gangster running a protection racket—play by His rules, and He won't burn your house down. Or at least

He'll save those members of your household who do play by His rules while leaving the rest to burn. I am reminded of an internet meme with a picture of Jesus knocking on a door and conversing with the homeowner:

JESUS: Let me in.

HOMEOWNER: Why?

JESUS: So I can save you.

HOMEOWNER: From what?

JESUS: From what I'm going to do to you if you don't let me in.

Does that make Jesus a hero? Does that even leave open the possibility of him being considered good?

Some apologists have argued that God is enslaved to an ideal of justice that requires payment once He has been disrespected, like the code of Omerta in *The Godfather*. But why would God be bound by such a code or any code? We don't require payment to forgive, so why must God? A modern approach to forgiveness is to have people do good works (restitution) to make up for wrongs they have done or to receive punishment proportional to their crime or both. Why wouldn't God do something like this? Is there something wrong with such an approach, employed by just about every civilized society?

Other apologists have argued, with virtually no scriptural support, that rather than a hereditary curse, sin represents either a natural consequence of our actions or violation of God's rules requiring punishment. For example, driving your car into a tree is a natural consequence of driving drunk. But being pulled over and sentenced to six months of a suspended license is an externally imposed punishment for violating a rule enacted by an authority. If sin is a punishment, then the objection arises that God has created a problem only to solve it. He has arbitrarily defined something as punishable that would otherwise have no negative consequences. If it is a natural consequence, then why does God need to act at all? Shouldn't the natural worldly consequences of our sins be punishment enough?

God demands belief. But as I've discussed, belief is not something we are free to give. For the intellectually honest, belief is not a choice. It must be compelled by good reasons to believe—by good evidence. If God has not provided such evidence, then it would be unjust to punish people for failing to believe. If God is really interested in every person getting into Heaven and Jesus is the only path to salvation, then why should a baby born into a family of Christian Evangelicals in South Carolina enjoy an extraordinary advantage over a baby born into a Muslim or Hindu family in Yemen or Mumbai? Why don't all people have equal access to the sources most likely to lead to Christian belief? Most will never even consider becoming a Christian because of their upbringing. The kindest and most loving of them will have no compulsion to become Christian because they already feel they are doing the right thing.

To summarize, the biblical view of sin and salvation is that God sacrificed Himself to Himself to set aside a curse He imposed and prevent Himself from punishing mankind for the disobedience of an ancient ancestor, which He orchestrated, according to rules He set for Himself and which requires a payment by all that some cannot give. That is more than incoherent. It is nonsense. And it is the core of Christianity.

3. What Do Philosophers Think?

Philosophers academically investigate and pursue the very questions theologians ask about the nature of truth and being. Were the philosophical arguments of apologists and theologians convincing, we would expect philosophers to be lining up behind them in record numbers. But this is not what we see. In a comprehensive study of philosophy faculty members from ninety-nine institutions, only 14.6 percent identified as theists.[75] This is comparable to the 7 percent of prestigious scientists identifying as theists and signifying a similarly overwhelming preference for atheism. The apologetics industry hasn't failed to win over the experts because it lacks money and resources to get the word out. It has failed because its arguments just aren't very good. The more you know about the subjects relevant to the truth of Christianity, the less likely you are to be a Christian or even a theist.

The logical inconsistencies inherent in Christianity are legion. Adherence to Christianity is only possible by consciously ignoring those inconsistencies or seeking to reconcile them with a string of contrived, ad hoc rationalizations, which can only lead to cognitive dissonance. You can understand the appeal of Christianity to someone who loves to be correct, though. They get to say, "I can't even begin to explain it, but I'm absolutely right." That's not enough for me, and I don't think it's enough for most people, either. I must agree with Christopher Hitchens:

The only position that leaves me with no cognitive dissonance is atheism. It is not a creed. Death is certain, replacing both the siren-song of Paradise and the dread of Hell. Life on this earth, with all its mystery and beauty and pain, is then to be lived far more intensely: we stumble and get up, we are sad, confident, insecure, feel loneliness and joy and love. There is nothing more; but I want nothing more.[76]

HISTORICALLY, THE BIBLE GETS MORE WRONG THAN RIGHT

> Through the reading of popular scientific books I soon reached the conviction that much in the stories of the Bible could not be true. The consequence was a positively fanatic orgy of freethinking coupled with the impression that youth is intentionally being deceived by the state through lies; it was a crushing impression.
>
> —Albert Einstein, *Autobiographical Notes*[77]

> The word God is for me nothing more than the expression and product of human weakness, the Bible a collection of honorable, but still purely primitive, legends which are nevertheless pretty childish. No interpretation no matter how subtle can (for me) change this. . . . For me the Jewish religion like all other religions is an incarnation of the most childish superstition.
>
> —Albert Einstein, from his letter to philosopher Erik Gutkind[78]

We would expect that a divinely inspired work would get everything right. At a minimum, we would expect it to get *most everything* right. We would not expect it to be flooded with factual errors on just about every page. And yet that is just what we find. The Bible is plagued with claims we know to be untrue. It is more often wrong than right.

Most Christians assume the Bible is historically accurate. Most similarly believe the historicity of the Bible is integral to, or at least heavily bolsters, its theological credibility. While it doesn't follow that historical accuracy leads to the legitimacy of theological claims, it is true that widespread historical inaccuracies must severely undercut such claims. This is especially true of the Jewish and Christian texts, in which the theological claims are so closely tied to the historical events the texts narrate. Historical validity is a necessary, though not sufficient, condition of theological legitimacy. If we can't trust the things we can verify, then why should we trust the things we can't?

Apologists take an ad hoc approach to biblical inaccuracies and inconsistencies, trotting out one convoluted rationalization after another to justify interpretations that defy the plain language of the text. They largely get away with this because, as Thomas Paine correctly notes, "The Bible is a book that has been read more and examined less than any book that ever existed."[79] But such arguments fall apart with the most cursory scrutiny, for they depend on an absurd assumption—that God purposely made His word obtuse and unintelligible to all but a select few.

Could God really have intended it to be so complicated to figure out what He was saying that He would require a PhD in theology and ancient languages? As a parent, would you require your child to understand particle physics before she could interpret your instructions on how to safely cross the street? Yet this is just the level of foundational knowledge many apologists claim people must have to properly understand the Bible when apparent falsehoods and contradictions arise. Even with such knowledge, they endlessly trip over themselves in disagreements over every issue under the sun, providing competing rationalizations that contradict not only the plain meaning of the text but also each other.

Their endless rationalizations, furthermore, miss the point, which is that if Christianity were true, *no such explanations would be necessary*. The text would be simple, straightforward, and clear to all. Its perfect accuracy would be instantly apparent to everyone and thus the ultimate evidence of its truth. That the Bible contains so many passages that must be rationalized away points in only one direction. The Bible resulted not from divine inspiration but from the all-too-fallible minds of man. Once again, Ockham's razor leads us to the most parsimonious explanation.

Even with such rationalizations, however, no apologist can effectively rebut the growing volume of conciliant evidence flatly contradicting the Bible's historical claims regarding both minor and major events. We have enough evidence today to dismiss most of those claims beyond a reasonable doubt. With its historical foundations uprooted, the Bible's theological claims wither on the vine.

A. The Old Testament

Jesus was a Jew. This often gets lost in theological discussions about Christianity, but it is nonetheless true and important to acknowledge that Jesus lived and died as a Jew. Jesus's God was YHWH, the God of the Jews. It is clear from Jesus's teachings that he completely believed everything written in Jewish Scripture and reaffirmed its accuracy and relevance in various ways. Jesus evidenced his literal belief in many Old Testament stories, including that of Noah and the destruction of Sodom (Luke 17:26–32; Matthew 11:21–24, 12:40, 24:37). Jesus spoke with apparitions of Moses and Elijah during the transfiguration (Mark 9:2–8; Matthew 17:1–8; Luke 9:28–36). Jesus reaffirmed some of the harshest Old Testament laws, such as requiring the murder of children who curse their parents (Mark 7:10; Matthew 14:4). In the most famous sermon ever given, the Sermon on the Mount, Jesus said, "Do not think that I have come to abolish the Law or the

Prophets; I have not come to abolish them but to fulfill them. I tell you the truth, until heaven and earth disappear, not the smallest letter, not the least stroke of a pen, will by any means disappear from the Law until everything is accomplished" (Matthew 5:17–18).

The law Jesus referred to is the Torah—what Christians call the Old Testament or the Hebrew Bible. According to Jesus, the Torah is all true *to the letter*.[80] It is to be followed verbatim until the end of time. Jesus and his disciples interpreted the events of his lifetime as fulfilling certain Old Testament prophecies. Jesus often used events recorded in the Torah to illustrate key points of his ministry, examples premised on those events being historically accurate. Jesus saw his story as a continuation of the historical drama recounted in the Torah. Jesus patterned his ministry around the Old Testament. He supposedly represented the culmination of what those Scriptures were leading toward. Accordingly, one can assess the claim of Jesus's divinity by analyzing the historical accuracy of the Old Testament. If the Old Testament is false, then Jesus was a false prophet. He could not have been who he claimed to be.

The Old Testament contains thirty-nine (Protestant), forty-six (Catholic), or more (Orthodox and other) books, divided broadly into the Pentateuch (meaning "five books"), the historical books, the "wisdom" books, and the prophets. The Pentateuch and the historical books represent the history of the Israelite people, from the creation of the universe through their defeat and exile in Babylon. These comprise the core of the Hebrew Bible. Because these books make verifiable scientific and historical claims, that is where my analysis focuses.

Scholars have long questioned why the Pentateuch seems to tell stories covering the same subject matter in different and often-contradictory ways. The leading theory to explain these inconsistencies is the documentary hypothesis.[81] According to the documentary hypothesis, the books of the Pentateuch, traditionally ascribed to Moses, were actually based on four independent, stand-alone sources, known as J, E, P, and D. Though roughly parallel, each was written by a different author under unique historical circumstances to express often-contradictory religious or political viewpoints. These sources were redacted several times and finally compiled into a single set of books during the Babylonian exile, between 597 and 538 BCE.

The final book of the Pentateuch, Deuteronomy, differs from the other four in that it bears a distinct voice, using unique terminology, and maintains a consistent focus. It condemns the worship of other gods, portrays God as transcendent rather than anthropomorphic, and strongly prohibits worship anywhere except the Temple in Jerusalem. The historical narratives that follow Deuteronomy—Joshua, Judges, 1 and 2 Samuel, and 1 and 2 Kings—are so closely related to Deuteronomy in style and theological content that they have long been considered to have common authorship and are thus referred to by scholars collectively as the Deuteronomistic History. Critical scholars have concluded that the Deuteronomistic History was likely compiled in the time of King Josiah of Judah (649–609 BCE) to justify his political ambitions and religious reforms.

Today, we are finally in a position to reliably assess the historicity of the Old Testament. While archeologists use physical evidence to determine what happened in the past, historians use documents. To analogize to a crime scene, the testimony of witnesses would be the tool of the historian. Of course, that testimony can be mistaken, biased, or intentionally misleading. The archeologist's role would be equivalent to that of the modern-day forensic examiner, using the gun, carpet fibers, bullet holes, and so on. The archeologist/forensic examiner is the only one of the two who can provide an objective picture. The physical evidence speaks for itself. Where such evidence exists, it is the superior means of determining the past.

Archeological finds of the last century have provided us unprecedented insight into the history of the Jewish people. Archeologists Israel Finkelstein and Neil Asher Silberman summarize the state of affairs: "[I]t is now evident that many events of biblical history did not take place in either the particular era or the manner described. Some of the most famous events in the Bible clearly never happened at all."[82]

1. A Timeline of Important Old Testament Events

The Old Testament begins with the creation of the universe but quickly moves on to the story of the Jewish people through approximately the third century BCE. Modern archeology has demonstrated that it is a mix of fact and fiction, with a heavy emphasis on the fiction. Here are the highlights.

God created all there is in six days. The first humans, Adam and Eve, disobeyed God, so He cursed mankind with original sin. Humanity flourished, but God didn't like how things were going. He therefore decided to kill every living creature in a flood, except for a single family and the animals they could take aboard their boat. Apparently, the ancestors of every living creature lived within walking distance of Noah's ark.

God started over with this boat and its passengers, and after a while, humanity was flourishing again. But the people got cocky. At Babel, they began building a tower they hoped to reach God. Despite His omnipotence, God became anxious that humans would become too powerful for Him to control if they learned to work together and reach the sky. To prevent such human cooperation, He destroyed the tower and made it so that no one could understand each other, giving rise to all the languages of the world. Luckily, the International Space Station has to date apparently escaped God's notice.

Eventually, God found a man He really liked—Abraham. Abraham had the quality God prized most: unconditional loyalty. To be on the safe side, God tested Abraham's loyalty by directing him to kill his own beloved child, Isaac. Abraham passed the test, standing ready to murder his child at God's command, demonstrating his unwavering obedience to God. In return, God promised Abraham he would father a great people and that God would give them a land of their own, Canaan. Abraham's descendants became the Jews.

Following a series of misfortunes most entertainingly chronicled by Andrew Lloyd Webber in his famous technicolor musical, Abraham's great-grandson Joseph got in tight with the Egyptian pharaoh as his most trusted advisor. After a famine struck, Joseph brought all the Jews from Canaan to Egypt, where, thanks to Joseph's brilliant foresight and planning, food was abundant. The Jews stayed in Egypt and grew numerous until a subsequent pharaoh became frightened of their growing numbers and enslaved them all.

After many years of slavery, Moses (as directed by God) convinced the Egyptian pharaoh to free the Jews by inflicting devastating plagues upon all the people of Egypt. The Jews, numbering more than 600,000, escaped Egypt in the Exodus. God then made a new covenant with the Jews. They would be His chosen people if they would worship God alone and obey His laws. In return, He would return Canaan to the Jews and make them prosperous there.

Unfortunately, the Jews failed to hold up their side of the bargain. Almost immediately, they began worshiping other gods and breaking the laws God had just given them. God therefore punished them in various ways, including, most significantly, requiring them to wander aimlessly for forty years so that no one of the generation who left Egypt would reach the promised land of Canaan.

Once the Exodus generation of Jews died out, God allowed their descendants to enter Canaan. Unfortunately, it was already occupied. This wasn't a problem for God, though. He simply gave the Jews permission to wipe out all the inhabitants of Canaan and agreed to assist with the genocide. Apparently getting rid of the Canaanites was too big a job for God to handle alone, but with God's help, the Jews succeeded in battle after battle.

Ultimately, the Jews killed all the inhabitants of Canaan and settled in, forming a loose confederation of tribes, and all was well. Except that suddenly, the Canaanites were back from extinction in record numbers, and for the next century or so, the Jews, now in the minority, were led by ad hoc leaders and heroes known as judges. This led to a cyclical pattern in which the Jews rejected God, were punished and delivered into the hands of their Canaanite enemies, and then were rescued by a judge.

This pattern apparently grew tiresome to God, so he appointed a king. God chose Saul to be the first king of Israel, ruling over a united monarchy. Saul disappointed God, however, so God chose Saul's armor bearer and musician, David, to replace Saul. David turned out to be a great king, popular and successful in battle. Under David, Israel became a major power in the known world.

David's son Solomon was equally popular and even more successful. Under Solomon, the kingdom of Israel grew to one of the grandest and wealthiest in the world. Solomon built the first temple in Jerusalem and many other important buildings. During his reign, Israel enjoyed a golden age. Ultimately, though, under the influence of his many pagan wives, Solomon began to worship other gods and incurred God's wrath. God therefore arranged for Solomon's kingdom to be split in two—Judah and Israel—after his death.

What we know as modern Israel remained a divided monarchy (Israel in the north, Judah in the south) until Judah fell to Babylon and its Jewish inhabitants were exiled. We know from extrabiblical sources that approximately fifty years later, the Babylonian Empire fell to the Persians, who allowed the Jews to return to their homeland. Between the end of the Old Testament and the beginning of the New Testament, Israel was occupied by the Romans.

2. The Creation

The first book of the Torah, Genesis, explains the Creation of the universe. It actually contains two inconsistent versions, redacted together into a single narrative. Both accounts, however, conflict entirely with the scientific consensus. Genesis claims that God created *everything* in six days. We know from science that the universe is 13.75 billion years old. The Earth was formed 4.54 billion years ago over at least millions of years. Life first arose between 3.65 and 3.85 billion years ago. Anatomically modern humans did not arrive on the evolutionary scene until approximately 200,000 years ago.

Genesis begins by describing the creation of the first day, defined as light followed by darkness, morning and evening. These terms only make sense using a specific geographical location on Earth as a point of reference, but according to the Bible, the Earth did not yet exist. It is a reasonable attempt at identifying the first moments of Creation by someone living in the prescientific world but makes no sense from a cosmic perspective. In space, there is no night or day. The source of daylight on Earth is our Sun, one of billions of stars in the universe, which was formed only 4.57 billion years ago. According to Genesis, the Sun didn't come into existence until days later. The Genesis account is exceptionally parochial for a God who created the entire universe.

Genesis describes the creation of Heaven and Earth according to the following model: The Earth is flat. Above it is a dome (firmament). The dome holds out water. Above the dome and beyond the water is Heaven. God gathers water from above the dome and makes it into our seas. This model might help to explain to ancient people why the sky appears blue and why rain comes from the sky. But scientifically, it is preposterous.

On the third day, God creates plants and trees. On the fourth, He finally creates the Sun, the Moon, and the stars. On the fifth day, God creates water creatures and birds. On the sixth, He creates land animals. According to Genesis, all living creatures were created in their present forms "according to their kinds." Finally, God creates Adam and Eve, the first man and woman.

Scientists are in broad agreement that human life evolved over billions of years from the first primitive forms of life. This was a slow and gradual process in which every link along the unbroken chain from single-celled organism to modern man was of the same species as its parent and, genetically, virtually identical. The only reason we have distinct species today is that various intermediate lines became extinct. The notion of animals being created in their present forms contradicts everything we know about biological development. Even the order of Creation in Genesis is wrong based on what we know from science. The Earth being created before the rest of the universe, for example, conflicts so starkly with everything we know from cosmology that it cannot be taken seriously.

3. Noah and the Flood, the Tower of Babel

According to Genesis, after humankind has taken over the Earth, God becomes angry with virtually all of humanity. God therefore sends a flood to kill every man, woman, and child and virtually every animal on Earth. God spares just one man, Noah, and his family. Noah is ordered to build a great ark; to take two (or more, depending on the version) of every animal on Earth; and to, after the flood has subsided, repopulate the Earth. This seems a wildly convoluted approach completely unnecessary for an omnipotent God.

According to the Bible, then, every human on Earth can trace their lineage to Noah—the genetic bottleneck of mankind. This would be easily verifiable but starkly conflicts with current scientific knowledge. We know from archeological and genetic evidence that humans have lived for hundreds of thousands of years. Population dispersal patterns show us man has lived all over the Earth since well before the supposed time of Noah and that no great disaster such as a worldwide flood interrupted that process. There is no genetic bottleneck anywhere near the time of Noah. Mankind did not descend from a contemporaneous pair of human ancestors. This raises the question of why Noah would need to take *any* animals on the ark. Couldn't God have just created them again as He created them the first time? Only in a world in which genetic lines must be maintained naturalistically does it make any sense to require Noah to collect two of every animal.

According to Genesis, we could also trace the lineage of every *animal* to a single point in history—the aftermath of the great flood. Once again, science demonstrates no such thing. We can trace animal evolution back millions of years in a roughly uninterrupted pattern to the first creatures capable of creating fossils. Evidence from biology, geology, and archeology, among many other disciplines, uniformly contradicts anything approaching the worldwide mass extinction detailed in the story of Noah.

If Noah's story is not true, then where did it come from? The story of Noah was long preceded by the *Epic of Gilgamesh* (approximately 1800 BCE), which is among the earliest surviving works of literature. The epic focuses on a Sumerian king who lived around 2500 BCE. Part of the epic follows a character named Utnapishtim, who, like Noah, was told by the gods to build a great boat, taking the animals of Earth upon it. Afterward, a great flood destroys all mankind, leaving only Utnapishtim to continue the human race. This may have been copied from another Babylonian creation/flood myth of the same vintage known as Atra-Hasis.

Both of these preceded the book of Genesis (sixth century BCE) *by more than one thousand years* and closely parallel the story of Noah. The word used for *pitch* in Genesis is closely related to the Babylonian word used in the Atra-Hasis story rather than the Hebrew word, strongly suggesting that the latter was taken directly from the former. There is substantial additional evidence the story of Noah came straight from the Atra-Hasis. It was simply a retelling of this ancient myth.

Likewise, the Tower of Babel story bears all the signs of an etiological myth intended to explain the variety of languages encountered by the ancient Jews, who must have thought it a great mystery. As with genealogy, we know today how languages evolve and can trace the development of most modern languages far into the past—long before the Tower of Babel was destroyed according to established biblical timelines. All languages originating independently of one another from a single point in time, is completely at odds with everything we know about linguistic development.

4. The Exodus

The Exodus refers to the period beginning with the enslavement of the Israelites in Egypt following the death of Joseph, proceeding to their escape through the leadership of Moses, the Revelations to Moses at Sinai, and their forty years of wanderings in the desert east of Egypt before reaching Canaan. It is considered the charter myth of Israel and is so important that roughly 80 percent of the central Israelite Scriptures are devoted to the events of this relatively brief period. The Gospels are filled with allusions to the Exodus and its constituent events.

And yet no archeological evidence has ever been found to support the Exodus.[83] If it occurred as the Bible claims, then we would expect to see truckloads of evidence for it. After decades of attempts to corroborate these events, most archeologists have abandoned the investigation of the Exodus altogether as a "fruitless pursuit."[84] The consensus among modern biblical scholars and archeologists is that there was never any Exodus remotely resembling that described in the Bible.

By using the dates provided in the Old Testament and working backward, we arrive at a biblical date of around 2100 BCE for Abraham's original departure for Canaan, the promised land that roughly corresponds with modern-day Israel. Perhaps unsurprisingly, there is no archeological evidence of Abraham, Isaac, Jacob, or Joseph. Quite surprising, however, neither is there any archeological evidence of the events surrounding the story of Joseph in Egypt, despite the biblical claim of seven years of unprecedented famine and the revolutionary first use of wide-scale rationing.

According to biblical scholars, the Exodus would have begun around 1440 BCE. At that time, Egypt was a relatively advanced society. Egyptians had writing and copiously recorded events of the day. Egypt was the dominant power in the world and traded extensively. We have records not only of significant events but also of mundane daily activities. We know all the kings of Egypt, in succession, from well before this period onward. Yet there is absolutely no Egyptian record of any Israelite captivity, any plagues (including the death of *every first-born male in Egypt*), a daring escape through the miraculously parted Red Sea, or any of the other momentous events claimed by the author of Exodus.

According to the books of the Pentateuch, at the time of the Exodus, the Israelites numbered more than 600,000 men, plus their wives, children, and livestock. Biblical scholars have estimated the total fleeing Egypt would have been *two million*, which, marching ten abreast, would have formed a line 150 miles long. By way of comparison, the entire Egyptian population in 1250 BCE was between 3 and 3.5 million, so this clearly would have been an event of unprecedented significance in Egyptian history. And yet it isn't reflected in any contemporaneous accounts from Egypt or the surrounding countries.[85] Neither is there evidence of Egyptians enslaving an entire race of people or any other similarly large group. We know from extensive contemporaneous documentation that the workers who built all the large Egyptian monuments were well-paid Egyptian citizens.

The Bible claims these two million Jews wandered in the "wilderness" between Egypt and Canaan for forty years. This region, the Sinai Peninsula, is a short land bridge bounded on three sides by water. The distance from Cairo to Jerusalem is 265 miles. At a speed of 2.8 miles per hour (the average walking speed of a sixty-five-year-old man), this distance could be traversed in *less than four days*. At any point in their journey, the line of Jews would stretch more than half the distance between Egypt and Canaan.

If two million Israelites spent forty years in this small area, we would expect millions of artifacts evidencing their stay. We would expect cooking utensils, campsites, animal bones, and many other indicia of an extended occupation. We would expect the area to be archeologically dense with remnants. Instead, we find nothing. There is absolutely no evidence of any large group of people roaming the Sinai Peninsula anywhere near this period or, for that matter, ever. And it has not been for lack of trying. There have been dozens of archeological surveys of the peninsula to find just this type of evidence. Modern archeological techniques are capable of tracing the most minute remains of ancient wandering tribes, and still such evidence remains nonexistent.[86]

Another problem is that the Exodus account is littered with anachronisms. Camels are mentioned repeatedly as beasts of burden. But we now know camels were not domesticated until hundreds of years later and were not widely used as beasts of burden for hundreds more.[87] Likewise, there are many references to the Philistines and their cities, but the Philistines established no settlements until after 1200 BCE, which would be like claiming that Steve Jobs lived at the same time as George Washington.[88]

The Exodus account describes encounters and battles with the people of specific cities or states, such as Heshbon or Edom. We now know this area was only sparsely populated during this period. While these places existed *by the seventh century BCE*, they either did not exist or were unoccupied at the very time they reportedly played a significant role in the Exodus story hundreds of years earlier.[89]

5. The Conquest of Canaan

Following the Exodus, the Bible describes the conquest of Canaan. The tale begins with the death of Moses, who turns over command of the Israelites to his longtime lieutenant, Joshua. Moses conveys God's instruction that the land be cleansed of all traces of idolatry, requiring the extermination of all existing Canaanites.[90] The book of Joshua follows, describing the astonishingly successful military campaign in which Joshua follows God's instruction to the letter. He defeats all the kings of Canaan in battle, leaving no survivors and allowing the Israelites to take the land for themselves.

The book of Joshua recounts numerous battles at specific locations. It details Joshua's thorough destruction of twenty Canaanite cities and walled towns by name. In each case, the Bible reports all the structures as being torn down and every last man, woman, child, and animal slaughtered. It reflects a *complete and thorough victory* over all of Canaan (Joshua 10:40, 11:16, 11:23), after which the Israelites move in and occupy the land for themselves with God's blessing.

If Joshua presents a historical account, then we would find several things. We should find, for instance, (1) references to the invasion and conquest from sources outside the Bible; (2) evidence there were walled cities and towns in Canaan at the time; (3) evidence that the cities and towns mentioned were in fact destroyed during this period; and (4) evidence of new people taking over from people of a different, rapidly exterminated culture.

We find none of these. No other ancient source mentions anything resembling Joshua's campaign. Archaeologists have revealed that few of the places mentioned were walled cities or towns when these battles supposedly occurred. Many of the cities supposedly conquered by Joshua did not even exist as cities at the time. This includes, most notably, Jericho, which was not inhabited until the fourteenth century BCE and, even then, only sparsely. The same applies to Ai and Heshbon, which were neither occupied, conquered, nor reinhabited in the days of Joshua.

Only two of the twenty towns claimed to have been destroyed by Joshua, Hazor and Bethel, have shown evidence of destruction in the right time period. But this would not be surprising for any similar time frame from this period, as it was not uncommon for ancient towns to be destroyed, burned, or otherwise abandoned for various reasons. The cities with evidence of destruction show it took place over an extended period—perhaps more than a century but certainly not in a single military campaign, as the Bible recounts.[91]

Throughout the period Joshua was supposedly conquering Canaan, it was an Egyptian province, closely controlled and monitored by the Egyptian administration. Archeologists have uncovered hundreds of contemporaneous Egyptian texts detailing the daily events and affairs of Canaan, most notably the Tell el-Amarna letters. These primarily include letters to Egypt from the rulers of Canaanite such city-states as Jerusalem, Schechem, Megiddo, Hazor, and Lachich. None mention any conquest by a foreign group or anything that would suggest the dramatic upheaval that would result from such a conquest. They describe merely a continuation of everyday life. Likewise, the book of Joshua mentions no Egyptians.[92] Finally, archeological evidence has revealed no evidence of a rapid influx of a new culture into Canaan at the time of Joshua's conquest. The settlements uncovered in Canaan from before, during, and after the supposed conquest demonstrate no major cultural shifts. Indigenous Canaanites remained fully in control throughout this period, living as they had always done. Archeology would ultimately reveal Israelites developed from within indigenous Canaanite culture, only gradually distinguishing themselves into a separate ethnic group.

Given the vast disparity between the biblical text and our knowledge from archeology, it is no wonder that virtually all critical scholars agree that the book of Joshua does not recount actual events and as a fictional work holds little historical value.

6. Judges

The book of Judges continues the story from the point at which Joshua's victory was complete, every last Canaanite was dead, and the Israelites controlled all of Canaan—except that now, in a bewildering contradiction, we learn that Joshua's victory was not complete after all. Judges identifies such great Canaanite cities as Megiddo, Dor, and Gezer as unconquered, even though the book of Joshua described their thorough destruction and the complete extermination of their inhabitants. We learn that large areas of Canaan still contain hostile tribes. In a *Twilight Zone*–like twist, Judges inexplicably describes the Israelites as a distinct *minority* among a much larger and stronger Canaanite majority. It is as though Joshua's conquest never happened.

These suddenly appearing Canaanites pose both military and cultural threats, for besides the physical dangers they present, there is the added risk that the Israelites will forsake their own traditions for those of their neighbors. This latter threat is especially acute because it endangers the Israelite's special covenant with God. The Canaanite gods are presented as very real and the Canaanite culture as highly enticing. The stage is set for a protracted struggle of heart and soul with the highest of stakes.

Judges tells some of the most colorful stories in the Bible—stories of individual valor and daring resourcefulness. Underlying all these is a recurrent theological theme: The people of Israel must remain separate and distinct from the indigenous Canaanite population. If they do so, then they will be rewarded. If they assimilate, then God will punish them brutally. This book, more than any other, describes the repeating cycle of the Israelites' sin, divine retribution, and salvation.

In Judges, we see the following cycle repeated six times: (1) The Israelites do evil in the sight of the Lord, often by assimilating with Canaanites; (2) God becomes angry and sells them into slavery; (3) the Israelites cry out to the Lord; (4) God hears their prayers, appoints a "judge," and through this judge slaughters the people to whom He arranged for the Israelites to be sold; (5) repeat. This happens with Othniel, Ehud, Deborah, Gideon, Jephthah, and Samson. God's ultimate slaughter often takes place with the aid of the all-powerful Israelite army, always stationed just offstage, waiting for the call. This begs the question of how the Jews could be repeatedly enslaved and yet maintain a massive, well-equipped army on standby to assist the intermittent judges. As with most poorly written fiction, I suppose it is best not to ask too many questions.

The events of Judges are set between the late fourteenth and early eleventh centuries BCE. There is no archeological or extrabiblical documentary evidence for these events. Further undermining the historical reliability of Judges is the writing and style. The book is permeated with literary devices and a lack of detail that betray fictional narrative rather than historical reporting. The stories appear designed to make a limited number of theological points through sparse but colorful storytelling. The characters are two-dimensional cutouts, typically with one defining trait that bears directly on the theological point to be made. The narratives are lean, like fairytales, focusing solely on the facts necessary to illustrate the moral of each tale before moving on to the next one.

And that moral is a consistent one. Judges reflects a retrospective view, attempting to justify the institution of a monarchy by telling cautionary tales of the disastrous consequences of living without one. Repeatedly, one finds the same type of phrase: "In those days, there was no king in Israel; every man did what was right in his own eyes" (Judges 21:25). The entire book is an *argument* for the institution and maintenance of a monarchy because only a monarchy can break the pernicious cycle. According to story after story, only a king could ensure the people remained loyal to the one true God. The book of Judges is followed by the story of the first Israelite king. It has long been clear to critical historians that Judges contains little, if any, actual history. It is instead an extended argument supported by the repeated telling of the same story with only the details changed.

7. The Empires of David and Solomon

The next chapter of the Deuteronomistic History begins in the first book of Samuel. Samuel was a prophet who also served as Israel's final judge. His sons are dishonest, and the Israelites become concerned of a crisis if the sons succeed Samuel as their leader. This concern leads Israelites to demand that Samuel appoint a king, and God, finally seeing the futility of this judge system He's been propping up so long, supports their demand. Though skeptical, Samuel dutifully follows God's command and appoints Saul as Israel's first true king.

Saul initially shows God's confidence in him to be well-placed. He seems a good king and achieves many military victories. Ultimately, however, Saul runs afoul of God's good graces by exercising *mercy*. Saul displeases God by failing to thoroughly annihilate a neighboring tribe, the Amalekites. Though God ordered Saul to kill every Amalekite man, woman, child, and animal, Saul allows the Amalekite king and a few animals to live. Because of Saul's "weakness" in failing to massacre all the Amalekites, God realizes He made a mistake in choosing Saul and goes about finding a more suitable king.

He finds one in the young shepherd boy David from Bethlehem, who was serving as Saul's armor bearer. After defeating the giant Goliath (in one version of the story), David goes on a God-inspired killing spree, after which he is heralded as single-handedly killing *tens of thousands*. Once, David kills two hundred Philistines, collecting their foreskins in the process, simply to obtain the hand of Saul's daughter in marriage, and then joins the Philistines as a mercenary and does more killing *for them*. God is thoroughly pleased with David's devotion, and after Saul's death at Gilboa (the Bible tells two conflicting stories of how he died, both by God's design), David is anointed Israel's new king.

The Bible describes David as a righteous king in the eyes of God due to his willingness to follow God's orders without question. David captures Jerusalem and makes it his capital. Afterward, God unconditionally promises David that he and his offspring will rule *forever*, regardless of what David does (2 Samuel 7:16). David significantly expands the Israelite kingdom, defeating the Philistines, Ammonites, Moabites, Edomites, and Arameans. By the time of his death, David's empire is legendary throughout the world.

David is succeeded by his son, Solomon, to whom God gives "wisdom and understanding beyond measure."[93] Solomon consolidates David's kingdom and organizes the empire, which now stretches from the Euphrates to the land of the Philistines to the border of Egypt (1 Kings 4:24). Solomon builds many extravagant buildings throughout Israel, including the first temple at Jerusalem. Solomon's reputation is summarized in 1 Kings: "Thus King Solomon excelled all the kings of Earth in riches and in wisdom. And the whole Earth sought the presence of Solomon to hear his wisdom, which God had put into his mind" (1 Kings 10:23–24). The Bible contains many tales of Solomon's vast riches, including a visit from the enigmatic queen of Sheba just to witness Solomon's prodigious fortune and wisdom.

In the summer of 1993, archeologists unearthed a fragment of a monument at Tel Dan in northern Israel. Written in Aramaic, it contains details of what scholars have concluded was the successful assault of Hazael, king of Damascus, on northern Israel around 835 BCE. In the inscription, Hazael boasts, "[I killed Jeho]ram son of [Ahab] king of Israel, and [I] killed [Ahaz]iahu son of [Jehoram kin]g of the House of David. And I set [their towns into ruins and turned] their land into [desolation]." This would appear to be evidence that a Davidic dynasty existed less than a hundred years after the reign of Solomon. The question is whether the biblical claims about David's kingdom and that of his successors accord with the historical record.

Given the vast empires the Bible attributes to David and Solomon, we would expect contemporaneous accounts to be littered with references. But they aren't. Neither David nor Solomon is mentioned in a single known Egyptian or Mesopotamian text. Furthermore, archeologists have found no evidence whatsoever for Solomon's famous building projects. Not a trace has been uncovered of Solomon's temple or palace complex in Jerusalem.

Judah, the southern region of Israel in which Jerusalem is located, was virtually empty of permanent settlements throughout the supposed reigns of David and Solomon in the late Bronze Age. It contained no major urban centers or even a hierarchy of hamlets, villages, or towns. Jerusalem has been excavated many times, frequently focusing on Bronze and Iron Age remains. Archeologists have failed to find any evidence for a significant population during the time of David or Solomon. Archeologists Finkelstein and Silberman conclude, "The most optimistic assessment of this negative evidence is that the tenth century Jerusalem was rather limited in extent, perhaps not more than a typical hill country village."[94]

Granting that David and Solomon existed and ruled over Judah in the tenth century, archeological remains suggest they were no more than local chieftains of a sparsely populated region. Judah contained only about twenty small villages and a few thousand inhabitants, many of whom were nomads. There is no archeological evidence of the resources required to support large armies in the field or to administer even the smallest empire. It would appear that the biblical accounts of the early Davidic Empire are, at best, grossly exaggerated.

8. The Fall of the Judaic Empire

According to the book of Kings, everything falls apart for the Judaic Empire after the death of King Solomon. Despite his great, God-given wisdom, Solomon foolishly marries many foreign wives, foolishly allows them to lead him away from God, and foolishly begins worshiping other gods. God retains a soft spot for Solomon, though, and so doesn't act against him during his lifetime. But in response to Solomon's betrayal, God ensures that his empire will not long survive his death.

Solomon's son, Rehoboam, imposes crushing taxes that soon drive the northern territories to break away. For the next two hundred years, the northern kingdom of Israel and the southern kingdom of Judah remain constantly at odds, a house divided against itself. The North falls under the sway of competing religions and cults, until it ultimately must pay the price for its idolatry—destruction of its cities and the exile of its people by the Assyrians. Throughout this period, the Jews loyal to God and the promise of the Davidic dynasty maintain their unwavering desire for reunification.

But the archeological evidence rebuts this account. There is no evidence that a united monarchy *ever existed*, especially one ruled from Jerusalem. Instead, it strongly suggests there were *always two distinct kingdoms*—one in the north and one in the south, with the southern kingdom, supposedly ruled by David and Solomon, being by far the poorer, weaker, and less influential. Only after the northern kingdom fell to the Assyrians did the southern tribes rise to prominence, taking advantage of the power vacuum.

The Deuteronistic History continues by recounting the reigns of a string of kings who rule from Judah over the next 150 years. Some are considered good in the eyes of God, but most are considered evil. Two kings from this period are singled out for exceptionally positive treatment: Hezekiah (727–698 BCE) and Josiah (639–609 BCE), with Josiah being proclaimed the most righteous of all kings, before or after him.[95] After Josiah's death, Judah declines rapidly into apostasy.

In 587 BCE, Judah is taken by the Babylonians, who kill the last descendant of the Davidic dynasty, burn Jerusalem, and destroy the temple. The remaining inhabitants of Judah are sent into exile. Luckily for the exiles, the Persians defeat the Babylonians fifty years later. Cyrus, the Persian king and only foreign "messiah," decrees that the Jews may return to their homeland and restore their temple. They do so, completing the second temple in 516 BCE. Over the next five hundred years, the Jews struggle with rebuilding and maintaining their culture in the face of numerous foreign occupiers, ultimately the Romans.

9. What Really Happened?

If the archeological record does not support the biblical account of events, then what does it support? We know that a people self-identified as a separate and unique group came to occupy the region now known as Israel by at least the seventh century BCE. How did they get there? What is their history? And why was the Deuteronomistic History written as it was? Luckily, finds of the last century have allowed us to reliably reconstruct much of that history and to know with confidence what really happened.

The Bible tells us that the Israelite people were all descended from one man, Jacob, and his twelve sons. Over four hundred years of bondage in Egypt, they grew from twelve nuclear families to more than two million people, before invading Canaan and displacing its indigenous inhabitants around 1400 BCE. The biblical account identifies the Israelites as a separate and distinct people with unique customs, who, after the invasion, were forced to deal with a neighboring Canaanite culture, entirely alien to them.

The prevailing opinion among archeologists, however, is that the Israelites emerged gradually from indigenous Canaanites sometime around the twelfth century BCE. These Canaanites were polytheistic, believing in an entire pantheon of gods, with a view of creation very similar to that of their Babylonian neighbors. The Israelites were never aliens to Canaanite culture. They were Canaanites from the beginning. They had been nomadic herders but, around this time, were forced by changing economic conditions to settle in the highlands and start farming.

The remains from these early farming villages are identical to those from other Canaanite settlements except for one thing—the absence of pig bones. This suggests that one particular community of Canaanites set itself apart by banning the cooking or eating of pork, perhaps as the result of some outbreak of sickness, such as trichinosis. Otherwise, it appears they worshipped the same gods as the neighboring Canaanites and followed the same customs.

Whatever the reason for the ban on pork, it is likely this development was instrumental in the proto-Israelites beginning to think of themselves as unique. Distinctive culinary practices are one way ethnic boundaries are formed. Modern-day Jews who avoid pork are continuing one of the oldest cultural practices of their people.

The name *Israel* first appears in the historical record in 1209 BCE, at the end of the late Bronze Age, in an inscription of the Egyptian pharaoh Merneptah, reading simply, "Israel is laid waste and his seed is not." The context suggests that *Israel* referenced a people living in the highlands of Samaria.[96] Israel may have been the name of a tribal leader from whom the tribe itself took its name. The inscription suggests the tribe was defeated in some conflict with Egypt, which administered Canaan at the time.

Over the next two hundred years, the number of villages in this area increased from twenty-five to more than three hundred, and the settled population increased to 45,000.[97] Ninety percent of these settlements were in the northern highlands, the region known in the Bible as Israel and encompassing Samaria. The southern highlands, by contrast, were only sparsely settled. This is the area known in the Bible as Judah, in which Jerusalem was located, as well as the kingdoms of David and Solomon.

The reasons for this difference in settlement patterns are obvious to archeologists today, as the two regions differed markedly in many respects. Israel had fertile land, rich resources, and a gentle climate. Judah had none of these. Israel had relatively easy access to the coastal regions, through which inhabitants could transport their goods by boat and access the major trade route between Egypt and Mesopotamia, while Judah did not. Israel had enormous advantages over Judah, geographically, environmentally, and economically.

By the tenth century BCE (1000–900 BCE), a rudimentary state had developed in Israel. During this same period, the population of Judah was no greater than five thousand and was widely dispersed. Until this time, the primary regional power had been the Canaanite city-states of the coastal plain. But at the end of the tenth century BCE, the Egyptian pharaoh Shishak launched an attack on Canaan to reassert his power. Shishak likely destroyed the majority of the Canaanite city-states before returning to Egypt, leaving a power vacuum in the region.

A tremendous opportunity arose for the fledgling state of Israel, and they took it. In the aftermath of the destruction, the Israelites expanded into the adjoining lowlands. From there, they set up new trade alliances, increasing their economic power exponentially. It was not long before a full-fledged kingdom developed. This kingdom was sometimes known as Israel by its neighbors but more commonly as "House (or Land) of Omri."[98] As for the southern region of Judah, settlement remained minimal from the twelfth through tenth centuries BCE.

The House of Omri, which ruled in the ninth century BCE, was likely the first true kingdom of Israel. Omri and his successors expanded their territory significantly, maintained one of the largest armies in the region, and were unsurpassed as builders and administrators. The capital city of the Omrides was Samaria, the ruins of which indicate a massive and opulent palace. The Omrides also constructed elaborate complexes at Meggido, Hazor, Jezreel, and Dan.[99]

The Omrides ruled over a multiethnic state with many competing customs. It appears the Omrides were content to allow such diversity rather than seeking to impose any common culture or religious practices. There is evidence that many gods were worshipped in Israel during the rule of the Omrides, which allowed the Omrides to successfully integrate diverse groups into the machinery of a growing empire. The Omrides appeared to succeed largely because they remained open and cosmopolitan rather than closed and insular.

The rise of the Omride Empire was advanced and benefitted by the contemporaneous revival of eastern Mediterranean trade. The Greeks and Phoenicians were actively seeking trade partners, and Israel was at the right place at the right time. The Omrides were also militarily successful in their heyday, conquering surrounding lands to expand their empire.

In the mid-ninth century, Israel was invaded by King Hazael of Syria, and the last Omride king was killed. The kingdom of Israel continued, however, most likely reaching the peak of its prosperity between 788 and 747 BCE under King Jeroboam II. During that period, Israel could finally boast the full complement of statehood: literacy, bureaucratic administration, specialized economic production, and a professional army. Throughout this period, Judah to the south remained a rural and stagnant collection of tribes. It was, as candidly reported in 2 Kings 14:9, a "thistle" compared to the "cedar" of Israel.

After the death of Jeroboam II in 747 BCE, the Israelite kingdom started to fall apart. This disintegration was accelerated by the aggressive tactics of the Assyrian Empire, which began to forcibly annex Israelite territory at an alarming rate. The last king of the northern kingdom made a final, desperate attempt to stand up to Assyria, but it was ultimately in vain. In 722 BCE, the Assyrians captured Samaria. The Assyrians deported Israel's inhabitants to the far reaches of the Assyrian Empire. For all practical purposes, the northern kingdom of Israel ceased to exist.

Though devastating for Israel, this was a golden opportunity for Judah. Having relatively little strategic or economic worth, Judah had been ignored by Assyria. The fall of Israel created another power vacuum in the region. Until the eighth century, the population of Judah was about one-tenth that of Israel. But that was all about to change. At the end of the eighth century BCE, Jerusalem's population exploded. Refugees from Israel poured into the town, and within a single generation, it was transformed into a city of 150 acres of closely packed buildings. Archeologists have estimated the population may have increased fifteen times—from 1,000 to 15,000 inhabitants.

The entire region of Judah also increased substantially in prosperity. Archeologists have described as "inescapable" the conclusion that Judah suddenly cooperated with the Assyrian Empire, became a vassal state, and integrated itself into the Assyrian economy, resulting in an economic revolution. Judah went from a village and clan-based culture to state-centralized industrialization. This all occurred during the reign of King Hezekiah.

Prior to the fall of Israel, religious ideas in Judah had been all over the map. Though there had been a cult of YHWH, it competed with many religions, including countless fertility and ancestor cults. There had never been any concerted effort to limit worship to YHWH alone, but with the increasing centralization of Jerusalem came a new political agenda—the unification of all Israel under a more unified religious ideology. These changes have caused such biblical scholars as Baruch Halpern to suggest that over the course of "no more than a few decades in the late eighth century and early seventh century BCE, the monotheistic tradition of Judeo-Christian civilization was born."[100]

Sometime in the late eighth century BCE, a particular religious movement began to gain steam in Judah. This movement urged people to abandon the worship of all gods except YHWH. Until that time, YHWH had been but one of a pantheon of Canaanite gods, essentially the Canaanite god of war. This "YHWH-alone movement," as it has been dubbed by historian Morton Smith, was also intensely nationalistic.[101] It desired a "restoration" of the Davidic dynasty. It also hoped for this dynasty to extend its rule over the conquered lands of Israel to the north, which would bring about a unification of the northern and southern highlands. It wanted the kingdom's political power and religious worship to be centralized in Jerusalem, with all competing cult centers destroyed.

The evidence suggests that King Hezekiah was receptive to the movement and initiated religious reforms consistent with its goals, such as banning countryside worship. But Hezekiah also made a disastrous mistake by revolting against Assyria. The Assyrians quickly crushed his rebellion and destroyed all the cities of Judah, except for Jerusalem. Hezekiah's son Manasseh appears to have reversed Hezekiah's religious reforms and allied himself with the Assyrians, resulting in a peaceful reign of fifty-five years, in which Judah largely recovered from the results of Hezekiah's rebellion. Manasseh died in 642 and was succeeded by his son Amon. Within two years, however, Amon was assassinated in a coup, resulting in Amon's eight-year-old son, Josiah, ascending to the throne.

Under Josiah, the YHWH-alone movement took off. Josiah appears to have embraced it fully, initiating unprecedented religious reforms to cleanse the land of any worship except for YHWH. He destroyed the shrines of foreign cults throughout Judah and outlawed sacrifices except in Jerusalem. Josiah's rule also ushered in a new wave of nationalism benefitted by the withdrawal of Assyrian forces from Israel for unrelated reasons. The time seemed right for Judah to expand its kingdom to the north and create a pan-Israelite state—if only Josiah could secure the will of the people behind his ambitious religious and military campaigns. Josiah needed something to convince them that his campaign was not only warranted but also divinely demanded and that victory was a foregone conclusion.

At this very time, in Josiah's eighteenth year of rule, the Bible reports a momentous and stunningly fortuitous discovery. It is claimed that in 622 BCE, as Josiah's high priest Hilkiah was renovating the temple, he found a long-lost text. The text was regarded as God's definitive law code, given directly to Moses at Mount Sinai. Luckily for Josiah, this Book of Law confirmed that he and the YHWH-alone movement had been right all along *about everything*. And more to the point, it provided a compelling argument for Josiah's proposed military campaign to take Israel.

By the eighteenth century, biblical scholars had recognized the many similarities between the Book of Law described in the biblical account of Josiah and Deuteronomy as we know it today. Later discoveries only reinforced this view. Today, critical historians agree that the Book of Law represents the original version of Deuteronomy. Rather than an ancient book discovered by Josiah's high priest, "it seems safe to conclude that Deuteronomy was written in the seventh century BCE, just before or during Josiah's reign."[102]

This, of course, casts new light on the entire Deuteronomistic History, which bears distinctive signs of identical authorship. With the writing of the history (Deuteronomy, Joshua, Judges, 1 and 2 Samuel, and 1 Kings) established during Josiah's reign, biblical scholars could finally make sense of unique themes and vast historical inaccuracies contained therein.

Josiah needed to rally the people of Judah to his cause. He needed to justify and validate his often-violent religious reforms and his military campaign. And he had a great new tool at his disposal. The rise of industrialization had dramatically increased the literacy rate in Judah. For the first time, people could read in substantial numbers.[103] If he could engage someone to write a history of the Jewish people, then he could ensure it was told so as to support his goals. And for that purpose, Josiah appears to have conscripted the Deuteronomistic Historian (DH).

The first book penned by the DH was likely Deuteronomy. Deuteronomy legitimized Josiah's religious and political reforms. It established a list of laws, straight from God, that required exclusive and centralized worship in Jerusalem. It delegitimized local power structures by stripping them of their most essential functions. It explicitly authorized a monarchy such as Josiah's. As Christian scholar Thom Stark recognizes, "What's taking place here in the Deuteronomistic History is that all of the events of the past are reinterpreted according to the ideology underwriting the Josianic reforms, and that ideology is legitimated by the forged Deuteronomy legislation which was said to have been 'lost' in the temples walls and conveniently found by Josiah's high priest."[104]

The literary character of Joshua represents a direct parallel to Josiah and his political ambitions. Like Josiah, Joshua faces an uncertain military campaign against people with religious practices he opposes. Joshua's campaign has God's clear blessing and assistance, for God promises the entire land of Canaan to the Jews. The end of the stories of Noah and of Sodom and Gomorrah appear intended as slanders against neighboring peoples, the Canaanites, Moabites, and Ammonites, who threatened Judah when the

Old Testament was written. Noah cursed his son Canaan. Lot slept with his daughter, producing two bastard incestuous sons, Moab and Ammon. These stories appear to have had a clear political purpose—delegitimizing Josiah's enemies.

Joshua's campaign was a complete success, most notably at the very cities that Josiah would need to take first and in which he could expect to face his greatest opposition. If God supported Joshua in his righteous cause, then why would He not support Josiah in his? As archeologist and biblical scholar Israel Finkelstein says,

> [T]he towering figure of Joshua is used to paint a metaphorical portrait of Josiah, the seventh century would-be savior of all the people of Israel. Josiah is the new Joshua, and the past, mythical Conquest of Canaan is the battle plan for the present fight and the conquest to be. The first two battles—at Jericho and Ai (i.e., the area of Bethel)—were pitched in territories that were the first targets of the Josianic expansion after the withdrawal of Assyria.[105]

The book of Judges would have provided Josiah two very important rhetorical tools: (1) practical arguments justifying a monarchy such as his and (2) horrifying accounts of the dangers of assimilating with Canaanites of other religions, which was one of his greatest concerns. A primary theme that recurs continuously in Judges is the importance of the Israelites maintaining racial, ethnic, and cultural purity. As biblical scholar John Collins explains,

> Josiah's reform was, among other things, an assertion of national identity. Judah was emerging from the shadow of Assyria and laying claim to sovereignty over the ancient territory of Israel. The assertion of identity entails differentiation from the "others," especially from those who are close, but different. The ferocity of the Deuteronomic rhetoric toward the Canaanites may be due in part to the fact that Israelites were Canaanites to begin with. Moreover, Josiah promoted a purist form of Yahwism that tolerated the worship of no other deities. The Canaanites were perceived as a threat to the purity of Israelite religion.[106]

Perhaps the most important aspect of the History came next: the myth of a great, united Davidic Empire. As we have seen, David was, at best, no more than a hill-country chieftain living in the shadow of the far more prosperous Israel to the north. The DH, however, recasts him as brilliant, unparalleled leader uniting all of Canaan under one kingdom, during which it experienced a golden age. This provided the Jews a nostalgic ideal that

Josiah could aspire to restore. It also justified Josiah's proposed unification of Israel and Judah as a *reunification* because this was the way God had always intended things to be.

But actual history presents a problem. If the kingdoms of David and Solomon were so great, then the DH had to make sense of why the Davidic monarchy split and was quickly overshadowed by the House of Omri. How could the DH explain the power, wealth, and dominance of the Omrides and their successors, which, being relatively recent in time, would have been well known among Josiah's subjects? The cultural and religious tolerance of the Omrides conflicted sharply with the exclusivist philosophy of the YHWH-alone movement. As Finkelstein and Silberman note, "The possibility that the Israelite kings who consorted with the nations, married foreign women, and built Canaanite-type shrines and palaces would prosper was both unbearable and unthinkable."[107]

The DH explains the kingdom's split as resulting from Solomon's failure to maintain the racial, ethnic, and cultural purity demanded by God. This would feed directly into Josiah's message by demonizing the cultures of his enemies and allowing him to claim he was simply nullifying the transgressions that led to the breakdown of the Davidic "Empire," so the Israelites could reclaim the glory of the past.

As for the Omrides, the DH has nothing but scorn for them. The DH portrays them and their successors, without exception, as evil in the eyes of God. From his vantage point looking back in time, however, the DH knew that the northern kingdom was destined to fall, so he simply portrays this as God's inevitable divine justice—delayed, yes, but no less complete when it finally arrives. The story of the northern kingdom, therefore, becomes a morality tale supporting Josiah's reforms—a grim reminder of what could happen if the people of Judah fail to heed Josiah's call: "The older and once powerful kingdom of Israel, though blessed with fertile lands and productive people, had lost its inheritance. Now, the surviving kingdom of Judah would soon act the part of a divinely favored younger brother—like Isaac, Jacob, or their own ancestral king David—eager to snatch up a lost birthright and redeem the land and the people of Israel."[108]

In marked contrast to its portrayal of the northern kings, the DH presents Josiah himself only in glowing terms: "For the author of the Deuteronomistic History, Josiah's reign marked a metaphysical moment hardly less important than those of God's covenant with Abraham, the Exodus from Egypt, or the divine promise to King David."[109] Josiah is portrayed not just as a worthy successor to Moses, Joshua, and David but also as their apotheosis. The second book of Kings 23:25 proclaims, "Before him there was no king like him, who turned to the *Lord* with all his heart and with all his soul and with all his might, according to all the law of Moses; nor did any like him arise after him." Josiah was the pinnacle of kingly perfection.

The original Deuteronomistic History, as historians have been able to reconstruct it, ends with Josiah's destruction of the idolatrous high places and the celebration of the first national Passover in Jerusalem, symbolically replaying the original Passover in the time of Moses. Josiah has been given a new law and a new purpose. With these, the stage is set for Josiah to fulfill his destiny and reclaim the lost glory of the Israelites, a perfect background for Josiah's bold initiatives. It was to be a perfect ending to phase 1 of his story and the perfect lead-in to his military campaign.

But then, the unthinkable happened. In 610 BCE, before he could complete his reforms or initiate his military campaign, Josiah was killed in a dispute with the Egyptian pharaoh at Megiddo. In the wake of Josiah's death, his reform movement fell apart. Soon thereafter, the Babylonians destroyed Jerusalem, took its people off into exile, and ended the Davidic dynasty. How was one to make sense of these disastrous events in light of the Deuteronomistic History? How could this story setting up the greatest hero Judah had ever known, and the most glorious victory to come, end like this?

While in exile, a new writer or set of writers began updating and revising the Deuteronomistic History through a source known to scholars as Dtr2 (as opposed to the original work of the DH, known as Dtr1). The apparent goal was to harmonize the Deuteronomistic History with recent events and to put the whole story into a new context. The authors of Dtr2 reframed Josiah's righteousness as merely *postponing* the destruction of Jerusalem, which had been rendered inevitable by the evil actions of Manasseh, the enemy of the YHWH-only movement. Josiah's righteousness had spared him seeing Jerusalem fall, but it would be the righteousness of the people who would determine the future of Israel: "Thus the rewritten Deuteronomistic History brilliantly subordinated the covenant with David to the fulfillment of the covenant between God and the people of Israel at Sinai. Israel would henceforth have a purpose and an identity, even in the absence of a king."[110]

The entire Deuteronomistic History represents a sophisticated form of political propaganda. The DH weaves local stories and legends into a rich drama, combining some history but mostly fiction, to support Josiah's aims, political, ideological, and theological. Its many anachronisms can be explained as the DH retrojecting his contemporary knowledge into stories from the past. Why did the book of Joshua identify towns and cities that didn't even exist when the events of the book supposedly took place? Because those towns *did exist* during the reign of Josiah. In fact, many of them were occupied *only during Josiah's reign*. And they were to be prime targets of Josiah's upcoming campaign.

So I've addressed Deuteronomy and the remaining books of the Deuter-onomistic History, but what about the first four books of the Pentateuch? Biblical tradition maintains that these, as well as Deuteronomy, were all written by Moses. But critical scholars rejected this premise long ago. The current scholarly consensus is that these books were compiled from at least four sources, which were edited into the books we know today by several redactors.

The primary sources are known as J, E, P, and D. J was composed by an author living in Judah, most likely between 800 and 722 BCE. E was composed somewhat later during this same time period but by a person living in the northern kingdom of Israel. P was composed after J and E by someone from the Jerusalem priesthood as a deliberate alternative to the history presented in J and E. D, the last to be written, includes both Dtr1 and Dtr2, which I discussed in previous sections.

Separating and identifying these biblical sources took centuries, and refinements are ongoing. The delineations are based on differences in linguistics, terminology, consistent content, narrative flow (continuity), and connections with other parts of the Bible. That these delineations so often converge has allowed modern scholars to reliably conclude with consilience that the final texts were indeed originally made up of these distinct sources.

What is so interesting is that once these sources are isolated, they can each be read as a cohesive whole. When this is done, it is apparent that, as with Josiah and the DH, each author had unique agendas and ideologies. This explains why there are so many contradictions throughout the ulti-mately redacted final books. It also explains why so many stories are told more than once, often with significant changes between the versions.

The authors of J and E (to whom I also refer as J and E, respectively) lived during roughly the same time period, but J lived in Judah, and E, in Israel. J always uses the term *YHWH* to describe God, while E refers to God exclusively as *Elohim*. The J narrative portrays the native royal family of David, Solomon, and Rehoboam favorably, while in E, their treatment is relatively succinct and implicitly critical.

The J narrative provides a significant role for the character of Judah and addresses many issues unique to the southern kingdom, such as tribes that bordered its territory. The E narrative minimizes the role of Judah and deals with issues of unique interest to the northern kingdom of Israel, especially to certain factions of the priesthood there. J focuses on the theme of the Jews being YHWH's people, under his protection so long as they remain loyal and faithful. E focuses on the religious aspects of prayer, sacrifice, and prophetic revelation, especially within the northern kingdom.

The P (Priestly) narrative was likely created by an Aaronid priest (priest from the line of Aaron) during the time of King Hezekiah of Judah and, like D, was edited during the Babylonian exile. It places great importance on the divisions between priestly classes and resulting privileges, divisions initially assigned by Hezekiah. Access to God is limited to Aaronid priests; there are no dreams, angels, judges, or prophets with direct pipelines to God. P is highly concerned with the centralization of worship and the importance of the Tabernacle, neither of which is ever mentioned in J or E. The God portrayed in P is far more interested in justice than in mercy and will forgive only if one brings a sacrifice to an Aaronid priest. While in both J and E, God is anthropomorphized, with human qualities both good and bad, the God of P is transcendent and mysterious, only accessible indirectly through the priesthood. The entire book seems primarily designed to justify and promote the unique value of the Aaronid priests.

While the book of Leviticus can be traced exclusively to the P source, and Deuteronomy, to the D source(s), Genesis, Exodus, and Numbers reflect a melting pot of source material. Genesis and Exodus in particular reveal a thorough mixing of the J, E, and P sources, resulting in narratives replete with repetition and contradictions (see figure 5.1). At times, the very nature of God appears to change from verse to verse.

When the sources are separated, it is clear that the "history" they recount is cohesive only from a high-level perspective. Each represents a form of propaganda in its own right. J advocates for positions of importance to the people of early Judah. E advocates for positions of importance to Levite priests in early Israel. P advocates for positions of importance to Aaronid priests in the time of Hezekiah, while D and the Deuteronomistic History advocate for positions of importance to Josiah and like-minded reformers of his day.

These are not documents that should be taken as historical in any traditional sense. While they surely preserve the kernels of many stories passed down orally among Bronze Age Israelites, there are no compelling reasons to consider such accounts reliable and many reasons not to. In light of what textual criticism has revealed of these texts, furthermore, the idea that they were inspired by a perfect, divine being is fraught with difficulties. What possible reason would such a being have for deliberately compiling the most important story ever told in such a convoluted fashion? Why suffuse it

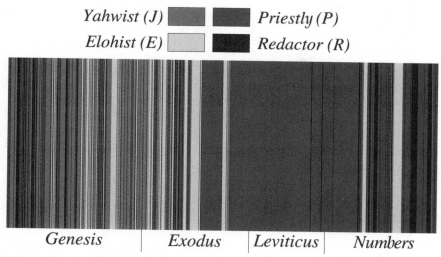

Distribution of materials of Jahwist, Elohist and Priestly sources, as well as Redactor's contribution in the first four books, following Richard Friedman.

Figure 5.1. Distribution of materials of Jahwist, Elohist, and Priestly sources and Redactor's contribution in the first four books, following Richard Friedman. *Wikipedia—public domain.*

with factual and theological contradictions that are explicable only through understanding local squabbles between factions living in pre-exilic Israel or the ambitions of a single king?

10. The History of God through the Old Testament

Former Catholic nun Karen Armstrong has written an amazing book titled *A History of God*.[111] In it, she details how concepts of God evolved over time to what we have today. Of particular interest is God's history through the Old Testament. Armstrong details how the characteristics and stories we associate with the Christian God originated with earlier traditions, assigned to earlier gods. These would ultimately be grafted together in piecemeal fashion to form the Jewish god, YHWH.

The story begins with the Babylonian epic the *Enuma Elish*, written in approximately 1750 BCE. In the *Enuma Elish*, Marduk, champion of the Babylonian gods, defeats chaos in the form of the dragon Tiamat, after which the Babylonian gods form the world. In the Babylonian story, the pre-Creation world is described as a formless void. The gods create light, the firmament, dry land, the Sun and Moon, and mankind in order, details that are edited into the books of Genesis and Isaiah while the Israelites are exiled in Babylon.

The next point of interest is the Canaanite religion, which, like that of the Babylonians, was thoroughly polytheistic. From our first records of this religion, around 1200 BCE, we know that three of the most important Canaanite gods were El Elyon ("God Most High"), who was believed to be the father of the other gods; El Elyon's wife Asherah, a fertility goddess; and Baal, the god of storms and fertility.

The writer of J begins his story with what is now chapter 2 of Genesis. This version of Creation bears little resemblance to the Babylonian or Canaanite creation myths, representing a separate tradition. But this changes with chapter 12 of Genesis, the story of Abraham. Abraham is said to worship El Shaddai, one name of the Canaanite god El Elyon. Abraham and his son Jacob interact with El Elyon in personal ways that mirror the other pagan religions of the time.

Ultimately, Jacob makes El Elyon his Elohim, which was a term used by the Canaanites to represent their *primary god*. Using this term only makes sense if Jacob considered El Elyon to be one god of many, for to be primary requires a hierarchy. It entails the existence of lesser gods in the same pantheon. It is clear from the language of J that Abraham and Jacob were polytheistic pagans like their Canaanite brethren.

The worship of El Elyon fades from the Hebrew text in Exodus, where he is replaced by YHWH. Even in the English translation, however, there is ample evidence that YHWH was considered only one of many gods.[112] The Bible also contains ample evidence that YHWH was initially considered *subordinate* to El Elyon. Deuteronomy 32:8–9 states, "When Elyon gave the nations as an inheritance, when he separated the sons of man, he set the boundaries of the peoples according to the number of the sons of God. For YHWH's portion was his people, Jacob his allotted inheritance." In other words, El Elyon initially divided the nations and assigned them to his children, other divine beings. One of these beings was YHWH, to whom El Elyon assigned the descendants of Jacob. These descendants were to occupy what we now call Israel, which would thereafter be the region of YHWH's control and influence. This is often obscured by certain English translations in which *Elyon* is translated as *God* or *Most High*, while *YHWH* is translated as *Lord*, rendering the passage nonsensical.

Exodus 15:3 establishes YHWH as Israel's war god, the warrior who delivered the Israelites from the Egyptians. YHWH's full name, Yahweh Sabaoth, means "the god of the armies." YHWH was the Canaanite equivalent of the Greek god Aries and like Aries was worshipped most fervently when war was threatened or waged. Once the Israelites saw their war with the Egyptians as over, they began to once again worship the Canaanite fertility gods Baal and Asherah, whose powers were more relevant to daily concerns.

As with the Greek pantheon of gods, factions aligned themselves with different gods. A certain group of Canaanites were primarily devoted to the war god, YHWH. This group understandably rose in prominence during times of political upheaval when war appeared to loom on the horizon. One such time was 747 BCE, as war with Assyria seemed imminent. The Bible preserves the writings of three "prophets" from this era, Isaiah, Amos, and Hosea, each of whom describe YHWH from his own unique perspective.

To Isaiah, a member of the royal family, YHWH was a king. Amos, a shepherd, saw YHWH as empathetic to the suffering poor. Hosea, who was suffering through marriage problems, saw YHWH as a jilted husband who continued to hold tenderness for his cheating wife, Israel. All three believe that Israel's problems stemmed from a lack of focused devotion to YHWH. Unfortunately, their words were not heeded in their own time, and Israel fell.

During the reign of Josiah, his reformers rewrote Israelite history. The books of Joshua, Judges, Exodus, Samuel, and Kings were written or revised according to the new YHWH-alone ideology. The Deuteronomist interpretation of the Exodus myth was edited into the older narratives of J and E. Even at this point, however, YHWH was recognized as one of many gods, though clearly superior to them all and the only one worthy of worship. For example, see Deuteronomy 5:7, 6:14–15, and 10:17 and Psalms 86:8: "You shall have no other gods before me"; "your lord is God of gods and Lord of lords"; "Among the gods there is none like unto thee"; "the Lord . . . will famish all the gods of the earth." These passages make no sense unless the writers believed in other gods.

The final stage came during the Babylonian exile, when the Israelites were at the deepest point of their despair with the threat of their religion dying completely. Under such extreme circumstances, the religion evolved. A new author, Second Isaiah, arose, and his words were appended to those of First Isaiah. Second Isaiah was the first to claim that YHWH was the *one and only god*. He wrote, "I am the first and I am the last; besides me there is no god" (Isaiah 44:6). Monotheism had been introduced, and things would never again be the same.

From this culture and period, the Priestly source P arises. Israelite history is rewritten once again. Exodus is edited to say that the El Shaddai worshipped by Abraham and the YHWH worshipped by Moses *were the same god* (Exodus 6:2–3). All references to El Elyon are explained by P as merely different names for YHWH, though these had always been distinct deities. The entire book of Leviticus is authored. Genesis chapter 1 is written as an improved version of the Babylonian Creation account. Second Isaiah rewrites the Babylonian myths attributed to Marduk, such as his defeat of the dragon Tiamat, attributing Marduk's exploits instead to YHWH (Isaiah 51:9–10). The Torah is edited by P to make it appear as if it were always monotheistic. In 600 BCE, the God of Judaism, Christianity, and Islam is born.

Once one knows where to look, this gradual evolution from polytheism to monotheism is readily apparent from reading the Old Testament. One can see the Hebrew God we know today taking form over the course of centuries, as different authors reinterpreted the texts and traditions of their people to address changing circumstances. This God is a work of man rather than the other way around.

11. Thoughts on the Old Testament

If the historical faith of Israel is not founded in real history, such faith is erroneous and, therefore, our faith is also.

—Roland de Vaux, Catholic theologian and archeologist (1903–1971),
The Early History of Israel

The historical saga contained in the Bible from Abraham to Moses is nothing more than a brilliant product of the human imagination. . . . We cannot talk about it as though it represents historical reality.

—Israel Finkelstein, *The Bible Unearthed*

Christian theology is inextricably tied to the texts of the Old Testament. Without the original sin of Adam and Eve, the Exodus of Moses, or the conquest of Canaan, Christianity has no context. Moreover, the historical accuracy and reliability of these accounts was a prerequisite to the validity of Jesus's claims. After all, Jesus claimed to be a *fulfillment* of the Old Testament texts and the prophecies contained therein. To Jesus, the history as recounted within the Old Testament *was all leading inextricably straight to him.*

Jesus's movement, furthermore, was grounded on the Old Testament. He confirmed the continued application of the laws within it and based many of his parables and advice on its teachings. Jesus, for instance, refers to himself as the lamb to be slaughtered in honor of the first Passover, as recounted in Exodus. If there was no Exodus, then there was no lamb. If there was no lamb, then Jesus was talking nonsense. Throughout Matthew, multiple parallels are drawn between the life of Jesus and that of Moses. If there was no Moses, then those parallels lose all theological significance. Roland de Vaux was correct to point out that if the Old Testament is false, then the foundation of Christianity crumbles beneath it.

We now know beyond any reasonable doubt that the Old Testament is, as de Vaux says, "not founded in real history." Archeology and textual criticism alone have demonstrated there is little that can be salvaged of any historical value. Divorced of any anchor to the historical record, the Old Testament texts retain their value only as myth and allegory. But as Christianity insists on strict historicity as an anchor, this must be acknowledged for what it is—a fatal blow. Christianity without the Old Testament to ground it is a charade.

B. The New Testament

I've addressed many of the problems for Christianity raised by the Old Testament, but how does the New Testament fare? We must first recognize that the New Testament represents a very different collection of documents than the Old. The New Testament comprises four Gospels, attributed by tradition to four of Jesus's disciples; a narrative of the apostles' ministries in the early church; letters from the apostle Paul of Tarsus to fledgling Christian congregations; letters from various other authors dealing with early Christian doctrine, instruction, and conflict resolution; and a book of prophecy known as Revelation. All twenty-seven books, arguably excluding Revelation, deal with Christianity in the first century, from roughly 33 CE to 70 CE.

There is no sprawling narrative covering centuries of geopolitical turmoil. The focus is far more limited and intimate in both time and scope. To the extent actual events are recounted, they are generally not of the type we would expect to be recorded by contemporary historians or to leave behind archeological evidence. They reflect the goings on of a relatively insignificant religious sect in a remote area of the world.

That is not to say that we wouldn't expect to see parallel contemporary accounts of *some* of the events detailed in, for instance, the Gospels. They make some truly extraordinary claims of events that occurred in or around Jerusalem, which is the subject of detailed historical accounts by contemporary historians. We cannot expect, however, the same level of extrabiblical sources and hard archeological evidence against which to evaluate the New Testament as we have for the Old.

But that does not mean we must simply accept the New Testament texts at face value. Historians use many objective criteria to assess the reliability of ancient texts. The entire field of textual criticism is based on these techniques. Today, we know much about the writing styles and conventions in the first and second centuries. We also know much about the zeitgeist of the period—what issues were being discussed and debated at different times and among different groups. We can compare the New Testament texts with other writings from the period and with each other to identify inconsistencies and anachronisms. Finally, we know much about the development of the New Testament, how it came about, and what forces shaped it. Critical historians have many tools at their disposal to assess these texts.

When we look at the New Testament critically, assessing it objectively for reliability rather than devotionally for guidance, there are good reasons to be highly skeptical of many claims central to modern Christianity. As a whole, the New Testament provides weak evidence for those claims. Given all the available evidence, alternative explanations are far more probable.

1. The Historical Jesus: What Is the Evidence?

What evidence do we have for the historical Jesus, by which I mean some genuine historical figure upon which the Gospel stories are based? Very little, as it turns out—at least as compared to such known historical events as the Civil War or even such historical figures as Julius Caesar. Jesus allegedly lived almost two thousand years ago in a relatively sparsely populated area of the world. He left no writings of his own. Though he is thought to have been executed around 30–35 CE, no writings exist from prior to or within that time even referencing him.

The first reference to Jesus comes in the letters of Paul of Tarsus, which most scholars date to the period from roughly 50 to 60 CE, at least *fifteen years and up to thirty years* after Jesus's alleged death and supposed Resurrection. For those not familiar with them, it will be surprising to learn that Paul says *almost nothing* about the life or teachings of Jesus in those letters. As New Testament scholar Bart Ehrman explains, everything Paul wrote about Jesus's life could be written on one 3x5 note card.[113] Paul's letters focus primarily on theological and practical issues in the early Christian churches.

Though he briefly references the Resurrection of Jesus in 1 Corinthians, Paul does not claim to have been an eyewitness to Jesus's life, death, or Resurrection. His letters suggest that Paul obtained his knowledge of Jesus through a chain of unknown verbal sources. The only thing that might arguably be classified as a personal experience of Jesus comes from a single vision at the beginning of his ministry.

Virtually everything we know about the life of Jesus comes from the four Gospels, known today by their titles: Matthew, Mark, Luke, and John. It is widely agreed by historians that the first of these, Mark, was authored around 70 CE, at least *thirty years* after the events it describes. Matthew and Luke were written between 70 and 100 CE. Matthew and Luke borrowed heavily from Mark and possibly another document of sayings, now lost, commonly known as Q. The Gospel of John was likely written between 90 and 110 CE and differs markedly from the other three (synoptic) Gospels in many significant respects.

All four Gospels were authored anonymously. It was not until at least a century later that Christians began assigning authors to them, at a time when spurious apostolic association was a popular means of claiming authority for a favored tract or artifact. Modern critical scholars agree that none of the Gospels were written by the apostles to whom they are attributed and that the actual authors were not eyewitnesses to the events described.

The Gospels are *hearsay*, at best secondhand accounts (and possibly many times removed) of events that allegedly happened decades earlier. Even the earliest, Mark, would be the equivalent of someone writing a book in 2015 about something that happened in 1985 from unknown oral sources. And this earliest Gospel doesn't mention Jesus's Resurrection!

If we were in a court, applying modern rules of evidence shortly after the final Gospel was written, and were attempting to establish the accuracy of the events detailed within, none of the Gospels would be admissible. Being based on hearsay, they would all be presumed unreliable—so unreliable as to not even merit the jury's attention. But the situation is worse than that, for we don't even have the originals. None of the original Gospels or other New Testament documents has survived to the present day. As Bart Ehrman says,

In fact we do not have the original copies of any of the books of the New Testament or of any of the other Christian writings. . . . Nor do we have copies made directly from the originals, copies made from the copies of the originals, or copies made from the copies of the first copies. Our earliest manuscripts (i.e., handwritten copies) of Paul's letters date from around 200 C.E., that is, nearly 150 years after he wrote them. The earliest full manuscripts of the Gospels come from about the same time, although we have some fragments of manuscripts that date earlier. . . . Even our relatively full manuscripts from around the year 200 are not preserved intact, however. Pages and entire books were lost from them before they were discovered in modern times. Indeed, it is not until the fourth century, nearly 300 years after the New Testament was written that we begin to find complete manuscripts of all of its books.[114]

This would not be a terrible problem if we could be sure these copies were accurate. But that is not the case. There were no Xerox machines in the first century, so all the copies were done by hand. We know that during the very period between the initial writing of the Gospels and the copying of our first manuscripts, the copyists freely added to or changed the materials they were copying. The manuscripts were seen as "living texts," unlike the Hebrew Old Testament, which was subject to strict controls because it was considered holy. Ehrman explains,

> Even for later scribes . . . the parallel passages of the Gospels were so familiar that they would adapt the text of one gospel to that of another. They also felt themselves free to make corrections in the text, improving it by their own standards of correctness, whether grammatically, stylistically, or more substantively. This was all the more true of the early period, when the text had not yet attained canonical status, especially in the earliest period when Christians considered themselves filled with the Spirit.[115]

Sometimes, scribes deliberately made changes for substantive reasons, such as to harmonize different accounts or to fabricate scriptural support for theological positions advocated in later intra-Christian disputes. According to Ehrman, "One of the most common kinds of intentional changes involved the 'harmonization' of one text to another, that is, changing one passage of the book to make it conform to a similar passage in another. This kind of change is particularly common in the Synoptic Gospels, since these three books tell so many of the same stories in slightly (or significantly) different ways."[116]

Copyists removed words and sentences that contradicted emerging orthodox beliefs. They added entire sections and stories to make theological points. These additions are known as interpolations. One of the most famous tales in the New Testament begins in John 7:53. It involves an adulteress brought before Jesus by a group of Pharisees. The Pharisees, recognizing that Mosaic law requires that the woman be stoned to death, ask Jesus what should be done with her, hoping to embarrass Jesus by forcing a choice between the Mosaic law and his own teachings on forgiveness. Jesus cleverly sidesteps the trap, however, replying, "He that is without sin among you, let him first cast a stone." The group leaves, and Jesus tells the woman to sin no more.

This is a powerful story widely recognized by those with even a passing familiarity with the Bible. It is told thousands of times each year in Christian churches. It features prominently in Mel Gibson's enormously popular film *The Passion of the Christ*. Unfortunately, John didn't write it, and we can say this with confidence. While we now have many copies of John's Gospel, this story does not appear in any version *until the Middle Ages*. The writing style differs markedly from the remainder of John and uses words not commonly in use until centuries after John's Gospel was written. The event never happened. It was an interpolation invented by a copyist hundreds of years later.

Copyists also added other passages that came to have great theological significance for later Christians. The ending of Mark, in which Jesus makes many post-Resurrection appearances (Mark 16:9–20), and the only explicit description of the Trinity in the Bible (John 5:7–8), are both recognized by critical scholars as later interpolations. Many modern Bibles omit these passages for this reason. For every interpolation we can clearly identify, such as by reviewing earlier manuscripts in which they are absent, dozens, if not hundreds, likely exist for which we can't. The interpolations we know of severely undercut the reliability of every story in the Gospels.

It was also common during this period for people to create forgeries and entirely fraudulent documents to manufacture fake authority for favored theological positions. We know of many letters, supposedly authored by Paul and other well-known early Christian leaders, that modern scholars widely agree were not authored by the people whose names they bear. Even the most conservative Christian scholars agree on this. We cannot know with any certainty how many such documents snuck into the New Testament canon or influenced it.

We can see that our evidence for the mere existence of Jesus is shaky. It rests on a fragmented collection of copies of copies of hearsay reports dating from the second and third centuries, hundreds of years after Jesus supposedly lived. We know that many of these were substantially altered over time or even initially created under false pretenses. They can tell us little, with any reliability, about the earliest Christian sources, written thirty to ninety years after Jesus's death.

2. Canon by Committee

There is yet another problem with assuming the reliability of the Gospels and other New Testament texts as a coherent whole: selection bias. Assume that you are asked to investigate a vehicle accident involving a car and van at an intersection and to prepare a report. In conducting that investigation, you interview ten witnesses. Four witnesses say that when the car entered the intersection, the light was red. The remaining six say the light was green. Assume that when you prepare your report, you include only some of these statements, destroying the others.

Failing to include or reference all ten witness statements provides a misleading picture. By including only the four who claimed the light was red, you present a blatantly false one. The key point is that once someone knows there were originally ten statements, from which you selected a mere subset for the report, unless you can demonstrate a legitimate, principled rationale for your selection criteria, the reliability of your report is destroyed. No valid conclusions can be drawn from it, *regardless of how credible we might deem the reports you did include*, because we don't have the others and therefore can't get the full picture.

Assume further that this accident resulted in a lawsuit, that you were an attorney representing the party benefitted by the light being red, and that you actively destroyed the statements of the witnesses claiming the light was green. Under these circumstances, the judge would likely tell the jury it could conclude that all the destroyed statements said the light was green, even if the judge had no idea what they said. This is known as an adverse inference instruction. The fact that you destroyed the documents alone makes it reasonable for the jury to believe they would have hurt your case because these are the very documents you would have had reason to destroy.

The same problem exists with the New Testament texts. The twenty-seven books of the New Testament were selected from hundreds, *if not thousands*, of documents that circulated among the early Christians. We now know these differed dramatically from one another and took inconsistent positions on issues of theological significance. In the last century alone, we have uncovered texts and references to texts that present wildly divergent views of who Jesus was, what he taught, whether he was resurrected, and even whether he ever walked the Earth in human form.

In the first two centuries of the Common Era, there were many churches across the Roman Empire that identified as Christian but that based their beliefs on different sets of documents and viewpoints. Church leaders would copy the documents that reflected or supported their views and share them with other churches. Likewise, they would ignore or even destroy documents that contradicted them. Unlike today, if documents were not actively copied, then they were likely to disintegrate under the harsh conditions of the region, leaving no record of their existence.

By the third or fourth centuries, certain influential groups sharing theological views began a deliberate and systematic attempt to separate the documents in circulation into those they found acceptable and those they did not. Through this process, they began to settle on a collection to be considered canonical and that would eventually become the New Testament. Many criteria drove this process. Some writings were looked at favorably on ideological grounds, while others were looked at unfavorably and deemed heretical. Long-forgotten political, social, and religious disputes also led to the propagation of some and the suppression of others.

Irenaeus of Lyon, who lived during the second century, claimed there could be only four Gospels for mystical reasons: There were four zones in the world, four winds, four elemental forces, and so on. This appears to have led to a search for four Gospels that accorded with the views of the growing orthodoxy and destruction of all others. We know of more than thirty gospels written about Jesus, only four of which made it into the New Testament. These noncanonical gospels were cited by early fathers of the Christian Church, such as Clement of Alexandria, Origen, Eusebius, Epiphanius, and Jerome. Many were Jewish gospels, written in Hebrew or Aramaic, but these were ultimately destroyed, replaced by Greek gospels written by Hellenized Christians. We can only speculate on why, but it seems a reasonable assumption that these noncanonical gospels did not reflect the preferred theology of the "winning" Christian faction—the Proto-Orthodox Church.

One competing vision of Christianity came from an early Christian known as Marcion. Marcion believed that Paul was the only true apostle. He believed that the Jewish texts of the Old Testament dealt with a Creator God distinct from Jesus's father, whom he called "God the Father." Marcion used the Gospel of Mark, an older version of Luke's Gospel, and many of Paul's letters to conclude that Christianity was a new religion entirely distinct from Judaism. God the Father had been hidden before Jesus arrived, and one of Jesus's primary missions was to announce his presence to the world. Marcion felt that the apostles identified in Mark failed to understand Jesus's message of a new God the Father, instead continuing to mistakenly believe that Jesus was referring to the Jewish Creator God, which is why Jesus started over with Paul after his death and Resurrection.

Marcionism became very popular, and the leaders of the fledgling Catholic Church believed it must be aggressively challenged, as it was becoming an active threat to their teachings. The church added (1) additional material to Luke disputing Marcion's teachings; (2) a new book, Acts, that clarified that Peter and Paul were both equally important apostles of the new church; and (3) letters falsely attributed to Paul to make it appear that Paul disagreed with Marcion. The leaders of the Catholic Church did, however, believe Marcion had a good point about creating a new book uniquely Christian rather than Jewish, which resulted in the New Testament.

In 367 CE, Athanasius, the bishop of Alexandria, took a firm position regarding the sources that should be officially recognized as authoritative. He listed the twenty-seven works with which modern churches are familiar as the only ones that should be considered legitimate. This list became canonized by leaders of the Proto-Orthodox Church, resulting in other Christian writings of the same period being excluded as heretical and systematically destroyed. After centuries of additional debate, the New Testament canon was formally recognized as authoritative at the Second Council of Trullan in 692 CE.

The group that ultimately won the right to tell the Christian story was, unlike other Christian sects of the day, historicist. It maintained that Jesus was an actual living man who interacted in the physical world. We now know that other contemporary sects rejected a historical Jesus altogether in favor of a being who existed solely in a separate divine realm as spirit rather than flesh. Because the writings of these "spirit" sects were destroyed or never copied and thus left to disintegrate, we cannot know how prevalent this view was, what evidence they relied on in rejecting a historical Jesus, and even whether a historical Jesus existed.[117] We know they existed, however, from the contemporary writings of others.

The exclusion of these other sources fatally undermines the credibility of the selected works in the same way as excluding those witnesses who claimed the light was red, undermining the lawyer's argument. In a textbook example of the Texas sharpshooter fallacy, it paints a false picture of consistency when biblical scholars now know the opposite was true. There was little consistency among early Christians, even on matters considered well-settled by Christians today, such as the existence of a historical Jesus. No other area of ancient literature or history is characterized by such a level of ideological and historical conflict affecting the texts. This selection bias is a very serious problem for anyone claiming the New Testament to be a reliable source of historical knowledge.

The most significant event for Christianity's future, however, was yet to come. Christianity as we know it would not exist if not for Emperor Constantine and his conversion in the early 300s CE. Before that, Christians were a relatively minor sect within the Roman Empire. They fought among themselves, with different groups of Christians taking radically divergent positions on just about every theological issue imaginable. But then Constantine declared himself a follower of Jesus, and things quickly changed.

Despite his later canonization by the Catholic Church, Constantine was no saint. He was, by all accounts, a brutal sociopath who murdered his own son, decapitated his brother-in-law, and killed his wife by boiling her alive—all *after converting to Christianity*. He was, however, politically astute and pragmatic. Historians have long suspected a political motivation for Constantine's conversion, as he continued to worship and patronize other gods long afterward. Constantine likely saw Christianity as a way of unifying his empire but only if he could reconcile the disputes among the Christian sects.

The main dispute of the day revolved around whether Jesus and God represented the same being. The bishop of Alexandria maintained that they were, while a popular priest named Arius disagreed, arguing that God had created Jesus as a separate and distinct entity—more in line with a traditional father-son relationship. Constantine convened a meeting of all the Christian leaders at Nicaea to settle the issue. Though Arius had the writings of Paul and much of the synoptic Gospels on his side, Constantine sided with the bishop that Jesus and God were the same being. Constantine arranged for a statement to be drawn up, known as the Nicene Creed, to formalize this position. Those refusing to sign the creed were banished or killed, thus settling the matter.

Fifty years later, in 381 CE, another meeting was held, at which a new agreement was reached. Jesus was declared to be not just two entities but three—the Father, Son, and Holy Ghost. The Nicene Creed was rewritten, and once again, those refusing to sign were banished or killed. This is the version presently recited every Sunday by Christians throughout the world. Thus was born the Trinity, a concept of committee in which no one apparently believed or even recognized just fifty years earlier. Under threat of the sword, however, it was suddenly orthodoxy.

Interestingly, Constantine is also responsible for several other Christian traditions taken for granted today. Both before and after his conversion to Christianity, Constantine openly worshipped the Roman Sun god. Though the Bible proclaims the seventh day of the week (Saturday) to be the Sabbath, the holy day of rest in which to honor God, Constantine declared *Sunday* to be the day of rest in honor of the pagan Sun god. At Nicaea, the Christian Sabbath was officially changed from Saturday to Sunday. Jesus's birthday also came to be celebrated on December 25, the traditional day of celebration for the Roman Sun god. Christians' modern observation of the Sunday Sabbath and Christmas owe themselves entirely to paganism.

3. The Non-Gospel Books of the New Testament

In assessing the reliability of the Jesus story, one must look to each of the sources in turn, which isn't hard to do because there are only a few. Our oldest sources of information regarding Christianity are the letters (epistles) of Paul of Tarsus, written in the mid-first century. Paul was an early Christian evangelist who traveled through much of the Roman Empire, establishing and consulting with fledgling Christian churches. Fourteen of the twenty-seven books of the New Testament are letters traditionally attributed to Paul.[118] These letters, written to churches he had visited, deal with various aspects of Christianity, such as doctrinal disputes and practical considerations of early Christian congregations.

What is often surprising to Christians reading Paul's letters for the first time is that they provide virtually no historical information about Jesus. Paul provides no details of Jesus's life. He mentions no teachings of Jesus, even when discussing disputed issues upon which the Gospels record Jesus taking clear positions. Paul either knew nothing about Jesus's teachings or found them unimportant and irrelevant to his own preaching. He never even mentions that Jesus was a teacher or had disciples. He scoffs at the idea that Jesus performed miracles (1 Corinthians 1:22–23). Paul never suggests that Jesus lived or died in the recent past or at any particular time in history. Paul denies that he obtained his knowledge of Jesus from any man. Instead, he claims it came to him directly through revelation and visions.

The Gospels reflect that, as stated in Matthew 3:2, the primary message preached by Jesus was to repent and be baptized, for the Kingdom of Heaven was at hand. Jesus repeatedly urged his disciples to follow the law, commit good acts, and repent of their sins so as to be prepared for the imminent arrival of the kingdom. This, according to Jesus, was the path to salvation. Paul had a *very different* idea, as reflected in 1 Corinthians 15:1–4. For Paul, the Gospel was that "Christ died for our sins according to the scriptures; and that he was buried, and that he rose again the third day according to the scriptures." According to Paul, the *belief in these things* was what led to salvation. Thus Paul transformed Christianity from the religion *of Jesus* to a religion *about Jesus*.

There is ample evidence from the Scriptures that Jesus did not share Paul's views. In Matthew 25:31–46, for instance, Jesus shares a parable of sheep and goats, the import of which is that salvation comes from one's acts alone, as opposed to professions of faith. Furthermore, it is clear from Matthew 16:21–28 that the disciples were *shocked and dismayed* when Jesus revealed that he would have to die and be resurrected. How, then, could this have been the Gospel they had been preaching throughout Jesus's ministry? This simply could not have been the case.

Paul was concerned exclusively with the theological effects of Jesus's death and Resurrection, things Jesus never said anything about. To Paul, these were events of monumental importance to mankind. Paul preached that Jesus's death represents an atonement for the original sin of Adam and that his Resurrection brought the promise of salvation to believers. Paul taught that Jesus would arrive very soon, almost certainly within Paul's life-time and definitely within the lifetimes of Paul's contemporaries, at which point those with the proper faith would meet him and share in God's king-dom. Paul's writings were not about Jesus's life but about what his death and Resurrection *meant for mankind.*

Of Paul's thirteen epistles, scholars identify only seven or eight as le-gitimate, and the majority of critical scholars believe even these include interpolations from later copyists. The letters of Paul are therefore almost worthless as evidence regarding a historical Jesus. They provide virtually no support for any related historical claims.

The remaining non-Gospel books of the New Testament also provide little if any historical information about Jesus. None discuss Jesus's life or death. Like Paul's letters, they are concerned solely with theological or eschatological issues.

4. The Four Gospels

It is not until decades after the letters of Paul that we get the first nar-rative account of Jesus—the Gospel of Mark. Mark would be followed by three additional Gospels. The four Gospels tell a roughly consistent story but contain many inconsistencies. The problem with treating these accounts as different interpretations of actual historical events is not that they contain inconsistencies but that *these inconsistencies follow deliberate, contrived patterns.* They unfailingly adhere to the unique ideological mo-tives of the authors or to recognizable patterns of legendary accretion or both. These patterns undermine the claim that the inconsistencies reflect differing good-faith interpretations of the same events, suggesting instead that they result from intentional fabrication.[119]

Suppose that two individuals, Max and Bill, each describe recent events they claim to have experienced—events that, if they happened at all, must have occurred at the same place and time. Both are leaders of radical leftist groups opposed to the operations of BigCorp, Inc., but Alex hates BigCorp for its support of animal testing, while Bill hates BigCorp for its support of genetically modified crops. In Alex's story, BigCorp claimed in a mysteriously unrecorded press conference that its top priority for the next year was to implement a crueler form of animal testing. In Bill's account, BigCorp claimed in the same conference that its top priority was to unleash a potentially deadly strain of GMO crops. Both Alex and Bill deny any other revelations from the conference. How can you reconcile these accounts?

There are several options: (1) Alex may be right, and Bill, wrong; (2) Bill may be right, and Alex, wrong; (3) they may both be wrong but innocently mistaken; or (4) they may both be deliberately lying. Given they both hate BigCorp, both certainly have an incentive to lie. Their agreement that BigCorp said *something* self-incriminating, therefore, cannot be used to argue that it in fact did so. If that had been the case, we would expect general agreement or at least significant overlap on the details. That the details they do relate so closely adhere to their own respective ideologies renders both stories highly unreliable, even on the more general point that BigCorp incriminated itself in some way.

Another way of saying this is that we can't justifiably ignore the differences in the details of Alex's and Bill's stories to conclude that the gist of the combined stories is accurate. Agreement in their overall message ("BigCorp is bad") would be expected even if they wholly fabricated their stories, so the fact that the core message of both stories is the same does not suggest that the details of either story is more likely to be true or even that the shared message is true. The inconsistency in the details severely undermines both stories and the core message. There is a saying that the "Devil is in the details," and that is all the more true when comparing reported accounts. It is agreement on the details that matters.

Critical biblical scholars are unanimous in concluding that each of the Gospels was compiled from various source materials and that none were independent accounts. The authors of Matthew and Luke had a version of Mark to work from and used it as their primary source. Eighty-five percent of the material in Matthew and Luke is copied directly from Mark, *word for word*. That is why these three Gospels seem so closely related and are referred to as the Synoptic Gospels. They can and should be read together, side by side, comparing them passage by passage to more clearly understand how and why they differ.

When we do this, several things become immediately apparent. The first is that the Synoptic Gospels agree fairly closely from Jesus's baptism through the discovery of the empty tomb—the precise period covered by Mark. By contrast, there is virtually *no agreement* between Matthew and Luke about the events before or after this period. Matthew and Luke tell wildly different and often inconsistent stories regarding Jesus's birth and his post-Resurrection appearances.

To demonstrate Jesus's legitimacy as the Jewish Messiah, for example, both Matthew and Luke must establish that Jesus was born in Bethlehem to fulfill a messianic prophecy found in the book of Micah. It appears, however, there existed a strong tradition that Jesus was from the town of Nazareth, which was nowhere near Bethlehem. Accordingly, both Matthew and Luke record Nativity stories that place Jesus's birth in Bethlehem before moving him to Nazareth. The stories differ, however, in just about every other detail and cannot be plausibly harmonized.

The fact that virtually none of these details agree suggests fabrication for the same reason as the BigCorp example. As committed proselytizing Christians, Matthew and Luke would have had similar goals, such as tying Jesus's ancestry to the Davidic line to accord with Old Testament prophecies or confirming to potential converts that Jesus did return to Earth in human form following his death. That they accomplished their goals by telling contradictory accounts strongly suggests these marketing goals drove the creation of the stories rather than historical accuracy.

The second thing one notices when reading the Synoptic Gospels side by side is that, within the time frame encompassed by Mark, both Matthew and Luke change or add to Mark in unique and deliberate ways. Matthew, for instance, includes many more Old Testament prophecies, with explanations of how Jesus fulfilled them. Luke, by contrast, actually eliminates some of Mark's references to Old Testament prophecies, significantly deemphasizing them. From these differences and others, scholars have concluded that Matthew was writing to a Jewish audience, to whom such prophecies would be highly relevant, while Luke was primarily writing to Gentiles. With these motivations in mind, one can anticipate where Matthew and Luke might be expected to add to or change Mark's account, and such changes are just what we find.

The third thing one notices is that Matthew and Luke include many of the same sayings of Jesus not found in Mark—but in very different places and under different circumstances. These sayings are identical word for word, suggesting a written rather than oral source. For example, at Matthew 6:24, Jesus says, "No one can serve two masters; for a slave will either hate the one and love the other or be devoted to the one and despise the other. You cannot serve God and wealth." At Luke 16:13, Jesus says these same words, but it occurs in a different conversation and context. This happens many times in the course of Matthew and Luke's Gospels. It has led most critical scholars to conclude that both worked off a common list of Jesus's sayings, known among scholars as Q. Because Q contains no narrative or context for the sayings, Matthew and Luke had to find their own ways to insert them into Mark's narrative and did so at different points and by very different means.

The fourth thing one notices is a pattern of legendary accretion, the tendency of stories to become more amazing and fantastical over time. The classic example is the fish story, in which each time a fisherman tells the story of a great catch, the tale becomes taller. With every telling, the fish becomes bigger, the battle to reel him in fiercer, the ultimate accomplishment more glorious. This has been a recognized feature of oral storytelling for centuries.

Two examples from the Synoptic Gospels involve the moment of Jesus's death and the discovery of the empty tomb. In Mark, Jesus cries out and abruptly dies, at which point the veil, a massive wall that separates God's holy chamber from the rest of the Jewish temple, splits in two. In Matthew, the temple veil also splits, but Jesus's death is additionally accompanied by an earthquake, the opening of graves, and the resurrection of many saints, who then leave their graves and, "[go] into the city and appear to many."[120] Matthew appears to have taken Mark's account, found it to be pedestrian by contemporary standards, and so embellished it into something even more incredible. Both accounts include three hours of worldwide darkness, an incredible event that somehow escaped the notice of everyone else on the planet because it is referenced nowhere outside the Gospels.

Regarding the empty tomb, Mark simply reports that the women who arrived saw a "young man,"[121] wearing white and sitting inside the tomb. There is no suggestion this man is exceptional. In Luke, there are *two men* inside the tomb, arrayed in "shining garments"[122] who tell them Jesus has risen. In Matthew, there is another earthquake, after which the "angel of the Lord descend[s] from Heaven," rolls away the stone, and causes the "keepers" to shake with fear and "become as dead men."[123] The angel has a face like lightning and clothes "as white as snow."[124] What begins as merely a young man in Mark has by the time of Matthew's account become a full-fledged, terrifying angel.

As to this last example, apologists often argue that it reflects no more than differing emphases placed by the Gospel authors. Mark, they argue, did not consider the additional details of Matthew central to the story he was trying to tell, so he left them out. While this explanation is, of course, possible, it is undercut by the stories always becoming *more fantastical* over time. The legendary elements increase in number from Mark to Matthew or Luke and never the other way around. This follows a pattern of legendary accretion, and legendary accretion indicates we're not talking about history.

The Gospel of John does not follow the parallel approach of the Synoptics. John was written much later, when various Christian communities and an established Christian Church existed. Theological disputes were circulating among the communities, evidence of which can be found in John's text. It is likely that John had access to one or more of the Synoptic Gospels but did not slavishly copy from them, as Matthew and Luke so often did from Mark.

John was concerned with expressing certain theological themes and ideological positions—so much so that he changed the events and chronologies in the Synoptic Gospels. For example, in the Synoptics, the Last Supper was a Passover meal, and Jesus was killed the day afterward. For John, however, Jesus represented the Passover lamb, who likewise had to die so others could live. This symbolism was crucial throughout John's Gospel, representing a running theme. In John, the Last Supper occurs before the day of the Passover meal, so Jesus dies *on Passover Eve, when the Passover lambs are slaughtered.* By converting a figurative symbolism into a literal event (Jesus becomes the Passover lamb), John dramatically strengthens the weight of his analogy and distinguishes his theology. In doing so, however, he abandons any claim to historicity by creating an irreconcilable conflict. There may be no better example of marketing goals overwhelming any attempt at historical accuracy.

All four Gospels were written in Greek by educated writers, despite the fact that Jesus's disciples would have spoken Aramaic and been unschooled peasants. Critical scholars have concluded the writers were likely Hellenized Jews or even Gentiles from that branch of Christians tracing their origins to Paul's teachings and organized churches. While it is possible that some of Jesus's original disciples later became educated Hellenized Jews, this seems highly unlikely for even one, based on what we know of demographics of the time, much less all four. All contain anachronisms and errors, showing they were written long after the events they describe, most likely far from the places in which their stories are set.

Among the four Gospel writers, the most important by far is Mark. This is because Mark was the first, and his Gospel was used as a source by the authors of the remaining Synoptic Gospels, Matthew and Luke. The Gospels of Matthew and Luke are not independent sources. They depend heavily on Mark and cannot be meaningfully discussed without first discussing Mark's Gospel.

One can see from figure 5.2 the unparalleled influence of Mark on our current understanding of Jesus. Of Mark's 666 original verses, some 600 appear in Matthew, and some 300, in Luke. Most everything we know about Jesus's life goes back to this single source, the Gospel of Mark, most of which was then recopied and supplemented by the authors of Luke and Matthew. This is why critical scholars often refer to the "Mark bottleneck" when discussing the Gospels. If Mark exhibits cracks in the foundation, then all of Christianity crumbles with it.

a. Mark   Mark is the shortest Gospel and the most straightforward. It contains no account of Jesus's birth and no post-Crucifixion appearances, beginning instead with Jesus's baptism by a well-known preacher, John the Baptist (JTB), living contemporaneously with Jesus. It is widely accepted among scholars that the original Gospel of Mark ends at chapter 16, verse 8 with the women fleeing Jesus's tomb. The remaining eleven verses contained in some versions of the Bible, such as the King James version, in which a resurrected Jesus returns and visits his followers, were added during the copying process by an unknown author decades, if not centuries, later.

In Mark, Jesus is presented as a normal human being. There is no hint he was the offspring of a virgin mother or divine father or that he existed as a divine being prior to his earthly life. It apparently never occurred to Mark that Jesus was the incarnation of God when he walked into the Jordan to be baptized, as evidenced by Jesus's reply to an onlooker: "Why do you call me good? No one is good but God alone" (Mark 10:17–18). If Jesus understood himself to be God, as he states repeatedly in the Gospel of John, then he would never say such a thing.

Throughout Mark's Gospel, Jesus is never called God or recognized as anything other than human. While the term *son of God* is used often, there is nothing to suggest this was intended literally as a supernatural parent-child relationship. *Son of God* was a term of art among both Jews and Gentiles of the period that commonly referred to a legendary hero or someone figuratively legitimized by God as a person of authority or significance. Many Jewish kings, Egyptian pharaohs, Roman emperors, and Greek heroes were known as sons of God.

Mark's Jesus is a miracle-working, apocalyptic prophet, preaching an imminent end to the secular world and establishment of the Kingdom of God. Jesus's message is that this Kingdom is at hand and that everyone must repent to be prepared and share in its glory (Mark 1:14–15). Jesus performs many miracles and healings (twenty in all) but vehemently denies these should be taken as signs he is divine or of anything in particular. The meth-

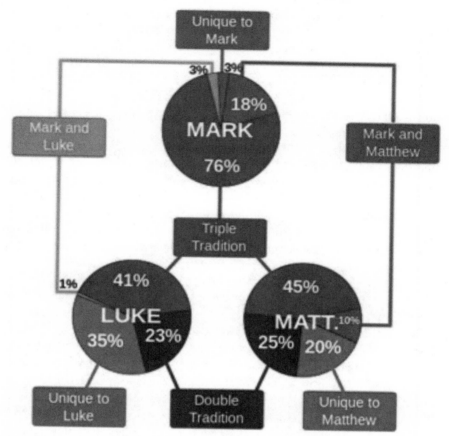

Figure 5.2. Relationships between the Synoptic Gospels.

ods used by Jesus to heal are those common to faith healers and magicians of the day, such as spittle to cure blindness and magic spells (Mark 7:33, 8:23). For Mark, Jesus's miracles did not demonstrate divinity but rather confirmed that he had been sent as a special but entirely human emissary for God, which was Mark's understanding of the Messiah.

While it is clear from the narrative that the author considers Jesus to have been the Messiah prophesied by Jewish Scripture, Jesus rarely acknowledges this himself, typically treating it as an unspoken secret, to which even the disciples are not privy. Whenever anyone calls him "Messiah" or claims him to be so, Jesus immediately silences them so no one will hear. Jesus speaks in vague parables, for the stated purpose that people *not understand his message* (Mark 4:11–12).[125]

While Jesus believes that he is fated to suffer and die, in Mark alone he questions that fate. Following the Last Supper, Jesus begs God to spare him the suffering and death to come, as if this were a real possibility. Jesus also appears forlorn and unsure of himself at the Crucifixion. His last words are to ask God, "Why have you forsaken me?" which makes absolutely no sense if Jesus was divine, as he would later be portrayed. Throughout, Jesus is portrayed as God's human emissary and prophet. Never is it suggested that Jesus and God are the same.

Mark ends with three of Jesus's female disciples arriving at his tomb to find the stone rolled away and a young man who instructs them to tell the disciples that Jesus has gone to Galilee. Unfortunately, according to the author, the women leave afraid and *never tell anyone*, thereby preserving the messianic secret. This would have explained to the reader why no one had ever before heard of Jesus rising from the dead. Presumably, following the ending to its logical conclusion, the disciples would never have met up with Jesus because they would never have learned that he had risen. By the end of Mark's Gospel, they all believed him to remain buried in the cave. The gospel ends in a mystery: "What happened to Jesus?" Mark's readers were never to know.

The author of Mark wrote in Greek for a Gentile audience, which is clear by his need to explain Jewish traditions and translate Aramaic terms. While at least superficially familiar with Judaism, he was far less so with the geographic areas in which his tale supposedly takes place. He commits many mistakes regarding the geography of the region, which the authors of Matthew and Luke felt obliged to correct in their accounts. It is clear that Mark was not an eyewitness to the events he describes. It is doubtful he ever visited Israel.

Mark is unmistakably a hagiography rather than a simple historical bi-ography as we know them today. It is intended to idealize its subject and engender devotion rather than to present objective historical truth. Scholar Dennis McDonald makes what many feel to be a very strong case that Mark was intended as a reinterpretation of the *Iliad* and *Odyssey*, updating Homer's outdated Greek values and presenting the story through a Jewish lens.[126] According to McDonald, Mark was not writing a biography at all but rather a fictional novel in the tradition of Homer's works, in which the realm of the divine is grounded in human, historical drama.[127]

Many elements of Mark suggest fiction rather than fact. One of these is the character of Barabbas. According to Mark, the Romans offered to free one prisoner on Passover and gave the Jewish crowd the option of freeing Jesus or a violent criminal named Barabbas. There is absolutely no historical support for such a Roman custom, which would have been antithetical to what we know of Roman rule. The Romans would *never* willingly release a known revolutionary and murderer like Barabbas. Preventing these very things was the reason Romans were stationed in Jerusalem to begin with.

While historically implausible, this story would have served an important persuasive function as an instrument of propaganda. It would have resonated with contemporary Jews, who had an annual custom in which one goat was sacrificed to atone for another. They would have immediately grasped the theological significance of this event, placing Jesus into the position of the sacrificial goat even before his Crucifixion. The story therefore grafts a well-known Jewish custom onto the Romans, to which this custom would have been anathema.

Also, there is no other contemporary account of *Barabbas* as a proper name. The word *Barabbas* literally means "son of the father," suggesting a literary device rather than a common proper name. It would be like naming your characters "good guy," "bad guy," "love interest," and so on, as in the opening credits of the 2015 film *Deadpool*. Barabbas had no real name because he wasn't a real person. He was a character given a name to specifically identify *his role in the story*. He was placed in the story to offer a parallel to Jesus, the son of the greatest father of all. Mark was clarifying to anyone paying attention that his account was intended as myth—not history.

Another example is the character of Joseph of Arimathea, the member of the Jewish Sanhedrin who apparently joined in the decision to condemn Jesus but then had a change of heart and donated his prepared tomb for Jesus's burial following his Crucifixion. Mark 14:64 is clear that the Sanhedrin's vote was unanimous ("They all condemned him to be guilty of death"), though Luke attempts to rehabilitate Joseph by claiming that he had "not consented" to the Sanhedrin's sentence (Luke 23:50–51). By the time of John's Gospel, Joseph has been elevated to a "secret disciple" of Jesus. The traditional rule of historical interpretation is to prefer the earlier source to the later one, which seems especially appropriate here, where Luke and John had clear incentives to make Joseph into a more sympathetic character than Mark's relatively sparse Gospel allowed. Joseph's role in the story was so compelling that it needed to be expanded.

Many critical scholars have pointed out the extreme implausibility of donating a tomb to Jesus for a proper burial, in part because this story contradicts the well-known tradition, preserved in Mark and Luke, of women going to the tomb to anoint the corpse, which presupposes a burial *without the proper rites and ceremonies*. Had Joseph buried the body honorably in accordance with Jewish custom, as the Gospel burial pericopes imply (and as John states outright, at John 19:40), there would have been *no reason* for the women to visit the tomb to anoint the corpse because this would have been done already.

By contrast, it is common in fiction for one of the bad guys to develop sympathy for the hero and then aid his cause. Just consider any of the James Bond films, in which agent 007 enlists the help of a beautiful member of the villain's team, who then plays a crucial role in taking down her former boss. This change of loyalties organically demonstrates the hero's righteousness without having to spell it out. A true hero's virtue is apparent to all and can even convert the wicked. Joseph of Arimathea would have played a similar role in Jesus's story—demonstrating that Jesus's cause was just and his message was persuasive beyond the "in group" of his dedicated followers. Like Barabbas, his presence in the story makes far more sense from a literary standpoint than a historical one. Joseph's inclusion would also have served another purpose—reimagining what was likely a dishonorable end to Jesus's corpse as a far more palatable coda. The Messiah deserved a better fate than to have the meat picked off his bones by scavengers and be thrown to rot in a common grave, the fate mandated by Roman custom of those executed by crucifixion.

Perhaps Mark completely invented his tale of Jesus's life on Earth to correspond with a mythical figure understood to exist entirely within a spiritual realm. It may also be that Mark began with the skeleton of a story about a historical or spiritual figure and fleshed it out with fictional details to satisfy his literary agenda. Unfortunately, there is no way to ever know. What is clear, however, is that Mark's Gospel is far more consistent with a fictional narrative than a historically accurate account. I now turn to the remaining Synoptic Gospels, which, if Mark's Gospel is considered unreliable, must be considered fruit of a poisonous tree.

b. Matthew   The author of Matthew is thought to have been a highly educated Jew, familiar with the technical aspects of Jewish law. He likely wrote for a group of Greek-speaking Jewish Christians living in Syria, though he was familiar with the geography of Israel, as reflected by the many times he corrects geographical mistakes made by Mark. Scholars believe that Matthew was composed from Mark (55 percent), Q (25 percent), and a unique source known as M (20 percent), which may have been a separate written source, one or more oral sources, or even originally composed by the author himself.

Matthew is chiefly concerned that the Jewish Christians in his community not abandon their traditions, especially given the increasing influence of Gentiles. Accordingly, in Matthew, Jesus makes it crystal clear that the

Jewish law remains in full force and effect (in marked contrast to, for instance, the teachings of Paul). Matthew tones down Mark's ban on divorce and limits Marks's apparent abolition of the Jewish food laws to handwashing alone. It is clear, however, that Matthew's community was at odds with other Jewish factions, such as the Pharisees.

Matthew is also more concerned than Mark with establishing Jesus's divine nature. Whereas in Mark, Jesus is portrayed as a purely human prophet, Matthew repeatedly modifies or adds to Mark to make the point that Jesus was more than that. This may have been in response to "Christian" factions who were happy to consider Jesus a moral teacher but denied his divinity. Even Matthew, however, never goes so far as to openly declare Jesus's divinity, remaining content to merely suggest it.

Matthew includes many more references to Jewish Scripture than Mark. It seems especially important to him to demonstrate a connection between Jesus and the Old Testament, explicitly claiming that Jesus fulfilled many Old Testament prophecies. Matthew makes this claim almost a dozen times, usually in what scholars call "formula quotations" (e.g., Matthew 1:22–23, 2:5–6, 2:15, 2:17–18). He is especially fond of the book of Isaiah, the most popular of the prophetic books among early Christians. Scholars have long recognized that many passages identified by Matthew as messianic prophecies were never intended to be anything of the sort. The people most familiar with the Old Testament, Jewish biblical scholars, disagree with Matthew's interpretations across the board.

Given Matthew's proclivities, it would be understandable for him to look for ways to market Jesus that would better appeal to potential Jewish converts. If proselytism were more important to him than historical accuracy, then we would not find it surprising for him to scour the Old Testament for ambiguous passages that could be reinterpreted out of context as messianic prophecies and then add to Mark stories of Jesus fulfilling those very "prophecies," thereby confirming that Jesus was both divine and the Messiah. It is significant that according to Matthew and consistent with Old Testament prophesies, Jesus was sent only to save the Jews (the "lost sheep of Israel"; Matthew 10:5–6, 15:24), not the Gentiles.

Matthew begins his Gospel with a genealogy of Jesus back through Abraham, the father of the Jewish race. Through this genealogy, Matthew shows how Jesus is descended from King David and therefore within the Davidic line of succession. This is important for Matthew because Jewish Scripture provides that the Messiah must be descended from David. Matthew is the only Gospel writer to call Jesus "son of David." Interestingly, Matthew's genealogy is traced through Joseph, who was not even Jesus's biological father. While logically nonsensical, this was traditional within Jewish culture, creating a quandary for Matthew he apparently just hoped everyone would overlook. Interestingly, the Gospels of Mark and John acknowledge that Jesus was *not* of Davidic lineage, providing alternate paths to messianic legitimacy (Mark 12:35–37; John 8:12–58). For Matthew, Mark's approach simply wouldn't do, so he changes it.

Matthew next tells his version of the Nativity story, something entirely absent in Mark. Matthew's Nativity closely parallels the infancy of Moses, the greatest of the Jewish heroes. Like Moses, Jesus must flee his homeland after a massacre of the innocents is ordered by a murderous tyrant. Like Moses, the tyrant (Pharaoh/Herod) is informed of his birth by Magi. Like Moses, Jesus lives in the adopted land (Egypt in both) until he can return to his homeland after his persecutor is dead. Following his return, both Moses and Jesus become saviors for their people. For Matthew, Jesus was the second Moses, a connection that would immediately appeal to prospective Jewish converts.

Matthew begins his tale with Mary and Joseph. Immediately after their marriage but somehow before they can consummate their vows, Mary becomes pregnant. Joseph is understandably troubled but is assured by an angel that Mary remains a virgin; her child was conceived by the Holy Spirit. Matthew claims this is the fulfillment of a prophecy found in Isaiah 7:14 ("Therefore, the Lord himself will give you a sign: behold, a *young woman/virgin* shall conceive, and bear a son, and shall call his name Immanuel").

Several points here are representative of Matthew's overall approach. First, no Hebrew scholar or critical scholar considers Isaiah 7:14 a messianic prophecy. It occurs in a story about King Ahaz of Judah, who is concerned that Jerusalem will soon be conquered. The prophet Isaiah promises Ahaz that God will destroy his enemies *before a child named Immanuel ("God-with-us"), not yet conceived, reaches the age of reason.* The point of mentioning the child is to establish the immediacy by which the destruction will commence. It is a secondary prophecy supporting a primary prophecy. Both prophecies come to pass, as Ahaz's enemies are destroyed and disaster is averted. The Immanuel prophecy is made and fulfilled within the same story, leaving nothing for Jesus or anyone else to fulfill.

While the original Hebrew word used in Isaiah 7:14, *almah*, simply means "young woman," this word was subsequently translated into the Greek word *parthenos* in a Greek version of the Old Testament known as the Septuagint. While *almah* does not imply virginity, *parthenos* does. The translator of the Septuagint therefore inadvertently changed the meaning of the word, resulting in a natural occurrence being transformed into a miraculous one. Matthew, a Greek speaker, used the Septuagint as a source and thus read Isaiah 7:14 as referencing a *virgin birth*, when no such virgin birth was originally intended. Matthew surely would have recognized that virgin births were seen by many pagan religions as signs of divinity, noting this would provide a great selling point for Christian missionaries preaching to pagans. And so he wrote one into the story.

Assume the original text of a document identifies the birth of a three-legged goat as a portentous sign. Assume further that in translating that text into another language, "three-legged goat" somehow becomes "talking cow." Finally, assume that a later writer supports his claims by representing that the sign was fulfilled, through the birth of a talking cow. You would no doubt dismiss his claim because (1) talking cows don't exist in nature and (2) the original prophesy said nothing about a talking cow, so how can a talking cow fulfill that prophecy or signify anything?

Matthew misidentifies scriptural authority for a virgin birth and shoe-horns it into a prophecy never intended as messianic by its author. He then works such a virgin birth into his Nativity narrative, specifically to demonstrate that such a prophecy had been fulfilled and that Jesus was at least partially divine. For people willing to accept Matthew's claims regarding the Old Testament prophecy at face value and buy into his narrative, this must have seemed like powerful confirmation. Once one recognizes how Matthew misrepresents the original prophecy, however, his story of an actual virgin birth is easily dismissed.[128] In fact, it undermines the legitimacy of the remainder of Matthew's Gospel because it betrays Matthew's willingness to engage in pious fraud.

Matthew records that Jesus is born in his hometown of Bethlehem during the time of Herod and, sometime thereafter, visited by Magi ("wise men") from the East, who bring him gifts and worship him as the "king of the Jews," referencing Isaiah 60. This terse passage (Matthew 2:1), succinctly indicating the grandest of entrances, is the *entire coverage* Matthew gives to Jesus's birth. Those familiar with the Nativity story primarily from Christmas pageants or other dramatizations may be surprised that Matthew mentions none of the familiar settings. There is no stable and no manger. There are no shepherds. There is no indication that Jesus's family suffered any hardship in connection with his birth. These are all unique contributions of Luke.

After being informed of Jesus's birth by the Magi, King Herod, like the Egyptian pharaoh during the infancy of Moses, orders a "slaughter of the innocents," in which all boys under the age of two are to be killed. Joseph and his family flee to Egypt, where they remain until Herod's death. When they return, it is not to their home in Bethlehem because Herod's son rules Judea. Instead, they settle in their *new home* of Nazareth.

No critical scholars consider Matthew's Nativity account historical. Herod's rule was extensively chronicled by contemporary historians who had no qualms presenting him in a bad light. While these historians mentioned many incidents of cruelty, *none mention any slaughter of the innocents*. It is inconceivable this act of wide-scale genocide would have escaped their attention. Moreover, Matthew's account is chock full of scriptural allusions and fulfilled prophecies, as if every event that occurred had theological significance. This is not characteristic of a writer preserving history. Instead, Matthew's account reads like a CliffsNotes version of Moses's birth story with the names, places, and dates changed.

Matthew was apparently not happy with Mark's ending. Rather than the women at Jesus's tomb fleeing the young man they encounter and telling no one what they saw, Matthew describes two splendidly attired men and then *Jesus himself* meeting the women and telling them to advise the disciples to meet him in Galilee. *They then do so*, explicitly contradicting Mark. Jesus next makes a single brief appearance to the eleven disciples in Galilee and commissions them to teach and baptize all nations of the Earth. One would presume from this account that Jesus thereafter accompanies them on their journeys. There is no ascension to Heaven. This is how Matthew concludes his Gospel, suggesting a sequel detailing Jesus's many journeys with his apostles and their misadventures along the way.

The places in which Matthew modifies or adds to Mark are explicable when one considers the audience for whom Matthew was writing and acknowledges that he may have considered acquiring new Jewish converts more important than historical accuracy. If one assumes instead that Matthew was attempting to write history, it becomes impossible to plausibly explain the inconsistencies away.

c. Luke   The author of Luke is thought to have been a well-educated and well-traveled Gentile writing to a Gentile community. Like Matthew, he used Mark as his primary source and Q as a secondary source. Around 35 percent of Luke's Gospel is original to him. Virtually all biblical scholars believe that Luke is also the author of Acts, with the books having been originally intended to be read together as a two-volume set.

Unlike Matthew, Luke's Gospel is not focused on Judaism but appears directed toward an international, cross-cultural audience. To Luke, Jesus is a savior not just to the Jews *but to all mankind*. Luke therefore presents a Jesus unshackled by the Jewish Scriptures. Luke wishes to show that

Christianity is free from Mosaic law, either as a means to salvation or as a required set of principles that Christians must obey.

Luke is also uniquely concerned with *social justice* and the treatment of those marginalized by society. Luke substantively references women forty-five times and presents many stories, such as the birth narratives of Jesus and JTB, from female perspectives. Luke includes eighteen unique parables, most of which involve themes of social justice and outcasts, such as the Good Samaritan, the Lost Sheep, and the Prodigal Son. Luke also emphasizes those things of highest importance to the marginalized: food and community. As portrayed by Luke, Jesus would be reviled by modern social conservatives and considered a communist if he lived and taught these same things today.

Luke's Jesus is calm and comfortable with his nature. Unlike in Mark, Jesus sets his sights on Jerusalem early in his ministry and marches inexorably to his fate. Luke's Jesus never expresses any doubts or registers any pain or discomfort, physical or emotional. Luke's Jesus is also not nearly as concerned with an imminent apocalypse as he appears in Mark and Matthew. Luke seems more open than Matthew to the possibility that Jesus's Second Coming might be somewhat delayed, perhaps because by the time Luke's Gospel was written, it had been.

Like Matthew, Luke also provides a genealogy connecting Jesus to David. Luke's genealogy also runs through Joseph but goes *all the way back to Adam, the first man*, signifying Jesus's status as a savior for all mankind. Matthew's stops at Abraham, signifying a connection only to the Jews. Strikingly, Luke's genealogy bears nothing in common with Matthew's. It disagrees with Matthew not only on the name of Joseph's father but also on the entire lineage back to David. *Every single name is different.* The obvious explanation is that Matthew, Luke, or both fabricated the genealogies to provide legitimacy to their claims that Jesus was the Messiah. Apologists have fumbled over themselves attempting to explain this embarrassing fact, such as positing, in direct contradiction to the text itself, that either Matthew or Luke has provided the genealogy of Mary. Critical scholars have unanimously rejected these desperate attempts at harmonization, as the Bible contains no support for them.

Luke's Nativity account begins by describing parallels between the birth of Jesus and JTB. JTB had a following of his own in Luke's time, so Luke would have had strong reasons to co-opt his followers by connecting him to Jesus. It may also very well be that Jesus started as a follower of JTB before leaving to start his own ministry and that their connection was preserved in the oral tradition. This is suggested by Mark.

According to Luke alone, the mothers of JTB and Jesus were cousins, both of whom received angelic visitations to announce their upcoming births. JTB supposedly "leapt in his mother's womb" to recognize his superior, Jesus. It would be hard to come up with a clumsier attempt to subordinate one popular figure to his rival. Such critical scholars as Raymond Brown and Geza Vermes describe this familial connection as "of dubious historicity," "artificial and undoubtedly Luke's creation."[129]

Like Matthew, Luke also places Jesus's birth in Bethlehem, thereby fulfilling the messianic birth prophecies, but he does so by completely different means. In Luke's account, Mary and Joseph live in Nazareth during her pregnancy and only travel to Bethlehem *temporarily* to comply with a worldwide census ordered by Emperor Augustus. Unfortunately for the apologists, we know from contemporary historical accounts there *was no such census*, and even if there had been, Joseph would not have had to travel to Bethlehem, the home of a long-dead relative, to register for it.

No historical sources, including renowned Jewish historian Josephus, who chronicled this period in great detail, mention a comprehensive census of the Roman world that would cover Joseph and his family. Any census ordered by Augustus would have covered only Roman citizens, which Joseph was not. There was no practice of requiring individuals to travel to the towns of their ancestors to register for a census. This would have been nonsensical, given the intended purpose of the census, which was to measure the population *of existing towns*. Even had he been required to travel to Bethlehem, furthermore, there would have been no plausible reason for Joseph's pregnant wife to accompany him on the journey. This story can only be reasonably understood as a tortured contrivance.

The governor of Syria, Quirinius, did conduct a limited census many years later, though it was not ordered by Augustus, as the Bible claims, and would be subject to the same objections mentioned here. Quirinius did not even become governor until long after the reign of King Herod, which means this could not have been the census referenced by Luke. If it were and Luke simply had all the details wrong, then it would mean the entire timeline of Jesus's life would need to be moved at least ten years ahead, and there could be no possible reconciliation with the Nativity story of Matthew because Herod would have been long dead by the time of Jesus's birth. In *The Birth of the Messiah*, a detailed study of the infancy narratives of Jesus, American scholar Raymond E. Brown concludes that "this information is dubious on almost every score, despite the elaborate attempts by scholars to defend Lucan accuracy."[130]

Unlike Matthew, Luke describes Jesus's birth as one of abject humility. Jesus's family is forced to take refuge in a stable after being turned out of the local inn. After his birth, Jesus is placed in a feeding trough meant for animals, a manger. Unlike in Matthew, where Jesus is visited by traveling kings, in Luke his birth is attended by those of the lowliest occupation—shepherds. Where Matthew describes a birth of a great and respected monarch, accompanied by circumstances that parallel Israel's greatest hero, Luke describes the birth of a humble peasant. For Luke, it was crucial that Jesus be firmly grounded, of humble origin, and accessible to all. In these respects, the versions could not be more different.

Luke's account of Jesus's post-Resurrection appearances also bears no resemblance to Matthew's. According to Luke alone, Jesus first appears to two men on the path to a village known as Emmaus. The men do not recognize Jesus and so explain to him the goings on of the past few days about Jesus's death and empty tomb. This appears suspiciously similar to literary exposition, in which the reader is caught up on the story thus far before proceeding to the next chapter. Jesus chastises the travelers for not believing in his Resurrection and then reveals himself to them, only to magically vanish immediately afterward.

Jesus next appears to the eleven remaining disciples but does so *in Jerusalem rather than Galilee*, as reported by Matthew. Jesus eats with the disciples and has a lengthy conversation with them, none of which is reported by Matthew, and then tells them to remain in Jerusalem until they be "imbued with power from on high."[131] Jesus leads them out of the city, where he is carried up to Heaven, after which they return to Jerusalem, where they praise God "continuously."

There is simply no way to square Luke's post-Resurrection account with Matthew's. They share nothing in common. Jesus could not have simultaneously appeared to the same disciples in two places (Galilee and Jerusalem). Likewise, there is no plausible reason that Matthew would have omitted Jesus's other appearances or his extended conversation with the apostles in Jerusalem. The obvious explanation is that, once again, with no guidance from Mark, Matthew, Luke, or most likely both, fabricated their accounts of Jesus's post-Resurrection appearances.

As with Matthew, the changes and additions made by Luke make the most sense when Luke is acknowledged as an author with a marketing mission—a social reformer using the story of Jesus to preach his unique message and values to Gentiles. According to Luke alone, Jesus's social justice agenda was a major theme of Jesus's teachings. Luke is also the most polished writer of the Gospel authors and so uses such literary devices as expository sequences and extended conversations to more effectively convey his themes. Luke was not a historian. He was a propagandist, creating something new and politically useful from his available sources.

d. John   The Gospel of John is unlike the Synoptic Gospels in a great many respects. It does not follow the same order or timeline. The teachings of Jesus in John are very different and, in the view of the majority of biblical scholars, largely irreconcilable with those found in the Synoptics. Unlike the relatively direct biographical accounts of the Synoptics, John elaborates on the theological significance of events as they occur and presents a Jesus very much aware of and willing to comment on theological concerns. John's Gospel reflects a period in which a Christian Church had been established for some time and was embroiled in theological debates, many of which are reflected in the text.

John is thought to have been written in two or three distinct phases by multiple authors from a community that associated itself with the apostle John. Most scholars agree it was the latest written, at least in its final form, probably between 90 and 100 CE. Unlike Matthew and Luke, which appear to have been primarily cut and pasted from other sources, much of John's text cannot be traced to any known written source and may be original to the author(s). Nonetheless, most modern scholars agree that John worked from a version of Luke.

Throughout the Synoptics, Jesus's divine nature remains obscured and even deliberately kept secret. In John, however, it seems that is *all Jesus wants to talk about*. Jesus openly discusses his divinity and repeatedly identifies himself with metaphors conveying it through "I am" statements (e.g., "the bread of life," "the light of the world," "the good shepherd," "the way, the truth, and the life"). These statements are reminiscent of those used by YHWH to discuss his own nature in the Old Testament. Jesus's divinity is his main message.

Where in the Synoptics Jesus's miracles were explicitly not intended as signs of his divinity, in John, that is the *only reason he performs miracles*. The miracles he performs, furthermore, are more public and more impressive. John characterizes them as the *seven signs*—leading to the most incredible of all, raising Lazarus from the dead, which is not mentioned in any other Gospel. In John, it is this event, rather than turning the tables of the temple money changers, that leads to Jesus's execution.

John presents a Jesus constantly making the case that he was what the Christians of the late first century claimed him to be, over the objections of their opponents—a fully divine Messiah. There is little discussion of the coming Kingdom of God, a persistent theme throughout the Synoptics. Jesus tells no parables. Jesus's iconic speeches, the Sermon on the Mount and the Olivet discourse, are never mentioned. John's Jesus is not concerned about practical advice for living a good life. He is not concerned with social justice or talk of forgiveness. He is not concerned with teaching or imparting wisdom or with preparing for the imminent Kingdom of Heaven. He is concerned only that people know who he is and follow him.

John begins his Gospel with a prologue in which he identifies Jesus as the "Logos," an eternal companion of God who was also, paradoxically, the same as God. John thus immediately confirms Jesus's divine nature, directly challenging the arguments of competing Christian sects of the late first century to the contrary. As with Mark, John includes no Nativity story but begins his account with JTB. Unlike in Mark, in which JTB baptizes Jesus, in John, JTB *merely witnesses to Jesus*, who then goes on to lead a ministry larger than JTB's, beating JTB at his own game. John thereby explicitly subordinates JTB to Jesus. The theological concerns are already clear, as given Jesus's clearly divine nature, John could not justify a baptism by JTB, as the baptizer was considered spiritually superior to the baptized, so he removes it from the story.

In John's Gospel, Jesus's ministry extends over two years, unlike the Synoptic Gospels, in which it covers less than one. In John's Gospel, Jesus travels back and forth to Jerusalem at least four times throughout his ministry rather than making a single fateful visit, as he does in the Synoptics. In John, Jesus overturns the tables of the temple money changers at the beginning of his ministry rather than the end, as the Synoptics record.[132]

John treats the Jews, collectively, as the enemies of Jesus. This is in marked contrast to the other Gospels and especially Matthew, in which only a small group of Jewish priests and politicians seek Jesus's death. In John, the Jews en masse demand his death. In his Jerusalem speeches, furthermore, John's Jesus makes disparaging references to the Jews not found in the other Gospels. Passages from John have been used to support Christian anti-Semitism through the modern day.[133] These passages are easily explained if viewed as rebuttals to Jewish criticism of the Johannine movement and its insistence on a fully divine Jesus, which did not occur until many decades after Jesus's death.

Further evidencing John's anti-Semitic bent, John describes the Roman procurator Pilate as repeatedly proclaiming Jesus innocent and deserving of release. Pilate ultimately orders Jesus's death, but only reluctantly after his hand is forced by bloodthirsty Jews. In Mark, by contrast, Pilate never proclaims Jesus innocent. In John, Jesus engages in extended conversations with Pilate, contrary to the mere two words Jesus utters in Mark. This all makes sense if John was attempting to shift responsibility for Jesus's death from the Romans to the Jews, as we might expect of a sect trying to curry Roman favor and scapegoat a bitter politically weak adversary.

As previously stated, John records the Last Supper and Jesus's Crucifixion to have occurred a day earlier than the Synoptics, a change with tremendous theological significance to John. John's account of the empty tomb, moreover, differs from all the Synoptics. In John, Mary Magdalene visits the tomb *alone*. Jesus makes his first post-Resurrection appearance to her as she is weeping, though inexplicably, she does not recognize him.

As in Luke, and contrary to Matthew (and implicitly Mark), Jesus appears to the disciples in Jerusalem alone. John includes an extended sequence, not contained in any of the Synoptics, in which Jesus proves that he is flesh and blood by allowing Thomas, who initially doubts this, to touch Jesus and insert his hand into Jesus's wound. This would have been instrumental in countering the claims of many early Christians, such as the Docetists, that Jesus was an entirely spiritual being without physical form.

John ends his Gospel with a final miracle, also unattested in the Synoptics—the "draft of fishes."[134] Jesus brings about a catch of exactly 153 fish, where there were previously none. This story parallels a well-known tale about famous philosopher and mathematician Pythagoras, who lived six hundred years earlier and used 153 because of its unique mathematical qualities. Jesus invests this miracle with both theological and practical significance, directing his disciples to feed his sheep as he had fed them and to follow him. As in Matthew, we are led to believe Jesus continued to preach his Gospel across the known world thereafter.

e. Conclusions   A side-by-side comparison of the Gospels reveals several important points. First, they are not primary sources. They are at best secondhand and most likely far more removed than that. Primary sources are, of course, the gold standard for historians attempting to establish that events actually happened. Anything else is hearsay, which becomes exponentially more unreliable with every intervening source. And even this analysis gives the Gospels the benefit of the doubt—that they reflect good-faith attempts by their authors to pass along accurate information. As I've shown, this is a premise we have ample reason to doubt.

Second, they do not represent independent accounts. Matthew and Luke, in particular, borrowed heavily from Mark and most likely from another common source, Q. A trial witness shown to have cribbed most of his testimony from another witness will not be looked upon favorably by a jury—and with good reason. Simply pointing this out on cross-examination would typically be devastating, especially if the witness were considered crucial.

Third, the Gospels contradict each other repeatedly, often on points of great theological significance. If you doubt this, simply attempt to create a comprehensive timeline of the events of the Passion incorporating all four Gospel accounts. The Easter story is the core narrative of Christianity but is impossible to accurately reconstruct because the sources conflict on virtually every detail. The same applies to Jesus's post-Resurrection appearances. This is especially surprising given that we know the Gospels were deliberately harmonized in various ways over the years by copyists to make them appear more consistent.

Fourth, the Gospel inconsistencies often correspond to unique motivations of the authors and suggest agendas more important than ensuring historical accuracy. Historical standards were not nearly as exacting as they are now. Fact checking and corroborating sources weren't required. Elaboration was acceptable and even expected. Even well-known historians commonly made up dialogue for their subjects, which might explain why Jesus's final words vary from Gospel to Gospel.[135] Some of these motivations, such as demonstrating that Jesus's Resurrection was not merely spiritual, make sense only in the context of a specific time period in which that particular theological issue was hotly debated among competing Christian groups, such as the late first century.

John, for instance, is written exactly as one would expect if the author was primarily attempting to prove that Jesus was divine. Assume you are a member of the Johannine community who believes in the divinity of Jesus. You attempt to argue your point from the existing Gospels of Mark, Matthew, and Luke but find they are unclear on the subject, at times even suggesting the contrary. It would be invaluable to have an account that is crystal clear on this point. This would account for the wildly different tone of and teachings in John, where Jesus appears concerned with nothing more than establishing his divinity and his role in facilitating salvation.

And this brings us to the next point—the genre of the Gospels is unclear. If I walk into the history section of a bookstore, I can reasonably presume that the authors of those books *at least claim* they are accurately describing what happened in the past. While I have no guarantee that their books are accurate, the genre in which they have written represents a claim that they intended it to be so.

But now assume that I pick up *Abraham Lincoln, Vampire Hunter* at a garage sale. The story describes a historical figure with whom I am familiar, and many of the names, places, and events are likewise familiar from my high school history class. Am I then justified in believing the author to have intended the remainder of the story to be historical? Obviously not, as the genre of this book is not history but something more like historical fiction or even horror. Even if the cover of the book were torn off, with no evidence of its genre, we could probably deduce fairly quickly that it was not intended to be strictly historical from other clues found within the story itself, such as its inclusion of tropes unknown to histories but common in fiction. Or perhaps simply because it deals with vampires.

And this is the problem with the Gospels—we don't know what genres were intended. It is very possible that the authors never envisioned them to be considered historical and thought no one would read them as such.[136] In fact, there is ample evidence they were not intended as histories as we understand that genre today. If the Gospels were written as historical fiction, then we have no good reason to accept any of their claims, much less the more fantastic ones.

The next problem, somewhat related to the previous one, is that the Gospels all share a common, openly stated bias. They were written to proselytize—to proclaim the "good news." This is, in fact, what *gospel* means. They were written as marketing tracts for the fledgling Christian religion. It should go without saying that most people are rightly skeptical of the claims of advertisers. Our skepticism is justified because advertisers are highly motivated to lie about their products. The success of the advertiser is inextricably tied to the success of the product, so he has little incentive to be objective.

It is the same with the authors of the Gospels. They were engaged in fierce market competition with many other religions and philosophies making competing claims in their attempts to win converts. Others advocated their own gods and demigods, claiming theirs to be bigger or better in some way than the competitors. Many of these figures were claimed to perform miracles or heal the sick. Some had virgin births. Would it be that surprising for the Gospel authors to exaggerate or even fabricate claims regarding their own founder to gain a competitive advantage? This type of legendary accretion is just what we see.

For all these reasons, it is simply not reasonable to take the Gospel accounts at face value. There are many very good reasons to believe they do not accurately reflect history. They are best understood as impassioned arguments for certain, often mutually exclusive points of view based around a possibly historical core—the life and death of a beloved leader.

5. Jesus's Miracles and Proof of the Resurrection

No discussion of biblical reliability would be complete without a discussion of its miracle claims. Before we ever get to whether an anciently attested miracle occurred, we must first determine whether the report itself is reliable, for with history, we are only required to explain the report—not the thing reported. It should be clear from the preceding discussion that both the Old and New Testaments were written in superstitious times, when miracle claims were abundant. These were prescientific eras filled with con artists, gullible believers, and reputed wonders of every variety. People wondered where the Sun went at night. The authors are largely unknown to us, as is the basis by which they acquired their information. We have no current means to assess their reliability. As demonstrated previously, much of the Bible is demonstrably false. The Bible, in short, falls light-years short of the standard required to justify belief in miracle claims.

As for Jesus in particular, it is noteworthy that the miracles with which he is credited during his ministry are not so different from magic tricks performed by modern-day magicians. Such performers as David Blaine have even presented their own versions of Jesus's reported miracles in television specials. Professional magicians Penn and Teller have throughout their long and distinguished careers developed unparalleled expertise in the methods of professional conjuring. This is in fact the premise of their hit television show *Fool Us*, in which magicians compete to deceive the duo. Despite Penn and Teller's encyclopedic knowledge, contestants often succeed in fooling them with their performances. If Penn and Teller can be fooled, then why would we expect Bronze Age peasants to do any better at ferreting out trickery?

And why does Jesus almost always perform miracles for people already convinced? If Jesus's miracles were intended as important signs, as the Gospel of John claims, then why doesn't he perform them primarily for people who are skeptical and have good critical-thinking skills? It is noteworthy that Paul, who describes himself as a skeptic before converting to Christianity, attributes no miracles to Jesus in his writings and, in 1 Corinthians 1:22–24, suggests that Jesus performed no miracles.[137] If miracles are to inspire belief, then who needs them more than skeptics and atheists? And yet there is no account outside the Bible of any such skeptic witnessing a Christian miracle. This is especially surprising, given Jesus's promise in John 14:12 that anyone believing in him would perform miracles even greater than his, in which case there should be no skeptics left.

There are numerous *biblical stories* of skeptics witnessing miracles, almost all before the time of Jesus. In the Old Testament, the message of such events is always the same: A true god provides readily observable evidence of his power and majesty; a god who fails to do so is false and does not deserve belief. In Kings, readers are presented with the challenge of Elijah. Elijah sets a test for the Canaanite god Baal to demonstrate that Baal is the "true God." Elijah challenges Baal to set an alter aflame, but Baal fails to do so. Elijah then calls upon YHWH to meet the challenge. When YHWH succeeds, the people fall to the ground, crying, "The Lord is God!" For the failure of their god to provide similarly compelling miraculous evidence, Elijah proclaims Baal discredited and kills his prophets (Kings 18:18–40).

Obviously, YHWH felt it was appropriate to set a test for Baal and for the Canaanites to discard belief in Baal if he failed to meet that test. Likewise, YHWH understood the importance of providing clear evidence supporting His claims. Under YHWH's logic, anyone doubting the truth of Christianity should simply set a test for God like that of Elijah, and if God fails the test, then they should abandon Christianity. Scientists have been effectively doing this for centuries, during which God's success rate has been a solid . . . zero. Isn't it time to follow Elijah's logic and move on?

Arguably, the most important event in all of Christianity is the Resurrection of Jesus. It was the miracle of all miracles, justifying Jesus's disciples in their belief that Jesus was in fact the divinely appointed Messiah. Paul found it so significant that he wrote, "If Christ be not raised, your faith is in vain" (1 Corinthians 15:17). The Resurrection would definitely qualify as a miracle, requiring extraordinarily strong evidence in its favor. That the only such evidence we have comes from the Gospel accounts and Paul, therefore, should immediately give us pause. The limited collection of sources that say Jesus's tomb was empty are the same limited sources that say he was resurrected, and they are hardly objective. We've already seen many reasons the Gospels cannot be accepted as reliable historical accounts of the events leading up to Jesus's Resurrection. There is even less reason to accept them regarding the post-Resurrection appearances of Jesus, on which they are thoroughly inconsistent.

The first, Mark, records no appearances at all. As discussed, Matthew and Luke differ on just about every point after Jesus's Crucifixion. John provides his own unique post-Crucifixion content that would appear important enough for either Matthew or Luke to have included if it had happened that way. You might say it is the equivalent of four witnesses telling inconsistent stories regarding an inherently implausible event, except that none even claim to be witnesses, so it is far worse than that. This alone is enough to discount the Gospel accounts of the Resurrection.

Assume a group of twelve poor people stop you on the street and tell you that their friend Jeb just rose from the dead and that he wants you to sell everything you own and follow him because he is the true God. Assume that they present you with a videotape showing Jeb lying still and then suddenly standing. Assume that one of them tells you he is sure Jeb was dead for three days before he got up, and they all claim to have seen him walking around afterward. Under these circumstances, would you immediately believe them, sell everything, and follow Jeb—or would you be more skeptical? If you would not believe them, then what type of evidence would you need to do so?

Now, assume you don't actually meet these twelve individuals but instead read about their claims in the newspaper. Next, assume the paper is fifty years old, and there is no video. Assume the story about Jeb actually occurred forty years before the article was written. Assume that instead of twelve accounts, you have only four. Assume that none of the individuals claim to be eyewitnesses to the events of Jeb's resurrection. Assume their stories differ on several important details, including when the resurrection took place and whether Jeb was ever seen after his death.

Next, assume there were no interviews but that the reporter just uncovered four manuscripts written anonymously about the incident. Assume that though their accounts involve stupendous miracles and major confrontations with the authorities, no contemporary reports confirm their stories or mention the events of their narrative. Now, assume the manuscripts were written not one hundred years ago but two thousand, in an area of great poverty and illiteracy and when there was little understanding about science but many stories of miracles and miracle makers. Further assume that the manuscripts aren't originals but were produced centuries later and that these manuscripts are but one set of such copies among hundreds that differ in thousands of ways. Would these factors make the claims more compelling or less?

All the evidence we have for the Resurrection comes from the four Gospels and, arguably, a couple letters from Paul. Paul recounts only a single vision of Jesus. Everything else in Paul's letters and the Gospels attesting to a Resurrection represents hearsay from unidentified sources. These are ancient documents, of which we have only much later copies that may have been altered substantially from the originals.

Compare this to the evidence supporting Mormonism. Mormon founder Joseph Smith claimed that in 1823 he was visited by an angel named

Moroni, who told him of a book written on golden plates buried in a stone box near his home. Smith claimed he found these plates and transcribed them to paper, creating what would become known as the Book of Mormon. Eleven witnesses signed affidavits attesting to having seen these golden plates, the angel, or both. They all claimed to have handled the plates. Their testimonies are found in the front of every modern edition of the Book of Mormon and at the time would have been admissible evidence in a court of law. This represents evidence far better than anything supporting the Resurrection of Jesus, and yet no non-Mormon Christian apologist accepts it.

An even more compelling case can be made for claims of black magic leading to the Salem witch trials of 1692 and 1693. Today, these trials are widely considered examples of mass hysteria and a cautionary tale of how false stories can take on lives of their own in certain circumstances. They have served as fodder for many literary takes on these issues, such as Arthur Miller's *The Crucible*, which used the trials as an allegory for McCarthyism and anti-Communist panic in the 1950s. No reasonable person living today takes these claims seriously or honestly believes the accused women were performing sorcery.

As philosophy professor Matthew McCormick points out, however, the evidence for actual witchcraft at Salem is *much stronger* than the historical argument for the Resurrection:

> In the case of Salem, the trials were a mere three hundred years ago, not two thousand. For Salem, we have thousands of actual documents surrounding the incidences, including the sworn testimonies from people claiming to have seen the magic performed. . . . The events in Salem were actively investigated by thoughtful, educated, (relatively) modern people. A large number of people devoted a great deal of time and energy to carefully examine the cases, and they concluded that whatever was going on must be of supernatural origin. . . . [T]he Gospel stories are only a few anecdotal, hearsay stories from passionate and committed religious followers passed by word of mouth for decades through an unknown number of people before being written down. All that remains of those stories are copies of copies from decades or even centuries later that were actively culled and patched together from a wider range of more varied writings. By reasonable measures of quantity and quality, the evidence we have for witchcraft at Salem is vastly better than the evidence we have for the magical return from the dead by Jesus. . . . You cannot consistently accept Jesus' returning from the dead while rejecting the magical power of the Salem witches.[138]

Apologists try to saddle nonbelievers with the burden of explaining the Resurrection naturalistically, as if it were an undisputed fact that Jesus died and rose again, and it is this "fact" for which naturalists must account. But that is unjustified. We never reach the point of requiring an explanation for the Resurrection because there is no agreed-upon Resurrection to explain. It is only necessary to plausibly explain *stories of the Resurrection* that circulated near the end of the first century, becoming the basis for various inconsistent accounts, for that is the only thing for which we have evidence. And that is relatively simple to do, as there are only a handful. Unless the apologist can demonstrate that all-natural explanations *for the Gospel accounts* of the Resurrection are logical impossibilities, then he has demonstrated no good reason to believe it was an actual event.

Consider the lottery paradox: a fair, one-thousand-ticket lottery that has one winning ticket. Given this information, it is rational to accept that some ticket will win. It is also presumed rational, however, to accept that for any individual ticket i, ticket i will not win. However, accepting that ticket i-1 won't win, accepting that ticket i-2 won't win, and so on, until accepting that ticket i-1,000 won't win suggests that it is rational to believe *no* ticket will win. One should believe the contradictory propositions that one ticket wins and no ticket wins, creating a paradox.

The flaw in this reasoning is that it limits one's options to a false dichotomy: winner or loser, with attendant probabilities of 100 percent or 0 percent assigned. It is indeed true that any one ticket has a less than 50 percent chance of winning and therefore is an unlikely winner. But that does not mean you can assign its chances as zero, for in fact, each ticket has a one-thousandth chance of winning. If you add these up, ticket by ticket, you reach a 100 percent chance by the end. Each ticket adds to a cumulative probability.

It is the same with naturalistic explanations of the Resurrection. While no one explanation may be more than 50 percent likely, you may add their probabilities together when presented with an alternate, supernatural explanation, the base probability of which must be assigned extremely low due to its inherent implausibility. Even if you feel that intuition supports the supernatural explanation, you cannot compare their probabilities unless and until you have identified all naturalistic explanations and added their probabilities together. While each may be individually highly unlikely on its own, they should be considered together when deciding between the probabilities of a natural versus supernatural explanation.

Once you recognize that we are dealing only with ancient stories and that fabrication and legendary accretion are possibilities, many naturalistic explanations are plausible. Such apologists as Lee Strobel, who claim the Resurrection is the best explanation, must create for themselves a huge head start—assuming a cherry-picked selection of Gospel claims to be historical. But we need not take the Gospel accounts at face value, as devotional Christians do. Given the many demonstrable factual inaccuracies of the Gospels, we probably aren't even justified in doing so.

a. The Tradition of the Empty Tomb The most common place for apologists to begin discussing the Resurrection is with the empty tomb. They identify this as the evidential foundation upon which to build their argument for the Resurrection, claiming such widespread agreement on Jesus's tomb being empty that it can be taken as historical fact.

Unfortunately for the apologists, this simply isn't true. Paul, for example, our earliest Christian source, never mentions an empty tomb. There is good reason to believe Paul wasn't even talking about a bodily Resurrection that would have required an empty tomb. Paul's language suggests only a spiritual Jesus, with no corporeal form. When describing his vision of Jesus, Paul uses the Greek word for spiritual visions rather than bodily appearances. A primary point of Paul's first letter to the Corinthians is to discredit the possibility of a bodily Resurrection. There he distinguishes between natural bodies, such as those of men, and the "spiritual body," which is of a different kind altogether: "It is sown a natural body; it is raised a spiritual body. There is a natural body, and there is a spiritual body" (1 Corinthians 15:44). For someone so concerned with the world-changing theological impact of Jesus's Resurrection, it would be surprising for Paul to mention nothing about Jesus's death or bodily Resurrection if he knew about them.

History provides no parallels for Romans even allowing a common criminal like Jesus to be buried in a tomb. Roman criminals were left on their crosses until their bodies decayed, often for weeks, as a warning to others, rendering any burial highly implausible. Another point against an actual empty tomb is that there is no evidence that Jesus's tomb was venerated during the first century CE. Apologist James Dunn expresses this argument this way:

> Christians today of course regard the site of Jesus' tomb with veneration, and that practice goes back at least to the fourth century. But for the period covered by the New Testament and other earliest Christian writings there is no evidence whatsoever for Christians regarding the place where Jesus had been buried as having any special significance. No practice of tomb veneration, or

even of meeting for worship at Jesus' tomb is attested for the first Christians. Had such been the practice of the first Christians, with all the significance which the very practice itself presupposes, it is hard to believe that our records of Jerusalem Christianity and of Christian visits thereto would not have mentioned or alluded to it in some way or at some point.[139]

The site of Jesus's tomb clearly would become a site of veneration and pilgrimage among early Christians regardless of whether it was full or empty. The factors of nagging doubt, pious curiosity, and liturgical significance would all contribute toward the empty tomb becoming a site of intense interest among Christians. Elvis Presley's tomb in Memphis, Tennessee, has been visited by tens of thousands of devotees every year since his death. Should we expect less of Jesus's followers? The obvious explanation is that early Christians had no idea where Jesus was buried or *if he was even buried*.

It might be objected that Paul did not mention the empty tomb story because it would not be useful if Paul understood the Resurrection to be of a spiritual rather than physical type, as his writings suggest. It is unlikely that Paul and other early Christians would have believed the Resurrection to be of a spiritual type if they knew Jesus's body was missing from the tomb after the Resurrection. Either Paul believed in a physical Resurrection but inexplicably didn't mention the empty tomb story, or Paul believed in a spiritual Resurrection only, which suggests he had never heard of the empty tomb. Either way, Paul's writings strongly undermine the claim of an empty tomb.

The only accounts of an empty tomb occur in the Gospels, which depend to varying degrees on Mark. Mark's account of the empty tomb story is, in turn, eerily similar to that of Daniel in the Old Testament. Mark mentions no bodily appearances by Jesus. Matthew goes further than Mark and actually uses specific passages from Daniel to make the connection more explicit. This strongly suggests a literary reworking of an Old Testament story rather than a historical event.

Some apologists point to Matthew's references to rebuttals from contemporary Jewish skeptics of Christianity, known as polemics. For example, Matthew claims these skeptics attempted to explain the empty tomb naturally, such as by claiming that Jesus's body must have been stolen, so as to deny the possibility of a Resurrection. Christian apologists suggest these polemics would only make such arguments if there were in fact an empty tomb to explain. But this gets the cart before the horse.

First, only Matthew mentions these arguments. We don't have the polemics themselves. Nor do we have any other sources for anyone attempting to explain an empty tomb outside Jerusalem, which is very surprising if
contemporary polemics existed. Another point against the apologists is that
Matthew was writing long after Jesus's death and would have been responding to Jewish skeptics *of his day*. By the time Matthew was written, circa
85–90 CE, any Jewish memory of the details of Jesus's burial would have
been long forgotten. There is no reason to think the Jews by that time were
aware of where Jesus's tomb had been and that it had been found empty.

Why not interpret the skeptics' arguments as conceding, *purely for the
sake of argument*, that there was an empty tomb, as people commonly do
today? They might have said, for example, "If there was in fact an empty
tomb, *as you guys say*, then how do we know the disciples didn't steal the
body away?" This is not a concession of the underlying assumption but
rather a rhetorical device to demonstrate that even if the assumption is
presumed valid, the argument still fails. This is a common debating tactic
when evidence is lacking or inconclusive on a point of contention but other
points may be argued that would themselves be dispositive of the issue in
question. One might reasonably choose to rush past the more contentious
and ultimately moot point to get to one that quickly settles the argument.

It is also enlightening to see how the Gospel writers respond to contemporary critiques of their claims. Matthew includes a unique story about a
Roman guard assigned to watch over Jesus's tomb to prevent theft of the
body (28:11–15), an account conceded by William Lane Craig as "nearly
universally rejected as an apologetic legend."[140] To the argument that experiences of the risen Jesus were mere ghost stories, Luke (24:39–43) has the
risen Jesus eat a piece of fish and invite the disciples to touch him, showing
he is not an immaterial wraith. These later additions to the primitive Mar-
kan account strongly suggest fabrications created by the later evangelists
specifically to answer the critics of their day. They indicate a legend that
continued to evolve in response to its detractors rather than a stable historical tradition.

The conclusion of many modern critical scholars is that the empty tomb
tradition was a late invention, originating around the time of Mark and
using Old Testament sources for inspiration. Scholars are increasingly concluding that the empty tomb tradition is a metaphorical interpretation of a
presumed spiritual event—a way of saying "Jesus is risen!"—rather than a
historical description of the event itself.

b. Possibilities Other than Fabrication   Though there are good reasons to believe the Gospel writers intentionally fabricated their accounts,

we need not reach this conclusion to discount their testimony as historically inaccurate. Another possibility is that one or more authors or their sources were honestly mistaken. This is especially plausible in relation to their accounts of the resurrected Jesus.

Psychologists have long recognized that people devoted to a powerful movement will often avoid facing reality when the movement fails. They look for any way to keep the dream alive, reinterpreting failed prophecies of a religious leader, for example, to avoid acknowledging that they dedicated their lives to a mistake. It may be that certain followers of Jesus manufactured post-Crucifixion appearances of Jesus that they conveyed to others. Or perhaps one or more followers innocently mistook someone for the resurrected Jesus, giving rise to the rumor of his Resurrection. The Gospel of Luke provides support for this view, with its story of two followers of Jesus who converse with him at some length without ever recognizing him. Could this perhaps preserve the oral tradition of travelers who talked to a man they only in retrospect thought *might* have been Jesus? There is no way to know, but these are plausible explanations.

It is even possible that an imposter claimed to be the resurrected Jesus, with Jesus's grief-stricken followers accepting his claim rather than face the reality of the end of their movement. The pain and guilt associated with losing a loved one is enormous. Many studies have shown how our perceptions can be affected and distorted in the wake of such an event, leaving us exceptionally open to trickery. Psychics have a long and notorious history of preying on the survivors of recently departed relatives by claiming to channel the dead, relying on the survivors' strong emotional needs to mask their deception.

For anyone who doesn't believe people can make mistakes about the identities of those with whom they have been close, I would refer them to the case of Nicholas Barclay. Barclay was a Texas boy who disappeared at the age of thirteen in 1994. Three years later, a twenty-two-year-old Spanish con man, Frederic Bourdin, showed up, claiming to be Barclay. Though the two looked and sounded nothing alike, Barclay's entire family accepted Bourdin as Barclay, fully believing him *to actually be Barclay*. They continued to believe until confronted with rock-solid proof by the FBI that Bourdin was not Barclay. This story was presented in the 2012 documentary film *The Imposter*. It is a testament to how easily people can allow themselves to be deceived in the right circumstances—even on the identity of their own family members. I do not claim this is the most probable theory or even that it is likely—only that it is plausible. The imposter theory is just one of many that could reasonably explain the post-Crucifixion appearances of Jesus without accusing the Gospel writers of intentional deception.

What about Paul, who claims that Jesus appeared to five hundred people? First, it must be acknowledged that Paul claims to have obtained all his information from visions, and there is no way to verify the accuracy of a man's visions. These are subjective experiences and need not be taken as fact. We know today, however, that many people of all religions claim to have religious visions and revelations, for which no basis has been found in objective reality. Many of these people suffer from mental illness, which can sometimes be episodic. One cannot rule out the possibility that Paul's visions were mere delusions.

There is, furthermore, no good reason to believe that Paul was referring to bodily appearances. Perhaps he was referring to visions of Jesus like he himself reported. These may have simply been dreams or hallucinations by devoted followers that later made their way to Paul second- or thirdhand. A study of more than 13,000 people revealed that almost 39 percent reported hallucinatory experiences, suggesting that such hallucinations are far more common than most people assume and are not limited to the "insane."[141] Another possibility is that rumors circulated that reached Paul's ears, but those rumors were, like a game of "Telephone," based on distortions of the original story or even an initial legitimate mistake. Once again, because we don't know the original sources, there is no way to tell.

Finally, one cannot ignore the possibility that Paul was simply lying because he thought no one would follow a dead Messiah. Paul was clearly a great salesman, devoted to spreading Christianity throughout the known world. Perhaps he fabricated the post-Crucifixion appearances to keep the movement alive and bolster his message. It would not be the first time, or last, that a proponent of a religious movement made things up to help sell his faith. This practice has been so common throughout history that it has been given a unique name: pious fraud.

Let's once again consider the principle of parsimony. There are several plausible explanations for Paul's claim. He could have hallucinated or been fooled by the sensed-presence effect, in which our brains make us think there is someone there when there is not.[142] Because he didn't meet Jesus when Jesus was purportedly alive, he might have just met some guy who claimed to be Jesus. Or he could be lying. *All* of those explanations are more plausible than the claim that the bodily form of a resurrected God appeared to a traveling Jew. Christopher Hitchens made this point in his 2010 debate with Al Sharpton: "Which is more likely: That the whole natural order is suspended, or that a Jewish minx should tell a lie?"[143] The same sentiment could be applied to Paul.

Some apologists have argued that Paul could not have gotten away with claiming that five hundred people had seen the risen Jesus if it were not true. But that is ridiculous. First, the claim is vague, with no names named. The communities to which Paul preached were scattered across the Roman Empire, hundreds of miles from one another. Paul lived in a time before the internet or any mass communication. Most people lived their entire lives within a few miles of their birthplace and never interacted with people from faraway lands. The idea that they could have effectively fact-checked Paul's claims with people living decades earlier in Jerusalem or Galilee is absurd.

Even if we accept at face value the claim that there were "hundreds of witnesses" to Jesus's resurrected body, this may sound impressive until you consider that many more people than that have claimed to have "seen" UFOs, Bigfoot, or the Loch Ness Monster. How many people claim to see ghosts *each year*? Thousands? Millions? And yet no solid evidence has ever supported any of these claims. The scientific community remains unimpressed. Anonymous reports from ancient times, no matter how many, are not a credible source of evidence. And where the claim is as fantastic as a man rising from the dead, such reports fall far below the threshold that would justify a reasonable person in believing it.

Keep in mind that the Jews of Jesus's own day overwhelmingly refused to believe that Jesus rose from the dead, despite sharing Jesus's faith and being familiar with all the Old Testament prophecies he supposedly fulfilled. It has been estimated there may have been 2.5 million Jews in Palestine at the time of Jesus's Crucifixion. According to Catholic New Testament scholar David C. Sim, throughout the first century, the total number of Jews in the Christian movement probably never exceeded 1,000, and by the end of the century the Christian church was largely Gentile.[144] That is less than 0.5 percent, meaning that well over 99 percent rejected the Christian claims of a resurrected Jesus. Because the Jews of Jesus's day didn't believe, why should we?

Assume you and I are walking out of your house one day and see an unusual rock in your yard that we know was not there when we walked in. We both speculate as to how the rock got there. I come up with mundane examples, such as perhaps someone left it there or, more exotically, it could've been a meteorite. Your explanation is a genie popped it into existence through magic. Now it's true that I may not have any specific evidence for either of my proposals, but can you see why either would be more probable than yours? Can you see why *any* naturalistic explanation that draws on things we know to exist are more probable than a supernatural one that draws on things we don't?

The biblical skeptic need only point out there are many plausible natural explanations for the stories in the Gospels and Paul's letters regarding Jesus' post-Crucifixion appearances, such as those mentioned previously. As with the lottery paradox, it is unnecessary to prove any of them with certainty or even probability. All are more likely than a supernatural explanation because we have no shortage of precedents from our collective experience. Improbable nonmiraculous things happen every day. What evidence there is for a supernatural explanation must be weighed against the inherent improbability of such, which is off the charts. Unless the apologist can negate the possibility of *every possible natural explanation* for these stories and show that all the "improbable" natural explanations are more improbable than a miracle, he cannot be justified in concluding that Jesus actually rose from the dead.

With all these problems, it should not be surprising to anyone that the Jesus Seminar, a cross-disciplinary group of more than two hundred religious scholars tasked with assessing the historical truth of biblical sayings about Jesus, ultimately concluded there was no credible, reliable evidence for either the Resurrection, the empty tomb, or Jesus's postmortem appearances.[145] If the experts found the proof unconvincing, then why should anyone else be convinced?

6. The "Cumulative Approach" Argument

Some apologists acknowledge the prior probability problem of Bayes' theorem, effectively conceding that something as inherently improbable as the Resurrection should generally be rejected if treated like any other unlikely event. They go on, however, to claim that such an approach shouldn't apply to the Resurrection because it occurred in a unique context and is therefore supported by a "cumulative approach" to the evidence. They claim that the prior probability problem can be addressed by appealing to other evidence for God, such as the cosmological, fine-tuning, and moral arguments, which increase the prior probability of a Resurrection. William Lane Craig, for example, states,

> Therefore, it seems to me that of the three alternatives before us—physical necessity, chance, or design—the most plausible explanation of the fine-tuning of the universe is design. That gives us a transcendent, super-intelligent

Designer of the cosmos who has fixed the values of nature's laws. Incredible! So now we have a third argument contributing to a cumulative case for the existence of God.[146]

Craig argues that once one accepts those arguments, resurrecting someone from the dead seems like small potatoes. Any God who can create the universe could surely accomplish something so trivial.

This approach is a nonstarter, however, because even if one accepts these "foundational" arguments at face value, despite all the problems previously presented, they would support a wide variety of mutually exclusive supernatural entities, including a Deist God unable or unwilling to resurrect. These arguments do not necessarily lead to the personal, intervening, miracle-working God required to bring about Jesus's Resurrection, *which they must to support the argument.*

Thomas Jefferson believed in a Deist God and would have been persuaded by these big three arguments but would have rejected the interventionist God of Christianity because there was no good evidence *for that type of God.* Those arguments are necessary but far from sufficient to support the type of God we could reasonably expect to resurrect Jesus. Even taken together, they only start the apologists' ball rolling, with all the hard, uphill work still ahead. The gulf between the philosopher's god and the God of Christianity is vast.

7. Jesus Was Wrong

If Jesus were indeed God, as Christians maintain, then we would not expect him to make mistakes. In fact, for Jesus to be wrong about anything would be inconceivable. I have discussed biblical inaccuracies, including those in the Gospels, and how these undercut the claim of Jesus's divinity. But there is a more direct response to this claim, for Jesus was clearly wrong on a central point of his ministry: "Verily I say unto you, this generation shall not pass, till all these things be fulfilled" (Matthew 24:34; also Mark 13:30 and Luke 21:32). This verse, part of the Olivet discourse, is found in all three of the Synoptic Gospels.[147] By the plain meaning of these words, Jesus explicitly claimed that all the events prophesied in the Olivet discourse would take place within the lifetimes of the generation living in Jesus's day.

The subject of the Olivet discourse is the Second Coming.[148] The events described lead up to and include God's establishment of his kingdom on Earth and the Last Judgment. Jesus describes the end of the world as we know it. In these passages Jesus is unambiguous about his return. He says that he will ride the clouds with angels to judge the world and will send his angels to gather his chosen ones from the Earth with the sound of a trumpet. The whole world would see him in the sky, just as the whole world sees the light of the Sun.

The remainder of the Synoptic Gospels, the writings of Paul, and the writings of the other books of the New Testament support this view, as it is clear that these authors *all believed Jesus would return in their lifetimes*. See, for example, Hebrews 1:1–2; 1 John 2:18; 1 Corinthians 7:27, 7:29–31; 1 Peter 4:7; 1 Thessalonians 4:15–17; James 5:8–9; Revelation 1:3, 22:6–7, 22:10, 22:12, 22:20; Mark 1:15; Matthew 10:23, 23:29–36; and Luke 12:49–50. To make it clear to his listeners these events would be happening *very soon*, Jesus confirmed that some of them would still be alive to see his return: "[S]ome of those who are standing here . . . will not taste death until they see the Son of Man coming in his kingdom" (Matthew 16:27–28). He could not have been any clearer.

But that isn't what happened. Nothing in either the Bible or contemporary historical writings suggests these fantastical events occurred. Had they actually taken place two thousand years ago, as Jesus predicted, someone surely would have noticed. It would be tough to hide an army of angels, widespread resurrections of the dead, and the complete destruction and remaking of the secular world. The only reasonable explanation is that Jesus was wrong.

This error is even more disconcerting because this was Jesus's *central message*. The majority of New Testament scholars agree that according to the earliest and most reliable sources, Jesus was an apocalyptic prophet preaching first and foremost the imminent arrival of the Kingdom of God, a lens through which virtually all his other teachings must be viewed. Throughout Mark, for instance, Jesus returns to this theme repeatedly.

Religious skeptics have pointed this out for centuries without ever receiving a satisfactory response from Christian apologists. Matthew 24:34 and its counterparts in Mark and Luke are described by revered apologist C. S. Lewis as the "most embarrassing verse(s) in the Bible."[149] Lewis finds this so troubling that he can think of no solution other than to reluctantly concede, against the weight of orthodox Christian theology, that Jesus was in fact mistaken. He writes,

> "Say what you like," we shall be told, "the apocalyptic beliefs of the first Christians have been proved to be false. It is clear from the New Testament that they all expected the Second Coming in their own lifetime. And, worse still, they had a reason, and one which you will find very embarrassing. Their Master had told them so. He shared, and indeed created, their delusion. He

said in so many words, 'This generation shall not pass till all these things be done.' And he was wrong. He clearly knew no more about the end of the world than anyone else." It is certainly the most embarrassing verse in the Bible.[150]

Lewis's "solution" to this problem was to acknowledge that Jesus was wrong but to find solace in a subsequent passage, by which, he claimed, Jesus negated the Olivet discourse and claimed ignorance: "Yet how teasing, also, that within fourteen words of it should come the statement 'But of that day and that hour knoweth no man, no, not the angels which are in heaven, neither the Son, but the Father.' The one exhibition of error and the one confession of ignorance grow side by side."[151]

This is a puzzling and unsatisfactory solution because it maintains that Jesus would state something with supreme confidence ["Heaven and Earth shall pass away, but my words shall not pass away" (Matthew 24:25)], of which he actually had *no confidence or knowledge*. Lewis posits that Jesus built his ministry around convincing people of something that he had no good reason to believe himself—something of which in one Gospel he would even claim ignorance. This merely constitutes a lie of a different sort, making Jesus into the liar Lewis elsewhere insists he cannot be.[152]

But there are greater problems with Lewis's solution. First, it ignores the implications of the Trinity, by which Jesus and God are one. How can Jesus confidently make a claim that God the Father knows to be false? This seems especially absurd when that claim is central to Jesus's ministry, which was designed by the unified trinitarian God as part of His divine plain. Lewis's position simply cannot be reconciled with mainstream Christianity.

Second, it makes Jesus into a false prophet by the biblical standard. This standard appears in Jeremiah 28:9, in which we are told that we can only know a prophet is of the Lord when his prophecies come true. God ensures that the prophecies made by His true prophets do not fail (Isaiah 44:24–26). The Bible condemns false prophets to death (Jeremiah 28:1–17; Zechariah 13:3). If Jesus was indeed wrong, as Lewis concedes, then he must have been a false prophet and not of the Lord. The Bible says so.[153] And yet neither Lewis nor any of his apologist contemporaries followed this to its logical conclusion.

More important, it renders Jesus unreliable on all his teachings. If we cannot accept what Jesus says about the Second Coming and the Kingdom of Heaven, then which of his statements can we accept? By what means can mere humans discern the true statements of Jesus from the false ones? If apologists concede that Jesus was wrong about even his most firm, forceful, and fundamental claims, then what justification can they possibly provide for us to take anything said by Jesus as true? It is an insoluble dilemma.

Apologists other than Lewis have attempted to address this quandary in ways equally ad hoc and thus no more satisfactory. One group, known as preterists, maintains these prophecies were fulfilled—but no one noticed. Preterists claim that Jesus did return within the lifetime of the disciples, but his return was a purely *spiritual* one, with no discernible impact on the material world. *Full* preterists maintain that the other events of the Olivet discourse said to occur at the same time as Jesus's Second Coming, such as the resurrection of dead Christians, also took place, but these also went unnoticed because, for example, the resurrected bodies remained in their graves so as not to disturb anyone. To accommodate their position, preterists must reject long-accepted tenets of orthodox Christianity taught in both the Old and New Testaments, such as the resurrection of the body, and to reduce many straightforward predictions of Jesus to allegory.

The more mainstream apologetic view is represented by the futurists, who agree that the events prophesied in the Olivet discourse did not occur within the disciples' lifetimes but claim through creative interpretation that *Jesus never actually said they would*. Futurists contend, for example, that by "this generation," Jesus was not referring to those living when he spoke but to some other undefined future generation. Some claim that Jesus used *generation* to mean the entire race of Jews, despite the fact that throughout the remainder of the Gospels, he consistently used *generation* to refer to people living in a particular era and never to an entire race of people. Futurists must twist Jesus's words well outside their ordinary meaning to arrive at such contrived conclusions. They must redefine *generation* to mean "race" and *this* to mean "that."

Futurists also must explain why God would delay the Second Coming for so long. What could He possibly be waiting on at this point? Hundreds of generations have come and gone since Jesus's day. No plausible rationale has ever been proposed for God postponing Judgment Day almost two thousand years and counting. Why the urgency of first-century Christians getting their houses in order if they weren't to see Judgment Day? If the delay was supposed to have some positive effect on humanity, then why wait so many generations? Whatever effect the threat of imminent judgment may have had on early generations was surely lost on successive ones, becoming more attenuated as that threat became increasingly remote and implausible.

Both the preterists and the futurists take positions far from intellectually defensible simply to preserve the integrity of Christianity.[154] Reason and logic have allowed them no quarter—no legitimate response to what apolo-gist Marshall Entrekin calls "perhaps the most powerful challenge to our faith that has ever been presented."[155] They are left with only desperate but dishonest rationalizations.

This leaves perhaps the most common explanation for the failure of Jesus's prophesies: the appeal to mystery. Perhaps, it is argued, our feeble human understanding cannot comprehend what Jesus meant when he said, "this generation will not pass away," or that some "will not taste death until they see the Son of Man coming in His kingdom." After all, he couldn't have meant what he seemed to be saying—that he would return in the first cen-tury—because he didn't return, and that would make him a false prophet.

All I can say in response is that to look at these extremely clear prophe-cies and claim they are beyond human understanding must be one of the most obvious possible examples of motivated reasoning. Only a mind sin-gularly dedicated to maintaining the illusion of faith could twist and mangle Jesus's words in such a way that his credibility is not destroyed. An honest mind would have no choice but to admit that Jesus's prophesy simply failed. He was wrong, plain and simple, and therefore could not have been the man Christians claim him to be.

8. What Really Happened?

So, you may be thinking, what does explain the writings of the New Testament? If, as you claim, Jesus was no more than a failed apocalyptic prophet, then how did he come to be revered and worshipped as God? How did he inspire a new religion that would within several centuries be one of the most powerful forces in the world?

As previously indicated, the early sources reveal that Jesus was an apoca-lyptic prophet and perhaps a teacher and philosopher of the cynic school.[156] He believed that God had temporarily allowed the world to be governed by evil forces, but this was all about to change. He preached that a figure known as the Son of Man, referenced in the Old Testament book of Daniel, would soon arrive in fanfare from Heaven and usher in a new kingdom on Earth.

This kingdom would ultimately be governed by God, but God would appoint an earthly king to administer it. That king was to be Jesus. Jesus would be in charge of separating the righteous, who could remain in the Kingdom of God, from the wicked, who would be banished forever to Hell. Jesus considered himself the Messiah, meaning that like messiahs before him, he would deliver the Jewish people (at least, the righteous ones) out of their suffering (in the world governed by evil forces) to a new and better existence (in the Kingdom of God).

In the meantime, Jesus had been tasked with notifying everyone he could of the coming apocalypse so they could prepare. Such preparation involved giving up their worldly possessions, abandoning their families, and urgently helping Jesus spread his message to the remainder of the Roman Empire. Jesus considered these extreme measures justified, given the imminent coming of the Son of Man. There was no time to lose.

Within a year or two of beginning his ministry, however, tragedy struck. One of his followers likely informed the Roman authorities that Jesus considered himself to be a king. The Romans, ever vigilant for anyone challenging the authority of the Roman emperor, captured Jesus and crucified him for sedition. Jesus meant that he would soon be a king *in the coming Kingdom of God*, but such subtleties would have been irrelevant to the Romans. Any perceived challenge to the emperor's legitimacy had to be dealt with quickly and decisively.

Jesus's followers were devastated. Their leader had been taken from them just as the ministry was gaining momentum. Psychology tells us this state of affairs would have predisposed Jesus's followers to fantasize about him, and indeed some did. These fantasies may have manifested as dreams or waking visions, but either way, at least some believed they had seen Jesus. In this superstitious and credulous community, rumors spread that Jesus's spirit had returned to Earth and was visiting his followers in visions. As the rumors circulated, the second- and thirdhand accounts of visions multiplied. Had God allowed Jesus's spirit to return to Earth, his followers likely reasoned, God must have been so pleased with Jesus that God exalted him to a position higher than any man had ever attained. Jesus had, in a spiritual sense, been resurrected, and this resurrection was a sign that Jesus had obtained a status greater than he ever had on Earth.

This was the state of affairs approximately twenty years after Jesus's Crucifixion, when Paul entered the picture. Perhaps, as stated in his letters, Paul was initially skeptical of the claims of the Jesus movement until he himself experienced a vision of Jesus, after which he became a believer. It also may be, as I've speculated, that Paul became a believer first and fabricated the vision, based on rumors of similar visions among the faithful, to increase his own credibility in his ministry. The story of a spectacular conversion from skeptic to believer would have further gilded the lily.

In either event, Paul's view, as expressed in his legitimate letters, was that Jesus was an angel who had voluntarily debased himself to become human. Jesus had then lived a righteous, earthly life so that his death served as an atonement for the sins of mankind. God was so pleased with this that He exalted Jesus and resurrected his spiritual body, which is what Paul claims he witnessed. Paul believed God had effectively decreed a new system, whereby redemption could be obtained through faith in Jesus. Paul knew and cared little about Jesus's earthly life because that simply wasn't important to his message.

Paul met with the leaders of the Jesus movement, Peter and James, but parted ways with them over several issues, including the importance of faith and the scope of the ministry. While the original Jesus movement focused on existing Jews and the actual teachings of the living Jesus, Paul believed his mission was to preach to Gentiles, as well, and to preach his own view of the significance of Jesus's death and spiritual Resurrection. Paul became an incredibly dynamic, prolific, and well-traveled missionary. Paul's version of Christianity, therefore, became very influential very quickly, rapidly overtaking Peter's and James's brand based on Jesus's own teachings.

The earliest Christians were monotheistic Jews, whose traditions did not include divinizing people. But as the Christian movement spread into the Roman Empire, it encountered a very different ethos, by which it was transformed. In the Greco-Roman world, unlike in the Jewish world, the line between humanity and divinity was frequently crossed and blurred, not only by mythological heroes like Hercules, but also by flesh-and-blood humans like the Roman Caesars. There actually was a fine and permeable line between divinity and humanity in the Greek and Roman worlds. Consider the myth of Hercules. His father was a god (Zeus), while his mother (Alcmene) was a human. Hercules lived as a sort of god-man, with superior strength and other abilities but bound to Earth and mortal. After his death, however, he became a full-on god.

In basic outline, this story sounds much like early Christian belief about Jesus. This isn't to say that the story of Jesus was based on the story of Hercules but rather that familiarity with the pagan stories greased the wheel for elevating Jesus from man to God, as the concept was no longer a foreign one. So it was only natural that formerly pagan Christians, competing for religious allegiance against a slew of Greco-Roman cults, would divinize Jesus. Pagans had no problem incorporating a new divine being into their pantheon, even one previously mortal. Therefore, the one who was once only an inspired human redeemer and teacher became *the One* regarded as divine.

In the pagan world, there were many mythological beings whose stories shared elements of what would soon be Jesus's story. Horus and Mithras, for example, were miraculously conceived or born, were half-god and half-man, performed miracles, and were saviors required to make extreme sacrifices. The healing miracles of the Synoptic Gospels bear similarities to

Greek stories of Asclepius, the god of healing and medicine. The narrative pattern of a story skipping over childhood and adolescence and then proceeding through the same basic "hero" structure is repeated in many stories predating Jesus, such as Jason, Bellerophon, Pelops, Joseph, Elijah, and Siegfried. The narrative tropes of the Gospels would be familiar to anyone hearing these stories.

In the thirty to forty years following Jesus's death, different traditions developed regarding his death and Resurrection. Some people felt that Jesus had been raised in spirit only, while others thought that, given the reports of Jesus sightings, his physical body must have been resurrected, as well. That would have required a body not previously desecrated, as was typical of Crucifixions. Jesus must then have been removed from the cross shortly after his death and entombed. It followed that if Jesus had been entombed, then he must have left his tomb once resurrected. Stories therefore spread about an empty tomb. By the time such stories spread, decades may have passed, so there would have been no way to verify them. Stories also circulated about miracles Jesus performed during his ministry. Perhaps Jesus engaged in faith healing and casting out of demons, as did many others of his day. Upon the basis of these stories, people may have extrapolated to believing he performed even greater miracles.

Sometime shortly after 70 CE, following the destruction of the Jewish temple, Mark wrote his Gospel. The Jews were in despair, with the intense need for a new hope. Mark, who was a Pauline Christian, did not intend his work to be a strictly historical account and did not expect his audience to consider it so. He used some oral traditions about Jesus, some Old Testament stories, and his knowledge of Homer's works to come up with a narrative account of Jesus's ministry and death. Mark created what scholar Joseph Campbell calls a "monomyth," a tale common in the ancient world involving a hero's journey with an adventure, a decisive crisis, a victory, and a transformation leading to the hero's power to bestow boons on mankind. Mark incorporated circulating traditions about the empty tomb but none regarding any post-Resurrection appearances. Perhaps he wasn't aware of them or found them untrustworthy.

By the time of Mark's Gospel, the views of Jesus's exaltation had evolved. People felt that if Jesus was resurrected by God, then perhaps he had been exalted to a higher, semidivine, status *during his lifetime*. Mark identified this point as Jesus's baptism, when God adopted Jesus as His son. This would explain why Jesus was able to perform miracles and cast out demons during his ministry, but Mark provides no account of Jesus's life before his baptism. Before that time, Mark's Jesus was just an ordinary man.

By the time Matthew and Luke were written, certain Christians believed Jesus must have had a special status *since his conception*. Matthew and Luke therefore either wholly fabricated or adapted from late traditions an infancy narrative explaining how Jesus came to acquire this status. Virgin births were common signs of divinity among pagan religions. Matthew found a prophecy from the Greek translation of the Old Testament that appeared to suggest the Messiah would be born of a virgin and so added this detail to his narrative to make it more compelling. Luke may have inherited this same tradition or come up with it independently.

By this time, Daniel's Son of Man and Jesus had been so conflated that many thought Jesus himself would be ushering in the new kingdom. Matthew and Luke therefore added passages suggesting that Jesus and the Son of Man were the same while retaining many passages from Mark indicating they were separate and distinct entities. Matthew and Luke also either incorporated existing conflicting traditions or fabricated their own of post-Resurrection appearances. Each included details to directly rebut those Christians arguing in their day that God raised only Jesus's spirit rather than his physical body.

By the time John wrote his Gospel, the Christology of Jesus had developed even further. Many Christians believed Jesus had *always been equal to God*, from the very beginning of time. Rather than being a mortal exalted to a higher status by God, Jesus was always the incarnation of a specific aspect of God, the Logos. The Johannites believed that Jesus was fully divine. If so, they reasoned, then Jesus must have proclaimed this during his ministry. The Synoptic picture of Jesus hiding his light under a bushel couldn't be squared with the view of the Johannite community.

John used existing traditions to create such a picture of Jesus. John also included even more details making it explicit that Jesus's body was raised physically rather than just spiritually, such as an account of doubting Thomas being invited to touch Jesus's open wounds. By the time of Matthew and Luke's Gospels, and certainly by the time of John's, it had become increasingly clear that the Kingdom of God was not as imminent as Jesus had claimed. Accordingly, those prophecies were dropped or substantially toned down.

The evolution of Jesus's story from Mark through John reflects what comic book fans call a "retcon."[157] Aspects of Jesus's story from early sources that were no longer plausible, such as Jesus's prediction of an imminent apocalypse, were written out, deemphasized, or reinterpreted in later sources. There is no hint in reading Mark, or even Paul, that Jesus did not mean these ubiquitous prophecies literally. It is only in reading the later works, written after they failed to materialize, that we see attempts to reinterpret the prophecies to avoid embarrassment.

By the end of the first century CE, those people lumped under the term *Christians* by their contemporaries had a wide variety of mutually exclusive beliefs, many of which conflicted starkly with those of modern Christians. Some believed that Jesus's Resurrection had been merely a spiritual one. Some did not believe Jesus has been resurrected at all. In the following two hundred years, early Christian theologians attempted to harmonize the many competing traditions and accounts of Jesus. They likely used early versions of the Gospels and other sources unavailable to us today. The views of the "winners" of the debates became that Jesus was an incarnation of God rather than an exalted human and that he had been bodily raised from the dead rather than just spiritually.

This explanation suggests that the story of Jesus as told in the Gospels is a legend. *Legend* is defined by *American Heritage Dictionary* as an "unverified story, handed down from earlier times, esp. one popularly believed to be historical."[159] How early can legends develop? As the expression "a legend in his own time" implies, very little time need pass. In fact, there are numerous instances of legends that have grown around historical events just since World War II.

It is easy to show that legends can and do arise and spread within a few decades of a remarkable person's death, despite the opposition of eyewitnesses. Consider the famous Darwin legend. Charles Darwin died on April 19, 1882. Almost immediately, stories began to circulate suggesting that Darwin, the agnostic and author of the godless theory of evolution, had repudiated his theories and confessed his faith in a dramatic deathbed conversion. With meticulous scholarship, historian James Moore has shown how quickly these false stories spread. His research revealed that *one week* after Darwin's burial, a Welsh minister preached a sermon claiming that Darwin had confessed his faith on his deathbed.[159]

We can also look to the mythology around what UFO enthusiasts call the "Roswell incident." In 1947, an Air Force weather balloon crashed at a ranch near Roswell, New Mexico. There was little to no interest in this incident for more than thirty years, but in 1980, a book was written by two sensationalist writers claiming the balloon was actually a crashed alien spaceship, from which aliens were recovered and autopsied, followed by a massive government cover-up. Within ten years, other authors joined the fray and began producing their own, often-conflicting accounts of the Roswell incident. From there, the mythology took on a life of its own, spawning an entire industry of UFO-related books, stories, and merchandise around Roswell, despite no compelling evidence of extraterrestrial visitation. And this was in an age of photographs, videos, and newspapers.

The point is that it is entirely plausible that legendary elements were added onto the story of Jesus's life and death almost immediately and certainly by the time Paul started writing his epistles fifteen to twenty years later. The legends had time to evolve considerably by the time Mark's Gospel was written and further still by the writing of the remaining Gospels.

We know from experience that people lie and distort the truth. We know that disappointed believers in a cause find ways to go on after hope seems lost, even to the extent of distorting reality and rewriting history. These are not extraordinary events or claims. They are common occurrences. The principle of analogy tells us they are far more probable than the alternative demanded by Christian apologists—that the Gospels record actual miraculous events.

6

WHAT IS THE HARM
OF CHRISTIANITY?

The most heinous and the most cruel crimes of which history has record have been committed under the cover of religion or equally noble motives.

—Mohandas K. Gandhi, *Young India*, 1927

Men never commit evil so fully and joyfully as when they do it for religious conviction.

—Blaise Pascal, *Pensees*

The three monotheisms share a series of identical forms of aversion: hatred of reason and intelligence; hatred of freedom; hatred of all books in the name of one book alone; hatred of sexuality, women, and pleasure; hatred of feminine; hatred of body, of desires, of drives. Instead Judaism, Christianity, and Islam extol faith and belief, obedience and submission, taste for death and longing for the beyond, the asexual angel and chastity, virginity and monogamous love, wife and mother, soul and spirit. In other words, life crucified and nothingness exalted.

—Michel Onfray, *The Atheist Manifesto*

Previously, I demonstrated many of the reasons I am an atheist and given what I believe to be many compelling reasons to reject Christianity. Still, some will say that that they simply choose to be Christians despite the lack of good evidence in its favor. They find it intuitively appealing and see no harm in it. What's more, they may wonder why I would write a book like this, pointing out all the problems with a religion they see as a positive force in the world. I maintain there is no good evidence that Christianity represents a net positive force. Christianity has done and continues to do substantial harm in the world and serves as the cause of great misery. The burden is on those Christians defending their faith to demonstrate other-wise, and this they have not done.

At this point, I will make an exception to my general rule so as not to implicitly give the wrong impression. So far, I have largely avoided com-parisons of Christianity with other religions. Some might take my focus on Christianity to suggest that I think it to be the religion of greatest harm. This is not the case. In fact, I believe certain forms of Islam to be a far greater threat to the modern world than the most virulent forms of Christi-anity. After all, you don't see suicidal Christian jihadists or Christians forc-ibly setting up caliphates under religious rule.

As with Christianity, Islam does not represent a monolithic system of belief. There are moderates and extremists, with the far greater danger ly-ing with the latter group. But Islam has nothing analogous to liberal Chris-tianity. Even moderate Muslims take their holy books literally, considering them to be infallible, and are far less willing than liberal Christians to make allowances for changing moral views on such issues such as homosexuality. There has been nothing like the Enlightenment in the Muslim world. Islam today is more analogous to Christianity three centuries ago, and in a world filled with weapons of mass destruction, that is exceptionally dangerous.

Self-proclaimed atheist Muslim Ali Rizvi says, "The left is wrong on Islam. The right is wrong on Muslims."[1] Rizvi's point is that Islam can and should be criticized for its doctrines without demonizing Muslims who are mostly good people trying to live morally righteous lives. Rizvi defends what he sees as positive aspects of Muslim culture while holding the religion accountable for the doctrines that promote intolerance, bigotry, and violence. Rizvi was critical of Donald Trump's Muslim ban because it painted all Muslims with the same brush, but he feels that the "failure of liberals to address Islamism from an honest and moral position left a void that allowed the Trumpian right to opportunistically address [it] from a position of xenophobia and big-otry."[2] Rizvi calls for a distinction between religion and people:

> You can't say, hey, I have a lot of Jewish friends who eat bacon, so Judaism must be okay with pork. It doesn't make sense. So when I say that most Mus-lims I know are very peaceful and law-abiding, that they wouldn't dream of

violence, that doesn't erase all of the violence and the calls for martyrdom and jihad and holy war against disbelievers in Islamic scripture. Most of my Muslim friends, both in Pakistan and here, had premarital sex and drank alcohol too. That doesn't mean Islam allows either of those things. The hard truth is there is a lot of violence endorsed in the Quran, and there are other terrible things, as there are in the Old Testament. But there are more people in the world—even if it's a minority of Muslims—who take their scripture seriously. It's dishonest to say that violent Muslim groups like ISIS are being un-Islamic.[3]

My goal is to take the same approach to Christianity. The doctrines of Christianity can account for harm and should be held accountable, but I do not intend to simultaneously demonize Christians. Bad ideas can lead good people to rationalize bad acts as well as good ones. In such cases, the ideas are the problem. This chapter addresses those ideas.

THE SUBVERSIVE EFFECTS OF DOGMA

People of faith often claim that the crimes of Hitler, Stalin, Mao and Pol Pot were the inevitable product of unbelief. The problem with fascism and communism, however, is not that they are too critical of religion; the problem is that they are too much like religions. Such regimes are dogmatic to the core and generally give rise to personality cults that are indistinguishable from cults of religious hero worship. Auschwitz, the gulag and the killing fields were not examples of what happens when human beings reject religious dogma; they are examples of political, racial and nationalistic dogma run amok. There is no society in human history that ever suffered because its people became too reasonable.

—Sam Harris, *Letter to a Christian Nation*

Looking back at the worst times, it always seems that they were times in which there were people who believed with absolute faith and absolute dogmatism in something. And they were so serious in this matter that they insisted that the rest of the world agree with them.

—Richard P. Feynman, *The Meaning of it All:
Thoughts of a Citizen-Scientist*

Much of the harm attributable to Christianity is due to its reliance on dogma. Dogma refers to beliefs or doctrines established by an authority within a particular group or organization. Acceptance and implementation of the beliefs are of paramount importance. The beliefs are not to be disputed, doubted, or diverged from—only followed. Those who do dispute, doubt, or diverge are to be marginalized, demonized, or ostracized. Where beliefs cannot be supported with evidence, adherents are directed to simply accept them anyway. Within a dogmatic institution, conformity is encouraged and often enforced. Dogma has no error-correcting mechanism and by its nature precludes such a mechanism. It is static, rigid, and impervious to reasoned argument. It may be altered only by the recognized authority that has a vested interest in maintaining the status quo. Accordingly, it is generally dismissive of new information or evidence, which is considered threatening.

One way to understand dogma is to look at its opposite. Science represents the antithesis of a dogmatic belief system. All "truths" of science are understood to be provisional, subject to modification based on sufficient evidence. Such truths obtain their respective places in the hierarchy by being proven through the processes of science. Reason and debate are always welcomed and encouraged. There is no equivalent of heresy or blasphemy, for as Robert Ingersoll says, "blasphemy is what an old mistake says of a newly discovered truth."[4] The highest accolades in science are reserved for those who successfully challenge conventional scientific wisdom and create a new paradigm. If even a cherished and highly respected scientific belief is demonstrated to be incorrect, it is abandoned without fanfare.

Religions "of the book," such as Christianity, Judaism, and Islam, are by definition dogmatic because of the privilege they grant to Scripture. They each consider certain scriptural texts as ultimate authorities. Such texts may be interpreted by the church itself but are not to be genuinely questioned by individual members, and while interpretation is acceptable, outright denial is not. There are always core beliefs not to be seriously doubted. Within Christianity, different denominations may be distinguished by their degree of dogmatism, with conservatives being less tolerant of dissent than liberals, but all are dogmatic to some extent.

Religious dogma is admittedly a mixed bag. Some aspects are positive, while others are negative. All major religions, however, have passages within their canon that can reasonably be read to justify hatred and intolerance—especially against those of different religions or values. When misguided, dogma provides convenient excuses to those inclined to act on their baser instincts, just as it requires those who would ordinarily act charitably to sublimate those positive instincts and act against them, encouraging bad behaviors while discouraging good ones.

Religions are not, of course, the only dogmatic institutions or belief systems, though they are certainly the most prolific and successful today.

As recognized by the previous Sam Harris quote, Communism and certain forms of fascism are also dogmatic. They invoke the same methods of indoctrination and thought control as religions. They insist on the same commitment to authority.

Without dogma, humans are left to their own human natures. Some are bad, and some are good, and their behavior is likely to reflect that. Because evolution has endowed humans with empathy, however, I believe that most people are generally good, with a strong desire to do the right thing, a finding supported by decades of psychological research. People may act contrary to this desire based on such fleeting emotions as fear, frustration, and anger, but this does not mean their overall natures are evil. Without dogma, there is very good reason to believe that people would typically do the right thing, and it would be very difficult to systematically convince them otherwise.

The only way to get someone to do something they would otherwise consider wrong is to convince them it is right. And the only reliable way to do this is to use dogma. Without dogma, it would be impossible to get large numbers of people to perform terrible acts or to accept them. An individual who subscribes to a dogma, however, can turn off or at least sublimate her own internal ethical filter and accept things she would otherwise find objectionable because they advance the greater good of the dogma. Dogma can cause people to ignore their intuitive feelings of empathy and justify acting against them. As Voltaire observes, "Those who can make you believe absurdities can make you commit atrocities."[5] This is why dogma and dogmatic belief systems are so dangerous: They can cause good people to do or accept very bad things.

The final problem with dogma is that it gives rise to a certainty unjustified by reason and evidence. The typical role of doubt and conscience in moderating one's morally questionable actions is minimized or even eliminated. For those inspired by dogma to do bad things, that same dogma makes them bold and exceptionally determined in doing them.

CHRISTIANITY SUPPORTS TRIBALISM AND JUSTIFIES BIGOTRY AND PREJUDICE

People don't simply wake up one day and commit genocide. They start by setting themselves apart from others, diminishing the stature of those adhering to dissenting beliefs in small, insidious steps. They begin by saying, "We're the righteous, and we'll tolerate those others." And as the toleration diminishes over time, the inevitable harms are overlooked.

—Michael Newdow, *In His Name*

The Bible has been quoted throughout Western history to justify the violence done to racial minorities, women, Jews and homosexuals. It might be difficult for some Christians to understand, but it is not difficult to document the terror enacted by believers in the name of Christianity.

—Bishop John Shelby Spong, *The Sins of Scripture*

You can safely assume that you've created God in your own image when it turns out that God hates all the same people you do.

—Anne Lamott, *Traveling Mercies: Some Thoughts on Faith*

Imagine there's no heaven. It's easy if you try. No hell below us. Above us only sky. Imagine all the people, living for today. . . . Imagine there's no countries. It isn't hard to do. Nothing to kill or die for. And no religion too. Imagine all the people. Living life in peace. . . . I hope someday you'll join us. And the world will be as one.

—John Lennon, "Imagine"

Evolution has bred humans to be naturally tribal. In Jared Diamond's book *The World until Yesterday,* he demonstrates how man evolved in an environment in which he might never meet anyone outside his tribe. If he did, then it was almost certain that they would be hostile. There was no common language among tribes and great competition for resources. When tribes came into contact, the most common response was open warfare.

Powerful incentives existed to freeload on others by posturing as a member of another's tribe. As such freeloading would quickly deplete the tribe's resources if unchecked, tribes were incentivized to develop countermeasures. These included unique rituals or bodily modifications, like circumcision or tattoos, to distinguish the members of one tribe from those of others. Tribes were likewise incentivized to root out these imposters and banish or even kill them so they couldn't freeload again.

While tribalism had definite survival benefits for our ancient ancestors, it is highly problematic in the modern world. No longer can people expect to live their lives in isolation from those of different races, religions, or cultures. Today, the world is highly interconnected. The old lines of demarcation become less and less useful or even less relevant. Such tribalistic traits as prejudice and xenophobia are far more often counterproductive. They can even be deadly. And yet, as Bertrand Russell so cogently recognizes, many people today cannot be happy "unless they hate some other person, nation, or creed."[6]

Religions, including Christianity, legitimize tribalism. They perpetuate and encourage the in-group/out-group thinking that leads to hatred and distrust among people of different "tribes."[7] Religions like Christianity privilege ancient texts that recognize tribal differences and enforce segregation and marginalization of certain groups. This can involve the indoctrination of children into xenophobic hatred and to the rationalization of existing prejudices held by adults. In the worst cases, it can lead to horrific violence. As Thomas Paine observes, "Belief in a cruel God makes a cruel man."[8] You don't need religious Scripture to justify love, but no better tool has been invented to justify hate.

Deviancy is defined as a break from the social norm. It represents what societies deem unacceptable. But the writers of the Bible had a relatively infantile system of social norms. Acts identified as evil represented subjective definitions of deviancy rather than absolute truths. In fact, many of these are rightly disregarded by civilized societies today as barbaric. The biblical authors were biased against other cultural groups and did not recognize how individual and social well-being could be effectively harmonized. Accordingly, they demonized societal deviants through a form of institutionalized prejudices.

Jack David Eller, in his seminal work on religion and hostility, explains how the lack of empathy toward "other" groups engendered by religious teachings can systematically lead otherwise peaceful people to violence:

> A person does not have to be a sociopath to feel good about causing harm and suffering—or to feel little or nothing at all about it. Rather what we have discovered is that a human needs only a belief system that teaches that he or she is acting for a good reason (even a "higher cause"), under someone else's authority. . . . Along the way, if the individual can learn, by way of gradual escalation, to commit violence against someone who is worth less—or completely worthless, less than a human being—then violence becomes not only possible but likely, if not certain.[9]

The results of this mind-set are reflected in the history of Christianity. As retired bishop John Shelby Spong writes, "Embarrassing as it may be to those of us who call ourselves Christians, the fact is that more people have been killed in the history of the world in conflicts over and about religion than over any other single factor."[10] And as Charles Kimball acknowledges, "A strong case can be made that the history of Christianity contains considerably more violence and destruction than that of most other major religions."[11]

Multiple studies demonstrate the effect of human emotion on prejudices. Researchers have been able to reliably predict such prejudices based on how strongly people register feelings of discomfort and disgust in response to new or different stimuli. A person with an immediate sense of discomfort with new foods, new places, and new people is more likely to hold negative biases against people of different cultures, ethnicities, and religions. The feelings and associations are automatic and unconscious in the individual but, importantly, cannot be rationally justified. This makes it difficult for someone holding these feelings to persuade others to adopt them or to defend them if challenged.

Religions of Scripture, such as Christianity, provide reasons and instruments of persuasion. They allow prejudices and superstitions to be elevated to the status of moral truths, which must be applied universally and enforced. People are easily divided into "right" and "wrong" based on their beliefs and affiliations. The Scripture allows adherents to validate and justify their own preexisting beliefs by projecting them onto God. It licenses their prejudices and provides warrant to defend them and persuade others to their views.

For others, the Scripture shapes their beliefs. A child begins with no prejudices or biases. These are learned behaviors, though for reasons discussed previously some might be more predisposed than others to adopting them. Any religious Scripture that validates treating others differently based on immutable characteristics creates adults who treat people differently based on immutable characteristics. For many, religion requires them to sublimate their natural moral instincts to conform with scriptural rules and commands, which, as we've seen of Christian Scripture, can be malignant. Besides the effect these scriptural proscriptions have on the moral norms of individual believers, they also have a broader impact. The religious often feel compelled to interfere with society's naturally evolving norms of morality, which has a retarding effect on those norms.

Religion, furthermore, is uniquely immunized to the critical thought processes and social pressures that marginalize and eradicate other misguided traditions. This is why religion is the last bastion for sexists, racists, homophobes, and others who hold to hate without rational justifications. Religion says you need no rational reason if you can justify your tribalism by an appeal to religious tradition, be that Scripture or otherwise. "God told me to hate you" is the only justification required. As many have implicitly argued, it's not prejudice if you call it religion.

RACE

> Frederick Douglass told in his Narrative how his condition as a slave
> became worse when his master underwent a religious conversion that
> allowed him to justify slavery as the punishment of the children of Ham.
> Mark Twain described his mother as a genuinely good person, whose
> soft heart pitied even Satan, but who had no doubt about the legitimacy
> of slavery, because in years of living in antebellum Missouri she had
> never heard any sermon opposing slavery, but only countless sermons
> preaching that slavery was God's will. With or without religion, good
> people can behave well and bad people can do evil; but for good people
> to do evil—that takes religion.
>
> —Steven Weinberg, "A Designer Universe"

> It is appalling that the most segregated hour of Christian America is
> eleven o'clock on Sunday morning.
>
> —Martin Luther King Jr., *Stride Toward Freedom*

Race, religion, and nationalism may seem like distinct concepts to us today, but they were not so distinct in the days of the Bible. God's chosen people, the Jews, represented a distinctive race, religion, *and* national identity. God's clear preference for the Jews over all other tribes in the Old Testament is the very essence of tribalism. The United Nations defines racism, in part, as "any distinction, exclusion, restriction or preference based on race, color, descent, or national or ethnic origin or religious intolerance motivated by racist considerations."[12] It is difficult to find a page of the Old Testament that is not replete with racism. After recognizing the Jews as His chosen people, God repeatedly instructs them to destroy without mercy the people of other tribes.

God repeatedly forbids intermarriage or intercultural exchanges with people of other tribes and endorses killing those who disregard these rules (Numbers 25:1–13; Nehemiah 13:23–30). Jesus himself degrades a woman of a different tribe, comparing her to a dog and refusing to help her until finally she grovels before him (Matthew 15:22–28). Tribal intolerance is one of the most recurring themes of the Old Testament, which is never explicitly rejected by Jesus and occasionally even reflected in his own words.

One of the greatest problems with the Bible, at least where it comes to race relations, is its many passages condoning slavery, either explicitly or

implicitly by establishing codes of conduct for slaveholders. These include
the following:

- Leviticus 25:44–46: "Your male and female slaves are to come from the
  nations around you; from them you may buy slaves. You may also buy
  some of the temporary residents living among you and members of
  their clans born in your country, and they will become your property.
  You can bequeath them to your children as inherited property and
  can make them slaves for life, but you must not rule over your fellow
  Israelites ruthlessly."
- Exodus 21:1–21: "These are the laws you are to set before [masters
  of Hebrew slaves]. If you buy a Hebrew servant, he is to serve you
  for six years. But in the seventh year, he shall go free, without paying
  anything. If he comes alone, he is to go free alone; but if he has a wife
  when he comes, she is to go with him. If his master gives him a wife
  and she bears him sons or daughters, the woman and her children
  shall belong to her master, and only the man shall go free. But if the
  servant declares, 'I love my master and my wife and children and do
  not want to go free,' then his master must take him before the judges.
  He shall take him to the door or the doorpost and pierce his ear with
  an awl. Then he will be his servant for life. If a man sells his daughter
  as a servant, she is not to go free as male servants do. If she does not
  please the master who has selected her for himself, he must let her be
  redeemed. He has no right to sell her to foreigners, because he has
  broken faith with her. . . . Anyone who beats their male or female slave
  with a rod must be punished if the slave dies as a direct result, but they
  are not to be punished if the slave recovers after a day or two, since the
  slave is their property."
- Ephesians 6:5: "Slaves, obey your earthly masters with respect and
  fear, and with sincerity of heart, just as you would obey Christ."
- 1 Timothy 6:1–2: "All who are under the yoke of slavery should consider their masters worthy of full respect, so that God's name and our
  teaching may not be slandered. Those who have believing masters
  should not show them disrespect just because they are fellow believers. Instead, they should serve them even better because their masters
  are dear to them as fellow believers and are devoted to the welfare of
  their slaves."
- Titus 2:9–10: "Teach slaves to be subject to their masters in everything,
  to try to please them, not to talk back to them, and not to steal from

them, but to show that they can be fully trusted, so that in every way they will make the teaching about God our Savior attractive."
- 1 Peter 2:18: "Slaves, in reverent fear of God submit yourselves to your masters, not only to those who are good and considerate, but also to those who are harsh."

It is clear from the New Testament that neither Jesus nor Paul ever envisioned a world without slavery and that neither considered slavery inherently evil or unjust. Like their contemporaries, they saw it as the natural order of things. Contrary to the claims of apologists that the slavery referenced in the Bible was voluntary, temporary, or entirely unlike the African slave trade, such passages as Leviticus 25:44–46 make it crystal clear that non-Israelite slaves were *permanent possessions*, with whom their masters could do as they pleased, including beating or killing them if necessary. The same passage blesses the buying of slaves. Numbers 31:17–18 blesses the kidnapping of young virgins, presumably to be sex slaves.

It was Christopher Columbus, a devout Christian, who immediately upon arrival in the New World forced Native Americans into forced servitude and laid the seeds for the transatlantic slave trade, officially started by fellow Christian Nicolas de Ovando in 1501, through which *more than ten million* Africans would be forcibly removed to the United States in chains. Around two million died on the voyage. This practice was endorsed by the Catholic Church, which maintained that slavery was divinely sanctioned. Pope Nicholas V declared in 1455 that the Portuguese, to whom had been granted exclusive rights to territories along the West African coast, had the right to invade, plunder, and "reduce their persons to perpetual slavery."[13]

Slavery in the American colonies officially began in Virginia in 1619 and would persist for 246 years, meaning slavery has been an American institution far longer than not. From the beginning, Christian churches worked hand in hand with local governments to support slavery. It had been a long-standing custom in England that Christians, being spiritual brothers and sisters, could not enslave one another. The sacrament of baptism conferred one with the rights and duties of a Christian. The Virginia General Assembly, however, passed a law holding that the "conferring of baptism does not alter the condition of the person as to his bondage or freedom."[14] Similar laws, representing overt coordination between church and state, were rapidly passed in other states. From this point forward, there would be two tiers of Christians with very different rights: the free and the enslaved. When Christianity was taught to incoming slaves, the message was consistent: Jesus could save one's soul but not break one's chains.

Ultimately, African Americans started their own Christian congregations and parishes, but White churches refused to allow them in. The story of St. Philip's, the first Black Episcopal parish in New York City, formed in 1809, is typical. St. Philip's faced repeated rejection from the Episcopal diocese until 1846, when the church's status was formally addressed at the annual diocesan convention. Their request for inclusion was denied, as well as prospectively "any other colored congregation" on the basis that Blacks did not possess the "qualities which would render their intercourse with the members of a Church Convention useful."[15] In other words, the position of the American Christian community was that Blacks were subhuman and unworthy. The first American Black Catholic priest, Augustus Tolton, had to study in Rome, after saving ten years to travel there from his home state of Missouri, because no Catholic seminary in the United States would accept a Black student.

Black Christians and their churches did work with White abolitionists to eliminate slavery, but their efforts were constantly frustrated by Christian Scripture. The overwhelming majority of Christian churches interpreted the Scripture as supporting slavery:

> [A]bolitionist claims were mostly met with skepticism because they advanced arguments based on the "spirit" rather than the "letter" of the law. Even when abolitionists made their case from the Bible, they were criticized because they were not able to cite a specific passage that explicitly condemned slavery. Instead, they had to argue from broader principles such as "love of neighbor" and the unity of humankind. Southern theologians, by contrast, appealed to a "plain meaning" of Scripture which they claimed clearly showed righteous and godly people who enslaved people with apparently no rebuke or accusation of sinfulness. Proslavery advocates grew confident in the Confederate cause because it seemed like the proslavery theological arguments respected the Bible's authority and employed a straightforward method of scriptural interpretation. . . . For most Christians, even those sympathetic to the plight of black people, the southern proslavery advocates seemed to have a clearer and simpler biblical argument, one that did not require sources outside of Scripture or employ unfamiliar interpretations.[16]

Southern White Christians consistently affirmed that God sanctioned slavery in Scripture and that bondage under White authority was the natural state for people of African descent. The president of the Confederacy, Jefferson Davis, justified the Confederacy's position in the Civil War as follows: "[Slavery] was established by decree of Almighty God. . . . [I]t is sanctioned in the Bible, in both Testaments, from Genesis to Revelation."[17]

Following the Civil War, the defeated Southerners blended painful memories of the war with Christian dogma into a new mythology of the Lost Cause. The narrative of the Lost Cause portrayed the pre–Civil War South as a virtuous, patriotic group of Christian communities wanting only to maintain their peaceful way of life until the godless and aggressive federal government of the North attacked to destroy it out of sheer jealousy. In this interpretation, the South was only defending itself and its uniquely Christian culture. The most prominent purveyor of the Lost Cause mythology was *Confederate Veteran* magazine, printed by the Southern Methodist publishing house.

Perhaps the most well-known organization peddling the Lost Cause narrative was the Ku Klux Klan, founded in the 1860s. The violence and terror it caused became such a problem that in 1871 Congress passed the Ku Klux Klan Act to criminalize its activities federally. The Klan morphed through various iterations over the next 150 years but maintained its unique fusion of Christianity, nationalism, and White supremacy.[18] In *The Gospel According to the Klan*, Kelly Baker concludes the Klan "was not just an order to defend America but also a campaign to protect and celebrate Protestantism. It was a *religious order*."[19] As recently as 2014, the leader of the Klan confirmed that it was, first and foremost, a Christian organization.[20]

Biblical endorsements of racial purity and prohibitions against intermarriage have provided ample ammunition to racists and segregationists. According to historian Jane Dailey, concern about cross-racial sexual activity was at the heart of the religious case for segregation, which was spearheaded by conservative Christians.[21] Christian segregationists regularly cited the Bible to support their positions, claiming, for example, that "God Himself" had drawn boundary lines to keep races and peoples separate, that "miscegenation and amalgamation are sins of man in direct defiance with the will of God," and that "God created and established the color line."[22]

In 1867, just two years after the American Civil War brought an end to slavery, the Pennsylvania Supreme Court upheld segregated railway cars on the grounds that the "natural law which forbids [racial intermarriage] and that social amalgamation which leads to a corruption of races, *is as clearly divine as that which imparted to [the races] different natures*."[23] This same divinity rationale was later adopted by state supreme courts in Alabama, Indiana, and Virginia to justify bans on interracial marriage and by justices in Kentucky to support residential segregation and segregated colleges.[24] There is no evidence that any Christians of the time found these views to be controversial.

Following the seminal 1954 Supreme Court case *Brown v. the Board of Education of Topeka*, requiring racial integration of public schools, backlash was swift and virulent. The backlash was led by prominent pastors of the day, including G. T. Gillespie; Carey L. Daniel; and W. A. Criswell, pastor of the largest Southern Baptist congregation in the country. Each quoted Christian Scripture to argue segregation was sanctioned by God.

Ross Barnett won Mississippi's governorship in a landslide in 1960 after claiming that the "good Lord was the original segregationist."[25] Senator Harry Byrd of Virginia relied heavily on passages from Genesis, Leviticus, and the Gospel of Matthew when he spoke out against the civil rights laws on the Senate floor. Churches across the South started private schools that came to be known as "segregation academies" because they did not have to abide by the *Brown v. Board of Education* integration mandate. Most of these schools, heavily subsidized by Christian churches, used *Christian* or *Church* in their names, making the connection explicit that segregation was God's way. A 1972 report found that "individual Protestant churches in most cities have participated and often led the private school movement during desegregation."[26]

Christian apologists respond to charges of systemic Christian racism by pointing to Martin Luther King Jr. or other African American Christian leaders of the 1950s and 1960s, as if these represented Christian attitudes generally. But as historian Jemar Tisby writes, these individuals represented the exception rather than the rule:

> All too often, Christians name a few individuals who stood against the racism of their day and claim them as heroes. They fail to recognize how rarely believers made public and persistent commitments to racial equality against the culture of their churches and denominations. . . . [O]ur collective memory of the proportion of Christians involved [in the Civil Rights movement] may be somewhat skewed. In reality, precious few Christians publicly aligned themselves with the struggle for black freedom in the 1950s and 1960s. Those who did participate faced backlash from their families, friends, and fellow Christians. At a key moment in the life of our nation, one that called for moral courage, the American church responded to much of the civil rights movement with passivity, indifference, or even outright opposition.[27]

Martin Luther King Jr. was rebuked even by the Black pastor of his own church, Reverend Joseph H. Jackson of Olivet Baptist Church in Chicago, leading King and two thousand others to leave and form the Progressive National Baptist Convention in 1961. When he spoke at the Southern Baptist Theological Seminary that same year, churches across the South rescinded their regular donations to the seminary in a fierce backlash. Even King's calls for peaceful racial equality were too much for them.

Billy Graham, the effective leader of the Evangelical community in the 1960s and 1970s, is often hailed as a religious moderate sympathetic to the cause of civil rights. When criticisms are made of systemic Evangelical racism, Graham is offered up as the rebuttal. But Graham refused to endorse the Civil Rights Act and, as King's message became increasingly popular, directed King to "put the brakes on a little bit."[28] Graham held back from declaring solidarity with protesting Blacks or from demonstrating alongside activists during the march on Selma. In each case, Graham stood with the racially oppressive status quo. That is hardly a show of courage.

Richard Nixon won the presidency in 1969 with 68 percent of the Evangelical vote, the highest ever for a Republican presidential candidate, based on an approach known today as the Southern strategy. The Southern strategy, which Republicans continued to employ for the next forty years, exploited racial backlash against the civil rights movement. In 2010, Republican National Convention chairman Michael Steele explained the Southern strategy as alienating minority voters by focusing on White male votes in the South and exploiting their prejudices. The goal was to demonize Blacks and ride the wave of White anger and resentment to victory. One of Nixon's closest advisors, H. R. Haldeman, said of the Southern strategy, "[Nixon] emphasized that you have to face the fact that the whole problem is really the blacks. The key is to devise a system that recognizes this while not appearing to."[29]

Perhaps the most significant event in Republican politics of the last century was the development of a politically active group of Evangelical Christians who came to be known as the Religious Right. For those who associate the Religious Right with abortion, it may be surprising that the original issue motivating it into existence was segregation—specifically the IRS's decision to withdraw tax exemption from "segregation academies."[30] In 1971, the Supreme Court held, in *Green v. Connally*, that "racially discriminatory private schools are not entitled to federal tax exemption provided for charitable, educational institutions." Because the IRS did not actively pursue enforcement of this mandate, its effects were limited. In 1976, however, the IRS revoked the tax-exempt status of Bob Jones University, a fundamentalist Christian school with a tradition and policy of segregation. The IRS issued new guidelines in 1978 that clarified it would be actively enforcing this mandate going forward.

In 1979, Jerry Falwell met with top religious leaders from across the country to discuss the IRS guidelines and what should be done about them. Falwell had in mind a religious coalition that would become a powerful political influence. Paul Weyrich, who would later go on to cofound conservative think tank the Heritage Foundation, used the phrase *moral majority*, and that's what Falwell decided to call it. The Moral Majority courted conservative Mormons, Jews, and Catholics, as well as Pentecostals and many Protestant denominations. In reflecting on the creation of the Moral Majority, the most effective organization of the Religious Right, Weyrich says, "What galvanized the Christian community was not abortion, school prayer, or the [Equal Rights Amendment]. . . . What changed their minds was Jimmy Carter's intervention against the Christian schools, trying to deny them tax-exempt status on the basis of so-called *de facto* segregation."[31] In short, the members of the Moral Majority were initially driven to action by the federal government's attempt to stop a Christian university from segregating Black students based on Christian Scripture.

In 1980, Ronald Reagan, a man who unapologetically called Black people "monkeys," won the presidency with full enthusiastic support from the Religious Right. That same year, President Reagan spoke at Bob Jones University and called it a "great institution," despite its persistent and well-publicized refusal to change its stance on race. On the national stage, Bob Jones University's segregation policy was its claim to fame. Shortly afterward, Reagan led his administration to reverse the IRS's ruling against Bob Jones University and restore its tax-exempt status. Unfortunately for Reagan, this led to a public backlash, causing him to reverse course and allow the IRS to revoke the tax-exempt status of racially discriminatory schools.

There is ample evidence that Christian Scripture has led to racial division and stood in the way of reconciliation and healing. Our current political divisions can be traced in part to the legacy of racism that grew in significant ways out of that Scripture and those who interpreted it to support slavery, segregation, and discrimination based solely on the color of one's skin.

RELIGIOUS INTOLERANCE

We despise all reverences and all the objects of reverence which are outside the pale of our own list of sacred things. And yet, with strange inconsistency, we are shocked when other people despise and defile the things which are holy to us.

—Mark Twain, *Follow the Equator* (1897)

And whoever would not seek the Lord, the God of Israel, should be put to death, whether young or old, man or woman.

—2 Chronicles 15:13

Religious intolerance is failing to respect the rights of other people to hold religious beliefs different from your own. This does not mean academically critiquing a belief system in good faith but rather pushing to punish people for their beliefs or coercing them into different beliefs. It would include forcing one's religious beliefs or practices on others, restricting human rights of people of an identifiable religious group, devaluing the religious beliefs of others as evil so they are ostracized, and inhibiting the freedom of people to change their religion. Christianity has a long history of all these.

Many times in the Bible, God acknowledges that He is a jealous god, by which He means jealous of His people following other deities and religions (Exodus 20:5, 34:14; Deuteronomy 4:24; Joshua 24:19). The first commandment in all versions of his Ten Commandments is the prohibition against worshipping any other gods. Again and again, God and His prophets characterize the religions of other tribes as evil and order their followers destroyed. The overwhelming theme of the Old Testament is religious exclusivity and intolerance. Having discussed this earlier, I do not revisit it here.

Religious exclusivity and intolerance also permeate the New Testament. A frequent message is those holding beliefs inconsistent with Christianity are not simply wrong but *immoral*. Paul considers the gods of all other religions "devils," with whom Christians must not associate (1 Corinthians 10:20–21; 2 Corinthians 6:14–17; Romans 16:17). John calls nonbelievers "deceivers" and warns Christians from allowing them into their homes (2 John 1:7–10). Paul curses with blindness a Jew who tries to turn people away from Christianity, calling him a "child of the devil" and an "enemy of righteousness" (Acts 13:6–11). Paul even preaches intolerance toward other Christians if they don't agree with Paul's specific teachings (Galatians 1:8–9). The clear message is that those without the proper belief must be shunned and treated as vile enemies.

Jesus himself calls for the murder of anyone who doesn't follow him: "But those mine enemies, which would not that I should reign over them, bring hither, and slay them before me" (Luke 19:27).[32] Jesus clarifies whom he considers such enemies in Matthew 12:30: "Whoever is not with me is against me and whoever does not gather with me scatters." In other words, Jesus's enemies include anyone not actively working to gather followers for him. Jesus claims as part of his mission to pit family members against each other, so believers and nonbelievers kill each other (Matthew 10:21, 34–37). Jesus also preaches that the wrath of God is on all nonbelievers, who will be condemned to eternal torture (John 3:36, 12:48). According to Jesus, anyone who rejects his religious movement or stands in its way doesn't deserve to flourish or even live.[33] Should it be a surprise when Christians, like Jesus, view nonbelievers as not worthy of coexisting on the same planet?

With the conversion of Constantine in 312 CE, Christianity became the dominant religion in the Roman Empire. Before long, the previously persecuted Christians became the persecutors, and the views of anyone not adhering to the orthodox Christian faith were actively suppressed. One of the earliest examples occurred in 383 CE with the burning of the heretic Priscillian and six of his followers at the stake. Later Christian emperors officially sanctioned attacks on pagan worship, leading to the destruction of innumerable pagan temples, with *pagan* defined as any religion other than Christianity.

Arguably the most influential of the Christian Church Fathers, Saint Augustine of Hippo, was a strong supporter of religious persecution. He developed a theological defense of it, which was undisputed for the next thousand years in Western Christianity. The only disagreement among Christian leaders concerned the *extent* to which heretics should be persecuted. Augustine himself advocated fines, imprisonment, banishment, and moderate floggings. Others presumably thought light floggings would suffice.

After the decline of the Roman Empire, encounters between Christians and pagans became increasingly confrontational. Such Christian kings as Charlemagne and Olaf I of Norway were well known for their violence against pagans. The Catholic Church established the Inquisition to counter any religious teachings or ideas contrary to orthodox Christianity, resulting in the torture and death of thousands. The Fourth Council of Lateran (1215 CE) codified the theory and practice of persecution, declaring that all secular authorities be compelled by church authority to exterminate "all heretics pointed out by the Church."[34] Saint Thomas Aquinas summed up the standard medieval position, declaring that obstinate heretics deserved "not only to be separated from the Church, but also to be eliminated from the world by death."[35]

During the late middle ages, the Crusades pitted Christians against pagans throughout Europe. Christians massacred thousands of Muslim and Jewish civilians when they took Jerusalem in 1099. The Baltic Crusades saw the systematic extermination of pagan tribes and customs throughout Northern Europe. Because of the enormous death toll of the Crusades, the pagan religions in Europe disappeared almost entirely.

European colonialism led to the suppression of indigenous religions in virtually all the territories conquered or usurped by the Europeans. The Spanish colonization of the Americas, for example, largely destroyed the Aztec and Inca civilizations. Through the Goa Inquisition, hundreds were persecuted, even killed, in colonial India between 1560 and 1812 CE for practicing their ancestral religions. By the eighteenth century, European persecutions of unsanctioned beliefs, having largely met their primary goals of eradication, had softened to mere overt religious discrimination in the form of legal restrictions on those who did not accept the official Christian faith.

With the Enlightenment, Europe and the Americas finally took significant steps to reject religious intolerance, which required a rejection of biblical authority. Such Enlightenment thinkers as Thomas Jefferson, James Madison, and John Adams extended religious toleration even to atheists. The tolerationist movement arguably reached its fulfillment in the Virginia Statute for Religious Freedom and the First Amendment to the US Constitution.[36]

More than two hundred years later, Christian intolerance of those not sharing their religious views is no longer as overt but still exists. It is perhaps most extreme in Christian views toward atheists. A survey by the University of Minnesota put atheists atop the list of minorities considered least American, least desirable to join one's family through marriage, and least acceptable as a political candidate.[37] Despite up to 25 percent of the American public being nonbelievers, not a single member of Congress, the federal judiciary, or the executive branch openly identifies as atheist.[38] Atheists are viewed more negatively than Muslims and gays.

Clearly, large numbers of Christians consider atheism to indicate a serious flaw in character. If this were true, then we would expect atheists to fall short of believers whenever moral behavior is studied, but as discussed elsewhere in this book, studies consistently show the opposite. These widespread prejudices are clearly irrational and based on false premises and bigotries. Considering the large number of American atheists, these prejudices affect many people, whose full views are effectively shut out of political and moral discussions. Considering the prominence and high representation atheists enjoy among just philosophers and scientists, America has been deprived of many distinctive and well-informed voices through Christian intolerance.

Lending to the wave of intolerance today is the false narrative of Christian persecution. Consider the following: A young boy is disciplined for praying over this school lunch; another is forced to submit to a psychological exam after drawing a picture of Jesus; a Veterans Hospital bans Christmas cards with religious messages; a high school track team is disqualified after a team member thanks God for the team's victory; an Air Force sergeant is fired because he opposes same-sex marriage; two middle school girls are forced to perform a lesbian kiss as part of an antibullying program.

These stories have two things in common. First, they were reported and re-reported extensively within the past decade by Christian broadcasters, activists, elected officials, and social media sites. Second, they are all false.[39] Many have gone viral, despite a complete lack of evidence in their favor, likely because they fit within a larger narrative systematically hammered by right-wing media—that Christians, the largest and most influential religious group in the United States, actually represent a persecuted minority, being driven underground in their own country. The courts, the media, academia, and the scientific establishment are all, if you buy into the argument, besieging Christianity on every front, while Christianity valiantly struggles to hold its own. A recent Pew study found that White, Evangelical Christians believed they experienced more discrimination than Blacks, Hispanics, Jews, atheists, or even Muslims![40]

Evidence of this Christian persecution complex is easy to find. The most notorious example may be the so-called War on Christmas, which has enjoyed extensive coverage by conservative media since the mid-2000s. Such popular commentators as Bill O'Reilly and Sean Hannity would annually sound off against merchants that dared to use inclusive seasonal greetings, such as "Happy Holidays" or "Seasons Greetings," rather than "Merry Christmas." The argument appears to be that by refusing to expressly acknowledge Jesus as the "reason for the season," merchants have thrown down the gauntlet and set their vast commercial machines firmly against the forces of Christianity. The possibility this might simply be a wise and empathetic commercial decision in an increasingly multicultural marketplace is never entertained.

Catholic bishop Daniel Jenky publicly equated the Obama administration's advocacy of the Affordable Care Act with governments that "have tried to force Christians to huddle and hide within the confines of their churches," including explicit comparisons to Stalinism and Nazism.[41] Republican Texas governor and presidential candidate Rick Perry identified Satan as behind President Obama's alleged "war on religion."[42] Senator Ted Cruz and Governor Mike Huckabee, 2016 presidential candidates, made the "liberal war on religion" central tenets of their campaigns. Even relatively moderate 2012 Republican presidential candidate Mitt Romney accused President Obama as waging a war on religion with no supporting evidence.

In 2013, Phil Robertson of the A&E reality show *Duck Dynasty* was briefly suspended by the network after making antigay and racist comments in an interview with *GQ* magazine.[43] Such right-wing heavyweights as Glen Beck, Sean Hannity, and Sarah Palin wasted no time reframing the issue as one of Christian persecution. Robertson received rousing support from such organizations as the American Family Association, the Family Research Council, and the National Organization for Marriage. One Republican congressional candidate called Robertson the "Rosa Parks of our generation."[44]

Three major motion pictures within the last ten years, *God's Not Dead* (2013), *Persecuted* (2014), and *God's Not Dead 2* (2016), are premised on the myth of Christian "persecution." *God's Not Dead* tells the story of a Christian college student forced into a debate by his arrogant atheist philosophy professor after refusing to declare God dead. The student ultimately prevails, forcing the professor to admit he really just hated God all along because of his mother's death. In *Persecuted*, a minister is framed for the rape and murder of a young girl after standing up to a government plot to marginalize Christians. *God's Not Dead 2* tells of a high school teacher vilified and sued by a zealous civil liberties group after she cites Scripture in class. Despite being roundly panned by critics (Rotten Tomatoes and Metacritic reveal scores for all three films evidencing "overwhelming dislike"), all three films were heavily promoted by Christian churches. *God's Not Dead* alone made $62 million at the box office, giving rise to two sequels.

Prominent Christian leaders have been especially scathing and consistent in their assaults on so-called new atheists, such as Richard Dawkins, Sam Harris, and Christopher Hitchens, who have challenged religious beliefs more directly and publicly than others of the recent past. Although they are only raising questions and making arguments like those found in this book, they are demonized as the epitome of evil, mounting an attack on all that is good and right in the world. Within the Christian media, the new atheists are commonly referred to as "militant," as though mere words were bullets or arguments were hand grenades.

I believe this narrative of persecution stems directly from conservative Christians being on the losing end of many significant cultural shifts. Within the past ten years, Americans have increasingly parted ways with right-wing Christians on such issues as gay rights, reproductive freedom, and religious liberty for minority groups. The basic assumptions they make regarding moral behavior are no longer the cultural consensus—and often even viewed as barbaric and bigoted. Globalization has broken the insular barriers to pluralistic ideas from other cultures. The internet has provided unparalleled access to dissenting views, frustrating the efforts of fundamentalist parents to control the information flowing to their children. And those dissenting views are growing in number, as Christian claims become less tenable with each new scientific or historical discovery.

By reframing their losses as religious oppression, the Religious Right galvanizes its members to close ranks, shutting their ears to outside voices, so as to "hear no evil." Followers are thereby encouraged to treat anyone outside the fold as a dangerous enemy, intent on doing them harm. Followers are recast as soldiers for Christ doing the good work. By fetishizing suffering and linking it to Scripture, the Right reassures its followers that they remain on the correct path, with victory right around the corner. Perhaps most important, followers are encouraged to contribute their resources, such as time and money, to the righteous cause until these progressive currents can be righted and the political and social advances of their enemies rolled back.[45]

Of course, this requires a drastic redefinition of *persecution*. Anything resembling traditional persecution is absurd to claim when your religion represents the largest in the country—with control of all branches of government; complete tax exemption; freedom from government reporting requirements; and immunity from numerous laws relating to health and safety, discrimination, and lobbying activity. Every US president of the modern age, as well as more than 90 percent of Congress, has identified as Christian. Christianity has through most of American history enjoyed a vast network of hospitals, secondary schools, colleges, social services, and other entities, many of which are subsidized directly by taxpayers. As Jon Stewart explained on the *Daily Show*,

> I have to say, as someone who is not a Christian, it's hard for me to believe Christians are a persecuted people in America. God-willing, maybe one of you one day will even rise up and get to be president of this country—or maybe forty-four times in a row. But that's my point, is they've taken this idea of no establishment as persecution, because they feel entitled, not to equal status, but to greater status.[46]

Rather than oppression, Christianity has experienced vast privileges and enormous governmental accommodation. This isn't exactly the Spanish Inquisition, when members of religious groups other than Christianity were habitually tortured and killed. Now that was persecution.

In fact, once the false stories are set aside, the issues that conservative Christians characterize as persecution suggest the real problem as the failure to accord Christians *special treatment*. Christian conservatives have purposefully conflated persecution with mere criticism. They should take the advice of Ralph Waldo Emerson, who said, "Let me never fall into the vulgar mistake of dreaming that I am persecuted whenever I am contradicted."[47] They claim, for example, that secularists are trying to "silence" Christians, when in fact secularists are simply refusing to show undue respect for beliefs they consider untrue.

Those who decry "strident" atheists are really asking that people silence and censor these critical voices through social ostracism and disapproval. But there is no constitutional right for one's views to be free from criticism or commercial censure. Nor is there any right to require American taxpayers, who are drawn from across the religious spectrum, to fund the erection and maintenance of uniquely Christian monuments or Christian proselytizing in public schools or the military. The Christian Right, however, demands both and takes to the airwaves when they are not forthcoming.

The thinking seems to be that because Christians represent a majority in the United States and a supermajority in many discrete regions, they should be allowed to use public resources as they see fit. But the Constitution was designed to protect the rights of religious *minorities* by keeping the government neutral on these issues. Those working to hold the government accountable to the Constitution are not persecuting Christians. They are keeping the government true to its founding principles.

When I've been drawn into discussions of school prayer, I have offered the example of an American community in which Islam has become the dominant religion and its followers have insisted on daily Muslim prayers at the local public schools. Most Christians are aghast at such a prospect, perhaps not recognizing this would be the required result of the very system they advocate, in which public resources are allocated according to the whims of whichever faith can demonstrate the highest head count.

As evidenced by the issues they have chosen to take on, the Religious Right aims to carve out broad exemptions to generally applicable civil laws, to shield certain religiously tinged speech from any form of criticism or censure, and to silence those who do not share their specific brand of conservative "Christian" values. What they really want is a government-enforced theocracy. The persecution narrative helps them accomplish all these goals by framing those pushing back as villainous oppressors out to destroy the faith.

American Christians have *never* been systematically oppressed or denied religious liberty. The irony is that all this talk of persecution within the United States, just as with "The Boy Who Cried Wolf," has devalued the reports from other countries in which Christians *really are being persecuted*. In North Korea and Saudi Arabia, for example, Christians risk imprisonment or even death for their faith. Such groups as ISIS and the Taliban actively seek out Christians for public displays of cruelty. There are indeed Christians experiencing real persecution in the world, but they are not the right-wing American variety, which are the ones protesting the loudest. We should all stand up against real persecution while ignoring those who continue to hawk the imagined kind.

THE JEWS

> Nazi anti-Judaism was the work of godless, anti-Christian criminals. But it would not have been possible without the almost two thousand years' pre-history of "Christian" anti-Judaism.
>
> —Hans Küng, Catholic priest, theologian,
> and author, *On Being Christian*

The Jews represent a special case when discussing Christian intolerance. They were, after all, God's chosen people throughout the Old Testament. In the New Testament, however, things changed dramatically. With Paul's focus on converting Gentiles and premising salvation on grace and belief, the Jews would lose their special status. In fact, due to their collective rejection of Jesus and complicity in his death, as recounted most explicitly in John's Gospel, they were to become seen as disfavored by God and vilified. The thoroughly Jewish religion of Jesus and his followers quickly became an anti-Jewish religion—that of the Christian Church.

As recorded in the Book of Acts, the members of the first Christian community in Jerusalem were strict Jews who observed the law to the last detail and had every intention of continuing to do so. They followed all the requirements of the law, including the observance of Shabbat, circumcision, and the dietary rules. New recruits came only from among fellow Jews. These earliest Christians thought only of being good Jews and were not even called Christians until after the middle of the first century at Antioch. Until that time, they were known by various names, including the Nazarenes, Ebionites, the Brethren, Followers of the Way, Sons of Light, and

Galileans, each representing a diverse viewpoint and theology. These were all, however, considered sects of Judaism rather than separate religions.

From the accounts in Acts, it is clear it was the Greek-speaking Jews of the Diaspora, the Hellenists, whose attitude toward the Gentiles was one of openness and tolerance, who were considered by the leaders in Jerusalem the greatest threat to the fledgling group of Nazarenes. After his conversion, Paul was such a Jew. As recorded in Acts, the first great conflict in the history of the church was a clash between these Hellenized Jews and the more orthodox followers of Jesus.

The main issues in the conflict were the following: (1) Did salvation through Christ supersede or make optional obedience to the Mosaic law? and (2) if Gentiles were already God-fearing and converted to Christ, should they be required to follow the whole of Jewish law? Because Jesus's teaching had been strictly directed toward Jews in Israel, the question had not previously arisen. The Nazarenes, who were led by Peter and James, said, "Yes." They presided over the synagogue of Nazarenes in Jerusalem. The Hellenists said, "No," and they were led by a man we've already met, the religious genius and outstanding missionary known as Paul of Tarsus.

Those in Jerusalem held strictly to the Mosaic law, maintaining that circumcision was a necessity for all followers of Christ. This is what Jesus had taught (see Matthew 5:17–19; Luke 16:17). Paul, however, had undertaken missionary journeys where he had converted Greeks to Christianity. He maintained that the law was unnecessary for Greek converts. For Paul, the only requirement was to be baptized into the faith. Law or no law, he considered his Greek converts to be bona fide Christians. James and Peter, however, who had actually known Jesus and were personally familiar with his teachings, remained insistent that a Gentile had to become a Jew before becoming a Christian.

Paul set up his headquarters in Antioch, a Syrian city. Here the segregation barriers of Jews and Gentiles began to fall, and the Jewish sect of Nazarenes began to be called in Greek *Christianoi*, or "followers of Christ" (Acts 11: 19–26). Because the conflict remained unresolved, the Hellenized Christian community of Antioch sent Paul and Barnabas to Jerusalem for a conference with Peter and James. There are two accounts of this conference. Galatians 2 is Paul's own account, in which he describes taking Titus, an uncircumcised Gentile, along with him to prove his point. Here he claims an unqualified victory over the orthodox viewpoint in Jerusalem.

The second account is by Luke (Acts 15), who reports that an arrangement was worked out between the Hellenized and Jerusalem Christian factions. In both accounts, there is agreement that Paul won his argument. As a result, Paul and Barnabas became accredited as missionaries to the Gentiles. And so in 48 CE, the Council of Jerusalem established the legitimacy of Gentile Christianity and freed it from the Jewish law. From that time on, Christianity would develop its own vocabulary in Greek and Latin and also uniquely Christian modes of expression that would make it increasingly divergent from those of Judaism and its origins.[48]

Leon Poliakov points out that when Paul "made the crucial decision to exempt Christian proselytes from the commandments of the Law, and from circumcision, [he] changed the course of the world's history."[49] And so Paul became known not only as the Apostle of the Gentiles but also among his fellow Jews as the Apostate of the Law: "He had opened the door to the Gentiles without requiring from them obedience to the Law, and they in turn had introduced into the new religion all their abominations—deification of Christ, the cult of the Virgin Mary harking back to the great pagan goddesses, the setting up of images in Churches, which was an open infringement of the second Commandment, and so on."[50]

Although Paul and other missionaries continued to preach in the synagogues, the gulf gradually widened between "Christian" church and "Jewish" synagogue. While Christianity had been birthed in Judaism and was at its inception powerfully influenced by it, it nonetheless ceased to be Jewish in language and outlook. Judaism, threatened by the popularity of this new religion, increasingly reacted by closing its ranks. The Jews established a canon of the Hebrew Bible and condemned the writings of the Nazarenes. The final break occurred near the end of the first century, when the Jewish patriarch Gamaliel II included an imprecation against the Christians in the Shemoneh Esreh (Eighteen Benedictions), an important prayer to guard against apostates.[51] At this point, Christians were no longer seen as harmless followers of Judaism but as grave heretics.

As mainline Jews rejected Paul's mission, so, too, did Paul begin to reject *them* and their religion. In the Pauline letters, Judaism is reflected as a joyless mechanical means of earning salvation by doing the works of the law. The God of the Jews is portrayed as a remote and gloomy tyrant who lays the burden of the law on men. Against this portrayal of Judaism, the gospel of freedom from the law is welcomed as good news. And only a people who were stubborn and stiff-necked would refuse to be liberated from this burden.

We can see examples of Paul's attitude toward the Jews in his letters. Paul claims that Jews are the enemies of Christians, as they have incurred

God's wrath (Romans 11:28). He further complains that the Christian churches in Judea had been persecuted by the Jews *who killed Jesus* and that such people displease God, oppose all men, and had prevented Paul from speaking to the Gentile nations about the New Testament message (1 Thessalonians 2:14–16).

The Gospels were written by Pauline Christians. It is not surprising, then, that they contain anti-Jewish sentiment, as well. The Gospel of John, written the latest, is the most virulent in its anti-Semitism. John calls the Jews "sons of Satan" who were responsible for Jesus's persecution and death and places words into Jesus's mouth to the same effect (John 5:16, 5:18, 7:1, 8:37–44, 19:7, 19:12, 19:14–16). In Acts, Peter also blames the Jews for Jesus's death (Acts 3:14–15, 5:30). In Matthew, Jesus condemns the Jews as descendants of murderers and curses them to be cast out into darkness and suffering (Matthew 8:12, 23:31–38). Matthew also reports that the Jews acknowledged responsibility for Jesus's death on behalf of themselves and all future generations, prospectively justifying any harm that might befall them (Matthew 27:25).[52]

The war of the Christian Church against the Jews took off, however, in the second century with the Church Fathers. For their role in bringing about Jesus's death (that is, fulfilling a necessary role in God's divine pan), the Church Fathers denounced the Jews as a "condemned race and hated of God."[53] As the power of the church grew, the Church Fathers would become increasingly obsessed with Jewish guilt. Origen (185–254 CE) echoes the growing hostility:

> On account of their unbelief and other insults which they heaped upon Jesus, the Jews will not only suffer more than others in the judgment which is believed to impend over the world but have even already endured such sufferings. For what nation is in exile from their own metropolis, and from the place sacred to the worship of their fathers, save the Jews alone? And the calamities they have suffered because they were a most wicked nation, which although guilty of many other sins, yet has been punished so severely for none as for those that were committed against our Jesus.[54]

If the new Christian Church was to establish its role as the "new Israel," it had to discredit the *old Israel*. It did so by incorporating anti-Jewish theology as an integral part of Christian apologetics. The Church Fathers turned out volumes of literature to prove that Christians were the true people of God and that Judaism had been only a prelude to Christianity. Justin Martyr (100–165 CE) and Saint Hippolytus (170–236 CE) were obsessed with the belief that the Jews were receiving and would continue to receive God's punishment for having murdered Jesus. Hippolytus writes,

> Now then, incline thine ear to me and hear my words, and give heed, thou Jew. Many a time does thou boast thyself, in that thou didst condemn Jesus of Nazareth to death, and didst give him vinegar and gall to drink; and thou dost vaunt thyself because of this. Come, therefore, and let us consider together whether perchance thou dost boast unrighteously, O, Israel, and whether thou small portion of vinegar and gall has not brought down this fearful threatening upon thee and whether this is not the cause of thy present condition involved in these myriad of troubles.[55]

As the church came into power in the fourth century, it turned on the synagogues with even greater furor. Jewish civil and religious status was deteriorating, thanks to the increasing political influence of Christian bishops. Laws were passed making it a capital offense for any Jew to make a convert. Jews were excluded from various professions and denied all civil honors. They were being discriminated against at every turn. Christians felt that their belief in divine punishment was now supported by this growing evidence.

Saint Hilary of Potieres (300–368 CE) spoke of the Jews as a "people who had always persisted in iniquity and out of its abundance of evil glorified in wickedness."[56] Saint Ambrose (340–397 CE) defended a fellow bishop for burning a synagogue at Callinicum and asked, "Who cares if a synagogue—home of insanity and unbelief—is destroyed?"[57] Saint Gregory of Nyssa (331–396 CE) gave the following indictment, calling the Jews "Slayers of the Lord, murderers of the prophets, adversaries of God, men who show contempt for the Law, foes of grace, enemies of their fathers' faith, advocates of the Devil, brood of vipers, slanderers, scoffers, men whose minds are in darkness, leaven of the Pharisees, assembly of demons, sinners, wicked men, stoners, and haters of righteousness."[58]

The strongest attacks on Jews and Judaism by the Church Fathers are found in the Homilies of Saint John Chrysostom (347–407 CE). He is considered among the most beloved and admired writers in church history. His name translates in Greek as St. John the Golden Mouthed. His Antioch discourses were prompted by the fact that many Christians were meeting on friendly terms with Jews, visiting Jewish homes, and attending their synagogues. This infuriated Chrysostom:

> The Jews sacrifice their children to Satan. . . . [T]hey are worse than wild beasts. The synagogue is a brothel, a den of scoundrels, the temple of demons

devoted to idolatrous cults, a criminal assembly of Jews, a place of meeting for the assassins of Christ, a house of ill fame, a dwelling of iniquity, a gulf and abyss of perdition.

The Jews have fallen into a condition lower than the vilest animal. Debauchery and drunkenness have brought them to the level of the lusty goat and the pig. They know only one thing: to satisfy their stomachs, to get drunk, to kill, and beat each other up like stage villains and coachmen.

The synagogue is a curse, obstinate in her error, she refuses to see or hear, she has deliberately perverted her judgment; she has extinguished with herself the light of the Holy Spirit.[59]

Chrysostom further claimed the Jews had become a degenerate race because of their "odious assassination of Christ for which crime there is no expiation possible, no indulgence, no pardon, and for which they will always be a people without a nation, enduring a servitude without end."[60] He elaborated further on God's punishment of the Jews:

But it was men, say the Jew, who brought these misfortunes upon us, not God. On the contrary, it was in fact God who brought them about. If you attribute them to men, reflect again that even supposing men had dared, they could not have had the power to accomplish them, unless it had been God's will. . . . Men would certainly not have made war unless God had permitted them. . . . Is it not obvious that it was because God hated you and rejected you once for all?[61]

On another occasion Chrysostom is quoted as saying, "I hate the Jews because they violate the Law. I hate the synagogue because it has the Law and the prophets. It is the duty of all Christians to hate the Jews."[62] Chrysostom's Homilies were to be used in seminaries and schools for centuries as model sermons, so his message of Jewish hatred passed down to succeeding generations of theologians. The great nineteenth century theologian Cardinal John Henry Newman described Chrysostom as an exceptionally eloquent speaker, known as the "Mouth of Gold," whose "unrivaled charm" won followers and riveted affections far and wide. He further described Chysostom as "a bright, cheeful gentle soul" with a "sensitive heart."[63] If this accurately describes Chrysostom, then one can only imagine what his Christian contemporaries were saying.

Saint Augustine was also guilty of the growing anti-Jew sentiment. In a sermon on Catechumens, he said, "The Jews hold him, the Jews insult him, the Jews bind him, crown him with thorns, dishonor him with spitting, scourge him, overwhelm with revilings, hang him upon the tree, pierce him with a spear. . . . The Jews killed him. But when the Jews killed Christ, though they knew it not, they prepared the supper for us."[64] In another sermon Augustine characterized the Jews as "willfully blind to Holy Scripture," "lacking in understanding," and "haters of truth."[65] These views represented the overwhelming consensus of the Christian Church. The Church Fathers had sown the seeds of intolerance through which Jews were to become the object of hatred and persecution throughout Europe for centuries to come.

The church would soon institutionalize the segregation of Jews through marriage laws, professional restrictions, special separation in ghettos, and distinctive clothing. When Pope Paul IV issued his bull, *Cum nimis* (1555), which established a ghetto for Jews, his rationale was that the Jews' "own guilt has consigned them to perpetual servitude."[66] Jews were expelled from England in 1290, from France in 1306, and from Spain by 1492.

German theologian Martin Luther (1483–1546 CE), the father of all Protestant religions, wrote the following in his treatise *On the Jews and Their Lies*:

> What then shall we Christians do with this damned, rejected race of Jews? Since they live among us and we know about their lying and blasphemy and cursing, we cannot tolerate them if we do not wish to share in their lies, curses, and blasphemy. . . . We must prayerfully and reverentially practice a merciful severity. . . . Let me give you my honest advice:
>
> First, to set fire to their synagogues or schools and to bury and cover with dirt whatever will not burn, so that no man will ever again see a stone or cinder of them. This is to be done in honor of our LORD and of Christendom, so that God might see that we are Christians. . . .
>
> Second, I advise that their houses also be razed and destroyed. . . .
>
> Third, I advise that all their prayer books and Talmudic writings, in which such idolatry, lies, cursing, and blasphemy are taught, be taken from them.
>
> Fourth, I advise that their rabbis be forbidden to teach henceforth on pain of loss of life and limb. . . .
>
> Fifth, I advise that safe conduct on the highways be abolished completely for the Jews. . . . Let them stay at home.
>
> Sixth, I advise that usury be prohibited to them, and that all cash and treasure of silver and gold be taken from them, and put aside for safe keeping. . . .
>
> Seventh, I recommend putting a flail, an ax, a hoe, a spade, a distaff, or a spindle into the hand of young, strong Jews and Jewesses and letting them earn their bread in the sweat of their brow, as was imposed on the children of Adam.[67]

Luther rarely encountered Jews during his life. His attitudes toward them reflect the long-standing theological and cultural traditions of seeing Jews as a rejected people guilty of murdering Jesus. Luther argued that the Jews were the "devil's people," citing Deuteronomy 13, in which Moses commands killing idolators and burning their cities as an offering to God. Luther wrote, "We are at fault in not slaying them," which, as historian Robert Michael recognizes, amounts to a sanction for murder.[68] After Luther's death, riots led to the expulsion of Jews from several German Lutheran states. Modern Christians generally acknowledge Luther as anti-Semitic but fail to acknowledge that his anti-Semitism was the rule rather than the exception within Christianity of his time. In fact, Luther was simply carrying on one of the longest traditions of Christianity—marginalizing and oppressing Jews.

Luther was the most widely read author of his generation, acquiring the status of a prophet within Germany. The prevailing scholarly view since the Second World War is that Luther's views had a major and persistent influence on German attitudes toward Germany's Jewish citizens between the Reformation and the Holocaust. The first physical violence against the Jews came on Luther's birthday, November 10—Kristallnacht (Crystal Night)— when the Nazis killed Jews, shattered glass windows, and destroyed hundreds of synagogues, just as Luther had proposed. The Nazis displayed Luthor's treatise prominently during their Nuremberg rallies. Just about every anti-Jewish book in the Third Reich contained references to and quotations from Luther. Hitler revered Luther, placing him aside Frederick the Great and Richard Wagner in his seminal work, *Mein Kampf*.[69]

Every point in Luther's plan was faithfully implemented by Nazi policy. Martin Bertram, a Lutheran scholar, states, "It is impossible to publish Luther's treatise today without noting how similar his proposals were to the actions of the Nationalist Socialist regime in Germany in the 1930s and 1940s."[70] Hitler states in *Mein Kampf*, "Hence today I believe that I am acting in accordance with the will of the Almighty Creator; by defending myself against the Jew, I am fighting for the work of the Lord."[71] In a conversation with the bishop of Osnabruck, Germany in 1933, Hitler justified his actions against the Jews: "I am only doing what the church has done for fifteen hundred years, only more effectively."[72]

Hitler's arguments would have had no force if the people of Germany were not receptive to his arguments and his appeals to authority. A Nazi report indicates that by 1938, 99.8 percent of SS members identified as Christians.[73] According to historian Christopher Probst, German clergy and theologians commonly used Luther's publications to justify the Nazis' violence against the Jews.[74] Catholic historian Jose M. Sanchez acknowledges, "There is little question that the Holocaust had its origin in the centuries-long hostility felt by Christians against Jews."[75] In the Holocaust, this long history of Christian anti-Semitism had reached its horrific culmination.[76]

NATIONALISM

> Today we are engaged in a final, all-out battle between communistic atheism and Christianity. The modern champions of communism have selected this as the time, and ladies and gentlemen, the chips are down—they are truly down.
>
> —Senator Joseph McCarthy, speech in Wheeling,
> West Virginia, February 9, 1950

There is nothing wrong with loving one's country of origin or adoption. But that love can become a negative, destructive force when taken to extremes. Sociologists have long recognized a strong correlation between religion and intense nationalism. That correlation is especially strong in America. American Christians have inculcated a powerful and pervasive cultural connection between being a good Christian and being a loyal American.

This connection became especially tight and sinister in the 1950s during the Communist scare. Such political demagogues as Joseph McCarthy conflated Christianity with American patriotism. Anyone who expressed opinions critical of Christianity stood in danger of being labeled a Communist sympathizer, blacklisted from gainful employment, or worse. President Herbert Hoover captured the political zeitgeist of the period: "What the world needs today is a definite, spiritual mobilization of the nations who believe in God against this tide of Red agnosticism. . . . And in rejecting an atheistic other world, I am confident that the Almighty God will be with us."[77]

The nationalistic link strengthened yet again with the rise of the Christian Right in the late 1970s. The Christian Right is profoundly tied to American exceptionalism—the belief that America is the greatest country in the history of the world. This belief is often coupled with the revisionist view that America is a "Christian nation," with God's full blessing behind it. If God unequivocally supports your country, then it is hard to imagine it doing anything wrong. America's actions become morally right simply because they are American.

There is a great deal to love about America, but it is not perfect. America has arrived at its place in the world through many good deeds but also through many that were less than good. Those who equate patriotism with their Christian faith are far more likely to deny America's failures and to support American causes without question. Their commitment to American exceptionalism causes too much cognitive dissonance to assess American policies critically. Blind faith in their religion translates into blind faith in their governmental leaders—at least those who share their religious and political views.

Conservative Christian commentators have a name for people willing to think critically about American actions and talk frankly about America's moral failings: the "hate America crowd." Anyone not expressing unqualified, 100 percent loyalty and support, buying into the "Everything Is Awesome" chorus, is systematically demonized. This was no more apparent than in the lead-up to the ill-advised Iraq War, when even the mainstream press was cowed into abdicating its traditional role as a check on nationalistic fervor. Detailing all the connections between Christianity, American nationalism, and disastrous decision making would require a book of its own. For present purposes, it is enough to say that strong correlations exist that must be weighed when assessing the net effects of Christianity. There is ample evidence that these intertwined beliefs make for a dangerous, potentially destructive combination.

SEXISM AND THE SUBJUGATION OF WOMEN

Man enjoys the great advantage of having a god endorse the code he writes; and since man exercises a sovereign authority over women it is especially fortunate that this authority has been vested in him by the Supreme Being. For the Jews, Mohammedans and Christians among others, man is master by divine right; the fear of God will therefore repress any impulse towards revolt in the downtrodden female.

—Simone de Beauvoir, *The Second Sex* (1949)

The bible teaches that woman brought sin and death into the world, that she precipitated the fall of the race, that she was arraigned before the judgment seat of Heaven, tried, condemned and sentenced. Marriage for her was to be a condition of bondage, maternity a period of suffering and anguish, and in silence and subjection, she was to play the role of a dependent on man's bounty for all her material wants, and for all the information she might desire. . . . Here is the Bible's position of woman briefly summed up.

—Elizabeth Cady Stanton, *The Woman's Bible*

Social reformer Elizabeth Cady Stanton aptly summarizes the Bible's views on women—overwhelmingly negative, condescending, and misogynistic. Women are vilified from their very introduction into the biblical narrative and remain deserving targets of scorn, derision, and reproach throughout the remainder. While a few Old Testament stories portray women favorably and the Gospels report a few women as among Jesus's followers, these stand out as exceptional islands among an ocean of disempowering messages. Mostly, biblical women are superfluous or malevolent. Among the most common biblical descriptions of women are "harlot," "whore," and "unclean."

According to the Old Testament, Israelite customs reflected God's laws. It is highly disturbing, then, to read how ancient Israelites treated their women. The social and legal position of an Israelite wife was inferior to the position of wives in surrounding countries. They were not educated or allowed to take leadership roles. Husbands could marry many wives, but women could have only one husband. Husbands could divorce their wives, but women could not ask for divorce. The wife called her husband "Lord" and addressed him as a slave addressed his master.

There are several places in the Old Testament in which relationships with God are analogized to that of wives to their husbands. In such cases, the husband, representing God, is a polygamist, a predator, and a rapist. The Bible explains what God the husband would do to his sexually promiscuous wives: strip them naked, stone them, and hack them to death with swords, indicating this is how Jewish men should handle similar situations with their own wives (Ezekiel 16:23). In a further example of the value God places on female dignity, God explicitly gives his blessing to raping female captives of war (Exodus 21:7–11; Deuteronomy 21:10–14).

The Decalogue includes a man's wife *among his possessions.* A father had the God-given right to sell his daughter. If a young woman was raped, then she was forced to marry her rapist (Deuteronomy 22:28–29). If a man's wife was raped by another man in a city, then the woman was to be stoned to death for not crying loudly enough (Deuteronomy 22:23–24). A woman was also to be stoned to death if she did not bleed on her wedding night, suggesting she was not a virgin. Women did not inherit unless there was no male heir. Women could not make vows or oaths except with the consent of their fathers or husbands, thus being treated as children regardless of their age.[78]

Whenever women are addressed collectively in the New Testament, the tone remains consistently negative. Paul has much to say about how women are to behave. They are to dress modestly, be submissive, and learn in silence. They are not to teach or exercise authority over any man (1 Timothy 2:9–12).[79] Paul admonishes women to keep silent in church, where they may not speak (1 Corinthians 14:34–35). They are to be obedient to their husbands (Titus 2:5) and submit to them as they do the Lord (Ephesians 5:22; Colossians 3:18; 1 Corinthians 11:3). Even Jesus jumps on the misogyny bandwagon, such as when he refuses to allow Mary Magdalene to touch him before his ascension but has no problem with a similar request from male disciple Thomas (John 20:17, 20:27), reinforcing the biblical description of women as inherently unclean and "lesser" than men by nature.

The Catholic Bible contains a book, Ecclesiasticus,[80] that contains several additional words of "wisdom" about women, including the following:

- "Give me any plague, but the plague of the heart: and any wickedness, but the wickedness of a woman."—Ecclesiasticus 25:13
- "Of the woman came the beginning of sin, and through her we all die."—Ecclesiasticus 25:22
- "If she go not as thou wouldest have her, cut her off from thy flesh, and give her a bill of divorce, and let her go."—Ecclesiasticus 25:26
- "The whoredom of a woman may be known in her haughty looks and eyelids. If thy daughter be shameless, keep her in straitly, lest she abuse herself through overmuch liberty."—Ecclesiasticus 26:9–10
- "A silent and loving woman is a gift of the Lord: and there is nothing so much worth as a mind well instructed. A shamefaced and faithful woman is a double grace, and her continent mind cannot be valued."—Ecclesiasticus 26:14–15
- "A shameless woman shall be counted as a dog; but she that is shamefaced will fear the Lord."—Ecclesiasticus 26:25
- "For from garments cometh a moth, and from women wickedness. Better is the churlishness of a man than a courteous woman, a woman, I say, which bringeth shame and reproach."—Ecclesiasticus 42:13–14

Within the Bible, there are approximately *three hundred* Bible verses or stories that explicitly mandate women's inequality, inferiority, or subservience.

It is not as if all these passages are harmless or haven't had horrific effects. Biblical passages have been used by Christians for centuries to justify the subjugation of women. As early as the fourth century, it was decreed by a synod that women should neither send nor receive letters in their own name.[81] They were confined to minor orders and forbidden to sing in church. Later, they would be deprived of holy orders altogether. In some Christian meetings, they had to sit apart at the back of the congregation. By 581 CE, a church council at Mâcon was debating whether women even had souls.

The great Catholic theologian Thomas Aquinas taught, based on his reading of Scripture, that women were defective in both body and soul. Leading scholars accepted Aquinas's biblically based teachings, and it became a fundamental premise of canon law that women were inferior beings. Following Aquinas, canon law decreed that women could not testify in will disputes or criminal proceedings. They suffered under the same legal disabilities as children and the mentally ill. They could not practice medicine, law, or any other profession. Nor could they hold any public office.

Protestant Churches were no better than the Catholic Church. It was Martin Luther who coined the phrase "A woman's place is in the home," and in strongly Protestant areas of Germany, it is still commonplace to hear that women should concern themselves only with *Kinder*, *Kirche*, *Küche* (children, the church, and cooking). Luther also insisted on a man's Christian right to beat his wife and held firmly to the traditional line on a woman's duty to bear children, even if it killed her: "If they become tired or even die, it does not matter. Let them die in childbirth—that is why they are there."[82]

Under canon law a woman's husband was both her lord and her guardian. In practical terms this meant she could not legally own property or make contracts. Her property came under her husband's control upon marriage. She could not sue at common law without his consent, which meant she could not sue him for any wrong done to her. If she deliberately killed him, then she was guilty not merely of murder but also, because of the feudal relationship, treason.

In England, pursuant to Christian Scripture, husband and wife were considered a single person, with the husband as the decision maker. This doctrine enabled an Englishman to lock up his wife and escape liability for false imprisonment. He could beat her and not be guilty of battery. He could sexually assault her and not be guilty of rape. A wife could not proceed against her husband nor be called to give evidence in court against him. Most such constraints were ultimately done away with by Acts of Parliament but not until 1935 and 1945 and against fierce opposition from the organized churches. It remained impossible for an Englishman to be charged with the rape of his wife until the 1990s!

Unmarried women were also inferior beings or, as the Bible puts it, "weaker vessels" (1 Peter 3:7). Fathers could legally treat them as their personal property and swap them for other goods or for political advantage, which is what arranged child marriages often amounted to. Unmarried adult women were not permitted many privileges allowed by law to men, nor were they thought capable of fulfilling the duties expected of men. Like married women, they were prohibited from practicing all professions and all but a few trades. In 1588, Pope Sixtus V even forbade them to appear on the public stage. Soon the whole of Western Christendom had banned actresses and female singers.

Well into the twentieth century, women weren't allowed to sit on juries. They were permitted only a few select jobs, such as school teaching and nursing, and even these they were generally obliged to give up when they married. All these restrictions were justified by reference to Christian Scripture. Women were so little regarded that until the twentieth century they were often excluded from church membership rolls.

Throughout their histories, the established Christian churches have consistently opposed women's right to vote. Only after the church's influence seriously weakened did women obtain this right. In England this happened in 1918, when the franchise was extended to women over the age of thirty.

The traditional position of the church, that women are mere chattels of their husbands, was challenged by such freethinkers as Thomas Paine (1737–1809) and Jeremy Bentham (1748–1832). The atheist Mary Wollstonecraft (1759–1797) published her *Vindication of the Rights of Women* in 1792. Her husband, the philosopher William Godwin (1756–1836), was a campaigner for women's rights, and so was their atheist son-in-law, the poet Percy Bysshe Shelley (1792–1822). Other prominent proponents included the unbelieving Mary Ann Evans (George Eliot, 1819–1880) and Harriet Law (1832–1897).

The utilitarian atheist John Stuart Mill (1806–1873) launched the women's suffrage movement in England with a petition to the House of Commons on June 7, 1866. He attempted to amend the 1867 Reform Bill to extend the franchise to women and to stop discrimination under the infamous Contagious Diseases Acts. He published the *Subjugation of Women* in 1869. Other active campaigners included the atheists George Holyoake (1817–1906), Charles Bradlaugh (1833–1891), and Annie Besant (1847–1933).

In France the argument for women's rights was led by opponents of the church like Denis Diderot (1713–1784) and the Marquis of Condorcet (1743–1794) and much later in the United States by atheists like

Ernestine Rose (1810–1892), Matilda Gage (1826–1898), Elizabeth Cady Stanton (1815–1902), and Susan B. Anthony (1820–1906), who was ultimately commemorated on an American dollar coin. Without atheists pushing back against Christian dogma, women would not enjoy the status they have today. At the time of writing, there are areas of Europe where "traditional Christian values" prevail and women still do not have full voting rights.

A sociological study in 1962 revealed that religious orthodoxy correlated with views that denied women equal rights. It is notable that the church itself continued to discriminate against women for years after such discrimination was abandoned outside the church. It was not until 1970 that a woman was authorized to teach Catholic theology, and throughout the world churches are still exempted from sex discrimination legislation. In England, the taxation laws and laws of inheritance still discriminate against women.

Today, Christian Scripture continues to provide support for those who would oppress, subjugate, and violate women. As former president and Evangelical Christian Jimmy Carter acknowledges, the interpretation of Scripture by male religious leaders

> provides the foundation or justification for much of the pervasive persecution and abuse of women throughout the world. . . . At their most repugnant, the belief that women are inferior human beings in the eyes of God gives excuses to the brutal husband who beats his wife, the soldier who rapes a woman, the employer who has a lower pay scale for women employees, or parents who decide to abort a female embryo.[83]

Many major Christian denominations, including the Catholic and Mormon Churches, still exclude women from the priesthood. As recently as June 2014, the Mormon Church excommunicated the founder of a group seeking priesthood for women, human rights lawyer Kate Kelly. The church suggested it might welcome her back if she "stopped teachings and actions that undermine the church" and claimed its action was taken "out of love."[84] Ms. Kelly's reaction was instructive: "That's classic language of an abusive relationship."[85]

Many people believe that the equality of women is ensconced in the US Constitution, but this is not so. The Constitution speaks only of the rights of men. To correct this, the Equal Rights Amendment (ERA) was introduced in Congress in 1923 to clarify that women shall have the same rights as men. Despite what most people today consider noncontroversial, the ERA was bitterly resisted by Christian groups from the beginning, only being approved by the US Congress in 1972. Today, the ERA still is not law though ratified by a supermajority of states. The fifteen states that oppose it are the most solidly Christian in the United States. The anti-ERA movement is today based on strong backing among Evangelical Christians, Mormons, Orthodox Jews, and Roman Catholics, each opposing the same rights for women the Constitution affords men.[86]

One final example involves contraception. Easy and effective contraception, a product of the late twentieth century, has freed women from a lifetime of raising children. It has enabled women around the world to complete their educations, pursue their dreams, and create more egalitarian relationships. It has allowed women to enter the workforce in unprecedented numbers. It has been heralded as perhaps the greatest invention of the modern age, in terms of its net positive benefit to society.

The Catholic Church, as well as many Protestant sects, has consistently opposed contraception on the basis of Scripture, holding to the position that, as Monty Python so cleverly quipped, "Every sperm is sacred." This has no doubt resulted in millions of unwanted pregnancies, leading to women abandoning promising careers and being forced to raise children for which they were not prepared, either emotionally or financially.

In 2014, corporate retailer Hobby Lobby won a case before the US Supreme Court claiming the Affordable Care Act violated the owners' Christian principles because it would require the company to indirectly pay for its employees' contraceptives. Thousands of women were thereby stripped of their insurance coverage for contraceptives through an interpretation of Christian Scripture. This issue is still alive and well today.

LGBTQ ISSUES

Christian opposition to women's rights and racial equality might seem like ancient history to younger readers. In recent headlines, however, one can find the past repeated with similar opposition to homosexuality and gay marriage. Organized opposition has been almost exclusively religious in nature. As with past civil rights movements, Christian opponents rely on Scripture to support their views that homosexuality is immoral and that marriage must be restricted to unions between men and women.

Biblical verses cited by those opposing gay rights include the following:

- "You shall not lie with a male as with a woman; it is an abomination." (Leviticus 18:22)
- "If a man lies with a male as with a woman, both of them have committed an abomination; they shall surely be put to death; their blood is upon them." (Leviticus 20:13)
- "For this cause God gave them up unto vile affections: for even their women did change the natural use into that which is against nature: And likewise also the men, leaving the natural use of the woman, burned in their lust one toward another; men with men working that which is unseemly, and receiving in themselves that recompense of their error which was meet." (Romans 1:26–27)

Relying on passages such as these, Christian groups have, beginning in the 1970s, mounted a systematic worldwide war on gay rights.[87] Such groups include Save Our Children, the Christian Broadcasting Network, Focus on the Family, Concerned Women for America, the American Family Association, and the Christian Coalition. All have built strong lobbying and fundraising organizations to assist in their efforts. Combatting the LGBTQ rights movement and its "gay agenda" has been a central theme of these organizations and their fundraising efforts. In the words of Focus on the Family founder James Dobson, the Christian battle against LGBTQ rights represents a second civil war.[88]

Christian groups have promoted the idea that homosexuality is an immoral choice. This has led to a multitude of conversion programs, in which Christian parents involuntarily place their children until they repent of their gay lifestyle. This contradicts the overwhelming consensus of medical science that sexuality is not a choice but rather epigenetic and therefore immutable. There is no way to calculate the psychological harm such programs have caused.

The relentless antigay rhetoric of Christian groups and churches has resulted in widespread suffering by LGBTQ teens, as reflected in their increased rates of suicide. LGBTQ youth are up to four times more likely to attempt suicide than their heterosexual peers. An LGBTQ youth commits suicide once every five hours, and for every one who succeeds, twenty attempt it. LGBTQ youth who come from highly rejecting families are more than eight times as likely to have attempted suicide than LGBTQ peers who reported no or low levels of family rejection.[89] Religious beliefs represent one of the primary sources of such rejection.[90] In these cases, religious dogma kills.

On August 4, 2014, sixteen-year-old Sergio Urrego of Bogota, Colombia, jumped to his death from the roof of a shopping center after Catholic school officials witnessed him kissing another boy, outed both boys to their parents, threw them out of school, blocked Sergio's transfer to another school, forced him to undergo psychological counseling, and accused him of sexual harassment. Before taking his life, Sergio wrote on his Facebook page, "My sexuality is not my sin."

Christian blogger John Shore writes,

> It's a fact that gay teenagers are about thirty percent more likely than straight teenagers to take their own lives. It's a fact that the vast majority of Christians believe that being gay is a profound moral failing, a foul aberration, a repelling, unnatural offense against God that fully warrants as punishment an eternity spent in hell. Asserting that those two facts have no relationship cannot possibly be anything but intellectually dishonest. It's like someone who sews robes for the Klan asserting that they personally don't contribute to the harming of African Americans.[91]

Another source of much pain and suffering among the LGBTQ community has been systemic discrimination encoded into the laws of many nations, including the United States. A prominent example is legal prohibition of same-sex marriage. Such prohibitions have made it more difficult, if not impossible, for gays to adopt children, share health benefits, and attend their dying or disabled loved ones.

In the late twentieth century, LGBTQ rights groups began publicly pressing to change these laws. They advocated for marriage to be extended to all people, regardless of sexual orientation. The only organized opposition came from religious groups and institutions. Of those opposed to same-sex marriage, almost half specifically cited their religious beliefs, interpretation of biblical passages, or both as the reason.[92]

Christian groups were exceptionally united in their hostility to gay marriage, including the Roman Catholic Church, the Southern Baptist Convention, and the United Pentecostal Church International. In 2009, a group of Christian leaders from various denominations issued the Manhattan Declaration, an "influential statement that united evangelicals and Catholic leaders in fighting abortion and gay marriage."[93] The declaration has been signed by more than a half-million people.

Proposition 8 was a narrowly successful 2008 California ballot proposition for a state constitutional amendment that effectively banned gay marriage in the state. Though the amendment was ultimately stricken as unconstitutional, it delayed California's ultimate adoption of gay marriage for several years. Two of the largest fundraisers and supporters of Proposition 8 were the Catholic and Mormon Churches. Mormons alone contributed more than a third of the money raised to support Proposition 8, totaling nearly $25 million.[94] Mormons also contributed significantly in nonmonetary ways, such as providing manpower, making up 80 to 90 percent of the early door-to-door volunteers.

Gays and lesbians finally secured the fundamental right to marry in the 2015 Supreme Court opinion *Obergefell v. Hodges*. The judges were divided five to four, with all four dissenters being male and Catholic. The majority opinion was written by Justice Anthony Kennedy, the only remaining male Catholic justice on the court, who retired in 2018 to be replaced by Catholic Brett Kavanaugh.

Donald Trump, with the strong support of Christian conservatives, took an openly hostile positions toward the LGBTQ community. He directed his justice department to argue that employers should be allowed to openly discriminate against or even fire lesbian, gay, or bisexual employees due simply to their sexual orientation. Trump rescinded Obama-era policies protecting transgendered students from discrimination and announced a ban on transgender soldiers serving openly in the US military, despite no evidence they served any less effectively than nontransgendered soldiers.

One final example of Christian influence on antigay policies and practices involves hate crimes in Africa. Predominantly Christian countries Uganda, Malawi, and Kenya have seen a dramatic increase in violence against gays over the past fifteen years, as Christian organizations have increased their presence and their focus on antigay propaganda. Such groups have also pushed for stronger laws and penalties against homosexuality. These efforts have resulted in such countries as Ethiopia enacting draconian laws against homosexuality, such as making it punishable by up to fifteen years in prison.

In both Uganda and Ethiopia "Kill the Gays" bills, making homosexuality punishable by death, passed at the express urging of such Christian groups as United for Life Ethiopia, though at the last minute, life imprisonment was substituted for the death penalty, and the act was ultimately found invalid for procedural grounds. Such Western Christian groups as Campus Crusade for Christ have actively promoted speakers advocating that Ethiopia become a "graveyard for homosexuality."[95] As antigay rhetoric heats up in these African countries and violence increases, we must acknowledge the substantial role of Christian doctrine.

Christian doctrine has likewise been the primary source of objection to extending civil rights to transgendered men and women. Evangelical Christians are three times as likely as the typical American to believe identifying with a different gender is morally wrong.[96] This is despite the widespread agreement among medical and psychological experts that transgendered individuals are not simply making voluntary choices to cross-identify but are compelled by their biology. Those citing Christian doctrine reference passages from Genesis describing the creation of men and women, often arguing that God decided on a binary separation of the sexes and God doesn't make mistakes.

The Southern Baptist Convention in 2014 denounced hormone therapy, transition-related procedures, and anything else that would "alter one's bodily identity."[97] At the same time, it announced its opposition to government efforts to "validate transgender identity as morally praiseworthy," consistent with the 2006 statements of then president Alber Mohler that any attempt to alter one's gender was an "act of rebellion against God."[98] Pope Benedict XVI likewise denounced gender theory, warning that it blurs the God-ordained distinction between male and female and thus could lead to the "self-destruction" of the human race.[99] Such hyperbolic language and positions can only incite intense opposition among Christians to transgendered people, just as it has to gays. The results are likely to be the same.

HEALTH AND SAFETY

Christian Scripture has also undermined health and safety throughout the world. There are many examples, but one in which the connection is especially clear involves Christian opposition to efforts to curb the spread of the deadly HIV virus. Research by UNAIDS estimates there are 42 million people in the world diagnosed with HIV, with about 15,000 new infections per day.[100] The condom is widely accepted by medical and administrative authorities as the most reliable way to stop the spread of AIDS. The Catholic Church, however, has maintained since 1968 that all forms of artificial contraception, including the use of condoms, are prohibited because they directly oppose God's will.[101]

In the 1980s, HIV spread across the world, resulting in widespread casualties from AIDS. As it became clear that the church's anticontraceptive position was directly undermining AIDS prevention efforts, doctors and AIDS activists harshly criticized the church and said that its position led to countless deaths and millions of AIDS orphans.[102] The church, however, remained steadfast, maintaining that condoms were a sin in all circumstances, regardless of how many deaths or how much suffering such a position might cause.[103] Even providing information about condoms was discouraged, as resulting in the "facilitation of evil."[104]

In addition to demonizing their use, the church has also systematically lied about the effectiveness of condoms. In 2003, the president of the Vatican's Pontifical Council for the Family falsely claimed that condoms were permeable to the AIDS virus; these claims were echoed by an archbishop in Nairobi and by Catholics as far away as Asia and Latin America. Pope Benedict XVI claimed that condoms actually *increase the spread of AIDS*. Afterward, the governments of Germany, France, and Belgium released statements criticizing the pope's views. Julio Montaner, president of the International AIDS Society, called the pope's statement "irresponsible and dangerous."[105] The Catholic Church's position has resulted in thousands of unnecessary deaths and unimaginable suffering.[106]

The devastating effects of the church's anticontraceptive position are not limited, however, to the spread of such deadly diseases as AIDS. Overpopulation is a terrible problem in many underdeveloped countries, in which poverty is rampant and government social programs are nonexistent. Such overpopulation often leads to starvation, as parents cannot afford to feed their numerous children. The World Health Organization reports that providing greater access to contraception in developing countries would prevent 54 million unintended pregnancies, 26 million abortions (the majority of which would be unsafe), 79,000 maternal deaths, and 1.1 million infant deaths.[107] By merely increasing the availability of and education regarding contraception methods, an enormous amount of gratuitous suffering could be prevented.

The influence of the Catholic Church, however, is so strong and so pervasive that it can block or at least substantially undermine any such initiatives. A 2014 report by the UN Committee on the Rights of the Child called on the church to "overcome all the barriers and taboos surrounding adolescent sexuality that hinder their access to sexual and reproductive information, including on family planning and contraceptives."[108] To date, the church has failed to do so.

The Catholic Church also perpetuates long-outdated views of treating mental illness. When the Bible was written, such illnesses were believed to result from possession by evil spirits. Today, of course, we know better and effectively treat such illnesses through methods like cognitive and drug therapy. The Catholic Church, however, officially holds to the demon possession theory of causation and treatment. The Vatican has an official exorcist—Gabriele Amorth, who claims to have performed more than 70,000 exorcisms. The church has formally recognized the International Association of Exorcists, comprising 250 priests in thirty countries. If each were as active as Mr. Amorth, more than 17.5 million mentally ill people will be treated by exorcism rather than modern medicine. As exorcism has a demonstrated effectiveness rate of *zero*, that means more than 17.5 million people will go untreated.

Some may object that at least such Catholics as Mother Teresa actively worked to alleviate suffering. But let us look at what Mother Teresa actually said on that issue: "I think it is very beautiful for the poor to accept their lot, to share it with the passion of Christ. I think the world is being much helped by the suffering of the poor people."[109] Adhering to this biblically based belief, Mother Teresa actively resisted any efforts to provide the sick people in her care with modern medical care or pain relief. She felt it perfectly appropriate for them to suffer, subject to God's will, though she herself had no problem accepting modern medical treatment after she was diagnosed with an aggravated heart condition. Even the Catholic most famous for her compassion single-handedly brought about an enormous amount of misery.

Another Christian group responsible for much unnecessary suffering and death are Christian Scientists. They believe, based on Scripture, that sickness is merely an illusion that can be corrected by prayer alone.[110] Since the 1880s, when the movement arose, the deliberate avoidance of medical treatment by Christian Scientists has resulted in many deaths and much extreme agony. Likewise, Jehovah's Witnesses, with members numbering nearly eight million worldwide, are directed to refuse blood transfusions based on their leaders' interpretations of biblical passages.[111] Those who die because of such refusal, many of whom are children deprived of deciding for themselves, are considered martyrs by the church.

CHRISTIANITY AND CHILDREN

Much is made among Christians of their commitment to children. Children are the most defenseless of our species and within each generation represent the promise of the next. We would expect the Christian God to protect children above all else. We would also expect Christian children to be the happiest, most successful, and well provided for on Earth. But that is not what we see. At all.

As discussed previously, millions of children die horribly of starvation and disease each year as part of an ongoing tragedy that must be acknowledged as sanctioned by God. Many have intentionally been deprived of lifesaving medical care by parents who base their reasoning on interpretations of Christian Scripture. Perhaps the most notorious example of recent vintage is the pedophilia scandal within the Catholic Church. It is now apparent that thousands of Christian children were raped and otherwise sexually preyed upon by Catholic priests, while the church systematically covered up the abuses, often moving the perpetrators to other parishes, where they could prey on new victims. Recent investigations of Protestant churches have resulted in similar findings. Since 1998, for example, more than four hundred Southern Baptist leaders, from youth pastors to top ministers, have pleaded guilty or been convicted of sex crimes against more than seven hundred victims. The leader of the Southern Baptist Convention, the largest Protestant denomination in the United States, called for repentance for a "culture that has made abuse, cover-ups and evading accountability far too easy."[112]

The trust and authority accorded these men, which allowed them regular access to their victims, discouraged reporting of their deeds, and effectively silenced those who did report, were granted by the Bible. According to Christian doctrine, they came from God Himself. Though the priests, ministers, and youth pastors continued to operate by the apparent authority accorded them by Christian Scripture, neither God nor the Church took any action to divest them of that authority or stop the abuses *for decades* as incalculable damage was done. Clearly, a primary function of the Catholic Church, which represented the only organized Christian Church for centuries, is to serve as a model of righteousness and moral rectitude for the world. Here, the church failed spectacularly in its mission. For the continued abuse of children under the care of the Catholic Church and Protestant churches, Christianity itself must accept the blame.

Another wave of child sex abuse scandals has recently hit the Boy Scouts of America, a quasi-religious organization that requires belief in God and denies admission to atheists. In 2019, hundreds of plaintiffs sued the organization, alleging abuse spanning decades, with hundreds more threatened. A trial expert testified in 2019 that through 2016, 7,819 troop leaders molested 12,254 victims. Once again, there can be little doubt that the trust and confidence inspired by the organization's open religiosity and common affiliation with Christianity and Christian churches, in which a large percentage of scout meetings are held, encouraged many parents to leave their children with sexual predators. Like the Catholic Church, the Boy Scouts have long hidden their records of sex abuse. In 2010, the Boy Scouts held the honor of being hit with the largest punitive damage award ever to a single plaintiff in a sex abuse case.

Although the consensus of psychologists has long been that hitting children is highly detrimental, causing harm similar to sexual abuse, such as antisocial behavior, aggression, mental health problems, and cognitive difficulties, this practice is very common in Christian communities, which can point to the Bible for justification.[113] Such passages as Proverbs 22:15 and 23:13–14 have been widely interpreted to explicitly condone and even demand parents beat their children with rods, so long as they do not die. While not found in the Bible, the well-known adage "Spare the rod, spoil the child" derives from it. Eighty-five percent of Evangelical Christians support corporal punishment for children. The Christian Parents Network maintains that parents have a religious duty to beat their children, as such punishment gives children a "foretaste of the potential terror and pain of eternal separation from God."[114] Darrel Reid, head of Focus on the Family–Canada explains, "[T]he theological underpinning for family corporal punishment is tied up with the responsibility that God gives families for raising the young."[115]

One hundred twenty-eight countries have outlawed corporal punishment, despite opposition from Christian churches. Forty Christian schools sued to overturn the United Kingdom's ban on school corporal punishment, charging that it prevented them from teaching morals to their students and interfered with religious freedom. The European Court of Human Rights and UK courts ruled against them. In South Africa, 196 Christian schools brought a similar challenge; the South African Constitutional Court ruled against them.

The United States is one of the few modern democracies to allow beating children for punishment. Every state allows corporal punishment by parents. Eighteen states, mostly in the South, allow "paddling" in public and private schools. In 2014, Texas alone recorded 49,000 such incidents, despite the practice being banned in the state's major metropolitan school districts. It is estimated that 1 to 2 percent of these students is seriously injured, including permanent nerve damage, brain injury, and even death.[116] While corporal punishment is more prevalent among poor families, studies have repeatedly found religious belief to be a better predictor than socioeconomic status.

In the previous section, I discussed Christian denominations avoiding medical treatment based on biblical teachings. While it is certainly tragic when an adult dies needlessly for such a belief, it is far worse when the victim is a child. The adult has a choice in the matter, but for the child, that choice is in the hands of his or her parents. In 1998, Seth Asser and Rita Swan published a paper in the medical journal *Pediatrics* showing the horrific effects of denying children medical care on religious grounds. Of the 172 children who died between 1975 and 1995 after being denied care for religious reasons, 140 (81 percent) had conditions with more than a 90 percent chance of recovery, and another 18 (10 percent) would have had between 50 and 90 percent chance of recovery. Only 3 of the 172 would not have benefitted from medical attention. The vast majority of these children, well over one hundred, died needlessly based on their parents' religious beliefs. Such parents have used the Free Exercise Clause of the First Amendment as a shield to protect them from prosecution, arguing that their choices were proscribed by their Christian faith.

The US government is also complicit in perpetuating this needlessly high death toll and abuse of children. Forty-three states confer civil or criminal immunity for parents who injure their children by withholding medical care on religious grounds. Forty-five US states maintain religious exemption laws that allow parents to avoid vaccinating their children, which has resulted in several outbreaks of preventable diseases and at least one death. Exemptions such as these were actually *required* by the US government from 1974 through 1983 as a condition for states to receive federal aid for child protection, during which the states with religious exemptions exploded from ten to forty-three. Even today, the US government subsidizes Christian Scientist "prayer practitioners" through Medicare and tax exemptions, despite their failure to provide *any medical care*.

Some point to Christian missionaries traveling to third-world countries to help malnourished children. To those people I would refer the story of Renee Bach, an American missionary who, between 2010 and 2015, "treated" such children in Uganda through her ministry, Serving His Children. Ms. Bach and her fellow missionaries lacked proper medical training but allegedly represented that they did, resulting in the death of at least 105 children. Journalist Sarabeth Caplin, who covered the story, writes,

> Bach "playing doctor" is a symptom of a larger problem with many Christian missionary groups coming from the U.S.: They promote "voluntourism" over actual help. Even if they mean well, the missions often serve as little more than backdrops for Facebook photos. The missionaries siphon money from local economies. Even when hospitals and schools are needed in those communities, the people sent there often lack experience and are primarily driven by a "calling" from God rather than a desire for justice and a willingness to monitor their projects in the long term.[117]

In other words, for children in the developing world, Christian missionaries often do more harm than good. In the case of Ms. Bach, far more.

What about the teaching of children? Recent research has seriously called into question the party line among Christians that a religious up-bringing is necessary to instill positive values. Children raised in secular households exhibit less racism than their religious counterparts and are less vengeful, less nationalistic, less militaristic, less authoritarian, more toler-ant, more empathetic, and less susceptible to peer pressure.[118] Nonreligious family life is more likely to focus on values common to secular culture, such as rational problem solving, personal autonomy, and independent thought.

If one is interested in her child staying out of jail and being a constructive member of society, then she can do no better than to raise them without religion. Atheists are almost absent from the prison population, comprising less than 0.5 percent of those behind bars. It has been widely documented that the unaffiliated and nonreligious engage in far fewer crimes than their religious brethren. Democratic countries with the lowest levels of religious faith and participation, such as Sweden, Denmark, Japan, Belgium, and New Zealand, have among the lowest violent crime rates in the world and enjoy extremely high levels of well-being.

For a stark comparison between a Christian country and a nonreligious country, look at the United States versus Japan. Japan is believed to have one of the highest rates of atheism in the world—65 percent according to one study. Approximately 1 percent are Christian. Table 6.1 reveals the relative rates of three acts considered by most Christians to indicate im-morality. In short, children raised without religion have not been shown to suffer for their lack of indoctrination but rather to thrive, exhibiting no shortage of positive traits and values.

Table 6.1.   Biblically Immoral Acts: Japan v. USA

	Japan	USA	Percent Difference
Murder (per 10K)	0.3	4.7	1,567 percent
Auto Theft (per 100K)	28.3	390.2	1,379 percent
Divorce (per 1K)	0.62	4.95	798 percent

UNDERMINING SCIENCE AND REASON

Question with boldness even the existence of a God; because, if there be one, he must more approve of the homage of reason, than that of blind-folded fear.

—Thomas Jefferson, Letter to Peter Carr, Paris, Aug. 10, 1787

Give me the storm and tempest of thought and action, rather than the dead calm of ignorance and faith. Banish me from Eden when you will; but first let me eat of the fruit of the tree of knowledge.

—Robert G. Ingersoll, *The Works of Robert G. Ingersoll, Vol. 3*

If a man, holding a belief which he was taught in childhood or persuaded of afterwards, keeps down and pushes away any doubts which arise about it in his mind, purposely avoids the reading of books and the company of men that call into question or discuss it, and regards as impious those questions which cannot easily be asked without disturbing it—the life of that man is one long sin against mankind.

—William Kingdon Clifford, *The Ethics of Belief and Other Essays*

The fact that religions can be so shamefully dishonest, so contemptuous of the intelligence of their adherents, and still flourish does not speak very well for the tough-mindedness of the believers. But it does indicate, if a demonstration was needed, that near the core of the religious experience is something remarkably resistant to rational inquiry.

—Carl Sagan, *Broca's Brain: Reflections on the Romance of Science*

Science threatens religion in several ways. First, it breaks down and blurs categories most people have held since childhood. We all instinctively divide things into discrete categories, such as male and female, human and animal, mind and body, good and evil. But one consistency of science has been its revelations that these categories are not as clearly delineated as we thought. Gender identity, for example, appears to be far more fluid than people have assumed throughout recorded history. To the extent Christian Scripture is premised on strict adherence to these categories, it is to a large extent undermined by science.

Second, the very concept of the scientific method, with its implicit refutation of dogma and insistence on following the evidence wherever it leads, is the antithesis of Christian epistemology, which relies on divine revelation. Science and reason don't allow one to control the end result of an inquiry, which always stands the risk of invalidating some or all of what came before. Third, there are many occasions in which the findings of science directly contradict the teachings or implications of Christianity. For all these reasons, Christian apologists have consistently worked to undermine science and reason.

A national poll appearing in *Time* magazine revealed that when asked what they would do if science showed that one of their religious beliefs was wrong, nearly two-thirds of the respondents—64 percent—said they would reject the scientific findings for their faith. Only 23 percent said they would consider changing their beliefs. Even those Christian denominations generally favorable to science draw the line where some key doctrinal point is concerned. The clear message is that ultimately, science must defer to religion. Not surprisingly, a 2018 survey by Christian research firm Barna found that more than half of churchgoing Christian teens believe that the "church seems to reject much of what science tells us about the world."[119]

The 2016 election of Donald Trump brought to the forefront the concept of the "postfacts" worldview. With his reliance on "alternative facts" and repeated attacks on so-called fake news, meaning any news critical of Trump, Trump and his surrogates openly attacked all the institutions Americans had relied on to provide them accurate information, suggesting that no authority was reliable except the president himself. But to Trump's Evangelical supporters, this was nothing new. Christian writer Rachel Held Evans, who attended Bryan College, an Evangelical school in Dayton, Ohio, describes how she was taught to distrust information coming from the scientific or media elite because these sources did not hold a "biblical worldview": "It was presented as a cohesive worldview that you could maintain if you studied the Bible. Part of that was that climate change isn't real, that evolution is a myth made up by scientists who hate God, and capitalism is God's ideal for society."[120]

The phrase *Christian worldview* is ubiquitous in the Evangelical world, in which it is considered a badge of virtue. Though it sounds harmless, what this really means is a worldview informed first and foremost by the Bible, in which anything that challenges Scripture is to be dismissed out of hand. Cornelius Van Til, the theologian quoted earlier in support of presuppositionalism, explains the concept of the Christian worldview as one that rejects the premise that all humans have access to objective reality. In a pamphlet to non-Christians, he writes, "We really do not grant that you see any fact in any dimension of life truly."[121] In other words, no one can or should trust what they see, hear, or otherwise observe. They must in all things defer to the Bible.

The Christian worldview doesn't just describe the views of a large number of Christians. It also represents a network of institutions and experts versed in presenting "alternative-fact" versions of climate change, biology, and other scientific fields that may hold positions at odds with Christian Scripture. A 2017 *New York Times* article includes a profile of Nathaniel Jeanson, a research biologist at the creationist ministry Answers in Genesis in Petersburg, Kentucky:

Dr. Jeanson is as important an asset for the ministry as its life-size replica of Noah's Ark in Williamstown, Ky. He believes the earth was created in six days—and he has a Ph.D. in cell and developmental biology from Harvard. Home-schooled until high school, Dr. Jeanson grew up going to "Worldview Weekend" Christian conferences. As an undergraduate at the University of Wisconsin, Parkside, he dutifully studied evolutionary biology during the day and read creationist literature at night.

This "reading double," as he calls it, equipped him to personify the contradictions that pervade this variety of Christian worldview. At Harvard Medical School, he chose a research topic that steered clear of evolution. "My research question is a present-tense question—how do blood cells function," he told me. "So perhaps it was easier to compartmentalize."

Dr. Jeanson rhapsodized about the integrity of the scientific method. Before graduate school, "I held this quack idea of cancer," he said. "But that idea got corrected. This is the way science works." Yet when his colleagues refuse to read his creationist papers and data sets, he takes their snub as proof that they can find no flaws in his research. "If people who devote their lives to it can't point anything out, then I think I may be on to something," he said.

Dr. Jeanson calls himself a "presuppositionalist evidentialist"—which we might define as someone who accepts evidence when it happens to affirm his nonnegotiable presuppositions. "When it comes to questions of absolute truth, those are things I've settled in my own mind and heart," he told me. "I couldn't call myself a Christian if I hadn't."[122]

Christianity is strongly correlated with denial of scientifically accepted facts, such as the age of the universe, and robust scientific theories, such as evolution and anthropogenic (man-made) global warming (AGW). Despite such facts and theories being so well accepted as to be noncontroversial within the relevant scientific communities, they remain hugely controversial among Christians. Within the United States, 64 percent of White Evangelical Protestants believe that humans have existed in their present forms since the beginning of time.[123] Even for those believing in evolution, 33 percent believe it was guided by a supreme being, thereby denying the scientifically accepted mechanism of natural selection.[124] Less than one in five Americans accept evolution as evolutionary biologists do.[125] By contrast, between 97 percent and 99.9 percent of scientists accept evolution by natural selection, including those with no expertise in biology.[126] When asked why they did not accept evolution in 2007, most Americans identified religious reasons, with only 14 percent citing "not enough scientific evidence."[127]

A similarly strong scientific consensus, more than 97 percent, supports the existence of AGW.[128] Among American Evangelical Christians, however, less than 50 percent believe in AGW, and only 33 percent consider it a major problem.[129] Despite the overwhelming scientific consensus, only 36 percent of churchgoing Catholics, 36 percent of nonmainline Protestants, and 45 percent of mainline Protestants say they are "very sure" climate change is occurring.[130]

AGW conflicts with the biblically based concept of "dominionism," that God has given humans the planet to use for their benefit (to have "dominion" over it), and nothing they do will ever harm it. Such influential Christians as Senator James Inhofe and former senator Rick Santorum adhere to this view, as does 38 percent of the general public.[131] Santorum actually believes that global warming, as part of God's mandate, is a positive event to be openly encouraged, a view shared by 65 percent of White Evangelical Christians and 36 percent of the general public.

Another conflict, raised by Evangelical congressman John Shimkus of the House Energy and Commerce Committee of the US House of Representatives, is that any disastrous effects of global warming would violate God's promise to Noah to never again destroy the Earth. Because God would never violate that promise, there must be nothing to worry about from AGW. Many believe that even if global warming is happening, we should expend no resources on it because the most disastrous consequences will be decades away, and the apocalypse is imminent. In light of the impending Second Coming, there is simply no need to take AGW seriously. For those who consider these beliefs harmless, consider that in 2016, 72 percent of the members of the congressional committee tasked with addressing global warming issues were either AGW denialists or had voted against measures to alleviate AGW.[132]

In 2017, President Donald Trump appointed Scott Pruitt to head the Environmental Protection Agency. Mr. Pruitt is a staunchly committed conservative Christian who founded Christian Legal Services, which focused on defending Christians in religious liberty cases. Mr. Pruitt's most well-known position at the time was his outright denial of the scientific consensus on AGW, claiming that carbon dioxide is not a pollutant, and his promises to undo all the work done by the Obama administration to combat it.[133] Pruitt's nomination was notoriously supported by the Evangelical group the Cornwall Alliance, which claimed the following in its "Evangelical Declaration on Global Warming": "Earth and its ecosystems—created by God's intelligent design and infinite power and sustained by His faithful providence—are robust, resilient, self-regulating, and self-corrective, admirably suited for human flourishing, and displaying His glory. Earth's climate system is no exception."[134] Trump ultimately replaced Pruitt with Andrew Wheeler, long-time aide to Senator Jim Inhofe, who waged a successful war on all AGW initiatives for years while maintaining that God "promised to maintain the seasons and that cold and heat would never cease as long as the earth remains."[135]

A further motivation that plays into the picture is general distrust by religious authorities of scientists and science due to clashes over evolution, cosmology, and other related issues. History and recent opinion polls reveal that whenever science reveals something at odds with Christian teachings, Christianity works to undermine the science. When a religiously controversial theory, such as evolution, serves as a foundation for entire fields of scientific inquiry and applied science, it can only result in the retardation of Christian intellectual development throughout these fields. Princeton economist Roland Benabou and two colleagues revealed that across countries, and even across US states, higher levels of religiosity correlated with lower levels of scientific innovation.[136] Millions of potential Einsteins will be lost, along with all their potential contributions, because their parents raised them as Christians. There is no way to calculate these costs to society.

When a religiously controversial theory, such as AGW, requires quick and decisive political action, the effect of Christian biases on public policy can be devastating. Global warming denialists may already have cost the world the only chance it had of avoiding catastrophe by irrationally sowing doubt and resisting reasonable options throughout the short window in which something meaningful could have been done.[137] Millions will likely die or face unprecedented hardship over the next century because of a potentially avoidable disaster. Such Christian doctrines as dominionism are far from the only factors in AGW opposition and denialism, but neither are they trivial ones.

In 2005, journalist Chris Moony documented how the George W. Bush administration, motivated largely by the substantial representation of Evangelical Christians in virtually all federal offices and dominating most advisory panels, suppressed reports by government scientists, not only on AGW, but also on other "culture war" issues, such as birth control and stem-cell research.[138] Each year from 2015 through 2019, the GOP Congress voted to slash funding for further AGW research. As president, flanked by Evangelicals opposing any action on AGW, Donald Trump made it a priority to turn back all progress the United States had made in combatting AGW, setting the planet on an irreversible track to environmental disaster. This is not hyperbole. It is the consensus opinion of knowledgeable experts across the globe.

President Trump called AGW a hoax invented by the Chinese and publicly dismissed the findings of his own interagency task force on AGW because he didn't believe them. Trump appointed a cabinet and administration replete with denialists and fossil fuel insiders. Trump withdrew the United States from the Paris Agreement and rolled back the gains Barack Obama made in addressing this issue. In 2019, Trump officials deleted all mentions of "climate change" from US Geological Survey press releases and buried studies from the Department of Agriculture revealing the devastating effects of AGW to hide the looming emergency. Trump's EPA chief eliminated the EPA's science advisor, systematically reduced the role of scientists in the agency's policy-making process, and dramatically limited the scientific studies the agency could consider. Trump consistently undermined alternative sources of energy, such as renewables, while offering full-throated support to the industries most responsible for AGW: fossil fuels and coal. All these actions were heralded, and arguably driven, by Trump's Evangelical Christian supporters.

One way Christianity negatively affects science and reason is its disparagement of doubt. It is fair to say that in general, atheists do not criticize Christians for their beliefs so much as for their unwarranted *certainty* in those beliefs, which often lead to overplaying their hands. Within Christianity, doubt is generally treated not as an integral component of rational inquiry but as a dangerous obstacle to be overcome because, in the end, the preservation of the faith is valued over all else. By insisting on quick, easy answers to difficult questions and by devaluing doubt and critical analysis of those easy answers, Christianity undermines the very foundation of scientific inquiry.

Christianity also has a history of anti-intellectualism, which has recently manifested itself in a new populism among many conservative Christians, in which intuition, gut instinct, and common sense are hailed as far superior to higher forms of education. This hostility to the educated finds biblical support, mostly in the writings of Paul ("Where is the one who is wise? Where is the scribe? Where is the debater of this age? Has not God made foolish the wisdom of the world?" [1 Corinthians 1:20]). Noting the corrosive effect that increased knowledge of history and the sciences have on Christian belief, such Christians have waged a relentless attack on all methods of formal education other than that of the strictly Christian variety. Recognizing further that analytic thinking leads people to abandon their religious beliefs, politically minded Christian conservatives have likewise sought to demonize any academic field, such as philosophy, that would lead to critical thinking.[139]

An example of Christian anti-intellectualism is the previously referenced film *God's Not Dead*. This film actively perpetuates the myth that secular colleges are engaged in a concerted conspiracy to turn their students away from God and indoctrinate them against Christianity. The villain is a philosophy instructor at a "typical" secular university. The movie ends with a long list of court cases in which on-campus religious groups purportedly argued their First Amendment rights were violated, none of which, the movie fails to acknowledge, succeeded.[140] The message is that higher education is stacked against Christianity and best to be avoided at all cost.

In a review for *Variety*, critic Scott Foundas writes,

> Though you wouldn't exactly guess it from the surveys that repeatedly show upwards of 80% of Americans identifying themselves as Christians, "God's Not Dead" wants us to know that Christianity is under attack in the old U.S. of A.—attack from the liberal, "Duck Dynasty"-hating media, from titans of industry leading lives of wanton decadence, from observers of non-Christian faiths, and worst of all from the world of academia, with its self-important evolutionary scientists and atheistic philosophies.[141]

The problem with this film and others like it is the complete lack of evidence for any anti-Christian conspiracy or systemic bias against Christianity. The real issue for many Christians is that academia fails to support and legitimize Christian claims, and the more people learn, the more they come to recognize this. Absent better arguments or evidence, Christian apologists can only attack secular academia itself in an attempt to poison the well by suggesting it is just an anti-Christian sham.

Secular, college-level academia is designed to teach people how to think. It is designed to focus on the "whys" of belief rather than the "whats," under the assumption that having the right whys will lead people in the right direction, whatever that is. But this is not something with which religions, with their singular focus on "whats," will ever be comfortable. Religious faith requires its adherents to relinquish their ability to freely question—perhaps the most beautiful aspect of who we are as human beings.

ATTACKS ON CONSTITUTIONAL PROTECTIONS

> I contemplate with sovereign reverence that act of the whole American people which declared that their legislature should "make no law respecting an establishment of religion, or prohibiting the free exercise thereof," thus building a wall of separation between Church & State.

> —Thomas Jefferson, Letter to the Danbury Baptist Association, 1802

At a time when we see around the world the violent consequences of the assumption of religious authority by government, Americans may count themselves fortunate: Our regard for constitutional boundaries has protected us from similar travails, while allowing private religious exercise to flourish. . . . Those who would renegotiate the boundaries between church and state must therefore answer a difficult question: Why would we trade a system that has served us so well for one that has served others so poorly?

> —Sandra Day O'Conner, Supreme Court justice,
> *McCreary County, Kentucky v. American Civil*
> *Liberties Union of Kentucky*, 545 U.S. 844, 882 (2005)

[Separation of church and state] is a recent thing that is unhistorical and unconstitutional.

> —Jeff Sessions, US attorney general,
> *Opposing Censorship in Public Schools* (2018)

The First Amendment to the US Constitution states, "Congress shall make no law respecting an establishment of religion or prohibiting the free exercise thereof." This language was drafted by James Madison, whose contemporary writings advocated a "perfect separation" between church and state.[142] In summarizing the Establishment Clause, Madison said that it prohibited Congress from acting so that "one sect might obtain a pre-eminence."[143] In 1947, the US Supreme Court addressed the scope of the Establishment Clause in *Everson v. Board of Education*, in which Justice Hugo Black held,

The "establishment of religion" clause of the First Amendment means at least this: Neither a state nor the federal government can set up a church. Neither can pass laws which aid one religion, aid all religions, or prefer one religion over another. Neither can force nor influence a person to go to or to remain away from church against his will or force him to profess a belief or disbelief in any religion. No person can be punished for entertaining or professing religious beliefs or disbeliefs, for church attendance or non-attendance. No tax in any amount, large or small, can be levied to support any religious activities or institutions, whatever they may be called, or whatever form they may adopt to teach or practice religion. Neither a state nor the Federal Government can, openly or secretly, participate in the affairs of any religious organizations or groups and vice versa. In the words of Jefferson, the clause against establishment of religion by law was intended to erect "a wall of separation between church and State.[144]

The Establishment Clause was written and approved within a very specific context. The American founders had seen the dangers of a state religion and of excessive entanglements between government and religion. The Anglican Church of England and its influence on the British Crown were the subjects of much criticism in the writings of our Founding Fathers. In their view, America was to be a melting pot of many different faiths, with none exercising direct influence over government affairs. The founders were well aware of the history of religious majorities oppressing religious minorities and found a separation of church and state to be the best way to avoid this result.

As Justice Black's opinion makes clear, the Establishment Clause was not limited to the formal establishment of a state religion. If that were all they wanted to do, the founders could have simply banned an official national church, such as that in England, something proposed in an early draft. But they recognized this would not be enough to address the evils of which they wrote. The founders understood that by simply favoring one religion or sect over another, a government would accomplish the same thing de facto. A government that limits or heavily weights the allocation of its resources to one religion or sect to the exclusion of others or to religion over nonreligion will have brought about the very dangers the founders feared and sought to guard against. This would constitute an implicit endorsement, sending the clear message that those not of the favored religion were of a lesser status. This is why the founders ultimately settled on more expansive language that would prohibit the mere *favoring* of religion or religious sects.

This view of the Establishment Clause was noncontroversial for most of American history. Though most Americans remained Christian, there was no organized push for government endorsement or support of their faith. It was understood that among American values was the separation between government and religion and neutrality on religious matters. Consistent with the clear statement to the world expressed in the 1797 Treaty of Tripoli, Americans understood that regarding its government, America was not a Christian nation any more than it was a Muslim nation. It was a secular nation without religious affiliation.

In the 1950s, however, there was a marked change in the national zeitgeist. This was the beginning of the Cold War, in which the Soviet Union was perceived as an existential threat to not only the United States but also the entire world. Populist politicians used nationalism and anti-Soviet fear as highly effective paths to power and influence. Chief among these was Wisconsin senator Joseph McCarthy, who claimed to know of large numbers of Communists and Soviet spies and sympathizers in prominent positions of government and industry within the United States. McCarthy started a witch hunt, in which thousands were blacklisted and millions lived in fear of being branded a Soviet sympathizer.[145]

Prior to 1957, the Christian God was officially absent from government documents, proceedings, and US currency. Neither the dollar bill nor the Pledge of Allegiance mentioned God. During this period of McCarthyism, however, atheism was explicitly associated with Communism, and Christianity with American patriotism. Politicians stepped all over themselves trying to be more pious than the next guy, wearing their Christianity on their sleeves to avoid suspicion. Not wanting to risk any association or sympathy for Communists, frightened politicians supported every measure they could that would conspicuously align themselves and the US government with Christianity. This is the period in which "under God" was inserted into the previously Godless Pledge of Allegiance, and "In God we Trust" became the motto of the United States, replacing "E Pluribus Unum." It was thereafter added to paper money.

Conservative Christians today cite these very things as evidence of America's "core Christian identity," either unaware or deliberately ignoring their dark origins and the sea change they represented.[146] This was a period not of America adhering to its core values but rather of departing from them in response to fear and intimidation. While legislatures were often in thrall to the "tyranny of the majority," the role of safeguarding constitutional protections fell, as it so often does, to the courts. Where legislatures pushed laws that favored Christianity, the courts were there to remind them that the Establishment Clause remained the supreme law of the land, and in its shadow, their laws could not stand.

In the early 1960s, challenges were raised by a Jew and an atheist, respectively, to the mandatory daily recitation of the Lord's Prayer and Bible readings by teachers in public classrooms. The Supreme Court ruled both unconstitutional, holding that a law must have a valid secular purpose and not be used to promote or inhibit a particular religion. Laws requiring all children, regardless of religious belief, to recite a Christian prayer or submit to Christian proselytizing while attending a school paid for by tax dollars failed this test.

In 1971, the Court provided further guidance on the Establishment Clause, holding in *Lemon v. Kurtzman* that government may not "excessively entangle" with religion. The case struck down two Pennsylvania laws, one that permitted the state to purchase services in secular fields from religious schools and the other permitting the state to pay a percentage of the salaries of private school teachers, including teachers in religious institutions. The problem with these arrangements was that they would often result in governments providing disproportionate aid to one religious group over others.

Over the past forty years, conservative Christian groups have intensified their attacks on protections guaranteed by the Establishment Clause. School prayer and the public erection or maintenance of Christian monuments have been the primary lightning rods for their indignation. They adhere to an absurdly narrow reading of the Establishment Clause, maintaining that it prohibits only the formal establishment of a national religion, and argue that Christianity and Christians *should receive favored treatment*, as Christianity remains the predominant religion in America.

To Christians who advocate such positions, I would ask how they would feel if (1) lawmakers wanted to use their tax dollars to support private Muslim schools to teach children Islamic beliefs; (2) police cars and courthouses had "Allah be praised" on them; (3) their children were forced to recite Islamic prayers to be on a public school sports team; or (4) presidential candidates said that the US Constitution should be ignored in favor of Islamic teachings? This is the situation every non-Christian living in America must deal with every day.

On many occasions, ordinary citizens living in staunchly Christian communities have challenged practices that violated the First Amendment. In each case, they have endured severe harassment by Christians. Many involve teenagers challenging unconstitutional practices at their own schools. For example, in 2010, high school junior Jessica Ahlquist protested the hanging of a banner listing an official school prayer in the auditorium of Cranston High School in Rhode Island—a banner raised the same year the Supreme Court struck down official prayer programs. When officials at the school refused to remove the banner, Ahlquist contacted the ACLU, which in 2011 sued on her behalf. The suit succeeded, and the district court judge praised Ahlquist for having the courage to take the case on at the age of sixteen.

Unfortunately, many members of the community didn't agree. Ahlquist was subjected to a torrent of abuse. The day after the ruling, Rhode Island state representative Peter G. Palumbo spoke on a local radio show and referred to Ahlquist an "evil little thing" and a "clapping seal."[147] A Twitter user said, "[T]his girl honestly needs to be punched in the face," and an anonymous commenter posted Ahlquist's home address on the *Providence Journal*'s website. She received numerous death threats and was shadowed by police for a time at school. Ahlquist was even blasted by the 1970s rock star and avowed Christian Meat Loaf, who cited her as an example of why the "world's gone to hell in a handbasket."[148] Things got so out of hand that when the Freedom from Religion Foundation tried to send flowers to Ahlquist, it couldn't find a local florist willing to deliver to her house.

There will be those who resort to the "no true Scotsman" fallacy and say that those who attacked Ahlquist were not "true Christians."[149] But there can be little doubt that Ahlquist's attackers felt justified by their Christian faith or that the entire sordid affair, from the initial unconstitutional hanging of the banner through all the vicious attacks on this young girl, would never have occurred if not for the widespread acceptance of Christianity within Ahlquist's community. Other teenagers who have, like Ahlquist, recently protested the unconstitutional imposition of Christianity in public schools include Zach Kopplin of Louisiana, Krystal Myers of Tennessee, and Corwyn Schulz and Mark Reyes of Texas. All have been subjected to various forms of harassment and abuse by Christians—simply for standing up for their constitutional rights.

The administration of Donald Trump took square aim at the protections afforded to non-Christians by the Establishment Clause. In 2017 Trump appointed Jeff Sessions, a staunch Christian conservative who believes the separation of church and state is "unconstitutional," to serve as US attorney general. On May 4, 2017, the National Day of Prayer, Sessions announced new guidance on "Protections for Religious Liberty," which prioritized religious exemptions over all other rights. In 2018, Sessions implemented a Religious Liberty Task Force within the Justice Department to combat the "dangerous movement, undetected by many" he claimed to be eroding traditional religion.[150] Sessions's view of religious liberty, like many religious conservatives, is characterized by objection to same-sex marriage, transgender identity, birth control, and abortion, and he never disguised that his intent was to allow religious people to openly discriminate against those with whom they disagree on religious principles.

After appointing Sessions, Trump issued an executive order directing regulatory agencies to effectively cease enforcement against organizations that discriminate on religious grounds, which the ACLU denounced as a "broadside to our country's long-standing commitment to the separation of church and state."[151] The same year, Trump's Department of Health and Human Services announced a new Conscience and Religious Freedom Division to be housed within the agency's Office for Civil Rights. Trump's director, Roger Severino, said the objective was to allow workers and institutions to deny patients access to health care if they claim providing such care would conflict with their religious beliefs. The Trump administration announced foster agencies may discriminate on the basis of religion, even if they receive federal funding, meaning, for example, that LGBTQ parents can be denied adoptions on grounds of religious objections.

Finding Sessions insufficiently loyal, Trump replaced him with William Barr. Barr is a staunchly Roman Catholic who disdains the separation of church and state and has called for the imposition of a moral consensus based on God's "natural law." Before his appointment, Barr referred to secularists as "fanatics," whose undermining of the "Judeo-Christian moral tradition" had led to widespread cultural decay.[152] Following his appointment, Barr repeated these themes, warning that "militant secularists" were behind a "campaign to destroy the traditional moral order" and were responsible for every form of social pathology, including drug abuse, rising suicide rates, and illegitimacy.[153] C. Colt Anderson, a Roman Catholic theologian and professor of religion at Jesuit-run Fordham University, has said that Barr sought to demolish the wall between church and state and, as such, represented a "threat to American democracy."[154]

Following the firing of former Exxon executive Rex Tillerson, Trump picked Mike Pompeo as his secretary of state. Mr. Pompeo is an evangelical Christian who wears his faith on his sleeve. He claims the Bible informs everything he does and said he would continue to fight Christian battles as part of the never-ending struggle until the Rapture.[155] In addressing a Muslim audience in Cairo in his official capacity as secretary of state, Pompeo described the importance of his Evangelical faith and made a point of stating he keeps a Bible open on his desk to remind him "of God, his word, and the truth."[156] Before becoming secretary of state, Pompeo described the war on terror as an Islamic battle against Christianity.[157] As secretary of state, Pompeo took a hard line against Iran and in favor of expanding Israel's territory at the expense of Palestinian interests.[158] These positions are directly aligned with Christian Zionists, who believe God promised the land to the Jews and that the gathering of Jews in Israel is a precondition to the Rapture and the ascent of Christians into the Kingdom of God. The most important biblical book to Christian Zionists is the book of Esther, in which the interests of the Jews and Persia, now Iran, are placed in stark contrast. A reporter noted the Bible in Pompeo's office was open and bookmarked to the book of Esther. When asked if Pompeo thought President Trump had been "raised for such a time as this, just like Queen Esther, to help save the Jewish people from the Iranian menace," Pompeo responded, "As a Christian, I certainly believe that's possible."[159] There can be little doubt that Pompeo's foreign policy was guided in large part by his interpretation of Christian Scripture.

Trump nominated Neil Gorsuch to the Supreme Court, despite Gorsuch authoring dissenting opinions in two separate appeals court cases, in which he argued that displays of the Ten Commandments and twelve-foot crosses on public lands did not violate the Establishment Clause. Trump's Department of Justice submitted numerous amicus briefs in cases before the Supreme Court supporting the privileging of Christian beliefs over non-Christian and weaponizing the concept of religious freedom embodied in the 1993 Religious Freedom Restoration Act to allow religious-based discrimination.[160] Trump banned travel and entry for individuals from certain predominantly Muslim countries, calling it a "Muslim ban."

Trump also vowed to repeal the Johnson Amendment, which prohibits churches from endorsing or opposing political candidates from the pulpit to maintain their tax-exempt status. Tax exemptions represent government subsidies. The Johnson Amendment was designed to avoid turning churches into government-funded political action committees, maintaining church-state separation. Trump, by executive order, directed the IRS to effectively end enforcement of the Johnson Amendment, which was not rigorous to begin with—encouraging churches to charge into the political fray.

Trump gave Evangelical Christian leaders what Richard Land, president of the Southern Evangelical Seminary, calls "unprecedented access."[161] Jerry Falwell Jr., former president of one of the largest Christian universities in the world, called Trump Evangelicals' "dream president," explaining that Christians were tired of electing "nice guys" and needed "street fighters" like Trump to go after the "liberal fascist Dems."[162] Ralph Reed, founder and chairman of the Faith and Freedom Coalition, said, "There has never been anyone who has defended us and who has fought for us, who we have loved more than Donald J. Trump. No one!"[163]

Trump's pandering to Christian leaders succeeded in garnering him unprecedented levels of support, despite behavior traditionally viewed by "family values" Evangelicals as highly immoral, such as multiple divorces, serial lying and adultery, paying hush money to porn stars, and boasts of sexually assaulting women. His approval rating among White Evangelical Protestants was in 2019 twenty-five points higher than the national average and five points higher for those attending church at least once per week. Such Christian leaders as Falwell and Franklin Graham followed Trump's lead in supporting Roy Moore in his Alabama Senate campaign after being credibly accused of sexual misconduct with numerous children. Consider that not a single Evangelical publicly criticized Trump for his lavish praise of Kim Jong Un, considered the worst persecutor of Christians in the world.

This can be explained by the fact that these politically active Christians see themselves locked in an existential struggle with the forces of liberalism and the Left. They see their religious beliefs and values being challenged by more secular ones and the withdrawal of public endorsement for their rituals and symbols, such as school prayer and monuments to Christianity, along with the elephant constantly in the room—abortion. Their true enemy in these struggles is the Establishment Clause, with its demands for equal treatment of all religious sects and an equal playing field for religion and nonreligion, as well as its prohibition of religious-based justifications for limiting abortion access or limiting marriage rights. Trump's sustained attacks on the Establishment Clause caused his Evangelical supporters to overlook his flagrant immorality and become his most ardent defenders.

In 2017, Fox News host Tucker Carlson had Amanda Knief of American Atheists on his show to respond to his own outrage, and presumably those of his viewers, about the removal of a Pennsylvania public park bench at a veteran's memorial, upon which was inscribed, through public funding, "Men Who Aren't Governed by God Will Be Governed By Tyrants."[164] This pointed dig at nonbelievers had, not surprisingly, generated a complaint by a nonbelieving resident of the town to American Atheists, which brought it to the attention of the town council, resulting in the removal of the bench. Carlson's machine gun arguments in that segment are representative of the attacks directed today against atheists who invoke the Establishment Clause to defend their rights. In order:

- Atheists are the tyrants because they are trying to remove something many people like.
- Atheists must want this bench gone because they find the word *God* or Christian symbols offensive, not because they are really concerned about the Constitution or find the message itself offensive.
- Theists are in the majority (and so implicitly should get their way for that reason alone).
- Threatening legal action is heavy-handed extortion against poor Christians meant to "crush" them and humiliate Christianity.
- The atheist complainant is a coward for wishing to remain anonymous and should be forced to reveal his identity or not be allowed to complain.
- The bench did not "establish a state religion" and therefore could not violate the Establishment Clause.
- American currency has "In God We Trust" on it, American politicians are often sworn in on Bibles, and American politicians use the word

"God" frequently.[165] The Declaration of Independence refers to the "Creator," which is a synonym for *God*. This selection of cherry-picked facts implicitly makes the point that America is a "Christian nation," in which Christianity should receive favored treatment by the government.

- The offer of American Atheists to pay for a replacement bench bearing a plaque stating "Paid for by American Atheists" would be equivalent to the original inscription accusing nonbelievers of being ruled by tyrants. It would also violate the Establishment Clause, making the atheists who objected to the bench hypocrites. The mere words *American Atheists* would demean all Christians and be offensive to them.

Carlson's arguments play into the false narrative of Christian persecution—that atheists are thugs attempting to eradicate all vestiges of Christianity, strong-arming poor Christians into submission with the threat of expensive legal proceedings. Carlson conveniently ignores the fact that none of the letters from American Atheists complaining of mandatory school prayers, Christian monuments, or government-funded pro-Christian messages would have any effect if American courts had not virtually unanimously found these things to violate the Constitution. Atheists who raise these issues are the patriots supporting American values. It is those standing in opposition to their removal who have forsaken those values.

Christianity, at its core, stands contrary to the core principles of the Constitution. In 1776, there was a serious question of whether people should be considered citizens or subjects. Should they be responsible for the acts of their governments, involved in governing, or subjects of an "all-powerful" monarch? With the US Constitution, our Founding Fathers came down firmly on the side of the former. The great achievement of the West was that it made citizens of its people, replacing ideas of "power" with those of "responsibility." Christianity, however, makes subjects of us all. It is these very values that conservative Christians today are threatening to destroy.

HUMAN GUILT, EMOTIONAL SUFFERING, AND MENTAL HEALTH

Living in sin, with sin, by sin, for sin, every hour, every day, year in, year out. Waking up with sin in the morning, seeing the curtains drawn on sin, bathing it, dressing it, clipping diamonds to it, feeding it, showing it round, giving it a good time, putting it to sleep at night with a tablet of Dial if it's fretful.

—Evelyn Waugh, *Brideshead Revisited*

Christianity is a religion built on guilt. It teaches that all humans are unclean, stained with sin inherited as their birthright. God has made a great sacrifice on our behalf by sending Jesus to suffer and die on the cross, for which we must be forever indebted. To take advantage of this sacrifice, we must acknowledge our insignificance and our inability to make good decisions on our own. To be saved, we must give up control and turn our lives over to Jesus.

It is difficult to square these teachings with the importance psychologists place on self-esteem as an intrinsic motivator. While science instructs us that those who feel good about themselves will be more confident and successful, Christianity teaches the opposite. It tells children they can obtain worth only through something outside their control. They must live forever in service to a being they have never met for a debt they did not incur. They cannot trust themselves but must rely on the teachings of men interpreting an ancient book to guide their every decision.

Christianity also places a unique emphasis on thought control and sexual activity, castigating such natural impulses as envy and sexual desire as wicked and evil. Religious traditions such as Catholicism identify even masturbation as a sinful act. The result is millions of Christians living in psychological torment for much of their lives for having harmless thoughts and emotions beyond their conscious control. Always looming over them is the threat of horrific, eternal torture in Hell. A 1988 study revealed that Christian religious belief was the best overall predictor of total guilt, with a strong correlation between the belief and the guilt.[166]

Psychologists have recognized a specific psychological disorder associated with the anxiety, depression, and social dysfunction caused or exacerbated by religious indoctrination: religious trauma syndrome (RTS). Dr. Marlene Winnell explains that the emotional and mental damage with RTS results from "(1) toxic teachings like eternal damnation or original sin; (2) religious practices or mindset, such as punishment, black and white thinking, or sexual guilt; and (3) neglect that prevents a person from having the information or opportunities to develop normally"—the teachings of many Christian traditions.[167]

There is no way to accurately quantify the psychological and emotional toll Christian teachings have inflicted over the last two-thousand-plus years, but given the billions of Christians who have lived by those teachings, it must be considered astronomical.

ANIMAL RIGHTS

> Man is to be understood only in his relation to God. The beasts are to be understood only in their relation to man and, through man, to God. . . . Atheists naturally regard the co-existence of man and the animals as a mere contingent result of interacting biological facts . . . but a Christian must not think so. Man was appointed by God to have dominion over the beasts, and everything a man does to an animal is either a lawful exercise, or a sacrilegious abuse, of an authority by Divine Right.
>
> —C. S. Lewis, *The Problem of Pain*

No discussion of the harms of Christianity would be complete without discussing the harm to all nonhuman animals. No one who has seen a dog or cat in pain can deny that animals experience intense suffering much like, if not identical to, human beings. Any legitimate system of ethics must take some account of such suffering and hold as an ideal to prevent needless animal suffering. Christianity, however, has long stood in the way of efforts to address such suffering and often has been the direct cause of otherwise unnecessary harm.

Science tells us that man and all other animals are part of the same tree of life, having descended from the same ancestors. Their differences are in degree rather than kind. While modern man is certainly capable of things that no other animal has demonstrated, no one has shown those things to be of sufficient moral significance to justify wanton disregard of animal rights. The tree of life demonstrates that while no nonhuman animal possesses all human traits, they all rest on a continuum, with chimpanzees the closest, sharing 99 percent of our DNA. One thing we know for certain is that these animals experience suffering and pain much like humans. To the extent humans have intrinsic value, so, too, must at least a significant portion of the animal kingdom based on how much they share with us.

But the Bible does not treat them that way. It is clear right from the beginning, in Genesis, that all animals were created *for* man. Genesis states that animals were created to serve man, whose duty it is to "subdue" every living thing.[168] The wording makes clear that animals are to be the slaves of men, who may use them for whatever purpose they wish, including their own amusement. This "dominion mandate," which has driven opposition to such environmental issues as AGW, has likewise led Christians to devalue animals and their feelings. Whatever value animals may have, it is not intrinsic but solely based on the use they can serve to humans. Such reasoning caused such Christian apologists as René Descartes to see animals as machines, whose cries of pain were the sounds of "broken machinery."[169]

God commanded the Israelites to sacrifice animals for no other purposes than that God enjoyed the smell of burning flesh and that these sacrifices demonstrated the loyalty of God's subjects. Such sacrifices did not atone for sins or serve any other theological purpose. They did not provide food or serve any other practical earthly purpose, for the meat itself was burned. These sacrifices signified that the lives of animals were so worthless that they could be killed, even when that killing served no purpose other than potentially the momentary sensory pleasure of a deity. We must keep in mind that the Bible sets God up as the ultimate role model, imparting morals by actions as well as commands. The message to God's subjects about how they should treat animals is perfectly clear.

Many passages from the Old Testament demonstrate God's complete disregard for animal life. On numerous occasions, God kills animals for the sins or decisions of humans. The animals might belong to the humans making the offensive decisions or may simply reside on the same land. One particularly egregious example is the plagues visited on Egypt, ravaging humans and animals alike, for the decision of Pharaoh to refuse the Israelites to leave Egypt. God commanded Joshua to cut the Achilles tendons of captured horses, inhumanely crippling them, and condoned David doing the same repeatedly (Joshua 11:6; 2 Samuel 8:4; Chronicles 18:4). Proverbs 12:10 does instruct treating the animals *one owns* humanely, though the underlying assumption is that animals are mere property. The limitation to *owned* animals betrays that the true concern is for the animal's owner, as the usefulness to the owner is diminished by mistreated animals. If God recognized all animals as having intrinsic value, then *He would have instructed them all to be treated humanely*, but He does not.

The New Testament fares little better when it comes to animal rights. Ethicist Peter Singer explains that while the Old Testament "did at least show flickers of concern for their sufferings," the New Testament is "completely lacking in any injunction against cruelty to animals, or any recommendation to consider their interests."[170] Jesus himself, with the power to dispose of a group of demons however he wished, sent them into a group of pigs, knowing they would drive the pigs off a cliff to their deaths. The message: Pigs are intrinsically worthless and therefore appropriate vessels for demons. Jesus, as a good Jew, would have participated in the regular ritual slaughter of animals for, as demonstrated previously, no reason of benefit to any human.

Animal charities are overwhelmingly secular. Of the top fifty animal charities worldwide, not a single one is associated with Christianity. Compare this to the charitable groups tasked with stopping abortion or promoting gay conversion therapy. In the Christian worldview, a one-day-old group of cells on the uterine wall of a human is more important than an entire family of chimpanzees. Money is better spent on the pointless shaming of gays than preventing cruelty to dogs, cats, dolphins, or elephants, each shown to have remarkably complex social lives.

The Bible is entirely anthropocentric. It is concerned only with humans, which it presents as so different in kind from every other creature as to exclusively deserve fair and just treatment (as that standard is inconsistently defined within its pages). It demonstrates no concern with animal welfare, and accordingly, neither does Christianity as a religion. Anyone who values animal welfare must acknowledge this value is not reflected within the seminal work of Christianity's perfect and loving God. Such value can come only from secular morality.

THE APOLOGETIC RESPONSE

Christian apologists will complain that I have not properly accounted for the "other side of the story." They will argue that Nazis and the KKK do not represent "true" Christians or "true" Christian values. They will say that alongside those passages promoting hatred and intolerance, the Bible contains many positive passages, as well, such as the direction to love one's neighbor as oneself. Some of these can be read to negate the more destructive passages. Some of the negative passages, furthermore, can be interpreted to be not so negative if read in the proper context. Christianity, they will further claim, has undoubtedly been responsible for much good in the world that this analysis fails to reflect.

A. The Racists and Homophobes Do Not Represent "True" Christians; They Have Interpreted the Bible Incorrectly

As to the first point, those keeping up with logical fallacies will recognize this as the "no true Scotsman" fallacy. The problem is there is no official definition of a Christian and no objective method of identifying "true" Christian values. KKK members can cite Christian Scripture to support their views, along with interpretations that have been well accepted by legitimate Christian scholars for more than a thousand years.

You would have to say that Augustine was not a true Christian—or Luther—or virtually all the popes through the modern age, as they all held similar views. You can certainly criticize the Nazis as being horrible human beings, but you cannot say with any legitimate authority they were not true Christians. Did they focus on some passages while ignoring others? Of course. But every Christian does that. The problem, many will say, is that they focused on the *wrong passages* and interpreted them the wrong way. But what source would one use to back this up?

If God exists, then He gave us no way to arbitrate such disputes. He provided no method to distinguish the "right" forms of Christianity from the "wrong" ones—no common standard for determining the "proper" interpretation of Christian Scripture. Abraham Lincoln acknowledged in his second inaugural address that both antislavery Northerners and proslavery Southerners "read the same Bible and pray to the same God and each invokes his aid against the other."[171]

To say that the "right" interpretations are the ones that happen to agree with one's own internal sense of right and wrong is begging the question—assuming that God's moral sense accords with your own, so God must have intended the interpretation that intuitively appeals to you. If everyone took this position, then each would follow a separate and unique standard, claiming it to be God's will. How is this any better than what Christian apologists claim atheists do in arriving at a moral code? It is no better. Due to the certainty Christians generally ascribe to their interpretations and the divine mandate they accept to live and spread their beliefs, it is actually much worse.

The New Testament undoubtedly contains many admirable teachings. Jesus taught much about helping the less fortunate, preventing needless suffering, and treating others with respect. The problem is that these teachings exist alongside others, often more specific, that teach the opposite. The Bible does not speak with a single voice on such issues. Jesus's teachings, moreover, when understood in the apocalyptic context of his overall message, lose many of their admirable qualities. Jesus was focused on the short term, crash-coursing for the big exam, not a long-term proscription for living one's life.

So when apologists claim that racists or sexists have misinterpreted Christian Scripture or failed to consider certain passages, I say that is precisely the point! The Bible is so open to interpretation that it can be used to support many inconsistent positions—from love to hatred and everything in between. Why would a loving God allow this? Why would He include so many passages that can be used by intelligent and knowledgeable people to support hateful positions? If God truly had the qualities apologists assign to him, then He wouldn't.

Christianity is at its core problematic because its Scripture is problematic. No one can legitimately lay claim to "true" Christianity. We must recognize that as long as we treat the Scriptures as magically special, there will be people doing violence and spreading hatred and bigotry in the name of Christianity. The real problem is privileging a set of ambiguous texts so people can justify their own hatred and call it the will of God. This renders their position immune from rational argument. It also grounds any actions taken in furtherance of their hatred with legitimacy that feeds on itself, stoking their prejudices and anger to ever greater intensity.

B. Christianity Has Been Responsible for Much Good in the World, Outweighing Any Bad

The second response is to claim that Christianity brings about an enormous amount of good in the world. My initial reply is skepticism. This claim is so firmly entrenched in Western society that it is rarely challenged, but it is rare to find any attempt to support it with solid evidence. Such evidence would initially need to demonstrate that the "goods" attributed to Christianity would not exist without it.

For example, Christian churches are involved in many charitable activities with broad outreach. But unlike private charities, churches are typically tax exempt. They avoid billions of dollars in taxes each year that are paid by nonreligious charitable organizations. To the extent such money is used to fund their charitable activities, it would be more accurate to say those activities are funded by taxpayers. Who is to say that such nonreligious organizations as Doctors without Borders or UNICEF would not do as good a job, if not better, if funded to the same degree with tax subsidies? At a minimum, their outreach would be expanded enormously.

Secular organizations benefit from a much narrower focus—providing tangible benefits to the needy. Christian charities, by contrast, are sidetracked by the need to proselytize and the additional resources that requires. The specious value of such proselytizing was pointed out no more brilliantly than in Matt Parker and Trey Stone's Broadway musical *The Book of Mormon* and, specifically, the song "Hasa Diga Eebowai," whose lyrics I do not print here, but you can look them up.

Nor do secular charities need to spend their money on real estate and religious art, as churches do. Writer Avro Manhattan concludes that the Catholic Church alone is the "biggest financial power, wealth accumulator and property owner in existence. She is a greater possessor of material riches than any other single institution, corporation, bank giant trust, government or state of the whole globe."[172] Gaudy buildings, jewels, art, and fine clothing are among the substantial assets of the church. Nonreligious nonprofits do not engage in such wealth accumulation.

Unlike secular nonprofits, furthermore, churches need not publicly account for their finances. Every year, church leaders are indicted for stealing church funds, in cases that must come to light through circuitous means. There is undoubtedly far more financial fraud among churches than nonprofit charities, meaning that much of the money they collect is going into the pockets of the wrong people. With their opacity and complete lack of accountability, churches are perfectly structured to facilitate massive fraud. One cannot reliably say that the charitable contributions of churches represent a "good" attributable to Christianity, for this avoids the enormous opportunity costs of outsourcing these charities to churches.

Even if we ignore opportunity costs, it is impossible to trace the positive acts of Christian churches, groups, and individuals to teachings unique to Christianity. Many positive Christian teachings simply reflect widespread moral intuitions common to Christians and non-Christians alike. Others reflect the teachings of secular ethical philosophies or even religions that long predated Christianity. Humanist principles were widely incorporated into Christian teachings as a result of the Enlightenment, causing certain antihumanist teachings to be marginalized or ignored altogether. Many Christians have chosen to promote humanist values from within their existing religious tradition and then co-opt them as "Christian values." Christianity cannot claim credit for actions ultimately based on secular grounds just because the actors consider themselves Christians. One thing that can be said for certain about the evolution of social norms among mainstream Christians is that they did not result from a closer reading of Christian Scripture.

Christian apologists may point to the fact that many Christians were involved in, say, the abolitionist movement as an argument that Christianity was responsible for positive social change. But so, too, were Christians on the opposite side, as well. And wouldn't it have been easier for the abolitionists if one of the Ten Commandments had been "Don't keep slaves?" Wouldn't this have been infinitely more helpful than the one about graven images? It could even have been included as one of the other six hundred prohibitions, maybe in place of the one about boiling a baby goat in its mother's milk. And wouldn't abolitionists' jobs have been easier if the Bible didn't contain so many rules for keeping slaves? There is not a single passage of the Bible that clearly denounces slavery. Abolitionists did not make their case because of their Scripture but in spite of it.

Apologists also claim that Christianity provides meaning and purpose for billions of believers. But as I discuss elsewhere in this book, Christianity has no monopoly on either. Atheists find meaning and purpose in their own lives, even if it is of a different character than that of Christians. Things need not be permanent or significant on a cosmic scale to be meaningful. There is no evidence that atheists' lives are any less fulfilled simply because they do not subscribe to the Christian view of a transcendent purpose for humanity. Nor is there evidence that atheists are less likely to appreciate beauty, to experience transcendence, or to act more selfishly than Christians.

What about those stories of drunks or drug addicts who turned their lives around after embracing Christianity? Much research has concluded that social support systems and accountability to a set of standards improve the quality of people's lives, regardless of the source. Christianity in many cases supplies these very things. But it is not unique in this regard. Secular support groups serve the same functions, helping people turn their lives around and get back on their feet. Without evidence demonstrating Christian support systems to be more effective than non-Christian systems, Christianity cannot claim such "success stories" as evidence of its value. Christian support services may be more abundant, but this is hardly surprising, given their greater access to funds and tax subsidies. A leveling of the playing field would certainly result in a substantial narrowing of the gap between religious and nonreligious support groups.

Many Christians cite their faith as a source of emotional strength and support. I do not doubt that such faith can be comforting, but it is a false comfort. It serves the same function as a placebo prescribed by a doctor. Just as a placebo can provide one with actual relief from pain based solely on psychological factors, so, too, can faith provide relief from emotional pain. But as a placebo is to effective medicine, so is faith to evidence-based treatments of psychological fatigue and damage. Evidence-based treatments have the distinct advantage of being tailored based on what works best in unique circumstances of emotional turmoil. Such treatments have the added benefit of not being based on false assumptions and not perpetuating the range of societal ills detailed in this book.

Even if apologists could identify a large sum of public good uniquely attributable to Christianity, however, this is not the question with which we should be concerned. The real question is whether, when the bad caused by Christianity is weighed against the good, the *net result* is negative or positive. Does it do more good than harm? Only then could Christianity be considered a positive force in the world, regardless of its truth.

I have yet to see any Christian apologist make a compelling case that Christianity represents a net good, and I don't believe such a case is possible.[173] I think it likely that the limited good Christianity accomplishes is not worth it. Anyone making such a claim must present evidence to establish a positive case without begging the question (such as by assuming the truth of the Bible to argue that Jesus forgives human sin, which is a problem of the Bible's making). I would challenge the reader to come up with even ten examples of societal goods uniquely attributable to Christianity. The apologist must then account for all the evils I have identified and justify them in relation to the goods, demonstrating that the goods more than balance the scales. No apologist of who I am aware has seriously attempted this, much less accomplished it. Given the ample opportunity they have had, I believe we can comfortably assume none ever will.

C. Conclusion

There is overwhelming evidence that Christianity has caused and continues to cause great suffering and societal harm. Jesus reportedly said, "by their fruits ye shall know them" (Matthew 7:20), and the fruits of Christianity are bitter indeed. These effects are typically ignored or glossed over in Western discourse but must be considered in determining whether Christianity, when netted out against its harm, provides the world with any value. There are good reasons to believe it does not.

In June 2013, the humor website The Onion published a parody article titled "Eminem Terrified as Daughter Begins Dating Man Raised on His Music." The article lampoons famed rapper Eminem's sudden anxiety as he realized his daughter's boyfriend was a huge fan of his: "Citing lyrics where he discussed raping a woman with an umbrella to 'make her p***y wider,' the visibly shaken multi-platinum artist said he can't imagine sitting by while his oldest daughter spends time alone with a man whose worldview could have been even slightly influenced by any of his songs."[174]

As I read this, I could not help but think of family-values-spouting Evangelical Christians, whom I would expect to be just as appalled to find their daughter dating someone raised on literature that justifies rape, incest, misogyny, and so on. Instead, they find this desirable, so long as the literature in question is the Bible. The mental gymnastics required to harmonize their worldview must be exhausting.

Christian beliefs regarding what God wants and expects have led to much human suffering. I am generally ambivalent about people's religious *beliefs*, but when the rights, privileges, and happiness of living, breathing human beings are compromised by those beliefs, I feel compelled to take sides. The rights of a gay person to marry or a critically ill person to receive lifesaving stem-cell treatment must never be considered equal to the rights of the faithful to adhere to the regulations of their chosen deity. You can believe what you want, but when that belief collides with the very real rights of others, it is the beliefs that must give way.

One might argue that neither Christianity nor any other religion should be singled out. One could argue that secular ideologies and doctrines have caused much misery, as well. I would agree with that. But such religions as Christianity are capable of causing far more harm than secular ideologies for one reason: They are based on the revealed will of invisible and undetectable beings and events in a world to which we will never have access. They therefore have no reality check. Their principles are announced by human "prophets," who cannot be questioned or subjected to checks and balances. They cannot be evaluated by their consequences. They are uniquely armored against criticism, questioning, and self-correction—against anything that could prevent them from spinning into extreme immorality. As writer Greta Cristina so colorfully puts it, "religion takes the human impulses towards evil, and cuts the brake line, sending them careening down a hill and into the center of town."[175]

7

WHAT ABOUT
LIBERAL CHRISTIANITY?

Liberal Christian: "I don't support hate, violence or discrimination. I just devote my life to the teachings of a book that supports hate, violence and discrimination."

—Anonymous internet meme

Perhaps you have read so far and think, "Okay, I understand what you're saying, and I don't necessarily disagree with most of it. I don't take the Bible literally. I don't believe it represents perfectly accurate history or science. I accept it as a product of its time. I believe it speaks primarily in metaphor and allegory and to broader truths. I believe in evolution and oppose teaching biblical Creation in public schools. I oppose racism, sexism, and other forms of tribalism. I don't see God as some bearded old man surrounded by harp-playing angels but more as a cosmic force representing love and tolerance. I can accept Jesus as a wise teacher without insisting that he performed miracles or was born of a virgin. I believe the main messages of the Bible, as conveyed by Jesus, were positive ones, such as loving one's neighbor. I leave the complicated doctrinal issues to theologians." In short, you are a liberal or moderate Christian.[1] What, you may ask, is the problem with that?

In many respects, I would say I have no problem with it. Moderate Christians are not wedded to restrictive religious doctrines or strict positions on social issues based on dogma. They are relatively open to the teachings of science and history and less likely to impose their religious beliefs on others or to support political parties and candidates who do. Many could be classified as cultural Christians, meaning they identify as Christians based more on a shared culture than agreement with the doctrinal positions of Christianity. As to many of their practical values and day-to-day activities, they are virtually indistinguishable from secular humanists. If all Christians were moderates, then we would not be faced with the interminable culture wars that continue to dominate American society. If all Christians were moderates, then most of the problems I detail in the previous chapter would not exist.

But that is not to say that liberal Christianity is entirely innocuous. While direct harm is far less prevalent, there are many areas in which liberal Christianity causes indirect harm or harm simply disguised. Many of these are effects of liberal Christianity on the way people think and the values they hold. For example, liberal Christianity has no clear rules and no firm foundation—no intellectually defensible core. It represents an ad hoc system of theology based on subjective cherry-picking of Scripture that can be all things to all people. It also continues to privilege the Bible and to accord unwarranted value to faith. It aids the spread of more extreme forms of Christianity, inhibits critical thinking, and contributes to the perpetuation of a worldview that fails to reflect reality. It further undercuts critical thought by marking off areas of inquiry and guarding the door. For these reasons, it is not an adequate solution to the problems discussed.

USEFUL DEFINITIONS

For this section, I reference a continuum of Christian belief, with fundamentalism on the far right and liberal Christianity on the far left. Those falling to the right of the midpoint of this continuum I call conservatives, while those falling to the left I call moderates or liberals. To the far right are fundamentalists. The vast majority of Christians fall somewhere between these extremes.

Fundamentalism in its purest form reflects a literal interpretation of the Bible with every passage taken at face value whenever possible. When interpretation is necessary, the fundamentalist defers to traditional church dogma and the opinions of established theologians recognized by their church as authoritative. If conflicts arise between Scripture as traditionally interpreted and modern scientific or historical findings, then fundamentalists insist the latter give way. For the fundamentalist, acceptance of the Bible is an all-or-nothing affair.

By contrast, there is no pure form of liberal Christianity. The left pole of the continuum represents those willing to accept highly idiosyncratic interpretations of Scripture but who nonetheless identify as Christians. Liberals typically maintain certain core Christian beliefs, such as in the God of the Old Testament, the divine inspiration of the Bible, and a historical Jesus who lived approximately two thousand years ago. They differ significantly, however, on everything else.

Due to their tendency to selectively pick and choose the church doctrines they accept and follow, liberals are often referred to pejoratively by their more conservative brothers as "cafeteria Christians." Their views vary widely, as they don't feel constrained by any particular creed. They often attend the church in which they feel *most comfortable* rather than systematically comparing their beliefs with the established doctrines of that church. At some point, the views of these individuals veer so far afield of church doctrine and theological creeds that it is a stretch to call them Christians at all.

A BRIEF HISTORY

To understand the problems with liberal Christianity, one must appreciate the historical context in which it arose. Until the late eighteenth century, there was no such thing. All organized Christian denominations would be considered conservative by today's standards. In the late 1700s, however, Western civilization was rocked by the Enlightenment. Enlightenment thinkers emphasized reason and individualism rather than tradition and faith. They sought to promote scientific thought, skepticism, and free intellectual interchange.

Many Christians of the time sought to reform their faith by bringing it more in line with Enlightenment ideals. Such philosophers as John Locke and David Hume advocated an "unprejudiced examination" of Scripture and a focusing on the essence of Christianity, which Locke believed to be a belief in Christ as redeemer. Thomas Jefferson went further, dropping all passages dealing with miracles, visitations of angels, and the Resurrection of Jesus to extract a practical moral code from the New Testament, which he felt was the only thing about it of true value.

Higher criticism was a term initially applied to a scholarly movement out of Germany that picked apart the human sources and development of ancient texts, including the Bible. This movement would call into question the roots, accuracy, and historicity of the bedrock of Christian Scripture. These were the first scholars to deliberately engage in systemic critical analysis rather than the devotional approach that came before. They made it possible for people to seriously doubt whether the Bible was a divinely inspired work.

Liberal Christianity picked up steam in the 1800s with the widespread success of science in answering questions traditionally reserved for theologians, including the publication of Darwin's *Origin of the Species*, which undermined many core beliefs of Christian fundamentalists. As science marched forward, many Christians observed irreconcilable conflicts between scientific findings and traditional Christian teachings. Rather than rejecting their faith of birth, however, they took a different approach. Heavily invested in Christianity through both tradition and emotion, they continued the quest of the Enlightenment thinkers to work within the system to make Christianity more compatible with science.

In the early 1900s, a conflict arose within Christianity known as the fundamentalist-modernist controversy. This schism resulted in much heated discussion and a more formal taking of sides among denominations and congregations. Ernestine van der Wall, a professor of the history of Christianity at Leiden University in the Netherlands, introduces his discussion of the origins of the disagreement in the early 1900s:

> All in all, the new scientific approach to the Bible caused men and women to ask themselves whether the Bible was merely a collection of myths, legends, and folklore, whether there was a kernel of history in it—and if so, what that kernel contained. The imagery of the "kernel" and the "husk" was immensely popular in modernist discourse. Actually, it was a modern rephrasing of a much older distinction in religious history, that between the "necessaria" and "non-necessaria," the fundamentals and non-fundamentals of faith. The "fundamentals," of course, was the term Christian conservatives in the United States made their own in the anti-modernist crusade in the early twentieth century, and "fundamentalist," a term coined in 1920, is merely a label derived from this notion.[2]

This controversy first arose in the Presbyterian Church, resulting in a denominational split in 1936, but quickly spread to other Protestant denominations.

During the twentieth century, liberal Christianity was shaped further by social justice movements. The most influential manifestation was the Christian Social Gospel, which sought to replace such "spiritual evils" as capitalism, nationalism, and militarism with socialism, internationalism, and pacifism. Other liberal theological movements of this period included liberation theology, postmodern Christianity, and Christian existentialism. Mainline Protestant churches were heavily influenced by liberal Christianity throughout the twentieth century, believing it to be the future of the faith.

By the end of the twentieth century, every major Protestant denomination had accommodated liberalism to one degree or another. The tent of liberal Christianity covered a wide diversity of belief. One thing they had in common, however, was that their beliefs would have been deemed heretical throughout virtually the entire history of the Christian Church. If a liberal Christian of the late twentieth century had been transported back to the Middle Ages, he most likely would have been burned at the stake. Times had certainly changed.

AD HOC THEOLOGY

> There is no harmony between religion and science. When science was a child, religion sought to strangle it in the cradle. Now that science has attained its youth, and superstition is in its dotage, the trembling, palsied wreck says to the athlete: "Let us be friends." It reminds me of the bargain the cock wished to make with the horse: "Let us agree not to step on each other's feet."
>
> —Robert Green Ingersoll, *The Truth Seeker* (1885)

Liberals distinguish themselves from fundamentalists by their willingness to "interpret" Scripture, such as determining whether a passage should be read literally or metaphorically. But this is not entirely fair. Fundamentalists, too, acknowledge the occasional need for interpretation, but they handle it differently. Fundamentalists are more likely to defer to the extensive writings of the Church Fathers, who took the messy puzzle pieces of Scripture and attempted to systematically build from them a coherent, intellectually defensible faith. They worked to create a model in which internal inconsistencies were minimized, to the extent possible, without sacrificing the big picture. They also appreciated Ockham's razor, generally preferring the most parsimonious interpretation.

The approach of Christian liberals, by contrast, has been more pragmatic and idiosyncratic. Rather than building a comprehensive system from the ground up, moderates have selectively modified more traditional Christian theology reactively based on an evolving scientific and moral landscape. They have rejected interpretations that conflict with accepted scientific knowledge and widely shared moral principles. They have relaxed rules that would otherwise not allow for views according with modern sensibilities. They have ignored or written out anything in the Scripture that would prove embarrassing or difficult to explain.[3] In doing so, however, they have largely abandoned any attempt to maintain systematic integrity and coherence.[4] The result is a Gordian knot of internal contradictions.

One example involves the Garden of Eden. Because of our current scientific knowledge, liberals generally reject a literal Adam and Eve. Neither evolution nor anthropology allows for any interpretation other than a purely allegorical one. This story, however, provides the basis of the Fall and Original Sin, which in turn justifies Jesus's entire mission. Without Adam and Eve as historical figures and their account as a historical narrative, there would have been no reason for Jesus to suffer or die. One cannot justifiably reject the former without also rejecting the latter.

Well-known apologist Tim Keller, author of *The Reason for God*, aptly summarizes the issue:

> [Paul] most definitely wanted to teach us that Adam and Eve were real historical figures. When you refuse to take a biblical author literally when he clearly wants you to do so, you have moved away from the traditional understanding of the biblical authority. . . . If Adam doesn't exist, Paul's whole argument—that both sin and grace work "covenantally"—falls apart. You can't say that Paul was a "man of his time" but we can accept his basic teaching about Adam. If you don't believe what he believes about Adam, you are denying the core of Paul's teaching.[5]

The New Testament contains much more evidence that a literal interpretation is required to make sense of Christianity. Paul speaks of Adam as the first man in Romans 5:14 and explicitly bases his teaching on literally interpreting Genesis 1–3 (See 1 Timothy 2:12–14). Paul's landmark teaching on Resurrection in 1 Corinthians 15 includes these statements: "For as in Adam all die, so also in Christ all will be made alive" (15:22) and "The first *man*, Adam, *became a living soul*. The last Adam became a life-giving spirit" (15:45). Jude also takes Genesis 1–11 literally: "Enoch, in the seventh generation from Adam, prophesied" (Jude 1:14). Luke explicitly traces Jesus's genealogy back to Adam and no further, clearly indicating that Adam was literally the first man. To argue otherwise is to render all these passages false or incomprehensible.

If some belief D is premised on beliefs A, B, and C, then you cannot simply disregard beliefs A–C while embracing some variant of D. Having renounced the very foundation on which D rests, you must now erect a new foundation for D from scratch. To do otherwise is to engage in the fallacy of the stolen concept. Likewise, one cannot simply accept certain core teachings of Christianity while rejecting the interpretations that led to those teachings. You can't just gerrymander your own version of God without regard to the theological consequences.

Liberal Christians lack the orderly, disciplined approach known as systematic theology. Systematic theologians understand the need to account for all sacred Christian Scripture in a coherent way. They recognize the hypocrisy of openly cherry-picking Scripture or personalizing interpretations without regard to how those interpretations may affect others or fit into the larger whole. They understand that to garner legitimacy, biblical interpretations and doctrines must be based on neutral principles that apply universally and systematically. Those principles must apply on the front rather than the back end. They must apply consistently and prospectively rather than reactively and capriciously. They must guide readers in how to interpret other Scripture, allowing us to successfully make predictions about how similar passages will be read in other books of the Bible.

Liberal theology does none of these things. It is inherently ad hoc, as variable and mercurial as the reader and his or her opinions. There are no right answers because there is no standard by which to judge the validity of another's interpretations. Within reason, everyone gets the interpretation he or she desires, and the church authorities rarely push back. Liberal theology is brilliant from a sales perspective, especially to the more independently minded, but lacks an intellectually rigorous foundation.

Liberals who embrace modern science but wish to hold onto their biblical faith must reconcile the following: God has existed forever for no apparent reason; for some unknown purpose, 14 billion years ago, God created our known universe, did nothing for 10 billion years, created the Earth as the third planet from an unremarkable star in an unremarkable galaxy among billions of others, resumed doing nothing for billions of years, and created life and caused it to evolve gradually over millions more years through fits and starts down innumerable dead ends until one path gave rise to humans. I have never seen a comprehensive explanation that attempts to account for these points in any coherent way. Liberal Christians eschew the hard work of coming up with such explanations, leaning heavily into the appeal to mystery.

One argument by liberal Christians is that the more miraculous stories in the Bible may have been intended as metaphor or symbolism (see figure 7.1). But the Bible uses no identifiable method to distinguish symbolic from actual events. All these events are presented as literal history and were generally interpreted as such until modern science rendered such interpretations untenable. If God used a metaphorical fairy tale to begin the Bible, then why shouldn't we also consider other similarly fantastical stories to be fairy tales, as well, such as Jonah and the big fish, talking donkeys, the flood,

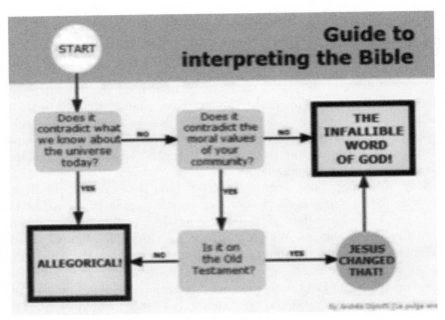

Figure 7.1.   Guide to Interpreting the Bible.

the Sun standing still, and the virgin birth? If one is willing to reject the literal truth of any of these, then why not every other implausible claim for which the only evidence comes from Scripture? Why not, for example, the Resurrection itself? No one holds a reliable metaphor detection device that could distinguish, say, the seven-day Creation from the virgin birth. Unless a consistent standard is employed, such interpretations must be treated as what they are: ad hoc rationalizations.

Another example of ad hoc rationalization is the strong, ecumenical outlook embraced by many liberal churches in which other religions are to be not only tolerated but also embraced. Perhaps the most extreme organized example is the Unitarian Universalist Church, which maintains that all religions are valid, merely representing different paths to the great spiritual truths. Whether you worship Jesus or Vishnu, you will get to the same place if you are sincere. This philosophy was represented narratively in the best-selling book (and movie) by Yann Martel, *Life of Pi*.

I sympathize with and commend Unitarian Universalists and other similarly minded moderates on their inclusive attitudes toward other religions. Many of their beliefs are indistinguishable from nonreligious humanists. But there is simply no way to harmonize such a position with a defensible reading of Christian Scripture. The tenets of Islam, for example, do not allow for Jesus to be God. If any clear chord resonates through the entire Bible, it is that faith in God and Jesus is the *one and only path to salvation*. Christianity is, if nothing else, an exclusivist religion. One can respect the tenets of all religions, or one can respect truth, but one cannot have it both ways.

Countless other examples exist, but the point is that liberal theology is simply incoherent. It can be characterized only negatively—in terms of what aspects of fundamentalist theology it rejects. It does not represent a valid, theologically sound model of its own. It would be as though someone tried to sell you a beautiful concept home but could not articulate how the home would hold together or how it would be constructed. It is one thing to claim an idiosyncratic interpretation, but that interpretation must be grounded on something solid. Unfortunately, that is just what liberal theology lacks.

UNDEFINED STANDARDS

> "Religion is a metaphor" is a floating plank of wood to which a castaway on the sea of reality desperately clings after the good ship "religion" has been dashed to pieces on the rocks of reason.
>
> —*Jesus and Mo* comic strip

Related to the first issue is another problem: Moderate Christianity employs no clear, defined standards to determine which scriptural interpretations should be considered valid and which should be rejected. The process is an individual and entirely relativistic one based on comparing the traditional interpretation with one's own moral instincts or understanding of science and rejecting those interpretations that result in serious conflicts. The very term *interpretation* becomes synonymous with "reading it to say whatever you want it to say." But such a subjective interpretive framework cannot legitimately ground a belief system. One might as well ignore Scripture altogether and simply decide on gut instinct.

The American legal system employs specific rules to interpret ambiguous laws. One such rule is that every word that appears in a statute must be considered in interpreting it. None can be ignored as superfluous, for the courts must assume that if the legislators decided to include it, then they had good reasons to do so. Another rule is that statutory language is to be taken at face value based on its ordinary meaning unless there is a very compelling reason this cannot be done—an application of Ockham's razor. In summary, American law prevents judges from ignoring or redefining the words of statutes without substantial justification. Such a practice is no more defensible when dealing with interpretation of Scripture.

Subjectively cherry-picking interpretations of supposedly divinely inspired Scripture to create a more theologically palatable picture, furthermore, is epistemically indefensible. One cannot justifiably argue for a nonliteral interpretation without appealing to an objective interpretive framework. Pragmatically conforming the meaning to shifting social norms does not represent such a framework. If the terrain doesn't agree with the map, then the only reasonable approach is to assume the map is wrong and throw it away. You can't rewrite reality to conform to the map or ignore large segments of the map to conform it to reality. Likewise, one should not have to resort to mental gymnastics to conform the Bible to our knowledge of science, history, or morality.

If the biblical text is indeed divinely inspired, as Christianity requires it to be, then who are we to second-guess it? If fallible humans can determine by whim which passages to accept and how they should be interpreted, then they must forfeit the right to treat any of it as somehow "special" or authoritative, for how can they reliably know what represents valid authority and what doesn't? The Bible renders this dilemma insoluble because it rejects the idea that human reason can even be trusted.

A system in which everyone's interpretation is to be treated as equally valid, furthermore, renders Christianity arbitrary. With no objective means of determining how the Bible should be read, one person's opinion is as valid as any other. Christianity becomes a meaningless label and a justification for following one's own desires. Moderates have succeeded in creating a loophole for avoiding conflicts, but that loophole is so large as to covalidate every competing belief system. There becomes no principled way to distinguish the legitimacy of Christianity from other religions or no religion at all.

The left turn of many liberal churches on same-sex romantic relation-ships, admirable as it may be, is a perfect example of this. The position of the churches did not budge until public opinion on same-sex romantic relationships changed and it came into the societal mainstream. Leading up to and immediately following the Supreme Court's 2015 *Obergefell* opin-ion, many liberal congregations suddenly extended the olive branch to the LGBTQ community. If your church's interpretation of its most sacred texts depends on popular opinion or court decisions, then perhaps those texts should not have been treated as sacred in the first place. Wouldn't it be more intellectually honest to simply admit these passages (and, even more so, the entire book) were never divinely inspired to begin with? Ockham's razor rears its head yet again.

To follow and promote a belief system, one must take it seriously. Dif-ficult issues must be dealt with in a way that is intellectually honest. Assume your teenage daughter comes to you and describes a boy she's been dat-ing and plans to marry. She says the guy is easygoing, has a great job, and makes her feel fantastic. He is super cool in every way, except for one thing: the slaves he keeps chained in the basement. Would you recommend she simply ignore this troubling fact or rationalize it and marry him anyway? Whenever biblical morality conflicts starkly with our common moral intu-itions, we must resolve those conflicts before moving forward, and not in a glib or superficial way, as liberal Christianity attempts to do.

Likewise, moderates typically employ definitions of *God*, the *Trinity*, and other foundational Christian concepts that are so vague as to be unintel-ligible. In doing so, they reject objectively verifiable criteria for assessing Christian claims. They rob words of their traditional meanings, turning solid to gas. This keeps their critics from pinning them down, as the arrows of legitimate criticism pass harmlessly through. Arguing with someone em-ploying such an approach is like playing chess with a chicken. You can make all the right moves according to the rules of the game, as they simply knock pieces over and declare victory. When words can be endlessly redefined to mean anything, the rules of debate no longer apply.

But this approach comes at a hefty cost, for liberal Christians have hol-lowed their claims of substance or meaning. Critical scholar Robert Price offers the following analogy:

> [I]f I claim that my wife is faithful to me, but then you show me photographs of her having sex with other men, this would be so incompatible with the notion of her fidelity as to debunk it. If she is indeed faithful to me, which is my claim, then no such liaisons or photos will exist. But suppose you can

produce the incriminating pictures, and I confront my wife with them, saying "You said you were being faithful to me! What about *this*?" And suppose she says, "Oh, but I *am* being faithful—in my own way." Yeah, that really helps. She has smuggled in a private definition of "faithfulness" that may make sense to *her*, but not to me. But let's say I am desperate to believe the best of her, and I adopt her version of fidelity, so that I no longer object to her escapades. Then some friend, hearing about her scandalous behavior, confronts me, saying, "Have you no self-respect at all, man? She is grossly unfaithful to you!" But I say "It's okay. She is faithful—in her way." My friend will shake his head in disgust and walk away, rightly convinced that I am a bigger fool than he thought. What he will have seen that I haven't is that, *by adopting a definition of "fidelity" that is so broad and flexible as to be compatible with any and every state of affairs, I have evacuated my claim of any sense whatever.* If my claim that my wife is being faithful to me is compatible with her sleeping with every man she meets, then my claim does not mean much at all, does it? What is it I am even asserting anymore? I *am* communicating *something*, though: I am signaling that my loyalty to my wife, however, undeserved, is nonetheless unwavering, even to the point of my making a hopeless and pathetic fool of myself.[6]

Likewise, Christians faced with overwhelming evidence that their existing view of God cannot be correct are often willing to relax that definition or related ones to the point of meaninglessness. If you define *God* by saying, in effect, "He is God in his own way" or "He is God in some unknowable, abstract way," then you have succeeded only in signaling your unwillingness to engage in an honest discussion of the issue. Creating or accepting such hopelessly vague definitions suggests that one is more interested in protecting his belief system from criticism than confirming that it is true. It communicates that the *need* to continue believing outweighs all other factors.

POOR EXEGESIS AND FALLACIOUS ARGUMENTS

> No man ever believes that the Bible means what it says: He is always convinced that it says what he means.
>
> —George Bernard Shaw, "The Living Pictures"

Whether a cause or result of the problems mentioned earlier, liberal Christianity is plagued by poor exegesis and fallacious arguments.[7] One example is the claim that the seven days described in Genesis (including the seventh, when the all-powerful God of the universe had to take a breather) should be interpreted as millions of years. Such an interpretation might bring the biblical Creation account more in line with science, but there is one big problem. It is scripturally indefensible. The argument usually begins by claiming the Creation account to be metaphorical. But saying the universe was created in seven days is not the same as saying "The moon is a pizza pie." The writers of the Bible certainly understood long periods of time and ways to express such things.

Those arguing for such an interpretation use Psalm 90:4 and 2 Peter 3:8, comparing a day to a thousand years. In both verses, however, the comparisons are rhetorical devices used to describe God's nature. There is nothing in Genesis to suggest that God intended the days of Creation to be interpreted metaphorically. Such an interpretation, furthermore, conflicts with every other use of the word *day* with an associated number in the Bible (e.g., three days). This combination occurs 357 times outside of Genesis 1. The combination is used in different ways, but each time it is used, it means a twenty-four-hour period of time without exception.

Another problem with this argument is that Genesis explicitly *defines day* as the evening followed by the morning. *Evening* and *morning* are found together thirty-eight times within the Old Testament, and each time, they refer to a normal day. Any possible uncertainty is resolved in the Ten Commandments, in which God commands humans to work six days and rest one day, *just as He did during the Creation.* (Exodus 20:11). Does God expect human Sabbaths to last millions of years? If not, then he must have meant the same thing in Genesis as he did in Exodus.

Most important, however, is that for virtually the entire history of Christianity, the greatest minds in the world—philosophers, theologians, and scientists—all interpreted Genesis literally. Interpreting seven days as anything other than seven twenty-four-hour periods never occurred to any of them until the late twentieth century, when Scripture came into conflict with modern science. It wasn't as if anyone looked at the text and said, "Oh wait. We missed something. The first line of Genesis actually says, 'Don't take any of this stuff seriously!'" Revised interpretations were forced on a reluctant Christian establishment by the scientific community. This is rationalizing from a conclusion rather than reasoning to one.

Another example of interpretive rationalization is the argument that Old Testament Scriptures appear false or barbaric to us only because we do not understand the unique historical context in which they were written. According to this argument, God was primarily focused on producing a contemporaneously *understandable* work and was therefore constrained to "write" in a way that would not go over the heads of Bronze Age desert dwellers.

But there are two big problems with this argument. The first is that Bronze Age desert dwellers were not the only audience for God's magnum opus. God would have recognized His inspired words would be read and studied for more than *two thousand years*. With all His power, He could have either written the initial text in a more "age-neutral" way or amended it over time to render it understandable to succeeding generations.

More significantly, however, is that the Bible isn't just dumbed down. It is factually wrong. And it includes rules that are immoral for people living in *any age*. Does anyone believe there was a time when it was morally acceptable to stone women to death for premarital sex? This would be like teaching young children that 2 plus 2 equals 5 because they can't understand arithmetic. Or that they should just smack anyone they don't like because they aren't ready for all the nuanced rules of proper social behavior. If this wouldn't be acceptable for us, then why should we find it acceptable for God in any age?

Another example is the attempt of liberal Christianity to hand-wave away troubling Old Testament rules and passages by claiming these were all invalidated by Jesus. This argument is usually premised on something said by Paul but in each case is invalidated by Jesus's own words, as in Matthew, where he could not have been clearer that the Jewish law of the Torah remained in effect and always will (Matthew 5:17–18). As important as Paul was to the Christian Church, to cherry-pick his words and elevate them over those of Jesus is something I've yet to see justified.

The tendency to ignore or interpret away troubling passages is entirely understandable, but the reasoning applied is backward. Liberal Christians begin with a strong conviction that their God is good. If a biblical passage appears on its face to contradict that conviction, then they conclude that the plain meaning cannot be correct. To preserve their view of a benevolent God, they must find and embrace an alternate interpretation. An intellectually honest approach would be to take the plain meaning on its face, consistent with the plain-meaning rule used by lawyers, unless it appears incorrect based on neutral principles applied systematically to all ancient literature.

Today, there is an unparalleled diversity of thought among liberal apologists on many theological issues. In each situation, a strong case can be made that apologists were forced into taking new positions because the evidence did not validate the old ones. This forces one to acknowledge one of two possibilities—one absurd and one highly embarrassing. Either

(1) the most brilliant theologians of the last two thousand years all had the wrong interpretation of Scripture, or (2) the recent crop has reached their conclusions based not on good-faith exegesis but on political expediency.

As liberal interpretations splinter into millions of idiosyncratic and increasingly pragmatic ones, it becomes more and more difficult to justify liberal Christianity as a worthwhile exercise. Rather than converging on some universal Truth, it moves in the opposite direction, demonstrating there is no Truth in the biblical texts, only reflections of our own minds, needs, and desires.

INDOCTRINATION OF CHILDREN

> I am now convinced that children should not be subjected to the frightfulness of the Christian religion. . . . If the concept of a father who plots to have his son [tortured and] put to death is presented to children as beautiful and as worthy of society's admiration, what types of human behavior can be presented to them as reprehensible?
>
> —Ruth Hurmence Green, *The Born Again Skeptic's Guide to the Bible*

> Should schools teach atheism? No. There's no need to teach atheism. It's the natural result of education without indoctrination.
>
> —Ricky Gervais, Tweet of October 9, 2012

Like their more conservative counterparts, liberal churches continue to indoctrinate children rather than responsibly teach them. Indoctrination involves presenting a proposition as the only reasonable possibility and demanding belief in that proposition, without acknowledging the appropriate level of uncertainty. Responsible teaching would involve giving children the facts about all religions, including how they started, what their adherents believe, and what arguments support and undermine them, with major religions getting roughly equal time and placed on equal footing. If liberals believe it is important for their children to have beliefs that transcend the material world, then they should allow their children to decide freely, with no coercion or thumbs on the scales.

Needless to say, Christian churches don't follow such an approach. They typically focus exclusively on Christianity, rarely even acknowledging other religions and never allowing for the possibility that the conflicting beliefs of these religions might have some legitimacy. This creates a systemic bias and tunnel vision, in which only a specific viewpoint is ever seriously considered. And they teach their church doctrine as if it were fact. Serious questioning is not encouraged, if even allowed. As Sam Harris observes, the doors to this type of religion don't open from the inside.[8] They have to be bashed open from the outside.

In science, concepts are taught according to and in proportion with the degree of acceptance they have attained within the relevant scientific community and the evidence supporting them. Where there is widespread disagreement regarding various hypotheses, as there is among the broader religious community on just about every religious issue under the Sun, that is reflected in the instruction. Where scientists teach certain concepts as being relatively certain, that is because those concepts have successfully run the gauntlet of the scientific method, so such certainty is warranted. Science has, accordingly, earned the modest level of certainty with which it teaches. Religions, by contrast, teach with *absolute certainty*, with the warrant for that certainty being exactly zero.

Liberal denominations are generally better about allowing some questioning and doubt, but there is always the understanding it can only go so far. One must ultimately accept certain core beliefs, reflected in regularly recited creeds, or be rejected from the fold. Unfortunately, given the wide variety of idiosyncratic beliefs found in most liberal denominations, many children are likely not being taught what their parents believe. Ironically, moderates regularly allow their children to be indoctrinated in a religion they don't fully understand based on a book they have never fully read.

UNJUSTIFIED FOCUS ON JESUS AND THE BIBLE

Many liberal Christians claim to attend church for its morally instructive value. It provides an hour each week to reflect on what's right and wrong and to gain important life lessons and guidance. A person who attends church weekly for 70 years will log more than 3,500 hours of such lessons, not including Sunday school, which amounts to almost 450 eight-hour workdays. This has always seemed to me an admirable motive, but it raises an important question: Why should the church focus so narrowly on the Bible and particularly on Jesus? Thousands of morally instructive stories are available outside the Bible. Discounting these seems an enormous waste of opportunity.

Is there a principled reason that churches should largely ignore such secular literature as fables or such pagan literature as the Greek myths? Shakespeare cleverly deals with many moral and ethical quandaries in greater depth and with more relevant context than that found in the Bible. Ethical philosophers have written brilliant treatises addressing even modern-day moral conundrums, such as those posed by evolving technology. Science fiction has always been prescient in tackling such issues, even before they manifested themselves in the real world. By comparison, the ethical principles espoused in the Bible are crude and antiquated. Liberal Christian churches, however, for the most part continue to limit their discussions to a select group of theologically homogenous writers living two to three thousand years ago, poring endlessly over a few select texts.[9]

The largest single contributor to the New Testament by far is Paul, whose views on many social issues of today would be considered, to put it mildly, out of touch. Among other things, Paul was a dedicated misogynist and apologist for slavery. Why should this man's writings be venerated far above those of social reformers like Robert Ingersoll, Frederick Douglass, or Susan B. Anthony?

And why should churches primarily focus on Jesus as a role model? While exemplary in many ways, his teachings conflict with modern moral norms in others, such as instructing children to hate their parents (Luke 14:26), breaking up families (Matthew 10:35–37, 19:29; Luke 12:51–53, 18:29–30), encouraging self-mutilation (Mark 9:43–48; Matthew 19:12), justifying eternal torture (Matthew 13:41–42, 25:41–46), and implicitly condoning slavery (Luke 7:2–10, 12:47; Matthew 18:23–25). Those extolling Jesus for saying, "Peace on Earth," rarely include the context: "Do not suppose that I have come to bring peace on to the Earth. I did not come to bring peace, but a sword" (Matthew 10:34). Even Jesus's positive moral messages were not unique or original to him. Every moral teaching of Jesus can be found in earlier works of the ancient world. Jesus never addressed many of the moral hot-button issues of the modern age—even those of great interest to Christian conservatives, such as abortion and gay rights. There are thousands of real-life role models whose words and stories are far more relevant to audiences of today. Why not use a good part of that 3,500 hours to talk about them?

UNWARRANTED PRIVILEGING OF THE BIBLE AND RELIGION IN GENERAL

While moderates quietly ignore much of the Bible, they continue to lay a veneer of privilege over the entire thing and treat it as if it were unique and special. They grant it an unjustified presumption of accuracy, assuming passages that seem obscure must be deep and insightful, if only we could understand them better. They speak of it in reverential tones, assign it special places in their homes, and reflexively defend it on principle alone.

The Bible presents acts committed, endorsed, or overtly permitted by God, covering an entire moral spectrum, from vicious to virtuous. Assume you knew of a person whose actions covered the same broad moral spectrum. He was a mass murderer but also gave massive amounts of time and money to charity. Would anyone hold this mass-murdering charity worker up as a role model? If he were tried in a court, his charity work would not negate his mass murders. The murders would clearly overwhelm any good acts done. Likewise, it is the cruelties in the Bible that should most concern any decent person.

The Bible warrants treatment no different than other ancient literature. It lacks any compelling evidence of divine inspiration and must be acknowledged as a work of men—some intelligent, some less so, but all fallible. Sometimes the authors were confused, sometimes politically opportunistic, and sometimes just wrong. Some passages are beautiful, and some, ugly. Some convey admirable moral messages, and others, despicable ones. It is possible to champion the former without legitimizing the latter but only if this cloak of biblical privilege is cast aside.

Privileging the Bible prevents moderates from clearly and openly denouncing the hundreds of biblical teachings at odds with human dignity and compassion. Even if the church focuses only on the more humanist, progressive, and life-affirming biblical teachings, it has failed its ethical duties, for rather than clearly repudiating the remaining teachings, it has merely ignored them. If the church is to adopt the role of moral teacher, then it must first tend to its own garden, which includes pulling the weeds.

Moderates also defend Christianity and religion in general from criticism. They exhibit what philosopher Daniel Dennett calls "belief in belief"—the belief that it is desirable and good for people to have religious beliefs, regardless of their content.[10] Dennett claims that far fewer people believe in supernatural gods than the number of self-identified theists would suggest, and most think that trying to believe, promoting belief, and telling others they believe is honorable and advantageous. Accordingly, they claim, criticism of any religious belief should be discouraged, even those beliefs at odds with the moderate's own theology and worldview.

The first problem with this position is that there is no good evidence religious belief is superior to nonbelief or offers any clear benefits. For many of the reasons discussed elsewhere in this book, the opposite is more likely true. Second, this belief protectionism creates many of the problems that free markets were designed to solve. An environment open to new and challenging ideas has the advantages of a capitalistic economy—the best ideas thrive, while the rest wither and die. This is the concept of the free marketplace of ideas.

But churches are not free marketplaces. They are more like communist systems, in which there is but a single seller whose goods are accorded preferential treatment well beyond what is warranted by their worth. It is a system in which bad ideas can survive and even thrive in perpetuity because competition is effectively squelched. This problem becomes more pronounced in a society such as America, which privileges religion, effectively subsidizing it by shielding it from criticism. Atheism has far more in common with capitalism than organized religion.

ADVOCATING FAITH AS A VIRTUE AND LEGITIMATE SOURCE OF KNOWLEDGE

> [I]f we offer too much silent assent about mysticism and superstition—even when it seems to be doing a little good—we abet a general climate in which skepticism is considered impolite, science tiresome, and rigorous thinking somehow stuffy and inappropriate.
>
> —Carl Sagan, *The Demon-Haunted World*

> It is time we admitted, from kings and presidents on down, that there is no evidence that any of our books was authored by the Creator of the universe. The Bible, it seems certain, was the work of sand-strewn men and women who thought the earth was flat and for whom a wheelbarrow would have been a breathtaking example of emerging technology. To rely on such a document as the basis for our worldview—however heroic the efforts of redactors—is to repudiate two thousand years of civilizing insights that the human mind has only just begun to inscribe upon itself through secular politics and scientific culture. We will see that the greatest problem confronting civilization is not merely religious extremism: rather, it is the larger set of cultural and intellectual accommodations we have made to faith itself.
>
> —Sam Harris, *The End of Faith*

Elsewhere, I discuss in some detail the myriad problems with faith. Liberal Christians almost universally promote faith. In doing so, they discount the value of reason and evidence, for these are mutually exclusive concepts. Moderate religion conveys the message that believing things without evidence is okay. It encourages people to trust in invisible beings, undetectable forces, and events beyond any hope of confirmation. Like its more extreme sibling, it therefore disables human reality checks, rendering people more vulnerable to oppression, fraud, and their own baser instincts. Once you endorse a style of thinking, you can't control how far it goes or to what it extends.

Writer Greta Christina references a useful analogy of two people who get their instructions for how to live from their hair dryers. Person 1 thinks his hair dryer is telling him to murder redheads. Person 2 thinks his is telling him to volunteer at a homeless shelter. Is it better, she asks, to volunteer at a homeless shelter than to kill redheads? Of course:

> But you still have a basic problem—which is that you think your hair dryer is talking to you. You are still getting your ethics from a hair dryer. You are still getting your perception of reality and your ideas about how you live your life, not from the core moral values that most human beings seem to share, not from any solid evidence about what decreases suffering and increases happiness, not from your own experience of what makes the world a better place . . . but from a household appliance. . . . If you don't have a better reason for what you do than "The hair dryer told me to," you're in trouble.[11]

Relying on faith is a bad idea, even if it sometimes leads to good results. Even if one's views are moderate and tolerant, the very principle will ultimately betray you. And if not you, then those guided by your endorsement of an approach that employs no rules and no rails, such as your children or anyone else who looks to you as an authority. Computer programmers use the phrase *Garbage in, garbage out* to capture the idea that a computer's output depends wholly on its input. Anyone making room for faith as a valid input cannot be surprised when the resulting outputs cover the spectrum from love and kindness to the depths of human depravity.

CONTRIBUTION TO MORE EXTREME FORMS OF CHRISTIANITY

> Religious moderates tend to imagine that there is some bright line of separation between extremist and moderate religion. But there isn't. Scripture itself remains a perpetual engine of extremism: because, while He may be many things, the God of the Bible and the Qur'an is not a moderate.
>
> —Sam Harris, *Letter to a Christian Nation*

In religious and in secular affairs, the more fervent beliefs attract followers. If you are a moderate in any respect—if you're a moderate on abortion, if you're a moderate on gun control, or if you're a moderate in your religious faith—it doesn't evolve into a crusade where you're either right or wrong, good or bad, with us or against us.

—Jimmy Carter, "A Statesman and a Man of Faith"

Christian moderates seek to preserve a legitimate role for Christianity in modern society by condemning interpretations that are no longer serviceable. By focusing solely on interpretations, however, they never get to the heart of the problem, which is the scriptural text itself. The very words are toxic. Claiming that "stone all gays to death" must be tempered by the direction to "love your neighbor" is like mixing a light-colored paint with a dark one. The dark color may be muted slightly, but it still dominates the picture. Scripture like this involving rules and proscriptions can't reasonably be taken other than literally because they're meant as *instructions* to be followed. Every time a moderate argues valiantly for a strained interpretation while insisting the Scripture must ultimately be deferred to as the word of God, he legitimizes the same text used by KKK members to peddle their message of hatred. He's saying, "I hope you accept my interpretation of the Scripture, but if you don't, you still have to follow it."

By insisting on convoluted interpretations to rationalize offensive passages, moderates will always be fighting an uphill battle with fundamentalists. The fundamentalists, who simply take the passages at face value, have Ockham's razor on their side. Moderates will never be able to establish a superior claim because they are arguing from a weaker position. Fundamentalist interpretations are, overall, simply more parsimonious with the text. The battle of interpretations will, at best, be a draw, allowing the extremists to go unchecked.

Meanwhile, moderates continue to accord the Bible special status and authority, even as they take its Scripture less and less seriously. They guard the text from criticism, insisting that it not be mocked or ridiculed, even when it promotes the most dehumanizing behaviors. They will take their places on the front lines with the extremists in protecting the very basis of extremist rhetoric, even if they disagree with the rhetoric itself. They lend credibility to the very things that allow Christianity to be used so destructively.

I've identified numerous examples in which fundamentalists have negatively influenced American public policy. Due to their narrow focus, intense dedication, and ability to mobilize followers through fear and common purpose, it is they rather than moderates who set the issues, language, and tone of political debate within the United States. Moderates often express indignation that they are painted with the same brush as the fundamentalists, but this results from their own failure to aggressively take the wheel. Where are prominent leaders of moderate denominations publicly denouncing fundamentalist claims? By failing to take them on directly, moderates have allowed fundamentalists to hijack the Christian brand.

Where there are moderates, furthermore, zealots will never be far behind. Fundamentalists will always excel at identifying and exploiting the abundant holes in moderate theology. Many moderates will be troubled by the resulting cognitive dissonance and seek to reconcile it by conforming their actions and beliefs more closely to the more parsimonious interpretations of the Bible. Some will go so far as to become fundamentalists and zealots themselves. Fundamentalists will always have a strong claim on "true Christianity," as moderate versions ultimately represent shifting temporizations. The flawed epistemology of moderate Christianity will continue to grease the path for many from the latter to the former.

OTHER PROBLEMS

> The improver of natural knowledge absolutely refuses to acknowledge authority, as such. For him, skepticism is the highest of duties; blind faith the one unpardonable sin. And it cannot be otherwise, for every great advance in natural knowledge has involved the absolute rejection of authority, the cherishing of the keenest skepticism, the annihilation of the spirit of blind faith.
>
> —Thomas Henry Huxley, *On the Advisableness of Improving Natural Knowledge* (1866)

> The civilization of man has increased just to the same extent that religious power has decreased. The intellectual advancement of man depends upon how often he can exchange an old superstition for a new truth. The Church never enabled a human being to make even one of these exchanges; on the contrary, all her power has been used to prevent them.
>
> —Robert Ingersoll, *The Gods and Other Lectures*

According to Sam Harris, "Religious moderation is the product of secular knowledge and scriptural ignorance."[12] To these I would add the inertia of culture and tradition. Moderates fail to understand what is in their Scripture and its theological implications but are wedded through their cultural heritage to the idea that it must be accepted, exalted, and defended.

Unfortunately, the moderates' attachment to Christian Scripture and tradition has an enormous opportunity cost, for it prevents society from exploring new approaches to areas commonly reserved for religion, such as ethics and transcendent experience. Just as evolution must modify existing designs rather than starting fresh, so, too, must any philosophy advocated by moderates be constrained by an ancient framework. As Harris recognizes, "Religious moderates seem to believe that what we need is not radical insight and innovation in these areas but a mere dilution of Iron Age philosophy."[13]

There is no good justification for circumscribing our conversations on ethics, for example, around views espoused by uneducated fisherman living more than two thousand years ago. This is like attempting to build the best state-of-the-art boat by retrofitting a two-thousand-year-old schooner, piece by piece—while it remains afloat. Much of the Bible is simply useless baggage that should be quickly discarded before we begin any serious discussion involving policy or ethics. We've progressed significantly since then and must acknowledge this.

It is clear from a review of history that liberal Christians have always been playing catch-up to secularists in the realm of progressive ethics. Slavery, women's rights, and gay rights, among similar causes, have been first championed by secularists before liberal denominations got onboard the train, with conservatives only occasionally, and even then reluctantly, pulling up the rear. While it is admirable that they got onboard at all, wouldn't it have been better had they first abandoned the beliefs that held them back in the first place? With so much at stake and so little time, wouldn't it be better if they abandoned them now?

CONCLUSION

The time has come to summarize my argument, which essentially is this: There are no good, compelling reasons to accept the claims of Christianity and many compelling reasons to reject them for naturalism. The evidence supporting Christianity is too weak; its foundational premises and doctrines, too often contradictory or incoherent. Rather than logically sound answers and explanations, it generates only an endless parade of questions and endless confusion. It is logically indefensible. When held to the same standards as all other disciplines, Christianity fails at every turn.

When well-accepted scientific facts are applied, the Christian hypothesis is that God created the universe billions of years ago, waited billions more to create the Earth, and then created life. Millions of years later, there arose a small tribe of people in which God took a special interest, taking their side in local skirmishes, punishing and rewarding their leaders for fidelity to Him, and making a unique covenant with them. With God's help, His favored tribe eventually conquered a relatively small tract of largely arid land in the Middle East.

Later, God arranged for a blood sacrifice of one aspect of Himself to another aspect of Himself to lift a curse on mankind He Himself had levied. Rather than directly proclaiming His existence and message to the world, God chose to speak to only a handful of Jews, whom He commissioned to write down everything of true importance to future generations. Unfortunately, their work was riddled with inconsistencies, incoherencies,

and blatantly false statements on just about every scientifically and historically verifiable claim. God decreed that if one was not convinced to believe
and follow Him by this "evidence," then they would be banished to eternal
torture.

But consider the naturalist alternative. Our universe was created through
the interplay of purely natural physical laws, possibly part of a far greater
cosmos. Life, too, arose naturally and proceeded through the unguided
process of natural selection, by which simple origins gradually brought
about increasing complexity. Rather than the culmination of a divine plan,
man represents merely one branch of a vast and ancient evolutionary tree.
The Bible and the entire Christian religion are products of humans, many
of whom were ignorant of the historical and scientific truths we take for
granted today but were trying to make sense of the world they saw around
them while maintaining social order.

Isn't the latter explanation by far the more plausible? It creates no paradoxes, results in no absurdities, and violates no known laws of physics or
logic. It actually *explains* the world we see and does so in the most parsimonious manner. And it does not require us to accept or rationalize away
dogma that on its face supports bigotry, sexism, and the rejection of reason.
As Sean Carroll notes, God is an "untenable hypothesis," as "it's not well-
defined, it's completely unnecessary to fit the data, and it adds unhelpful
layers of complexity without any corresponding increase in understanding."[1]

If one is being intellectually honest, then he must acknowledge that
virtually nothing science has revealed of the universe in the modern age
would or could reasonably have been predicted by anyone relying solely on
Christian Scripture. Such findings as the age and scale of the universe or
evolution would be extremely surprising to well-read Christians of the first
and second centuries precisely because they contradict a straightforward
reading of Christian Scripture. Each such finding has therefore undercut
and delegitimized Christianity as a worldview.

In America you *can* believe what you want to believe. But that is not the
same as saying you *should* believe what you want or that it is socially desirable to do so. Society works best if people believe things for good reasons
rather than bad ones. If you defend your beliefs simply by claiming a right
to your opinion, then you are referring to a political or legal right rather
than an epistemic one. You have epistemic justification only if there are
good reasons and evidence to support your claim. Fideism—basing one's
beliefs exclusively on faith—makes belief arbitrary. There becomes no way
to distinguish the respective validity of one belief over another. If I must
accept your beliefs without evidence, then you must accept mine, no matter

how absurd they may seem to you. Is belief without reason and evidence worthy of human beings?

I consider it unethical to believe on insufficient evidence because the pleasure one obtains is a stolen one. It stands in defiance of our duty to humankind. When we believe for unworthy reasons, we weaken our powers of critical thought and reliable assessment. The danger to society is not just in believing the wrong ideas but also in forgetting how to discern the good ideas from the bad ones.

Progress depends on discarding outdated, destructive ideas and embracing new, more constructive ones. Christianity is filled with outdated destructive ideas. The only way we can move forward as a civilization is to permanently relegate them to the scrap heap of history. We can keep the more progressive teachings of Christianity without holding onto the baggage of scriptural authority on which they now rest. Ideas that can be justified without resort to Scripture are the ones we should maintain.

Some who cannot deny this wisdom will nevertheless resist discarding Christianity due to the feeling that they will lose something of great value—that their lives will afterward lose meaning and purpose. To these people, I refer to the words of Stephen Fry:

> Some people believe that there is one single meaning of life. They think that the universe was created for a purpose and that human beings are part of some larger cosmic plan. They think our meaning comes from being part of this plan, and is written into the universe, waiting to be discovered. A humanist's view of the meaning of life is different. Humanists do not see that there is any obvious purpose to the universe, but that it is a natural phenomenon with no design behind it. Meaning is not something out there, waiting to be discovered, but something we create in our own lives. And although this vast and incredibly old universe was not created for us, all of us are connected to something bigger than ourselves, whether it is family and community, a tradition stretching into the past, an idea or cause looking forward to the future, or the beautiful wider natural world on which we were born and our species evolved. This way of thinking means that there is not just one big meaning of life, but that every person will have many different meanings in their life. Each one of us is unique and our different personalities depend on a complex mixture of influences from our parents, our environment, and our connections. They change with our experience and changing circumstances. There are no simple recipes for living that are applicable to all people. We have different tastes and preferences, different priorities and goals. One person may like drawing, walking in the woods and caring for their grandchildren. Another may like cooking, watching soap operas, savoring a favorite wine or a new food. We may find meaning through our family, our career, making a

commitment to an artistic project or a political reform—in simple pleasures such as gardening and hobbies or in a thousand other ways giving reign to our creativity or our curiosity, our intellectual capacities or our emotional life. The time to be happy is now, and the way to find meaning in life is to get on and live it as fully and as well as we can.[2]

If Mr. Fry's words are not sufficient, then I leave you with these from the great agnostic, Robert Green Ingersoll:

When I became convinced that the universe is natural, that all the ghosts and gods are myths, there entered into my brain, into my soul, into every drop of my blood the sense, the feeling, the joy of freedom. The walls of my prison crumbled and fell. The dungeon was flooded with light and all the bolts and bars and manacles became dust. I was no longer a servant, a serf, or a slave. There was for me no master in all the wide world, not even in infinite space. I was free—free to think, to express my thoughts—free to live my own ideal, free to live for myself and those I loved, free to use all my faculties, all my senses, free to spread imagination's wings, free to investigate, to guess and dream and hope, free to judge and determine for myself. . . . I was free!

Reason, Observation and Experience—the Holy Trinity of Science—have taught us that happiness is the only good; that the time to be happy is now, and the way to be happy is to make others so. This is enough for us. In this belief we are content to live and die. If by any possibility the existence of a power superior to, and independent of, nature shall be demonstrated, there will then be time enough to kneel. Until then, let us stand erect.[3]

APPENDIX:
LOGICAL FALLACIES COMMON
TO CHRISTIAN APOLOGETICS

I. SPECIAL PLEADING

Special pleading is creating or allowing an exception to a generally applicable rule (a double standard) without first justifying the exception. The principled approach, by contrast, is to set or recognize prescriptive rules on the front end and then apply those rules consistently. A special pleader will set ad hoc rules or exceptions after the fact, based on whatever argument he is making. Special pleading is often used to immunize one's position from criticism by claiming that the rules applicable to everyone and everything else simply don't apply to *this claim*. His claim, the proponent argues, involves special considerations and must be treated differently. Why, you may ask? Because.

Special pleading is often seen in paranormal research, where those claiming such powers as ESP fail to demonstrate it under controlled conditions. They will claim, for instance, that the testing procedures themselves interfered with their abilities. When repeated tests fail to confirm their paranormal claims, they may explain that their ability is not amenable to testing at all. In this way, they render their claims unfalsifiable. Special pleading is perhaps the most common logical fallacy used by apologists, who routinely create double standards for God.

Example 1: Because all things must have a cause, the cause of the universe must be God.

This argument sets up a rule that is consistent with our common experience but then exempts God without justification. If the universe must have a cause, then why must God not have a cause? If God can be uncaused (eternal), then why could the universe not be uncaused? The first premise of the cosmological argument is often written as "Everything *except God* has a cause," but of course that gives away the game because the exemption is written into the premise. There is no justifiable basis for simply defining God as the only thing in existence not requiring a cause just so one can prove the existence of God. It is a circular argument.

Example 2: While it is true that throughout the Old Testament, God engages in behavior we would deem horrific by modern standards of morality, we cannot judge God by those standards.

Here, the apologist has attempted to do an end run around the obvious conflict between God's behavior, as most notoriously reflected in the Old Testament, and modern standards of common morality by claiming that no such standard applies to God. No rationale is ever offered for why we shouldn't expect God's behavior to conform to virtually universal moral sentiments on such issues as rape, slavery, and arbitrary murder. Nor is any standard ever offered by which we might assess or classify God's actions on an ethical scale. God's actions are defined to be good simply because He took them—another circular argument.

Related to this argument, many apologists also claim that God, being omniscient, has ultimately beneficent goals and strategies we could not hope to imagine. Accordingly, they say, we cannot assess God's motivations by our own limited reasoning and understanding. This has been called the Omniscience Escape Clause because it would effectively immunize any act of God from critical inquiry.

The problem, once again, is that there is no verifiable basis for concluding that an omniscient God even exists, much less that His actions follow altruistic motives. If God did exist and were omniscient, then His motives would be inaccessible to us. Such a position, therefore, has no explanatory value.[1] To the extent it is used to rebut an argument against God, it is useless because it must assume the existence of the very God it is attempting to prove. (See "5. Begging the Question.")

Example 3: While there might appear to be conflicts between scientific consensus and the Bible on numerous points, that is only because we do not adequately understand either the true nature of the universe, the Bible, or both. If we only had better understanding, then we would see how they could be harmonized.

This argument, common among religious moderates, tries to deflect the parsimonious conclusion that conflicts between science and religion must mean that one or both are wrong. As scientific consensus is always based on a solid foundation of empirically testable and repeatable experiments, religious claims must yield where such conflicts arise. The apologist argues, however, that despite all appearances to the contrary, no such conflicts exist.

The special pleading here is that some undetectable fog intrudes to distort our observations in *only those areas in which science and religion appear to conflict*. Presumably, we can trust our observations in other areas, but an exception occurs once apparent conflicts are identified with religious claims. No standards are ever offered by which we can proscriptively identify situations in which our observations are trustworthy and those in which they are not. The claims subject to exception can only be identified after the fact, once a conflict becomes apparent. As such, the argument is entirely ad hoc. (See ad hoc explanations.)

The only reason the apologist has to doubt the scientific consensus or biblical interpretation is that he cannot accept that they would irrevocably conflict. He therefore creates his own set of rules, having no internal consistency or proscriptive value, by which he can dismiss any conflicts in retrospect as purely theoretical but retain all observations and interpretations that appear in accord.

Apologists can get away with these strategies because they staunchly refuse to agree to any meaningful definition of God or even of Christianity. This is perhaps the greatest example of special pleading of all. An endlessly malleable definition provides one's position with immunity from all forms of criticism. It renders that position unfalsifiable, thus serving the apologists' immediate goal of deflecting attack. Unfortunately for them, however, it also renders their position epistemologically worthless.

2. NO TRUE SCOTSMAN

A subcategory of special pleading is the "no true Scotsman" fallacy. When faced with a counterexample to a universal claim, rather than denying the counterexample or conceding the original claim, the proponent modifies the claim just enough to account for the exception in an ad hoc manner. The use of the term was advanced by British philosopher Antony Flew:

> Imagine Hamish McDonald, a Scotsman, sitting down with his *Glasgow Morning Herald* and seeing an article about how the "Brighton Sex Maniac Strikes Again." Hamish is shocked and declares that "No Scotsman would do such a thing." The next day he sits down to read his *Glasgow Morning Herald* again; and, this time, finds an article about an Aberdeen man whose brutal actions make the Brighton sex maniac seem almost gentlemanly. This fact shows that Hamish was wrong in his opinion but is he going to admit this? Not likely. This time he says, "No *true* Scotsman would do such a thing."[2]

A simple rendition of the fallacy would be:

> PERSON A: No Scotsman puts sugar on his porridge.
>
> PERSON B: I am Scottish, and I put sugar on my porridge.
>
> PERSON A: Then you are not a true Scotsman.

Apologists use this argument to deflect criticisms of Christian atrocities, church scandals, or the vast body of evidence revealing Christians to behave less morally than non-Christians. They merely wave away these criticisms by claiming those behaving badly could not have been true Christians in the first place because no true Christian would behave like that. They identify no standard by which one can identify a true Christian from a false Christian proscriptively but only, once again, after the fact, based on whether that person's behavior supports the Christian hypothesis or undermines it.

If the claims of Christianity are true, then it represents a moral system superior to all others. We would reasonably expect Christians as a group to behave better than non-Christians. We would expect there to be statistically significant differences in their behavior, whereby the Christians acted with more charity, love, compassion, and justice than non-Christians. But, as discussed elsewhere herein, that is not what we find in the world. We generally find the opposite. The logical conclusion is that the claims of Christianity are not true. Rather than face this conclusion, however, apologists cling to the "no true Scotsman" fallacy.

3. EQUIVOCATION

Equivocation occurs when one uses the same word to mean different things in an argument without acknowledging the tactic. This is especially common among apologists when using words that are naturally vague or ambiguous or poorly understood outside of technical applications, such as *objective* or *theory*.

Apologists regularly equivocate when using *faith*, sometimes equating it to trust generated by reliable evidence ("I have faith the Sun will rise tomorrow morning") and then, having induced acceptance in faith as a valid epistemological approach, using it to mean belief *in the absence of reliable evidence* ("You just have to have faith that God will provide"). No one can seriously equate belief in gravity with belief in angels. The former is based on mountains of testable evidence, notably lacking among those who believe in the latter. Referring to the basis of both beliefs as *faith* without distinguishing between how that term is being used is an intellectually dishonest means of manufacturing credibility from thin air.

At times, apologists may tap into a widely understood meaning for such a term as *good* but use it in a way that is necessarily inconsistent with that meaning. For example, they might describe God's command to slaughter all Canaanite children as good simply because God commanded it, despite that killing children does not comport with any modern understanding of *good*. We are clearly talking about very different concepts.

Another common source of equivocation would be descriptions of God. When apologists describe God, they often do so in vague terms that allow them cover if their arguments are attacked. If characteristic X is criticized, then they can claim they never explicitly stated God to have characteristic X. They can reinstate characteristic X into their definition if it later becomes strategically advantageous to do so. This tactic improperly uses inherent or even manufactured ambiguity in people's concepts of God.

While insisting on a vague and nebulous definition may appear to shield the apologist's claim from atheist attacks, that is just an illusion. This version of God bears little resemblance to the being in which most Christians believe, which has such measurable qualities as love for humanity and acts in such predictable ways as regularly intervening in response to prayer and rewarding those who follow His commands. If God has no measurable qualities, then it makes little sense to talk about proving His existence. A claim that cannot be defined cannot be defended, and an argument to an incoherent position must be rejected as incoherent itself.

Equivocation is related to a fallacy known as "failure to elucidate," in which one makes a claim based on an obscure term that one fails to define in a meaningful way. Calling a *spirit* an incorporeal entity or an *aura* a mystical field of psychic energy provides no useful information because the definitions themselves lack a clear meaning. While we might understand the individual words in isolation, stringing them together results in nonsense. Definitions of Christian *souls* run into this same problem.

Apologists regularly use definitions for *God* and such theological concepts as the *Trinity* that fail to elucidate. How can we meaningfully discuss God's existence if we can't agree on a definition for *God*? In such cases, skeptics often resort to ridiculing the vague claim for, as Thomas Jefferson recognizes, "Ridicule is the only weapon that can be used against unintelligible propositions. Ideas must be distinct before reason can act upon them."[3] When evaluating an argument, the key terms must be adequately defined, and those definitions must be used consistently. Unless the terms are clearly understood by all involved, no reasoned argument is possible.

4. ARGUMENT OF THE BEARD

When one argues as if no useful distinction can be made between two extremes simply because no clearly definable point exists on the spectrum between them, he is making the fallacious argument of the beard. The name comes from a philosophical paradox that posits the arguably rhetorical question, "When does a man go from clean shaven to having a beard?" Presumably, everyone would agree that at some point, he will develop a beard, but it may be impossible to reach a consensus on the exact moment that occurs. One could say that a beard is a fuzzy concept.

Another example would be defining the point at which a person reaches adulthood, purely legal definitions aside. It seems absurd that on any single day a person would magically transform from child to adult, and so it would be difficult to get people to agree on a specific date when this occurs. We can all agree, however, that by the time people reach their early twenties, they are adults. Though no single day makes a demonstrably meaningful difference, there is certainly a real difference that becomes more noticeable as the gap widens. The lack of a clear demarcation point wouldn't justify us refusing to distinguish a six-year-old from a twenty-six-year-old.

This argument often arises in discussing the moral argument for God. Many apologists subscribe to the position that any valid ethical system must incorporate a set of absolute rules. This is known as deontological ethics. It can be contrasted with consequentialist ethics, by which the moral value of a choice is determined by evaluating its consequences. Consequentialist ethics are necessarily context based. Where a deontologicalist might insist on the absolute scope of such a command as "Thou shalt not kill" and condemn anyone who violates it, a consequentialist would need further information. He would need to know, for example, the consequences of the killing in question, such as whether it served a greater good, to determine whether the killing warrants condemnation.

Most secular ethical systems are consequentialist in nature. Apologists often attempt to delegitimize such systems by arguing that the lack of clearly defined rules determining right from wrong renders the entire systems relativistic and therefore worthless. Such arguments commit the fallacy of the beard by failing to acknowledge that useful and legitimate distinctions can be made even where it is difficult or even impossible to agree on specific points of demarcation.

The fallacy of the beard also comes into play in debates over abortion. Strict abortion opponents argue that human lives begin at conception and are thereafter all of identical intrinsic value. This would treat the thousands of fertilized eggs in a lab conducting in vitro fertilizations equal in value to a six-year-old child. If forced to choose between destroying the egg or killing the child, then this position would offer no guidance as to the correct moral choice. A coin flip would be as moral a decision-making method as any.

One who is prochoice would presumably see a just-fertilized egg as different in kind from a six-year-old child, just as day-old stubble differs from a chest-length beard, entailing different moral considerations. This is the approach taken by the Supreme Court cases governing abortion in the United States today, such as *Roe v. Wade* and *Planned Parenthood v. Casey*, which recognize stronger rights to abortion based on the length of pregnancy and viability of the fetus. An advocate of abortion rights would treat a "human being accorded full human rights and intrinsic value" as something analogous to a beard—something that emerges over time, even if a clear point of demarcation cannot be pinpointed.

Categories are human constructs we create to help us make sense of things. They can often lead to confusion, however, by tricking us into thinking these abstract concepts exist as concrete things with clear boundaries. In fact, category boundaries can and often should be fluid. The important thing is that our categories be useful, at least representing conditions with meaningful differences. When discussing issues of morality, they must be morally significant. To deny a moral distinction simply because one cannot identify the demarcation point is to commit the fallacy of the beard.

5. BEGGING THE QUESTION

Begging the question is assuming the very thing you are trying to prove as a premise of your argument. One must accept the conclusion to accept the premises, resulting in circular reasoning.

Christian apologists often beg the question when discussing biblical authority. If you've ever heard someone say when describing the Bible, "God said it. I believe it," then you've witnessed begging the question. Apologists called on to support some claim found in the Bible often feel they need point only to the Bible itself. After all, they say, it is the word of God. Apparently, it does not occur to them that when attempting to establish that something is X (with X representing whatever claim the apologist is making), one cannot assume from the outset it is X. While the apologist may consider the Bible to be the inerrant and inspired work of a divine author, that assumption would not extend to the outsider, for whom any reasoned argument must be persuasive and who may not believe that author even exists. The assumption itself must be supported by evidence before it can support the argument.

An example that demonstrates the circularity of begging the question is as follows:

1. We know that the Bible is true because Jesus performed a miracle witnessed by five hundred people.
2. We know that Jesus performed a miracle witnessed by five hundred people because it is in the Bible (which is true—see number 1).

Any outsider would immediately recognize that neither claim may be assumed. Biblical inerrancy can only be proven by independently verifying *every claim in the Bible*, for which we could begin by using the empirical findings of science and archaeology. Even a divinely *inspired* book would get virtually everything correct. Only if it is demonstrated to be exceedingly accurate regarding all verifiable claims would we arguably be justified in accepting its accounts of such unverifiable *extraordinary* claims as miracles or such purely theological claims as the correct path to salvation. We must begin by reading the Bible as we would read any other book written in the same time period with the same skepticism and see if it makes a compelling case for its claims.

Another example comes from apologists who cite as support for their Christian beliefs experiences that can "only be described as divine," such as William Lane Craig's "self-authenticating witness of the holy spirit."[4] By beginning with the assumption that any unusual experience of transcendence, calm, or clarity must necessarily have been generated by the God they already believe in, the experience becomes evidence for that God in their minds. Their failure to consider other plausible alternatives (or to acknowledge the similar claims of the practitioners of thousands of other mutually exclusive religions) renders their conclusions wholly uncompelling to anyone who doesn't already share their beliefs.

Rather than starting with the *known* to determine the unknown, the foundation of logical reasoning, one who begs the question assumes something *unknown* to establish or reinforce belief in something else that is unknown. In the immediately preceding example, Dr. Craig must assume the existence of an ineffable God to provide meaning and significance to his experiences, which then serve as evidence for that same God. At no point in this process has useful information been injected, so it results in no increase in clarity. It is merely a closed, self-reinforcing feedback loop that may just as accurately be characterized as "I feel what I feel" or "I believe what I believe."

An approach to argument that systematically incorporates begging the question is known as presuppositional. A presuppositionalist begins with the assumption that Christianity is true and should be accepted *unless definitively proven impossible*. As Darius and Karin Viet of apologist website Answers in Genesis acknowledge, "We agree that presuppositional apologetics is the ultimate biblical approach to apologetics. The common accusation that the presuppositionalist uses circular reasoning is actually true."[5] Being a presuppositionalist means never having to admit you're wrong because you begin with the non-negotiable premise that you are right. The Viets defend this obviously flawed approach by inexplicably claiming that "everyone uses some degree of circular reasoning when defending his ultimate standard."[6]

Contrary to the Viets' claim, no circular reasoning is required when advocating or defending claims based on sufficient evidence. Take evolution, for example.[7] The theory of evolution is based on billions of known observations and repeatable experiments that consistently demonstrate its validity. Evolution does not require as a premise anything that is not known or self-evident.[8] Evolution allows for future predictions, which have, when tested, consistently verified the theory. No circular reasoning or begging the question has ever been required to prove evolution or many other scientific claims. Circular reasoning is only necessary when one has no evidence to support their claims from the ground up.

Some may have noticed that begging the question and special pleading are related. When people engage in special pleading on God's behalf, they are usually begging the question, as well. For example, apologists claim that all God's actions must be considered good, even those that would be deemed atrocities by any modern civilized society, because God by nature is good. This provides God an unwarranted exception but also depends on the unproven assumption, which is also part of the ultimate argument, that God is indeed good.

6. ARGUMENT FROM AUTHORITY

I'll be the first to acknowledge this one can be tricky. The idea is that citing another person or authority who agrees with you does not *necessarily* support your argument. Your argument must stand on its own merits, and the agreement of others doesn't directly go to the merits. While there may be some people who agree with you, there are likely others who don't. We don't determine who is right and who is wrong on a factual issue by adding up those who agree with each of the two sides. Reality is not decided by majority rule.

There are situations, however, in which the agreement of others may legitimately help decide an issue—when fully understanding it requires *specialized expertise*. That is why American courts allow expert witnesses to provide their opinions to juries, while nonexperts cannot. These opinions, which would otherwise be excluded as hearsay, are allowed if they are shown to be reliable and helpful. The reasoning of the courts is that without expertise relevant to the issue at hand, one person's opinion should be accorded no more weight than any other. As juries determine what happened in a case, their task is not made any easier or more reliable by hearing the opinions of others with no more understanding of the issue than themselves. That is why generally witnesses may not give their *opinions*. Their testimony is limited to facts of which they have firsthand knowledge.

But the courts treat experts differently. Experts are allowed to provide their opinions specifically because they have unique knowledge that is likely to assist the jury in making better decisions. To qualify as an expert, however, the witness must demonstrate specialized knowledge related to a matter at issue. The great minds who developed our system of laws determined that such people should be treated differently from nonexperts and their opinions accorded more weight.

Presumably relevant expert opinions should be given even more weight when they converge in general agreement—especially in the scientific fields. The agreement of true scientific experts is not based on whims or arbitrary factors, as would be the case when people choose their favorite singers on *American Idol*, but on mutually agreed-upon standards and empirically verifiable evidence. That makes all the difference.

As an example, a full understanding of evolutionary theory requires specialized expertise. One must have a solid background in biology and relatively strong knowledge of other scientific fields, such as chemistry. We would expect, furthermore, someone with an advanced degree, such as a PhD, in biology to have a greater level of knowledge and expertise than someone with merely a BS degree. All other things being equal, their opinions should be accorded different weights.

The difference between a true subject matter expert and a nonexpert is analogous to that between a professional and amateur athlete. Just as my Uncle Joe would fare pathetically poorly in a golf game against Tiger Woods, so, too, do nonexperts have no business being on the same playing field as experts in established fields of scientific study. When I see Christian apologists objecting to the conclusions of professional physicists on physics, I always picture my Uncle Joe duffing away, while Tiger absent-mindedly glances at his watch. If a layman perceives something erroneous about an expert's opinion, then his first thought should be "What mistake am I making?" rather than "This expert must have it all wrong."

Likewise, just because someone is an expert in one field doesn't render him qualified to give an opinion in an unrelated field. Michael Jordan was one of the greatest basketball players who ever lived, but when he turned his attention to professional baseball, he was, so to speak, way out of his league. Even someone with all the athletic gifts of Michael Jordan couldn't effectively compete with players who had dedicated their lives to baseball. Likewise, no number of professional degrees renders one competent to speak in an area on which she has had no formal training.

Where a solid consensus has emerged among those with the highest levels of scientific expertise, that opinion should be accorded the greatest weight. Because of the self-correcting nature of science, the formation of a consensus around a particular theory or idea represents something significant—the successful and confirming results of thousands, if not millions, of tests and observations and the analysis of those results by people with the expertise to understand them.

A crucial component of useful expertise is that it be disinterested. The opinion of a person with a strong incentive to take one position or another should not be given special (if any) weight. Bias is always relevant in American courts, as it is directly germane to the credibility of the testifying witness. Outside of the hard sciences, expertise also has value, but it becomes more difficult to weed out bias because there may be fewer, if any, objective measures or self-correcting mechanisms in place. Where bias can be demonstrated, the weight of "expert" opinion is reduced.

One area rife with biased "expert" opinion is apologetics. Apologists are notorious for supporting their arguments by citing the support of the *majority of biblical scholars*. The problem is that the majority of biblical scholars are lifelong Christians. They were raised as Christians, took on Christian beliefs as children, maintained them into adulthood, and likely decided to pursue a study of the Bible at least in part to strengthen and support their preexisting religious views. Their early views were not shaped by the evidence but do provide them a particular lens for viewing that evidence. Such individuals can hardly be called disinterested.

Even more troubling are the large number of such "scholars" employed by religious institutions explicitly dedicated to perpetuating a particular faith. Many such institutions have purpose statements that confirm their commitment to the inerrancy of Christian Scripture or something similar. Faculty members are often required to sign these statements, allowing the institution to ensure that no employee strays too far from party line. The institutions can and do use these statements to force out anyone who publishes something contrary to the purpose statements.

In a 2010 book, New Testament scholar and professor Michael Licona from Southern Evangelical Seminary (SES) said that the events of Matthew 27:52, in which thousands of corpses reportedly roamed the land following Jesus's Resurrection, didn't literally happen. This caused quite a controversy within the scholarly Evangelical community. According to *Christianity Today*, prominent Christian theologian Norman Geisler accused Licona of denying the full inerrancy of Scripture and called for him to recant.[9] Licona was ultimately pressured out of his job as professor at SES, and his position as apologetics coordinator for the North American Mission Board was eliminated.

Religious institutions are not subject to the same religious discrimination laws as other businesses, so they may punish their employees for taking positions contrary to established doctrine. To call this a potential source of bias would be a monumental understatement. These people are under threat of losing their entire careers just for expressing the "wrong" opinion. In such an environment, no room is left for intellectual honesty. They might as well have a gun to their heads or to the heads of their entire families, who rely on them for support.

Many Christian scholars are "devotional," meaning they begin with the assumption that the Bible is divinely inspired and allow only for interpretations that support its credibility and integrity. They consider it their job to harmonize difficult facts and deliberately avoid any interpretation that might undermine the Christian faith. Devotional scholars begin with biases so profound that none of their conclusions can be taken seriously. Their aims are identical to those of the apologists, which is why it is disingenuous for apologists to cite them for authority. The apologists might just as well cite each other.

The remainder are considered critical scholars. Despite the somewhat misleading name, it is not the goal of critical scholars to find fault with Scripture. Unlike devotional scholars, they simply *allow* for interpretations that do not tow the Christian party line. They take an impartial, disinterested approach to Christian Scripture, applying the same standards to religious Scripture as to other historical documents. They do not privilege Scripture over other ancient texts and are at least willing to entertain the possibility it was not divinely inspired. They do not begin with the assumption that every passage of the Bible is true in some respect. They consider that a particular passage may simply be wrong. In other words, they may be critical and even dismissive *when the evidence demands it*, which is the only intellectually defensible approach. Critical scholars can be identified by their disinterested, principled use of the same tools to assess all historical documents, regardless of content. The common component to legitimate philosophy and history is criticism. One must take a critical approach, treating everything as an open question, to distinguish truth from falsity and to thereby uncover what is genuinely true.

We all use sources for information we treat as true. The key question is how do we determine which sources are trustworthy? Which should be relevant to our assessments of truth? It is irrelevant and unreliable authority that should be disregarded. The opinions of devotional scholars are worthless because, having their minds made up before they begin, their opinions tell us nothing about the relative weight of the evidence, which is precisely the reason we depend on experts. A devotional scholar, like an apologist, could be presented with the strongest possible argument against a Christian claim, but he will always find a way to rationalize it away to arrive at his preset conclusion. What good is a conclusion that bears no relation to the supporting evidence?

Any time you hear an apologist cite the "majority of biblical historians or philosophers," insist that all lifelong Christians be identified so their opinions can be placed into proper context and that all devotional scholars be removed from the equation entirely. Otherwise, you are falling for a fallacious appeal to authority.

7. ARGUMENT FROM POPULARITY

An argument from popularity suggests a position is more likely true if it is held by many people. While you rarely see this argument made explicitly, there can be little doubt that it comforts a great many Christians that billions of other people share their views. With so many people believing the same thing, there must be something to it, right? Strength in numbers represents a powerful psychological support for any belief.

Any historian can tell you that history is littered with beliefs extraordinarily popular in their day that ultimately proved false. At one time, belief in the Roman gods was widespread among the Western world, but today they are universally acknowledged as myth. False medical theories were ubiquitous until the 1800s, when advances in science swept them into the dustbins of irrelevance. As Bertrand Russell points, "The fact that an opinion has been widely held is no evidence whatever that it is not utterly absurd; indeed in view of the silliness of the majority of mankind, a widespread belief is more likely to be foolish than sensible."[10]

8. POISONING THE WELL

Consider the following: A person who mocks something the church considers sacred is called a blasphemer. One who questions or openly criticizes church doctrine is known as a heretic. To leave a church for another or no church at all will get one branded an apostate. Now, try to come up with a word outside the religious context for someone who mocks, criticizes, or abandons an idea, set of ideas, or ideology. There is none.

Religion has such a rich history of suppressing critical inquiry that it has developed names to marginalize people with dissenting views, names that can have very serious consequences. For most of recorded history, being labeled a blasphemer, heretic, or apostate has been sufficient grounds for imprisonment, torture, or even execution. In some countries, it remains so. Even where penalties are not so severe, being assigned one of these labels instantly tags you as a dangerous outsider, someone whose views should be avoided at all costs.

This argumentative strategy, known as *poisoning the well*, involves priming one's audience with adverse information about the opponent to preemptively undermine the opponent's credibility. It is a form of the ad hominem fallacy, by which one attacks his opponent's personal character rather than the merits of the opposing claims. Through its branding of dissenters, religion has taken this strategy and institutionalized it.

These attacks can be effective because humans are inclined to put disproportionate weight on whether the person addressing them is within their "tribe." Once someone has been branded an outsider, those within the tribal group will erect cognitive barriers, such as confirmation bias, to shield themselves from the outsider's arguments. The mere perception of outsider status may be enough for people to shut their ears entirely.

Good ideas don't require demonizing those who disagree. Good ideas stand on their own merits and do not shrink from critical inquiry. Those seeking the best ideas actually invite such inquiry, for without it, how would we ever hope to approximate truth? When one sees this strategy being employed, it should send up a red flag that the proponent of the strategy is operating out of desperation rather than strength.

9. APPLYING INCONSISTENT STANDARDS OF PROOF

Apologists regularly apply inconsistent *standards* of proof to claims that support their version of Christianity versus those that do not. Philosophers call these epistemic standards. Such standards set an evidential bar for those claims that people are justified in believing. If one is being intellectually honest, then he must apply the same standard to all comparable claims, accepting only those that meet the standard while rejecting those that don't. With the strong emotional pull of religion, this is often difficult for people to do, as their cognitive biases strongly incline them to judge their own religion far less stringently than others. As Mark Twain wryly observes, however, "The easy confidence with which I know another man's religion is folly teaches me to suspect that my own is also."[11]

It is common for the religious to apply inconsistent standards to claims of religious miracles. Many religions make miracle claims, usually based on the same type of evidence, such as anecdotal hearsay. Christian apologists regularly accept the miracle claims that accord with their views while rejecting those that don't. Rarely, if ever, do they attempt any justification for treating miracle claims differently.

Needless to say, these are all extraordinary claims, to which a high standard of proof must apply. One cannot justifiably lower that standard when faced with a claim he favors. But this is just what Christian apologists do. They adopt whatever epistemic standard they need to justify accepting or rejecting a particular claim, based on whether that claim supports or undermines their version of Christianity. Such an ad hoc approach is intellectually indefensible.

10. CHERRY-PICKING AND STRAW-MAN ARGUMENTS

Also known as the fallacy of exclusion or incomplete evidence, cherry-picking refers to selectively using only information that supports one's position and ignoring that which contradicts it while representing or suggesting that one has presented a more or less complete picture. Unless someone relying on a subset of data that supports his preconceived opinions can provide principled objective criteria for excluding other data that does not, he is likely engaging in cherry-picking.

Apologists regularly employ cherry-picking when interpreting Scripture. They cite biblical passages that support the positions they already recognize as valid and aligned with their values while ignoring those that contradict those positions. Conservative politicians regularly cherry-pick biblical prohibitions that accord with their political ideologies. They may, for example, freely cite passages condemning homosexuality while ignoring those that condemn speaking against the government, bringing lawsuits, and public prayer. When citing Leviticus on homosexuality, conservatives also conveniently ignore Paul's proclamation that Jesus abolished the Jewish law, only to turn around and cite Paul when anyone suggests the politicians would be bound by the same code.

Those who compiled and preserved both the Old and New Testaments also engaged in cherry-picking when selecting, translating, and copying documents for inclusion. Many of their decisions were based not on principled, objective criteria but on a desire to endorse certain viewpoints and to promote their versions of the faith.

Apologists also cherry-pick when presenting arguments of natural theology defending Christianity. They will, for example, present evidence of the universe's life-supporting qualities while ignoring that the vast majority of the universe is violently hostile to life. Another example is offered by Stephen Fry:

> You can't just say there is a God because well, the world is beautiful. You have to account for bone cancer in children. You have to account for the fact that almost all animals in the wild live under stress with not enough to eat and will die violent and bloody deaths. There is not any way that you can just choose the nice bits and say that means there is a God and ignore the true fact of what nature is. The wonder of nature must be taken in its totality and it is a wonderful thing. It is absolutely marvelous and the idea that an atheist or a humanist if you want to put it that way, doesn't marvel and wonder at reality, at the way things are, is nonsensical. The point is we wonder all the way. We don't just stop and say that which I cannot understand I will call God, which is what mankind has done historically.[12]

A good way to understand the problem with this approach is to look at how philosophical and religious discussions differ from lawsuits in the American legal system. America has adopted the adversary system. Each side of a dispute may select an attorney of his or her choice, who then has the discretion to present that side's case as he or she chooses, within the bounds of ethics. Mostly, one's attorney can ignore any evidence that undermines her client's position and present only evidence that advances that position. The opposing attorney may do the same.

The American system assumes that both lawyers are competent and that, through this approach, the most important evidence relevant to the dispute will be presented. Each side has a substantial incentive to ferret out all information supporting his position and present it favorably. A competent and impartial jury considering this evidence should more often than not reach a decision reflecting truth and justice. The system does not require an attorney to present evidence that weakens his case, though it is often strategically advisable to do so because one can reasonably expect the opposition will present it if you don't, and it will sound worse coming from them.

Such rules don't apply to philosophical arguments, and apologists regularly take advantage of this. Because many spend most of their time "preaching to the choir," there is often no reason for them to expect that their audiences will ever be presented with strong arguments or evidence that undercut the positions they advocate. Accordingly, they simply ignore such arguments and evidence. For many reading this book, it will be the first time they have been exposed to certain arguments and information. Most preachers never present them to their congregations, conveying a false sense that Christianity rests on solid intellectual foundations. Because there is no opposing counsel to present the other side of the story, the preachers can be secure that they will get away with such a strategy. But that doesn't make it right.

I find this to be a point of much frustration in reading apologetics, as apologists so often present arguments that have been demolished many times over, as if no one has ever offered an adequate response. Obviously, it is impossible when discussing a complex issue, such as religion, to address every possible argument that might be mounted in opposition, but it becomes fallacious and disingenuous when one ignores well-known rebuttals or strong proof undercutting one's position. The stronger the disconfirming evidence withheld, the more fallacious (and dishonest) one's argument becomes.

It is not just those arguing for a position who cherry-pick but also those to whom the argument is being addressed. Due to inherent biases for one position over another, people are inclined to focus on and more readily remember and incorporate those facts and arguments that support their preconceived position (the hits) rather than those that don't (the misses). Francis Bacon claims, "The root of all superstition is that men observe when a thing hits, but not when it misses."[13]

Related to cherry-picking is erecting a straw man. Here, rather than simply ignoring an opponent's argument, one mischaracterizes it in such a way that it becomes easier to defeat and then mount an attack on the new weakened argument, thus securing an easy victory. This can occasionally result from misunderstanding an opponent's argument but at some point almost always requires intentional misrepresentation.

Any cursory review of apologetic literature will reveal straw-man arguments abounding. Creationists continue to rhetorically inquire, "If man evolved from monkeys, then why are there still monkeys?" mischaracterizing the claim of evolutionary biologists that men and monkeys both evolved *from a common ancestor*. Proponents of the cosmological argument propose false analogies of cows or cars "popping into existence" to demonstrate the apparent absurdity of an uncaused universe, ignoring the very real difference recognized by physicists between occurrences within the known universe and those outside it. Proponents of the moral argument regularly characterize all secular humanists as wedded to an arbitrary "anything goes" scheme of morality, taking no account of the many secular ethical systems long recognized by philosophers that are anything but arbitrary.

I I. APPEAL TO INTUITION (COMMON SENSE)

Another fallacy common among apologists is the appeal to intuition or common sense. This argument maintains that anything that is counterintuitive or not readily understandable by the common man must be rejected in favor of a simple, easy-to-understand, and intuitive explanation. An appeal to intuition is essentially an argument that for something to be true, it must accord with what one already believes or feels to be true. This argument gives intuition far more credit than it deserves.

Intuition refers to a particular mode of thinking that involves mental shortcuts based on preconceived assumptions rather than systematic, ground-up, rational analysis. Intuitive thinking is rapid and almost effortless. Some describe it as "going with your gut" or following your hunch. It is the default mode for many everyday tasks with which we have become intimately familiar and for which comprehensive analytical scrutiny would be a waste of time and mental resources.

Intuition is often applauded by populist politicians and others who rail against intellectuals and established ways of doing things. It was even the subject of Malcolm Gladwell's bestselling book *Blink*, which found it to have legitimate highly specialized uses in certain situations. But science has shown us repeatedly that many truths are counterintuitive, and intuition is deeply flawed as a general indicator of truth. While it may be useful in limited circumstances, in many others it is worthless or even counterproductive.

We must recall how our intuitions originated. Scientists believe the intuitive mode developed to conserve precious mental resources. Thinking hard requires energy, energy requires food, and food was in short supply for our primitive ancestors. Not every situation requires a full, deep-dive analysis. Many routine matters could be accomplished on mental autopilot, so the human brain developed one.

If we have an innate tendency toward certain intuitive beliefs, then it's likely because they were useful to our ancestors. The autopilot may have directed them to certain plants and berries that proved to be safe and nutritious and away from such animals as snakes that proved to be dangerous. It's easy to see how moral intuitions favoring fairness and generosity would have been crucial to the survival of our ancestors' tribes, as would the intuition to condemn tribe members who betrayed those reciprocal norms.[14]

This autopilot mode, however, is limited. It can serviceably handle familiar situations and certain new situations highly analogous to familiar ones. But it is poorly equipped to handle entirely novel problems with no analogous precedent. Intuition simply doesn't have the tools for the job. The only way to deal with those is to switch to the brain's systematic, analytical mode and take the problem step by step.

Human intuition is ill suited to deal with many problems of the modern age entirely foreign to our ancient ancestors. They enjoyed a perspective far more limited, with no access to the vast cosmos or the microscopic world but only to that narrow, intermediate range of medium-sized objects moving at relatively medium speeds, than that to which we have access today. They did not know of higher math or the sciences—no experience with pulsars, neutrinos, or quarks. Their brains developed to create models of the world that were useful rather than necessarily true and in doing so carved into our thinking many false assumptions. Scientists have come to realize that human common sense is useless to formulate something like a theory of quantum gravity.

This is not to imply there is no relation between useful and true. A true model, for example, would almost always be useful, but a model need not be 100 percent true to have utility. An understanding of quantum gravity, for example, would have been useless to our ancient ancestors. It would, however, have been very helpful to have accurate models by which to judge the speed and direction of moving objects, so there we should expect substantial overlap between what is useful and what is true. Many optical illusions excellently demonstrate the disconnect between how our minds visually model the world and how it actually is.

The history of science is replete with evidence that appeals to intuition but do not reliably yield truth. Modern science has shown that virtually every time we examine some part of the world distant from those experiences we share with our ancestors, we discover that our intuitions do not match reality. Who, for instance, would have concluded from intuition and common sense that all of humanity lives on a giant rock hurtling through space at 70,000 miles per hour? Scientific findings that contradicted virtually universal intuitive beliefs include the following:

- Absent wind resistance, heavy weights fall at the same speed as a feather.
- Solid matter is more than 99 percent empty space.
- Subatomic particles regularly teleport and in unpredictable ways.
- It is possible for something to be both a wave and a particle.
- There is an upper limit on how fast things can go.
- Despite there being an infinite amount of rational numbers between any two positive integers, the set of rational numbers is the same size as the set of positive integers.
- What appears as the absolute, constant passage of time is in fact relative to the observer.

None of these findings could be said to correspond with human intuitions. In each case, scientists were required to make observations and conduct experiments that would have been impossible for our ancient ancestors. These examples were simply unavailable for inclusion in the evolutionary data bank on which intuition draws. One final example is probability theory. Very little in this field aligns with our intuitive predictions. Las Vegas is a testament to this. It is an object lesson that when we rely on our intuitions to seek wealth, we are likely to be left far poorer.

The advantages of intuition are speed and mental resource cost. The disadvantages are inaccuracy and unreliability, especially in new, unfamiliar areas. Even where intuition may more directly align with ancient human experience and thus yield more reliable results, it is no match for analytical reasoning, for intuition is still fuzzy and prone to many of the biases and reasoning foibles of the human mind.

As Daniel Simons and Christopher Chabris report, "The most troublesome aspect of intuition may be the misleading role it plays in how we perceive patterns and identify causal relationships."[15] Unfortunately, this is the very use to which is most often put by apologists. It is common to see apologists appealing to intuition to support claims that the universe requires a creator, that life requires a designer, and that morality requires a lawgiver.

These conclusions seem so natural to us precisely because we instinctively analogize them to common situations involving personal agents. We are immediately familiar with people designing and creating complicated items and with people writing and enforcing laws. But we have no experience with, for example, the vast periods of time and space necessary for evolutionary change or the complex mathematical and statistical analyses inherent in theoretical physics. On what basis must we conclude that the ways of the universe are human ways? We have no good reasons to conclude that such "agency" analogies even apply. Though these assumptions come easily to us and are shared by many, that is just the type of assumption we should be wary of, precisely because of its tendency to be taken for granted. As Paul Broca recognizes, "The least questioned assumptions are often the most questionable."[16]

Intuitions can assist us in constructing hypotheses that can thereafter be tested with empirical evidence. It would be entirely unjustified, however, to use them to reach conclusions where no such evidence is available, such as the objectivity of morality. For example, cultures throughout history and around the world have engaged in ritual human sacrifice. Only in the modern era has this practice been widely criticized. Evidently, human intuition led millions of humans throughout history to believe something was right that we now all agree is wrong. On what basis can we legitimately say that the latter intuition is the "right" one?

Of more immediate relevance to Christians, if one's intuition tells you that the massacre of the Amalekites, as found in 1 Samuel 15, was wrong, then either God was wrong, or human moral intuition is untrustworthy. As virtually no Christians would countenance the first option, they are led necessarily to the second. And how would one resolve a conflict between two people whose intuitions were at odds—who each argued that common sense favored their mutually exclusive position over the other? There is no common ground to resolve competing intuitions.

Although appeals to intuition can be found in many philosophical sub-fields, their validity as evidence has come under increasing scrutiny over the last two decades, from such philosophers as Hilary Kornblith, Robert Cummins, Stephen Stich, Jonathan Weinberg, and Jaakko Hintikka. The severity of their criticisms varies from Weinberg's warning that we don't know enough about how intuitions work to Cummins's wholesale rejection of philosophical intuition as "epistemologically useless."[17]

Intuition is a poor method for resolving issues of metaphysical truth. To appeal to intuition is to appeal to a faulty and inherently unreliable approach to problem solving. That may be a practical necessity where intuition is the *only approach available*, such as when you must make a quick decision about whether to trust a stranger giving you directions. But where one has alternatives, such as the far superior scientific method and reasoned analysis, and accuracy is imperative, it is nothing less than irresponsible to rely on one's intuition. An appeal to intuition should, in such cases, be rejected as fallacious reasoning.

12. APPEAL TO EMOTION

Occasionally, I have heard that one who appeals to logic and reason be branded a "logic Nazi" or some similar derogatory epithet. The implication is that "cold" logic and reason are suspect and must be complemented, if not replaced, by "warm" human emotion to reach a valid result.[18] Inadvertent enablers of this position, I'm afraid, are science-fiction writers. Who better exemplifies the humanity-impaired logician than Spock of *Star Trek* or any other number of robots or androids who supposedly think entirely logically but lack emotion. In such stories, humans are invariably portrayed as superior *because* they have emotions, leading to the conclusion that emotions are better than logic. The primary quest of the android is typically to understand human emotion and therefore become more human. That this would be an advancement is never questioned.

All humans possess the capacity for both reason and emotion, and each plays an important role in decision making. But in good decision making, the role of each is limited to what it does best. Emotion allows us to assess the respective *weights* of various options, which logic does not. When we talk about values, that is really what we mean—value, as in how much does something mean to us? How do we prioritize one interest over the other when those interests come into conflict? Those who have lost their emotions (as with brain injuries) typically become so indecisive that they cannot function in the real world. They are paralyzed because they cannot assign relative values to things. Assigning valuative weight is something only our emotions can do.

So emotions help us formulate our goals. They identify the points on the map to where we should be heading. Determining the best route, however, is typically best left to reason and logic. If I want to go from Washington to Buffalo as quickly as possible, then I need only a map, a ruler, and some general concept of math. No emotion, whether anger, sadness, or giddy joy, will aid me in reaching the correct result more quickly or accurately. This rule applies to other decisions in our lives, as well. Anyone who makes all buying decisions primarily on emotion is likely to quickly end up in bankruptcy court.

Evaluating truth claims regarding issues on which we have empirical evidence requires a firm, rational approach. In this area, there is little room for emotion. That is why scientists require strict testing and research protocols. They know that simply wanting a particular result to occur can too often infect the testing process and make it more likely to bias the results. Science seeks to remove emotion from the equation precisely because emotion brings about invalid results in an area in which valid results are the name of the game.

Religious beliefs are so resistant to change precisely because of the strong emotional attachment people have to them. They are typically learned by children from their loving parents and authority figures and often nurtured in a secure environment. They satisfy emotional needs and concerns. But these factors do not represent valid reasons to hold onto them. As neurologist and well-known science communicator Dr. Stephen Novella observes,

> Questioning our own motives, and our own process, is critical to a skeptical and scientific outlook. We must realize that the default mode of human psychology is to grab onto comforting beliefs for purely emotional reasons,

and then justify those beliefs to ourselves with post-hoc rationalizations. It takes effort to rise above this tendency, to step back from our beliefs and our emotional connection to conclusions and focus on the process. The process (i.e. science, logic, and intellectual rigor) has to be more important than the belief.[19]

It is unnecessary to incorporate emotion into decision-making processes past the goal-development phase. The entire history of scientific inquiry has consistently demonstrated it to be counterproductive.

13. APPEAL TO NARRATIVE AND ANECDOTES

Stories activate human brains like nothing else. They engage our senses, our emotions, our memories, and our reasoning centers and, because of this, engrain ideas in our minds more effectively than any other method. People who hear something in a story are far more likely to remember it than those who don't. Cave paintings from 27,000 years ago tell us storytelling is one of our oldest and most fundamental methods of communicating. Our minds have been honed by years of evolution to gravitate to stories. There is a good reason that Jesus's parables are so well known, both within and outside Christian circles.

Pagan mythology is full of stories used to explain such observations as the rising of the Sun or the changing of the seasons. These stories make narrative sense and can even be placed within a broader context of coherence. Just because a story is coherent, however, does not mean it provides the best explanation. We know from the history of science that virtually all these stories have proven false explanations, regardless of the additional levels of meaning they provided.

Research has also shown that we consistently treat stories and the information they impart as more accurate and as deserving more weight than they deserve. People are more likely to be convinced by a short anecdote from a common stranger than from pages of data by knowledgeable experts. Charities know this and therefore highlight the plight of one or a few individuals rather than relying on numbers alone because stories speak louder than statistics. There is a saying among scientists to keep them on guard from falling prey to this very strong cognitive bias: "The plural of anecdote is not data." In other words, no volume of mere stories should ever be considered equivalent to responsibly collected scientific data.

Rarely is there any way to ensure that stories are even remotely reliable. They often come to us from second- or thirdhand sources, if that. Even if from firsthand sources, we typically have little to go on in determining whether the teller is truthful. Even if the teller is telling the truth as he sees it, there are almost always many reasons he might be mistaken. Faulty memories, perceptions, or interpretations all may undermine a story's trustworthiness. Likewise, we cannot know that the person who used this story to prove his point did not cherry-pick it, ignoring or rejecting other stories that provided inconsistent or contradictory views of the same events.

Unfortunately, our minds work in such a way that "sticky" information, such as that conveyed in a story, is likely to be considered more accurate over time as we lose track of its source. This often makes it impossible for us to analyze the reliability of such information, even if we understood when we received it that the source was untrustworthy! This is the unique power of stories.

Anyone can come up with a narrative frame that gives meaning to otherwise meaningless data, but that doesn't increase their likelihood of being correct. Scientific findings and explanations are often counterintuitive and do not fit within any familiar narrative frame. Religious explanations often do, but that reflects only ample opportunity to draft explanations to fit that frame and not that the proposed explanations enjoy any privileged claim to truth.

14. APPEAL TO PERSONAL INCREDULITY

The appeal to personal incredulity is related to the appeal to intuition and common sense but sufficiently distinct as to deserve its own brief section. An apologist appeals to personal incredulity when he claims he finds the proposition in question incredible or absurd. The implication is that if *he* finds it absurd, then *you* should find it absurd, as well. This approach often leaves one's opponents at a loss for words, as it is hard to argue with an incredulous stare.

While there is nothing wrong with providing one's personal opinion of another's position (I do it myself within these pages), no one should mistake such opinions for a sound rebuttal. Opinions are not evidence. Only the opinions of disinterested experts with expertise in relevant fields should be accorded any value and then only because their opinions can generally (though not always) be considered informed distillations of relevant data.

These arguments are common in discussing such scientific theories as evolution. Many claim, for instance, that they find it absurd that humans could develop through a process, evolution, incorporating so many random variables. The inability to grasp science, however, is not an argument against it. To such a person, I could only recommend that they learn the science and study the theory so they can properly understand it before rendering an opinion regarding its viability. Opinions offered with no such foundation are of negligible value.

The appeal to personal incredulity may also be thought of as a disguised appeal to intuition. It asks that one run the proposition through his commonsense filter (also known as a bullshit detector) and, if the proposition appears counterintuitive, reject it out of hand. However, we simply cannot rely on our intuitions to provide reliable bullshit filters in areas in which we have no expertise. In those situations, we must defer to those who actually know what they are talking about—no matter how counterintuitive their conclusions may appear to us or the person making the opposing argument.

We must also keep in mind that even views that seem common to us because they are shared by many people we know and interact with are not necessarily true. Sometimes, things you and your peers accept as universal truths are simply true within your own limited social or cultural sphere. We can only hope to accurately assess these views by getting outside our spheres and looking to disinterested expert opinion.

15. APPEAL TO MARTYRDOM

Apologists often point to the martyrdom of early Christians as evidence for the truth of Christianity. They argue, for example, that no one would die for something they knew to be a lie, and so Christianity must have been true. I have spoken with Christians who claim this as one of the strongest arguments for Christianity.

The argument rests on several unstated premises that are highly questionable. The first is that there were any Christian martyrs who witnessed Jesus's miracles and Resurrection. The second is that these were executed specifically for being Christians rather than some unrelated reason. The third is that they were given an opportunity to recant but chose not to. The final premise is the most problematic: that willingness to die for a belief makes it more likely to be true.

There is very little contemporary evidence of any Christians executed in the first century and none suggesting that they were killed for failing to renounce Christianity. Virtually all stories of Christian martyrdom appear to have originated in the third and fourth centuries, by which time no potential Christian martyr could critically assess the claims of Jesus's miracles and Resurrection. Modern scholars have concluded that very few of even the earliest accounts of Christian martyrdom are historically reliable.[20]

Even if we assume all Christian martyr accounts to be historically accurate, however, they do not count as evidence for the truth of Christianity. Throughout history, people have been willing to die for beliefs we now know to be false. We know that a great many of these people were sincerely mistaken. The concept of a "good death" long predates Christianity and has been used by ideological, secular, and religious movements throughout history to motivate followers to make the ultimate sacrifice. That every major religion can point to its own willing martyrs, despite making irreconcilable claims, demonstrates that willingness to die for a belief is no reliable indicator of truth. An argument that can be made on behalf of multiple contradictory belief systems cannot substantially advance any one of them.

16. ARGUMENT FROM THE DESIRABLE OR FROM FINAL CONSEQUENCES

It should go without saying that what may be desirable is not necessarily true. Likewise, just because the consequences of accepting a hypothesis may seem undesirable doesn't suggest the hypothesis is faulty. That we may *want things to be a certain way* is no indication they are or will be that way. As President John Adams observes, "Facts are stubborn things; and whatever may be our wishes, our inclinations, or the dictates of our passions, they cannot alter the state of facts and evidence."[21] And yet, many apologists argue as if they can.

For example, many object to naturalism because it doesn't allow for an external purpose—either individually or for humanity as a whole. They claim that life would not be worth living without some cosmic significance and goals given to us by an intelligent agent. Pastor Rick Warren, for example, in his runaway best-seller *The Purpose-Driven Life*, claims, "Without God, life has no purpose, and without purpose, life has no meaning. Without meaning, life has no significance or hope."[22] William Lane Craig puts it this way: "If all the events are meaningless, then what can be the ultimate meaning of influencing any of them? Ultimately it makes no difference."[23]

While millions of atheists would argue vehemently with these claims, the important point is that they have nothing to do with whether naturalism represents an accurate view of the universe. The *desire* of some people to believe in an external purpose makes it no more likely that one exists, though it might explain why people would rationalize their religious beliefs in the face of disconfirming evidence.

Another example would be the desire for an objective basis for morality. In a world swimming with complex moral problems, it is not surprising that many would like to think there is an objective code by which every moral question can be definitively answered. But as with the previous example, that desire does not translate into increased likelihood that such a code actually exists. This is a subcategory of the human desire for certainty and cognitive closure, which is discussed elsewhere herein.

Two additional examples relate to evolution. A common sentiment of evolution deniers is their distaste for the idea that they share a relatively recent common ancestor with monkeys. They feel it diminishes the status and role of human beings and threatens the biblical claim that man was created in God's image. Creationists also argue that acceptance of evolution will lead to eugenics, citing Nazi scientists who referenced Darwinian principles, such as "survival of the fittest," to justify genocide of races they believed to be inferior. But this merely demonstrates that people can use otherwise neutral scientific findings to justify their own bad ideas, not that the findings themselves are flawed.

As a caveat, this argument is often disguised as an argument from intuition. The apologist will claim that if many people feel that something should be so, then that alone suggests that it is so. But this is a non sequitur. There is no evidence that reality is related to human wishes, no matter how common they may be. Humans desire many things that do not reflect reality. Our desires remain merely desires, regardless of how many people share them.

There is one more important point to make on this subject. Psychologists have demonstrated that when humans want things to be a certain way, they are likely to overlook information suggesting they are not and to interpret ambiguous data so it supports their desire. This is known as motivated reasoning, one of the cognitive weaknesses the scientific method is designed to address. We have good reason to be skeptical when a particular theory or explanation lines up with *how we would want things to be*. As physicist Brian Greene observes, "When you know the answer you want, it is often all too easy to figure out a way of getting it."[24] This is especially true when large groups of people have a common desire.

17. ARGUMENT FROM UTILITY

Related to the argument from final consequences is the argument from utility, which suggests that an idea is more likely to be true if it will be useful or lead to positive results. A typical example is the claim that religion leads to more prosocial behavior. Putting aside whether there is any truth to this claim, consider the following.

Assume we all have a colleague who believes an invisible cricket sits on his shoulder, whispering advice that keeps him in line. Assume that everyone has humored him for years, agreeing to his face that they can hear the cricket talking, just as he does. Further assume that one day, I decide to break his spell by revealing I have in fact never heard the voices and no one else has either. Assume this causes him to abandon belief in the invisible cricket and embark on a wild killing spree, murdering everyone he sees because he no longer recognizes any moral anchor. You may argue in hindsight that my choice was not wise, and with such knowledge, I would have to agree with you. You must acknowledge, however, that the man's killing spree does not suggest that the invisible cricket *ever actually existed*. Likewise, an argument that religion has social utility renders it no more likely that it reflects reality.

18. FALSE EQUIVALENCE

A common approach to defending against arguments hitting a little too close to home is to paint your opponent's position as equivalent to yours in some crucial respect, even if it isn't. This false equivalence suggests that any weaknesses your opponent has pointed out in your position apply equally to his without saying as much. It allows you to implicitly bring your opponent's position down to the level of your own without explicitly undermining any of his arguments.

Tu quoque is a term meaning literally "you as well," and it describes a common argument based on false equivalence. It is used to deflect criticism of a position by reflecting those criticisms back on one's opponent. It allows the proponent to avoid actually addressing the criticism by attempting to establish equivalence between the position one is defending and one he opposes. It has also been called the appeal to hypocrisy, as it can be used to attack the validity of a position by arguing that one's opponent has failed to act consistently with belief in that position.

The first problem with this argument is that it doesn't advance the ball for the proponent. To say "You're as bad as I am" isn't exactly a ringing endorsement. Likewise, to attack the personal behavior of one's opponent doesn't undermine their argument in any way—just their personal commitment to it. Perhaps it was a legitimate criticism of Vice President Al

Gore *the person* that he flew around the world on jet aircraft to promote his global warming documentary *An Inconvenient Truth*. One might argue, for example, that Gore allowed his desire for comfort and convenience to outweigh the commitment to ideals he championed. But Gore's behavior is irrelevant to the science-based arguments made in that film, which must stand or fall on their own merits, regardless of Gore's behavior. This is just another form of the ad hominem fallacy.

The second problem is that tu quoque arguments are prone to the fallacies of false equivalence and straw manning. To make an effective tu quoque argument, one must first establish that the opposing position is directly equivalent to one's own. If I am going to attack you for promoting a position with the same flaws you attack in mine, then I must first demonstrate that the two positions do indeed suffer from the same flaws. I cannot hope to legitimately advance my position where I present only a caricature of yours. Where this argument has been made by apologists, such equivalence is typically assumed rather than demonstrated.

Perhaps the most common apologetic use of a tu quoque argument is the charge that naturalists are wedded to their own "religion," which apologists call "scientism." As with most terms crafted for argumentative rather than explanatory purposes, *scientism* is poorly and inconsistently defined. In general, however, it is used to reference an unreasonably enthusiastic embrace of science; an unwarranted reliance on it to guide all aspects of one's life, such as in morality and the arts; and a blind deference that does not sufficiently acknowledge its limitations and potential dangers. In short, apologists claim, scientism is the replacement of religion with science as the all-encompassing worldview, thus rendering the two equivalent.

This scientism construct is nothing more than a straw man. It is a caricature of scientists and scientifically minded individuals that bears little resemblance to their actual beliefs. The *Oxford Companion to Philosophy* has this to say:

> Scientism is a term of abuse. Therefore, perhaps inevitably, there is no one simple characterization of the views of those who are thought to be identified as prone to it. . . . A successful accusation of scientism usually relies upon a restrictive conception of the sciences and an optimistic conception of the arts as hitherto practiced. Nobody espouses scientism; it is just detected in the writings of others.[25]

Scientism is an insult used to denigrate others rather than an actual position held by anyone—an insult that can only be justified by redefining science and the arts for purposes of the argument. It carries a pejorative connotation, building lack of legitimate justification into its every meaning.

Of all the atheists I have known and the atheist writers whose works I've read, I have never known one whose views I would recognize as consistent with scientism as apologists use it. None see science as an all-encompassing worldview equivalent to religion, and none are blind to its limitations. If anything, science as a discipline is *obsessed with its own limitations*, always finding better ways to address them. Naturalists view scientific methodology as a tool with a specific purpose—assessing truth claims regarding observable phenomena. Broadly construed to include a commitment to rationality and empirical observation, we claim science is the only reliable way to obtain *objective knowledge* about the universe. This claim is not intended to encompass areas of *subjective knowledge* or value-based disciplines, such as art and morality.[26] No one claims that science can determine the most beautiful painting or emotionally moving song.

While it can justifiably be said that science is better than religion at certain tasks that religion has traditionally carved out for itself (such as explaining natural phenomena), that does not render science and religion broadly equivalent, and there are scarce few on the science side who argue it does. More specifically, it does not imply that science is vulnerable to the same criticisms as religions—especially the criticism that beliefs should be only held with certainty proportionate to the evidence supporting them.

19. FALSE DICHOTOMY/DILEMMA

Briefly referenced earlier, an argument based on a false dilemma begins by providing a misleadingly limited number of options (usually two or three) as if they were the only possibilities, when in fact they are not. Assume that Alex points to a rock and asks you whether it is an animal or a vegetable. Alex then demonstrates why one of these options should be eliminated from consideration. For instance, he may show that the rock has no nervous system, so it cannot be an animal. Alex claims that having eliminated the first option, the second must be true. Therefore, the rock must be a vegetable. Here, the fallacious nature of the argument is clear, but it is not always so, for it depends on you recognizing that other options are available.

The value of this approach is that it avoids having to provide positive evidence for your favored proposition. You need only show that the other alternative(s) (all of which you have conveniently supplied) fail. Notice how Alex has provided no affirmative support for the claim that rocks are vegetables. The structure of his argument doesn't require him to. Once you have bought into the premise that only two options are possible, Alex need only discredit one for the other to win by default.

The problem is that the initial premise is invalid. Alex never allowed for the possibility that the rock might be a mineral and so never had to address it. Unless all available options are presented, no valid inference may be drawn. Only possibilities that are collectively exhaustive can reasonably point in a single direction when all but one have been eliminated, as reflected in Sherlock Holmes's famous statement, "When you have eliminated the impossible, whatever remains, however, improbable, must be the truth."[27] The difficulty here is in being confident that one has collected and addressed all options.

From the world of apologetics, a well-known example of this fallacy in action is the alliterative "trilemma" of C. S. Lewis, positing that Jesus must have been either "Liar, Lunatic, or Lord."[28] After providing arguments against the first two options, Lewis leaves his audience with the last as the only reasonable choice. Conveniently, Lewis fails to account for numerous other possibilities, such as, in keeping with the alliterative theme, "Legend." By omitting such possibilities, Lewis obviates the need to address them or even to provide positive evidence for his favored hypothesis. Win, win, win.

Another example is when Christian apologists argue as if the only options on the table are Christianity and atheism, such that poking holes in the latter must necessarily lead to the former. They conveniently ignore the vast array of other world religions, both actively practiced *and extinct*, as possibilities. For example, arguments based on establishing a first cause, such as the cosmological argument, would support thousands of other religions, as well as Deism, which in practice would be indistinguishable from atheism. Proving such arguments or merely undermining atheism would leave the apologists' work far from done.

A well-known prudential argument based on a false dichotomy is Pascal's wager. Blaise Pascal, a Christian philosopher living in the mid-1600s, acknowledged that the existence of God could not be proven by rational argument. He argued that such belief was nonetheless *justified* by comparing the advantages of believing versus disbelieving. Pascal claimed that if one believed in the Christian God but was mistaken, then nothing was lost. If one disbelieved and was mistaken, however, then one would lose an eternity of bliss and suffer an eternity in Hell. The cost of being wrong in the latter case is astronomical by comparison, far outweighing the risk of erroneous belief in God. Accordingly, it is prudent to believe because the false positive outweighs the false negative. Regarding Pascal's wager, Alan

Dershowitz says, "I have always considered Pascal's Wager a questionable bet to place, since any God worth believing in would prefer an honest agnostic to a calculating hypocrite."[29]

Aside from the unwarranted assumption that belief of this kind is voluntary and can be given or withheld based on prudential considerations or that God would even value such a tactically manufactured "belief," Pascal ignores all the possibilities other than Christianity and atheism, each of which would have its own cost/benefit analysis. A Hindu, Muslim, or Native American shaman, for instance, could claim their own version of Pascal's wager. If the Christian chooses the wrong god to believe in, then she may be subjected to eternal suffering in the Hell equivalent of whichever religion turns out to be correct. And what about the possibility there may be a god who is the subject of no existing religion but nonetheless horribly punishes those who don't worship him? As even Homer Simpson recognizes, "Suppose we've chosen the wrong god? Every time we go to church, we're just making him madder and madder."[30]

Arguments from ignorance can also be thought of as false dilemmas. They focus entirely on poking holes in a limited range of options presented by the proponent, under the premise that by undermining these options, you will be persuaded to reach their preferred conclusion, which is the one conveniently offered up by the proponent. An apologist who argues for a theistic origin to the universe in this way must effectively address all known naturalistic hypotheses as well as those that have not yet been proposed by his opponent. Otherwise, he can provide no assurance that he has exhausted all competing possibilities. Instead, however, they typically offer only one or two options as alternatives to Christianity, often straw men, hoping that disparaging those will result in a default win for their side.

An especially pernicious breed of false dilemma is known as "false in one, false in all." Also known as the Nirvana fallacy, it can be stated as "If it's not perfect, then it's worthless." One relies on this fallacy when she promotes position A *solely* by attempting to poke holes in position B under the notion that *any fault* in position B, no matter how minor, disqualifies it from consideration, resulting in a default victory for position A. Those who employ this line of argument typically rely exclusively on a negative inference derived from attacking position B.

The problem is that a theory need not be perfect to provide the best explanation. Competing theories can only be assessed by comparing how each explains all the available evidence. If theory A satisfactorily explains only six of ten pieces of evidence, then that does not mean it must immediately be discarded for theory B because it can't explain the remaining four. Perhaps theory A is simply incomplete or mistaken on some negligible points that do not undermine its main thrust. Theory B should only be preferred if it satisfactorily explains *more of the evidence than theory A*. But this first requires a thorough, independent analysis of theory B. Comparing testable theories to determine which best explains the observable evidence is the basis of scientific progress.

This fallacy is frequently employed by conspiracy theorists. They spend all their time attempting to find problems with the "official" position, preferring *any alternate explanations*—even those that are mutually exclusive. Rarely are conspiracy theorists willing to settle on a single alternate theory and compare it, point by point, with the official position to assess which theory best explains all the evidence.

Likewise, this strategy is favored by Christian apologists. The intelligent design (ID) movement, in particular, rests its entire case on trying to poke holes in evolution. It fails, however, to provide any true alternate explanations for all the evidence addressed by evolution. In contrast to the detailed explanations and predictions evolutionary biologists can provide for billions of observations science has made about terrestrial life, ID proponents offer only a bold conclusion: God did it. Such a conclusion, with no testable claims, provides no valid basis for comparison. Science may not be able to explain everything, but is religion able to explain anything?

20. ARGUMENT TO MODERATION

The argument to moderation argues for a middle ground by asserting that between any two positions, there must exist a compromise between them that is correct and, accordingly, that any compromise is more likely correct than either extreme. If person A argues for one unit and person B argues for one hundred units, then person C may argue for fifty, claiming his to be the superior position *simply because it rests between the "extremes" of A and B*.

While this argument has intuitive appeal in a society concerned with notions of fairness, it is based on a false assumption that a middle ground position is *necessarily* more likely to be correct than positions on either end of the spectrum. There is no valid basis for such a belief. Every position can be represented as an extreme on *some* spectrum. Just because you can assign positions along that spectrum doesn't mean that any is more likely to be true than any other. Their relative placements have no bearing on the truth of any position.

A negotiating strategy well known to lawyers is to frame the position you want so it appears to be the moderate position. This is why savvy negotiators engage in lowballing (or highballing), beginning with what they know to be an unreasonably low (or high) position, so their opponent finds it psychologically easier to move to the position the framer desires under the pretense that the parties are merely splitting the difference. The framer hereby exploits the human bias for moderation to manipulate the behavior of anyone who doesn't recognize this strategy.

This is an argument often used by liberal apologists to support their own brand of Christianity, which they strategically represent as a compromise between the "extremes" of fundamentalist theology and atheism. This argument is also used by creationists to inject ID into modern science classrooms. By characterizing ID as a compromise between Christian creationism and scientific evolution, they exploit people's moderation bias to make their position intuitively sound more reasonable.

Another example is anthropogenic global warming (AGW). That those fully accepting global warming and those wholly denying it represent opposite ends of a spectrum does not justify one in taking a "wait and see" attitude (presented as the moderate approach between immediate action and outright denial) when 97 percent of scientists accept it as fact. Nor does it justify treating the two positions as roughly equivalent. Why should the 3 percent that disagree with the scientific consensus be entitled to 50 percent of the time?

There is no compromise when it comes to truth. One must evaluate each claim independently based on the evidence supporting it rather than where it may fall along a spectrum of views. Various claims can always be placed on a continuum, with points arbitrarily assigned between them, but the relative placement of these claims does not affect their likelihood to be true. In such cases, we must actively guard against our intuitive preferences for moderation and look at each claim on its own merits.

21. APPEAL TO RELATIVISM

Relativism is the position that there is no one truth; what is legitimately true for one person can be legitimately false for someone else. By adopting relativism ad hoc to comparable objective facts, one commits the relativist fallacy. Religious moderates commonly fall back on the relativist fallacy when backed into a corner. Rather than directly address legitimate questions and arguments posed by nonbelievers, they simply end-run the argument with "While that may be true for you, it isn't necessarily for me." If their opponent's argument is based on logic and reason, however, then this is absurd, for logic and reason can only point to one truth.

In 1952, Mississippi politician Noah Sweat gave a speech on the controversial (at that time) subject of whiskey that by clever rhetoric, allowed him to effectively take no position on the topic. It represents a perfect example of the relativist fallacy in action. I have reworded Mr. Sweat's speech, known as "If by Whisky," to resemble the argument of a religious moderate invoking the fallacy:

> My friends, I had not intended to discuss this controversial subject at this particular time. However, I want you to know that I do not shun controversy. On the contrary, I will take a stand on any issue at any time, regardless of how fraught with controversy it might be. You have asked me how I feel about God. All right, here is how I feel about God.
>
> If when you say God, you mean the bloodthirsty tyrant of Israel (Isaiah 34:2–7); the wrathful being who calls Himself "jealous" (Exodus 34:14); the source of all evil, anguish, and misery (Amos 3:6; Lamentations 3:38; Isaiah 45:6–7); the sender of evil spirits (Judges 9:23; Samuel 16:14, 18:10) who engages in deliberate deceit (Ezekiel 14:9; 2 Thessalonians 2:11); the champion of war (1 Samuel 15:2–3); the enabler of rape (Exodus 21:2–7, 21:20–21; Leviticus 25:44–46; 2 Samuel 12:11–19; Numbers 31:32–35); and the murderer of children (Numbers 31:17–18), then certainly I am against Him.
>
> But if when you say God you mean the protector of the meek (Matthew 5:5), the voice of the outcasts (Luke 15:1–31), the champion of the poor and marginalized (Matthew 6:1), and the sponsor of peace and forgiveness (Matthew 5:9), then certainly I am for Him.
>
> This is my stand. I will not retreat from it. I will not compromise.

22. TEXAS SHARPSHOOTER

This refers to assigning unwarranted significance to data that has been cherry-picked specifically to advance the proponent's argument. The name comes from a joke about a Texan sharpshooter who earns his reputation by firing shots into the side of a barn blindfolded and then painting the target around the biggest cluster of hits. Apologists often invoke this fallacy when arguing for the reliability of the Bible, focusing on the apparent consistency of, for example, the four canonical Gospels. Their point is that we should not expect such consistency unless the Gospels were all working off a story with a strong factual basis.

Unfortunately, the apologists typically fail to account for the myriad of noncanonical, roughly contemporaneous Christian writings of which we now know and which demonstrate how *inconsistent* early Christians were on even core Christian beliefs. Such documents as the Nag Hamadi texts and the Gospel of Peter reveal that the consistency argued for by the apologists is largely an illusion achieved by the church systematically ignoring, suppressing, or actively destroying evidence of inconsistencies while compiling a text intentionally designed to appear consistent and reliable. Once one steps back and sees all the other holes in the barn, it becomes clear that the Gospels weren't written by literary sharpshooters. They were cherry-picked to promote a specific version of the faith.

23. COMPOSITION/DIVISION

The fallacy of composition involves inferring that something is true of the whole from the fact that it is true of some part of the whole. Apologists often argue, for example, that because items and actions within the universe appear to require causes, the universe itself (defined as everything potentially observable) requires a cause. Physicists have demonstrated through modeling that this is not necessarily true, as the qualities we have observed within the universe may not apply outside it.

Another example is consciousness. Apologists often claim that because the brain is made up of tissue that itself lacks consciousness, it cannot be the *source* of consciousness. This introduces the concept of emergent properties, whereby two things that lack a certain quality may develop that quality when combined. Requiring a supernatural explanation for consciousness simply because the components of the brain lack consciousness commits the fallacy of composition. The flip side of the fallacy of composition is division, through which one concludes something is true of a part because it is true of the whole. To assume that every member of a church reflects the doctrinal position of that church, for example, would be to commit the fallacy of division.

24. STOLEN CONCEPT

This is an interesting fallacy used by apologists in their attempts to undercut any basis for human knowledge other than divine revelation. It occurs when one assumes the truth or validity of some concept in attempting to disprove it. In other words, they steal a concept for the ad hoc limited purpose of supporting their argument, but if the position for which they argue were valid, then the concept supporting their argument would be invalid, thus rendering the argument itself incoherent. The argument becomes self-defeating.

This fallacy appears where apologists attempt to show that humans cannot trust reason, logic, or their senses to provide accurate information. But these arguments invariably rely on the same reason, logic, and appeal to sensory input they attempt to reveal as hopelessly flawed. They presuppose the truth of that which they are attempting to invalidate, resulting in an incoherent argument. Employing stolen concepts involves applying a *double standard*, by which your opponent's arguments are judged by criteria you abandon when presenting your own.

25. USE OF TAUTOLOGIES

Apologists love to use rhetorical tautologies. These are self-contained statements that are technically true but impart no information and thus are worthless as arguments. A simple example would be "The blue car is blue." Well, okay, but so what? If you *begin* with the premise that the car is blue, then it is merely circular *to conclude* that it is blue. We aren't learning anything or saying anything new about it. When presented as arguments, the truth of the proposition being argued for is guaranteed. Consequently, the argument is unfalsifiable but pointless.

One common example from apologetics is to claim we can believe the Bible because the Bible was inspired by God, as stated in the Bible. Another is that the Bible was written by man *but inspired by God*, relying on the Bible itself for support. This allows the apologist to shrug off any clearly false passages as human errors but still maintain divine inspiration for statements and claims that can't be verified or definitively falsified. Again, however, the argument is circular and completely unpersuasive. In fact, the accuracy of the Bible is a crucial question that can and should be assessed independently. It cannot merely be assumed but can only be evaluated by comparing biblical claims to external evidence. The Bible is not proof of anything. It is the claim.

All our "authoritative" information about the Christian God comes from the Bible. If the information in the Bible is questionable, then there is no reliable information upon which to base belief in God. All belief in God is founded on the premise that the Bible is, at least in some sense, true. It follows that in order to disprove the existence of the Christian God, it is sufficient to show that the Bible is not true. If the verifiable and falsifiable claims are falsified, then the job should be done, as there is no principled reason to assume the nonfalsifiable claims to be true.[31]

26. CATEGORICAL DISMISSAL OF THE ARGUMENT FROM SILENCE

An argument that arises fairly often in discussions of Christian apologetics is known as the argument from silence (AOS). According to the AOS, we are justified in inferring a claim to be false where we would reasonably expect to find evidence in its favor but no such evidence is found. The valid AOS represents an exception to the general rule that the "absence of evidence is not evidence of absence." This rule applies only where we would have no good reason to expect supporting evidence to be found, in which case relying on the AOS would constitute a fallacy. The key, therefore, is to identify situations in which the argument may be employed validly, as opposed to those in which it may not.

Assume Alex claims that President Bill Clinton was shot and almost killed on March 27, 1997. One would reasonably expect such an event to receive worldwide media coverage. If a review of all major news agencies revealed no reports of such an incident, then we would be justified in concluding that Alex's claim is false. This is a valid AOS. Assume, however, that Alex instead claims that on March 27, 1997, President Clinton stubbed his toe. Here, a lack of confirming reports from any major news agency would not, by itself, justify dismissing Alex's claim. In this latter case, the event would be of such minor significance that we would not reasonably expect it to be reported.

Another way to discuss this is to say that while the absence of evidence isn't *definitive proof* of absence, it can certainly be *evidence* of absence, depending on the circumstances. The strength of that evidence is proportional to how hard we've looked and the reasons we have to expect evidence to be there. The greater the length of time and the more people involved in the search, the more powerful an argument from silence becomes that the thing being claimed to exist in fact doesn't.

Christian apologists hate the AOS because it so often refutes Christian claims. For example, given that God desperately seeks a personal relationship with every person, why does He remain effectively hidden from mankind, affording no clear evidence of even His existence? Likewise, given the biblical claims of astounding miracles surrounding Jesus's life and Resurrection, why are there no contemporary accounts of these events? People have been looking in vain for two thousand years and have found no compelling proof of either. In both cases, we would expect to see solid evidence if Christianity were true, but in both cases, we see none. The parsimonious explanation is that Christianity is false.

The most common apologetic response to such polemics is to simply deny the legitimacy of all arguments from silence. One frequently sees an appeal to the general rule with no acknowledgment that the AOS can, when applied properly, represent a valid exception. The argument from silence is the perfect occasion to apply Bayes' theorem and the surprise factor, discussed earlier. Every contemporaneous historian who fails to mention Jesus or his miracles, every Israeli dig site that fails to turn up evidence for the vast dynasties of David and Solomon, and every year that passes with no archeological proof of a Jewish Exodus across the Sinai Peninsula represents yet another white marble of countless thousands supporting naturalism.

27. ESTABLISHING NECESSARY BUT NOT SUFFICIENT CONDITIONS

Several arguments are used by apologists that I categorize as necessary but not sufficient. This means they argue for something that would be required to establish God exists but is not sufficient on its own to make the case. The argument, even if successful, might not even advance the claim for the Christian God. They treat the success of each such claim as a winning touchdown, when it in fact indicates only that they are still in the game.

For example, assume I am trying to sell you a car. You agree to buy the car only if I can convince you it is the fastest on the planet. I agree to these terms. I get in the car, press the gas pedal, and show you that the car moves forward when I hit the gas. The car moves a few feet and stops. I get out, and I ask you to fork over the cash. Would you do so?

Certainly not, for I have not complied with our terms. For the car to be the fastest on the planet, it is indeed necessary that it move forward when the gas pedal is pressed. But this is by no means *all* that is necessary. It must also move faster than other cars—*all other cars*. My meager demonstration has, though establishing a necessary condition, made no headway on that claim. If I cannot even demonstrate that the car can move forward, however, then you may *immediately reject my grander claim* because I have failed to show a necessary condition.

Likewise, apologists attempt many arguments to establish something that would have to be true for the Christian God to exist but that does not, even if true, necessarily lead to the existence of God. It is crucial to keep these types of arguments in perspective and recognize that if any of these "necessary" arguments fail, then the entire case for the Christian God crumbles. Even if one finds them compelling, however, the apologist still has a long way to go to make his case.

28. UNDERSTATED EVIDENCE

The fallacy of understated evidence is a form of cherry-picking, in which one presents general data that supports one's hypothesis but fails to account for more specific data that would defeat it. One example would be that in which an apologist argues human consciousness is more likely given theism than naturalism because it is consistent with a preexisting mind. But we know more about consciousness than the mere fact that it exists, and these facts must be accounted for, as well. For example, we know that conscious states appear to depend entirely on the brain, so damage to the brain alters consciousness in predictable ways. The dualist view of Christianity posits that minds are independent of the brain, while naturalism posits that the conscious mind is just a description of something the brain does. All the brain research of the last century supports the naturalist view. An argument for theism that ignores the research on brain-mind dependency commits the fallacy of understated evidence.

Another way to commit this fallacy is to argue for one's hypothesis in isolated stages, as in the cumulative approach discussed previously, but failing to account for all the predictions one would expect to be true were one's hypothesis correct. A Christian apologist relying on the first-cause argument, for example, relies solely on the universe existing rather than nothing, which he posits is more consistent with a preexisting first mover than any naturalistic explanation. But we know far more about the universe than the mere fact that it exists. We know, for instance, that it is far vaster than any human could ever explore, that it is almost entirely inhospitable to life, and that it fails to conform to any description found in the Christian Bible. Any argument based on first cause must also account for these facts, demonstrating that the sum of the evidence, *taken as a whole*, supports theism over naturalism.

29. THE FALLACY FALLACY

No discussion of fallacies would be complete without mentioning this one. To reject one's position simply because he has employed an informal logical fallacy is itself fallacious. Recall that a fallacy doesn't render the proponent's argument false. It simply establishes that that argument fails to advance the position for which it argues. Establishing the fallacy invalidates the merit of only the specific argument being made—not the position itself.

Also, an argument that may be fallacious for one purpose may be entirely valid for another. If I argued, for example, that Christianity is false *because* many of its practitioners engage in immoral acts, that would be a fallacious argument. If, however, I used the same argument to counter a contention made in favor of Christianity that Christians are more moral than non-Christians, then the argument would be entirely valid. In the latter case, my argument goes to the heart of a particular claim made by my opponent.

If a position is warranted, then one would expect there to be arguments in its favor that do not employ fallacies or otherwise faulty reasoning. Given the history of Christianity, along with the resources and incentives available to construct the most compelling supporting arguments, one should expect many sound arguments confirming its validity. If the leading arguments are shown to be fraught with fallacious reasoning, then that should, at a minimum, give us great pause before accepting its claims.

NOTES

CHAPTER I

1. For the purpose of expediency, I use the term *jury* to refer to the finder of fact, though judges or juries can be fact finders, depending on the nature of the proceeding. In most cases, however, the jury serves as the fact finder, while the judge administers the trial and makes legal rulings on evidentiary and other house-keeping matters.

2. *Black's Law Dictionary* explains the parenthetical maxim as follows: "*Ei incumbit probatio, qui dicit, non qui negat; cum per rerum naturam factum negantis probatio nulla sit.* . . . The proof lies upon him who affirms, not upon him who denies; since, by the nature of things, he who denies a fact cannot produce any proof." Henry Campbell Black, *Black's Law Dictionary: Definitions of the Terms and Phrases of American and English Jurisprudence, Ancient and Modern*, 6th ed. (St. Paul, MN: West, 1990), 516.

3. The appropriate *standard of proof* in various situations, however, is a more fertile area of legitimate debate. But that discussion is beyond the scope of this book.

4. Oxford, "Science," Lexico, accessed March 6, 2021, https://en.oxforddictionaries.com/definition/science.

5. Oxford, "Scientific Method," Lexico, accessed March 6, 2021, https://en.oxforddictionaries.com/definition/scientific_method.

6. Wikipedia, "Scientific Method," last updated February 12, 2021, https://en.wikipedia.org/wiki/Scientific_method.

7. Valerie Tarico, "Christian Belief through the Lens of Cognitive Science," *The Christian Delusion: Why Faith Fails*, ed. John W. Loftus (Amherst, NY: Prometheus Books, 2010), 50.

8. Shane McKee, "Show me the Sausages," *Answers In Genes blog*, June 2, 2011, accessed March 16, 2021. http://www.answersingenes.com/2011/06/show-me-sausages.html

9. Admittedly, this is a bit of an oversimplification. Sometimes, one must gather facts before even forming a hypothesis. Sometimes, hypotheses are not tested by experiments but by observations they predict. In any event, the basic principle of scientific knowledge advancing through the formation and testing of hypotheses holds true.

10. Carl Sagan, *The Demon-Haunted World: Science as a Candle in the Dark* (New York: Ballantine Books, 1996).

11. David Elmes, Barry Kantowitz, and Henry Roediger, *Research Methods in Psychology*, 8th ed., (Belmont, CA: Thomson/Wadsworth, 2006), Chapter 2.

12. Richard P. Feynman, *The Meaning of It All: Thoughts of a Citizen-Scientist* (New York: Basic Books, 2005).

13. Religious apologists often attack the concept of attaching reliability to the scientific by referencing Galileo, who overturned the consensus of his day by proving that the Earth actually revolved around the Sun. This story merely demonstrates that the scientific consensus of Galileo's day was much less reliable than it is today. In Galileo's day, science was in its infancy. The expert consensus was based primarily on Christian Scripture rather than anything we would today recognize as science. Comparing that consensus to those of today is to compare apples and oranges. It also demonstrates, however, the great strength of science: its built-in controls for self-correction. When the data does not conform to the theory, the theory must be changed.

14. Isaac Asimov, "The Relativity of Wrong," *Skeptical Inquirer* 14, no. 1 (Fall 1998): 35–44, http://chem.tufts.edu/AnswersInScience/RelativityofWrong.htm.

15. Bertrand Russell, *ABC of Relativity*, 4th rev. ed. (New York: Routledge, 2009).

16. Jerry Coyne, *Faith versus Fact: Why Science and Religion Are Incompatible* (New York: Penguin Books, 2016), 26.

17. Tatjana Jevremovic, *Nuclear Principles in Engineering* (Springer 2005), 397 https://download.e-bookshelf.de/download/0000/0002/88/L-G-0000000288-0002339943.pdf

18. Artur Conan Doyle, "A Scandal in Bohemia," *The Adventures of Sherlock Holmes* (1891).

19. This is known as "theistic evolution" and addressed later herein.

20. Penn Jillette, *God, No! Signs You May Already Be an Atheist and other Magical Tales* (Simon & Schuster 2011).

21. J. B. S. Haldane, *Fact and Faith* (Neilson Press 1934), Preface vi–vii.

22. Steven Weinberg, *To Explain the World: The Discovery of Modern Science* (Harper Perennial, 2016). https://www.goodreads.com/book/show/22328555-to -explain-the-world.

23. James Randi, *The Mask of Nostradamus*, (Prometheus Books 1993), 66.

24. Edward J. Larson and Larry Witham, "Leading Scientists Still Reject God," *Nature* 394, no. 313 (July 23, 1998), https://www.nature.com/articles/28478; Pew Research Center, "Scientists and Belief," November 5, 2009, https://www.pewfo rum.org/2009/11/05/scientists-and-belief/.

25. Larson and Witham, "Leading Scientists"; Pew Research Center, "Scientists and Belief."

26. For this example, I must thank Robert Price.

27. The principle of analogy can be considered a specialized application of Ockham's razor, as the more analogous explanation will almost always be the most parsimonious one. Ockham's razor is discussed in more detail later in this book.

28. This pithy maxim is attributed to professional skeptic Marcello Truzzi and then later to Carl Sagan, who popularized it for the masses.

29. Gotthold Lessing, "On the Proof of the Spirit and of Power" (1777), in *Lessing's Theological Writings*, ed. Henry Chadwick (Stanford, CA: Stanford University Press, 1956), http://faculty.tcu.edu/grant/hhit/Lessing.pdf.

30. "If no historical truth can be demonstrated, then nothing can be demonstrated by means of historical truths. That is: accidental truths of history can never become the proof of necessary truths of reason. . . . That, then is the ugly, broad ditch which I cannot get across, however often and however earnestly I have tried to make the leap." Lessing, "On the Proof."

31. Lessing, "On the Proof."

32. The claim that Jesus died and was resurrected to satisfy the sense of justice of a Bronze Age god is perhaps one the most incredible claims possible, and it comes with a great many serious consequences.

33. W. K. Clifford, *Lectures and Essays, The Ethics of Belief* (Macmillan 1879).

34. We know that each of our senses can prove unreliable in certain situations. We have all seen or heard something, for example, that wasn't really there. It does appear, however, that most of the time, most of our senses reflect reality, which supports the assumption that our senses are generally reliable.

35. George H. Smith, *Atheism: The Case against God* (Amherst, NY: Prometheus Books, 2016), 99.

36. Ayn Rand defines *reason* as the "faculty that identifies and integrates the material provided by man's senses." Ayn Rand, *The Virtue of Selfishness: A New Concept of Egoism* (New York: Signet, 1964), 13. Reason incorporates evidence and logic and can be used as shorthand for all three.

37. Prior to the advent of the scientific method, describing things we could "see" was shorthand for those things detectible through empirical means. Augustine of Hippo, *Sermones (Sermons to the People)*, (Crown Publishing Group 2002), 4.1.1. https://en.wikiquote.org/wiki/Faith

38. Francois-Marie Arouet, *The Flood* (1764), alternatively translated as "Faith consists in believing what reason cannot." https://en.wikiquote.org/wiki/Voltaire

39. Bertram Russell, *Human Society in Ethics and Politics* (Routledge, 1954), Chapter 7.

40. Quoted in Walter Kaufmann, *Critique of Religion and Philosophy* (Princeton, NJ: Princeton University Press, 1979), 305–7.

41. Martin Luther, *Werke VIII.*

42. Tertullian, *De Carne Cristi. Church Fathers* is a term used within Christianity to refer to a group of highly influential Christian theologians who wrote in the early days of the church, generally prior to 700 CE, and substantially shaped its doctrines. Most were honored as saints. The earliest were known as the Apostolic Fathers because tradition describes them as having been taught by the original twelve apostles of Jesus.

43. Tertullian, "The Prescriptions Against the Heretics," trans. S. L. Greenslade, in *Early Latin Theology* (Vol. V in "The Library of Christian Classics"; Philadelphia: Westminster Press, 1956), 31–32; cited in Hugh T. Kerr, ed., *Readings in Christian Thought* (Nashville: Abingdon Press, 1989), 39.

44. Craig states, "[T]he way we know Christianity to be true is by the self-authenticating witness of God's Holy Spirit. Now what do I mean by that? I mean that the experience of the Holy Spirit is . . . unmistakable . . . for him who has it; . . . that arguments and evidence incompatible with that truth are overwhelmed by the experience of the Holy Spirit." William Lane Craig, *Reasonable Faith: Christian Truth and Apologetics*, 3rd ed. (Wheaton, IL: Crossway Books, 2008), 43.

45. Those keeping up with their logical fallacies will recognize this as an argument from ignorance.

46. Jerry A. Coyne, *Fact v. Faith: Why Science and Religion are Incompatible* (Penguin Books, 2015), preface, xii.

47. James Haugt, *2000 Years of Disbelief: Famous People with the Courage to Doubt* (Prometheus Books, 2010), 127. Quoted from Manford's Magazine.

48. Dan Barker, *Losing Faith in Faith: From Preacher to Atheist* (Freedom from Religion Foundation 1992), 102.

49. *God is Not Great: How Religion Poisons Everything* (New York: Twelve Books, 2007), 150.

50. The meaning of *objective* can be contextual. The philosophical objectivity discussed here distinguishes between things that exist only through conscious thought and those that exist independent of conscious thought. *Objective* can also mean "impartial or unbiased," in the sense that one is not influenced by personal feelings or opinions. This is a related but distinct concept.

51. Alvin Plantinga, *God and Other Minds: A Study of the Rational Justification of Belief in God* (Ithaca, NY: Cornell University Press, 1967).

52. I address the *sensus divinitatis* separately in a later chapter.

53. An eleventh white marble, however, will render B impossible, compelling the conclusion that your jar represents possibility A.

CHAPTER 2

1. In the English language, the primary meaning of the word *apology* has changed and now refers to a plea for forgiveness for a wrongful act. Implicit in this is an admission of guilt, thus turning on its head the original concept of the Greek root word, "speaking in defense." For purposes of this discussion, I use the word in a way that is consistent with its original meaning.

2. Keynote address at CSICOP conference (1987), as quoted in *Do Science and the Bible Conflict?* (2003) by Judson Poling, 30.

3. William Lane Craig, "Dealing with Doubt," video, https://www.youtube .com/watch?v=S-fDyPU3wlQ.

4. Julian Baggini, "How Science Lost Its Soul and Religion Handed it Back," in *The Blackwell Companion to Science and Christianity*, eds. J.B. Stump and A.G. Padgett (Oxford: Wiley-Blackwell 2012), 516–17.

5. Obviously, one cannot rationalize from a conclusion unless one has a conclusion in mind before beginning the reasoning process. Employment of scientific methodology ensures no such a priori conclusions. Employment of apologetic methodology ensures the opposite.

6. William Lane Craig, *Reasonable Faith: Christian Truth and Apologetics*, 3rd ed. (Wheaton, IL: Crossway Books, 2008), 36.

7. Lee Strobel quotes Craig as saying, "I think skeptics act in a closed-minded way [and] will not allow supernatural explanations even to be in the pool of live options." Lee Strobel, *The Case for Faith: A Journalist Investigates the Toughest Objections to Christianity* (Grand Rapids, MI: Zondervan, 2009), 66–67.

8. Increasing knowledge of science, history, and archeology increasingly provides conclusive refutations of apologetic arguments, but apologists rarely even acknowledge them. When they do acknowledge discoveries that challenge traditional Christian views, apologists are the first to attack those discoveries and the last to concede.

9. In 2018, Notre Dame, for example, ranked thirteenth on the National Association of College and University Business Officers' (NACUBO), ranking of endowments at more than $10.7 billion. Boston College ranked forty-first, with more than $2.4 billion. Baylor's was more than $1.3 billion (not including more than $1 billion for its medical school), while Wheaton's was more than $211 million. See National Association of College and University Business Officers, "US and Canadian Institutions Listed by Fiscal Year 2018 Endowment Market Value and Change in Endowment Market Value from FY17 to FY18," 2019, https://www.nacubo.org/ Research/2020/Public-NTSE-Tables.

10. 1949, The Dictionary of Humorous Quotations, ed. Evan Esar, Section: Upton Sinclair, Quote Page 185, Doubleday, Garden City, New York. (Verified on paper in 1989 reprint edition from Dorset Press, New York).

11. Jonathan Haidt, *The Righteous Mind*, (Pantheon Books 2012), Introduction.

12. Paul Z. Myers, "The Courtier's Reply," *Science Blogs* (blog), December 24, 2006, https://scienceblogs.com/pharyngula/2006/12/24/the-courtiers-reply.

13. In fact, as is discussed in greater detail herein, there are very good reasons to believe that version of God does not exist.

14. For example, the Oxford English Dictionary defines *religion* as "[a]ction or conduct indicating belief in, obedience to, and reverence for a god, gods, or similar superhuman power; the performance of religious rites or observances."

15. Sam Harris, *Letter to a Christian Nation* (London: Transworld Digital, 2011).

16. Richard Carrier, *Sense and Goodness without God: A Defense of Metaphysical Naturalism* (Authorhouse 2005).

17. Carl Sagan, *The Varieties of Scientific Experience: A Personal View of the Search for God* (New York: Penguin Press, 2006), 251.

18. David Seidman, *What if I'm an Atheist?: A Teen's Guide to Exploring a Life without Religion* (Simon Pulse 2015), 17.

19. The term *humanism* has had multiple meanings throughout history, but I use it in the sense that it has been equated with secular humanism.

20. Janet Fitch, *White Oleander: A Novel* (Boston: Little, Brown, 2000).

21. Avalon Project—The Barbary Treaties 1786-1816—Treaty of Peace and Friendship, signed at Tripoli November 4, 1796. https://avalon.law.yale.edu/18th_century/bar1796t.asp#art11

CHAPTER 3

1. Trey Parker and Matt Stone, *South Park*, "Chef Aid", Season 2, episode 14, aired October 7, 1998. https://www.youtube.com/watch?v=34Em8BkZYnI

2. John Landis, *National Lampoon's Animal House*, Universal Pictures (1978). https://www.moviequotedb.com/movies/animal-house/quote_2019.html

3. These two examples could both be categorized as "red herring" fallacies.

4. Alfred Mander, *Logic for the Millions*, (Philosophical Library 1947).

5. The intelligent design movement, for example, is essentially one enormous argument from ignorance. It is based on identifying (or, in some cases, completely fabricating) small areas of disagreement among evolutionary biologists and extrapolating that these discrete disagreements thereby falsify the entire theory of evolution. Intelligent design proponents hope that with evolution thus "discredited," they can fall back on what they posit to be the "default" explanation: the Christian God.

6. Henri René Albert Guy de Maupassant, *"The Horla"*, (Kessinger Publishing, LLC, 2010).

7. There are other justifications, as well. For example, naturalism is a simpler explanation than supernaturalism. Supernaturalists may incorporate scientific explanations inherent in naturalism but add such claims as the existence of unde-

tectable personal agents unbound by the laws of physics that bring about effects in unexplainable ways. It thus violates Ockham's razor.

8. Neil Degrasse Tyson, *The Sky Is Not the Limit: Adventures of an Urban Astrophysicist*, (Prometheus Books 2010), 183.

9. Apologists have rebranded the naturalistic default as the naturalistic *bias*. I consider this disingenuous because a bias is an improper or unjustified motive. For the reasons stated herein, preferring a naturalistic explanation is exceedingly well justified and thus cannot reasonably be considered a form of bias.

10. Robert M. Price, "Jesus: Myth and Method," in *The Christian Delusion: Why Faith Fails*, ed. John W. Loftus (Amherst, NY: Prometheus Books, 2010), 275.

11. Apologists do not use the term *explanation* as scientists do. Scientists mean something that clarifies and has predictive value. Apologists typically use it to mean "emotionally satisfying narrative." To call God an explanation is a bastardization of the term, for God ultimately explains nothing. It just adds another level of mystery. God simply becomes another term to describe the unexplainable.

12. Percy Bysshe Shelley, *The Necessity of Atheism* (1811).

13. Thanks to Ricky Gervais for this example.

14. Take, for example, the Gospel of John, which was written explicitly "so that you will believe" (John 20:31). A stated intent to induce belief in a particular religion seriously undercuts any claim that an author's account is reliable as history.

15. Albert Einstein Quotes. BrainyQuote.com, BrainyMedia Inc, 2021. https://www.brainyquote.com/quotes/albert_einstein_100017, accessed March 16, 2021.

16. This does not imply, however, that we can never have any means to assess whether one hypothesis is more probable than another without evidential support. Principles of analogy and parsimony, for example, allow us to compare natural to supernatural hypotheses and favor the natural one, given no further information regarding either.

17. This is not an absolute rule, but if one is going to argue for the violation of Ockham's razor, then he should have a very good argument as to why the violation is justified. In legal parlance, Ockham's razor creates a presumption in favor of the most parsimonious explanation. This presumption can be rebutted only with a strong, properly supported argument. Apologist arguments regularly violate Ockham's razor without any justification. They are content to show that the less parsimonious hypothesis remains *possible* and appeal to their audience's faith to carry them the rest of the way.

18. 1950 June, Poetry, Reviews section, Poetry in a Modern Age by Louis Zukofsky, [Review of the volume "William Carlos Williams" by Vivienne Koch (The Makers of Modern Literature Series)], Page 180, Volume 76, Number 3, Modern Poetry Association. (Google Books snippet view. Verified on paper).

19. The challenge was started in 1964 with a reward of one thousand dollars, which increased incrementally until 1996, when the pot reached one million dollars.

20. Daniel C. Dennett, *Intuition Pumps and Other Tools for Thinking* (New York: W. W. Norton, 2013).

CHAPTER 4

1. George H. Smith, *Atheism: The Case against God* (Amherst, NY: Prometheus Books, 2016), 222.

2. Brian Greene, *The Hidden Reality: Parallel Universes and the Deep Laws of the Cosmos* (New York: Knopf, 2011), 4.

3. Lawrence M. Krauss, *A Universe from Nothing: Why There Is Something Rather than Nothing* (New York: Atria Books, 2013), 125–26.

4. Not only do we have an example of virtual particles emerging from "nothing" (a quantum vacuum) without a cause, but also noted physicist Alex Vilenkin, in describing a quantum-tunneling model of the past boundary of the universe, has this to say in his book *Many Worlds in One*: "If there was nothing before the universe popped out, then what could have caused the tunneling? Remarkably, the answer is that no cause is required. In classical physics, causality dictates what happens from one moment to the next, but in quantum mechanics the behavior of physical objects is inherently unpredictable and some quantum processes have no cause at all." Alex Vilenkin, *Many Worlds in One: The Search for Other Universes* (New York: Hill and Wang, 2006), 181.

5. David Bourget and David J. Chalmers, "What Do Philosophers Believe?" PhilPapers, November 30, 2013, http://philpapers.org/archive/BOUWDP. In fact, for his theory to work, Craig must reject Einstein's theory of relativity, one of the most robust scientific theories ever developed. Craig promotes his own far more complex theory, which he calls the "Neo-Lorenzian" theory of time. He supports this competing theory in part by arguing that it is the only theory that is consistent with the existence of God, which is of course the epitome of a circular argument. William Lane Craig, ed., *Time and the Metaphysics of Relativity* (Dordrecht, Netherlands: Kluwer Academic, 2001), 179.

6. Yuri Balashov, review of *A Future for Presentism*, by Craig Bourne, *Notre Dame Philosophical Reviews* (July 4, 2007).

7. William Lane Craig and J. P. Moreland, *The Blackwell Companion to Natural Theology* (Chichester, UK: Wiley-Blackwell, 2009), 183–84.

8. Of course, they cannot really mean this because even they posit that God existed during this period of nothingness, and however one defines God, one must acknowledge that God is *something*.

9. Stephen W. Hawking, *A Brief History of Time: From the Big Bang to Black Holes* (Toronto: Bantam, 1988), 129.

10. Victor J. Stenger, *God: The Failed Hypothesis: How Science Shows That God Does Not Exist* (Amherst, NY: Prometheus Books, 2007), 133.

11. One might just as easily turn this question around to a Christian and inquire, "Why is there God rather than no God? How does one explain the existence of God?" To a Christian, there can be no principled reason for requiring the explanation of matter but not the creator of matter. One can only treat the second set of questions differently by engaging in special pleading.

12. Alan Guth, *Eternal Inflation*, talk given at Massachusetts Institute of Technology April 14–16, 1999. https://cds.cern.ch/record/485381/files/0101507.pdf.

13. Sean Carroll, "Why Time Is a Mystery," course 1, *Mysteries of Modern Physics: Time*, Great Courses video series, September 1, 2012.

14. William Craig rejects this possibility based on his contention that infinity, by definition, represents a logical contradiction, so nothing can be eternal. But this argument is nonsense. There is, for example, an infinite series of fractions between every integer, but we can nonetheless move from 1 to 2 with no difficulty. If you take a pentagram and continue adding sides to it, with S representing the number of sides, it will look more and more like a circle as S approaches infinity without ever actually becoming one. Craig's infinity argument is rebutted by the entire field of calculus.

15. Bertrand Russell, *Why I Am Not a Christian and Other Essays on Religion and Related Subjects*, (Touchstone 1937).

16. Other theories allowing for an uncaused universe include Vilenkin's quantum-tunneling model and several from string theory and loop quantum gravity. Even if the *observable* universe has a beginning at the big bang, a theory of quantum gravity may show that the universe evolved from a prior state that was timeless and causeless. The fact that we do not yet know demonstrates two things: that we must remain agnostic regarding the origin of the universe and that there is insufficient evidence to claim the universe requires an external, transcendent cause.

17. Hawking, *A Brief History of Time*, 140–41.

18. Edward J. Larson and Larry Witham, "Leading Scientists Still Reject God," *Nature* 394, no. 313 (July 23, 1998), https://www.nature.com/articles/28478. Eighty percent of NAS physicists and astronomers disbelieve in God—and as Larson and Witham's paper shows, this number has risen over the decades.

19. This has been persuasively argued by Sean Carroll in his paper "Why (Almost All) Cosmologists Are Atheists," God and Physical Cosmology: Russian-Anglo American Conference on Cosmology and Theology, Notre Dame, January–February 2003, http://preposterousuniverse.com/writings/nd-paper/.

20. A timeless being must necessarily be static and frozen as to all possibilities. Any change in state, either physical or mental, would require time, as time is implicit in the concept of change. A timeless being could not "create" time because time itself would be a prerequisite to its own creation. The concept of Creation requires the preexistence of time. The concept of a personal timeless creator of time, therefore, is incoherent.

21. Victor J. Stenger, *The Fallacy of Fine-Tuning: Why the Universe Is Not Designed for Us* (Amherst, NY: Prometheus Books, 2011), 122.

22. Some modern liberal apologists have attempted to reconcile the Genesis account(s) with big bang cosmology. All these attempts are characterized by very selective, metaphorical interpretations that apparently occurred to no one for more than two thousand years. The fact that these interpretations only appeared after the emergence of scientific consensus in contrast to the biblical view is stark evidence

that we are dealing with ad hoc rationalizations rather than good-faith interpretations of the text.

23. It should be noted that evolutionary theory has rendered the term *species* problematic. It has traditionally meant creatures incapable of interbreeding. Evolution tells us that everything we now consider a separate species arose from another species through a continuous chain of interbreeding. At some point, later generations became sufficiently distinct from their distant ancestors that if they were to travel back in time, the later generations could not interbreed with the earlier ones, thereby representing a new species. And yet, because of the continuous chain of interbreeding, there would be no clear point of demarcation between one species and another. The only reason our species today appear distinct is that the intermediate forms became extinct, leaving us with large gaps in the chain. We know they existed, however, due to transitional fossils and genetics.

24. David Powers's clever retort to this claim is "If God created man in his own image, how come I'm not invisible?"

25. This question seems especially vexing in light of the 2015 discovery of *Homo naledi*, a species separate from man that buried its dead in a ritualized fashion. This practice suggests a recognition and contemplation of death, previously considered one of the defining human characteristics.

26. Daniel Dennett, *Darwin's Dangerous Idea* (Simon & Schuster 1996).

27. John Rennie, "15 Answers to Creationist Nonsense," *Scientific American*, July 1, 2002.

28. Wikipedia, "Nothing in Biology Makes Sense Except in the Light of Evolution," updated November 26, 2020, https://en.wikipedia.org/wiki/Nothing_in_Biology_Makes_Sense_Except_in_the_Light_of_Evolution. Dobzhansky was advancing a form of theistic evolution in which God played an influencing role, something I take up later herein.

29. Michael Behe, *Darwin's Black Box: The Biochemical Challenge to Evolution*, 10th Anniversary ed. (Simon and Schuster 2006), 39.

30. *Kitzmiller v. Dover Area School District*, 400 F. Supp. 2d 707 (M.D. Pa. 2005).

31. Gallup, "Evolution, Creationism, Intelligent Design," accessed March 7, 2021, https://news.gallup.com/poll/21814/evolution-creationism-intelligent-design.aspx.

32. The National Academies, *Science and Creationism: A View from the National Academy of Sciences*, 2nd ed. (Washington, DC: National Academy Press, 1999), https://www.nap.edu/read/6024/chapter/1.

33. Karen Weekes, *Women Know Everything!: 3,241 Quips, Quotes, & Brilliant Remarks*, (Quirk Books 2007), 374.

34. Bill Maher, *The New New Rules: A Funny Look at How Everybody but Me Has Their Head up Their Ass*, (Plume 2012).

35. Gallup, "Evolution, Creationism, Intelligent Design."

36. Gallup, "Evolution, Creationism, Intelligent Design."

37. Alvin Plantinga, *Where the Conflict Really Lies: Science, Religion, and Naturalism* (New York: Oxford University Press, 2011), 4–5.

38. Rodolfo Llinas, *I of the Vortex: From Neurons to Self* (Bradford Books 2002).

39. This is not to say that there aren't discrete areas of evolutionary theory still debated by scientists, but the sufficiency of natural processes to explain the evolution of humans is not one of them.

40. Here, I am specifically talking about the local universe.

41. William Lane Craig, "#49 Design from Fine-Tuning," Reasonable Faith with William Lane Craig, March 24, 2008, http://www.reasonablefaith.org/design-from -fine-tuning.

42. Timothy Keller, *The Reason for God: Belief in an Age of Skepticism* (New York: Penguin Books, 2009), 134.

43. Credit for this analogy goes to Neil deGrasse Tyson.

44. Richard Carrier, "Why I Am Not a Christian," Secular Web, 2006, http:// infidels.org/library/modern/richard_carrier/whynotchristian.html.

45. The problem with Galileo's discoveries was that if the Earth truly moved, then it could no longer be the fixed center of God's creation and His plan of salvation. Nor could man be the central focus of the cosmos. The absolute uniqueness and significance of Christ's intervention into human history seemed to require a corresponding uniqueness and significance for the Earth.

46. William Lane Craig, "#49 Design from Fine-Tuning," Reasonable Faith with William Lane Craig, March 24, 2008. https://www.reasonablefaith.org/writings/ question-answer/design-from-fine-tuning/.

47. See Stenger, *Fallacy of Fine-Tuning*.

48. John Hudson Tiner, *Isaac Newton: Inventor, Scientist, and Teacher* (Mott Media 1981).

49. Douglas Adams, *The Salmon of Doubt: Hitchhiking the Galaxy One Last Time*, (Harmony 2002).

50. At least, according to Mr. Adams.

51. Richard Dawkins, "God's Utility Function," *Scientific American*, November 1995, 80–85. http://www.physics.ucla.edu/~chester/CES/may98/dawkins.html.

52. @iansample, Interview, *The Guardian*, May 15, 2011. https://www.theguard ian.com/science/2011/may/15/stephen-hawking-interview-there-is-no-heaven.

53. Sean Carroll, "Does the Universe Need God?" accessed March 7, 2021, https://www.preposterousuniverse.com/writings/dtung/.

54. Due to its speculative nature, some may see the multiverse hypothesis as a retreat to the possible. In this case, however, that isn't accurate. I am comparing two speculative theories where we have good grounds to treat one as the *more probable* of the two. It represents not a retreat to the possible but rather an appeal to most probable explanation. An inherently plausible hypothesis should always be preferred over an inherently implausible one.

55. Of course, one would also have to eliminate all supernatural models of other religions, living and dead. Just because a religion has gone out of favor doesn't mean its doctrines are necessarily untrue.

56. Logically, one would need to answer the question of "How?" before being in a position to answer "Who?" for unless one can demonstrate how life developed, he has no good basis for concluding who, if anyone, started it. It is the extent of the "how" details we do have, incomplete as they may be, that make the naturalist theory superior to that of the creationist, for these details would be very surprising if life were indeed seeded by God.

57. To be clear, dualism represents a broader concept of which substance dualism is only a subset. Related concepts include property dualism and predicate dualism. I limit the discussion to substance dualism, however, out of space limitations and because it is most relevant to the religious concept of souls, which forms a foundation of much religious faith.

58. René Descartes, *Meditations*, in The Philosophical Writings of Descartes, translated by J. Cottingham, R. Stoothoff, and Dugald Murdoch (Cambridge, 1984).

59. Fiddling with people's brains across the necessary large populations to study effects on consciousness is simply an ethical nonstarter.

60. Steven Novella, "What Is Consciousness? Another Reply to Kastrup," *Neurologica* (blog), May 17, 2012, http://theness.com/neurologicablog/index.php/what-is-consciousness-another-reply-to-kastrup/.

61. As of 1998, the belief in human immortality among scientists had slid from a high of 35 percent in 1914 to a mere 7.9 percent. Larson and Witham, "Leading Scientists."

62. William Lane Craig, *Reasonable Faith: Christian Truth and Apologetics*, 3rd ed. (Wheaton, IL: Crossway, 2008), 33.

63. Oxford, "Miracle," Lexico, accessed March 7, 2021, https://en.oxford dictionaries.com/definition/miracle.

64. Carl Sagan, Cosmos: A Personal Voyage, Episode 12. "Encyclopedia Galactica" (December 14, 1980).

65. Carrier, "Why I Am Not a Christian."

66. Isaac Asimov, *The Roving Mind*, New Edition, (Prometheus Books 1997).

67. This claim is entirely unwarranted, given the multitude of ancient documents attesting to miracles, including the texts of countless other religions.

68. David Hume, *An Enquiry Concerning Human Understanding*, 2d ed. (1902). https://iep.utm.edu/hume-rel/#:~:text=First%2C%20Hume%20tells%20 us%20that,its%20testimony%20(EHU%2010.15).

69. Thomas Paine, *The Age of Reason* (Watchmaker Publishing 2010).

70. Frans de Waal, *Primates and Philosophers: How Morality Evolved* (Princeton, NJ: Princeton University Press, 2016), 4.

71. Frans de Waal, *The Age of Empathy: Nature's Lessons for a Kinder Society* (New York: Broadway Books, 2010).

72. Felix Warneken, Brian Hare, Alicia P. Melis, Daniel Hanus, and Michael Tomasello, "Spontaneous Altruism by Chimpanzees and Young Children," *PLOS Biology* 5, no. 7 (June 26, 2007): e184, http://journals.plos.org/plosbiology/article?id=10.1371/journal.pbio.0050184.

73. Aristotle, *Aristotle's Nichomachean Ethics*, trans. Robert Bartlett and Susan Collins (University of Chicago Press, 2012).

74. Sam Harris, for example, has professed belief in "objective moral values," but he is talking about objectively valid reasons for behavior given such shared human goals as human happiness and flourishing. These values are not fixed ideals but contextually varying guidelines that provide best practices for achieving mutually beneficial objectives.

75. William Craig, *Reasonable Faith: Christian Truth and Apologetics*, (Crossway 2008), 173.

76. I explain in the previous section this would be so under a naturalistic model.

77. Richard Garner, *Beyond Morality* (Echo Point Books & Media, 2014).

78. Robert Sallin, Jack B. Sowards, Nicholas Meyer, William Shatner, Leonard Nimoy, Ricardo Montalbán, DeForest Kelley, *et al.*, Star Trek II: the Wrath of Khan (2009).

79. Craig is really arguing for something more akin to "universal" morality, moral principles that apply consistently within the global universe. Any source of such morality must necessarily transcend the universe by definition. In this way, Craig sets up an entirely circular argument, for once we grant this premise, the conclusion is foregone. The problem is that we have no evidence for universal morality. We don't even share a perspective by which such evidence would be possible.

80. Richard Swinburne, *The Existence of God*, 2nd ed. (New York: Oxford University Press, 2004), 215.

81. Robert G. Ingersoll, *The Best of Robert Ingersoll, Selections from his writings and speeches*, edited by Roger Greeley (1993), 7.

82. It is interesting and instructive that Craig and other proponents of DCT often appeal to those same moral intuitions as their primary, if not exclusive, support for the existence of objective moral values, rarely if ever acknowledging the obvious contradiction.

83. As presented by German philosopher Gottfried Leibniz, "It is generally agreed that whatever God wills is good and just. But there remains the question whether it is good and just because God wills it or whether God wills it because it is good and just; in other words, whether justice and goodness are arbitrary or whether they belong to the necessary and eternal truths about the nature of things." Gottfried Wilhelm Leibniz, *Discourse on Metaphysics, the Monadology and Theodicy* (n.p.: CreateSpace, 2014), 516.

84. William Craig, "#16 Slaughter of the Canaanites," *Reasonable Faith Blog*, Aug. 6, 2007, accessed March 16, 2021. https://www.reasonablefaith.org/writings/question-answer/slaughter-of-the-canaanites/.

85. William Craig, *The Indispensability of Theological Meta-Ethical Foundation of Morality,* accessed March 16, 2021. https://www.reasonablefaith.org/writings/scholarly-writings/the-existence-of-god/the-indispensability-of-theological-meta ethical-foundations-for-morality/.

86. Thomas Paine, *The Works of Thomas Paine: A Hero in the American Revolution,* (Moss Brothers & Co. 1858), 373.

87. The list commonly referred to as the Ten Commandments, known as the Decalogue, is found at Exodus 20:1–17. Unlike Exodus 34:10–28, however, the text confers it no special significance. It represents merely the first ten of hundreds of spoken proscriptions (see Exodus 21:1–23:31), the vast majority of which are routinely ignored by Christians today. The Decalogue makes a reappearance, in slightly revised form, in Deuteronomy 5:4–21, but this entire reimagining is seriously suspect, as discussed later in this book.

88. Also, what about the commandment against working on the Sabbath (the violation of which would result in your being put to death; Exodus 35:2)? Or what about the fact that the tenth commandment lists wives as among a man's property?

89. Alan Jeskin, *Outgrowing God: Moving beyond Religion*, Kindle ed. (n.p.: CreateSpace, 2010), at 2871.

90. Bill Puka, "The Golden Rule," Internet Encyclopedia of Philosophy, accessed March 7, 2021, http://www.iep.utm.edu/goldrule/.

91. As discussed in a later section, there is good reason to believe that much of the Nazi agenda was in fact inspired by, or at least consistent with, the writings of the father of Protestant Christianity, Martin Luther.

92. Nicholas Epley, Benjamin A. Converse, Alexa Delbosc, George A. Monteleone, and John T. Cacioppo, "Believers' Estimates of God's Beliefs Are More Egocentric than Estimates of Other People's Beliefs," *Proceedings of the National Academy of Sciences* 106, no. 51 (December 22, 2009): 21533–38, http://www.pnas.org/content/106/51/21533.abstract.

93. Fyodor Dostoevsky, *The Brothers Karamazov*, Part 4, Book 11, Chapter 4 (1880).

94. Those without this sense of empathy are classified as psychopaths, representing less than 1 percent of society. Jeremy Coid, Min Yang, Simone Ullrich, Amanda Roberts, and Robert D. Hare, "Prevalence and Correlates of Psychopathic Traits in the Household Population of Great Britain," *International Journal of Law and Psychiatry* 32, no. 2 (March–April 2009): 65–73, http://www.sciencedirect.com/science/article/pii/S0160252709000028. This argument of Christians presupposes that all atheists are psychopaths, for only then could they be unconcerned with the consequences of their actions and indeed act as if all things were permitted. Instead, however, atheists cry for starving children on television, just like everyone else. The almost universal presence of empathy, regardless of religious belief, contradicts the Christian hypothesis that a moral code is required for people to act ethically toward one another.

95. John Donne, Meditation 17 from *The Works of John Donne*, vol. III, ed. Henry Alford (1839) http://www.luminarium.org/sevenlit/donne/meditation17.php.

96. Albert Einstein, "Religion and Science," *New York Times Magazine*, November 9, 1930, http://www.sacred-texts.com/aor/einstein/einsci.htm.

97. Situational ethics is different from moral relativism, which states that no action is *ever* right or wrong. Situational ethics reflects moral principles that are provisionally true, applying to most people in most cultures in most circumstances most of the time.

98. Phil Zuckerman, *Society Without God*, (New York University Press 2008), 61.

99. Robert D. Putnam and David E. Campbell, *American Grace: How Religion Divides and Unites Us* (New York: Simon and Schuster, 2012), 473.

100. Paul Bloom, "Religion, Morality, Evolution," *Annual Review of Psychology* 63 (2012): 179–99.

101. A related claim is that the *body count* of such atheist dictators as these exceeds that attributable to Christian rulers or Christian-based conflicts. Even if body count were somehow relevant to the truth of a belief system and if a statistically significant difference could be observed, this could be due to many unrelated factors, such as the far greater potential for mass destruction available in the modern age that wasn't available in the more brutal centuries of Christian conflict. To say that the leaders of the Spanish Inquisition were somehow morally superior to Stalin because, though willing, they didn't have *the means* to murder as many people isn't exactly a compelling argument.

102. Stalin's brutal regime would have been entirely inconsistent with, for example, secular humanism. It would, however, have been consistent with Christian morality as interpreted by someone such as Martin Luther, as discussed elsewhere in this book.

103. Any argument that logic is independent of God is ultimately self-defeating because it must necessarily rely on logic itself, thereby committing the fallacy of the stolen concept.

104. The immediately apparent problem is the false assumption that survival and accuracy are two mutually exclusive evolutionary objectives selected for independently of each other. In fact, however, accurate perception will always be a survival advantage.

105. Plantinga, *Where the Conflict Really Lies*, 314.

106. C. S. Lewis, "Is Theology Poetry?" in *The Weight of Glory and Other Addresses* (New York: Macmillan, 1949).

107. Steven Pinker, *So How Does the Mind Work?* (Wiley Online Library 2005), 18. https://stevenpinker.com/files/pinker/files/so_how_does_the_mind_work.pdf.

108. John Calvin, *Institutes of the Christian Religion*, ed. John T. McNeill, trans. Ford Lewis Battles (Philadelphia: Westminster Press, 1960), 43, 45–46.

109. Philosopher A. C. Grayling amusingly identifies this "fault" among nonbelievers as *rationality*.

110. William Craig, *Interview with Kevin Harris*, August 17, 2014. https://www
.reasonablefaith.org/media/reasonable-faith-podcast/answering-critics-of-the-inner
-witness-of-the-spirit/.

111. Carl Sagan, *The Demon Haunted World: Science as a Candle in the Dark*
(New York: Ballantine Books, 1996), 45.

112. David Hume, *The Natural History of Religion*, from *Essays and Treatises
on Several Subjects in Two Volumes* (1784).

113. A 2012 Pew Research survey revealed the relative sizes of religions worldwide to be as follows: Christianity (31.5 percent), Islam (23.2 percent), unaffiliated
(16.3 percent), Hinduism (15.0 percent), Buddhism (7.1 percent), and other (6.9
percent). Pew Research Center, "The Global Religious Landscape," December 18,
2012, https://www.pewforum.org/2012/12/18/global-religious-landscape-exec/.

114. Dum Diversas Papal Bull from Pope Nicholas V to King Alfonso of Portu-
gal, 1452, quoted in article by Vinnie Rotondaro, *Doctrine of Discovery: A Scandal
in Plain Sight*, National Catholic Reporter, Sept. 5, 2015.

115. The discovery doctrine was adopted into US law by the US Supreme Court
in *Johnson v. McIntosh*, 21 U.S. (8 Wheat.) 543 (1823). Writing for a unanimous
court, Chief Justice John Marshall noted that Christian European nations had assumed "ultimate dominion" over America and that upon its "discovery," the Native
Americans had lost "their rights to complete sovereignty as independent nations."
In discussing the legal precedent for the decision, Marshall cited the English charter issued to explorer John Cabot, explaining that Cabot was authorized to take possession of the land, "notwithstanding the occupancy of the natives, who were hea-
thens, and, at the same time, admitting the prior title of any Christian people who
may have made a previous discovery." *Johnson v. McIntosh*, at 577. In other words,
the court concluded that the rights of Native Americans could be safely ignored because they were not Christians. A land would only be considered "discovered," for
the purpose of assigning property rights, once it was occupied by Christians, which
is why Columbus is credited for discovering America, even though America was
already populated by hundreds of thousands of people. This case would become the
cornerstone of US–Native American relations for more than a century.

116. Howard Zinn, *A People's History of the United States 1492-present*,
(Harper & Rowe 2009). The veneration with which Americans hold Columbus
today is a testament to the fact that America was ultimately settled by Christians,
and the victors write the history.

117. Ward Churchill, *A Little Matter of Genocide: Holocaust and Denial in the
Americas 1492 to the Present*, (City Lights Publishers 2001).

118. This resolution included acknowledgment of the "forcible removal of
Native children from their families to faraway boarding schools where their Native practices and languages were degraded and forbidden." Warren Throckmor-
ton, "Native American Apology Resolution 2009—Full Text," March 2, 2011,
https://www.wthrockmorton.com/2011/03/02/native-american-apology-resolution
-2009-full-text/.

119. Pope Francis Apologizes for Church's "Grave Sins," *Huffington Post*, accessed March 12, 2021. https://www.huffpost.com/entry/pope-francis-apologizes-for-churchs-grave-sins_n_5b578160e4b01e373aac2b1f.

120. Maria Konnikova, "Why We Need Answers," *New Yorker*, April 30, 2013, http://www.newyorker.com/tech/elements/why-we-need-answers.

121. The idea that many Christians make these claims and then a claim to abject humility in the same breath is absolutely astounding.

122. Mark Twain, "Satan's Letter," in *Letters from Earth*, 1909, http://www.online-literature.com/twain/letters-from-the-earth/2/.

123. William Craig, *The Absurdity of Life Without God*. https://www.reasonablefaith.org/writings/popular-writings/existence-nature-of-god/the-absurdity-of-life-without-god/.

124. William Craig, *On Guard: Defending Your Faith with Reason and Precision* (David Cook 2010).

125. The very question "What is the purpose of life?" improperly begs the question by presuming the existence of an intelligent creator, as only a designer can give purpose to his design. The term has meaning only in reference to an intelligent being and a goal assigned by that being. Without some good independent reason to believe such a being exists, the question is as meaningless as "What is the color of jealousy?" Our collective experience has demonstrated that purpose and meaning make sense only in human terms, in reference to human goals.

126. John Shedd, *Salt from My Attic*, (Mosher Press 1928), referenced in *The Yale Book of Quotations* by Fred R. Shapiro, Section: John A. Shedd (New Haven, CT: Yale University Press, 2006), 705.

127. Deepak Chopra, interview with Stephen Colbert, the Colbert Report Season 2, episode 160, December 19, 2006, https://www.cc.com/video/v81egv/the-colbert-report-deepak-chopra. Chopra goes on to explain that there is no creative impulse in the absences of discontent. Though Chopra is well-known for compulsively spouting strings of scientific-sounding mumbo-jumbo, even he occasionally hits one on the head.

128. Bertrand Russell, *Unpopular Essays* (1950).

129. Carl Sagan, *The Demon-Haunted World: Science as a Candle in the Dark* (Ballentine 1997).

130. Penny Edgell, Joseph Gerteis, and Douglas Hartmann, "Atheists as 'Other': Moral Boundaries and Cultural Membership in American Society," *American Sociological Review* 71, no. 2 (2006): 211–34.

131. Rob Sherman, *Rob Sherman Advocacy* (April 1, 2006), accessed March 16, 2021, https://web.archive.org/web/20161105012823/http://www.robsherman.com/advocacy/060401a.htm.

132. Justin McCarthy, "Less Than Half in U.S. Would Vote for a Socialist for President," *Gallup News* (May 9, 2019) https://news.gallup.com/poll/254120/less-half-vote-socialist-president.aspx. The constitutions of eight U.S. states—Arkansas, Maryland, Mississippi, North Carolina, South Carolina, Tennessee, Texas, and Pennsylvania—ban atheists from holding public office.

133. Will Gervais, Azim F. Shariff, Are Norenzayan, "Distrust is Central to Anti-Atheist Prejudice," *Journal of Personality and Social Psychology,* https://www2 .psych.ubc.ca/~ara/Manuscripts/Gervais%20et%20al-%20Atheist%20Distrust.pdf.

134. Dan Arel, "The Numbers Are In: America Still Distrusts Atheists and Muslims," Salon, July 21, 2014, http://www.salon.com/2014/07/21/the_numbers _are_in_america_still_distrusts_atheists_and_muslims_partner/.

135. Pew Research Center, "2007 U.S. Religious Landscape Survey," February 1, 2008, https://www.pewforum.org/2008/02/01/u-s-religious-landscape-survey-reli gious-affiliation/; Frank Newport, "American More Likely to Believe in God than the Devil, Heaven More than Hell," Gallup, June 13, 2007, http://www.gallup.com/ poll/27877/Americans-More-Likely-Believe-God-Than-Devil-Heaven-More-Than -Hell.aspx. A more recent set of surveys, conducted in 2018 and 2019, showed 2 percent identifying as atheist but 26 percent as religiously unaffiliated, up from 17 percent in 2009. Pew Research Center, "In U.S., Decline of Christianity Continues as Rapid Pace," October 17, 2019, https://www.pewforum.org/2019/10/17/in-u-s -decline-of-christianity-continues-at-rapid-pace/.

136. Tom Rees, "The War on Atheism—Bucking the Social Norm Leads to Social Rejection and Unhappiness," Patheos, September 4, 2012, http://epiphenom .fieldofscience.com/2012/09/the-war-on-atheism-bucking-social-norm.html.

137. George Bernard Shaw, *Androcles and the Lion* (1913), Preface, The importance of hell in the salvation scheme.

138. John F. Kennedy, Commencement Address at Yale University, June 11, 1962. https://www.americanrhetoric.com/speeches/jfkyalecommencement.htm.

139. Maurice Maeterlinck, as quoted in Optimum Sports Nutrition by Michael Colgan (1993), 144.

140. Phil Zuckerman, *Society Without God,* (New York University Press 2008), 61.

141. The four highest-ranking countries were Norway, Denmark, Sweden, and the Netherlands.

142. Gregory S. Paul, "Cross-National Correlations of Quantifiable Societal Health with Popular Religiosity and Secularism in the Prosperous Democracies: A First Look," *Journal of Religion and Society* 7 (2005): 1–17.

143. Paul, "Cross-National Correlations," 7.

CHAPTER 5

1. Thomas Paine, *The Age of Reason.*

2. Robert Ingersoll, *Some Mistakes of Moses,* from *The Works of Robert G. Ingersoll,* (Library of Alexandria 2012).

3. If you accept religious faith as a valid epistemology, then it does make sense to talk about beliefs as a matter of choice *within that framework.* Most people would recognize that believing in Santa Claus or leprechauns is not really a mat-

ter of choice because neither fits within a paradigm of religious faith. None would likely say they have "chosen" to disbelieve in leprechauns, but many Christians would simultaneously conclude that atheists have "chosen" to disbelieve in God. The key here is that your epistemology is not itself a matter of choice. It is an assumption that guides your beliefs. The problem is that an epistemology based on faith represents a double standard, which is itself unwarranted because it is based on special pleading.

4. For a different perspective, Rabbi Harold Kushner, in his book *How Good Do We Have to Be?* sees the story of Adam and Eve as a myth signifying the emergence of humankind as distinct from other animals rather than the Fall of Man. Rabbi Kushner does find the moral significance to Adam and Eve of disobeying God's commands vague because at the time those commands were given, they had no knowledge of good and evil. Rabbi Kushner sees Eve's decision to eat from the tree not as sinful but as "one of the bravest and most liberating events in the history of the human race" [Harold Kushner, *How Good Do We Have to Be?: A New Understanding of Guilt and Forgiveness* (New York: Back Bay Books, 1997), 31]. As a Jew, however, Rabbi Kushner need not harmonize his interpretation of the story with Paul's explanation of original sin and its foundational purpose as the justification of Jesus's death and Resurrection. While Rabbi Kushner makes excellent points, from a Christian perspective, Eve's decision must have been sinful.

5. Thomas Paine, *The Age of Reason.*

6. Alvin Plantinga, *The Nature of Necessity* (Oxford, UK: Clarendon Press, 1974), 166–67.

7. Goodreads, "William Lane Craig Quotes," accessed March 7, 2021, https://www.goodreads.com/author/quotes/72189.William_Lane_Craig.

8. This is a term coined by theologian Randal Rauser, who rejects the thesis. In his book *Is the Atheist My Neighbor?*, Rouser acknowledges the thesis as scripturally unjustified and inconsistent with what he believes to be core Christian values. Rauser also sees it as a formidable barrier to constructive dialogue between Christians and atheists, as it causes Christians to be dismissive of and condescending toward atheists and causes atheists to, understandably, take umbrage at such treatment.

9. Randal Rauser, *Is the Atheist My Neighbor? Rethinking Christian Attitudes toward Atheism* (Eugene, OR: Cascade Books, 2015), 6.

10. See, generally, Rauser, *Is the Atheist My Neighbor?*, 32–46.

11. Even if atheists were claiming disbelief disingenuously to rebel against God and justify continuing in their sinful ways, then why would they choose this particular approach? If you don't like your father's rules, would you find the easiest way to ignore them to be denying your father's very existence? That seems like using an elephant gun to kill a fly. Why not simply choose an interpretation of Scripture, from the countless interpretations available, that would allow or even condone your chosen behavior? You would then obtain the advantage of divine sanction.

12. For example, see accounts by Dan Barker, John Loftus, Julia Sweeny, Tim Short, Ryan Bell, Anthony Pinn, Andrew Johnson, Jerry DeWitt, and Teresa MacBain. DeWitt and MacBain are associated with the Clergy Project, which has aided hundreds of Christian clergy members who have, despite wanting to believe, nonetheless lost their faith.

13. Richard Carrier, "Why I Am Not a Christian," Secular Web, 2006, http://infidels.org/library/modern/richard_carrier/whynotchristian.html.

14. Alan Cooperman, "What Americans Do and Don't Know About Religion," interview with PBS News Hour, September 28, 2010.

15. The Dunning-Kruger effect is a cognitive bias shown to be fairly universal, whereby people tend to greatly overestimate their competence on tasks with which they have only general familiarity. It can be said that they are so confident precisely because they are incompetent to recognize their own incompetence.

16. Harold Kushner, *When Bad Things Happen to Good People*, 20th anniversary ed. (New York: Schocken Books, 2001).

17. Interestingly, Jesus spoke out very clearly against the type of public prayer seen in most churches today, which serve as affirmations of group identity at least equally as any other purpose (Matthew 6:5–7).

18. Beliefnet, "U.S. News and Beliefnet Prayer Survey," accessed March 7, 2021, http://www.beliefnet.com/Faiths/Faith-Tools/Meditation/2004/12/U-S-News-Beliefnet-Prayer-Survey-Results.aspx.

19. Herbert Benson, et al., "Study of the Therapeutic Effects of Intercessory Prayer (STEP) in Cardiac Bypass Patients: A Multicenter Randomized Trial of Uncertainty and Certainty of Receiving Intercessory Prayer," *American Heart Journal* 151, no. 4 (2006): 934–42.

20. The foundation awards an annual prize of $1.5 million to a "living person who has made an exceptional contribution to affirming life's spiritual dimension, whether through insight, discovery, or practical works." John Templeton Foundation, "Our Story," accessed March 7, 2021, https://www.templeton.org/about.

21. Phil Zuckerman, "Atheism and Societal Health," essay from *The Oxford Handbook of Atheism*, Oxford University Press, eds. Stephen Bullivant and Michael Ruse (2013).

22. George Carlin, "On Religion," 1999, http://www.rense.com/general69/obj.htm.

23. This can be distinguished from the "logical" problem of evil, which makes the far more ambitious claim that the existence of evil renders God *logically impossible* because no imaginable scenario can account for their coexistence. I find such an argument unjustified because an ad hoc scenario can be constructed to render just about anything *possible*. We should be concerned not with finding an explanation that renders God possible in the world we experience but instead whether this is the world we would expect to find if the perfectly good God of Christianity exists. The real question is whether any of these scenarios are plausible or, more

importantly still, *probable*. This is the question with which the evidential problem of evil is concerned.

24. The word *theodicy* derives from the Greek words for "God" and "just" or "right." Thus, *theodicy* literally means "justifying God." Patrick Sherry, "Theodicy," Britannica, accessed October 20, 2013, https://www.britannica.com/topic/theodicy theology.

25. Some apologists, such as Lee Strobel, argue that evil, defined in this way, represents positive evidence for God because it suggests a standard of goodness from which things deviate. If things are supposed to happen a certain way, then injustices or "evils" seem to suggest a moral/design independent of nature. Of course, no evidence has ever been offered to demonstrate this is the case. Isn't it far more likely that injustices we perceive are not intrinsic properties of the universe but qualities of human perception? We evaluate natural phenomena based on whether they have a harmful or beneficial effect *for us*. Often those effects are harmful, but this doesn't imply that the universe has deviated from an original plan of goodness. Instead, it shows only that natural phenomena don't take human needs into account. The randomness and amorality of nature is a much stronger argument for atheism than for theism.

26. John Mackie, "Evil and Omnipotence," in *The Philosophy of Religion*, ed. Basil Mitchell (London: Oxford University Press, 1971), 92.

27. Richard Swinburne, "Evil, the Problem Of," in *The Oxford Companion to Philosophy*, ed. Ted Honderich (Oxford, UK: Oxford University Press, 2005).

28. In fact, philosopher Stephen Law raises just this objection in his "Evil God" hypothesis. Law points out that virtually all the arguments presented for the Christian God would just as easily support the existence of a deity with every characteristic assigned to God but one. Instead of being supremely good, He would be supremely evil and thus known as "Evil God." The same rationalizations apologists use to justify evil in the world of a good God could be used to justify good in the world of Evil God. Law demonstrates that there is no principled way for apologists to render the Christian God more plausible than Evil God. The fact that most Christians are willing to dismiss the Evil God hypothesis out of hand suggests that their biases strongly slant their interpretation of the evidence.

29. C.S. Lewis, *The Problem of Pain* (HarperCollins Publishers 2001).

30. C. S. Lewis, *The Problem of Pain*, rev. ed. (New York: Harper One, 2015). One thing that should be immediately apparent is that God is not limited to the "natural order." He is not limited by fixed laws or causal necessity. The Christian God can violate these at will or do away with them entirely if He were to so choose. Life could survive under any conditions.

31. Gregory Boyd, *Letters from a Skeptic: A Son Wrestles with His Father's Questions about Christianity* (Colorado Springs, CO: David C. Cook, 2008).

32. Stephen Maitzen, "Ordinary Morality Implies Atheism," *European Journal for Philosophy of Religion* (2009), 122–23.

33. For those who point to contemporary claims of visiting Heaven, I would refer them to the story of Alex Malarkey. In 2010, Mr. Malarkey wrote a *New York Times* best-seller with his father titled *The Boy Who Came Back from Heaven*, detailing his trip to Heaven while in a coma. In January 2015 (actually well before that, but no one would give him a voice to stop the publishing juggernaut), Alex came clean and admitted that he had made the entire thing up to get attention. Believers had defended Alex's story by saying it would have been impossible for a young child to make up such a detailed account. Apparently it wasn't.

34. For well over a thousand years, kings and despots have appealed to this argument and to the clergy who helped spread it on their behalf to quell dissent among their long-suffering subjects. Parishioners were told not to complain about their lives, regardless of how awful they might seem, for in the afterlife, justice would prevail, and all would be made right. If you suffered, then it was because God meant for you to suffer. But your suffering would be temporary. Do not revolt. Accept things as they are in this life, and you will be rewarded in the afterlife. As so used, this argument has been the basis for an enormous amount of otherwise needless suffering. People who could have stood up and made their lives better were cowed into submission by the illusory promise of future rewards. It is a malicious and cruel lie used to justify tyranny.

35. Tim Keller, "Creation, Evolution, and Christian Laypeople," Biologos, February 23, 2012, www.biologos.org/uploads/projects/Keller_white_paper.pdf.

36. Genetic studies have clearly demonstrated that the human race did not descend from a single male-female couple. As Christian scientist Francis Collins acknowledges, all humans "descended from a common set of founders, approximately 10,000 in number, who lived about 100,000 to 150,000 years ago." Francis S. Collins, *The Language of God: A Scientist Presents Evidence for Belief* (New York: Free Press, 2006), 126.

37. Arthur C. Clarke, "Credo," published in *Greetings, Carbon-Based Bipeds!*, *Collected Essays 1934–1998* (Macmillan 2001).

38. National Catholic Almanac, Franciscan Clerics of Holy Name College (1943), 147–48. https://archive.org/details/nationalcatholic013833mbp/page/n149/mode/2up.

39. Thomas Nagel, *The Last Word* (New York: Oxford University Press, 1997), 174–75.

40. George H. Smith, *Atheism: The Case against God* (Amherst, NY: Prometheus Books, 2016), 71.

41. John Stuart Mill, *Three Essays on Religion*, (New York, H. Holt 1874). https://archive.org/details/threeessaysonrel00mill/page/176/mode/2up.

42. If God is timeless, then why would He have waited so long to send Jesus? If God is omnipotent, then why would He have needed to at all?

43. Richard Swinburne, *The Coherence of Theism*, 2nd ed. (Oxford, UK: Oxford University Press, 2016).

44. Letter to William Short, August 4, 1820. https://founders.archives.gov/docu ments/Jefferson/98-01-02-1438.

45. Albert Bigelow Paine, *Mark Twain, A Biography, 1935–1910, Complete Personal and Literary Life of Samuel Langhorne Clemons* (Gutenberg Press 2006).

46. See, for example, Exodus 20:2-9; Exodus 32:9-12; Deuteronomy 32:39-42; Jeremiah 46:10; Isaiah 49:26; Ezekiel 39:17-19; Revelation 17:6.

47. The manner of worshipping gods in the days of the Old Testament was to sacrifice animals to them.

48. Wells chose this title because this phrase is used to describe God within the Bible no less than five times.

49. William Lane Craig and Joseph Gorra, "A Reasonable Response: Answers to Tough Questions on God, Christianity, and the Bible," (Moody Publishers 2013).

50. This raises numerous issues, such as why is God's mind so easily changed? Doesn't He already have all the information Moses has and a billion times more? Furthermore, If Moses can question God's actions using human ethical principles (and persuade God accordingly), then why can't we?

51. Thomas Paine, *The Age of Reason*, part 1 (Gearhart, OR: Watchmaker, 2010), 18–19.

52. When I separate the Old Testament God from the New Testament God, it is because this is the way many Christians see them. According to orthodox Christian doctrine, however, they are one and the same being. This is implicit in the concept of the Trinity and explicit in such New Testament verses as John 14:9, John 10:30, and John 12:45.

53. D. A. Carson, "How Can We Reconcile the OT God and NT God?" 2014 https://www.thegospelcoalition.org/blogs/justin-taylor/d-a-carson-how-can-we-rec oncile-the-old-testament-god-and-the-new-testament-god/.

54. Ira Glass, "Heretics," *This American Life*, December 16, 2005, https://www .thisamericanlife.org/304/heretics.

55. Pope John Paul II, speech to general audience in Rome on July 28, 1999. http://www.vatican.va/content/john-paul-ii/en/audiences/1999/documents/hf_jp -ii_aud_28071999.html.

56. Billy Graham, "Heaven and Hell," from *The Challenge: Sermons from Madison Square Garden*, (New York: Doubleday 1969), 71.

57. According to Catholic theology, Limbo represents a sort of halfway house between Heaven and Hell, where souls are denied the eternal presence of God but spared the torments of damnation.

58. Augustine of Hippo, *City of God*, vol. 2 (Cambridge, MA: Harvard University Press, 1957).

59. Many will no doubt argue that Paul took a different view, but since when did Paul overrule Jesus?

60. This passage occurs in a parable about a king disappointed by his subjects, but it is clear from the context that the parable is about Jesus and his attitude toward those who choose not to follow him.

61. Dan Barker, *Losing Faith in Faith: From Preacher to Atheist* (Freedom from Religion Foundation 2006).

62. If God is indeed the standard for what is good, then saying God is good is the same as saying that God is God. It is a meaningless tautology of the form God = good; good = God.

63. Gottfried Wilhelm Leibniz, *Discourse on Metaphysics, the Monadoloy and Theodicy* (n.p.: Createspace, 2014), 1686.

64. *Oxford English Dictionary*, https://www.lexico.com/en/definition/perfect.

65. This is known as the documentary hypothesis or the Wellhausen hypothesis. It is currently the consensus view among critical biblical scholars concerning the origin of the Pentateuch.

66. Baruch Spinoza, *Theologico-Political Treatise (1670).* Quoted in Strauss, L., *Jewish Philosophy and the Crisis of Modernity: Essays and Lectures in Modern Jewish Thought*, (SUNY Press 1997), 206.

67. Todd Johnson, Peter Crossing, and Gina Zurlo, Center for the Study of Global Christianity at Godon-Conwell Theological Seminary, Status of Global Christianity 2021, accessed March 14, 2021. https://www.gordonconwell.edu/cen ter-for-global-christianity/wp-content/uploads/sites/13/2020/12/Status-of-Global -Christianity-2021.pdf

68. Definition of the Fourth Lateran Council, quoted in Catechism of the Catholic Church, Pope John Paul II (1992), 253.

67. It will surprise many to learn that the Trinity is mentioned in a recognizable form only once in the Bible—at 1 John 5:7, known as the Comma Johanneum: "For there are three that bear record in heaven, the Father, the Word, and the Holy Ghost: and these three are one." Most critical scholars agree that this passage did not appear in the original text but was added by a copyist hundreds of years later. An increasing number of modern Bibles therefore omit the Comma entirely or at least resign it to a footnote. In other words, the original biblical texts never mention the Trinity.

70. Alister E. McGrath, *Christian Theology: An Introduction*, 5th ed. (Hoboken, NJ: Wiley-Blackwell, 2011), 321.

71. F. L. Cross, ed., "Trinity, Doctrine of the," in *The Oxford Dictionary of the Christian Church*, 2nd ed. (London: Oxford University Press, 1974).

72. Over time, many have conflated this snake with Satan, but there is no evidence in the biblical text that Satan and the snake were in any way related.

73. As quoted by E. Christopher Reyes, *In His Name* (AuthorHouse 2010), 143.

74. PhilPapers, "The PhilPapers Surveys," accessed March 7, 2021, http://phil papers.org/surveys/results.pl. When you account for the fact that some portion of these are likely to be Christian devotional scholars, who have a priori commitments to Christianity such that they don't allow for even the possibility that atheism is true, it becomes evident that even this overstates the intellectual legitimacy of Christianity among philosophers.

75. Christopher Hitchens, ed., *The Portable Atheist: Essential Readings for the Nonbeliever*, 3rd ed. (Philadelphia: Da Capo Press, 2007).

76. Albert Einstein, letter to Eric Gutkind from Princeton dated January 3, 1954, translated from German by Joan Stambaugh.

77. Albert Einstein, letter to Erik Gutkind, January 1954, http://www.lettersof note.com/2009/10/word-god-is-product-of-human-weakness.html.

78. Thomas Paine, *The Theological Works of Thomas Paine* (Belford-Clarke Co. 1890).

79. Some of these Scriptures vary markedly between differing Christian denominations; Protestants accept only the Hebrew Bible's canon but divide it into thirty-nine books, while the Catholic, Eastern Orthodox, Coptic, and Ethiopian Churches recognize a considerably larger collection.

80. The Documentary hypothesis has evolved since its iconic formulation by Christian theologian Julius Wellhausen in 1883. I primarily discuss the version advocated by biblical scholar Richard Elliott Friedman, discussed at length in his two well-known works, *Who Wrote the Bible?* (San Francisco: HarperSanFrancisco, 1987) and *The Bible with Sources Revealed: A New View into the Five Books of Moses* (San Francisco: HarperSanFrancisco, 2003).

81. Israel Finkelstein and Neil Asher Silberman, *The Bible Unearthed: Archeology's New Vision of Ancient Israel and the Origin of Its Sacred Texts* (New York: Touchstone, 2001), 5.

82. The Bible contains yet another Creation story, referenced in the books of Isaiah, Psalms, and Job, in which the world is created in the aftermath of a great battle between God and a great sea dragon called Rahab. I don't think it is necessary to spend much time addressing the scientific plausibility of this one.

83. Carol Meyers, *Exodus* (Cambridge, UK: Cambridge University Press, 2005), 5.

84. Peter Enns, *The Evolution of Adam: What the Bible Does and Doesn't Say about Human Origins* (Grand Rapids, MI: Baker Books, 2012), 26.

85. For those who argue the Egyptian historians would not have recorded embarrassing information or events due to nationalistic concerns, what explanation could possibly account for the fact that the historians of neighboring countries, in competition with the Egyptians, also failed to record any of the events recorded uniquely in the Pentateuch? They had every incentive to embarrass the Egyptians and every reason to detail Egypt's every indignity. And yet none did so.

86. Finkelstein and Silberman, *Bible Unearthed*, 62–63.

87. Finkelstein and Silberman, *Bible Unearthed*, 37.

88. Finkelstein and Silberman, *Bible Unearthed*, 37.

89. Finkelstein and Silberman, *Bible Unearthed*, 64.

90. The Bible justifies this extermination by means of a curse placed on the ancestor of the Canaanites by Noah. Noah cursed his grandson Canaan after Canaan's father, Ham, witnessed Noah drunk and naked. Noah proclaimed that Canaan and

his descendants would forever be subservient to the descendants of Shem, who would ultimately become the Israelites (Genesis 9:20–27). Because all residents of Canaan were subject to this ancient curse, as their ancestor's father saw Noah naked, they were fair game for mass slaughter.

91. Finkelstein and Silberman, *Bible Unearthed*, 90.
92. Finkelstein and Silberman, *Bible Unearthed*, 76–77.
93. 1 Kings 4:29.
94. Finkelstein and Silberman, *Bible Unearthed*, 133.
95. 2 Kings 23:25.
96. Lester L. Grabbe, ed., *Israel in Transition: From Late Bronze II to Iron IIa (c. 1250–850 B.C.E.)* (New York: T&T Clark, 2008), 75.
97. Paula M. McNutt, *Reconstructing the Society of Ancient Israel* (Louisville, KY: Westminster John Knox Press, 1999), 70.
98. Philip R. Davies, *In Search of "Ancient Israel": A Study in Biblical Origins* (Sheffield, UK: Sheffield Academic Press, 1992), 63–64.
99. These complexes were initially dated incorrectly to the tenth century and pointed to by apologists as evidence for the Kingdom of Solomon. Subsequent discoveries, however, allowed archeologists to accurately redate them to the time of the Omrides.
100. Finkelstein and Silberman, *Bible Unearthed*, 246–47.
101. Morton Smith, Palestinian Parties and Politics that Shaped the Old Testament (Trinity Press 1971).
102. Finkelstein and Silberman, *Bible Unearthed*, 281.
103. This refers to the elite classes, as the poor and marginalized would have had no access to education.
104. Thom Stark, *Is God a Moral Compromiser?: A Critical Review of Paul Copan's "Is God a Moral Monster?"* 2nd ed. (n.p.: n.p., 2011), http://religionat themargins.com/2011/07/the-real-second-edition-is-god-a-moral-compromiser-a -critical-review-of-paul-copans-is-god-a-moral-monster/.
105. Israel Finkelstein, "Patriarchs, Exodus, Conquest: Fact or Fiction?" in *The Quest for the Historical Israel: Debating Archaeology and the History of Early Israel*, by Israel Finkelstein and Amihai Mazar, ed. Brian B. Schmidt (Atlanta, GA: Society of Biblical Literature, 2007), 54.
106. John J. Collins, *Introduction to the Hebrew Bible* (Minneapolis: Fortress Press, 2004), 194.
107. Finkelstein and Silberman, *Bible Unearthed*, 195.
108. Finkelstein and Silberman, *Bible Unearthed*, 225.
109. Finkelstein and Silberman, *Bible Unearthed*, 275.
110. Finkelstein and Silberman, *Bible Unearthed*, 305.
111. Karen Armstrong, *A History of God* (Alfred A. Knopf 1993).
112. For example, "Who is like you among gods, YHWH!" (Exodus 15:11) and "Now I know that YHWH is greater than all other gods!" (Exodus 18:11).

114. Bart Ehrman, How Jesus Became God: The Exaltation of a Jewish Preacher from Galilee (HarperOne 2014), 89.

114. Bart D. Ehrman, *The New Testament: A Historical Introduction to the Early Christian Writings* 6th ed. (New York: Oxford University Press, 2015), 479–80.

115. Ehrman, *New Testament*, 479–80.

116. Ehrman, *New Testament*, 479–80.

117. We can likewise be sure that if any document existed that reflected the historicity of Jesus, such as the writings of contemporary regional historians Josephus and Tacitus, they would have been lovingly preserved by the church leaders of the day. While a copyist of Josephus's works three hundred years later included a previously unknown passage testifying not only to Jesus's historical existence but also to his status as "the Christ," known as the *Testimonium Flavianum*, the passage is overwhelmingly recognized by historians as an interpolation.

118. Only seven of these are widely considered authentic by modern scholars. Some, such as the Epistle to the Hebrews, are almost universally rejected by scholars, while the authenticity of the remainder as works of Paul remains disputed to various degrees.

119. One must also keep in mind what inconsistencies represent. An inconsistency between two statements means that at least one must be false. It is possible for both to be false, but both cannot be true. Twenty inconsistencies mean at least twenty and perhaps up to forty false statements. Biblical inconsistencies are so damaging to the claims of apologists because they contradict the claim of divine authorship.

120. Matthew 27:51–27:53.

121. Mark 16:5.

122. Luke 24:4.

123. Matthew 28:2–28:4.

124. Matthew 28:3.

125. This is notably inconsistent with the lion's share of later Christian theology, which posits God as deeply concerned with humans clearly understanding Jesus's message so that they can be saved.

126. Dennis R. MacDonald, *The Homeric Epics and the Gospel of Mark* (New Haven, CT: Yale University Press, 2000). All educated Greek writers would have been familiar with these epics, so this would have been an obvious point of inspiration.

127. MacDonald, *Homeric Epics*, 7.

128. This problem is not unique to Matthew. There are many places in the New Testament in which some act of Jesus is announced as a fulfillment of Scripture, but the citation is clearly to the Greek translation, the Septuagint, rather than the original Hebrew or Aramaic. In such cases, it would be more accurate to say that Jesus's act was the fulfillment of a misinterpretation of Scripture not reflected in the original text. Of course, that wouldn't sound nearly as impressive.

129. Raymond E. Brown, *The Virginal Conception and Bodily Resurrection of Jesus* (New York: Paulist Press, 1973), 54; Geza Vermes, *The Nativity: History and Legend* (New York: Doubleday 2007), 14.

130. Raymond E. Brown, *The Birth of the Messiah: A Commentary on the Infancy Narratives in Matthew and Luke*, updated ed. (New York: Doubleday, 1999), 413.

131. Luke 24:49.

132. In either case, this event is wildly implausible, given that the area involved would have been enormous and overseen by a resident Roman legion tasked with preventing this very type of disturbance. Overturning even a significant number of the tables would have taken hours. Furthermore, any disturbance of the type described in the Bible would have been immediately quelled and the instigator arrested. It is especially inconceivable that Jesus could have gotten away with this twice, as some apologists argue in an attempt to reconcile John's Gospel with the Synoptics. It would be equivalent to the biggest bank robbery ever committed under the following conditions: (1) The bank spanned several football fields, (2) thousands of tellers were forced to turn over all they had, (3) hundreds of policemen were permanently stationed at that very bank but were somehow unable to prevent the robbery, and (4) the event was not recorded by any contemporary historian. A solo cleanout of Fort Knox with no media coverage would, in contemporary times, be roughly comparable.

133. It must be noted here, however, that it is Matthew that includes the New Testament verse that has perhaps caused the most Jewish suffering: "His [Jesus's] blood be on us and on our children!" (Matthew 27:25). The term *Jews* in Matthew, however, is applied selectively to those who deny the Resurrection of Jesus and believe the disciples stole Jesus's corpse (Matthew 28:13–15).

134. John 21:1–14.

135. Compare Mark and Matthew ("My God, my God, why hast thou forsaken me?") to Luke ("Father, into thy hands I commend my spirit") to John ("It is finished"). Each is consistent with the character of Jesus presented by that author but inconsistent with the character presented by the others.

136. Some argue that the genre can be determined from such passages as Luke 1:1–4 and John 24:24, in which the authors of Luke and John attest to the veracity of their Gospels. Putting aside the question of how one could ever be confident the writers were being truthful when they claimed they were being truthful, there is the very real question of what it meant to say you were being truthful when writing a document such as this in first-century Palestine. Other contemporary sources undermine the claim that "historians" of the period were objectively reciting known or vetted facts without embellishment. The recognized standards of "truthfulness" were far less exacting than what historians recognize today.

137. Early fathers of the Christian Church also mention no miracles. Many critical New Testament scholars believe the miracle stories were later additions to the text.

138. Matthew S. McCormick, *Atheism and the Case against Christ* (Amherst, NY: Prometheus Books, 2012), 59–60.

139. James D. G. Dunn, *The Evidence for Jesus: The Impact of Scholarship on Our Understanding of How Christianity Began* (Philadelphia: Westminster Press, 1985), 67–68. Dunn attempts to rationalize the lack of veneration as being because there were no bones in the tomb, which is completely nonsensical.

140. William Lane Craig, "The Guard at the Tomb," *New Testament Studies* 30 (1984): 273–81, http://www.leaderu.com/offices/billcraig/docs/guard.html.

141. M. M. Ohayon, "Prevalence of Hallucinations and Their Pathological Associations in the General Population," *Psychiatry Research* 97, nos. 2–3 (2000): 153–64.

142. See Michael Shermer, "The Sensed-Presence Effect," *Scientific American*, April 1, 2010, http://www.scientificamerican.com/article/the-sensed-presence -effect/.

143. Christopher Hitchens, November 26, 2010 debate with Al Sharpton. http:// hitchensdebates.blogspot.com/2010/11/hitchens-vs-sharpton-new-york-public .html.

144. David Sim, *How many Jews became Christians in the first century? The failure of the Christian mission to the Jews* (Hervormde Teologiese Studies 2009) 61. 10.4102/hts.v61i1/2.430.

145. Robert W. Funk and the Jesus Seminar, eds., *The Acts of Jesus: The Search for the Authentic Deeds of Jesus* (San Francisco: HarperSanFrancisco, 1998), 36. The Jesus Seminar was founded in 1985 and remained active through the early 2000s. The members published two other reports: Robert W. Funk, Roy W. Hoover, and the Jesus Seminar, eds., *The Five Gospels: The Search for the Authentic Worlds of Jesus: New Translation and Commentary* (New York: Macmillan, 1993), and Robert W. Funk and the Jesus Seminar, eds., *The Gospel of Jesus: According to the Jesus Seminar* (Santa Rosa, CA: Polebridge Press, 1999). The seminar members sought to reconstruct the historical Jesus using the methods of contemporary historians.

146. William Craig, *On Guard: Defending Your Faith with Reason and Precision* (David Cook 2010), 124.

147. The full accounts are found in Matthew 24:1–51, Mark 13:1–37, and Luke 21:5–33.

148. There are very compelling arguments that among the earliest traditions, Jesus's references to the "Son of Man" ushering in God's kingdom on Earth were not intended to refer to himself but to another cosmic being initially referenced in the book of Daniel. Accordingly, there would be no "Second Coming" per se because it was not Jesus who would return but another being that would arrive *for the first time*. Nonetheless, I assume for purposes of this discussion that Jesus did in fact consider himself to be the "Son of Man," as most Christians believe.

149. C. S. Lewis, "The World's Last Night" (1960), in *The Essential C. S. Lewis*, ed. Lyle W. Dorsett (New York: Collier Books, 1988), 385.

150. C. S. Lewis, "The World's Last Night" (1960), in *The Essential C. S. Lewis*, ed. Lyle W. Dorsett (New York: Collier Books, 1988), 385.

151. C. S. Lewis, "The World's Last Night" (1960), in *The Essential C. S. Lewis*, ed. Lyle W. Dorsett (New York: Collier Books, 1988), 385.

152. It also ignores the more obvious interpretation, which doesn't require Jesus to contradict himself or deliberately lie: that Jesus was certain of the *general time frame* (within the current generation) but only unsure of the *exact date and time* within that time frame. In either event, of course, Jesus remains wrong.

153. Anyone who claims the Bible as an authority and does not denounce Jesus as a false prophet without a principled way out of this dilemma must acknowledge their own hypocrisy.

154. While full preterists and full futurists represent two ends of the continuum, apologists fall all along that continuum, with some characterizing themselves as partial preterists, and others, as partial futurists. These intermediate positions believe that some of Jesus's prophesies have been fulfilled while others have not. It is beyond the scope of this work (and perhaps impossible in the space provided) to address all these positions. Each, however, is susceptible to the arguments against either the full preterists or the full futurists.

155. Marshall Entrekin, Did Jesus Wrongly Predict a First Century Return in Matthew 24:34?, Blog post accessed March 14, 2021. http://www.thingstocome.org/whatgen.htm.

156. While some apologists, taking C. S. Lewis's lead, would object that this isn't a viable option, their arguments depend on assuming that Jesus actually said everything attributed to him in the Gospels. Virtually no critical scholar takes such a position. The Jesus Seminar has concluded that no more than 20 percent of such sayings could reasonably be attributed to a historical Jesus.

157. Retroactive continuity, or retcon, is the alteration of previously established facts in the continuity of a fictional work, such as those in previous issues of a comic. It often involves reinterpreting crucial events by revealing "facts" that previously were not part of the narrative and were not contemplated by earlier writers, such as revealing that the villain who appeared to die in a previous work actually faked his death and secretly survived. Motivations for retcons include reintroducing popular characters or harmonizing story lines by different authors. One infamous retcon occurred when the writers of the popular 1980s show *Dallas* effectively erased an entire season by revealing it had all been a dream. Retcons are common in pulp fiction, especially comic books, but also in long-running stories, such as soap operas. They are often seen in sequels or prequels that weren't anticipated when the original tales were penned, such as when the writers of *Rogue One* explained why the Death Star in *Star Wars* had a design flaw that make it comically easy to destroy. One of the earliest well-known examples is the return of Sherlock Holmes after his apparent death in Arthur Conan Doyle's 1893 tale, "The Adventure of the Final Problem."

158. American Heritage Dictionary of the English Language, definition of "Legend" https://www.ahdictionary.com/word/search.html?q=legend.

159. Adrian Desmond and James Moore, *Darwin: The Life of a Tormented Evolutionist* (New York: W. W. Norton, 1994), 113–14.

CHAPTER 6

1. Tweet by Ali Rizvi dated June 19, 2017. https://twitter.com/aliamjadrizvi/status/876817219589722112?lang=en.

2. Interview with reporter Sean Illing, *Vox*, November 7, 2017 https://www.vox.com/conversations/2017/7/7/15886862/islam-trump-isis-terrorism-ali-rizvi-religion-sam-harris.

3. Sean Illing, "An Atheist Muslim on What the Left and Right Get Wrong about Islam," *Vox*, November 7, 2017, https://www.vox.com/conversations/2017/7/7/15886862/islam-trump-isis-terrorism-ali-rizvi-religion-sam-harris.

4. Robert Ingersoll, from his summation as defense lawyer in the trial of Charles B. Reynolds for blasphemy (1887).

5. Voltaire, *Questions sur les miracles* (1765).

6. Herbert Prochnow, *Speaker's Handbook of Epigrams and Witticisms*, (Harper & Brothers 1955), 132.

7. By tribes, I am here referring to people of different races, cultures, religions, sexual orientations, national origins, or other similar group characteristics by which people commonly define themselves.

8. Thomas Paine, "A letter: being an answer to a friend, on the publication of The Age of Reason," (Paris, May 12, 1797).

9. Jack David Eller, *Cruel Creeds, Virtuous Violence: Religious Violence across Culture and History* (Amherst, NY: Prometheus Books, 2010), 44.

10. John Shelby Spong, *The Sins of Scripture: Exposing the Bible's Texts of Hate to Reveal the God of Love* (San Francisco: HarperSanFrancisco, 2002), 217.

11. Charles Kimball, *When Religion Becomes Evil* (San Francisco: HarperSanFrancisco, 2002), 27.

12. Declaration on Race and Racial Prejudice, Adopted and Proclaimed by the General Conference of the United Nations Educational, Scientific and Cultural Organization at its twentieth session, on 27 November 1978.'" https://www.un.org/en/genocideprevention/documents/atrocity-crimes/Doc.11_declaration%20on%20race%20and%20racial%20prejudice.pdf

13. Romanus Pontifex, a papal bull issued by Nicholas V in 1455.

14. An act declaring that baptisme of slaves doth not exempt them from bondage, passed by the General Assembly in the session of September 1668, Hening's Statutes at Large, Volume 2, page 260. https://encyclopediavirginia.org/entries/an-act-declaring-that-baptisme-of-slaves-doth-not-exempt-them-from-bondage-1667/

15. Craig D. Townsend, *Faith in Their Own Color: Black Episcopalians in Antebellum New York City* (New York: Columbia University Press, 2015), 132.

16. Jemar Tisby, *The Color of Compromise: The Truth about the American Church's Complicity in Racism* (Grand Rapids, MI: Zondervan, 2019), 103–5.

17. Jefferson Davis, "Inaugural Address as Provisional President of the Confederacy," Montgomery, AL, Confederate States of America, February 18, 1861, *Congressional Journal* 1:64–66, http://funnelweb.utcc.utk.edu/~hoemann/jdinaug.html.

18. Contrary to popular belief, the Klan was active not only in the South but also in the North, where its membership has been estimated at between 3 and 5 million, including 40,000 Christian ministers. Olivia B. Waxman, "How the KKK's Influence Spread in Northern States," *Time*, October 24, 2017, http://time.com/4990253/kkk-white-nationalists-history/.

19. Kelly J. Baker, *The Gospel According to the Klan: The KKK's Appeal to Protestant America, 1915–1930* (Lawrence: University Press of Kansas, 2011), 6, italics original.

20. Shadee Ashtari, "KKK Leader Disputes Hate Group Label: 'We're a Christian Organization,'" HuffPost, March 21, 2014, http://www.huffingtonpost.com/2014/03/21/virginia-kkk-fliers_n_5008647.html.

21. Jane Dailey, "Sex, Segregation, and the Sacred after Brown", The Journal of American History, Vol. 91, No. 1 (Jun., 2004), Oxford University Press, pp. 119–44. https://www.jstor.org/stable/3659617?seq=1

22. Fay Botham, *Almighty God Created the Races: Christianity, Interracial Marriage, and American Law* (Chapel Hill: University of North Carolina Press, 2013), 106, 135.

23. West Chester & P. R. Co. v. Miles, 55 Pa. 209, 213 (1867), emphasis supplied.

24. For example, the trial judge who upheld Virginia's law against mixed marriages in the 1967 case of *Loving v. Virginia* cited the fact that God had put the races on separate continents as proof "that he did not intend for the races to mix." (*Loving v. Virginia*, 388 U.S. 1, 3 [1967].)

25. "Ross Barnett, Segregationist, Dies: Governor of Mississippi in 1960's," *The New York Times*, November 7, 1987. https://www.nytimes.com/1987/11/07/obituaries/ross-barnett-segregationist-dies-governor-of-mississippi-in-1960-s.html

26. The Alabama Council on Human Relations, American Friends Service Committee, Delta Ministry of the National Council of Churches, NAACP Legal Defense and Educational Fund, Southern Regional Council, and Washington Research Project, *It's Not Over in the South: School Desegregation in Forty-three Southern Cities Eighteen Years after Brown* (Atlanta, GA: Southern Education Foundation and Urban Coalition, May 1972), 142, https://eric.ed.gov/?q=ed065646&id=ED065646.

27. Tisby, *Color of Compromise*, 26, 160–61.

28. "Billy Graham Urges Restraint in Sit-Ins," *The New York Times*, April 18, 1963. https://www.nytimes.com/1963/04/18/archives/billy-graham-urges-restraint-in-sitins.html.

29. Michelle Alexander, *The New Jim Crow: Mass Incarceration in the Age of Colorblindness*, rev. ed. (New York: New Press, 2012), 44.

30. In 1971, the Southern Baptist Convention (SBC), the nation's largest Protestant denomination, passed a resolution on abortion that called upon Southern Baptists "to work for legislation that will allow the possibility of abortion under such conditions as rape, incest, clear evidence of fetal deformity, and carefully ascertained evidence of the likelihood of damage to the emotional, mental, and physical health of the mother." W. A. Criswell, pastor of the largest SBC congregation, said after *Roe v. Wade*, "I have always felt that it was only after a child was born and had life separate from its mother . . . that it became an individual person."(Randall Ballmer, *Thy Kingdom Come: How the Religious Right Distorts Faith and Threatens America* [Basic Books 2007].) A 1970 poll found that 70 percent of Southern Baptist pastors "supported abortion to protect the mental or physical health of the mother, 64 percent supported abortion in cases of fetal deformity and 71 percent in cases of rape." (David Roach, *How Southern Baptists Became Pro-Life*, Baptist Press, January 16, 2015, accessed March 16, 2021. https://www.baptistpress.com/resource-library/news/how-southern-baptists-became-pro-life/.)

31. Frances FitzGerald, *The Evangelicals: The Struggle to Shape America* (New York: Simon and Schuster, 2017), 304.

32. Jesus says this at the end of the parable of the Ten Minas, assigning the quote to a fictional nobleman who in the course of the story becomes a king. But the king is clearly intended to represent Jesus himself at the Final Judgment, which he believes and preaches to be coming soon. Jesus is commanding that once he returns to usher in the kingdom, those not willing to bend the knee to him are to be rounded up and killed violently.

33. While Jesus does speak broadly in other passages about loving one's enemies and treating others as one would himself like to be treated, these more general proscriptions surely do not overrule Jesus's more specific commands. These passages are easily harmonized if the general passages were intended to refer to personal slights and personal enemies, while the specific passages address how Christians should treat enemies of Jesus and the religion he promoted. In other words, if someone steals your shoe, forgive him and move on. But if someone tries to turn you away from Jesus, shun or even kill him, for opposition to Jesus is a capital offense.

34. *Medieval Sourcebook: Twelfth Ecumenical Council: Lateran IV 1215*. Fourth Lateran Council: Canon 3 on Heresy, Internet Medieval Sourcebook, Fordham University (1996). https://sourcebooks.fordham.edu/source/lat4-c3.asp.

35. Aquinas, *Summa Theologica*, in *Aquinas, Selected Political Writings*, ed. A. P. d'Entrèves, trans. J. G. Dawson (Oxford, UK: Oxford University Press, 1959), 77.

36. John Coffey, *Persecution and Toleration in Protestant England, 1558–1689*, Studies in History (London: Routledge, 2000), 208.

37. Penny Edgell, Joseph Gerteis, and Douglas Hartmann, "Atheists as 'Other': Moral Boundaries and Cultural Membership in American Society," *American Sociological Review* 71, no. 2 (2006): 211–34.

38. This suggests one of three options: (1) No atheists have chosen to run for federal office; (2) atheists have run for these positions and been roundly defeated; or (3) there are atheists currently in these positions who won't publicly identify as atheist. All three of these suggest that atheists are unelectable in the United States, which, given their prominence in such fields as philosophy and the sciences, suggests that America has lost out on a very distinctive and well-informed set of voices.

39. These stories, most reported by Todd Starnes of Fox News, have been repeatedly debunked by many sources. See, generally, Right Wing Watch Staff, "The Persecution Complex: The Religious Right's Deceptive Rallying Cry," Right Wing Watch, June 2014, http://www.pfaw.org/rww-in-focus/persecution-complex-reli gious-right-s-deceptive-rallying-cry. Christian commentator and founder of Christ and Pop Culture Alan Noble has written of Starnes, who has built a career almost exclusively around stories such as this, "Starnes tells us what we want to hear. We want to believe that we are the underdog. And Starnes sells us that story, wrapped in the language of patriotism and faith." Alan Noble, "The Evangelical Persecution Complex," *The Atlantic,* August 4, 2014, http://www.theatlantic.com/national/ archive/2014/08/the-evangelical-persecution-complex/375506/.

40. Pew Research Center, "Public Sees Religion's Influence Waning," Section 1: Religion in Public Life, accessed March 16, 2021. https://www.pewforum. org/2014/09/22/section-1-religion-in-public-life/.

41. Tom Dermody, "Heroic Catholicism Needed in Face of Threats, Bishop Tells Men," *The Catholic Post,* April 26, 2012, accessed March 16, 2021. https://the catholicpost.com/2012/04/26/heroic-catholicism-needed-in-face-of-threats-bishop -tells-men-2/.

42. Aaron Blake, "Rick Perry Ad Condemns Obama's 'War on Religion,'" *Washington Post*, December 7, 2011, https://www.washingtonpost.com/blogs/the-fix/ post/rick-perry-ad-condemns-obamas-war-on-religion/2011/12/07/gIQAZHpZcO _blog.html.

43. Among other things, Robertson equated gays with liars, thieves, and drunkards and claimed that African Americans in Jim Crow–era Louisiana must have been happy with their second-class status because he never heard any complain.

44. Amanda Terkel, Ian Bayne, "GOP Congressional Candidate: 'Duck Dynasty Star is Rosa Parks of our Generation.'" *Huffington Post*, December 20, 2013. https://www.huffpost.com/entry/ian-bayne-duck-dynasty_n_4480745.

45. According to researcher Jay Michaelson, the persecution narrative has been a centerpiece of the campaigns by conservative Christians to end desegregation, enforce school-sponsored prayer, and nullify abortion rights.

46. John Stewart, *The Ultimate Daily Show and Philosophy: More Moments of Zen, More Indecision Theory,* (John Wiley & Sons 2013).

47. Ralph Waldo Emerson from his personal journal of November 8, 1838, *Emerson in his Journals,* (Harvard University Press 1984), 206.

48. This is further evidence that the Gospels were not written by the Jewish disciples of Jesus but by Hellenized Christians from this later-developed faction.

Recall that the Gospels were written in Greek, with many reflections of Greek culture that would have been unknown to the Jewish followers of Jesus, who, if even literate, would have written in Aramaic.

49. Leon Poliakov, *The History of Anti-Semitism, vol. 1, From the Time of Christ to the Court Jews*, trans. Richard Howard, (New York: Vanguard Press 1965), 19.

50. Vamberto Morais, *A Short History of Anti-Semitism* (New York: Norton, 1976), 77.

51. Morais, *Short History of Anti-Semitism*, 77.

52. The irony is that, according to Christian doctrine, Christ's death was predetermined and integral to God's divine plan. Those responsible for bringing it about should, therefore, be praised rather than vilified, as they were necessary instruments in mankind's salvation. In light of God's extensive history of exerting mind control over people to bring His plans about, it is no stretch to assume He did the same in this case. In neither event would condemnation be warranted.

53. Fred Gladston Bratton, *The Crime of Christendom: The Theological Sources of Christian Anti-Semitism* (Boston: Beacon Press, 1969), 79.

54. *The Ante-Nicene Fathers Vol. 4*, eds. Alexander Roberts and James Donaldson, (W.B. Eerdmans 1956), quoted in Bratton, *The Crime of Christendom*, 80.

55. *The Ante-Nicene Fathers*, Vol. 4, cited by Bratton, 214.

56. "Tractatus in LI Psalmum," 6; J.P. Migne, ed., Patrologiae, Cursus Completus, Series Latina (1844).

57. Ambrose, *Epistolarum Classis I, XL.* 26 in *Patrologia*, ed. J.P. MIgne 15:1110–11. Reprinted in Jacob Marcus, ed., *The Jew in the Medieval World* (New York 1979).

58. *Europe and the Jews* (Boston: Beacon Press 1961), 26, quoted in Bratton, *The Crime of Christendom*, 8.

59. Saint Chrysostom, *Homilies against Judaizing Christians.* https://www.ccjr.us/dialogika-resources/primary-texts-from-the-history-of-the-relationship/chrysostom.

60. Saint Chrysostom, *Homilies against Judaizing Christians.*

61. Saint Chrysostom, *Homilies against Judaizing Christians.*

62. Saint Chrysostom, *Homilies against Judaizing Christians.*

63. Cardinal John Newman, "St. Chrysostom" profile, *The Newman Reader, Rambler* (1859). https://www.newmanreader.org/works/historical/volume2/saints/chrysostom/chapter2.html.

64. Quoted in Dennis Prager and Joseph Telushkin, *Why the Jews?: The Reason for Antisemitism* (New York: Simon and Schuster, 1983), 94.

65. Quoted in Bratton, 86; *Nicene and Post-Nicene Fathers of the Christian Church*, ed. Philip Schaff (Grand Rapids, MI: W. B. Eerdmans, 1956), 373–74.

66. Nicene and Post-Nicene Fathers of the Christian Church, ed. Philip Schaff.

67. Kenneth Stow, *Catholic Thought and Papal Jewry Policy, 1555–1593* (New York: Jewish Theological Seminary of America, 1977), 295.

68. Martin Luther, "On the Jews and Their Lies," trans. Martin H. Bertram, in *Luther's Works: The Christian in Society IV*, ed. Franklin Sherman (Minneapolis: Fortress Press, 1971), 268–72.

69. Robert Michael, "Luther, Luther Scholars, and the Jews," *Encounter* 46, no. 4 (Autumn 1985): 343–44.

70. Adolf Hitler, *Mein Kampf*, trans. Ralph Manheim (Boston: Houghton Mifflin, 1971), 213.

71. Martin Luther, *On the Jews and Their Lies*, trans. Martin Bertram (n.p.: Createspace, 2017).

72. Hitler, *Mein Kampf*, 65. It has been argued, based on certain writings late in Hitler's career, that he ultimately lost his Catholic faith and became an atheist. Usually, this is presented as part of an argument attempting to pin the blame for the Holocaust on atheism as a belief system. In discussing the culpability of Christianity as a belief system for the Holocaust, whether Hitler died as a believer or nonbeliever is ultimately beside the point. One can draw a direct tie to the Holocaust and the Christian teachings on which Hitler was raised. In other words, one can clearly show that Hitler's virulent anti-Semitism and initiation of a "final solution" very likely resulted from his early Christian worldview, regardless of whether he rejected belief in God later in life. Moreover, one can clearly show that the success of Nazi propaganda on the German public was intimately tied to the argument that Hitler was carrying out the will of the Christian God, which was supported by ample authority from prominent Christian theologians going back to the dawn of Christianity.

73. Peter De Rosa, *Vicars of Christ: The Dark Side of the Papacy* (New York: Crown, 1988), 6–7. See also Guenter Lewy, *The Catholic Church and Nazi Germany* (Boulder, CO: Da Capo Press, 2000), 51.

74. Richard Steigmann-Gall, *The Holy Reich: Nazi Conceptions of Christianity, 1919–1945* (New York: Cambridge University Press, 2003), 221.

75. Christopher J. Probst, *Demonizing the Jews: Luther and the Protestant Church in Nazi Germany* (Bloomington: Indiana University Press, 2012).

76. José M. Sánchez, *Pius XII and the Holocaust: Understanding the Controversy* (Washington, DC: Catholic University of America Press, 2002), 70.

77. The Christian contribution to anti-Semitism is detailed in such works as Lillian C. Freudmann, *Antisemitism in the New Testament* (Lanham, MD: University Press of America, 1994), and John Dominic Crossan (a former Catholic priest), *Who Killed Jesus?: Exposing the Roots of Anti-Semitism in the Gospel Story of the Death of Jesus* (San Francisco: HarperSanFrancisco, 1995). It is noteworthy that Hitler, who was baptized a Catholic, was never excommunicated from the Catholic Church.

78. Herbert Hoover, *Addresses Upon the American Road, 1948–1950* (Stanford University Press 1951).

79. Roland de Vaux, *Ancient Israel*, vol. 2, *Religious Institutions* (New York: McGraw-Hill, 1965).

80. Most critical scholars believe that none of 1 Timothy was actually written by Paul. This would get Paul off the hook but not God, for why would God allow 1 Timothy to be included within the Bible if it did not represent God's position on the subject? Whoever were the human authors of the Bible, the divine father, responsible for all its content, remains God.

81. Ecclesiasticus, also known as the Wisdom of Sirach, is one of the apocryphal or deuterocanonical books included in some Bibles but not in others. It was well known and widely read around the time of Jesus, having been written between 190 and 170 BCE, and part of the Greek translations of the Hebrew Bible used by the Gospel writers.

82. Synod of Elvira, Canon 81.

83. Martin Luther, *The Estate of Marriage* (1522).

84. Jimmy Carter, speech to the Parliament of the World's Religions, Melbourne, Australia, December 3, 2009.

85. "Mormon Women's Group Founder Kate Kelly Excommunicated," NBC News (June 23, 2014). https://www.nbcnews.com/news/us-news/mormon-womens -group-founder-kate-kelly-excommunicated-n138746.

86. Laurie Goodstein, "Mormons Expel Founder of Group Seeking Priesthood for Women," *New York Times*, June 23, 2014, http://www.nytimes.com/2014/06/24/ us/Kate-Kelly-Mormon-Church-Excommunicates-Ordain-Women-Founder.html? _r=1.

87. Donald T. Critchlow and Cynthia L. Stachecki, "The Equal Rights Amendment Reconsidered: Politics, Policy, and Social Mobilization in a Democracy," *Journal of Policy History* 20, no. 1 (January 2008): 160.

88. Sara Diamond, *Spiritual Warfare: The Politics of the Christian Right* (Boston: South End Press 1999), 49–50.

89. Colin Gorenstein, "Gay Marriage could lead to 'civil war': The Christian right's latest bigoted theory," Salon (April 10, 2015). https://www.salon .com/2015/04/10/gay_marriage_could_lead_to_civil_war_the_christian_rights_latest _bigoted_theory/.

90. Caitlin Ryan, David Huebner, Rafael M. Diaz, and Jorge Sanchez, "Family Rejection as a Predictor of Negative Health Outcomes in Whit and Latino Lesbian, Gay, and Bisexual Young Adults," *Pediatrics* 123, no. 1 (January 2009): 346–52.

91. Katherine Zeininger, "Religious Beliefs Among Family Members of Lesbian, Gay, and Bisexual (LGB) Individuals Examining Their Stability over Time," Thesis submitted to Ball State University (2014). http://cardinalscholar.bsu.edu/ bitstream/123456789/198504/1/Zeining-erK_2014-3_BODY.pdf.

92. John Shore, "The Gay Teen Suicide Rate and the Christian Condemnation of Gays," Patheos, September 26, 2010, http://www.patheos.com/blogs/john shore/2010/09/the-christian-condemnation-of-gays-and-the-teen-gay-suicide-rate/.

93. Frank Newport, "Religion Big Factor for Americans against Same-Sex Marriage," Gallup, December 5, 2012, http://www.gallup.com/poll/159089/religion -major-factor-americans-opposed-sex-marriage.aspx.

94. Dennis Coday, "The Manhattan Declaration," *National Catholic Reporter*, November 20, 2009. https://www.ncronline.org/blogs/ncr-today/manhattan-decla ration.

95. Fred Karger, "Mormongate—The Church's Cover-up of Its Prop 8 Funding," HuffPost, May 25, 2011, http://www.huffingtonpost.com/fred-karger/mor mongate----the-churchs_b_163016.html. One interesting point about this is that we know that the 27,000 or so poverty-related deaths of children worldwide could be ended within the next twenty years if enough people only provided a modest percentage of their income. Instead, these Mormons devoted $25 million dollars to stopping gay marriage. Apparently, this was their top religious priority.

96. Jay Michaelson, "The Christian Do-Gooders Secretly Attacking Gays," Daily Beast, April 14, 2017, http://www.thedailybeast.com/articles/2014/07/07/how-cam pus-crusade-for-christ-exports-homophobia-to-africa.html#.

97. Lisa Cannon Green, "Where Evangelicals Stand on Transgender Morality," *Christianity Today*, July 14, 2016, http://www.christianitytoday.com/glean ings/2016/july/where-evangelicals-stand-on-transgender-morality-lifeway.html.

98: Southern Baptist Convention First-Day SBC Bulletin Part 2, 91st volume. https://www.sbc.net/resource-library/resolutions/on-transgender-identity/.

99. "Southern Baptists Elect President, Approve Transgender Resolution," Associated Press, June 10, 2014, accessed March 16, 2021. https://www.clarionled ger.com/story/news/2014/06/10/new-southern-baptist-president/10286961/?utm _source=google&utm_medium=amp&utm_campaign=speakable.

100. BBC News, "Pope Attacks Blurring of Gender," December 23, 2008, http://news.bbc.co.uk/2/hi/europe/7796663.stm.

101. The AIDS virus is most virulent in Africa, where roughly 80 percent of the global population of AIDS patients resides. Despite being discovered three decades ago, AIDS continues to be a leading cause of death throughout Africa. Given the popularity of Catholicism throughout Africa and the fact that 25 percent of HIV and AIDS patients worldwide are being treated at Catholic facilities, the Vatican's doctrines and speeches have had significant impacts on the continent.

102. Pope Paul VI, 1968 "Humanae Vitae," Vatican, 1968.

103. Elisabeth Rosenthal, "Top Catholics question condom ban," *The New York Times*, April 16, 2005. https://www.nytimes.com/2005/04/16/world/europe/top -catholics-question-condom-ban.html.

104. Episcopal Conference of Madagascar, "AIDS: Imminent Danger for Man Today, for the Family and Society," May 14, 1990, in Speak Out on HIV and AIDS: Our Prayer Is Always Full of Hope, by the Catholic Bishops of Africa and Madagascar (Nairobi: Paulines Publications Africa, 2004), 32. John Paul's 1990 speech "sentenced millions to die." Jonathan Clayton, *"John Paul's 1990 Speech 'Sentenced Millions to Die,'" Sunday Times*, March 18, 2009, http://www.thetimes .co.uk/tto/faith/article2100295.ece.

105. Letter from Cardinal Joseph Ratzinger regarding the 1988 meeting of the National Conference of Catholic Bishops. https://www.ewtn.com/catholicism/ library/letter-of-cardinal-ratzinger-on-aids-2039.

106. "Redemption for the Pope?" *Lancet* 373, no. 9669 (March 28, 2009): p1054, http://www.thelancet.com/journals/lancet/article/PIIS0140-6736(09)60627-9/full text.

107. Yet another result of Catholic opposition to health-related science is its intense campaign against the availability of vaccines to prevent the human papillomavirus (HPV), the leading cause of cervical cancer in women. Despite studies showing the almost complete effectiveness of the vaccine, the Catholic Church, along with other right-wing religious groups, has continued to oppose it on the discredited basis that it will undermine the church's teachings on abstinence and chastity. The avoidable death of thousands of women is apparently an acceptable cost of keeping the party line on church doctrine.

108. World Health Organization, *Ensuring Human Rights in the Provision of Contraceptive Information and Services: Guidance and Recommendations* (World Health Organization, 2014), 12–13.

109. Cindy Wooden, "UN Committee Presses Vatican on Child Abuse, Some Church Teaching," *Catholic News Service*, February 5, 2014.

110. Christopher Hitchens, *The Missionary Position: Mother Teresa in Theory and Practice* (London: Verso, 1995), 11.

111. Christian Scientists base their practices on such passages as James 5:13–15: "Is any among you afflicted? Is any merry? Let him sing psalms. Is any sick among you? Let him call for the elders of the church; and let them pray over him, anointing him with oil in the name of the Lord. And the power of faith shall save the sick, and the Lord shall raise him up; and if he has committed sins, they shall be forgiven him."

112. For example, Genesis 9:4 ("But flesh with the life thereof, which is the blood thereof, shall ye not eat") and Leviticus 17:10 ("I will even set my face against that soul who eateth blood, and will cut him off from among his people").

113. Elizabeth Dias, "Southern Baptists Announce Plans to Address Sexual Abuse," *The New York Times*, Feb. 18, 2019. https://www.nytimes.com/2019/02/18/us/southern-baptists-sexual-abuse.html.

114. University of Texas at Austin, "Risks of Harm from Spanking Confirmed by Analysis of 5 Decades of Research," Science Daily, April 25, 2016, https://www.sciencedaily.com/releases/2016/04/160425143106.htm; University of New Hampshire, "College Students More Likely to Be Lawbreakeres If Spanked as Children," Science Daily, November 22, 2013, https://www.sciencedaily.com/releases/2013/11/131122103621.htm.

115. Rita Swan, "Religious Attitudes on Corporal Punishment," accessed March 7, 2021, http://childrenshealthcare.org/?page_id=146.

116. Catholic-Saints.net, "Spanking and Corporal Punishment," accessed March 7, 2021, http://www.catholic-saints.net/corporal-punishment/.

117. Steven R. Poole, Martin C. Ushkow, Philip R. Nader, Bradley J. Bradford, John R. Asbury, Daniel C. Worthington, Kathleen E. Sanabria, and Thea Carruth, "The Role of the Pediatrician in Abolishing Corporal Punishment in Schools," *Pediatrics* 88, no. 1 (July 1991): 162–67.

118. Beth Stoneburner, "An Untrained Christian Missionary 'Played Doctor' in Uganda . . . and 105 Kids Died," Patheos, August 15, 2019, https://friendlyathe ist.patheos.com/2019/08/15/an-untrained-christian-missionary-played-doctor-in -uganda-and-105-kids-died/.

119. Phil Zuckerman, "Op-Ed: How Secular Families Stack Up," *Los Angeles Times*, Jan. 14, 2015, accessed March 16, 2021. https://www.latimes.com/nation/ la-oe-0115-zuckerman-secular-parenting-20150115-story.html.

120. Barna, "Gen Z: Your Questions Answered," February 6, 2018, https://www .barna.com/research/gen-z-questions-answered/.

121. Molly Worthen, "The Evangelical Roots of Our Post-Truth Society," *New York Times*, April 13, 2017, https://www.nytimes.com/2017/04/13/opinion/sunday/ the-evangelical-roots-of-our-post-truth-society.html?emc=edit_th_20170414&nl= todaysheadlines&nlid=43032813&_r=0.

122. Worthen, "Evangelical Roots."

123. Worthen, "Evangelical Roots."

124. That number is 50 percent for Black Protestants, 31 percent for Hispanic Catholics, 26 percent for White Catholics, 20 percent for unaffiliated Christians, and 15 percent for White mainline Protestants.

125. Gallup, "Evolution, Creationism, Intelligent Design," accessed March 7, 2021, https://news.gallup.com/poll/21814/evolution-creationism-intelligent-design. aspx.

126. Gallup, "Evolution, Creationism, Intelligent Design."

127. Pew Research Center, "Public Praises Science; Scientists Fault Public, Media," July 9, 2009; Cynthia Delgado, "Finding the Evolution in Medicine," *NIH Record* 58, no. 15 (July 28, 2006): 1, 8–9.

128. Frank Newport, "Majority of Republicans Doubt Theory of Evolution," Gallup News Service, June 11, 2007.

129. John Cook, Dana Nuccitelli, Sarah A. Green, Mark Richardson, Bärbel Winkler, Rob Painting, Robert Way, Peter Jacobs, and Andrew Skuce, "Quantify-ing the Consensus on Anthropogenic Global Warming in the Scientific Literature," *Environmental Research Letters* 8, no. 2 (May 15, 2013): 024024.

130. N. Smith and A. Leiserowitz, "American Evangelicals and Global Warm-ing," *Global Environmental Change* 23, no. 5 (October 2013): 1009–17, http://www .trunity.net/files/235101_235200/235121/americanevangelicals-globalwarmingarti cle-1-.pdf. In 2008, a Pew Research Center survey reported that only 34 percent of White Evangelical Protestants believed in AGW, less than any other group mea-sured by the survey.

131. Barna, "Evangelicals Go 'Green' with Caution," September 22, 2008, www .barna.org/barna-update/culture/23-evangelicals-go-qgreenq-with-caution#.UswF-0NDna00.

132. Public Relations Research Institute, "Americans More Likely to Attribute Increasingly Severe Weather to Climate Change, Not End Times," December 2012, http://publicreligion.org/research/2012/12/prri-rns-december–2012-survey/.

133. The term *denialist* is admittedly loaded, but I define it as someone who holds to a position regardless of the evidence mustered against it—someone who simply will not engage with the opposing evidence.

134. Justin Worland, "EPA Chief Says Carbon Isn't a 'Primary Contributor' to Climate Change. Science Says He's Wrong," *Time*, March 9, 2017, http://time .com/4696658/scott-pruitt-epa-carbon-climate-change/.

135. Jay Michaelson, "Trump's EPA Pick Blends Conservative Christianity with Anti-Environmental Activism," Daily Beast, April 11, 2017, http://www.thedaily beast.com/articles/2017/01/23/trump-s-epa-pick-blends-conservative-christianity -with-anti-environmental-activism.html.

136. Ben Terris, "Jim Inhofe Is a Small-Plane-Flying, Global-Warming-Denying Senator. And Now He's Got a Gavel," *Washington Post*, January 8, 2015, https:// www.washingtonpost.com/lifestyle/style/the-senates-top-climate-change-denier-is flying-high-with-a-committee-chairmanship/2015/01/07/bf625fe0-9365-11e4-ba53 -a477d66580ed_story.html.

137. Chris Mooney, "Study: Science and Religion Really Are Enemies after All," *Mother Jones*, September 3, 2014, http://www.motherjones.com/environment/ 2014/09/religion-quashes-innovation-patents.

138. I do not mean to suggest that Christian ideology is the only or even the primary source of resistance to science supporting AGW. Such political ideologies as libertarianism are at least as much to blame. Nonetheless, there can be little doubt that Christian belief systems have played a substantial role in the public debate, even if that role is difficult to quantify.

139. Chris Mooney, *The Republican War on Science* (New York: Basic Books, 2005).

140. Marina Krakovsky, "Losing Your Religion: Analytic Thinking Can Undermine Belief," *Scientific American*, April 26, 2012, http://www.scientificamerican .com/article.cfm?id=losing-your-religion-analytic-thinking-can-undermine-belief.

141. The failure of these suits is indicative of the failure of their underlying assumptions. It is not that universities are censoring Christian professors based on the content of their writings. The professors are simply being held to the same standards as everyone else. The problem with these professors is that they refuse to engage in the processes by which academic writings earn the rights to publication, such as peer review.

142. Scott Foundas, "Film Review: 'God's Not Dead,'" *Variety*, March 22, 2014. https://variety.com/2014/film/reviews/film-review-gods-not-dead-1201142881/.

143. James Madison, Letter to Edward Livingston on July 10, 1822.

144. Debate over the Bill of Rights in the First Congress, Aug. 15, 1789.

145. *Everson v. Board of Education of the Township of Ewing*, 330 U.S. 1, 15–16 (1947).

146. The metaphorical was rendered literal in Arthur Miller's play *The Crucible*, detailing many of the tactics used by McCarthy and his supporters in the context of the Salem witch trials.

147. Unfortunately, this has resulted in many Christians promoting and believing in a revisionist history, in which American laws and policies were intended for the benefit of Christians and the flourishing of Christianity. Buoyed by such faux historians as David Barton, Christian values have been conflated with American values, resulting in anything not overly pro-Christian being considered anti-American. Many expressly advocate government policies that favor Christianity over other religions or no religion, seeing this as a uniquely American value. They are likely to see atheists not just as incorrect in their religious beliefs but also as political traitors.

148. Abby Goodnough and Jen McCaffery, "Student Faces Town's Wrath in Protest against a Prayer," *New York Times*, January 26, 2012.

149. Hemant Mehta, *Meat Loaf Says Jessica Ahlquist is What's Wrong with America,* Friendly Atheist, March 23, 2012.

150. To which one might reasonably offer the critique: "Then why isn't Christian Scripture clearer on issues such as this? Why would God allow for such ambiguity that otherwise reasonable people could believe they are acting in accordance with God's will?"

151. United States Department of Justice, Justice News, July 30, 2018. https://www .justice.gov/opa/speech/attorney-general-sessions-delivers-remarks-department -justice-s-religious-liberty-summit

152. John Wagner and Sarah Pulliam Bailey, "Trump signs order aimed at allowing churches to engage in more political activity," *Chicago Tribune*, May 4, 2017. https://www.chicagotribune.com/nation-world/ct-trump-political-limits-churches -20170504-story.html.

153. Rob Boston, "Seeking God's Law: Past Statements by Attorney General Nominee William Barr Are Cause for Concern, Americans United Says," Americans United for Separation of Church and State, January 2019, https://www .au.org/church-state/january-2019-church-state/featured/seeking-gods-law-past -statements-by-attorney.

154. Philip Shenon, "'A Threat to Democracy': William Barr's Speech on Religious Freedom Alarms Liberal Catholics," *Guardian*, October 20, 2019, https:// www.theguardian.com/us-news/2019/oct/19/william-barr-attorney-general-catholic -conservative-speech.

155. Shenon, "'Threat to Democracy.'"

156. Mattathias Schwartz, "Mike Pompeo's Mission: Clean up Trump's Messes," *New York Times Magazine*, February 26, 2019, https://www.nytimes .com/2019/02/26/magazine/mike-pompeo-translates-trump.html.

157. Edward Wong, "The Rapture and the Real World: Mike Pompeo Blends Beliefs and Policy," *New York Times*, March 30, 2019, https://www.nytimes .com/2019/03/30/us/politics/pompeo-christian-policy.html.

158. Lee Fang, "Trump CIA Pick Mike Pompeo Depicted War on Terror as Islamic Battle against Christianity," Intercept, November 23, 2016, https://thein tercept.com/2016/11/23/mike-pompeo-religious-war/.

159. According to the *Washington Post*, it was at the urging of Pompeo and fellow Evangelical Christian Mike Pence that President Trump ordered the 2020 drone strike on General Qassem Soleimani, considered by many an act of war. Josh Hudson, Josh Dawsey, Shane Harris, and Dan Lamothe, "Killing of Soleimani Follows Long Push from Pompeo for Aggressive Action against Iran, but Airstrike Brings Serious Risks," *Washington Post*, January 5, 2020, https://www .washingtonpost.com/world/national-security/killing-of-soleimani-follows-long -push-from-pompeo-for-aggressive-action-against-iran-but-airstrike-brings-serious -risks/2020/01/05/092a8e00-2f7d-11ea-be79-83e793dbcaef_story.html.

160. Wong, "Rapture and the Real World."

161. The Religious Freedom Restoration Act of 1993 (RFRA) was enacted to protect against religious discrimination—specifically in response to the firing of two Native American men over the ritual use of peyote, which the Supreme Court found was not protected activity. In the words of Representative Joseph Kennedy III of Massachusetts, however, RFRA "morphed from a shield of protection to a sword of infringement, allowing employers to undermine basic workplace protections, organizations to stonewall child labor investigations, and health providers to deny needed care for victims of sexual abuse." (Testimony by Congressman Joseph P. Kennedy, III for "Do No Harm: Examining the Misapplication of the 'Religious Freedom Restoration Act." https://edlabor.house.gov/imo/media/doc/RepKennedy-Testimony0625191.pdf.) This morphing was engineered and cheered by Christian conservatives, most evidently in the 2014 Hobby Lobby decision and its aftermath. With this new narrative of "religious freedom" replacing "religious discrimination," support from conservatives has more than doubled. Today, 47 percent of Republicans support the right of Christians to discriminate against gays on the basis of their religious beliefs, up from 21 percent in 2014. Paul Waldman, "Opinion: Why Republicans Are Growing More Willing to Embrace Discrimination," *Washington Post*, June 25, 2019, https://www.washingtonpost.com/opinions/2019/06/25/ why-republicans-are-growing-more-willing-embrace-discrimination/?utm_term= .da89abd9b3ed.

162. Adelle Banks, *Conservative Evangelicals revel in their "unprecedented" presidential access,* Religion News Service, July 19, 2017. https://religionnews .com/2017/07/19/conservative-evangelicals-revel-in-their-unprecedented-access -to-the-president/.

163. 2017 Fox News interview with Jeanine Pirro. https://www.huffpost.com/ entry/jerry-falwell-jr-dream-president-trump_n_5906950fe4b05c3976807a08. Josh Feldman, "Jerry Falwell Jr.: 'Nice Guys' May Make Great Christian Leaders, but we need more 'street fighters' like Trump," MediaIte, Sept. 29, 2018. https://www .mediaite.com/online/jerry-falwell-jr-nice-guys-may-make-great-christian-leaders -but-we-need-more-street-fighters-like-trump/.

164. Reed, speaking to attendees of the 2019 Road to Majority conference. Peter Wehner, The Deepening Crisis in Evangelical Christianity, *The Atlantic*, July 5, 2019.

165. Jake Bauer, "Oil City Bench Controversy in National Spotlight," *Explore Venango*, May 6, 2017, accessed March 16, 2021. https://explorevenango.com/oil-city-bench-controversy-in-national-spotlight/. I use Mr. Carlson as an example because he is currently one of the biggest names at Fox News, a network that is watched far out of proportion to any other by the Religious Right. I believe it is fair to conclude that his views are representative of many of his conservative Christian viewers. I have also seen many of these same arguments raised by other conservative Christians when addressing legal challenges by atheist groups.

166. "In God We Trust" has been challenged as a violation of the Establishment Clause, but like the inclusion of "Under God" in the Pledge of Allegiance, it has held not to be a violation. See *Lynch v. Donnelly*, 465 U.S. 668 (1984); *Elk Grove Unified School District v. Newdow*, 542 U.S. 1 (2004). Supreme Court justices William Brennan and Sandra Day O'Conner reasoned that these statements amounted to no more than "ceremonial deism," which "have lost through rote repetition any significant religious context." (*Lynch v. Donnelly*, 465 U.S. 668, 716 [1984] [Justice Brennan dissenting]; *Elk Grove Unified School District v. Newdow*, 542 U.S. 1, 42–44 [2004] [Justice O'Conner concurring].) In other words, these justices found these phrases to pass constitutional muster precisely because they have lost any religious meaning and therefore do not reflect government endorsement of any specific religious belief. It is ironic, then, that Christian conservatives cite the continued use of these phrases as evidence that America is a Christian nation that endorses Christianity.

167. Thomas Demaria and Howard Kassinove, "Predicting Guilt from Irrational Beliefs, Religious Affiliation and Religiosity," *Journal of Rational-Emotive and Cognitive-Behavior Therapy* 6 (1988): 259–72, http://link.springer.com/article/10.1007%2FBF01061292.

168. Interview of Dr. Marlene Winell by Valerie Tarico of Alternate, "Religious Trauma Syndrome: How Some Organized Religion Leads to Mental Health Problems," *Truthout*, March 27, 2013, accessed March 16, 2021. https://truthout.org/articles/religious-trauma-syndrome-how-some-organized-religion-leads-to-mental-health-problems/.

169. Genesis 1:26–28.

170. René Descartes, *Discourse on the Method of Rightly Conducting One's Reason and of Seeking Truth in the Sciences* (1637). https://www.gutenberg.org/files/59/59-h/59-h.htm.

171. Peter Singer, *Animal Liberation* (New York: Avon Books, 1990), 191.

172. Abraham Lincoln, "Second Inaugural Address," March 4, 1865, http://www.bartleby.com/124/pres32.html.

173. Avro Manhattan, *The Vatican Billions* (Ontario: Chick Pub, 1983).

174. It is likewise probably impossible to demonstrate conclusively that Christianity represents a net evil, though one can certainly tally the known goods and evils and reach a tentative conclusion. As this book demonstrates, I find it more plausible that the net effect of Christianity is a negative one.

175. "Eminem Terrified As Daughter Begins Dating Man Raised on his Music," *The Onion*, June 17, 2013, accessed March 16, 2021.

176. Greta Christina, *Why Are You Atheists So Angry? 99 Things that Piss Off the Godless* (Pitchstone 2012).

CHAPTER 7

1. I certainly recognize that liberal Christianity encompasses a wide spectrum of belief and that this example is not representative of all Christian moderates. It is, however, illustrative of how far liberal Christianity can depart from its conservative counterpart and still claim to fall under the same Christian umbrella.

2. Ernestine Van der Wall, "The Enemy Within: Religion, Science, and Modernism" (Wassenaar, Netherlands: Netherlands Institute for Advanced Study in the Humanities and Social Sciences, 2007).

3. Unicorns, for example, are mentioned eight times in the King James Bible but have been conspicuously purged from more contemporary versions, such as the New American Standard and the New International (Numbers 23:22, 24:8; Deuteronomy 33:17; Job 39:9; Isaiah 34:7; Psalms 22:21, 29:6, 92:10).

4. It is important to recognize that traditional theology was forged from the fires of pagan criticism. Theologians were forced to come up with plausible and coherent explanations to critiques leveled against the Christian faith. As I point out numerous times in this book, they often failed in this mission. But to cast aside all their work, as liberals so often do, is to throw the baby out with the bathwater. Accordingly, liberal theology often must begin at ground zero, addressing issues long ago parsimoniously addressed by the Church Fathers.

5. Tim Keller, "Creation, Evolution, and Christian Laypeople," *Biologos*, Feb. 23, 2012, accessed March 16, 2021. https://biologos.org/articles/creation-evolution-and-christian-laypeople/.

6. Robert M. Price, *The Reason-Driven Life: What Am I Here on Earth For?* (Amherst, NY: Prometheus Books 2006), 236.

7. *Exegesis* is the critical explanation or interpretation of a text, typically an ancient one written under very different cultural traditions than those of today. *Exegesis* is occasionally used interchangeably with *hermeneutics*.

8. Sam Harris, *The End of Faith: Religion, Terror, and the Future of Reason* (W.W. Norton 2005), 18–19.

9. Some liberal denominations with more of an intellectual tradition, such as the Episcopal Church, are more open to outside texts and discussions. But even Episcopal sermons usually treat these superficially as a way to tie their message back to Christian Scripture.

10. Daniel Dennett, *Breaking the Spell: Religion as a Natural Phenomenon* (Penguin Books 2007).

11. Greta Christina, *Why Are You Atheists So Angry? 99 Things That Piss off the Godless* (Charlottesville, VA: Pitchstone, 2012). The analogy originated with Sam Harris, *Letter to a Christian Nation* (New York: Vintage Books, 2008).

12. Sam Harris, *The End of Faith: Religion, Terror, and the Future of Reason* (W.W. Norton 2005), 21.

13. Sam Harris, *The End of Faith: Religion, Terror, and the Future of Reason* (W.W. Norton 2005), 21.

CONCLUSION

1. Sean Carroll, "Science and Religion are not Compatible," *Discover Magazine*, June 23, 2009, accessed March 16, 2021. https://www.discovermagazine.com/the-sciences/science-and-religion-are-not-compatible.

2. Stephen Fry, in video for the British Humanism Association titled "How Can I Be Happy?" https://www.irishtimes.com/life-and-style/health-family/stephen-fry-on-the-secret-of-happiness-1.1732416.

3. Robert Ingersoll, *The Gods and Other Lectures* (Cosimo Classics 2009).

APPENDIX

1. When scientists speak of explanatory value, they are referring to aspects of a hypothesis or theory that account for a wide variety of observed phenomena.

2. Anthony Flew, *Thinking about Thinking: Do I Sincerely Want to Be Right?* (Glasgow: Fontana/Collins, 1975).

3. Thomas Jefferson, Letter to Francis Adrian van der Kemp, July 30, 1816. https://founders.archives.gov/documents/Jefferson/03-10-02-0167.

4. William Craig, "#68 The Witness of the Holy Spirit," *Reasonable Faith Blog*, Aug. 4, 2008, accessed March 16, 2021. https://www.reasonablefaith.org/question-answer/P50/the-witness-of-the-holy-spirit/.

5. Darius and Karin Viet, "Circular Reasoning," *Answers in Genesis Blog*, May 27, 2011, accessed March 16, 2021. https://answersingenesis.org/apologetics/circular-reasoning/.

6. Darius and Karin Viet, "Circular Reasoning," *Answers in Genesis Blog*, May 27, 2011, accessed March 16, 2021. https://answersingenesis.org/apologetics/circular-reasoning/.

7. I reference evolution for many analogies throughout this book. There is no better example of something (design in nature) that once served as a powerful argument to ignorance for God that was dealt a crippling blow by scientific explanation.

8. Obviously, every explanation breaks down at some point. Like a precocious toddler, you can always ask, "Why?" until your inquiries are met with nothing more

than a blank stare. Ultimately, our beliefs are based on properly basic beliefs, which are simply necessary foundations for any useful knowledge.

9. SES had a purpose statement that said the institution assumes the "infallibility and inerrancy of the Scriptures." Bobby Ross, Jr., "Interpretation Sparks a Grave Theology Debate," *Christianity Today*, November 7, 2011, accessed March 16, 2021. https://www.christianitytoday.com/ct/2011/november/interpretation-sparks -theology-debate.html.

10. Bertrand Russell, *Marriage and Morals* (1929). https://russell-j.com/begin ner/MaM1929-TEXT.HTM. It is important to distinguish here between common popularity and scientific consensus, for the latter supports a valid argument for a proposition, while the former does not. Scientific consensus is based on the combined opinions of experts with relevant expertise analyzing volumes of appropriate data pursuant to objective, agreed-upon standards. Common popularity reflects none of these safeguards.

11. Mark Twain, *The Autobiography of Mark Twain* (University of California Press, 2010).

12. Stephen Fry, "The Importance of Unbelief," Interview on bigthink.com, December 8, 2009. https://bigthink.com/videos/the-importance-of-unbelief.

13. Francis Bacon, *Sylva Sylvarum: A Natural History, in Ten Centuries* (1627). https://openlibrary.org/books/OL24331806M/Sylva_sylvarum.

14. To say these intuitions were useful is not the same as saying they were true in some broader sense.

15. Daniel J. Simons and Christopher F. Chabris, "The Trouble with Intuition," *Chronicle of Higher Education*, May 30, 2010.

16. Paul Broca, *Quelques propositions sur les tumeurs dites cancéreuses* (1849).

17. Robert Cummins, "Reflections on Reflective Equilibrium," in *Rethinking Intuition: The Psychology of Intuition and Its Role in Philosophical Inquiry*, ed. Michael DePaul and William Ramsey, 113–28 (Lanham, MD: Rowman and Littlefield, 1998).

18. These very descriptions we commonly use to describe logic and emotion reveal the relative values our society has placed on them. One is devalued as uncaring and unfeeling, while the other is exalted as the opposite.

19. Steven Novella, "The Ultimate Argument from Authority," *Neurologica blog*, Dec. 1, 2009, accessed March 16, 2021. https://theness.com/neurologicablog/index .php/the-ultimate-argument-from-authority/.

20. See Candida R. Moss, *The Myth of Persecution: How Early Christians Invented a Story of Martyrdom* (New York: HarperCollins, 2013).

21. Argument in Defense of the British Soldiers in the Boston Massacre Trials (1770). https://founders.archives.gov/documents/Adams/05-03-02-0001-0004-0016.

22. Rick Warren, *The Purpose-Driven Life: What on Earth Am I Here For?* (Grand Rapids, MI: Zondervan, 2013).

23. William Lane Craig, "The Absurdity of Life without God," Reasonable Faith with William Lane Craig, accessed March 7, 2021, https://www.reasonablefaith.org/writings/popular-writings/existence-nature-of-god/the-absurdity-of-life-without-god/.

24. Brian Greene, *The Elegant Universe: Superstrings, Hidden Dimensions, and the Quest for the Ultimate Theory* (W.W. Norton & Co., 2010).

25. Ted Honderich, ed., *The Oxford Companion to Philosophy* (Oxford, UK: Oxford University Press, 2005).

26. This isn't to say that science can't be helpful in *informing such disciplines*, however, such as by providing objective knowledge that assists in determining how best to achieve a desired goal.

27. Arthur Conan Doyle, *The Sign of Four* (Garden City, NY: Doubleday, 1977), 111.

28. C. S. Lewis, *Mere Christianity* (HarperOne 2009).

29. Alan Dershowitz, *Letters to a Young Lawyer* (Basic Books 2005).

30. "Homer the Heretic," The Simpsons, Season 4, ep. 3, first aired October 8, 1992. https://www.youtube.com/watch?v=Rg-AjdCpsvo.

31. It is interesting to note that several, if not all, of William Lane Craig's apologetic arguments ultimately depend on treating the Bible as an authoritative historical source. Craig, however, has consistently refused to debate the issue of whether the Bible *should be treated as such*. One can only speculate as to his motives, but it is certainly a reasonable guess that Craig is fully aware of how this would undercut his other arguments, which he can't risk losing.

INDEX